SECURITIES REGULATION
STATUTORY SUPPLEMENT
2023 Edition

Securities Act – Statutes:

Section 1 – Short Title

This title may be cited as the "Securities Act of 1933."

Section 2 – Definitions; Promotion of Efficiency, Competition, and Capital Formation

a. **Definitions**

When used in this title, unless the context otherwise requires–

1. The term "security" means any note, stock, treasury stock, security future, security-based swap, bond, debenture, evidence of indebtedness, certificate of interest or participation in any profit-sharing agreement, collateral-trust certificate, preorganization certificate or subscription, transferable share, investment contract, voting-trust certificate, certificate of deposit for a security, fractional undivided interest in oil, gas, or other mineral rights, any put, call, straddle, option, or privilege on any security, certificate of deposit, or group or index of securities (including any interest therein or based on the value thereof), or any put, call, straddle, option, or privilege entered into on a national securities exchange relating to foreign currency, or, in general, any interest or instrument commonly known as a "security", or any certificate of interest or participation in, temporary or interim certificate for, receipt for, guarantee of, or warrant or right to subscribe to or purchase, any of the foregoing.

3.   The term "sale" or "sell" shall include every contract of sale or disposition of a security or interest in a security, for value. The term "offer to sell", "offer for sale", or "offer" shall include every attempt or offer to dispose of, or solicitation of an offer to buy, a security or interest in a security, for value. The terms defined in this paragraph and the term "offer to buy" as used in subsection (c) of section 5 shall not include preliminary negotiations or agreements between an issuer (or any person directly or indirectly controlling or controlled by an issuer, or under direct or indirect common control with an issuer) and any underwriter or among underwriters who are or are to be in privity of contract with an issuer (or any person directly or indirectly controlling or controlled by an issuer, or under direct or indirect common control with an issuer). Any security given or delivered with, or as a bonus on account of, any purchase of securities or any other thing, shall be conclusively presumed to constitute a part of the subject of such purchase and to have been offered and sold for value. The issue or transfer of a right or privilege, when originally issued or transferred with a security, giving the holder of such security the right to convert such security into another security of the same issuer or of another person, or giving a right to subscribe to another security of the same issuer or of another person, which right cannot be exercised until some future date, shall not be deemed to be an offer or sale of such other security; but the issue or transfer of such other security upon the exercise of such right of conversion or subscription shall be deemed a sale of such other security. Any offer or sale of a security futures product by or on behalf of the issuer of the securities underlying the security futures product, an affiliate of the issuer, or an underwriter, shall constitute a contract for sale of, sale of, offer for sale, or offer to sell the underlying securities. Any offer or sale of a security-based swap by or on behalf of the issuer of the securities upon which such security-based swap is based or is referenced, an affiliate of the issuer, or an underwriter, shall constitute a contract for sale of, sale of, offer for sale, or offer to sell such securities. The publication or distribution by a broker or dealer of a research report about an emerging growth company that is the subject of a proposed public offering of the common equity securities of such emerging growth company pursuant to a registration statement that the issuer proposes to file, or has filed, or that is effective shall be deemed for purposes of paragraph (10) of this subsection and section 5(c) not to constitute an offer for sale or offer to sell a security, even if the broker or dealer is participating or will participate in the registered offering of the securities of the issuer. As used in this paragraph, the term 'research report' means a written, electronic, or oral communication that includes information, opinions, or recommendations with respect to securities of an issuer or an analysis of a security or an issuer, whether or not it provides information reasonably sufficient upon which to base an investment decision.

4.   The term "issuer" means every person who issues or proposes to issue any security; except that with respect to certificates of deposit, voting-trust certificates, or collateral-trust certificates, or with respect to certificates of interest or shares in an unincorporated investment trust not having a board of directors (or persons performing similar functions) or of the fixed, restricted management, or unit type, the term "issuer" means the person or persons

performing the acts and assuming the duties of depositor or manager pursuant to the provisions of the trust or other agreement or instrument under which such securities are issued; except that in the case of an unincorporated association which provides by its articles for limited liability of any or all of its members, or in the case of a trust, committee, or other legal entity, the trustees or members thereof shall not be individually liable as issuers of any security issued by the association, trust, committee, or other legal entity; except that with respect to equipment-trust certificates or like securities, the term "issuer" means the person by whom the equipment or property is or is to be used; and except that with respect to fractional undivided interests in oil, gas, or other mineral rights, the term "issuer" means the owner of any such right or of any interest in such right (whether whole or fractional) who creates fractional interests therein for the purpose of public offering.

7. The term "interstate commerce" means trade or commerce in securities or any transportation or communication relating thereto among the several States or between the District of Columbia or any Territory of the United States and any State or other Territory, or between any foreign country and any State, Territory, or the District of Columbia, or within the District of Columbia.

10. The term "prospectus" means any prospectus, notice, circular, advertisement, letter, or communication, written or by radio or television, which offers any security for sale or confirms the sale of any security; except that (a) a communication sent or given after the effective date of the registration statement (other than a prospectus permitted under subsection (b) of section 10) shall not be deemed a prospectus if it is proved that prior to or at the same time with such communication a written prospectus meeting the requirements of subsection (a) of section 10 at the time of such communication was sent or given to the person to whom the communication was made, and (b) a notice, circular, advertisement, letter, or communication in respect of a security shall not be deemed to be a prospectus if it states from whom a written prospectus meeting the requirements of section 10 may be obtained and, in addition, does no more than identify the security, state the price thereof, state by whom orders will be executed, and contain such other information as the Commission, by rules or regulations deemed necessary or appropriate in the public interest and for the protection of investors, and subject to such terms and conditions as may be prescribed therein, may permit.

11. The term "underwriter" means any person who has purchased from an issuer with a view to, or offers or sells for an issuer in connection with, the distribution of any security, or participates or has a direct or indirect participation in any such undertaking, or participates or has a participation in the direct or indirect underwriting of any such undertaking; but such term shall not include a person whose interest is limited to a commission from an underwriter or dealer not in excess of the usual and customary distributors' or sellers' commission. As used in this paragraph the term "issuer" shall include, in addition to an issuer, any person directly or indirectly controlling or controlled by the issuer, or any person under direct or indirect common control with the issuer.

12. The term "dealer" means any person who engages either for all or part of his time, directly or indirectly, as agent, broker, or principal, in the business of offering, buying, selling, or otherwise dealing or trading in securities issued by another person.

19. The term 'emerging growth company' means an issuer that had total annual gross revenues of less than $1,000,000,000 (as such amount is indexed for inflation every 5 years by the Commission to reflect the change in the Consumer Price Index for All Urban Consumers published by the Bureau of Labor Statistics, setting the threshold to the nearest 1,000,000) during its most recently completed fiscal year. An issuer that is an emerging growth company as of the first day of that fiscal year shall continue to be deemed an emerging growth company until the earliest of—

   A. the last day of the fiscal year of the issuer during which it had total annual gross revenues of $1,000,000,000 (as such amount is indexed for inflation every 5 years by the Commission to reflect the change in the Consumer Price Index for All Urban Consumers published by the Bureau of Labor Statistics, setting the threshold to the nearest 1,000,000) or more;

   B. the last day of the fiscal year of the issuer following the fifth anniversary of the date of the first sale of common equity securities of the issuer pursuant to an effective registration statement under this title;

   C. the date on which such issuer has, during the previous 3-year period, issued more than $1,000,000,000 in non-convertible debt; or

   D. the date on which such issuer is deemed to be a 'large accelerated filer', as defined in Rule 12b–2 or any successor thereto.

Section 3 – Classes of Securities under this Title

a. **Exempted securities**

    Except as hereinafter expressly provided, the provisions of this title shall not apply to any of the following classes of securities:

    1. Reserved.

    2. Any security issued or guaranteed by the United States or any territory thereof, or by the District of Columbia, or by any State of the United States, or by any political subdivision of a State or territory, or by any public instrumentality of one or more States or territories, or by any person controlled or supervised by and acting as an instrumentality of the Government of the United States pursuant to authority granted by the Congress of the United States; or any certificate of deposit for any of the foregoing; or any security issued or guaranteed by any bank; or any security issued by or representing an interest in or a direct obligation of a Federal Reserve bank; or any interest or participation in any common trust fund or similar fund that is excluded from the definition of the term "investment company" under section 3(c)(3) of the Investment Company Act of 1940; or any security which is an industrial development bond (as defined in section 103(c)(2) of the Internal Revenue Code of 1954) the interest on which is excludable from gross income under section 103(a)(1) of such Code if, by reason of the application of paragraph (4) or (6) of section 103(c) of such Code (determined as if paragraphs (4)(A), (5), and (7) were not included in such section 103(c)), paragraph (1) of such section 103(c) does not

apply to such security; or any interest or participation in a single trust fund, or in a collective trust fund maintained by a bank, or any security arising out of a contract issued by an insurance company, which interest, participation, or security is issued in connection with (A) a stock bonus, pension, or profit-sharing plan which meets the requirements for qualification under section 401 of the Internal Revenue Code of 1954, (B) an annuity plan which meets the requirements for the deduction of the employer's contributions under section 404(a)(2) of such Code, (C) a governmental plan as defined in section 414(d) of such Code which has been established by an employer for the exclusive benefit of its employees or their beneficiaries for the purpose of distributing to such employees or their beneficiaries the corpus and income of the funds accumulated under such plan, if under such plan it is impossible, prior to the satisfaction of all liabilities with respect to such employees and their beneficiaries, for any part of the corpus or income to be used for, or diverted to, purposes other than the exclusive benefit of such employees or their beneficiaries, or (D) a church plan, company, or account that is excluded from the definition of an investment company under section 3(c)(14) of the Investment Company Act of 1940, other than any plan described in subparagraph (A), (B), (C), or (D) of this paragraph (i) the contributions under which are held in a single trust fund or in a separate account maintained by an insurance company for a single employer and under which an amount in excess of the employer's contribution is allocated to the purchase of securities (other than interests or participations in the trust or separate account itself) issued by the employer or any company directly or indirectly controlling, controlled by, or under common control with the employer, (ii) which covers employees some or all of whom are employees within the meaning of section 401(c)(1) of such Code, or (iii) which is a plan funded by an annuity contract described in section 403(b) of such Code. The Commission, by rules and regulations or order, shall exempt from the provisions of section 5 of this title any interest or participation issued in connection with a stock bonus, pension, profit-sharing, or annuity plan which covers employees some or all of whom are employees within the meaning of section 401(c)(1) of the Internal Revenue Code of 1954, if and to the extent that the Commission determines this to be necessary or appropriate in the public interest and consistent with the protection of investors and the purposes fairly intended by the policy and provisions of this title. For purposes of this paragraph, a security issued or guaranteed by a bank shall not include any interest or participation in any collective trust fund maintained by a bank; and the term "bank" means any national bank, or any banking institution organized under the laws of any State, territory, or the District of Columbia, the business of which is substantially confined to banking and is supervised by the State or territorial banking commission or similar official; except that in the case of a common trust fund or similar fund, or a collective trust fund, the term "bank" has the same meaning as in the Investment Company Act of 1940;

3.   Any note, draft, bill of exchange, or banker's acceptance which arises out of a current transaction or the proceeds of which have been or are to be used for current transactions, and which has a maturity at the time of issuance of not exceeding nine months, exclusive of days of grace, or any renewal thereof the maturity of which is likewise limited;

4.   Any security issued by a person organized and operated exclusively for religious, educational, benevolent, fraternal, charitable, or reformatory purposes and not for pecuniary profit, and no part of the net earnings of which inures to the benefit of any person, private stockholder, or individual, or any security of a fund that is excluded from the definition of an investment company under section 3(c)(10)(B) of the Investment Company Act of 1940;

5.   Any security issued (A) by a savings and loan association, building and loan association, cooperative bank, homestead association, or similar institution, which is supervised and examined by State or Federal authority having supervision over any such institution; or (B) by (i) a farmer's cooperative organization exempt from tax under section 521 of the Internal Revenue Code of 1954, (ii) a corporation described in section 501(c)(16) of such Code and exempt from tax under section 501(a) of such Code, or (iii) a corporation described in section 501(c)(2) of such Code which is exempt from tax under section 501(a) of such Code and is organized for the exclusive purpose of holding title to property, collecting income therefrom, and turning over the entire amount thereof, less expenses, to an organization or corporation described in clause (i) or (ii);

6.   Any interest in a railroad equipment trust. For purposes of this paragraph "interest in a railroad equipment trust" means any interest in an equipment trust, lease, conditional sales contract, or other similar arrangement entered into, issued, assumed, guaranteed by, or for the benefit of, a common carrier to finance the acquisition of rolling stock, including motive power;

7.   Certificates issued by a receiver or by a trustee or debtor in possession in a case under title 11 of the United States Code, with the approval of the court;

8.   Any insurance or endowment policy or annuity contract or optional annuity contract, issued by a corporation subject to the supervision of the insurance commissioner, bank commissioner, or any agency or officer performing like functions, of any State or Territory of the United States or the District of Columbia;

9.   Except with respect to a security exchanged in a case under title 11 of the United States Code, any security exchanged by the issuer with its existing security holders exclusively where no commission or other remuneration is paid or given directly or indirectly for soliciting such exchange;

10.   Except with respect to a security exchanged in a case under title 11 of the United States Code, any security which is issued in exchange for one or more bona fide outstanding securities, claims or property interests, or partly in such exchange and partly for cash, where the terms and conditions of such issuance and exchange are approved, after a hearing upon the fairness of such terms and conditions at which all persons to whom it is proposed to issue securities in such exchange shall have the right to appear, by any court, or by any official or agency of the United States, or by any State or Territorial banking or insurance commission or other governmental authority expressly authorized by law to grant such approval;

11.   Any security which is a part of an issue offered and sold only to persons resident within a single State or Territory, where the issuer of such security is a person resident and doing business within or, if a corporation, incorporated by and doing business within, such State or Territory.

12. Any equity security issued in connection with the acquisition by a holding company of a bank under section 3(a) of the Bank Holding Company Act of 1956 or a savings association under section 10(e) of the Home Owners' Loan Act, if–
    A. the acquisition occurs solely as part of a reorganization in which security holders exchange their shares of a bank or savings association for shares of a newly formed holding company with no significant assets other than securities of the bank or savings association and the existing subsidiaries of the bank or savings association;
    B. the security holders receive, after that reorganization, substantially the same proportional share interests in the holding company as they held in the bank or savings association, except for nominal changes in shareholders' interests resulting from lawful elimination of fractional interests and the exercise of dissenting shareholders' rights under State or Federal law;
    C. the rights and interests of security holders in the holding company are substantially the same as those in the bank or savings association prior to the transaction, other than as may be required by law; and
    D. the holding company has substantially the same assets and liabilities, on a consolidated basis, as the bank or savings association had prior to the transaction.

    For purposes of this paragraph, the term "savings association" means a savings association (as defined in section 3(b) of the Federal Deposit Insurance Act) the deposits of which are insured by the Federal Deposit Insurance Corporation.
13. Any security issued by or any interest or participation in any church plan, company or account that is excluded from the definition of an investment company under section 3(c)(14).
14. Any security futures product that is–
    A. cleared by a clearing agency registered under section 17A of the Securities Exchange Act of 1934 or exempt from registration under subsection (b)(7) of such section 17A; and
    B. traded on a national securities exchange or a national securities association registered pursuant to section 15A(a) of the Securities Exchange Act of 1934.

b. **Additional exemptions**
    1. Small Issues Exemptive Authority. The Commission may from time to time by its rules and regulations, and subject to such terms and conditions as may be prescribed therein, add any class of securities to the securities exempted as provided in this section, if it finds that the enforcement of this title with respect to such securities is not necessary in the public interest and for the protection of investors by reason of the small amount involved or the limited character of the public offering; but no issue of securities shall be exempted under this subsection where the aggregate amount at which such issue is offered to the public exceeds $5,000,000.
    2. Additional Issues. The Commission shall by rule or regulation add a class of securities to the securities exempted pursuant to this section in accordance with the following terms and conditions:

    A.   The aggregate offering amount of all securities offered and sold within the prior 12-month period in reliance on the exemption added in accordance with this paragraph shall not exceed $50,000,000.

    B.   The securities may be offered and sold publicly.

    C.   The securities shall not be restricted securities within the meaning of the Federal securities laws and the regulations promulgated thereunder.

    D.   The civil liability provision in section 12(a)(2) shall apply to any person offering or selling such securities.

    E.   The issuer may solicit interest in the offering prior to filing any offering statement, on such terms and conditions as the Commission may prescribe in the public interest or for the protection of investors.

    F.   The Commission shall require the issuer to file audited financial statements with the Commission annually.

    G.   Such other terms, conditions, or requirements as the Commission may determine necessary in the public interest and for the protection of investors, which may include

        i.   a requirement that the issuer prepare and electronically file with the Commission and distribute to prospective investors an offering statement, and any related documents, in such form and with such content as prescribed by the Commission, including audited financial statements, a description of the issuer's business operations, its financial condition, its corporate governance principles, its use of investor funds, and other appropriate matters; and

        ii. disqualification provisions under which the exemption shall not be available to the issuer or its predecessors, affiliates, officers, directors, underwriters, or other related persons, which shall be substantially similar to the disqualification provisions contained in the regulations adopted in accordance with section 926 of the Dodd-Frank Wall Street Reform and Consumer Protection Act.

3.   Limitation. Only the following types of securities may be exempted under a rule or regulation adopted pursuant to paragraph (2): equity securities, debt securities, and debt securities convertible or exchangeable to equity interests, including any guarantees of such securities.

4.   Periodic Disclosures. Upon such terms and conditions as the Commission determines necessary in the public interest and for the protection of investors, the Commission by rule or regulation may require an issuer of a class of securities exempted under paragraph (2) to make available to investors and file with the Commission periodic disclosures regarding the issuer, its business operations, its financial condition, its corporate governance principles, its use of investor funds, and other appropriate matters, and also may provide for the suspension and termination of such a requirement with respect to that issuer.

5.   Adjustment. Not later than 2 years after the date of enactment of the Small Company Capital Formation Act of 2011 and every 2 years thereafter, the Commission shall review the offering amount limitation described in paragraph (2)(A) and shall increase such amount as the Commission determines

appropriate. If the Commission determines not to increase such amount, it shall report to the Committee on Financial Services of the House of Representatives and the Committee on Banking, Housing, and Urban Affairs of the Senate on its reasons for not increasing the amount.

Section 4 – Exempted Transactions

a. The provisions of section 5 shall not apply to–
    1. transactions by any person other than an issuer, underwriter, or dealer.
    2. transactions by an issuer not involving any public offering.
    3. transactions by a dealer (including an underwriter no longer acting as an underwriter in respect of the security involved in such transaction), except–
        A. transactions taking place prior to the expiration of forty days after the first date upon which the security was bona fide offered to the public by the issuer or by or through an underwriter,
        B. transactions in a security as to which a registration statement has been filed taking place prior to the expiration of forty days after the effective date of such registration statement or prior to the expiration of forty days after the first date upon which the security was bona fide offered to the public by the issuer or by or through an underwriter after such effective date, whichever is later (excluding in the computation of such forty days any time during which a stop order issued under section 8 is in effect as to the security), or such shorter period as the Commission may specify by rules and regulations or order, and
        C. transactions as to securities constituting the whole or a part of an unsold allotment to or subscription by such dealer as a participant in the distribution of such securities by the issuer or by or through an underwriter.
        With respect to transactions referred to in clause (B), if securities of the issuer have not previously been sold pursuant to an earlier effective registration statement the applicable period, instead of forty days, shall be ninety days, or such shorter period as the Commission may specify by rules and regulations or order.
    4. brokers' transactions executed upon customers' orders on any exchange or in the over-the-counter market but not the solicitation of such orders.
    5. transactions involving offers or sales by an issuer solely to one or more accredited investors, if the aggregate offering price of an issue of securities offered in reliance on this paragraph does not exceed the amount allowed under section 3(b)(1) of this title, if there is no advertising or public solicitation in connection with the transaction by the issuer or anyone acting on the issuer's behalf, and the issuer files such notice with Commission as the Commission shall prescribe.
    6. transactions involving the offer or sale of securities by an issuer (including all entities controlled by or under common control with the issuer), provided that—
        A. the aggregate amount sold to all investors by the issuer, including any amount sold in reliance on the exemption provided under this paragraph during the 12-month period preceding the date of such transaction, is not more than $1,000,000;

B.   the aggregate amount sold to any investor by an issuer, including any amount sold in reliance on the exemption provided under this paragraph during the 12-month period preceding the date of such transaction, does not exceed—

  i.   the greater of $2,000 or 5 percent of the annual income or net worth of such investor, as applicable, if either the annual income or the net worth of the investor is less than $100,000; and

  ii.   10 percent of the annual income or net worth of such investor, as applicable, not to exceed a maximum aggregate amount sold of $100,000, if either the annual income or net worth of the investor is equal to or more than $100,000;

C.   the transaction is conducted through a broker or funding portal that complies with the requirements of section 4A(a); and

D.   the issuer complies with the requirements of section 4A(b).

7.   transactions meeting the requirements of subsection (d).

b.   Offers and sales exempt under Rule 506 under the Securities Act of 1933 (as revised pursuant to section 201 of the Jumpstart Our Business Start-ups Act) shall not be deemed public offerings under the Federal securities laws as a result of general advertising or general solicitation.

c.

1.   With respect to securities offered and sold in compliance with Rule 506 of Regulation D under this Act, no person who meets the conditions set forth in paragraph (2) shall be subject to registration as a broker or dealer pursuant to section 15(a)(1) of [the Securities Exchange Act of 1934], solely because—

A.   that person maintains a platform or mechanism that permits the offer, sale, purchase, or negotiation of or with respect to securities, or permits general solicitations, general advertisements, or similar or related activities by issuers of such securities, whether online, in person, or through any other means;

B.   that person or any person associated with that person co-invests in such securities; or

C.   that person or any person associated with that person provides ancillary services with respect to such securities.

2.   The exemption provided in paragraph (1) shall apply to any person described in such paragraph if—

A.   such person and each person associated with that person receives no compensation in connection with the purchase or sale of such security;

B.   such person and each person associated with that person does not have possession of customer funds or securities in connection with the purchase or sale of such security; and

C.   such person is not subject to a statutory disqualification as defined in section 3(a)(39) of this title and does not have any person associated with that person subject to such a statutory disqualification.

3. For the purposes of this subsection, the term 'ancillary services' means—
    A. the provision of due diligence services, in connection with the offer, sale, purchase, or negotiation of such security, so long as such services do not include, for separate compensation, investment advice or recommendations to issuers or investors; and
    B. the provision of standardized documents to the issuers and investors, so long as such person or entity does not negotiate the terms of the issuance for and on behalf of third parties and issuers are not required to use the standardized documents as a condition of using the service.

d. **Certain Accredited Investor Transactions**. The transactions referred to in subsection (a)(7) are transactions meeting the following requirements:
    1. Accredited Investor Requirement. Each purchaser is an accredited investor, as that term is defined in section Rule 501(a) of Regulation D (or any successor regulation).
    2. Prohibition on General Solicitation or Advertising. Neither the seller, nor any person acting on the seller's behalf, offers or sells securities by any form of general solicitation or general advertising.
    3. Information Requirements. In the case of a transaction involving the securities of an issuer that is neither subject to section 13 or 15(d) of the Securities Exchange Act of 1934, nor exempt from reporting pursuant to Rule 12g3–2(b) of the Securities Exchange Act of 1934, nor a foreign government (as defined in Rule 405 eligible to register securities under Schedule B, the seller and a prospective purchaser designated by the seller obtain from the issuer, upon request of the seller, and the seller in all cases makes available to a prospective purchaser, the following information (which shall be reasonably current in relation to the date of resale under this section):
        A. The exact name of the issuer and the issuer's predecessor (if any).
        B. The address of the issuer's principal executive offices.
        C. The exact title and class of the security.
        D. The par or stated value of the security.
        E. The number of shares or total amount of the securities outstanding as of the end of the issuer's most recent fiscal year.
        F. The name and address of the transfer agent, corporate secretary, or other person responsible for transferring shares and stock certificates.
        G. A statement of the nature of the business of the issuer and the products and services it offers, which shall be presumed reasonably current if the statement is as of 12 months before the transaction date.
        H. The names of the officers and directors of the issuer.
        I. The names of any persons registered as a broker, dealer, or agent that shall be paid or given, directly or indirectly, any commission or remuneration for such person's participation in the offer or sale of the securities.
        J. The issuer's most recent balance sheet and profit and loss statement and similar financial statements, which shall—
            i.   be for such part of the 2 preceding fiscal years as the issuer has been in operation;
            ii. be prepared in accordance with generally accepted accounting principles or, in the case of a foreign private issuer, be prepared in

> accordance with generally accepted accounting principles or the International Financial Reporting Standards issued by the International Accounting Standards Board;
>
> iii. be presumed reasonably current if—
>
>   I.   with respect to the balance sheet, the balance sheet is as of a date less than 16 months before the transaction date; and
>
>   II. with respect to the profit and loss statement, such statement is for the 12 months preceding the date of the issuer's balance sheet; and
>
> iv. if the balance sheet is not as of a date less than 6 months before the transaction date, be accompanied by additional statements of profit and loss for the period from the date of such balance sheet to a date less than 6 months before the transaction date.

K. To the extent that the seller is a control person with respect to the issuer, a brief statement regarding the nature of the affiliation, and a statement certified by such seller that they have no reasonable grounds to believe that the issuer is in violation of the securities laws or regulations.

4. Issuers Disqualified. The transaction is not for the sale of a security where the seller is an issuer or a subsidiary, either directly or indirectly, of the issuer.

5. Bad Actor Prohibition. Neither the seller, nor any person that has been or will be paid (directly or indirectly) remuneration or a commission for their participation in the offer or sale of the securities, including solicitation of purchasers for the seller is subject to an event that would disqualify an issuer or other covered person under Rule 506(d)(1) of Regulation D or is subject to a statutory disqualification described under section 3(a)(39) of the Securities Exchange Act of 1934.

6. Business Requirement. The issuer is engaged in business, is not in the organizational stage or in bankruptcy or receivership, and is not a blank check, blind pool, or shell company that has no specific business plan or purpose or has indicated that the issuer's primary business plan is to engage in a merger or combination of the business with, or an acquisition of, an unidentified person.

7. Underwriter Prohibition. The transaction is not with respect to a security that constitutes the whole or part of an unsold allotment to, or a subscription or participation by, a broker or dealer as an underwriter of the security or a redistribution.

8. Outstanding Class Requirement. The transaction is with respect to a security of a class that has been authorized and outstanding for at least 90 days prior to the date of the transaction.

e. **Additional Requirements**.

1. In General. With respect to an exempted transaction described under subsection (a)(7):

A. Securities acquired in such transaction shall be deemed to have been acquired in a transaction not involving any public offering.

B. Such transaction shall be deemed not to be a distribution for purposes of section 2(a)(11).

C. Securities involved in such transaction shall be deemed to be restricted securities within the meaning of Rule 144.

2.   Rule of Construction. The exemption provided by subsection (a)(7) shall not be the exclusive means for establishing an exemption from the registration requirements of section 5.

Section 4A – Requirements With Respect to Certain Small Transactions

a.   **Requirements on Intermediaries.** A person acting as an intermediary in a transaction involving the offer or sale of securities for the account of others pursuant to section 4[(a)](6) shall—
1.   register with the Commission as—
   A. a broker; or
   B. a funding portal (as defined in section 3(a)(80) of the Securities Exchange Act of 1934);
2.   register with any applicable self-regulatory organization (as defined in section 3(a)(26) of the Securities Exchange Act of 1934);
3.   provide such disclosures, including disclosures related to risks and other investor education materials, as the Commission shall, by rule, determine appropriate;
4.   ensure that each investor—
   A. reviews investor-education information, in accordance with standards established by the Commission, by rule;
   B. positively affirms that the investor understands that the investor is risking the loss of the entire investment, and that the investor could bear such a loss; and
   C. answers questions demonstrating—
      i.   an understanding of the level of risk generally applicable to investments in startups, emerging businesses, and small issuers;
      ii. an understanding of the risk of illiquidity; and
      iii. an understanding of such other matters as the Commission determines appropriate, by rule;
5.   take such measures to reduce the risk of fraud with respect to such transactions, as established by the Commission, by rule, including obtaining a background and securities enforcement regulatory history check on each officer, director, and person holding more than 20 percent of the outstanding equity of every issuer whose securities are offered by such person;
6.   not later than 21 days prior to the first day on which securities are sold to any investor (or such other period as the Commission may establish), make available to the Commission and to potential investors any information provided by the issuer pursuant to subsection (b);
7.   ensure that all offering proceeds are only provided to the issuer when the aggregate capital raised from all investors is equal to or greater than a target offering amount, and allow all investors to cancel their commitments to invest, as the Commission shall, by rule, determine appropriate;
8.   make such efforts as the Commission determines appropriate, by rule, to ensure that no investor in a 12-month period has purchased securities offered pursuant to section 4[(a)](6) that, in the aggregate, from all issuers, exceed the investment limits set forth in section 4[(a)](6)(B);

9. take such steps to protect the privacy of information collected from investors as the Commission shall, by rule, determine appropriate;

10. not compensate promoters, finders, or lead generators for providing the broker or funding portal with the personal identifying information of any potential investor;

11. prohibit its directors, officers, or partners (or any person occupying a similar status or performing a similar function) from having any financial interest in an issuer using its services; and

12. meet such other requirements as the Commission may, by rule, prescribe, for the protection of investors and in the public interest.

b. **Requirements for Issuers.** For purposes of section 4[(a)](6), an issuer who offers or sells securities shall—

1. file with the Commission and provide to investors and the relevant broker or funding portal, and make available to potential investors—

    A. the name, legal status, physical address, and website address of the issuer;

    B. the names of the directors and officers (and any persons occupying a similar status or performing a similar function), and each person holding more than 20 percent of the shares of the issuer;

    C. a description of the business of the issuer and the anticipated business plan of the issuer;

    D. a description of the financial condition of the issuer, including, for offerings that, together with all other offerings of the issuer under section 4[(a)](6) within the preceding 12-month period, have, in the aggregate, target offering amounts of—

        i. $100,000 or less—

            I.   the income tax returns filed by the issuer for the most recently completed year (if any); and

            II. financial statements of the issuer, which shall be certified by the principal executive officer of the issuer to be true and complete in all material respects;

        ii. more than $100,000, but not more than $500,000, financial statements reviewed by a public accountant who is independent of the issuer, using professional standards and procedures for such review or standards and procedures established by the Commission, by rule, for such purpose; and

        iii. more than $500,000 (or such other amount as the Commission may establish, by rule), audited financial statements;

    E. a description of the stated purpose and intended use of the proceeds of the offering sought by the issuer with respect to the target offering amount;

    F. the target offering amount, the deadline to reach the target offering amount, and regular updates regarding the progress of the issuer in meeting the target offering amount;

    G. the price to the public of the securities or the method for determining the price, provided that, prior to sale, each investor shall be provided in writing the final price and all required disclosures, with a reasonable opportunity to rescind the commitment to purchase the securities;

H. a description of the ownership and capital structure of the issuer, including—

    i. terms of the securities of the issuer being offered and each other class of security of the issuer, including how such terms may be modified, and a summary of the differences between such securities, including how the rights of the securities being offered may be materially limited, diluted, or qualified by the rights of any other class of security of the issuer;

    ii. a description of how the exercise of the rights held by the principal shareholders of the issuer could negatively impact the purchasers of the securities being offered;

    iii. the name and ownership level of each existing shareholder who owns more than 20 percent of any class of the securities of the issuer;

    iv. how the securities being offered are being valued, and examples of methods for how such securities may be valued by the issuer in the future, including during subsequent corporate actions; and

    v. the risks to purchasers of the securities relating to minority ownership in the issuer, the risks associated with corporate actions, including additional issuances of shares, a sale of the issuer or of assets of the issuer, or transactions with related parties; and

I. such other information as the Commission may, by rule, prescribe, for the protection of investors and in the public interest;

2. not advertise the terms of the offering, except for notices which direct investors to the funding portal or broker;

3. not compensate or commit to compensate, directly or indirectly, any person to promote its offerings through communication channels provided by a broker or funding portal, without taking such steps as the Commission shall, by rule, require to ensure that such person clearly discloses the receipt, past or prospective, of such compensation, upon each instance of such promotional communication;

4. not less than annually, file with the Commission and provide to investors reports of the results of operations and financial statements of the issuer, as the Commission shall, by rule, determine appropriate, subject to such exceptions and termination dates as the Commission may establish, by rule; and

5. comply with such other requirements as the Commission may, by rule, prescribe, for the protection of investors and in the public interest.

c. **Liability for Material Misstatements and Omissions.**

1. Actions authorized.

A. In general. Subject to paragraph (2), a person who purchases a security in a transaction exempted by the provisions of section 4[(a)](6) may bring an action against an issuer described in paragraph (2), either at law or in equity in any court of competent jurisdiction, to recover the consideration paid for such security with interest thereon, less the amount of any income received thereon, upon the tender of such security, or for damages if such person no longer owns the security.

           B.   Liability. An action brought under this paragraph shall be subject to the provisions of section 12(b) and section 13, as if the liability were created under section 12(a)(2).

    2.   Applicability. An issuer shall be liable in an action under paragraph (1), if the issuer—

           A. by the use of any means or instruments of transportation or communication in interstate commerce or of the mails, by any means of any written or oral communication, in the offering or sale of a security in a transaction exempted by the provisions of section 4(6), makes an untrue statement of a material fact or omits to state a material fact required to be stated or necessary in order to make the statements, in the light of the circumstances under which they were made, not misleading, provided that the purchaser did not know of such untruth or omission; and

           B. does not sustain the burden of proof that such issuer did not know, and in the exercise of reasonable care could not have known, of such untruth or omission.

    3.   Definition. As used in this subsection, the term 'issuer' includes any person who is a director or partner of the issuer, and the principal executive officer or officers, principal financial officer, and controller or principal accounting officer of the issuer (and any person occupying a similar status or performing a similar function) that offers or sells a security in a transaction exempted by the provisions of section 4(6), and any person who offers or sells the security in such offering.

d.   **Information Available to States**. The Commission shall make, or shall cause to be made by the relevant broker or funding portal, the information described in subsection (b) and such other information as the Commission, by rule, determines appropriate, available to the securities commission (or any agency or office performing like functions) of each State and territory of the United States and the District of Columbia.

e.   **Restriction on Sales**. Securities issued pursuant to a transaction described in section 4[(a)](6)—

    1.   may not be transferred by the purchaser of such securities during the 1-year period beginning on the date of purchase, unless such securities are transferred—

           A. to the issuer of the securities;

           B. to an accredited investor;

           C. as part of an offering registered with the Commission; or

           D. to a member of the family of the purchaser or the equivalent, or in connection with the death or divorce of the purchaser or other similar circumstance, in the discretion of the Commission; and

    2.   shall be subject to such other limitations as the Commission shall, by rule, establish.

f. **Applicability**. Section 4[(a)](6) shall not apply to transactions involving the offer or sale of securities by any issuer that—
1. is not organized under and subject to the laws of a State or territory of the United States or the District of Columbia
2. is subject to the requirement to file reports pursuant to section 13 or section 15(d) of the Securities Exchange Act of 1934;
3. is an investment company, as defined in section 3 of the Investment Company Act of 1940, or is excluded from the definition of investment company by section 3(b) or section 3(c) of that Act; or
4. the Commission, by rule or regulation, determines appropriate.

g. **Rule of Construction**. Nothing in this section or § 4[(a)](6) shall be construed as preventing an issuer from raising capital through methods not described under § 4[(a)](6).

h. **Certain Calculations**.
1. Dollar Amounts. Dollar amounts in section 4[(a)](6) and subsection (b) of this section shall be adjusted by the Commission not less frequently than once every 5 years, by notice published in the Federal Register to reflect any change in the Consumer Price Index for All Urban Consumers published by the Bureau of Labor Statistics.
2. Income and Net Worth. The income and net worth of a natural person under section 4[(a)](6)(B) shall be calculated in accordance with any rules of the Commission under this title regarding the calculation of the income and net worth, respectively, of an accredited investor.

Section 5 – Prohibitions Relating to Interstate Commerce and the Mails

a. **Sale or delivery after sale of unregistered securities**
Unless a registration statement is in effect as to a security, it shall be unlawful for any person, directly or indirectly–
1. to make use of any means or instruments of transportation or communication in interstate commerce or of the mails to sell such security through the use or medium of any prospectus or otherwise; or
2. to carry or cause to be carried through the mails or in interstate commerce, by any means or instruments of transportation, any such security for the purpose of sale or for delivery after sale.

b. **Necessity of prospectus meeting requirements of section 10**
It shall be unlawful for any person, directly or indirectly–
1. to make use of any means or instruments of transportation or communication in interstate commerce or of the mails to carry or transmit any prospectus relating to any security with respect to which a registration statement has been filed under this title, unless such prospectus meets the requirements of section 10; or
2. to carry or cause to be carried through the mails or in interstate commerce any such security for the purpose of sale or for delivery after sale, unless accompanied or preceded by a prospectus that meets the requirements of subsection (a) of section 10.

c. **Necessity of filing registration statement**
    It shall be unlawful for any person, directly or indirectly, to make use of any means or instruments of transportation or communication in interstate commerce or of the mails to offer to sell or offer to buy through the use or medium of any prospectus or otherwise any security, unless a registration statement has been filed as to such security, or while the registration statement is the subject of a refusal order or stop order or (prior to the effective date of the registration statement) any public proceeding or examination under section 8.

d. **Limitation**. Notwithstanding any other provision of this section, an emerging growth company or any person authorized to act on behalf of an emerging growth company may engage in oral or written communications with potential investors that are qualified institutional buyers or institutions that are accredited investors, as such terms are respectively defined in section Rule 144A and Rule 501(a) of Regulation D, or any successor thereto, to determine whether such investors might have an interest in a contemplated securities offering, either prior to or following the date of filing of a registration statement with respect to such securities with the Commission, subject to the requirement of subsection (b)(2).

e. Notwithstanding the provisions of section 3 or 4, unless a registration statement meeting the requirements of section 10(a) is in effect as to a security-based swap, it shall be unlawful for any person, directly or indirectly, to make use of any means or instruments of transportation or communication in interstate commerce or of the mails to offer to sell, offer to buy or purchase or sell a security-based swap to any person who is not an eligible contract participant as defined in section 1a(18) of the Commodity Exchange Act.

Section 6 – Registration of Securities

a. **Method of registration**
    Any security may be registered with the Commission under the terms and conditions hereinafter provided, by filing a registration statement in triplicate, at least one of which shall be signed by each issuer, its principal executive officer or officers, its principal financial officer, its comptroller or principal accounting officer, and the majority of its board of directors or persons performing similar functions (or, if there is no board of directors or persons performing similar functions, by the majority of the persons or board having the power of management of the issuer), and in case the issuer is a foreign or Territorial person by its duly authorized representative in the United States; except that when such registration statement relates to a security issued by a foreign government, or political subdivision thereof, it need be signed only by the underwriter of such security. Signatures of all such persons when written on the

said registration statements shall be presumed to have been so written by authority of the person whose signature is so affixed and the burden of proof, in the event such authority shall be denied, shall be upon the party denying the same. The affixing of any signature without the authority of the purported signer shall constitute a violation of this title. A registration statement shall be deemed effective only as to securities specified therein as proposed to be offered.

e. **Emerging growth companies**
    1. In general. Any emerging growth company, prior to its initial public offering date, may confidentially submit to the Commission a draft registration statement, for confidential nonpublic review by the staff of the Commission prior to public filing, provided that the initial confidential submission and all amendments thereto shall be publicly filed with the Commission not later than 15 days before the date on which the issuer conducts a road show, as such term is defined in Securities Act Rule 433(h)(4), or any successor thereto. An issuer that was an emerging growth company at the time it submitted a confidential registration statement or, in lieu thereof, a publicly filed registration statement for review under this subsection but ceases to be an emerging growth company thereafter shall continue to be treated as an emerging market growth company for the purposes of this subsection through the earlier of the date on which the issuer consummates its initial public offering pursuant to such registrations statement or the end of the 1-year period beginning on the date the company ceases to be an emerging growth company.
    2. Confidentiality. Notwithstanding any other provision of this title, the Commission shall not be compelled to disclose any information provided to or obtained by the Commission pursuant to this subsection. For purposes of section 552 of title 5, United States Code, this subsection shall be considered a statute described in subsection (b)(3)(B) of such section 552. Information described in or obtained pursuant to this subsection shall be deemed to constitute confidential information for purposes of section 24(b)(2) of the Securities Exchange Act of 1934.

Section 7 – Information Required in Registration Statement

a. **Information required in a registration statement**
    1. In general. The registration statement, when relating to a security other than a security issued by a foreign government, or political subdivision thereof, shall contain the information, and be accompanied by the documents, specified in Schedule A, and when relating to a security issued by a foreign government, or political subdivision thereof, shall contain the information, and be accompanied by the documents, specified in Schedule B; except that the Commission may by rules or regulations provide that any such information or document need not be included in respect of any class of issuers or securities if it finds that the requirement of such information or document is inapplicable to such class and that disclosure fully adequate for the protection of investors is otherwise required to be included within the registration statement. If any accountant, engineer, or appraiser, or any person whose profession gives authority to a statement made by him, is named as having prepared or certified

any part of the registration statement, or is named as having prepared or certified a report or valuation for use in connection with the registration statement, the written consent of such person shall be filed with the registration statement. If any such person is named as having prepared or certified a report or valuation (other than a public official document or statement) which is used in connection with the registration statement, but is not named as having prepared or certified such report or valuation for use in connection with the registration statement, the written consent of such person shall be filed with the registration statement unless the Commission dispenses with such filing as impracticable or as involving undue hardship on the person filing the registration statement. Any such registration statement shall contain such other information, and be accompanied by such other documents, as the Commission may by rules or regulations require as being necessary or appropriate in the public interest or for the protection of investors.

2. Treatment of emerging growth companies. An emerging growth company
   A. need not present more than 2 years of audited financial statements in order for the registration statement of such emerging growth company with respect to an initial public offering of its common equity securities to be effective, and in any other registration statement to be filed with the Commission, an emerging growth company need not present selected financial data in accordance with section 301 of Regulation S-K for any period prior to the earliest audited period presented in connection with its initial public offering; and
   B. may not be required to comply with any new or revised financial accounting standard until such date that a company that is not an issuer (as defined under section 2(a) of the Sarbanes-Oxley Act of 2002 is required to comply with such new or revised accounting standard, if such standard applies to companies that are not issuers.

c. **Disclosure requirements**
   1. In general. The Commission shall adopt regulations under this subsection requiring each issuer of an asset-backed security to disclose, for each tranche or class of security, information regarding the assets backing that security.
   2. Content of regulations. In adopting regulations under this subsection, the Commission shall—
      A. set standards for the format of the data provided by issuers of an asset-backed security, which shall, to the extent feasible, facilitate comparison of such data across securities in similar types of asset classes; and
      B. require issuers of asset-backed securities, at a minimum, to disclose asset-level or loan-level data, if such data are necessary for investors to independently perform due diligence, including—
         i. data having unique identifiers relating to loan brokers or originators;
         ii. the nature and extent of the compensation of the broker or originator of the assets backing the security; and
         iii. the amount of risk retention by the originator and the securitizer of such assets.

d. **Registration statement for asset-backed securities**
Not later than 180 days after the date of enactment of this subsection, the Commission shall issue rules relating to the registration statement required to be filed by any issuer of an asset-backed security (as that term is defined in § 3(a)(77) of the Securities Exchange Act of 1934) that require any issuer of an asset-backed security—
1. to perform a review of the assets underlying the asset-backed security; and
2. to disclose the nature of the review under paragraph (1).

Section 8 – Taking Effect of Registration Statements and Amendments Thereto

a. **Effective date of registration statement.** Except as hereinafter provided, the effective date of a registration statement shall be the twentieth day after the filing thereof or such earlier date as the Commission may determine, having due regard to the adequacy of the information respecting the issuer theretofore available to the public, to the facility with which the nature of the securities to be registered, their relationship to the capital structure of the issuer and the rights of holders thereof can be understood, and to the public interest and the protection of investors. If any amendment to any such statement is filed prior to the effective date of such statement, the registration statement shall be deemed to have been filed when such amendment was filed; except that an amendment filed with the consent of the Commission, prior to the effective date of the registration statement, or filed pursuant to an order of the Commission, shall be treated as a part of the registration statement.

b. **Incomplete or inaccurate registration statement.** If it appears to the Commission that a registration statement is on its face incomplete or inaccurate in any material respect, the Commission may, after notice by personal service or the sending of confirmed telegraphic notice not later than ten days after the filing of the registration statement, and opportunity for hearing (at a time fixed by the Commission) within ten days after such notice by personal service or the sending of such telegraphic notice, issue an order prior to the effective date of registration refusing to permit such statement to become effective until it has been amended in accordance with such order. When such statement has been amended in accordance with such order the Commission shall so declare and the registration shall become effective at the time provided in subsection (a) of this section or upon the date of such declaration, whichever date is the later.

c. **Effective date of amendment to registration statement.** An amendment filed after the effective date of the registration statement, if such amendment, upon its face, appears to the Commission not to be incomplete or inaccurate in any material respect, shall become effective on such date as the Commission may determine, having due regard to the public interest and the protection of investors.

d. **Untrue statements or omissions in registration statement.** If it appears to the Commission at any time that the registration statement includes any untrue statement of a material fact or omits to state any material fact required to be stated therein or necessary to make the statements therein not misleading, the Commission may, after notice by personal service or the sending of confirmed telegraphic notice, and after opportunity for hearing (at a time fixed by the Commission) within fifteen days after such notice by personal service or the sending of such telegraphic notice, issue a stop order suspending the effectiveness of the registration statement. When such statement has been amended in accordance with such stop order, the Commission shall so declare and thereupon the stop order shall cease to be effective.

e. **Examination for issuance of stop order.** The Commission is empowered to make an examination in any case in order to determine whether a stop order should issue under subsection (d) of this section. In making such examination the Commission or any officer or officers designated by it shall have access to and may demand the production of any books and papers of, and may administer oaths and affirmations to and examine, the issuer, underwriter, or any other person, in respect of any matter relevant to the examination, and may, in its discretion, require the production of a balance sheet exhibiting the assets and liabilities of the issuer, or its income statement, or both, to be certified to by a public or certified accountant approved by the Commission. If the issuer or underwriter shall fail to cooperate, or shall obstruct or refuse to permit the making of an examination, such conduct shall be proper ground for the issuance of a stop order.

f. **Notice requirements.** Any notice required under this section shall be sent to or served on the issuer, or, in case of a foreign government or political subdivision thereof, to or on the underwriter, or, in the case of a foreign or Territorial person, to or on its duly authorized representative in the United States named in the registration statement, properly directed in each case of telegraphic notice to the address given in such statement.

Section 10 – Information Required in Prospectus

a. **Information in registration statement; documents not required**
Except to the extent otherwise permitted or required pursuant to this subsection or subsections (c), (d), or (e)–
1. a prospectus relating to a security other than a security issued by a foreign government or political subdivision thereof, shall contain the information contained in the registration statement, but it need not include the documents referred to in paragraphs (28) to (32), inclusive, of Schedule A;
2. a prospectus relating to a security issued by a foreign government or political subdivision thereof shall contain the information contained in the registration statement, but it need not include the documents referred to in paragraphs (13) and (14) of Schedule B;
3. notwithstanding the provisions of paragraphs (1) and (2) of this subsection (a) when a prospectus is used more than nine months after the effective date of the registration statement, the information contained therein shall be as of a date not more than sixteen months prior to such use, so far as such information is known to the user of such prospectus or can be furnished by such user without unreasonable effort or expense;
4. there may be omitted from any prospectus any of the information required under this subsection (a) which the Commission may by rules or regulations designate as not being necessary or appropriate in the public interest or for the protection of investors.

b. **Summarizations and omissions allowed by rules and regulations.** In addition to the prospectus permitted or required in subsection (a), the Commission shall by rules or regulations deemed necessary or appropriate in the public interest or for the protection of investors permit the use of a prospectus for the purposes of subsection (b)(1) of section 5 which omits in part or summarizes information in the prospectus specified in subsection (a). A prospectus permitted under this subsection shall, except to the extent the Commission by rules or regulations deemed necessary or appropriate in the public interest or for the protection of investors otherwise provides, be filed as part of the registration statement but shall not be deemed a part of such registration statement for the purposes of section 11. The Commission may at any time issue an order preventing or suspending the use of a prospectus permitted under this subsection (b), if it has reason to believe that such prospectus has not been filed (if required to be filed as part of the registration statement) or includes any untrue statement of a material fact or omits to state any material fact required to be stated therein or necessary to make the statements therein, in the light of the circumstances under which such prospectus is or is to be used, not misleading. Upon issuance of an order under this subsection, the Commission shall give notice of the issuance of such order and opportunity for hearing by personal service or the sending of confirmed telegraphic notice. The Commission shall vacate or modify the order at any time for good cause or if such prospectus has been filed or amended in accordance with such order.

c. **Additional information required by rules and regulations**. Any prospectus shall contain such other information as the Commission may by rules or regulations require as being necessary or appropriate in the public interest or for the protection of investors.

d. **Classification of prospectuses.** In the exercise of its powers under subsections (a), (b), or (c), the Commission shall have authority to classify prospectuses according to the nature and circumstances of their use or the nature of the security, issue, issuer, or otherwise, and, by rules and regulations and subject to such terms and conditions as it shall specify therein, to prescribe as to each class the form and contents which it may find appropriate and consistent with the public interest and the protection of investors.

e. **Information in conspicuous part of prospectus.** The statements or information required to be included in a prospectus by or under authority of subsections (a), (b), (c), or (d), when written, shall be placed in a conspicuous part of the prospectus and, except as otherwise permitted by rules or regulations, in type as large as that used generally in the body of the prospectus.

f. **Prospectus consisting of radio or television broadcast.** In any case where a prospectus consists of a radio or television broadcast, copies thereof shall be filed with the Commission under such rules and regulations as it shall prescribe. The Commission may by rules and regulations require the filing with it of forms and prospectuses used in connection with the offer or sale of securities registered under this title.

Section 11 – Civil Liabilities on Account of False Registration Statement

a. **Persons possessing cause of action; persons liable.** In case any part of the registration statement, when such part became effective, contained an untrue statement of a material fact or omitted to state a material fact required to be stated therein or necessary to make the statements therein not misleading, any person acquiring such security (unless it is proved that at the time of such acquisition he knew of such untruth or omission) may, either at law or in equity, in any court of competent jurisdiction, sue–

    1. every person who signed the registration statement;
    2. every person who was a director of (or person performing similar functions) or partner in the issuer at the time of the filing of the part of the registration statement with respect to which his liability is asserted;
    3. every person who, with his consent, is named in the registration statement as being or about to become a director, person performing similar functions, or partner;
    4. every accountant, engineer, or appraiser, or any person whose profession gives authority to a statement made by him, who has with his consent been named as having prepared or certified any part of the registration statement, or as having prepared or certified any report or valuation which is used in connection with the registration statement, with respect to the statement in such registration statement, report, or valuation, which purports to have been prepared or certified by him;
    5. every underwriter with respect to such security.

    If such person acquired the security after the issuer has made generally available to its security holders an earning statement covering a period of at least twelve months beginning after the effective date of the registration statement, then the right of recovery under this subsection shall be conditioned on proof that such person acquired the security relying upon such untrue statement in the registration statement or relying upon the registration statement and not knowing of such omission, but such reliance may be established without proof of the reading of the registration statement by such person.

b. **Persons exempt from liability upon proof of issues.** Notwithstanding the provisions of subsection (a) of this section no person, other than the issuer, shall be liable as provided therein who shall sustain the burden of proof–

    1. that before the effective date of the part of the registration statement with respect to which his liability is asserted (A) he had resigned from or had taken such steps as are permitted by law to resign from, or ceased or refused to act in, every office, capacity, or relationship in which he was described in the registration statement as acting or agreeing to act, and (B) he had advised the Commission and the issuer in writing that he had taken such action and that he would not be responsible for such part of the registration statement; or
    2. that if such part of the registration statement became effective without his knowledge, upon becoming aware of such fact he forthwith acted and advised the Commission, in accordance with paragraph (1) of this subsection, and, in addition, gave reasonable public notice that such part of the registration statement had become effective without his knowledge; or

3.   that (A) as regards any part of the registration statement not purporting to be made on the authority of an expert, and not purporting to be a copy of or extract from a report or valuation of an expert, and not purporting to be made on the authority of a public official document or statement, he had, after reasonable investigation, reasonable ground to believe and did believe, at the time such part of the registration statement became effective, that the statements therein were true and that there was no omission to state a material fact required to be stated therein or necessary to make the statements therein not misleading; and (B) as regards any part of the registration statement purporting to be made upon his authority as an expert or purporting to be a copy of or extract from a report or valuation of himself as an expert, (i) he had, after reasonable investigation, reasonable ground to believe and did believe, at the time such part of the registration statement became effective, that the statements therein were true and that there was no omission to state a material fact required to be stated therein or necessary to make the statements therein not misleading, or (ii) such part of the registration statement did not fairly represent his statement as an expert or was not a fair copy of or extract from his report or valuation as an expert; and (C) as regards any part of the registration statement purporting to be made on the authority of an expert (other than himself) or purporting to be a copy of or extract from a report or valuation of an expert (other than himself), he had no reasonable ground to believe and did not believe, at the time such part of the registration statement became effective, that the statements therein were untrue or that there was an omission to state a material fact required to be stated therein or necessary to make the statements therein not misleading, or that such part of the registration statement did not fairly represent the statement of the expert or was not a fair copy of or extract from the report or valuation of the expert; and (D) as regards any part of the registration statement purporting to be a statement made by an official person or purporting to be a copy of or extract from a public official document, he had no reasonable ground to believe and did not believe, at the time such part of the registration statement became effective, that the statements therein were untrue, or that there was an omission to state a material fact required to be stated therein or necessary to make the statements therein not misleading, or that such part of the registration statement did not fairly represent the statement made by the official person or was not a fair copy of or extract from the public official document.

c.   **Standard of reasonableness.** In determining, for the purpose of paragraph (3) of subsection (b) of this section, what constitutes reasonable investigation and reasonable ground for belief, the standard of reasonableness shall be that required of a prudent man in the management of his own property.

d.   **Effective date of registration statement with regard to underwriters.** If any person becomes an underwriter with respect to the security after the part of the registration statement with respect to which his liability is asserted has become effective, then for the purposes of paragraph (3) of subsection (b) of this section such part of the registration statement shall be considered as having become effective with respect to such person as of the time when he became an underwriter.

e.   **Measure of damages; undertaking for payment of costs**. The suit authorized under subsection (a) of this section may be to recover such damages as shall represent the difference between the amount paid for the security (not exceeding the price at which the security was offered to the public) and (1) the value thereof as of the time such suit was brought, or (2) the price at which such security shall have been disposed of in the market before suit, or (3) the price at which such security shall have been disposed of after suit but before judgment if such damages shall be less than the damages representing the difference between the amount paid for the security (not exceeding the price at which the security was offered to the public) and the value thereof as of the time such suit was brought: *Provided,* that if the defendant proves that any portion or all of such damages represents other than the depreciation in value of such security resulting from such part of the registration statement, with respect to which his liability is asserted, not being true or omitting to state a material fact required to be stated therein or necessary to make the statements therein not misleading, such portion of or all such damages shall not be recoverable. In no event shall any underwriter (unless such underwriter shall have knowingly received from the issuer for acting as an underwriter some benefit, directly or indirectly, in which all other underwriters similarly situated did not share in proportion to their respective interests in the underwriting) be liable in any suit or as a consequence of suits authorized under subsection (a) of this section for damages in excess of the total price at which the securities underwritten by him and distributed to the public were offered to the public. In any suit under this or any other section of this title the court may, in its discretion, require an undertaking for the payment of the costs of such suit, including reasonable attorney's fees, and if judgment shall be rendered against a party litigant, upon the motion of the other party litigant, such costs may be assessed in favor of such party litigant (whether or not such undertaking has been required) if the court believes the suit or the defense to have been without merit, in an amount sufficient to reimburse him for the reasonable expenses incurred by him, in connection with such suit, such costs to be taxed in the manner usually provided for taxing of costs in the court in which the suit was heard.

f.   **Joint and several liability; liability of outside director**
1.   Except as provided in paragraph (2), all or any one or more of the persons specified in subsection (a) of this section shall be jointly and severally liable, and every person who becomes liable to make any payment under this section may recover contribution as in cases of contract from any person who, if sued separately, would have been liable to make the same payment, unless the person who has become liable was, and the other was not, guilty of fraudulent misrepresentation.
2.   A.   The liability of an outside director under subsection (e) shall be determined in accordance with section 21D(f) of the Securities Exchange Act of 1934.
     B.   For purposes of this paragraph, the term "outside director" shall have the meaning given such term by rule or regulation of the Commission.

g.   **Offering price to public as maximum amount recoverable.** In no case shall the amount recoverable under this section exceed the price at which the security was offered to the public.

Section 12 – Civil Liabilities Arising in Connection with Prospectuses and Communications

a. **In general**

Any person who–

1. offers or sells a security in violation of section 5, or

2. offers or sells a security (whether or not exempted by the provisions of section 3, other than paragraphs (2) and (14) of subsection (a) of said section), by the use of any means or instruments of transportation or communication in interstate commerce or of the mails, by means of a prospectus or oral communication, which includes an untrue statement of a material fact or omits to state a material fact necessary in order to make the statements, in the light of the circumstances under which they were made, not misleading (the purchaser not knowing of such untruth or omission), and who shall not sustain the burden of proof that he did not know, and in the exercise of reasonable care could not have known, of such untruth or omission,

shall be liable, subject to subsection (b), to the person purchasing such security from him, who may sue either at law or in equity in any court of competent jurisdiction, to recover the consideration paid for such security with interest thereon, less the amount of any income received thereon, upon the tender of such security, or for damages if he no longer owns the security.

b. **Loss causation.** In an action described in subsection (a)(2), if the person who offered or sold such security proves that any portion or all of the amount recoverable under subsection (a)(2) represents other than the depreciation in value of the subject security resulting from such part of the prospectus or oral communication, with respect to which the liability of that person is asserted, not being true or omitting to state a material fact required to be stated therein or necessary to make the statement not misleading, then such portion or amount, as the case may be, shall not be recoverable.

Section 13 – Limitation of Actions

No action shall be maintained to enforce any liability created under section 11 or section 12(a)(2) unless brought within one year after the discovery of the untrue statement or the omission, or after such discovery should have been made by the exercise of reasonable diligence, or, if the action is to enforce a liability created under section 12(a)(1), unless brought within one year after the violation upon which it is based. In no event shall any such action be brought to enforce a liability created under section 11 or section 12(a)(1) more than three years after the security was bona fide offered to the public, or under section 12(a)(2) more than three years after the sale.

Section 14 – Contrary Stipulations Void

Any condition, stipulation, or provision binding any person acquiring any security to waive compliance with any provision of this title or of the rules and regulations of the Commission shall be void.

Section 15 – Liability of Controlling Persons

a. **Controlling persons**

Every person who, by or through stock ownership, agency, or otherwise, or who, pursuant to or in connection with an agreement or understanding with one or more other persons by or through stock ownership, agency, or otherwise, controls any person liable under section 11 or 12, shall also be liable jointly and severally with and to the same extent as such controlled person to any person to whom such controlled person is liable, unless the controlling person had no knowledge of or reasonable ground to believe in the existence of the facts by reason of which the liability of the controlled person is alleged to exist.

b. **Prosecution of persons who aid and abet violations.**

For purposes of any action brought by the Commission under subparagraph (b) or (d) of section 20, any person that knowingly or recklessly provides substantial assistance to another person in violation of a provision of this Act, or of any rule or regulation issued under this Act, shall be deemed to be in violation of such provision to the same extent as the person to whom such assistance is provided.

Section 16 – Additional Remedies; Limitation on Remedies

a. **Remedies additional**

Except as provided in subsection (b), the rights and remedies provided by this title shall be in addition to any and all other rights and remedies that may exist at law or in equity.

b. **Class action limitations**

No covered class action based upon the statutory or common law of any State or subdivision thereof may be maintained in any State or Federal court by any private party alleging–

1. an untrue statement or omission of a material fact in connection with the purchase or sale of a covered security; or
2. that the defendant used or employed any manipulative or deceptive device or contrivance in connection with the purchase or sale of a covered security.

c. **Removal of covered class actions**

Any covered class action brought in any State court involving a covered security, as set forth in subsection (b), shall be removable to the Federal district court for the district in which the action is pending, and shall be subject to subsection (b).

d. **Preservation of certain actions**
    1.   Actions under State law of State of incorporation
        A. Actions preserved
            Notwithstanding subsection (b) or (c), a covered class action described in subparagraph (B) of this paragraph that is based upon the statutory or common law of the State in which the issuer is incorporated (in the case of a corporation) or organized (in the case of any other entity) may be maintained in a State or Federal court by a private party.
        B. Permissible actions
            A covered class action is described in this subparagraph if it involves–
            i.   the purchase or sale of securities by the issuer or an affiliate of the issuer exclusively from or to holders of equity securities of the issuer; or
            ii.   any recommendation, position, or other communication with respect to the sale of securities of the issuer that–
                I.   is made by or on behalf of the issuer or an affiliate of the issuer to holders of equity securities of the issuer; and
                II.   concerns decisions of those equity holders with respect to voting their securities, acting in response to a tender or exchange offer, or exercising dissenters' or appraisal rights.
    2.   State actions
        A. In general
            Notwithstanding any other provision of this section, nothing in this section may be construed to preclude a State or political subdivision thereof or a State pension plan from bringing an action involving a covered security on its own behalf, or as a member of a class comprised solely of other States, political subdivisions, or State pension plans that are named plaintiffs, and that have authorized participation, in such action.
        B. State pension plan defined
            For purposes of this paragraph, the term "State pension plan" means a pension plan established and maintained for its employees by the government of the State or political subdivision thereof, or by any agency or instrumentality thereof.
    3.   Actions under contractual agreements between issuers and indenture trustees
        Notwithstanding subsection (b) or (c), a covered class action that seeks to enforce a contractual agreement between an issuer and an indenture trustee may be maintained in a State or Federal court by a party to the agreement or a successor to such party.
    4.   Remand of removed actions
        In an action that has been removed from a State court pursuant to subsection (c), if the Federal court determines that the action may be maintained in State court pursuant to this subsection, the Federal court shall remand such action to such State court.

e. **Preservation of State jurisdiction**
The securities commission (or any agency or office performing like functions) of any State shall retain jurisdiction under the laws of such State to investigate and bring enforcement actions.

f.   **Definitions**
     For purposes of this section, the following definitions shall apply:
     1.   Affiliate of the issuer
          The term "affiliate of the issuer" means a person that directly or indirectly, through one or more intermediaries, controls or is controlled by or is under common control with, the issuer.
     2.   Covered class action
          A.   In general
               The term "covered class action" means–
               i.   any single lawsuit in which–
                    I.   damages are sought on behalf of more than 50 persons or prospective class members, and questions of law or fact common to those persons or members of the prospective class, without reference to issues of individualized reliance on an alleged misstatement or omission, predominate over any questions affecting only individual persons or members; or
                    II.   one or more named parties seek to recover damages on a representative basis on behalf of themselves and other unnamed parties similarly situated, and questions of law or fact common to those persons or members of the prospective class predominate over any questions affecting only individual persons or members; or
               ii. any group of lawsuits filed in or pending in the same court and involving common questions of law or fact, in which–
                    I.   damages are sought on behalf of more than 50 persons; and
                    II.   the lawsuits are joined, consolidated, or otherwise proceed as a single action for any purpose.
          B.   Exception for derivative actions
               Notwithstanding subparagraph (A), the term "covered class action" does not include an exclusively derivative action brought by one or more shareholders on behalf of a corporation.
          C.   Counting of certain class members
               For purposes of this paragraph, a corporation, investment company, pension plan, partnership, or other entity, shall be treated as one person or prospective class member, but only if the entity is not established for the purpose of participating in the action.
          D.   Rule of construction
               Nothing in this paragraph shall be construed to affect the discretion of a State court in determining whether actions filed in such court should be joined, consolidated, or otherwise allowed to proceed as a single action.
     3.   Covered security
          The term "covered security" means a security that satisfies the standards for a covered security specified in paragraph (1) or (2) of section 18(b) at the time during which it is alleged that the misrepresentation, omission, or manipulative or deceptive conduct occurred, except that such term shall not include any debt

security that is exempt from registration under this title pursuant to rules issued by the Commission under section 4(2).

Section 17 – Fraudulent Interstate Transactions

a. **Use of interstate commerce for purpose of fraud or deceit.** It shall be unlawful for any person in the offer or sale of any securities including any security-based swaps or any security-based swap agreement (as defined in section 3(a)78 of the Securities Exchange Act of 1934) by the use of any means or instruments of transportation or communication in interstate commerce or by use of the mails, directly or indirectly–

   1. to employ any device, scheme, or artifice to defraud, or

   2. to obtain money or property by means of any untrue statement of a material fact or any omission to state a material fact necessary in order to make the statements made, in light of the circumstances under which they were made, not misleading; or

   3. to engage in any transaction, practice, or course of business which operates or would operate as a fraud or deceit upon the purchaser.

Section 18 – Exemption from State Regulation of Securities Offerings

a. **Scope of exemption**

Except as otherwise provided in this section, no law, rule, regulation, or order, or other administrative action of any State or any political subdivision thereof–

   1. requiring, or with respect to, registration or qualification of securities, or registration or qualification of securities transactions, shall directly or indirectly apply to a security that–

     A. is a covered security; or

     B. will be a covered security upon completion of the transaction;

   2. shall directly or indirectly prohibit, limit, or impose any conditions upon the use of–

     A. with respect to a covered security described in subsection (b), any offering document that is prepared by or on the behalf of the issuer; or

     B. any proxy statement, report to shareholders, or other disclosure document relating to a covered security or the issuer thereof that is required to be and is filed with the Commission or any national thereof that is required to be and is filed with the Commission or any national securities organization registered under section 15A of the Securities Exchange Act of 1934, except that this subparagraph does not apply to the laws, rules, regulations, or orders, or other administrative actions of the State of incorporation of the issuer; or

   3. shall directly or indirectly prohibit, limit, or impose conditions, based on the merits of such offering or issuer, upon the offer or sale of any security described in paragraph (1).

b. **Covered securities**

For the purposes of this section, the following are covered securities:

   1. Exclusive federal registration of nationally traded securities.

     A security is a covered security if such security is–

A. listed, or authorized for listing, on the New York Stock Exchange or the American Stock Exchange, or listed, or authorized for listing, on the National Market System of the Nasdaq Stock Market (or any successor to such entities);

B. listed, or authorized for listing, on a national securities exchange (or tier or segment thereof) that has listing standards that the Commission determines by rule (on its own initiative or on the basis of a petition) are substantially similar to the listing standards applicable to securities describe in subparagraph (A); or

C. a security of the same issuer that is equal in seniority or that is a senior security to a security described in subparagraph (A) or (B).

2. Exclusive federal registration of investment companies

A security is a covered security if such security is a security issued by an investment company that is registered, or that has filed a registration statement, under the Investment Company Act of 1940.

3. Sales to qualified purchasers

A security is a covered security with respect to the offer or sale of the security to qualified purchasers, as defined by the Commission by rule. In prescribing such rule, the Commission may define the term "qualified purchaser" differently with respect to different categories of securities, consistent with the public interest and the protection of investors.

4. Exemption in connection with certain exempt offerings

A security is a covered security with respect to a transaction that is exempt from registration under this title pursuant to–

A. paragraph (1) or (3) of section 4, and the issuer of such security files reports with the Commission pursuant to section 13 or 15(d) of the Securities Exchange Act of 1934;

B. section 4[(a)](4);

C. section 4[(a)](6);

D. a rule or regulation adopted pursuant to section 3(b)(2) and such security is
    i.   offered or sold on a national securities exchange; or
    ii. offered or sold to a qualified purchaser, as defined by the Commission pursuant to paragraph (3) with respect to that purchase or sale;

E. section 3(a), other than the offer or sale of a security that is exempt from such registration pursuant to paragraph (4), (10) or (11) of such section, except that a municipal security that is exempt from such a registration pursuant to paragraph (2) of such section is not a covered security with respect to the offer or sale of such security in the State in which the issuer of such security is located; or

F. Commission rules or regulations issued under section 4(2), except that this subparagraph does not prohibit a State from imposing notice filing requirements that are substantially similar to those required by rule or regulation under section 4(2) that are in effect on September 1, 1996.

c. **Preservation of authority**
    1. Fraud authority
        Consistent with this section, the securities commission (or agency or office performing like functions) of any State shall retain jurisdiction under the laws of such State to investigate and bring enforcement actions, in connection with securities or securities transactions
        A. with respect to
            i.   fraud or deceit; or
            ii. unlawful conduct by a broker or dealer; and
        B. in connection to a transaction described under section 4[(a)](6), with respect to
            i.   fraud or deceit; or
            ii. unlawful conduct by a broker, dealer, funding portal, or issuer.
    2. Preservation of filing requirements
        A. Notice filings permitted
            Nothing in this section prohibits the securities commission (or any agency or office performing like functions) of any State from requiring the filing of any document filed with the Commission pursuant to this title, together with annual or periodic reports of the value of securities sold or offered to be sold to persons located in the State (if such sales data is not included in documents filed with the Commission), solely for notice purposes and the assessment of any fee, together with a consent to service of process and any required fee.
        B. Preservation of fees
            i.   In general
                 Until otherwise provided by law, rule, regulation, or order, or other administrative action of any State or any political subdivision thereof, adopted after the date of enactment of the National Securities Markets Improvement Act of 1996, filing or registration fees with respect to securities or securities transactions shall continue to be collected in amounts determined pursuant to State law as in effect on the day before such date.
            ii. Schedule
                 The fees required by this subparagraph shall be paid, and all necessary supporting data on sales or offers for sales required under subparagraph (A), shall be reported on the same schedule as would have been applicable had the issuer not relied on the exemption provided in subsection (a).
        C. Availability of preemption contingent on payment of fees
            i.   In general
                 During the period beginning on the date of enactment of the National Securities Markets Improvement Act of 1996 and ending 3 years after that date of enactment, the securities commission (or any agency or office performing like functions) of any State may require the registration of securities issued by any issuer who refuses to pay the fees required by subparagraph (B).

      ii. Delays

For purposes of this subparagraph, delays in payment of fees or underpayments of fees that are promptly remedied shall not constitute a refusal to pay fees.

    D. Fees not permitted on listed securities

Notwithstanding subparagraphs (A), (B), and (C), no filing or fee may be required with respect to any security that is a covered security pursuant to subsection (b)(1), or will be such a covered security upon completion of the transaction, or is a security of the same issuer that is equal in seniority or that is a senior security to a security that is a covered security pursuant to subsection (b)(1).

    F. Fees not permitted on crowdfunded securities.

Notwithstanding subparagraphs (A), (B), and (C), no filing or fee may be required with respect to any security that is a covered security pursuant to subsection (b)(4)(B), or will be such a covered security upon completion of the transaction, except for the securities commission (or any agency or office performing like functions) of the State of the principal place of business of the issuer, or any State in which purchasers of 50 percent or greater of the aggregate amount of the issue are residents, provided that for purposes of this subparagraph, the term 'State' includes the District of Columbia and the territories of the United States.

3.   Enforcement of requirements

Nothing in this section shall prohibit the security commission (or any agency or office performing like functions) of any State from suspending the offer or sale of securities within such State as a result of the failure to submit any filing or fee required under law and permitted under this section.

d. **Definitions**

For purposes of this section, the following definitions shall apply:

1.   Offering document

The term "offering document"–

    A. has the meaning given the term "prospectus" in section 2(a)(10), but without regard to the provisions of subparagraphs (a) and (b) of that section; and

    B. includes a communication that is not deemed to offer a security pursuant to a rule of the Commission.

2.   Prepared by or on behalf of the issuer

Not later than 6 months after the date of enactment of the National Securities Markets Improvement Act of 1996 [enacted October 11, 1996], the Commission shall, by rule, define the term "prepared by or on behalf of the issuer" for purposes of this section.

3.   State

The term "State" has the same meaning as on section 3 of the Securities Exchange Act of 1934.

4.   Senior security

The term "senior security" means any bond, debenture, note, or similar obligation or instrument constituting a security and evidencing indebtedness, and any stock of a class having priority over any other class as to distribution of assets or payments of dividends.

Section 24 – Penalties

Any person who willfully violates any of the provisions of this title, or the rules and regulations promulgated by the Commission under authority thereof, or any person who willfully, in a registration statement filed under this title, makes any untrue statement of a material fact or omits to state any material fact required to be stated therein or necessary to make the statements therein not misleading, shall upon conviction be fined not more than $10,000 or imprisoned not more than five years, or both.

Section 27 – Private Securities Litigation

a. **Private class actions**
    1. In general
        The provisions of this subsection shall apply to each private action arising under this title that is brought as a plaintiff class action pursuant to the Federal Rules of Civil Procedure.
    2. Certification filed with complaint
        A. In general
            Each plaintiff seeking to serve as a representative party on behalf of a class shall provide a sworn certification, which shall be personally signed by such plaintiff and filed with the complaint, that–
            i.   states that the plaintiff has reviewed the complaint and authorized its filing;
            ii.   states that the plaintiff did not purchase the security that is the subject of the complaint at the direction of plaintiff's counsel or in order to participate in any private action arising under this title;
            iii. states that the plaintiff is willing to serve as a representative party on behalf of a class, including providing testimony at deposition and trial, if necessary;
            iv.   sets forth all of the transactions of the plaintiff in the security that is the subject of the complaint during the class period specified in the complaint;
            v.   identifies any other action under this title, filed during the 3-year period preceding the date on which the certification is signed by the plaintiff, in which the plaintiff has sought to serve, or served, as a representative party on behalf of a class; and
            vi.   states that the plaintiff will not accept any payment for serving as a representative party on behalf of a class beyond the plaintiff's pro rata share of any recovery, except as ordered or approved by the court in accordance with paragraph (4).
        B. Nonwaiver of attorney-client privilege
            The certification filed pursuant to subparagraph (A) shall not be construed to be a waiver of the attorney-client privilege.
    3. Appointment of lead plaintiff
        A. Early notice to class members

     i.   In general

Not later than 20 days after the date on which the complaint is filed, the plaintiff or plaintiffs shall cause to be published, in a widely circulated national business-oriented publication or wire service, a notice advising members of the purported plaintiff class–

       I.   of the pendency of the action, the claims asserted therein, and the purported class period; and

       II.   that, not later than 60 days after the date on which the notice is published, any member of the purported class may move the court to serve as lead plaintiff of the purported class.

     ii.   Multiple actions

If more than one action on behalf of a class asserting substantially the same claim or claims arising under this title is filed, only the plaintiff or plaintiffs in the first filed action shall be required to cause notice to be published in accordance with clause (i).

     iii.   Additional notices may be required under Federal Rules

Notice required under clause (i) shall be in addition to any notice required pursuant to the Federal Rules of Civil Procedure.

B.   Appointment of lead plaintiff

     i.   In general

Not later than 90 days after the date on which a notice is published under subparagraph (A)(i) , the court shall consider any motion made by a purported class member in response to the notice, including any motion by a class member who is not individually named as a plaintiff in the complaint or complaints, and shall appoint as lead plaintiff the member or members of the purported plaintiff class that the court determines to be most capable of adequately representing the interests of class members (hereafter in this paragraph referred to as the "most adequate plaintiff") in accordance with this subparagraph.

     ii.   Consolidated actions

If more than one action on behalf of a class asserting substantially the same claim or claims arising under this title has been filed, and any party has sought to consolidate those actions for pretrial purposes or for trial, the court shall not make the determination required by clause (i) until after the decision on the motion to consolidate is rendered. As soon as practicable after such decision is rendered, the court shall appoint the most adequate plaintiff as lead plaintiff for the consolidated actions in accordance with this subparagraph.

     iii.   Rebuttable presumption

       I.   In general

Subject to subclause (II), for purposes of clause (i), the court shall adopt a presumption that the most adequate plaintiff in any private action arising under this title is the person or group of persons that-

         (aa) has either filed the complaint or made a motion in response to a notice under Subparagraph (A)(i);

(bb) in the determination of the court, has the largest financial interest in the relief sought by the class; and

(cc) otherwise satisfies the requirements of Rule 23 of the Federal Rules of Civil Procedure.

II.   Rebuttable evidence

The presumption described in subclause (I) may be rebutted only upon proof by a member of the purported plaintiff class that the presumptively most adequate plaintiff–

(aa) will not fairly and adequately protect the interests of the class; or

(bb) is subject to unique defenses that render such plaintiff incapable of adequately representing the class.

iv.   Discovery

For purposes of this subparagraph, discovery relating to whether a member or members of the purported plaintiff class is the most adequate plaintiff may be conducted by a plaintiff only if the plaintiff first demonstrates a reasonable basis for a finding that the presumptively most adequate plaintiff is incapable of adequately representing the class.

v.   Selection of lead counsel

The most adequate plaintiff shall, subject to the approval of the court, select and retain counsel to represent the class.

vi.   Restrictions on professional plaintiffs

Except as the court may otherwise permit, consistent with the purposes of this section, a person may be a lead plaintiff, or an officer, director, or fiduciary of a lead plaintiff, in no more than 5 securities class actions brought as plaintiff class actions pursuant to the Federal Rules of Civil Procedure during any 3-year period.

4.   Recovery by plaintiffs

The share of any final judgment or of any settlement that is awarded to a representative party serving on behalf of a class shall be equal, on a per share basis, to the portion of the final judgment or settlement awarded to all other members of the class. Nothing in this paragraph shall be construed to limit the award of reasonable costs and expenses (including lost wages) directly relating to the representation of the class to any representative party serving on behalf of the class.

5.   Restrictions on settlements under seal

The terms and provisions of any settlement agreement of a class action shall not be filed under seal, except that on motion of any party to the settlement, the court may order filing under seal for those portions of a settlement agreement as to which good cause is shown for such filing under seal. For purposes of this paragraph, good cause shall exist only if publication of a term or provision of a settlement agreement would cause direct and substantial harm to any party.

6.   Restrictions on payment of attorneys' fees and expenses

Total attorneys' fees and expenses awarded by the court to counsel for the plaintiff class shall not exceed a reasonable percentage of the amount of any damages and prejudgment interest actually paid to the class.

7.   Disclosure of settlement terms to class members

Any proposed or final settlement agreement that is published or otherwise disseminated to the class shall include each of the following statements, along with a cover page summarizing the information contained in such statements:

A. Statement of plaintiff recovery

The amount of the settlement proposed to be distributed to the parties to the action, determined in the aggregate and on an average per share basis.

B. Statement of potential outcome of case

   i.   Agreement on the amount of damages

If the settling parties agree on the average amount of damages per share that would be recoverable if the plaintiff prevailed on each claim alleged under this title, a statement concerning the average amount of such potential damages per share.

   ii. Disagreement on the amount of damages

If the parties do not agree on the average amount of damages per share that would be recoverable if the plaintiff prevailed on each claim alleged under this title, a statement from each settling party concerning the issue or issues on which the parties disagree.

   iii. Inadmissibility for certain purposes

A statement made in accordance with clause (i) or (ii) concerning the amount of damages shall not be admissible in any Federal or State judicial action or administrative proceeding, other than an action or proceeding arising out of such statement.

C. Statement of attorneys' fees or costs sought

If any of the settling parties or their counsel intend to apply to the court for an award of attorneys' fees or costs from any fund established as part of the settlement, a statement indicating which parties or counsel intend to make such an application, the amount of fees and costs that will be sought (including the amount of such fees and costs determined on an average per share basis) , and a brief explanation supporting the fees and costs sought.

D. Identification of lawyers' representatives

The name, telephone number, and address of one or more representatives of counsel for the plaintiff class who will be reasonably available to answer questions from class members concerning any matter contained in any notice of settlement published or otherwise disseminated to the class.

E. Reasons for settlement

A brief statement explaining the reasons why the parties are proposing the settlement.

F. Other information: Such other information as may be required by the court.

8.   Attorney conflict of interest

If a plaintiff class is represented by an attorney who directly owns or otherwise has a beneficial interest in the securities that are the subject of the litigation, the court shall make a determination of whether such ownership or other interest constitutes a conflict of interest sufficient to disqualify the attorney from representing the plaintiff class.

b. **Stay of discovery; preservation of evidence**

1.   In general

In any private action arising under this title, all discovery and other proceedings shall be stayed during the pendency of any motion to dismiss, unless the court finds, upon the motion of any party, that particularized discovery is necessary to preserve evidence or to prevent undue prejudice to that party.

2. Preservation of evidence

During the pendency of any stay of discovery pursuant to this subsection, unless otherwise ordered by the court, any party to the action with actual notice of the allegations contained in the complaint shall treat all documents, data compilations (including electronically recorded or stored data) , and tangible objects that are in the custody or control of such person and that are relevant to the allegations, as if they were the subject of a continuing request for production of documents from an opposing party under the Federal Rules of Civil Procedure.

3. Sanction for willful violation

A party aggrieved by the willful failure of an opposing party to comply with paragraph (2) may apply to the court for an order awarding appropriate sanctions.

4. Circumvention of stay of discovery

Upon a proper showing, a court may stay discovery proceedings in any private action in a State court as necessary in aid of its jurisdiction, or to protect or effectuate its judgments, in an action subject to a stay of discovery pursuant to this subsection.

c. **Sanctions for abusive litigation**

1. Mandatory review by court

In any private action arising under this title, upon final adjudication of the action, the court shall include in the record specific findings regarding compliance by each party and each attorney representing any party with each requirement of Rule 11(b) of the Federal Rules of Civil Procedure as to any complaint, responsive pleading, or dispositive motion.

2. Mandatory sanctions

If the court makes a finding under paragraph (1) that a party or attorney violated any requirement of Rule 11(b) of the Federal Rules of Civil Procedure as to any complaint, responsive pleading, or dispositive motion, the court shall impose sanctions on such party or attorney in accordance with Rule 11 of the Federal Rules of Civil Procedure. Prior to making a finding that any party or attorney has violated Rule 11 of the Federal Rules of Civil Procedure, the court shall give such party or attorney notice and an opportunity to respond.

3. Presumptions in favor of attorneys' fees and costs

A. In general

Subject to subparagraphs (B) and (C), for purposes of paragraph (2), the court shall adopt a presumption that the appropriate sanction—

i. for failure of any responsive pleading or dispositive motion to comply with any requirement of Rule 11(b) of the Federal Rules of Civil Procedure is an award to the opposing party of the reasonable attorneys' fees and other expenses incurred as a direct result of the violation; and

       ii.   for substantial failure of any complaint to comply with any requirement of Rule 11(b) of the Federal Rules of Civil Procedure is an award to the opposing party of the reasonable attorneys' fees and other expenses incurred in the action.

  B. Rebuttal evidence

The presumption described in subparagraph (A) may be rebutted only upon proof by the party or attorney against whom sanctions are to be imposed that–

       i.   the award of attorneys' fees and other expenses will impose an unreasonable burden on that party or attorney and would be unjust, and the failure to make such an award would not impose a greater burden on the party in whose favor sanctions are to be imposed; or

      ii.   the violation of Rule 11(b) of the Federal Rules of Civil Procedure was de minimis.

  C. Sanctions

If the party or attorney against whom sanctions are to be imposed meets its burden under subparagraph (B), the court shall award the sanctions that the court deems appropriate pursuant to Rule 11 of the Federal Rules of Civil Procedure.

d. **Defendant's right to written interrogatories.** In any private action arising under this title in which the plaintiff may recover money damages only on proof that a defendant acted with a particular state of mind, the court shall, when requested by a defendant, submit to the jury a written interrogatory on the issue of each such defendant's state of mind at the time the alleged violation occurred.

Section 27A – Application of Safe Harbor for Forward-Looking Statements

a. **Applicability.** This section shall apply only to a forward-looking statement made by–

1.   an issuer that, at the time that the statement is made, is subject to the reporting requirements of section 13(a) or section 15(d) of the Securities Exchange Act of 1934;

2.   a person acting on behalf of such issuer;

3.   an outside reviewer retained by such issuer making a statement on behalf of such issuer; or

4.   an underwriter, with respect to information provided by such issuer or information derived from information provided by the issuer.

b. **Exclusions.** Except to the extent otherwise specifically provided by rule, regulation, or order of the Commission, this section shall not apply to a forward-looking statement–

1.   that is made with respect to the business or operations of the issuer, if the issuer–

    A. during the 3-year period preceding the date on which the statement was first made–

        i. was convicted of any felony or misdemeanor described in clauses (i) through (iv) of section 15 (b)(4)(B) of the Securities Exchange Act of 1934; or

        ii. has been made the subject of a judicial or administrative decree or order arising out of a governmental action that–

            I. prohibits future violations of the antifraud provisions of the securities laws;

            II. requires that the issuer cease and desist from violating the antifraud provisions of the securities laws; or

            III. determines that the issuer violated the antifraud provisions of the securities laws;

    B. makes the forward-looking statement in connection with an offering of securities by a blank check company;

    C. issues penny stock;

    D. makes the forward-looking statement in connection with a rollup transaction;

    E. makes the forward-looking statement in connection with a going private transaction; or

2. that is–

    A. included in a financial statement prepared in accordance with generally accepted accounting principles;

    B. contained in a registration statement of, or otherwise issued by, an investment company;

    C. made in connection with a tender offer;

    D. made in connection with an initial public offering;

    E. made in connection with an offering by, or relating to the operations of, a partnership, limited liability company, or a direct participation investment program; or

    F. made in a disclosure of beneficial ownership in a report required to be filed with the Commission pursuant to section 13(d) of the Securities Exchange Act of 1934.

c. **Safe harbor**

    1. In general

    Except as provided in subsection (b), in any private action arising under this title that is based on an untrue statement of a material fact or omission of a material fact necessary to make the statement not misleading, a person referred to in subsection (a) shall not be liable with respect to any forward-looking statement, whether written or oral, if and to the extent that–

    A. the forward-looking statement is–

        i. identified as a forward-looking statement, and is accompanied by meaningful cautionary statements identifying important factors that could cause actual results to differ materially from those in the forward-looking statement; or

        ii. immaterial; or

        B.   the plaintiff fails to prove that the forward-looking statement–
           i.   if made by a natural person, was made with actual knowledge by that person that the statement was false or misleading; or
          ii.   if made by a business entity, was–
              I.   made by or with the approval of an executive officer of that entity, and
             II.   made or approved by such officer with actual knowledge by that officer that the statement was false or misleading.

2.   Oral forward-looking statements

In the case of an oral forward-looking statement made by an issuer that is subject to the reporting requirements of section 13(a) or section 15(d) of the Securities Exchange Act of 1934, or by a person acting on behalf of such issuer, the requirement set forth in paragraph (1) (A) shall be deemed to be satisfied–

        A.   if the oral forward-looking statement is accompanied by a cautionary statement–
           i.   that the particular oral statement is a forward-looking statement; and
          ii.   that the actual results could differ materially from those projected in the forward-looking statement; and
        B.   if–
           i.   the oral forward-looking statement is accompanied by an oral statement that additional information concerning factors that could cause actual results to differ materially from those in the forward-looking statement is contained in a readily available written document, or portion thereof;
          ii.   the accompanying oral statement referred to in clause (i) identifies the document, or portion thereof, that contains the additional information about those factors relating to the forward-looking statement; and
         iii.   the information contained in that written document is a cautionary statement that satisfies the standard established in para. (1) (A).

3.   Availability

Any document filed with the Commission or generally disseminated shall be deemed to be readily available for purposes of paragraph (2).

4.   Effect on other safe harbors

The exemption provided for in paragraph (1) shall be in addition to any exemption that the Commission may establish by rule or regulation under subsection (g).

d.   **Duty to update.** Nothing in this section shall impose upon any person a duty to update a forward-looking statement.

e.   **Dispositive motion.** On any motion to dismiss based upon subsection (c) (1), the court shall consider any statement cited in the complaint and cautionary statement accompanying the forward-looking statement, which are not subject to material dispute, cited by the defendant.

f.   **Stay pending decision on motion.** In any private action arising under this title, the court shall stay discovery (other than discovery that is specifically directed to the applicability of the exemption provided for in this section) during the pendency of any motion by a defendant for summary judgment that is based on the grounds that–

1.   the statement or omission upon which the complaint is based is a forward-looking statement within the meaning of this section; and
2.   the exemption provided for in this section precludes a claim for relief.

g.   **Exemption authority.** In addition to the exemptions provided for in this section, the Commission may, by rule or regulation, provide exemptions from or under any provision of this title, including with respect to liability that is based on a statement or that is based on projections or other forward-looking information, if and to the extent that any such exemption is consistent with the public interest and the protection of investors, as determined by the Commission.

h.   **Effect on other authority of Commission.** Nothing in this section limits, either expressly or by implication, the authority of the Commission to exercise similar authority or to adopt similar rules and regulations with respect to forward-looking statements under any other statute under which the Commission exercises rulemaking authority.

i.   **Definitions.** For purposes of this section, the following definitions shall apply:
1.   Forward-looking statement. The term "forward-looking statement" means–
    A.   a statement containing a projection of revenues, income (including income loss), earnings (including earnings loss) per share, capital expenditures, dividends, capital structure, or other financial items;
    B.   a statement of the plans and objectives of management for future operations, including plans or objectives relating to the products or services of the issuer;
    C.   a statement of future economic performance, including any such statement contained in a discussion and analysis of financial condition by the management or in the results of operations included pursuant to the rules and regulations of the Commission;
    D.   any statement of the assumptions underlying or relating to any statement described in subparagraph (A) , (B) , or (C) ;
    E.   any report issued by an outside reviewer retained by an issuer, to the extent that the report assesses a forward-looking statement made by the issuer; or
    F.   a statement containing a projection or estimate of such other items as may be specified by rule or regulation of the Commission.
2.   Investment company: The term "investment company" has the same meaning as in section 3(a) of the Investment Company Act of 1940.
3.   Penny stock: The term "penny stock" has the same meaning as in section 3(a)(51) of the Securities Exchange Act of 1934, and the rules and regulations, or orders issued pursuant to that section.
4.   Going private transaction: The term "going private transaction" has the meaning given that term under the rules or regulations of the Commission issued pursuant to section 13(e) of the Securities Exchange Act of 1934.
5.   Security laws: The term "securities laws" has the same meaning as in section 3 of the Securities Exchange Act of 1934.

6.   Person acting on behalf of an issuer: The term "person acting on behalf of an issuer" means an officer, director, or employee of the issuer.

7.   Other terms: The terms "blank check company", "rollup transaction", "partnership", "limited liability company", "executive officer of an entity" and "direct participation investment program", have the meanings given those terms by rule or regulation of the Commission.

Section 27B – Conflicts of Interest Relating to Certain Securitizations

a.   **In general**. An underwriter, placement agent, initial purchaser, or sponsor, or any affiliate or subsidiary of any such entity, of an asset-backed security (as such term is defined in section 3 of the Securities and Exchange Act of 1934, which for the purposes of this section shall include a synthetic asset-backed security), shall not, at any time for a period ending on the date that is one year after the date of the first closing of the sale of the asset-backed security, engage in any transaction that would involve or result in any material conflict of interest with respect to any investor in a transaction arising out of such activity.

b.   **Rulemaking**. Not later than 270 days after the date of enactment of this section, the Commission shall issue rules for the purpose of implementing subsection (a).

c.   **Exception**. The prohibitions of subsection (a) shall not apply to—
1.   risk-mitigating hedging activities in connection with positions or holdings arising out of the underwriting, placement, initial purchase, or sponsorship of an asset-backed security, provided that such activities are designed to reduce the specific risks to the underwriter, placement agent, initial purchaser, or sponsor associated with positions or holdings arising out of such underwriting, placement, initial purchase, or sponsorship; or
2.   purchases or sales of asset-backed securities made pursuant to and consistent with—
   A.   commitments of the underwriter, placement agent, initial purchaser, or sponsor, or any affiliate or subsidiary of any such entity, to provide liquidity for the asset-backed security, or
   B.   bona fide market-making in the asset backed security.

d.   **Rule of construction.** This subsection shall not otherwise limit the application of section 15G of the Securities Exchange Act of 1934.

Section 28 – General Exemptive Authority

The Commission, by rule or regulation, may conditionally or unconditionally exempt any person, security, or transaction, or any class of persons, securities, or transactions, from any provision or provisions of this title or of any rule or regulation issued under this title, to the extent that such exemption is necessary or appropriate in the public interest, and is consistent with the protection of investors.

Securities Act – Rules:

Rule 134 – Communications Not Deemed a Prospectus

Except as provided in paragraphs (e) and (g) of this section, the terms "prospectus" as defined in section 2(a)(10) of the Act or "free writing prospectus" as defined in Rule 405 shall not include a communication limited to the statements required or permitted by this section, provided that the communication is published or transmitted to any person only after a registration statement relating to the offering that includes a prospectus satisfying the requirements of section 10 of the Act (except as otherwise permitted in paragraph (a) of this section) has been filed.

    a. Such communication may include any one or more of the following items of information, which need not follow the numerical sequence of this paragraph, provided that, except as to paragraphs (a)(4), (a)(5), (a)(6) of this section, the prospectus included in the filed registration statement does not have to include a price range otherwise required by rule:

1. Factual information about the legal identity and business location of the issuer limited to the following: the name of the issuer of the security, the address, phone number, and e-mail address of the issuer's principal offices and contact for investors, the issuer's country of organization, and the geographic areas in which it conducts business;

2. The title of the security or securities and the amount or amounts being offered, which title may include a designation as to whether the securities are convertible, exercisable, or exchangeable, and as to the ranking of the securities;

3. A brief indication of the general type of business of the issuer, limited to the following:

    i. In the case of a manufacturing company, the general type of manufacturing, the principal products or classes of products manufactured, and the segments in which the company conducts business;

    ii. In the case of a public utility company, the general type of services rendered, a brief indication of the area served, and the segments in which the company conducts business;

    iii. In the case of an asset-backed issuer, the identity of key parties, such as sponsor, depositor, issuing entity, servicer or servicers, and trustee, the asset class of the transaction, and the identity of any credit enhancement or other support; and

    iv. In the case of any other type of company, a corresponding statement;

4. The price of the security, or if the price is not known, the method of its determination or the bona fide estimate of the price range as specified by the issuer or the managing underwriter or underwriters;

5. In the case of a fixed income security, the final maturity and interest rate provisions or, if the final maturity or interest rate provisions are not known, the probable final maturity or interest rate provisions, as specified by the issuer or the managing underwriter or underwriters;

6. In the case of a fixed income security with a fixed (non-contingent) interest rate provision, the yield or, if the yield is not known, the probable yield range, as specified by the issuer or the managing underwriter or underwriters and the yield of fixed income securities with comparable maturity and security rating;

7. A brief description of the intended use of proceeds of the offering, if then disclosed in the prospectus that is part of the filed registration statement;

8. The name, address, phone number, and e-mail address of the sender of the communication and the fact that it is participating, or expects to participate, in the distribution of the security;

9. The type of underwriting, if then included in the disclosure in the prospectus that is part of the filed registration statement;

10. The names of underwriters participating in the offering of the securities, and their additional roles, if any, within the underwriting syndicate;

11. The anticipated schedule for the offering (including the approximate date upon which the proposed sale to the public will begin) and a description of marketing events (including the dates, times, locations, and procedures for attending or otherwise accessing them);

12. A description of the procedures by which the underwriters will conduct the offering and the procedures for transactions in connection with the offering with the issuer or an underwriter or participating dealer (including procedures regarding account opening and submitting indications of interest and conditional offers to buy), and procedures regarding directed share plans and other participation in offerings by officers, directors, and employees of the issuer;

13. Whether, in the opinion of counsel, the security is a legal investment for savings banks, fiduciaries, insurance companies, or similar investors under the laws of any State or Territory or the District of Columbia, and the permissibility or status of the investment under the Employee Retirement Income Security Act of 1974;

14. Whether, in the opinion of counsel, the security is exempt from specified taxes, or the extent to which the issuer has agreed to pay any tax with respect to the security or measured by the income therefrom;

15. Whether the security is being offered through rights issued to security holders, and, if so, the class of securities the holders of which will be entitled to subscribe, the subscription ratio, the actual or proposed record date, the date upon which the rights were issued or are expected to be issued, the actual or anticipated date upon which they will expire, and the approximate subscription price, or any of the foregoing;

16. Any statement or legend required by any state law or administrative authority;

17. With respect to the securities being offered:
    i. Any security rating assigned, or reasonably expected to be assigned, by a nationally recognized statistical rating organization as defined in Rule 15c3-1(c)(2)(vi)(F) of the Securities Exchange Act of 1934 (Rule 15c3-1(c)(2)(vi)(F) of this chapter) and the name or names of the nationally recognized statistical rating organization(s) that assigned or is or are reasonably expected to assign the rating(s); and
    ii. If registered on Form F-9, any security rating assigned, or reasonably expected to be assigned, by any other rating organization specified in the Instruction to paragraph A.(2) of General Instruction I of Form F-9;

18. The names of selling security holders, if then disclosed in the prospectus that is part of the filed registration statement;

19. The names of securities exchanges or other securities markets where any class of the issuer's securities are, or will be, listed;

20. The ticker symbols, or proposed ticker symbols, of the issuer's securities;

21. The CUSIP number as defined in Rule 17Ad-19(a)(5) of the Securities Exchange Act of 1934 assigned to the securities being offered; and

22. Information disclosed in order to correct inaccuracies previously contained in a communication permissibly made pursuant to this section.

b. Except as provided in paragraph (c) of this section, every communication used pursuant to this section shall contain the following:
    1. If the registration statement has not yet become effective, the following statement:
    A registration statement relating to these securities has been filed with the Securities and Exchange Commission but has not yet become effective. These

securities may not be sold nor may offers to buy be accepted prior to the time the registration statement becomes effective; and

2. The name and address of a person or persons from whom a written prospectus for the offering meeting the requirements of section 10 of the Act (other than a free writing prospectus as defined in Rule 405) including as to the identified paragraphs above a price range where required by rule, may be obtained.

c. Any of the statements or information specified in paragraph (b) of this section may, but need not, be contained in a communication which:

1. Does no more than state from whom and include the uniform resource locator (URL) where a written prospectus meeting the requirements of section 10 of the Act (other than a free writing prospectus as defined in Rule 405) may be obtained, identify the security, state the price thereof and state by whom orders will be executed; or

2. Is accompanied or preceded by a prospectus or a summary prospectus, other than a free writing prospectus as defined in Rule 405, which meets the requirements of section 10 of the Act, including a price range where required by rule, at the date of such preliminary communication.

d. A communication sent or delivered to any person pursuant to this section which is accompanied or preceded by a prospectus which meets the requirements of section 10 of the Act (other than a free writing prospectus as defined in Rule 405), including a price range where required by rule, at the date of such communication, may solicit from the recipient of the communication an offer to buy the security or request the recipient to indicate whether he or she might be interested in the security, if the communication contains substantially the following statement:

No offer to buy the securities can be accepted and no part of the purchase price can be received until the registration statement has become effective, and any such offer may be withdrawn or revoked, without obligation or commitment of any kind, at any time prior to notice of its acceptance given after the effective date.

Provided, that such statement need not be included in such a communication to a dealer.

e. A section 10 prospectus included in any communication pursuant to this section shall remain a prospectus for all purposes under the Act.

f. The provision in paragraphs (c)(2) and (d) of this section that a prospectus that meets the requirements of section 10 of the Act precede or accompany a communication will be satisfied if such communication is an electronic communication containing an active hyperlink to such prospectus.

g. This section does not apply to a communication relating to an investment company registered under the Investment Company Act of 1940 or a business development company as defined in section 2(a)(48) of the Investment Company Act of 1940.

Rule 135 – Notice of Proposed Registered Offerings

a. **When notice is not an offer**. For purposes of section 5 of the Act only, an issuer or a selling security holder (and any person acting on behalf of either of them) that publishes through any medium a notice of a proposed offering to be registered under the Act will not be deemed to offer its securities for sale through that notice if:

   1. Legend. The notice includes a statement to the effect that it does not constitute an offer of any securities for sale; and

   2. Limited notice content. The notice otherwise includes no more than the following information:

      i. The name of the issuer;

      ii. The title, amount and basic terms of the securities offered;

      iii. The amount of the offering, if any, to be made by selling security holders;

      iv. The anticipated timing of the offering;

      v. A brief statement of the manner and the purpose of the offering, without naming the underwriters;

      vi. Whether the issuer is directing its offering to only a particular class of purchasers;

      vii. Any statements or legends required by the laws of any state or foreign country or administrative authority; and

      viii. In the following offerings, the notice may contain additional information, as follows:

         A. Rights offering. In a rights offering to existing security holders:

            1. The class of security holders eligible to subscribe;

            2. The subscription ratio and expected subscription price;

            3. The proposed record date;

            4. The anticipated issuance date of the rights; and

            5. The subscription period or expiration date of the rights offering.

         B. Offering to employees. In an offering to employees of the issuer or an affiliated company:

            1. The name of the employer;

            2. The class of employees being offered the securities;

            3. The offering price; and

            4. The duration of the offering period.

         C. Exchange offer. In an exchange offer:

            1. The basic terms of the exchange offer;

            2. The name of the subject company;

            3. The subject class of securities sought in the exchange offer.

         D. Rule 145(a) offering. In a Rule 145(a) offering:

            1. The name of the person whose assets are to be sold in exchange for the securities to be offered; The names of any other parties to the transaction;

            2. A brief description of the business of the parties to the transaction;

            3. The date, time and place of the meeting of security holders to vote on or consent to the transaction; and

      4.   A brief description of the transaction and the basic terms of the transaction.

b.   **Corrections of misstatements about the offering**. A person that publishes a notice in reliance on this section may issue a notice that contains no more information than is necessary to correct inaccuracies published about the proposed offering.

Rule 135c – Notice of Certain Proposed Unregistered Offerings

a.   For the purposes only of section 5 of the Act, a notice given by an issuer required to file reports pursuant to section 13 or 15(d) of the Securities Exchange Act of 1934 or a foreign issuer that is exempt from registration under the Securities Exchange Act of 1934 pursuant to Rule 12g3-2(b) of this chapter that it proposes to make, is making or has made an offering of securities not registered or required to be registered under the Act shall not be deemed to offer any securities for sale if:

   1.   Such notice is not used for the purpose of conditioning the market in the United States for any of the securities offered;

   2.   Such notice states that the securities offered will not be or have not been registered under the Act and may not be offered or sold in the United States absent registration or an applicable exemption from registration requirements; and

   3.   Such notice contains no more than the following additional information:

      i.   The name of the issuer;

      ii.   The title, amount and basic terms of the securities offered, the amount of the offering, if any, made by selling security holders, the time of the offering and a brief statement of the manner and purpose of the offering without naming the underwriters;

      iii.   In the case of a rights offering to security holders of the issuer, the class of securities the holders of which will be or were entitled to subscribe to the securities offered, the subscription ratio, the record date, the date upon which the rights are proposed to be or were issued, the term or expiration date of the rights and the subscription price, or any of the foregoing;

      iv.   In the case of an offering of securities in exchange for other securities of the issuer or of another issuer, the name of the issuer and the title of the securities to be surrendered in exchange for the securities offered, the basis upon which the exchange may be made, or any of the foregoing;

      v.   In the case of an offering to employees of the issuer or to employees of any affiliate of the issuer, the name of the employer and class or classes of employees to whom the securities are offered, the offering price or basis of the offering and the period during which the offering is to be or was made or any of the foregoing; and

      vi.   Any statement or legend required by State or foreign law or administrative authority.

b.   Any notice contemplated by this section may take the form of a news release or a written communication directed to security holders or employees, as the case may be, or other published statements.

c. Notwithstanding the provisions of paragraphs (a) and (b) of this section, in the case of a rights offering of a security listed or subject to unlisted trading privileges on a national securities exchange or quoted on the NASDAQ inter-dealer quotation system information with respect to the interest rate, conversion ratio and subscription price may be disseminated through the facilities of the exchange, the consolidated transaction reporting system, the NASDAQ system or the Dow Jones broad tape, provided such information is already disclosed in a Form 8-K on file with the Commission, in a Form 6-K furnished to the Commission or, in the case of an issuer relying on Rule 12g3-2(b) of this chapter, in a submission made pursuant to that Section to the Commission.

d. The issuer shall file any notice contemplated by this section with the Commission under cover of Form 8-K or furnish such notice under Form 6-K, as applicable, and, if relying on Rule 12g3-2(b) of this chapter, shall furnish such notice to the Commission in accordance with the provisions of that exemptive Section.

Rule 137 – Publications or Distributions of Research Reports by Brokers or Dealers that are not Participating in an Issuer's Registered Distribution of Securities.

Under the following conditions, the terms "offers," "participates," or "participation" in section 2(a)(11) of the Act shall not be deemed to apply to the publication or distribution of research reports with respect to the securities of an issuer which is the subject of an offering pursuant to a registration statement that the issuer proposes to file, or has filed, or that is effective:

a. The broker or dealer (and any affiliate) that has distributed the report and, if different, the person (and any affiliate) that has published the report have not participated, are not participating, and do not propose to participate in the distribution of the securities that are or will be the subject of the registered offering.

b. In connection with the publication or distribution of the research report, the broker or dealer (and any affiliate) that has distributed the report and, if different, the person (and any affiliate) that has published the report are not receiving and have not received consideration directly or indirectly from, and are not acting under any direct or indirect arrangement or understanding with:
    1. The issuer of the securities;
    2. A selling security holder;
    3. Any participant in the distribution of the securities that are or will be the subject of the registration statement; or
    4. Any other person interested in the securities that are or will be the subject of the registration statement.
    Instruction to Rule 137(b).
    This paragraph (b) does not preclude payment of:
    1. The regular price being paid by the broker or dealer for independent research, so long as the conditions of this paragraph (b) are satisfied; or
    2. The regular subscription or purchase price for the research report.

c. The broker or dealer publishes or distributes the research report in the regular course of its business.

d. The issuer is not and during the past three years neither the issuer nor any of its predecessors was:
    1. A blank check company as defined in Rule 419(a)(2);
    2. A shell company, other than a business combination related shell company, each as defined in Rule 405; or
    3. An issuer for an offering of penny stock as defined in Rule 3a51-1 of the Securities Exchange Act of 1934.

e. **Definition of research report**. For purposes of this section, research report means a written communication, as defined in Rule 405, that includes information, opinions, or recommendations with respect to securities of an issuer or an analysis of a security or an issuer, whether or not it provides information reasonably sufficient upon which to base an investment decision.

Rule 138 – Publications or Distributions of Research Reports by Brokers or Dealers about Securities other than those they are Distributing.

a. **Registered offerings**. Under the following conditions, a broker's or dealer's publication or distribution of research reports about securities of an issuer shall be deemed for purposes of sections 2(a)(10) and 5(c) of the Act not to constitute an offer for sale or offer to sell a security which is the subject of an offering pursuant to a registration statement that the issuer proposes to file, or has filed, or that is effective, even if the broker or dealer is participating or will participate in the registered offering of the issuer's securities:
    1. i. The research report relates solely to the issuer's common stock, or debt securities, or preferred stock convertible into its common stock, and the offering involves solely the issuer's non-convertible debt securities or non-convertible, non-participating preferred stock; or
        ii. The research report relates solely to the issuer's non-convertible debt securities or non-convertible, non-participating preferred stock, and the offering involves solely the issuer's common stock, or debt securities, or preferred stock convertible into its common stock.

    Instruction to paragraph (a)(1): If the issuer has filed a shelf registration statement under Rule 415(a)(1)(x) or pursuant to General Instruction I.D. of Form S-3 or General Instruction I.C. of Form F-3 with respect to multiple classes of securities, the conditions of paragraph (a)(1) of this section must be satisfied for the offering in which the broker or dealer is participating or will participate.
    2. The issuer as of the date of reliance on this section:
        i. Is required to file reports, and has filed all periodic reports required during the preceding 12 months (or such shorter time that the issuer was required to file such reports) on Forms 10-K, 10-Q and 20-F) pursuant to section 13 or section 15(d) of the Securities Exchange Act of 1934; or
        ii. Is a foreign private issuer that:
            A. Meets all of the registrant requirements of Form F-3 other than the reporting history provisions of General Instructions I.A.1. & I.A.2(a) of Form F-3;

        B. Either:
- (1) Satisfies the public float threshold in General Instruction I.B.1. of Form F-3; or
- (2) Is issuing non-convertible securities, other than common equity, and the issuer meets the provisions of General Instruction I.B.2. of Form F-3; and

        C. Either:
- (1) Has its equity securities trading on a designated offshore securities market as defined in Rule 902(b) and has had them so traded for at least 12 months; or
- (2) Has a worldwide market value of its outstanding common equity held by non-affiliates of $700 million or more.

3. The broker or dealer publishes or distributes research reports on the types of securities in question in the regular course of its business; and

4. The issuer is not, and during the past three years neither the issuer nor any of its predecessors was:
   - i. A blank check company as defined in Rule 419(a)(2);
   - ii. A shell company, other than a business combination related shell company, each as defined in Rule 405; or
   - iii. An issuer for an offering of penny stock as defined in Rule 3a51-1 of the Securities Exchange Act of 1934.

b. **Rule 144A offerings**. If the conditions in paragraph (a) of this section are satisfied, a broker's or dealer's publication or distribution of a research report shall not be considered an offer for sale or an offer to sell a security or general solicitation or general advertising, in connection with an offering relying on Rule 144A.

c. **Regulation S offerings**. If the conditions in paragraph (a) of this section are satisfied, a broker's or dealer's publication or distribution of a research report shall not:
   1. Constitute directed selling efforts as defined in Rule 902(c) for offerings under Regulation S; or
   2. Be inconsistent with the offshore transaction requirement in Rule 902(h) for offerings under Regulation S.

d. **Definition of research report**. For purposes of this section, research report means a written communication, as defined in Rule 405, that includes information, opinions, or recommendations with respect to securities of an issuer or an analysis of a security or an issuer, whether or not it provides information reasonably sufficient upon which to base an investment decision.

Rule 139 – Publications or Distributions of Research Reports by Brokers or Dealers Distributing Securities.

a. **Registered offerings**. Under the conditions of paragraph (a)(1) or (a)(2) of this section, a broker's or dealer's publication or distribution of a research report about an issuer or any of its securities shall be deemed for purposes of sections 2(a)(10) and 5(c) of the Act not to constitute an offer for sale or offer to sell a security that is the subject of an offering pursuant to a registration statement that the issuer proposes to file, or has filed, or that is effective, even if the broker or dealer is participating or will participate in the registered offering of the issuer's securities:

1. Issuer-specific research reports.

    i. The issuer either:

        (A)(1) At the later of the time of filing its most recent Form S-3 or Form F-3 or the time of its most recent amendment to such registration statement for purposes of complying with section 10(a)(3) of the Act or, if no Form S-3 or Form F-3 has been filed, at the date of reliance on this section, meets the registrant requirements of such Form S-3 or Form F-3 and:

        (i) either at such date meets the minimum float provisions of General Instruction I.B.1 of such Forms; or,

        (ii) At the date of reliance on this section, is, or if a registration statement has not been filed, will be, offering non-convertible securities, other than common equity, and meets the requirements for the General Instruction I.B.2 of Form S-3 or Form F-3; or

        (iii) At the date of reliance on this section is a well-known seasoned issuer as defined in Rule 405, other than a majority-owned subsidiary that is a well-known seasoned issuer by virtue of paragraph (1)(ii) of the definition of well-known seasoned issuer in Rule 405; and

        (2) As of the date of reliance on this section, has filed all periodic reports required during the preceding 12 months on Forms 10-K, 10-Q and 20-F pursuant to section 13 or section 15(d) of the Securities Exchange Act of 1934; or

        (B) Is a foreign private issuer that as of the date of reliance on this section:

        (1) Meets all of the registrant requirements of Form F-3 other than the reporting history provisions of General Instructions I.A.1. and I.A.2(a) of Form F-3 ;

        (2) Either:

        (i) Satisfies the public float threshold in General Instruction I.B.1. of Form F-3; or

        (ii) Is issuing non-convertible securities, other than common equity, and meets the provisions of General Instruction I.B.2. of Form F-3; and

        (3) Either:

        (i) Has its equity securities trading on a designated offshore securities market as defined in Rule 902(b) and has had them so traded for at least 12 months; or

        (ii) Has a worldwide market value of its outstanding common equity held by non-affiliates of $700 million or more;

    ii. The issuer is not and during the past three years neither the issuer nor any of its predecessors was:

        (A) A blank check company as defined in Rule 419(a)(2);

        (B) A shell company, other than a business combination related shell company, each as defined in Rule 405; or

(C) An issuer for an offering of penny stock as defined in Rule 3a51-1 of the Securities Exchange Act of 1934; and

iii. The broker or dealer publishes or distributes research reports in the regular course of its business and such publication or distribution does not represent the initiation of publication of research reports about such issuer or its securities or reinitiation of such publication following discontinuation of publication of such research reports.

2. Industry reports.

i. The issuer is required to file reports pursuant to section 13 or section 15(d) of the Securities Exchange Act of 1934 or satisfies the conditions in paragraph (a)(1)(i)(B) of this section;

ii. The condition in paragraph (a)(1)(ii) of this section is satisfied;

iii. The research report includes similar information with respect to a substantial number of issuers in the issuer's industry or sub-industry, or contains a comprehensive list of securities currently recommended by the broker or dealer;

iv. The analysis regarding the issuer or its securities is given no materially greater space or prominence in the publication than that given to other securities or issuers; and

v. The broker or dealer publishes or distributes research reports in the regular course of its business and, at the time of the publication or distribution of the research report, is including similar information about the issuer or its securities in similar reports.

b. **Rule 144A offerings.** If the conditions in paragraph (a)(1) or (a)(2) of this section are satisfied, a broker's or dealer's publication or distribution of a research report shall not be considered an offer for sale or an offer to sell a security or general solicitation or general advertising, in connection with an offering relying on Rule 144A.

c. **Regulation S offerings.** If the conditions in paragraph (a)(1) or (a)(2) of this section are satisfied, a broker's or dealer's publication or distribution of a research report shall not:

1. Constitute directed selling efforts as defined in Rule 902(c) for offerings under Regulation S; or

2. Be inconsistent with the offshore transaction requirement in Rule 902(h) for offerings under Regulation S.

d. **Definition of research report.** For purposes of this section, research report means a written communication, as defined in Rule 405, that includes information, opinions, or recommendations with respect to securities of an issuer or an analysis of a security or an issuer, whether or not it provides information reasonably sufficient upon which to base an investment decision.

Instruction to Rule 139

Projections. A projection constitutes an analysis or information falling within the definition of research report. When a broker or dealer publishes or distributes projections of an issuer's sales or earnings in reliance on paragraph (a)(2) of this section, it must:

1. Have previously published or distributed projections on a regular basis in order to satisfy the "regular course of its business" condition;

2. At the time of publishing or disseminating a research report, be publishing or distributing projections with respect to that issuer; and

3. For purposes of paragraph (a)(2)(iii) of this section, include projections covering the same or similar periods with respect to either a substantial number of issuers in the issuer's industry or sub-industry or substantially all issuers represented in the comprehensive list of securities contained in the research report.

Rule 144 – Persons Deemed Not to be Engaged in a Distribution and Therefore Not Underwriters

Preliminary Note

Certain basic principles are essential to an understanding of the registration requirements in the Securities Act of 1933 (the Act or the Securities Act) and the purposes underlying Rule 144:

1. If any person sells a non-exempt security to any other person, the sale must be registered unless an exemption can be found for the transaction.

2. Section 4[a](1) of the Securities Act provides one such exemption for a transaction "by a person other than an issuer, underwriter, or dealer." Therefore, an understanding of the term "underwriter" is important in determining whether or not the Section 4[a](1) exemption from registration is available for the sale of the securities.

The term "underwriter" is broadly defined in Section 2(a)(11) of the Securities Act to mean any person who has purchased from an issuer with a view to, or offers or sells for an issuer in connection with, the distribution of any security, or participates, or has a direct or indirect participation in any such undertaking, or participates or has a participation in the direct or indirect underwriting of any such undertaking. The interpretation of this definition traditionally has focused on the words "with a view to" in the phrase "purchased from an issuer with a view to . . . distribution." An investment banking firm which arranges with an issuer for the public sale of its securities is clearly an "underwriter" under that section. However, individual investors who are not professionals in the securities business also may be "underwriters" if they act as links in a chain of transactions through which securities move from an issuer to the public.

Since it is difficult to ascertain the mental state of the purchaser at the time of an acquisition of securities, prior to and since the adoption of Rule 144, subsequent acts and circumstances have been considered to determine whether the purchaser took the securities "with a view to distribution" at the time of the acquisition. Emphasis has been placed on factors such as the length of time the person held the securities and whether there has been an unforeseeable change in circumstances of the holder. Experience has shown, however, that reliance upon such factors alone has led to uncertainty in the application of the registration provisions of the Act.

The Commission adopted Rule 144 to establish specific criteria for determining whether a person is not engaged in a distribution. Rule 144 creates a safe harbor from the Section 2(a)(11) definition of "underwriter." A person satisfying the applicable conditions of the Rule 144 safe harbor is deemed not to be engaged in a distribution of the securities and therefore not an underwriter of the securities for purposes of Section 2(a)(11). Therefore, such a person is deemed not to be an underwriter when determining whether a sale is eligible for the Section 4[a](1) exemption for "transactions by any person other than an issuer, underwriter, or dealer." If a sale of securities complies with all of the applicable conditions of Rule 144:

1. Any affiliate or other person who sells restricted securities will be deemed not to be engaged in a distribution and therefore not an underwriter for that transaction

2. Any person who sells restricted or other securities on behalf of an affiliate of the issuer will be deemed not to be engaged in a distribution and therefore not an underwriter for that transaction; and

3. The purchaser in such transaction will receive securities that are not restricted securities.

Rule 144 is not an exclusive safe harbor. A person who does not meet all of the applicable conditions of Rule 144 still may claim any other available exemption under the Act for the sale of the securities. The Rule 144 safe harbor is not available to any person with respect to any transaction or series of transactions that, although in technical compliance with Rule 144, is part of a plan or scheme to evade the registration requirements of the Act.

a. **Definitions.** The following definitions shall apply for the purposes of this rule.

   1. An **affiliate** of an issuer is a person that directly, or indirectly through one or more intermediaries, controls, or is controlled by, or is under common control with, such issuer.

   2. The term **person** when used with reference to a person for whose account securities are to be sold in reliance upon this rule includes, in addition to such person, all of the following persons:

      i. Any relative or spouse of such person, or any relative of such spouse, any one of whom has the same home as such person;

      ii. Any trust or estate in which such person or any of the persons specified in paragraph (a)(2)(i) of this section collectively own ten percent or more of the total beneficial interest or of which any of such persons serve as trustee, executor or in any similar capacity; and

      iii. Any corporation or other organization (other than the issuer) in which such person or any of the persons specified in paragraph (a)(2)(i) of this section are the beneficial owners collectively of ten percent or more of any class of equity securities or ten percent or more of the equity interest.

   3. The term **restricted securities** means:

      i. Securities acquired directly or indirectly from the issuer, or from an affiliate of the issuer, in a transaction or chain of transactions not involving any public offering;

      ii. Securities acquired from the issuer that are subject to the resale limitations of Rule 502(d) under Regulation D or Rule 701(c);

      iii. Securities acquired in a transaction or chain of transactions meeting the requirements of Rule 144A;

      iv. Securities acquired from the issuer in a transaction subject to the conditions of Regulation CE;

      v. Equity securities of domestic issuers acquired in a transaction or chain of transactions subject to the conditions of Rule 901 or Rule 903 under Regulation S (Rules 901 through 905 and Preliminary Notes);

      vi. Securities acquired in a transaction made under Rule 801 to the same extent and proportion that the securities held by the security holder of the class with respect to which the rights offering was made were, as of the record date for the rights offering, "restricted securities" within the meaning of this paragraph (a)(3);

      vii. Securities acquired in a transaction made under Rule 802 to the same extent and proportion that the securities that were tendered or exchanged in the exchange offer or business combination were "restricted securities" within the meaning of this paragraph (a)(3); and

    viii.   Securities acquired from the issuer in a transaction subject to an exemption under section 4[a](5) of the Act.

4.   The term **debt securities** means:

    i.   Any security other than an equity security as defined in Rule 405;

    ii.   Non-participatory preferred stock, which is defined as non-convertible capital stock, the holders of which are entitled to a preference in payment of dividends and in distribution of assets on liquidation, dissolution, or winding up of the issuer, but are not entitled to participate in residual earnings

    iii.   Asset-backed securities, as defined in Rule 1101 of this chapter.

b.   **Conditions to be Met.** Subject to paragraph (i) of this section, the following conditions must be met:

1.   **Non-Affiliates**.

    i.   If the issuer of the securities is, and has been for a period of at least 90 days immediately before the sale, subject to the reporting requirements of section 13 or 15(d) of the Securities Exchange Act of 1934 (the Exchange Act), any person who is not an affiliate of the issuer at the time of the sale, and has not been an affiliate during the preceding three months, who sells restricted securities of the issuer for his or her own account shall be deemed not to be an underwriter of those securities within the meaning of section 2(a)(11) of the Act if all of the conditions of paragraphs (c)(1) and (d) of are met. The requirements of paragraph (c)(1) of this section shall not apply to restricted securities sold for the account of a person who is not an affiliate of the issuer at the time of the sale and has not been an affiliate during the preceding three months, provided a period of one year has elapsed since the later of the date the securities were acquired from the issuer or from an affiliate of the issuer.

    ii.   If the issuer of the securities is not, or has not been for a period of at least 90 days immediately before the sale, subject to the reporting requirements of section 13 or 15(d) of the Exchange Act, any person who is not an affiliate of the issuer at the time of the sale, and has not been an affiliate during the preceding three months, who sells restricted securities of the issuer for his or her own account shall be deemed not to be underwriter of those securities within the meaning of section 2(a)(11) of the Act if the condition of paragraph (d) of this rule is met.

2.   **Affiliates or persons selling on behalf of affiliates**. Any affiliate of the issuer, or any person who was an affiliate at any time during the 90 days immediately before the sale, who sells restricted securities, or any person who sells restricted or any other securities for the account of an affiliate of the issuer of such securities, or any person who sells restricted or any other securities for the account of a person who was an affiliate at any time during the 90 days immediately before the sale, shall be deemed not to be an underwriter of those securities within the meaning of section 2(a)(11) of the Act if all of the conditions of this section are met.

c. **Current Public Information**. Adequate current public information with respect to the issuer of the securities must be available. Such information will be deemed to be available only if the applicable condition set forth in this paragraph is met:

1. **Reporting Issuers**. The issuer is, and has been for a period of at least 90 days immediately before the sale, subject to the reporting requirements of section 13 or 15(d) of the Exchange Act and has:

    i. Filed all required reports under section 13 or 15(d) of the Exchange Act, as applicable, during the 12 months preceding such sale (or for such shorter period that the issuer was required to file such reports), other than Form 8-K reports; and

    ii. Submitted electronically and posted on its corporate Web site, if any, every Interactive Data File required to be submitted and posted pursuant to Rule 405 of Regulation S-T, during the 12 months preceding such sale (or for such shorter period that the issuer was required to submit and post such files); or

2. **Non-reporting issuers**. If the issuer is not subject to Section 13 or 15(d) of the Securities Exchange Act of 1934, there is publicly available the information concerning the issuer specified in paragraphs (b)(5)(i)(A) to (N), inclusive, and paragraph (b)(5)(i)(P) of Rule 15c2-11 of this chapter or, if the issuer is an insurance company, the information specified in Section 12(g)(2)(G)(i) of the Exchange Act.

Note to Rule 144(c). With respect to paragraph (c)(1), the person can rely upon:

1. A statement in whichever is the most recent report, quarterly or annual, required to be filed and filed by the issuer that such issuer has:

    a. Filed all reports required under section 13 or 15(d) of the Exchange Act, as applicable, during the preceding 12 months (or for such shorter period that the issuer was required to file such reports), other than Form 8–K reports, and has been subject to such filing requirements for the past 90 days; and

    b. Submitted electronically and posted on its corporate Web site, if any, every Interactive Data File required to be submitted and posted pursuant to Rule 405 of Regulation S-T, during the preceding 12 months (or for such shorter period that the issuer was required to submit and post such files); or

2. A written statement from the issuer that it has complied with such reporting, submission or posting requirements.

3. Neither type of statement may be relied upon, however, if the person knows or has reason to believe that the issuer has not complied with such requirements.

d. **Holding Period for Restricted Securities**. If the securities sold are restricted securities, the following provisions apply:

1. **General Rule**.

    i. If the issuer of the securities is, and has been for a period of at least 90 days immediately before the sale, subject to the reporting requirements of section 13 or 15(d) of the Exchange Act, a minimum of six months must elapse between the later of the date of the acquisition of the securities from the issuer, or from an affiliate of the issuer, and any resale of such securities in reliance on this section for the account of either the acquiror or any subsequent holder of those securities.

ii.   If the issuer of the securities is not, or has not been for a period of at least 90 days immediately before the sale, subject to the reporting requirements of section 13 or 15(d) of the Exchange Act, a minimum of one year must elapse between the later of the date of the acquisition of the securities from the issuer, or from an affiliate of the issuer, and any resale of such securities in reliance on this section for the account of either the acquiror or any subsequent holder of those securities.

iii.   If the acquiror takes the securities by purchase, the holding period shall not begin until the full purchase price or other consideration is paid or given by the person acquiring the securities from the issuer or from an affiliate of the issuer.

2.   **Promissory Notes, Other Obligations or Installment Contracts.** Giving the issuer or affiliate of the issuer from whom the securities were purchased a promissory note or other obligation to pay the purchase price, or entering into an installment purchase contract with such person, shall not be deemed full payment of the purchase price unless the promissory note, obligation or contract:

i.   provides for full recourse against the purchaser of the securities;

ii.   is secured by collateral, other than the securities purchased, having a fair market value at least equal to the purchase price of the securities purchased; and

iii. shall have been discharged by payment in full prior to the sale of the securities.

3.   **Determination of Holding Period**. The following provisions shall apply for the purpose of determining the period securities have been held:

i.   Stock Dividends, Splits and Recapitalizations. Securities acquired from the issuer as a dividend or pursuant to a stock split, reverse split or recapitalization shall be deemed to have been acquired at the same time as the securities on which the dividend or, if more than one, the initial dividend was paid, the securities involved in the split or reverse split, or the securities surrendered in connection with the recapitalization.

ii.   Conversions. If the securities sold were acquired from the issuer solely in exchange for other securities of the same issuer, the newly acquired securities shall be deemed to have been acquired at the same time as the securities surrendered for conversion or exchange, even if the securities surrendered were not convertible or exchangeable by their terms.

Note to Rule 144(d)(3)(ii). If the surrendered securities originally did not provide for cashless conversion or exchange by their terms and the holder provided consideration, other than solely securities of the same issuer, in connection with the amendment of the surrendered securities to permit cashless conversion or exchange, then the newly acquired securities shall be deemed to have been acquired at the same time as such amendment to the surrendered securities, so long as, in the conversion or exchange, the securities sold were acquired from the issuer solely in exchange for other securities of the same issuer.

iii. Contingent Issuance of Securities. Securities acquired as a contingent payment of the purchase price of an equity interest in a business, or the assets of a business, sold to the issuer or an affiliate of the issuer shall be deemed to have been acquired at the time of such sale if the issuer or affiliate was then committed to issue the securities subject only to conditions other than the payment of further consideration for such securities. An agreement entered into in connection with any such purchase to remain in the employment of, or not to compete with, the issuer or affiliate or the rendering of services pursuant to such agreement shall not be deemed to be the payment of further consideration for such securities.

iv.   Pledged Securities. Securities which are bona fide pledged by an affiliate of the issuer when sold by the pledgee, or by a purchaser, after a default in the obligation secured by the pledge, shall be deemed to have been acquired when they were acquired by the pledgor, except that if the securities were pledged without recourse they shall be deemed to have been acquired by the pledgee at the time of the pledge or by the purchaser at the time of purchase.

v.   Gifts of Securities. Securities acquired from an affiliate of the issuer by gift shall be deemed to have been acquired by the donee when they were acquired by the donor;

vi.   Trusts. Where a trust settlor is an affiliate of the issuer, securities acquired from the settlor by the trust, or acquired from the trust by the beneficiaries thereof, shall be deemed to have been acquired when such securities were acquired by the settlor;

vii. Estates. Where a deceased person was an affiliate of the issuer, securities held by the estate of such person or acquired from such an estate by the estate beneficiaries shall be deemed to have been acquired when they were acquired by the deceased person, except that no holding period is required if the estate is not an affiliate of the issuer or if the securities are sold by a beneficiary of the estate who is not such an affiliate.

Note to Rule 144(d)(3(vii). While there is no holding period or amount limitation for estates and beneficiaries thereof which are not affiliates of the issuer, paragraphs (c), and (h) of this section apply to securities sold by such persons in reliance upon this section.

viii. Rule 145(a) transactions. The holding period for securities acquired in a transaction specified in Rule 145(a) shall be deemed to commence on the date the securities were acquired by the purchaser in such transaction, except as otherwise provided in paragraphs (d)(3)(ii) and (ix) of this section.

ix.   Holding company formations. Securities acquired from the issuer in a transaction effected solely for the purpose of forming a holding company shall be deemed to have been acquired at the same time as the securities of the predecessor issuer exchanged in the holding company formation where:

A.   The newly formed holding company's securities were issued solely in exchange for the securities of the predecessor company as part of a reorganization of the predecessor company into a holding company structure;

      B. Holders received securities of the same class evidencing the same proportional interest in the holding company as they held in the predecessor, and the rights and interests of the holders of such securities are substantially the same as those they possessed as holders of the predecessor company's securities; and

      C. Immediately following the transaction, the holding company has no significant assets other than securities of the predecessor company and its existing subsidiaries and has substantially the same assets and liabilities on a consolidated basis as the predecessor company had before the transaction.

  x. Cashless exercise of options and warrants. If the securities sold were acquired from the issuer solely upon cashless exercise of options or warrants issued by the issuer, the newly acquired securities shall be deemed to have been acquired at the same time as the exercised options or warrants, even if the options or warrants exercised originally did not provide for cashless exercise by their terms.

      Note 1 to Rule 144(d)(3)(x). If the options or warrants originally did not provide for cashless exercise by their terms and the holder provided consideration, other than solely securities of the same issuer, in connection with the amendment of the options or warrants to permit cashless exercise, then the newly acquired securities shall be deemed to have been acquired at the same time as such amendment to the options or warrants so long as the exercise itself was cashless.

      Note 2 to Rule 144(d)(3)(x). If the options or warrants are not purchased for cash or property and do not create any investment risk to the holder, as in the case of employee stock options, the newly acquired securities shall be deemed to have been acquired at the time the options or warrants are exercised, so long as the full purchase price or other consideration for the newly acquired securities has been paid or given by the person acquiring the securities from the issuer or from an affiliate of the issuer at the time of exercise.

e. **Limitation on Amount of Securities Sold.** Except as hereinafter provided, the amount of securities sold for the account of an affiliate of the issuer in reliance upon this section shall be determined as follows:

  1. If any securities are sold for the account of an affiliate of the issuer, regardless of whether those securities are restricted, the amount of securities sold, together with all sales of securities of the same class for the account of such person within the preceding three months, shall not exceed the greatest of

      i. one percent of the shares or other units of the class outstanding as shown by the most recent report or statement published by the issuer, or

      ii. the average weekly reported volume of trading in such securities on all national securities exchanges and/or reported through the automated quotation system of a registered securities association during the four calendar weeks preceding the filing of notice required by paragraph (h), or if no such notice is required the date of receipt of the order to execute the transaction by the broker or the date of execution of the transaction directly with a market maker, or

iii. the average weekly volume of trading in such securities reported through the consolidated transaction reporting system contemplated by Rule 11Aa3-1 under the Securities Exchange Act of 1934 during the four-week period specified in subdivision (ii) of this paragraph.

2. If the securities sold are debt securities, then the amount of debt securities sold for the account of an affiliate of the issuer, regardless of whether those securities are restricted, shall not exceed the greater of the limitation set forth in paragraph (e)(1) of this section or, together with all sales of securities of the same tranche (or class when the securities are on-participatory preferred stock) sold for the account of such person within the preceding three months, ten percent of the principal amount of the tranche (or class when the securities are non-participatory preferred stock) attributable to the securities sold..

3. Determination of Amount. For the purpose of determining the amount of securities specified in paragraph (e)(1) of this section and, applicable, paragraph (e)(2) of this section, the following provisions shall apply:

   i. Where both convertible securities and securities of the class into which they are convertible are sold, the amount of convertible securities sold shall be deemed to be the amount of securities of the class into which they are convertible for the purpose of determining the aggregate amount of securities of both classes sold;

   ii. The amount of securities sold for the account of a pledgee of those securities, or for the account of a purchaser of the pledged securities, during any period of three months within six months (or within one year if the issuer of the securities is not, or has not been for a period of at least 90 days immediately before the sale, subject to the reporting requirements of section 13 or 15(d) of the Exchange Act) after a default in the obligation secured by the pledge, and the amount of securities sold during the same three-month period for the account of the pledgor shall not exceed, in the aggregate, the amount specified in paragraph (e)(1) or (2) of this section, whichever is applicable.

   Note to Rule 144(e)(3)(ii). Sales by a pledgee of securities pledged by a borrower will not be aggregated under paragraph (e)(3)(ii) with sales of the securities of the same issuer by other pledgees of such borrower in the absence of concerted action by such pledgees.

   iii. The amount of securities sold for the account of a donee of those securities during any three-month period within six months (or within one year if the issuer of the securities is not, or has not been for a period of at least 90 days immediately before the sale, subject to the reporting requirements of section 13 or 15(d) of the Exchange Act) after the donation, and the amount of securities sold during the same three-month period for the account of the donor, shall not exceed, in the aggregate, the amount specified in paragraph (e)(1) or (2), which is applicable.

   iv. Where securities were acquired by a trust from the settlor of the trust, the amount of such securities sold for the account of the trust during any period of three months within six months (or within one year if the issuer of the securities is not, or has not been for a period of at least 90 days immediately before the sale, subject to the reporting requirements of section 13 or 15(d) of the Exchange Act) after the acquisition of the securities by the trust, and the amount of securities sold during the same three-month period for the account of the settlor, shall not exceed, in the aggregate, the amount specified in paragraph (e)(1) or (2) of this section, whichever is applicable;

v.   The amount of securities sold for the account of the estate of a deceased person, or for the account of a beneficiary of such estate, during any three-month period and the amount of securities sold during the same three-month period for the account of the deceased person prior to his death shall not exceed, in the aggregate, the amount specified in subparagraph (1) or (2) of this section, whichever is applicable; *Provided,* That no limitation on amount shall apply if the estate or beneficiary thereof is not an affiliate of the issuer;

vi.   When two or more affiliates or other persons agree to act in concert for the purpose of selling securities of an issuer, all securities of the same class sold for the account of all such persons during any three-month period shall be aggregated for the purpose of determining the limitation on the amount of securities sold;

vii.   The following sales of securities need not be included in determining the amount of securities sold in reliance upon this section:
A.   securities sold pursuant to an effective registration statement under the Act;
B.   securities sold pursuant to an exemption provided by Regulation A under the Act;
C.   securities sold in a transaction exempt pursuant to Section 4 of the Act and not involving any public offering; and
D.   securities sold offshore pursuant to Regulation S under the Act.

f.   **Manner of Sale**.
1.   The securities shall be sold in one of the following manners:
i.   *brokers' transactions* within the meaning of section 4[a](4) of the Act;
ii.   transactions directly with a *market maker,* as that term is defined in section 3(a)(38) of the Exchange Act; or
iii.   *riskless principal transactions* where
A.   the offsetting trades must be executed at the same price (exclusive of an explicitly disclosed markup or markdown, commission equivalent, or other fee);
B.   the transaction is permitted to be reported as riskless under the rules of a self-regulatory organization; and the requirements of paragraphs (g)(2) (applicable to any markup or markdown, commission equivalent, or other fee, (g)(3), and (g)(4) of this section are met.

Note to Rule 144(f)(1)
For purposes of this paragraph, a riskless principal transaction means a principal transaction where, after having received from a customer an order to buy, a broker or dealer purchases the security as principal in the market to satisfy the order to buy or, after having received from a customer an order to sell, sells the security as principal to the market to satisfy the order to sell.

2.   The person selling the securities shall not:
     i.   solicit or arrange for the solicitation of orders to buy the securities in anticipation of or in connection with such transaction, or
     ii.   make any payment in connection with the offer or sale of the securities to any person other than the broker who executes the order to sell the securities.

3.   Paragraph (f) of this section shall not apply to:
     i.   Securities sold for the account of the estate of a deceased person or for the account of a beneficiary of such estate provided the estate or beneficiary thereof is not an affiliate of the issuer; or
     ii.   Debt securities.

g.   **Brokers' Transactions.** The term *brokers' transactions* in Section 4[a](4) of the Act shall for the purposes of this rule be deemed to include transactions by a broker in which such broker:

1.   does no more than execute the order or orders to sell the securities as agent for the person for whose account the securities are sold;

2.   receives no more than the usual and customary broker's commission;

3.   neither solicits nor arranges for the solicitation of customers' orders to buy the securities in anticipation of or in connection with the transaction; *provided,* that the foregoing shall not preclude
     i.   inquiries by the broker of other brokers or dealers who have indicated an interest in the securities within the preceding 60 days,
     ii.   inquiries by the broker of his customers who have indicated an unsolicited bona fide interest in the securities within the preceding 10 business days; **Note to Subparagraph (g)(3)(ii):** The broker should obtain and retain in his files written evidence of indications of bona fide unsolicited interest by his customers in the securities at the time such indications are received.
     iii.   the publication by the broker of bid and ask quotations for the security in an inter-dealer quotation system provided that such quotations are incident to the maintenance of a bona fide inter-dealer market for the security for the broker's own account and that the broker has published bona fide bid and ask quotations for the security in an inter-dealer quotation system on each of at least twelve days within the preceding thirty calendar days with no more than four business days in succession without such two-way quotations; or
     iv.   the publication by the broker of bid and ask quotations for the security in an alternative trading system, as defined in Rule 300 of this chapter, provided that the broker has published bona fide bid and ask quotations for the security in the alternative trading system on each of the last twelve business days; and

4.   after reasonable inquiry is not aware of circumstances indicating that the person for whose account the securities are sold is an underwriter with respect to the securities or that the transaction is a part of a distribution of securities of the issuer. Without limiting the foregoing, the broker shall be deemed to be aware of any facts or statements contained in the notice required by paragraph (h) below.

Notes
    i.   The broker, for his own protection, should obtain and retain in his files a copy of the notice required by paragraph (h).

    ii.   The reasonable inquiry required by paragraph (g)(4) of this section should include, but not necessarily be limited to, inquiry as to the following matters:

        a.   The length of time the securities have been held by the person for whose account they are to be sold. If practicable, the inquiry should include physical inspection of the securities;

        b.   The nature of the transaction in which the securities were acquired by such person;

        c.   The amount of securities of the same class sold during the past three months by all persons whose sales are required to be taken into consideration pursuant to paragraph (e) of this section;

        d.   Whether such person intends to sell additional securities of the same class through any other means;

        e.   Whether such person has solicited or made any arrangement for the solicitation of buy orders in connection with the proposed sale of securities;

        f.   Whether such person has made any payment to any other person in connection with the proposed sale of the securities; and

        g.   The number of shares or other units of the class outstanding, or the relevant trading volume.

h.   **Notice of Proposed Sale**.

    1.   Reporting issuers. If the issuer is, and has been for a period of at least 90 days immediately before the sale, subject to the reporting requirements of section 13 or 15(d) of the Exchange Act and the amount of securities to be sold in reliance upon this rule during any period of three months exceeds 5,000 shares or other units or has an aggregate sale price in excess of $50,000, a notice on Form 144 shall be filed electronically with the Commission.

    2.   *Non-reporting issuers*. If the issuer is not subject to the reporting requirements of section 13 or 15(d) of the Exchange Act, and the amount of securities to be sold in reliance upon this rule during any period of three months exceeds 5,000 shares or other units or has an aggregate sale price in excess of $50,000, three copies of a notice on Form 144 (§ 239.144 of this chapter) shall be filed with the Commission.

i.   **Unavailability to securities of issuers with no or nominal operations and no or nominal non-cash assets.**

    1.   This section is not available for the resale of securities initially issued by an issuer defined below:

        i.   An issuer, other than a business combination related shell company, as defined in Rule 405, or an asset-backed issuer, as defined in Item 1101(b) of Regulation AB, that has:

            A.   No or nominal operations; and

      B.   Either:
         1.   No or nominal assets;
         2.   Assets consisting solely of cash and cash equivalents; or
         3.   Assets consisting of any amount of cash and cash equivalents and nominal other assets; or

    ii.   An issuer that has been at any time previously an issuer described in paragraph (i)(1)(i).

2.   Notwithstanding paragraph (i)(1), if the issuer of the securities previously had been an issuer described in paragraph (i)(1)(i) but has ceased to be an issuer described in paragraph (i)(1)(i); is subject to the reporting requirements of section 13 or 15(d) of the Exchange Act; has filed all reports and other materials required to be filed by section 13 or 15(d) of the Exchange Act, as applicable, during the preceding 12 months (or for such shorter period that the issuer was required to file such reports and materials), other than Form 8-K reports; and has filed current "Form 10 information" with the Commission reflecting its status as an entity that is no longer an issuer described in paragraph (i)(1)(i), then those securities may be sold subject to the requirements of this section after one year has elapsed from the date that the issuer filed "Form 10 information" with the Commission.

3.   The term "Form 10 information" means the information that is required by Form 10 or Form 20-F, as applicable to the issuer of the securities, to register under the Exchange Act each class of securities being sold under this rule. The issuer may provide the Form 10 information in any filing of the issuer with the Commission. The Form 10 information is deemed filed when the initial filing is made with the Commission.

Rule 144A – Private Resales of Securities to Institutions

Preliminary Notes

1.   This section relates solely to the application of section 5 of the Act and not to antifraud or other provisions of the federal securities laws.

2.   Attempted compliance with this section does not act as an exclusive election; any seller hereunder may also claim the availability of any other applicable exemption from the registration requirements of the Act.

3.   In view of the objective of this section and the policies underlying the Act, this section is not available with respect to any transaction or series of transactions that, although in technical compliance with this section, is part of a plan or scheme to evade the registration provisions of the Act. In such cases, registration under the Act is required.

4.   Nothing in this section obviates the need for any issuer or any other person to comply with the securities registration or broker-dealer registration requirements of the Securities Exchange Act of 1934 (the *Exchange Act)*, whenever such requirements are applicable.

5.   Nothing in this section obviates the need for any person to comply with any applicable state law relating to the offer or sale of securities.

6. Securities acquired in a transaction made pursuant to the provisions of this section are deemed to be *restricted securities* within the meaning of Rule 144(a)(3).

7. The fact that purchasers of securities from the issuer thereof may purchase such securities with a view to reselling such securities pursuant to this section will not affect the availability to such issuer of an exemption under section 4(a)(2) of the Act, or Regulation D under the Act, from the registration requirements of the Act.

a. **Definitions**.

    1. For purposes of this section, **qualified institutional buyer** shall mean:

        i. Any of the following entities, acting for its own account or the accounts of other qualified institutional buyers, that in the aggregate owns and invests on a discretionary basis at least $100 million in securities of issuers that are not affiliated with the entity:

            A. Any *insurance company* as defined in section 2(a)(13) of the Act ;

                Note: A purchase by an insurance company for one or more of its separate accounts, as defined by section 2(a)(37) of the Investment Company Act of 1940, which are neither registered under section 8 of the Investment Company Act nor required to be so registered, shall be deemed to be a purchase for the account of such insurance company.

            B. Any *investment company* registered under the Investment Company Act or any *business development company* as defined in section 2(a)(48) of that Act;

            C. Any *Small Business Investment Company* licensed by the U.S. Small Business Administration under section 301(c) or (d) of the Small Business Investment Act of 1958 or any *Rural Business Investment Company* as defined in section 384A of the Consolidated Farm and Rural Development Act;

            D. Any *plan* established and maintained by a state, its political subdivisions, or any agency or instrumentality of a state or its political subdivisions, for the benefit of its employees;

            E. Any *employee benefit plan* within the meaning of title I of the Employee Retirement Income Security Act of 1974;

            F. Any trust fund whose trustee is a bank or trust company and whose participants are exclusively plans of the types identified in paragraph (a)(1)(i)(D) or (E) of this section, except trust funds that include as participants individual retirement accounts or H.R. 10 plans.

            G. Any *business development company* as defined in section 202(a)(22) of the Investment Advisers Act of 1940;

            H. Any organization described in section 501(c) (3) of the Internal Revenue Code, corporation (other than a bank as defined in section 3(a)(2) of the Act or a savings and loan association or other institution referenced in section 3(a)(5)(A) of the Act or a foreign bank or savings and loan association or equivalent institution), partnership, limited liability company, or Massachusetts or similar business trust; and

            I. Any *investment adviser* registered under the Investment Advisers Act; and

J.   Any institutional accredited investor, as defined in rule 501(a) under the Act, of a type not listed in paragraphs (a)(1)(i)(A) through (I) or paragraphs (a)(1)(ii) through (vi).

Note: An entity seeking qualified institutional buyer status under Rule 144A(a)(1)(i)(J) may be formed for the purpose of acquiring the securities being offered under this section.

ii.   Any *dealer* registered pursuant to section 15 of the Exchange Act, acting for its own account or the accounts of other qualified institutional buyers, that in the aggregate owns and invests on a discretionary basis at least $10 million of securities of issuers that are not affiliated with the dealer, *Provided,* That securities constituting the whole or a part of an unsold allotment to or subscription by a dealer as a participant in a public offering shall not be deemed to be owned by such dealer;

iii.   Any *dealer* registered pursuant to section 15 of the Exchange Act acting in a riskless principal transaction on behalf of a qualified institutional buyer;

Note: A registered dealer may act as agent, on a non-discretionary basis, in a transaction with a qualified institutional buyer without itself having to be a qualified institutional buyer.

iv.   Any investment company registered under the Investment Company Act, acting for its own account or for the accounts of other qualified institutional buyers, that is part of a family of investment companies which own in the aggregate at least $100 million in securities of issuers, other than issuers that are affiliated with the investment company or are part of such family of investment companies. *Family of investment companies* means any two or more investment companies registered under the Investment Company Act, except for a unit investment trust whose assets consist solely of shares of one or more registered investment companies, that have the same investment adviser (or, in the case of unit investment trusts, the same depositor), *Provided* That, for purposes of this section:

A.   Each series of a series company (as defined in Rule 18f-2 under the Investment Company Act) shall be deemed to be a separate investment company; and

B.   Investment companies shall be deemed to have the same adviser (or depositor) if their advisers (or depositors) are majority-owned subsidiaries of the same parent, or if one investment company's adviser (or depositor) is a majority-owned subsidiary of the other investment company's adviser (or depositor);

v.   Any entity, all of the equity owners of which are qualified institutional buyers, acting for its own account or the accounts of other qualified institutional buyers; and

vi.   Any *bank* as defined in section 3(a)(2) of the Act, any savings and loan association or other institution as referenced in section 3(a)(5)(A) of the Act, or any foreign bank or savings and loan association or equivalent institution, acting for its own account or the accounts of other qualified institutional buyers, that in the aggregate owns and invests on a discretionary basis at least $100 million in securities of issuers that are not affiliated with it and that has an audited net worth of at least $25 million as demonstrated in its latest annual financial statements, as of a date not more than 16 months preceding the date of sale under the Rule in the case of a U.S. bank or savings and loan association, and not more than 18 months preceding such date of sale for a foreign bank or savings and loan association or equivalent institution.

2. In determining the aggregate amount of securities owned and invested on a discretionary basis by an entity, the following instruments and interests shall be excluded: bank deposit notes and certificates of deposit; loan participations; repurchase agreements; securities owned but subject to a repurchase agreement; and currency, interest rate and commodity swaps.

3. The aggregate value of securities owned and invested on a discretionary basis by an entity shall be the cost of such securities, except where the entity reports its securities holdings in its financial statements on the basis of their market value, and no current information with respect to the cost of those securities has been published. In the latter event, the securities may be valued at market for purposes of this section.

4. In determining the aggregate amount of securities owned by an entity and invested on a discretionary basis, securities owned by subsidiaries of the entity that are consolidated with the entity in its financial statements prepared in accordance with generally accepted accounting principles may be included if the investments of such subsidiaries are managed under the direction of the entity, except that, unless the entity is a reporting company under section 13 or 15(d) of the Exchange Act, securities owned by such subsidiaries may not be included if the entity itself is a majority-owned subsidiary that would be included in the consolidated financial statements of another enterprise.

5. For purposes of this section, *riskless principal transaction* means a transaction in which a dealer buys a security from any person and makes a simultaneous offsetting sale of such security to a qualified institutional buyer, including another dealer acting as riskless principal for a qualified institutional buyer.

6. For purposes of this section, *effective conversion premium* means the amount, expressed as a percentage of the security's conversion value, by which the price at issuance of a convertible security exceeds its conversion value.

7. For purposes of this section, *effective exercise premium* means the amount, expressed as a percentage of the warrant's exercise value, by which the sum of the price at issuance and the exercise price of a warrant exceeds its exercise value.

b. **Sales by Persons Other than Issuers or Dealers.** Any person, other than the issuer or a dealer, who offers or sells securities in compliance with the conditions set forth in paragraph (d) of this section shall be deemed not to be engaged in a distribution of such securities and therefore not to be an underwriter of such securities within the meaning of sections 2(a)(11) and 4(a)(1) of the Act.

c. **Sales by Dealers.** Any dealer who offers or sells securities in compliance with the conditions set forth in paragraph (d) of this section shall be deemed not to be a participant in a distribution of such securities within the meaning of section 4(a)(3)(C) of the Act and not to be an underwriter of such securities within the meaning of section

2(a)(11) of the Act, and such securities shall be deemed not to have been offered to the public within the meaning of section 4(a)(3)(A) of the Act.

d. **Conditions to be Met.** To qualify for exemption under this section, an offer or sale must meet the following conditions:

1. The securities are sold only to a qualified institutional buyer or to a purchaser that the seller and any person acting on behalf of the seller reasonably believe is a qualified institutional buyer. In determining whether a prospective purchaser is a qualified institutional buyer, the seller and any person acting on its behalf shall be entitled to rely upon the following non-exclusive methods of establishing the prospective purchaser's ownership and discretionary investments of securities:

    i. The prospective purchaser's most recent publicly available financial statements, *Provided,* That such statements present the information as of a date within 16 months preceding the date of sale of securities under this section in the case of a U.S. purchaser and within 18 months preceding such date of sale for a foreign purchaser;

    ii. The most recent publicly available information appearing in documents filed by the prospective purchaser with the Commission or another United States federal, state, or local governmental agency or self-regulatory organization, or with a foreign governmental agency or self-regulatory organization, *Provided,* That any such information is as of a date within 16 months preceding the date of sale of securities under this section in the case of a U.S. purchaser and within 18 months preceding such date of sale for a foreign purchaser;

    iii. The most recent publicly available information appearing in a recognized securities manual, *Provided,* That such information is as of a date within 16 months preceding the date of sale of securities under this section in the case of a U.S. purchaser and within 18 months preceding such date of sale for a foreign purchaser; or

    iv. A certification by the chief financial officer, a person fulfilling an equivalent function, or other executive officer of the purchaser, specifying the amount of securities owned and invested on a discretionary basis by the purchaser as of a specific date on or since the close of the purchaser's most recent fiscal year, or, in the case of a purchaser that is a member of a family of investment companies, a certification by an executive officer of the investment adviser specifying the amount of securities owned by the family of investment companies as of a specific date on or since the close of the purchaser's most recent fiscal year;

2. The seller and any person acting on its behalf takes reasonable steps to ensure that the purchaser is aware that the seller may rely on the exemption from the provisions of section 5 of the Act provided by this section;

3. The securities offered or sold:

    i. Were not, when issued, of the same class as securities listed on a national securities exchange registered under section 6 of the Exchange Act or quoted in a U.S. automated inter-dealer quotation system; *Provided,* That securities that are convertible or exchangeable into securities so listed or quoted at the time of issuance and that had an effective conversion premium of less than 10 percent, shall be treated as securities of the class into which they are convertible or exchangeable; and that warrants that may be exercised for securities so listed or quoted at the time of issuance, for a period of less than 3 years from the date of issuance, or that had an effective exercise premium of less than 10 percent, shall be treated as securities of the class to be issued upon exercise; and *Provided further,* That the Commission may from time to time, taking into account then-existing market practices, designate additional securities and classes of securities that will not be deemed of the same class as securities listed on a national securities exchange or quoted in a U.S. automated inter-dealer quotation system; and

ii.   Are not securities of an open-end investment company, unit investment trust or face-amount certificate company that is or is required to be registered under section 8 of the Investment Company Act; and

4.   i.   In the case of securities of an issuer that is neither subject to section 13 or 15(d) of the Exchange Act, nor exempt from reporting pursuant to Rule 12g3-2(b) under the Exchange Act, nor a foreign government as defined in Rule 405 eligible to register securities under Schedule B of the Act, the holder and a prospective purchaser designated by the holder have the right to obtain from the issuer, upon request of the holder, and the prospective purchaser has received from the issuer, the seller, or a person acting on either of their behalf, at or prior to the time of sale, upon such prospective purchaser's request to the holder or the issuer, the following information (which shall be reasonably current in relation to the date of resale under this section): a very brief statement of the nature of the business of the issuer and the products and services it offers; and the issuer's most recent balance sheet and profit and loss and retained earnings statements, and similar financial statements for such part of the two preceding fiscal years as the issuer has been in operation (the financial statements should be audited to the extent reasonably available).

ii.   The requirement that the information be *reasonably current* will be presumed to be satisfied if:

A.   The balance sheet is as of a date less than 16 months before the date of resale, the statements of profit and loss and retained earnings are for the 12 months preceding the date of such balance sheet, and if such balance sheet is not as of a date less than 6 months before the date of resale, it shall be accompanied by additional statements of profit and loss and retained earnings for the period from the date of such balance sheet to a date less than 6 months before the date of resale; and

B.   The statement of the nature of the issuer's business and its products and services offered is as of a date within 12 months prior to the date of resale; or

C.   With regard to foreign private issuers, the required information meets the timing requirements of the issuer's home country or principal trading markets.

e. **Offers and Sales of Securities Pursuant to this Section** – shall be deemed not to affect the availability of any exemption or safe harbor relating to any previous or subsequent offer or sale of such securities by the issuer or any prior or subsequent holder thereof.

Rule 147 – "Part of an Issue," "Person Resident," and "Doing Business Within" for Purposes of Section 3(a)(11)

a. This section shall not raise any presumption that the exemption provided by section 3(a)(11) of the Act is not available for transactions by an issuer which do not satisfy all of the provisions of this section.

b. **Manner of offers and sales**. An issuer, or any person acting on behalf of the issuer, shall be deemed to conduct an offering in compliance with section 3(a)(11) of the Act, where offers and sales are made only to persons resident within the same state or territory in which the issuer is resident and doing business, within the meaning of section 3(a)(11) of the Act, so long as the issuer complies with the provisions of paragraphs (c), (d), and (f) through (h) of this section.

c. **Nature of the issuer**. The issuer of the securities shall at the time of any offers and sales be a person resident and doing business within the state or territory in which all of the offers and sales are made.

   1. The issuer shall be deemed to be a resident of the state or territory in which:
      i. It is incorporated or organized, and it has its principal place of business, if a corporation, limited partnership, trust or other form of business organization that is organized under state or territorial law. The issuer shall be deemed to have its principal place of business in a state or territory in which the officers, partners or managers of the issuer primarily direct, control and coordinate the activities of the issuer;
      ii. It has its principal place of business, as defined in paragraph (c)(1)(i) of this section, if a general partnership or other form of business organization that is not organized under any state or territorial law;
      iii. Such person's principal residence is located, if an individual.

      Instruction to paragraph (c)(1): An issuer that has previously conducted an intrastate offering pursuant to this section or Rule 147A may not conduct another intrastate offering pursuant to this section in a different state or territory, until the expiration of the time period specified in paragraph (e) of this section or paragraph (e) of Rule 147A, calculated on the basis of the date of the last sale in such offering.

   2. The issuer shall be deemed to be doing business within a state or territory if the issuer satisfies at least one of the following requirements:
      i. The issuer derived at least 80% of its consolidated gross revenues from the operation of a business or of real property located in or from the rendering of services within such state or territory;

         Instruction to paragraph (c)(2)(i): Revenues must be calculated based on the issuer's most recent fiscal year, if the first offer of securities pursuant to this section is made during the first six months of the issuer's current fiscal year, and based on the first six months of the issuer's current fiscal year or during the twelve-month fiscal period ending with such six-month period, if the first offer of securities pursuant to this section is made during the last six months of the issuer's

 ii. The issuer had at the end of its most recent semi-annual fiscal period prior to an initial offer of securities in any offering or subsequent offering pursuant to this section, at least 80% of its assets and those of its subsidiaries on a consolidated basis located within such state or territory;

 iii. The issuer intends to use and uses at least 80% of the net proceeds to the issuer from sales made pursuant to this section (§ 230.147) in connection with the operation of a business or of real property, the purchase of real property located in, or the rendering of services within such state or territory; or

 iv. A majority of the issuer's employees are based in such state or territory.

d. **Residence of offerees and purchasers.** Offers and sales of securities pursuant to this section shall be made only to residents of the state or territory in which the issuer is resident, as determined pursuant to paragraph (c) of this section, or who the issuer reasonably believes, at the time of the offer and sale, are residents of the state or territory in which the issuer is resident. For purposes of determining the residence of offerees and purchasers:

 1. A corporation, partnership, limited liability company, trust or other form of business organization shall be deemed to be a resident of a state or territory if, at the time of the offer and sale to it, it has its principal place of business, as defined in paragraph (c)(1)(i) of this section, within such state or territory.

  Instruction to paragraph (d)(1): A trust that is not deemed by the law of the state or territory of its creation to be a separate legal entity is deemed to be a resident of each state or territory in which its trustee is, or trustees are, resident.

 2. Individuals shall be deemed to be residents of a state or territory if such individuals have, at the time of the offer and sale to them, their principal residence in the state or territory.

 3. A corporation, partnership, trust or other form of business organization, which is organized for the specific purpose of acquiring securities offered pursuant to this section, shall not be a resident of a state or territory unless all of the beneficial owners of such organization are residents of such state or territory.

Instruction to paragraph (d): Obtaining a written representation from purchasers of in-state residency status will not, without more, be sufficient to establish a reasonable belief that such purchasers are in-state residents.

e. **Limitation on resales.** For a period of six months from the date of the sale by the issuer of a security pursuant to this section, any resale of such security shall be made only to persons resident within the state or territory in which the issuer was resident, as determined pursuant to paragraph (c) of this section, at the time of the sale of the security by the issuer.

Instruction to paragraph (e): In the case of convertible securities, resales of either the convertible security, or if it is converted, the underlying security, could be made during the period described in paragraph (e) only to persons resident within such state or territory. For purposes of this paragraph (e), a conversion in reliance on section 3(a)(9) of the Act does not begin a new period.

f.   **Precautions against interstate sales.**
  1. The issuer shall, in connection with any securities sold by it pursuant to this section:
      i.   Place a prominent legend on the certificate or other document evidencing the security stating that: "Offers and sales of these securities were made under an exemption from registration and have not been registered under the Securities Act of 1933. For a period of six months from the date of the sale by the issuer of these securities, any resale of these securities (or the underlying securities in the case of convertible securities) shall be made only to persons resident within the state or territory of [identify the name of the state or territory in which the issuer was resident at the time of the sale of the securities by the issuer].";
      ii.   Issue stop transfer instructions to the issuer's transfer agent, if any, with respect to the securities, or, if the issuer transfers its own securities, make a notation in the appropriate records of the issuer; and
      iii. Obtain a written representation from each purchaser as to his or her residence.
  2. The issuer shall, in connection with the issuance of new certificates for any of the securities that are sold pursuant to this section that are presented for transfer during the time period specified in paragraph (e), take the steps required by paragraphs (f)(1)(i) and (ii) of this section.
  3. The issuer shall, at the time of any offer or sale by it of a security pursuant to this section, prominently disclose to each offeree in the manner in which any such offer is communicated and to each purchaser of such security in writing a reasonable period of time before the date of sale, the following: "Sales will be made only to residents of [identify the name of the state or territory in which the issuer was resident at the time of the sale of the securities by the issuer]. Offers and sales of these securities are made under an exemption from registration and have not been registered under the Securities Act of 1933. For a period of six months from the date of the sale by the issuer of the securities, any resale of the securities (or the underlying securities in the case of convertible securities) shall be made only to persons resident within the state or territory of [identify the name of the state or territory in which the issuer was resident at the time of the sale of the securities by the issuer]."

g.   **Integration with other offerings.** To determine whether offers and sales should be integrated, refer to Rule 152.

Rule 147A – Intrastate Sales Exemption

a.   **Scope of the exemption.** Offers and sales by or on behalf of an issuer of its securities made in accordance with this section are exempt from section 5 of the Act. This exemption is not available to an issuer that is an investment company registered or required to be registered under the Investment Company Act of 1940.

b.   **Manner of offers and sales.** An issuer, or any person acting on behalf of the issuer, may rely on this exemption to make offers and sales using any form of general solicitation and general advertising, so long as the issuer complies with the provisions of paragraphs (c), (d), and (f) through (h) of this section.

c. **Nature of the issuer**. The issuer of the securities shall at the time of any offers and sales be a person resident and doing business within the state or territory in which all of the sales are made.

1. The issuer shall be deemed to be a resident of the state or territory in which it has its principal place of business. The issuer shall be deemed to have its principal place of business in a state or territory in which the officers, partners or managers of the issuer primarily direct, control and coordinate the activities of the issuer.

2. The issuer shall be deemed to be doing business within a state or territory if the issuer satisfies at least one of the following requirements:

    i. The issuer derived at least 80% of its consolidated gross revenues from the operation of a business or of real property located in or from the rendering of services within such state or territory;

    Instruction to paragraph (c)(2)(i): Revenues must be calculated based on the issuer's most recent fiscal year, if the first offer of securities pursuant to this section is made during the first six months of the issuer's current fiscal year, and based on the first six months of the issuer's current fiscal year or during the twelve-month fiscal period ending with such six-month period, if the first offer of securities pursuant to this section is made during the last six months of the issuer's current fiscal year.

    ii. The issuer had at the end of its most recent semi-annual fiscal period prior to an initial offer of securities in any offering or subsequent offering pursuant to this section, at least 80% of its assets and those of its subsidiaries on a consolidated basis located within such state or territory;

    iii. The issuer intends to use and uses at least 80% of the net proceeds to the issuer from sales made pursuant to this section in connection with the operation of a business or of real property, the purchase of real property located in, or the rendering of services within such state or territory; or

    iv. A majority of the issuer's employees are based in such state or territory.

Instruction to paragraph (c): An issuer that has previously conducted an intrastate offering pursuant to this section or Rule 147 may not conduct another intrastate offering pursuant to this section in a different state or territory, until the expiration of the time period specified in paragraph (e) of this section or paragraph (e) of Rule 147, calculated on the basis of the date of the last sale in such offering.

d. **Residence of purchasers**. Sales of securities pursuant to this section shall be made only to residents of the state or territory in which the issuer is resident, as determined pursuant to paragraph (c) of this section, or who the issuer reasonably believes, at the time of sale, are residents of the state or territory in which the issuer is resident. For purposes of determining the residence of purchasers:

1. A corporation, partnership, limited liability company, trust or other form of business organization shall be deemed to be a resident of a state or territory if, at the time of sale to it, it has its principal place of business, as defined in paragraph (c)(1) of this section, within such state or territory.

Instruction to paragraph (d)(1): A trust that is not deemed by the law of the state or territory of its creation to be a separate legal entity is deemed to be a resident of each state or territory in which its trustee is, or trustees are, resident.

2.   Individuals shall be deemed to be residents of a state or territory if such individuals have, at the time of sale to them, their principal residence in the state or territory.

3.   A corporation, partnership, trust or other form of business organization, which is organized for the specific purpose of acquiring securities offered pursuant to this section, shall not be a resident of a state or territory unless all of the beneficial owners of such organization are residents of such state or territory.

Instruction to paragraph (d): Obtaining a written representation from purchasers of in-state residency status will not, without more, be sufficient to establish a reasonable belief that such purchasers are in-state residents.

e.   **Limitation on resales**. For a period of six months from the date of the sale by the issuer of a security pursuant to this section, any resale of such security shall be made only to persons resident within the state or territory in which the issuer was resident, as determined pursuant to paragraph (c) of this section, at the time of the sale of the security by the issuer.

Instruction to paragraph (e): In the case of convertible securities, resales of either the convertible security, or if it is converted, the underlying security, could be made during the period described in paragraph (e) only to persons resident within such state or territory. For purposes of this paragraph (e), a conversion in reliance on section 3(a)(9) of the Act does not begin a new period.

f.   **Precautions against interstate sales**.

1.   The issuer shall, in connection with any securities sold by it pursuant to this section:

   i.   Place a prominent legend on the certificate or other document evidencing the security stating that: "Offers and sales of these securities were made under an exemption from registration and have not been registered under the Securities Act of 1933. For a period of six months from the date of the sale by the issuer of these securities, any resale of these securities (or the underlying securities in the case of convertible securities) shall be made only to persons resident within the state or territory of [identify the name of the state or territory in which the issuer was resident at the time of the sale of the securities by the issuer].";

   ii. Issue stop transfer instructions to the issuer's transfer agent, if any, with respect to the securities, or, if the issuer transfers its own securities, make a notation in the appropriate records of the issuer; and

   iii. Obtain a written representation from each purchaser as to his or her residence.

2.   The issuer shall, in connection with the issuance of new certificates for any of the securities that are sold pursuant to this section that are presented for transfer during the time period specified in paragraph (e), take the steps required by paragraphs (f)(1)(i) and (ii) of this section.

3.   The issuer shall, at the time of any offer or sale by it of a security pursuant to this section, prominently disclose to each offeree in the manner in which any

such offer is communicated and to each purchaser of such security in writing a reasonable period of time before the date of sale, the following: "Sales will be made only to residents of the state or territory of [identify the name of the state or territory in which the issuer was resident at the time of the sale of the securities by the issuer]. Offers and sales of these securities are made under an exemption from registration and have not been registered under the Securities Act of 1933. For a period of six months from the date of the sale by the issuer of the securities, any resale of the securities (or the underlying securities in the case of convertible securities) shall be made only to persons resident within the state or territory of [identify the name of the state or territory in which the issuer was resident at the time of the sale of the securities by the issuer]."

g. **Integration with other offerings.** To determine whether offers and sales should be integrated, refer to Rule 152.

Rule 152 – Integration

This section provides a general principle of integration and non-exclusive safe harbors from integration of registered and exempt offerings. Because of the objectives of this section and the policies underlying the Act, the provisions of this section will not have the effect of avoiding integration for any transaction or series of transactions that, although in technical compliance with the section, is part of a plan or scheme to evade the registration requirements of the Act.

a. **General principle of integration**. If the safe harbors in paragraph (b) of this section do not apply, in determining whether two or more offerings are to be treated as one for the purpose of registration or qualifying for an exemption from registration under the Act, offers and sales will not be integrated if, based on the particular facts and circumstances, the issuer can establish that each offering either complies with the registration requirements of the Act, or that an exemption from registration is available for the particular offering. In making this determination:

1. For an exempt offering prohibiting general solicitation, the issuer must have a reasonable belief, based on the facts and circumstances, with respect to each purchaser in the exempt offering prohibiting general solicitation, that the issuer (or any person acting on the issuer's behalf) either:

    i. Did not solicit such purchaser through the use of general solicitation; or

    ii. Established a substantive relationship with such purchaser prior to the commencement of the exempt offering prohibiting general solicitation; and

2. For two or more concurrent exempt offerings permitting general solicitation, in addition to satisfying the requirements of the particular exemption relied on, general solicitation offering materials for one offering that includes information about the material terms of a concurrent offering under another exemption may constitute an offer of securities in such other offering, and therefore the offer must comply with all the requirements for, and restrictions on, offers under the exemption being relied on for such other offering, including any legend requirements and communications restrictions.

b. **Safe harbors**. No integration analysis under paragraph (a) of this section is required, if any of the following non-exclusive safe harbors apply:

1.   Any offering made more than 30 calendar days before the commencement of any other offering, or more than 30 calendar days after the termination or completion of any other offering, will not be integrated with such other offering, provided that for an exempt offering for which general solicitation is not permitted that follows by 30 calendar days or more an offering that allows general solicitation, the provisions of Rule 152(a)(1) shall apply.

2.   Offers and sales made in compliance with Rule 701, pursuant to an employee benefit plan, or in compliance with Regulation S will not be integrated with other offerings;

3.   An offering for which a registration statement under the Act has been filed will not be integrated if it is made subsequent to:

   i.   A terminated or completed offering for which general solicitation is not permitted;

   ii. A terminated or completed offering for which general solicitation is permitted made only to qualified institutional buyers and institutional accredited investors; or

   iii. An offering for which general solicitation is permitted that terminated or completed more than 30 calendar days prior to the commencement of the registered offering; or

4.   Offers and sales made in reliance on an exemption for which general solicitation is permitted will not be integrated if made subsequent to any terminated or completed offering.

c.   **Commencement of an offering**. For purposes of this section, an offering of securities will be deemed to be commenced at the time of the first offer of securities in the offering by the issuer or its agents. The following non-exclusive list of factors should be considered in determining when an offering is deemed to be commenced. Pursuant to the requirements for registered and exempt offerings, an issuer or its agents may commence an offering in reliance on:

1.   Rule 241, on the date the issuer first made a generic offer soliciting interest in a contemplated securities offering for which the issuer had not yet determined the exemption under the Act under which the offering of securities would be conducted;

2.   Section 4(a)(2)), Rules 501 through 508 (Regulation D), or Rules 147 or 147A, on the date the issuer first made an offer of its securities in reliance on these exemptions;

3.   Rules 251 through 263 (Regulation A), on the earlier of the date the issuer first made an offer soliciting interest in a contemplated securities offering in reliance on Rule 255, or the public filing of a Form 1-A offering statement;

4.   Rules 100 through 503 of this chapter (Regulation Crowdfunding), on the earlier of the date the issuer first made an offer soliciting interest in a contemplated securities offering in reliance on Rule 206 of this chapter, or the public filing of a Form C offering statement; and

5.   A registration statement filed under the Act, in the case of:

   i.   A continuous offering that will commence promptly on the date of initial effectiveness, on the date the issuer first filed its registration statement for the offering with the Commission; or

       ii. A delayed offering, on the earliest date on which the issuer or its agents commenced public efforts to offer and sell the securities, which could be evidenced by the earlier of:

           A. The first filing of a prospectus supplement with the Commission describing the delayed offering; or

           B. The issuance of a widely disseminated public disclosure, such as a press release, confirming the commencement of the delayed offering.

Note 1 to paragraph (c)(5): Offers by the issuer, or persons acting on behalf of the issuer, limited exclusively to qualified institutional buyers and institutional accredited investors, including those that would qualify for the safe harbor in Rule 163B, will not be considered the commencement of a registered offering for purposes of this section.

d.   **Termination or completion of an offering**. For purposes of this section, the termination or completion of an offering is deemed to have occurred when the issuer and its agents cease efforts to make further offers to sell the issuer's securities under such offering. The following non-exclusive list of factors should be considered in determining when an offering is deemed to be terminated or completed including for offerings made in reliance on:

    1.   Section 4(a)(2), Regulation D, or Rules 147 or 147A, on the later of the date:

       i. The issuer entered into a binding commitment to sell all securities to be sold under the offering (subject only to conditions outside of the investor's control); or

       ii. The issuer and its agents ceased efforts to make further offers to sell the issuer's securities under such offering;

    2.   Regulation A, on:

       i.   The withdrawal of an offering statement under Rule 259(a);

       ii. The filing of a Form 1-Z with respect to a Tier I offering under Rule 257(a);

       iii. The declaration by the Commission that the offering statement has been abandoned under Rule 259(b); or

       iv. The date, after the third anniversary of the date the offering statement was initially qualified, on which Rule 251(d)(3)(i)(F) prohibits the issuer from continuing to sell securities using the offering statement, or any earlier date on which the offering terminates by its terms;

    3.   Regulation Crowdfunding, on the deadline of the offering identified in the offering materials pursuant to Rule 201(g) of this chapter, or indicated by the Regulation Crowdfunding intermediary in any notice to investors delivered under Rule 304(b) of this chapter; and

    4.   A registration statement filed under the Act:

       i.   On the withdrawal of the registration statement after an application is granted or deemed granted under Rule 477;

       ii.   On the filing of a prospectus supplement or amendment to the registration statement indicating that the offering, or particular delayed offering in the case of a shelf registration statement, has been terminated or completed;

       iii. On the entry of an order of the Commission declaring that the registration statement has been abandoned under Rule 479;

       iv. On the date, after the third anniversary of the initial effective date of the registration statement, on which Rule 415(a)(5) prohibits the issuer from continuing to sell securities using the registration statement, or any earlier date on which the offering terminates by its terms; or

v.   Any other factors that indicate that the issuer has abandoned or ceased its public selling efforts in furtherance of the offering, or particular delayed offering in the case of a shelf registration statement, which could be evidenced by:

A.   The filing of a Current Report on Form 8-K; or

B.   The issuance of a widely disseminated public disclosure by the issuer, or its agents, informing the market that the offering, or particular delayed offering, in the case of a shelf registration statement, has been terminated or completed.

Note 2 to paragraph (d)(4): A particular delayed offering may be deemed terminated or completed, even though the issuer's shelf registration statement may still have an aggregate amount of securities available to offer and sell in a later delayed offering.

Rule 153 – Definition of "Preceded by a Prospectus," as Used in Section 5(b)(2), in Relation to Certain Transactions

a.   **Definition of preceded by a prospectus**. The term preceded by a prospectus as used in section 5(b)(2) of the Act, regarding any requirement of a broker or dealer to deliver a prospectus to a broker or dealer as a result of a transaction effected between such parties on or through a national securities exchange or facility thereof, trading facility of a national securities association, or an alternative trading system, shall mean the satisfaction of the conditions in paragraph (b) of this section.

b.   **Conditions**. Any requirement of a broker or dealer to deliver a prospectus for transactions covered by paragraph (a) of this section will be satisfied if:

1.   Securities of the same class as the securities that are the subject of the transaction are trading on that national securities exchange or facility thereof, trading facility of a national securities association, or alternative trading system;

2.   The registration statement relating to the offering is effective and is not the subject of any pending proceeding or examination under section 8(d) or 8(e) of the Act;

3.   Neither the issuer, nor any underwriter or participating dealer is the subject of a pending proceeding under section 8A of the Act in connection with the offering; and

4.   The issuer has filed or will file with the Commission a prospectus that satisfies the requirements of section 10(a) of the Act.

c.   **Definitions**.

1.   The term national securities exchange, as used in this section, shall mean a securities exchange registered as a national securities exchange under section 6 of the Securities Exchange Act of 1934.

2.   The term trading facility, as used in this section, shall mean a trading facility sponsored and governed by the rules of a registered securities association or a national securities exchange.

3.   The term alternative trading system, as used in this section, shall mean an alternative trading system as defined in Rule 300(a) of Regulation ATS under

the Securities Exchange Act of 1934 registered with the Commission pursuant to Rule 301 of Regulation ATS under the Securities Exchange Act of 1934.

Rule 158 – Definitions of Certain Terms in the Last Paragraph of Section 11(a)

a.　An "earning statement" made generally available to security holders of the registrant pursuant to the last paragraph of section 11(a) of the Act shall be sufficient for the purposes of such paragraph if:

　　1.　There is included the information required for statements of comprehensive income (as defined in Rule 1-02 of Regulation S-X) contained either:

　　　　i.　In Item 8 of Form 10-K, part I, Item 1 of Form 10-Q, or rule 14a-3(b) under the Securities Exchange Act of 1934;

　　　　ii.　In Item 17 of Form 20-F, if appropriate; or

　　　　iii.　In Form 40-F; and

　　2.　The information specified in the last paragraph of section 11(a) is contained in one report or any combination of reports either:

　　　　i.　On Form 10-K, Form 10-Q, Form 8-K, or in the annual report to security holders pursuant to rule 14a-3 under the Securities Exchange Act; or

　　　　ii.　On Form 20-F, Form 40-F or Form 6-K.

　　　　A subsidiary issuing debt securities guaranteed by its parent will be deemed to have met the requirements of this paragraph if the parent's income statements satisfy the criteria of this paragraph and information respecting the subsidiary is included to the same extent as was presented in the registration statement. An "earning statement" not meeting the requirements of this paragraph may otherwise be sufficient for purposes of the last paragraph of section 11(a).

Note 1 to paragraph (a). A subsidiary issuing debt securities guaranteed by its parent will be deemed to have met the requirements of this paragraph (a) if the parent's statements of comprehensive income (as defined in Rule 1-02 of Regulation S-X) satisfy the criteria of this paragraph and information respecting the subsidiary is included to the same extent as was presented in the registration statement. An "earning statement" not meeting the requirements of this paragraph (a) may otherwise be sufficient for purposes of the last paragraph of section 11(a) of the Act.

b.　For purposes of the last paragraph of section 11(a) only, the "earning statement" contemplated by paragraph (a) of this section shall be deemed to be "made generally available to its security holders" if the registrant:

　　1.　Is required to file reports pursuant to section 13 or 15(d) of the Securities Exchange Act of 1934 and

　　2.　Has filed its report or reports on Form 10-K, Form 10-Q, Form 8-K, Form 20-F, Form 40-F, or Form 6-K, or has submitted to the Commission in electronic format, in accordance with the EDGAR Filer Manual, its annual report sent to security holders pursuant to Rule 14a-3(c) containing such information. A registrant may use other methods to make an earning statement "generally available to its security holders" for purposes of the last paragraph of 11(a).

A registrant may use other methods to make an earning statement "generally available to its security holders" for purposes of the last paragraph of section 11(a).

c.   For purposes of the last paragraph of section 11(a) of the Act only, the effective date of the registration statement is deemed to be the date of the latest to occur of:

1.   The effective date of the registration statement;

2.   The effective date of the last post-effective amendment to the registration statement next preceding a particular sale of the issuer's registered securities to the public filed for the purposes of:

i.   Including any prospectus required by section 10(a)(3) of the Act; or

ii.   Reflecting in the prospectus any facts or events arising after the effective date of the registration statement (or the most recent post-effective amendment thereof) which, individually or in the aggregate, represent a fundamental change in the information set forth in the registration statement;

3.   The date of filing of the last report of the issuer incorporated by reference into the prospectus that is part of the registration statement or the date that a form of prospectus filed pursuant to Rule 424(b) or Rule 497(b), (c), (d), or (e) is deemed part of and included in the registration statement, and relied upon in either case in lieu of filing a post-effective amendment for purposes of paragraphs (c)(2)(i) and (ii) of this section next preceding a particular sale of the issuer's registered securities to the public; or

4.   As to the issuer and any underwriter at that time only, the most recent effective date of the registration statement for purposes of liability under section 11 of the Act of the issuer and any such underwriter only at the time of or next preceding a particular sale of the issuer's registered securities to the public determined pursuant to Rule 430B.

Rule 159 – Information Available to Purchaser at Time of Contract of Sale

a.   For purposes of section 12(a)(2) of the Act only, and without affecting any other rights a purchaser may have, for purposes of determining whether a prospectus or oral statement included an untrue statement of a material fact or omitted to state a material fact necessary in order to make the statements, in the light of the circumstances under which they were made, not misleading at the time of sale (including, without limitation, a contract of sale), any information conveyed to the purchaser only after such time of sale (including such contract of sale) will not be taken into account.

b.   For purposes of section 17(a)(2) of the Act only, and without affecting any other rights the Commission may have to enforce that section, for purposes of determining whether a statement includes or represents any untrue statement of a material fact or any omission to state a material fact necessary in order to make the statements made, in light of the circumstances under which they were made, not misleading at the time of sale (including, without limitation, a contract of sale), any information conveyed to the purchaser only after such time of sale (including such contract of sale) will not be taken into account.

c.   For purposes of section 12(a)(2) of the Act only, knowing of such untruth or omission in respect of a sale (including, without limitation, a contract of sale), means knowing at the time of such sale (including such contract of sale).

Rule 159A – Certain Definitions for Purposes of Section 12(a)(2) of the Act

a. **Definition of seller for purposes of section 12(a)(2) of the Act.** For purposes of section 12(a)(2) of the Act only, in a primary offering of securities of the issuer, regardless of the underwriting method used to sell the issuer's securities, seller shall include the issuer of the securities sold to a person as part of the initial distribution of such securities, and the issuer shall be considered to offer or sell the securities to such person, if the securities are offered or sold to such person by means of any of the following communications:

1. Any preliminary prospectus or prospectus of the issuer relating to the offering required to be filed pursuant to Rule 424 or Rule 497;

2. Any free writing prospectus as defined in Rule 405 relating to the offering prepared by or on behalf of the issuer or used or referred to by the issuer and, in the case of an issuer that is an open-end management company registered under the Investment Company Act of 1940, any profile relating to the offering provided pursuant to Rule 498;

3. The portion of any other free writing prospectus (or, in the case of an issuer that is an investment company registered under the Investment Company Act of 1940 or a business development company as defined in section 2(a)(48) of the Investment Company Act of 1940, any advertisement pursuant to Rule 482) relating to the offering containing material information about the issuer or its securities provided by or on behalf of the issuer; and

4. Any other communication that is an offer in the offering made by the issuer to such person.

    Notes to paragraph (a) of Rule 159A:

1. For purposes of paragraph (a) of this section, information is provided or a communication is made by or on behalf of an issuer if an issuer or an agent or representative of the issuer authorizes or approves the information or communication before its provision or use. An offering participant other than the issuer shall not be an agent or representative of the issuer solely by virtue of its acting as an offering participant.

2. Paragraph (a) of this section shall not affect in any respect the determination of whether any person other than an issuer is a "seller" for purposes of section 12(a)(2) of the Act.

b. **Definition of by means of for purposes of section 12(a)(2) of the Act.**

1. For purposes of section 12(a)(2) of the Act only, an offering participant other than the issuer shall not be considered to offer or sell securities that are the subject of a registration statement by means of a free writing prospectus as to a purchaser unless one or more of the following circumstances shall exist:

    i.   The offering participant used or referred to the free writing prospectus in offering or selling the securities to the purchaser;

    ii. The offering participant offered or sold securities to the purchaser and participated in planning for the use of the free writing prospectus by one or more other offering participants and such free writing prospectus was used or referred to in offering or selling securities to the purchaser by one or more of such other offering participants; or

      iii. The offering participant was required to file the free writing prospectus pursuant to the conditions to use in Rule 433.

  2. For purposes of section 12(a)(2) of the Act only, a person will not be considered to offer or sell securities by means of a free writing prospectus solely because another person has used or referred to the free writing prospectus or filed the free writing prospectus with the Commission pursuant to Rule 433.

Rule 163 – Exemption from Section 5(c) of the Act for Certain Communications by or on Behalf of Well-Known Seasoned Issuers

Preliminary Note

Attempted compliance with this section does not act as an exclusive election and the issuer also may claim the availability of any other applicable exemption or exclusion. Reliance on this section does not affect the availability of any other exemption or exclusion from the requirements of section 5 of the Act.

  a. In an offering by or on behalf of a well-known seasoned issuer, as defined in Rule 405, that will be or is at the time intended to be registered under the Act, an offer by or on behalf of such issuer is exempt from the prohibitions in section 5(c) of the Act on offers to sell, offers for sale, or offers to buy its securities before a registration statement has been filed, provided that:

    1. Any written communication that is an offer made in reliance on this exemption will be a free writing prospectus as defined in Rule 405 and a prospectus under section 2(a)(10) of the Act relating to a public offering of securities to be covered by the registration statement to be filed; and

    2. The exemption from section 5(c) of the Act provided in this section for such written communication that is an offer shall be conditioned on satisfying the conditions in paragraph (b) of this section.

  b. **Conditions.**

    1. Legend

      i. Every written communication that is an offer made in reliance on this exemption shall contain substantially the following legend:

> The issuer may file a registration statement (including a prospectus) with the SEC for the offering to which this communication relates. Before you invest, you should read the prospectus in that registration statement and other documents the issuer has filed with the SEC for more complete information about the issuer and this offering. You may get these documents for free by visiting EDGAR … at www.sec.gov. Alternatively, the company will arrange to send you the prospectus after filing if you request it by calling toll-free 1-8[xx-xxx-xxxx].

      ii. The legend also may provide an e-mail address at which the documents can be requested and may indicate that the documents also are available by accessing the issuer's Web site, and provide the Internet address and the particular location of the documents on the Web site.

      iii. An immaterial or unintentional failure to include the specified legend in a free writing prospectus required by this section will not result in a violation of section 5(c) of the Act or the loss of the ability to rely on this section so long as:

(A) A good faith and reasonable effort was made to comply with the specified legend condition;

(B) The free writing prospectus is amended to include the specified legend as soon as practicable after discovery of the omitted or incorrect legend; and

I. If the free writing prospectus has been transmitted without the specified legend, the free writing prospectus is retransmitted with the legend by substantially the same means as, and directed to substantially the same prospective purchasers to whom, the free writing prospectus was originally transmitted.

2. Filing condition.

i. Subject to paragraph (b)(2)(ii) of this section, every written communication that is an offer made in reliance on this exemption shall be filed by the issuer with the Commission promptly upon the filing of the registration statement, if one is filed, or an amendment, if one is filed, covering the securities that have been offered in reliance on this exemption.

ii. The condition that an issuer shall file a free writing prospectus with the Commission under this section shall not apply in respect of any communication that has previously been filed with, or furnished to, the Commission or that the issuer would not be required to file with the Commission pursuant to the conditions of Rule 433 if the communication was a free writing prospectus used after the filing of the registration statement. The condition that the issuer shall file a free writing prospectus with the Commission under this section shall be satisfied if the issuer satisfies the filing conditions (other than timing of filing which is provided in this section) that would apply under Rule 433 if the communication was a free writing prospectus used after the filing of the registration statement.

iii. An immaterial or unintentional failure to file or delay in filing a free writing prospectus to the extent provided in this section will not result in a violation of section 5(c) of the Act or the loss of the ability to rely on this section so long as:

(A) A good faith and reasonable effort was made to comply with the filing condition; and

(B) The free writing prospectus is filed as soon as practicable after discovery of the failure to file.

3. Ineligible offerings. The exemption in paragraph (a) of this section shall not be available to:

i. Communications relating to business combination transactions that are subject to Rule 165 or Rule 166;

ii. Communications by an issuer that is an investment company registered under the Investment Company Act of 1940; or

iii. Communications by an issuer that is a business development company as defined in section 2(a)(48) of the Investment Company Act of 1940).

c. For purposes of this section, a communication is made by or on behalf of an issuer if the issuer or an agent or representative of the issuer, other than an offering participant who is an underwriter or dealer, authorizes or approves the communication before it is made.

d.   For purposes of this section, a communication for which disclosure would be required under section 17(b) of the Act as a result of consideration given or to be given, directly or indirectly, by or on behalf of an issuer is deemed to be an offer by the issuer and, if a written communication, is deemed to be a free writing prospectus of the issuer.

e.   A communication exempt from section 5(c) of the Act pursuant to this section will not be considered to be in connection with a securities offering registered under the Securities Act for purposes of Rule 100(b)(2)[(iii)] of Regulation FD under the Securities Exchange Act of 1934.

Rule 163A – Exemption From Section 5(c) of the Act for Certain Communications Made By or On Behalf of Issuers More than 30 Days Before a Registration Statement is Filed

Preliminary Note
Attempted compliance with this section does not act as an exclusive election and the issuer also may claim the availability of any other applicable exemption or exclusion. Reliance on this section does not affect the availability of any other exemption or exclusion from the requirements of section 5 of the Act.

a.   Except as excluded pursuant to paragraph (b) of this section, in all registered offerings by issuers, any communication made by or on behalf of an issuer more than 30 days before the date of the filing of the registration statement that does not reference a securities offering that is or will be the subject of a registration statement shall not constitute an offer to sell, offer for sale, or offer to buy the securities being offered under the registration statement for purposes of section 5(c) of the Act, provided that the issuer takes reasonable steps within its control to prevent further distribution or publication of such communication during the 30 days immediately preceding the date of filing the registration statement.

b.   The exemption in paragraph (a) of this section shall not be available with respect to the following communications:
    1.   Communications relating to business combination transactions that are subject to Rule 165 or Rule 166;
    2.   Communications made in connection with offerings registered on Form S-8, other than by well-known seasoned issuers;
    3.   Communications in offerings of securities of an issuer that is, or during the past three years was (or any of whose predecessors during the last three years was):
        i.   A blank check company as defined in Rule 419(a)(2);
        ii.   A shell company, other than a business combination related shell company, each as defined in Rule 405; or
        iii. An issuer for an offering of penny stock as defined in Rule 3a51-1 of the Securities Exchange Act of 1934; or
    4.   Communications made by an issuer that is:
        i.   An investment company registered under the Investment Company Act of 1940; or

        ii.   A business development company as defined in section 2(a)(48) of the Investment Company Act of 1940.

c.   For purposes of this section, a communication is made by or on behalf of an issuer if the issuer or an agent or representative of the issuer, other than an offering participant who is an underwriter or dealer, authorizes or approves the communication before it is made.

d.   A communication exempt from section 5(c) of the Act pursuant to this section will not be considered to be in connection with a securities offering registered under the Securities Act for purposes of Rule 100(b)(2)[(iii)] of Regulation FD under the Securities Exchange Act of 1934.

Rule 163B – Exemption from section 5(b)(1) and section 5(c) of the Act for certain communications to qualified institutional buyers or institutional accredited investors

a.   Attempted compliance with this rule does not act as an exclusive election, and the issuer also may claim the availability of any other applicable exemption or exclusion. Reliance on this rule does not affect the availability of any other exemption or exclusion from the requirements of section 5 of the Act.

b.

    1.   An issuer, or any person authorized to act on behalf of an issuer, may engage in oral or written communications with potential investors described in paragraph (c) of this section to determine whether such investors might have an interest in a contemplated registered securities offering, either prior to or following the date of filing of a registration statement with respect to such securities with the Commission. Communications under this rule will be exempt from section 5(b)(1) and section 5(c) of the Act.

    2.   Any oral or written communication by an issuer, or any person authorized to act on behalf of an issuer, made in reliance on this rule will be deemed an "offer" as defined in section 2(a)(3) of the Act.

    3.   Any oral or written communication by an issuer, or any person authorized to act on behalf of an issuer, made in reliance on this rule is not required to be filed with the Commission, including pursuant to Rule 424(a) or Rule 497(a) of Regulation C under the Act or section 24(b) of the Investment Company Act of 1940) and the rules and regulations thereunder.

c.   Communications under this rule may be made with potential investors that are, or that an issuer or person authorized to act on its behalf reasonably believes are:
    1.   Qualified institutional buyers, as defined in Rule 144A; or
    2.   Institutions that are accredited investors, as defined in Rules 501(a)(1), (a)(2), (a)(3), (a)(7), (a)(8), (a)(9), (a)(12), or (a)(13).
    Note: Though the definition of "family client" from Rule 501(a)(13) includes both natural persons and institutions, only family clients that are institutions may be considered institutional accredited investors.

Rule 164 – Post-filing Free Writing Prospectuses in Connection with Certain Registered Offerings

Preliminary Notes

1. This section is not available for any communication that, although in technical compliance with this section, is part of a plan or scheme to evade the requirements of section 5 of the Act.

2. Attempted compliance with this section does not act as an exclusive election and the person relying on this section also may claim the availability of any other applicable exemption or exclusion. Reliance on this section does not affect the availability of any other exemption or exclusion from the requirements of section 5 of the Act.

a. In connection with a registered offering of an issuer meeting the requirements of this section, a free writing prospectus, as defined in Rule 405, of the issuer or any other offering participant, including any underwriter or dealer, after the filing of the registration statement will be a section 10(b) prospectus for purposes of section 5(b)(1) of the Act provided that the conditions set forth in Rule 433 are satisfied.

b. An immaterial or unintentional failure to file or delay in filing a free writing prospectus as necessary to satisfy the filing conditions contained in Rule 433 will not result in a violation of section 5(b)(1) of the Act or the loss of the ability to rely on this section so long as:

    1. A good faith and reasonable effort was made to comply with the filing condition; and

    2. The free writing prospectus is filed as soon as practicable after discovery of the failure to file.

c. An immaterial or unintentional failure to include the specified legend in a free writing prospectus as necessary to satisfy the legend condition contained in Rule 433 will not result in a violation of section 5(b)(1) of the Act or the loss of the ability to rely on this section so long as:

    1. A good faith and reasonable effort was made to comply with the legend condition;

    2. The free writing prospectus is amended to include the specified legend as soon as practicable after discovery of the omitted or incorrect legend; and

    3. If the free writing prospectus has been transmitted without the specified legend, the free writing prospectus must be retransmitted with the legend by substantially the same means as, and directed to substantially the same prospective purchasers to whom, the free writing prospectus was originally transmitted.

d. Solely for purposes of this section, an immaterial or unintentional failure to retain a free writing prospectus as necessary to satisfy the record retention condition contained in Rule 433 will not result in a violation of section 5(b)(1) ... or the loss of the ability to rely on this section so long as a good faith and reasonable effort was made to comply with the record retention condition. Nothing in this paragraph will affect, however, any other record retention provisions applicable to the issuer or any offering participant.

e.   **Ineligible issuers.**
1.   This section and Rule 433 are available only if at the eligibility determination date for the offering in question, determined pursuant to paragraph (h) of this section, the issuer is not an ineligible issuer as defined in Rule 405 (or in the case of any offering participant, other than the issuer, the participant has a reasonable belief that the issuer is not an ineligible issuer);
2.   Notwithstanding paragraph (e)(1) of this section, this section and Rule are available to an ineligible issuer with respect to a free writing prospectus that contains only descriptions of the terms of the securities in the offering or the offering (or in the case of an offering of asset-backed securities, contains only information specified in paragraphs (a)(1), (2), (3), (4), (6), (7), and (8) of the definition of ABS informational and computational materials in Item 1101 of Regulation AB, unless the issuer is or during the last three years the issuer or any of its predecessors was:
i.   A blank check company as defined in Rule 419(a)(2);
ii. A shell company, other than a business combination related shell company, as defined in Rule 405; or
iii. An issuer for an offering of penny stock as defined in Rule 3a51-1 of the Securities Exchange Act of 1934.

f.   **Excluded issuers.** This section and Rule 433 are not available if the issuer is an investment company registered under the Investment Company Act of 1940 or a business development company as defined in section 2(a)(48) of the Investment Company Act of 1940.

g.   **Excluded offerings.** This section and Rule 433 are not available if the issuer is registering a business combination transaction as defined in Rule 165(f)(1) or the issuer, other than a well-known seasoned issuer, is registering an offering on Form S-8.

h.   For purposes of this section and Rule 433, the determination date as to whether an issuer is an ineligible issuer in respect of an offering shall be:
1.   Except as provided in paragraph (h)(2) of this section, the time of filing of the registration statement covering the offering; or
2.   If the offering is being registered pursuant to Rule 415, the earliest time after the filing of the registration statement covering the offering at which the issuer, or in the case of an underwritten offering the issuer or another offering participant, makes a bona fide offer, including without limitation through the use of a free writing prospectus, in the offering.

Rule 168 – Exemption from Sections 2(a)(10) and 5(c) of the Act for Certain Communications of Regularly Released Factual Business Information and Forward-Looking Information

Preliminary Notes
1.   This section is not available for any communication that, although in technical compliance with this section, is part of a plan or scheme to evade the requirements of section 5 of the Act.

2. This section provides a non-exclusive safe harbor for factual business information and forward-looking information released or disseminated as provided in this section. Attempted compliance with this section does not act as an exclusive election and the issuer also may claim the availability of any other applicable exemption or exclusion. Reliance on this section does not affect the availability of any other exemption or exclusion from the definition of prospectus in section 2(a)(10) or the requirements of section 5 of the Act.

3. The availability of this section for a release or dissemination of a communication that contains or incorporates factual business information or forward-looking information will not be affected by another release or dissemination of a communication that contains all or a portion of the same factual business information or forward-looking information that does not satisfy the conditions of this section.

a. For purposes of sections 2(a)(10) and 5(c) of the Act, the regular release or dissemination by or on behalf of an issuer (and, in the case of an asset-backed issuer, the other persons specified in paragraph (a)(3) of this section) of communications containing factual business information or forward-looking information shall be deemed not to constitute an offer to sell or offer for sale of a security which is the subject of an offering pursuant to a registration statement that the issuer proposes to file, or has filed, or that is effective, if the conditions of this section are satisfied by any of the following:

1. An issuer that is required to file reports pursuant to section 13 or section 15(d) of the Securities Exchange Act of 1934;

2. A foreign private issuer that:
   i. Meets all of the registrant requirements of Form F-3 other than the reporting history provisions of General Instructions I.A.1. and I.A.2.(a) of Form F-3;
   ii. Either:
      (A) Satisfies the public float threshold in General Instruction I.B.1. of Form F-3; or
      (B) Is issuing non-convertible securities, other than common equity, and meets the provisions of General Instruction I.B.2. of Form F-3; and
   iii. Either:
      (A) Has its equity securities trading on a designated offshore securities market as defined in Rule 902(b) and has had them so traded for at least 12 months; or
      (B) Has a worldwide market value of its outstanding common equity held by non-affiliates of $700 million or more; or

3. An asset-backed issuer or a depositor, sponsor, or servicer (as such terms are defined in Item 1101 of Regulation AB) or an affiliated depositor, whether or not such other person is the issuer.

b. **Definitions.**

1. Factual business information means some or all of the following information that is released or disseminated under the conditions in paragraph (d) of this section, including, without limitation, such factual business information contained in reports or other materials filed with, furnished to, or submitted to the Commission pursuant to the Securities Exchange Act of 1934:

        i.   Factual information about the issuer, its business or financial developments, or other aspects of its business;

        ii.   Advertisements of, or other information about, the issuer's products or services; and

        iii. Dividend notices.

2.   Forward-looking information means some or all of the following information that is released or disseminated under the conditions in paragraph (d) of this section, including, without limitation, such forward-looking information contained in reports or other materials filed with, furnished to, or submitted to the Commission pursuant to the Securities Exchange Act of 1934:

        i.   Projections of the issuer's revenues, income (loss), earnings (loss) per share, capital expenditures, dividends, capital structure, or other financial items;

        ii.   Statements about the issuer management's plans and objectives for future operations, including plans or objectives relating to the products or services of the issuer;

        iii. Statements about the issuer's future economic performance, including statements of the type contemplated by the management's discussion and analysis of financial condition and results of operation described in Item 303 of Regulation S-K or the operating and financial review and prospects described in Item 5 of Form 20-F; and

        iv. Assumptions underlying or relating to any of the information described in paragraphs (b)(2)(i), (b)(2)(ii) and (b)(2)(iii) of this section.

3.   For purposes of this section, the release or dissemination of a communication is by or on behalf of the issuer if the issuer or an agent or representative of the issuer, other than an offering participant who is an underwriter or dealer, authorizes or approves such release or dissemination before it is made.

4.   For purposes of this section, in the case of communications of a person specified in paragraph (a)(3) of this section other than the asset-backed issuer, the release or dissemination of a communication is by or on behalf of such other person if such other person or its agent or representative, other than an underwriter or dealer, authorizes or approves such release or dissemination before it is made.

c.   **Exclusion**. A communication containing information about the registered offering or released or disseminated as part of the offering activities in the registered offering is excluded from the exemption of this section.

d.   **Conditions to exemption**. The following conditions must be satisfied:

1.   The issuer (or in the case of an asset-backed issuer, the issuer and the other persons specified in paragraph (a)(3) of this section, taken together) has previously released or disseminated information of the type described in this section in the ordinary course of its business;

2.   The timing, manner, and form in which the information is released or disseminated is consistent in material respects with similar past releases or disseminations; and

3.   The issuer is not an investment company registered under the Investment Company Act of 1940 or a business development company as defined in section 2(a)(48) of the Investment Company Act of 1940.

Rule 169 – Exemption from Sections 2(a)(10) and 5(c) of the Act for Certain Communications of Regularly Released Factual Business Information

Preliminary Notes
1. This section is not available for any communication that, although in technical compliance with this section, is part of a plan or scheme to evade the requirements of section 5 of the Act.
2. This section provides a non-exclusive safe harbor for factual business information released or disseminated as provided in this section. Attempted compliance with this section does not act as an exclusive election and the issuer also may claim the availability of any other applicable exemption or exclusion. Reliance on this section does not affect the availability of any other exemption or exclusion from the definition of prospectus in section 2(a)(10) or the requirements of section 5 of the Act.
3. The availability of this section for a release or dissemination of a communication that contains or incorporates factual business information will not be affected by another release or dissemination of a communication that contains all or a portion of the same factual business information that does not satisfy the conditions of this section.

a. For purposes of sections 2(a)(10) and 5(c) of the Act, the regular release or dissemination by or on behalf of an issuer of communications containing factual business information shall be deemed not to constitute an offer to sell or offer for sale of a security by an issuer which is the subject of an offering pursuant to a registration statement that the issuer proposes to file, or has filed, or that is effective, if the conditions of this section are satisfied.

b. **Definitions.**
    1. **Factual business information** means some or all of the following information that is released or disseminated under the conditions in paragraph (d) of this section:
        i. Factual information about the issuer, its business or financial developments, or other aspects of its business; and
        ii. Advertisements of, or other information about, the issuer's products or services.
    2. For purposes of this section, the release or dissemination of a communication is by or on behalf of the issuer if the issuer or an agent or representative of the issuer, other than an offering participant who is an underwriter or dealer, authorizes or approves such release or dissemination before it is made.

c. **Exclusions.** A communication containing information about the registered offering or released or disseminated as part of the offering activities in the registered offering is excluded from the exemption of this section.

d. **Conditions to exemption.** The following conditions must be satisfied:
    1. The issuer has previously released or disseminated information of the type described in this section in the ordinary course of its business;
    2. The timing, manner, and form in which the information is released or disseminated is consistent in material respects with similar past releases or disseminations;

3.   The information is released or disseminated for intended use by persons, such as customers and suppliers, other than in their capacities as investors or potential investors in the issuer's securities, by the issuer's employees or agents who historically have provided such information; and

4.   The issuer is not an investment company registered under the Investment Company Act of 1940 or a business development company as defined in section 2(a)(48) of the Investment Company Act of 1940.

Rule 172 – Delivery of Prospectuses

a.   **Sending confirmations and notices of allocations**. After the effective date of a registration statement, the following are exempt from the provisions of section 5(b)(1) of the Act if the conditions set forth in paragraph (c) of this section are satisfied:

1.   Written confirmations of sales of securities in an offering pursuant to a registration statement that contain information limited to that called for in Rule 10b-10 under the Securities Exchange Act of 1934 and other information customarily included in written confirmations of sales of securities, which may include notices provided pursuant to Rule 173; and

2.   Notices of allocation of securities sold or to be sold in an offering pursuant to the registration statement that may include information identifying the securities (including the CUSIP number) and otherwise may include only information regarding pricing, allocation and settlement, and information incidental thereto.

b.   **Transfer of the security**. Any obligation under section 5(b)(2) of the Act to have a prospectus that satisfies the requirements of section 10(a) of the Act precede or accompany the carrying or delivery of a security in a registered offering is satisfied if the conditions in paragraph (c) of this section are met.

c.   **Conditions**.

1.   The registration statement relating to the offering is effective and is not the subject of any pending proceeding or examination under section 8(d) or 8(e) of the Act;

2.   Neither the issuer, nor an underwriter or participating dealer is the subject of a pending proceeding under section 8A of the Act in connection with the offering; and

3.   The issuer has filed with the Commission a prospectus with respect to the offering that satisfies the requirements of section 10(a) of the Act or the issuer will make a good faith and reasonable effort to file such a prospectus within the time required under Rule 424 and, in the event that the issuer fails to file timely such a prospectus, the issuer files the prospectus as soon as practicable thereafter.

4.   The condition in paragraph (c)(3) of this section shall not apply to transactions by dealers requiring delivery of a final prospectus pursuant to section 4[a](3) of the Act.

d.   **Exclusions**. This section shall not apply to any:

1.   Offering of any investment company registered under the Investment Company Act of 1940;

2. Offering of any business development company as defined in section 2(a)(48) of the Investment Company Act of 1940;
3. A business combination transaction as defined in Rule 165(f)(1); or
4. Offering registered on Form S-8.

Rule 173 – Notice of Registration

a. In a transaction that represents a sale by the issuer or an underwriter, or a sale where there is not an exclusion or exemption from the requirement to deliver a final prospectus meeting the requirements of section 10(a) of the Act pursuant to section 4[a](3) of the Act or Rule 174, each underwriter or dealer selling in such transaction shall provide to each purchaser from it, not later than two business days following the completion of such sale, a copy of the final prospectus or, in lieu of such prospectus, a notice to the effect that the sale was made pursuant to a registration statement or in a transaction in which a final prospectus would have been required to have been delivered in the absence of Rule 172.

b. If the sale was by the issuer and was not effected by or through an underwriter or dealer, the responsibility to send a prospectus, or in lieu of such prospectus, such notice as set forth in paragraph (a) of this section, shall be the issuer's.

c. Compliance with the requirements of this section is not a condition to reliance on Rule 172.

d. A purchaser may request from the person responsible for sending a notice a copy of the final prospectus if one has not been sent.

e. After the effective date of the registration statement with respect to an offering, notices as set forth in paragraph (a) of this section, are exempt from the provisions of section 5(b)(1) of the Act.

f. **Exclusions**. This section shall not apply to any:
1. Transaction solely between brokers or dealers in reliance on Rule 153;
2. Offering of any investment company registered under the Investment Company Act of 1940;
3. Offering of any business development company as defined in section 2(a)(48) of the Investment Company Act of 1940;
4. A business combination transaction as defined in Rule 165(f)(1); or
5. Offering registered on Form S-8.

Rule 174 – Delivery of Prospectus by Dealers; Exemptions Under Section 4[a](3) of the Act

The obligations of a dealer (including an underwriter no longer acting as an underwriter in respect of the security involved in such transactions) to deliver a prospectus in transactions in a security as to which a registration statement has been filed taking place prior to the expiration of the 40- or 90-day period specified in section 4[a](3) of the Act after the effective date of such registration statement or prior to the expiration of such period after the first date upon which the security was bona fide offered to the public by the issuer or by or through an underwriter after such effective date, whichever is later, shall be subject to the following:

a.   No prospectus need be delivered if the registration statement is on Form F-6.

b.   No prospectus need be delivered if the issuer is subject, immediately prior to the time of filing the registration statement, to the reporting requirements of section 13 or 15(d) of the Securities Exchange Act of 1934.

c.   Where a registration statement relates to offerings to be made from time to time no prospectus need be delivered after the expiration of the initial prospectus delivery period specified in section 4[a](3) of the Act following the first bona fide offering of securities under such registration statement.

d.   If –
1.   the registration statement relates to the security of an issuer that is not subject, immediately prior to the time of filing the registration statement, to the reporting requirements of section 13 or 15(d) of the Securities Exchange Act of 1934, and
2.   as of the offering date, the security is listed on a registered national securities exchange or authorized for inclusion in an electronic inter-dealer quotation system sponsored and governed by the rules of a registered securities association, no prospectus need be delivered after the expiration of twenty-five calendar days after the offering date. For purposes of this provision, the term *offering date* refers to the later of the effective date of the registration statement or the first date on which the security was bona fide offered to the public.

e.   Notwithstanding the foregoing, the period during which a prospectus must be delivered by a dealer shall be:
1.   As specified in section 4[a](3) of the Act if the registration statement was the subject of a stop order issued under section 8 of the Act; or
2.   As the Commission may provide upon application or on its own motion in a particular case.

f.   Nothing in this section shall affect the obligation to deliver a prospectus pursuant to the provisions of section 5 of the Act by a dealer who is acting as an underwriter with respect to the securities involved or who is engaged in a transaction as to securities constituting the whole or a part of an unsold allotment to or subscription by such dealer as a participant in the distribution of such securities by the issuer or by or through an underwriter.

g.   If the registration statement relates to an offering of securities of a "blank check company," as defined in Rule 419 under the Act, the statutory period for prospectus delivery specified in section 4[a](3) of the Act shall not terminate until 90 days after the date funds and securities are released from the escrow or trust account pursuant to Rule 419 under the Act.

h.   Any obligation pursuant to Section 4[a](3) of the Act and this section to deliver a prospectus, other than pursuant to paragraph (g) of this section, may be satisfied by compliance with the provisions of Rule 172.

Rule 176 – Circumstances Affecting the Determination of What Constitutes Reasonable Investigation and Reasonable Grounds for Belief Under Section 11 of the Securities Act

In determining whether or not the conduct of a person constitutes a reasonable investigation or a reasonable ground for belief meeting the standard set forth in section 11(c), relevant circumstances include, with respect to a person other than the issuer.

a.   The type of issuer;

b.   The type of security;

c.   The type of person;

d.   The office held when the person is an officer;

e.   The presence or absence of another relationship to the issuer when the person is a director or proposed director;

f.   Reasonable reliance on officers, employees, and others whose duties should have given them knowledge of the particular facts ;

g.   When the person is an underwriter, the type of underwriting arrangement, the role of the particular person as an underwriter and the availability of information with respect to the registrant; and

h.   Whether, with respect to a fact or document incorporated by reference, the particular person had any responsibility for the fact or document at the time of the filing from which it was incorporated.

Rule 193 – Review of underlying assets in asset-backed securities transactions

An issuer of an "asset-backed security" (as that term is defined in Section 3(a)(79) of the Securities Exchange Act of 1934), offering and selling such a security pursuant to a registration statement shall perform a review of the pool assets underlying the asset-backed security. At a minimum, such review must be designed and effected to provide reasonable assurance that the disclosure regarding the pool assets in the form of prospectus filed pursuant to Rule 424 of this chapter is accurate in all material respects. The issuer may conduct the review or an issuer may employ a third party engaged for purposes of performing the review. If the findings and conclusions of the review are attributed to the third party, the third party must be named in the registration statement and consent to being named as an expert in accordance with Rule 436 of this chapter.
Instruction to Rule 193: An issuer of an "asset-backed security" may rely on one or more third parties to fulfill its obligation to perform a review under this section, provided that the reviews performed by the third parties and the issuer, in the aggregate, comply with the minimum

standard in this section. The issuer must comply with the requirements of this section for each third party engaged by the issuer to perform the review for purposes of this section. An issuer may not rely on a review performed by an unaffiliated originator for purposes of performing the review required under this section.

Rule 215 – Accredited Investor

The term *accredited investor* as used in section 2(a)(15)(ii) of the Securities Act of 1933 shall have the same meaning as the definition of that term in rule 501(a) under the Act.

Rule 401 – Requirements as to Proper Form

a. The form and contents of a registration statement and prospectus shall conform to the applicable rules and forms as in effect on the initial filing date of such registration statement and prospectus.

b. If an amendment to a registration statement and prospectus is filed for the purpose of meeting the requirements of section 10(a)(3) of the Act or pursuant to the provisions of section 24(e) or 24(f) of the Investment Company Act of 1940, the form and contents of such an amendment shall conform to the applicable rules and forms as in effect on the filing date of such amendment.

c. An amendment to a registration statement and prospectus, other than an amendment described in paragraph (b) of this section, may be filed on any shorter Securities Act registration form for which it is eligible on the filing date of the amendment. At the issuer's option, the amendment also may be filed on the same Securities Act registration form used for the most recent amendment described in paragraph (b) of this section or, if no such amendment has been filed, the initial registration statement and prospectus.

d. The form and contents of a prospectus forming part of a registration statement which is the subject of a stop order entered under section 8(d) of the Act, if used after the date such stop order ceases to be effective, shall conform to the applicable rules and forms as in effect on the date such stop order ceases to be effective.

e. A prospectus filed as part of an amendment to an effective registration statement, or other amendment to such registration statement, on any form may be prepared in accordance with the requirements of any other form which would then be appropriate for the registration of securities to which the prospectus or other amendment relates, provided that all of the other requirements of such other form and applicable rules (including any required undertakings) are met.

f. Notwithstanding the provisions of this section, a registrant
    1. shall comply with the rules and forms as in effect at a date different from those specified in paragraphs (a), (b), (c) and (d) of this section if the rules or forms or amendments thereto specifically so provide; and
    2. may comply voluntarily with the rules and forms as in effect at dates subsequent to those specified in paragraphs (a), (b), (c) and (d) of this section, provided that

all of the requirements of the particular rules and forms in effect at such dates (including any required undertakings) are met.

g. 1. Subject to paragraphs (g)(2) and (g)(3) of this rule, except for registration statements and post-effective amendments that become effective immediately pursuant to Rule 462 and Rule 464, a registration statement or any amendment thereto is deemed filed on the proper registration form unless the Commission objects to the registration form before the effective date.

    2. An automatic shelf registration statement as defined in Rule 405 and any post-effective amendment thereto are deemed filed on the proper registration form unless and until the Commission notifies the issuer of its objection to the use of such form. Following any such notification, the issuer must amend its automatic shelf registration statement onto the registration form it is then eligible to use, *provided, however*, that any continuous offering of securities pursuant to Rule 415 that the issuer has commenced pursuant to the registration statement before the Commission has notified the issuer of its objection to the use of such form may continue until the effective date of a new registration statement or post-effective amendment to the registration statement that the issuer has filed on the proper registration form, if the issuer files promptly after notification the new registration statement or post-effective amendment and if the offering is permitted to be made under the new registration statement or post-effective amendment.

    3. Violations of General Instruction I.B.6. of Form S-3 or General Instruction I.B.5. of Form F-3 will also violate the requirements as to proper form under this rule notwithstanding that the registration statement may have been declared effective previously.

    4. Notwithstanding that the registration statement may have become effective previously, requirements as to proper form under this section will have been violated for any offering of securities where the requirements of General Instruction I.A. of Form SF-3 have not been met as of ninety days after the end of the depositor's fiscal year end prior to such offering.

Rule 405 – Definition of Terms

Unless the context otherwise requires, all terms used in Rule 400 to Rule 494, inclusive, or in the forms for registration have the same meanings as in the Act and in the general rules and regulations. In addition, the following definitions apply, unless the context otherwise requires:

Affiliate. An *affiliate* of, or person *affiliated* with, a specified person, is a person that directly, or indirectly through one or more intermediaries, controls or is controlled by, or is under common control with, the person specified.

Amount. The term *amount,* when used in regard to securities, means the principal amount if relating to evidences of indebtedness, the number of shares if relating to shares, and the number of units if relating to any other kind of security.

Associate. The term *associate,* when used to indicate a relationship with any person, means (1) a corporation or organization (other than the registrant or a majority-owned subsidiary of the registrant) of which such person is an officer or partner or is, directly or indirectly, the beneficial owner of 10 percent or more of any class of equity securities, (2) any trust or other estate in which such person has a substantial beneficial interest or as to which such person serves as trustee or in a similar capacity, and (3) any relative or spouse of such person, or any relative of such spouse, who has the same home as such person or who is a director or officer of the registrant or any of its parents or subsidiaries.

Automatic shelf registration statement. The term *automatic shelf registration statement* means a registration statement filed on Form S-3 or Form F-3 by a well-known seasoned issuer pursuant to General Instruction I.D. or I.C. of such forms, respectively.

Business development company. The term *business development company* refers to a company which has elected to be regulated as a business development company under sections 55 through 65 of the Investment Company Act of 1940.

Certified. The term *certified,* when used in regard to financial statements, means examined and reported upon with an opinion expressed by an independent public or certified public accountant.

Charter. The term *charter* includes articles of incorporation, declarations of trust, articles of association or partnership, or any similar instrument, as amended, affecting (either with or without filing with any governmental agency) the organization or creation of an incorporated or unincorporated person.

Common equity. The term *common equity* means any class of common stock or an equivalent interest, including but not limited to a unit of beneficial interest in a trust or a limited partnership interest.

Commission. The term *Commission* means the Securities and Exchange Commission.

Control. The term *control* (including the terms *controlling, controlled by* and *under common control with*) means the possession, direct or indirect, of the power to direct or cause the direction of the management and policies of a person, whether through the ownership of voting securities, by contract, or otherwise.

Depositary share. The term *depositary share* means a security, evidenced by an American Depositary Receipt, that represents a foreign security or a multiple of or fraction thereof deposited with a depositary.

Director. The term *director* means any director of a corporation or any person performing similar functions with respect to any organization whether incorporated or unincorporated.

Dividend or interest reinvestment plan. The term *dividend or interest reinvestment plan* means a plan which is offered solely to the existing security holders of the registrant, which allows such persons to reinvest dividends or interest paid to them on securities issued by the registrant, and also may allow additional cash amounts to be contributed by the participants in the plan, provided the securities to be registered are newly issued, or are purchased for the account of plan participants, at prices not in excess of current market prices at the time of purchase, or at prices not in excess of an amount determined in accordance with a pricing formula specified in the plan and based upon average or current market prices at the time of purchase.

Electronic filer. The term *electronic filer* means a person or an entity that submits filings electronically pursuant to Rules 100 and 101 of Regulation S-T.

Electronic filing. The term *electronic filing* means a document under the federal securities laws that is transmitted or delivered to the Commission in electronic format.

Emerging growth company.
1. The term *emerging growth company* means an issuer that had total annual gross revenues of less than $1,235,000,000 during its most recently completed fiscal year.
2. An issuer that is an emerging growth company as of the first day of that fiscal year shall continue to be deemed an emerging growth company until the earliest of:
   i. the last day of the fiscal year of the issuer during which it had total annual gross revenues of $1,235,000,000 or more;
   ii. the last day of the fiscal year of the issuer following the fifth anniversary of the date of the first sale of common equity securities of the issuer pursuant to an effective registration statement under the Securities Act of 1933;
   iii. the date on which such issuer has, during the previous three year period, issued more than $1,000,000,000 in non-convertible debt; or
   iv. the date on which such issuer is deemed to be a large accelerated filer, as defined in Rule 12b-2 of the Exchange Act, or any successor thereto.

Employee. The term *employee* does not include a director, trustee, or officer.

Employee benefit plan. The term *employee benefit plan* means any written purchase, savings, option, bonus, appreciation, profit sharing, thrift, incentive, pension or similar plan or written compensation contract solely for employees, directors, general partners, trustees (where the registrant is a business trust), officers, or consultants or advisors. However, consultants or advisors may participate in an employee benefit plan only if:
1. They are natural persons;
2. They provide bona fide services to the registrant; and
3. The services are not in connection with the offer or sale of securities in a capital-raising transaction, and do not directly or indirectly promote or maintain a market for the registrant's securities.

Equity security. The term *equity security* means any stock or similar security, certificate of interest or participation in any profit sharing agreement, preorganization certificate or subscription, transferable share, voting trust certificate or certificate of deposit for an equity security, limited partnership interest, interest in a joint venture, or certificate of interest in a business trust; any security future on any such security; or any security convertible, with or without consideration into such a security, or carrying any warrant or right to subscribe to or purchase such a security; or any such warrant or right; or any put, call, straddle, or other option or privilege of buying such a security from or selling such a security to another without being bound to do so.

Executive officer. The term *executive officer,* when used with reference to a registrant, means its president, any vice president of the registrant in charge of a principal business unit, division or function (such as sales, administration or finance), any other officer who performs a policy making function or any other person who performs similar policy making functions for the registrant. Executive officers of subsidiaries may be deemed executive officers of the registrant if they perform such policy making functions for the registrant.

Fiscal year. The term *fiscal year* means the annual accounting period or, if no closing date has been adopted, the calendar year ending on December 31.

Foreign government. The term *foreign government* means the government of any foreign country or of any political subdivision of a foreign country.

Foreign issuer. The term *foreign issuer* means any issuer which is a foreign government, a national of any foreign country or a corporation or other organization incorporated or organized under the laws of any foreign country.

Foreign private issuer.
1. The term *foreign private issuer* means any foreign issuer other than a foreign government except an issuer meeting the following conditions:
    i.   More than 50 percent of the outstanding voting securities of such issuer are directly or indirectly owned of record by residents of the United States; and
    ii. Any of the following:
         A. The majority of the executive officers or directors are United States citizens or residents;
         B. More than 50 percent of the assets of the issuer are located in the United States; or
         C. The business of the issuer is administered principally in the United States.
    Note to paragraph (1): To determine the percentage of outstanding voting securities held by U.S. residents:
    A. Use the method of calculating record ownership in Rule 12g3-2(a) of this chapter, except that:
        1. The inquiry as to the amount of shares represented by accounts of customers resident in the United States may be limited to brokers, dealers, banks and other nominees located in:
            i.   The United States,
            ii. The issuer's jurisdiction of incorporation, and
            iii. The jurisdiction that is the primary trading market for the issuer's voting securities, if different than the issuer's jurisdiction of incorporation; and
        2. Notwithstanding Rule 12g5-1(a)(8) of this chapter, the issuer shall not exclude securities held by persons who received the securities pursuant to an employee compensation plan.
    B. If, after reasonable inquiry, the issuer is unable to obtain information about the amount of shares represented by accounts of customers resident in the United States, the issuer may assume, for purposes of this definition, that the customers are residents of the jurisdiction in which the nominee has its principal place of business.

C.   Count shares of voting securities beneficially owned by residents of the United States as reported on reports of beneficial ownership provided to the issuer or filed publicly and based on information otherwise provided to the issuer.

Free writing prospectus. Except as otherwise specifically provided or the context otherwise requires, a *free writing prospectus* is any written communication as defined in this section that constitutes an offer to sell or a solicitation of an offer to buy the securities relating to a registered offering that is used after the registration statement in respect of the offering is filed (or, in the case of a well-known seasoned issuer, whether or not such registration statement is filed) and is made by means other than:

1.   A prospectus satisfying the requirements of section 10(a) of the Act, Rule 430, Rule 430A, Rule 430B, Rule 430C, Rule 430D, or Rule 431;

2.   A written communication used in reliance on Rule 167 and Rule 426;

3.   A written communication that constitutes an offer to sell or solicitation of an offer to buy such securities that falls within the exception from the definition of prospectus in clause (a) of section 2(a)(10) of the Act

4.   A written communication used in reliance on Rule 163B (§230.163B) or on section 5(d) of the Act.

Graphic communication. The term *graphic communication*, which appears in the definition of "write, written" in section 2(a)(9) of the Act and in the definition of written communication in this section, shall include all forms of electronic media, including, but not limited to, audiotapes, videotapes, facsimiles, CD-ROM, electronic mail, Internet Web sites, substantially similar messages widely distributed (rather than individually distributed) on telephone answering or voice mail systems, computers, computer networks and other forms of computer data compilation. Graphic communication shall not include a communication that, at the time of the communication, originates live, in real-time to a live audience and does not originate in recorded form or otherwise as a graphic communication, although it is transmitted through graphic means.

Ineligible issuer.

1.   An *ineligible issuer* is an issuer with respect to which any of the following is true as of the relevant date of determination:

     i.   Any issuer that is required to file reports pursuant to section 13 or 15(d) of the Securities Exchange Act of 1934 that has not filed all reports and other materials required to be filed during the preceding 12 months (or for such shorter period that the issuer was required to file such reports pursuant to sections 13 or 15(d) of the Securities Exchange Act of 1934), other than reports on Form 8-K required solely pursuant to an item specified in General Instruction I.A.2 of Form SF-3 (or in the case of an asset-backed issuer, to the extent the depositor or any issuing entity previously established, directly or indirectly, by the depositor (as such terms are defined in Item 1101 of Regulation AB are or were at any time during the preceding 12 calendar months required to file reports pursuant to section 13 or 15(d) of the Securities Exchange Act of 1934 with respect to a class of asset-backed securities involving the same asset class, such depositor and each such issuing entity must have filed all reports and other material required to be filed for such period (or such shorter period that each such entity was required to file such reports), other than reports on Form 8-K required solely pursuant to an item specified in General Instruction I.A.4 of Form S-3);

ii. The issuer is, or during the past three years the issuer or any of its predecessors was:

    A. A blank check company as defined in Rule 419(a)(2);

    B. A shell company, other than a business combination related shell company, each as defined in this section;

    C. An issuer in an offering of penny stock as defined in Rule 3a51-1 of the Securities Exchange Act of 1934;

iii. The issuer is a limited partnership that is offering and selling its securities other than through a firm commitment underwriting;

iv. Within the past three years, a petition under the federal bankruptcy laws or any state insolvency law was filed by or against the issuer, or a court appointed a receiver, fiscal agent or similar officer with respect to the business or property of the issuer subject to the following:

    A. In the case of an involuntary bankruptcy in which a petition was filed against the issuer, ineligibility will occur upon the earlier to occur of:

        (1) 90 days following the date of the filing of the involuntary petition (if the case has not been earlier dismissed); or

        (2) The conversion of the case to a voluntary proceeding under federal bankruptcy or state insolvency laws; and

    B. Ineligibility will terminate under this paragraph (1)(iv) if an issuer has filed an annual report with audited financial statements subsequent to its emergence from that bankruptcy, insolvency, or receivership process;

v. Within the past three years, the issuer or any entity that at the time was a subsidiary of the issuer was convicted of any felony or misdemeanor described in paragraphs (i) through (iv) of section 15(b)(4)(B) of the Securities Exchange Act of 1934;

vi. Within the past three years (but in the case of a decree or order agreed to in a settlement, not before [insert date 120 days after publication in the Federal Register]), the issuer or any entity that at the time was a subsidiary of the issuer was made the subject of any judicial or administrative decree or order arising out of a governmental action that:

    A. Prohibits certain conduct or activities regarding, including future violations of, the anti-fraud provisions of the federal securities laws;

    B. Requires that the person cease and desist from violating the anti-fraud provisions of the federal securities laws; or

    C. Determines that the person violated the anti-fraud provisions of the federal securities laws;

vii. The issuer has filed a registration statement that is the subject of any pending proceeding or examination under section 8 of the Act or has been the subject of any refusal order or stop order under section 8 of the Act within the past three years; or

viii. The issuer is the subject of any pending proceeding under section 8A of the Act in connection with an offering.

2. An issuer shall not be an ineligible issuer if the Commission determines, upon a showing of good cause, that it is not necessary under the circumstances that the issuer be considered an ineligible issuer. Any such determination shall be without prejudice

to any other action by the Commission in any other proceeding or matter with respect to the issuer or any other person.

3. The date of determination of whether an issuer is an ineligible issuer is as follows:
    i.   For purposes of determining whether an issuer is a well-known seasoned issuer, at the date specified for purposes of such determination in paragraph (2) of the definition of well-known seasoned issuer in this section; and
    ii. For purposes of determining whether an issuer or offering participant may use free writing prospectuses in respect of an offering in accordance with the provisions of Rules 164 and 433, at the date in respect of the offering specified in paragraph (h) of Rule 164.

Majority-owned subsidiary. The term *majority-owned subsidiary* means a subsidiary more than 50 percent of whose outstanding securities representing the right, other than as affected by events of default, to vote for the election of directors, is owned by the subsidiary's parent and/or one or more of the parent's other majority-owned subsidiaries.

Material. The term *material,* when used to qualify a requirement for the furnishing of information as to any subject, limits the information required to those matters to which there is a substantial likelihood that a reasonable investor would attach importance in determining whether to purchase the security registered.

Officer. The term *officer* means a president, vice president, secretary, treasurer or principal financial officer, comptroller or principal accounting officer, and any person routinely performing corresponding functions with respect to any organization whether incorporated or unincorporated.

Parent. A *parent* of a specified person is an affiliate controlling such person directly, or indirectly through one or more intermediaries.

Predecessor. The term *predecessor* means a person the major portion of the business and assets of which another person acquired in a single succession, or in a series of related successions in each of which the acquiring person acquired the major portion of the business and assets of the acquired person.

Principal underwriter. The term *principal underwriter* means an underwriter in privity of contract with the issuer of the securities as to which he is underwriter, the term *issuer* having the meaning given in sections 2(a)(4) and 2(a)(11) of the Act.

Promoter.
1. The term *promoter* includes:
    i.   Any person who, acting alone or in conjunction with one or more other persons, directly or indirectly takes initiative in founding and organizing the business or enterprise of an issuer; or
    ii. Any person who, in connection with the founding and organizing of the business or enterprise of an issuer, directly or indirectly receives in consideration of services or property, or both services and property, 10 percent or more of any class of securities of the issuer or 10 percent or more of the proceeds from the sale of any class of such securities. However, a person who receives such securities or

proceeds either solely as underwriting commissions or solely in consideration of property shall not be deemed a promoter within the meaning of this paragraph if such person does not otherwise take part in founding and organizing the enterprise.

2. All persons coming within the definition of promoter in paragraph 1 of this definition may be referred to as *founders* or *organizers* or by another term provided that such term is reasonably descriptive of those persons' activities with respect to the issuer.

Prospectus. Unless otherwise specified or the context otherwise requires, the term *prospectus* means a prospectus meeting the requirements of section 10(a) of the Act.

Registrant. The term *registrant* means the issuer of the securities for which the registration statement is filed.

Share. The term *share* means a share of stock in a corporation or unit of interest in an unincorporated person.

Significant subsidiary. The term *significant subsidiary* means a subsidiary, including its subsidiaries, which meets any of the following conditions:

1. The registrant's and its other subsidiaries' investments in and advances to the subsidiary exceed 10 percent of the total assets of the registrant and its subsidiaries consolidated as of the end of the most recently completed fiscal year (for a proposed business combination between entities under common control, this condition is also met when the number of common shares exchanged or to be exchanged by the registrant exceeds 10 percent of its total common shares outstanding at the date the combination is initiated); or

2. The registrant's and its other subsidiaries' proportionate share of the total assets (after intercompany eliminations) of the subsidiary exceeds 10 percent of the total assets of the registrants and its subsidiaries consolidated as of the end of the most recently completed fiscal year; or

3. The registrant's and its other subsidiaries' equity in the income from continuing operations before income taxes of the subsidiary exclusive of the amounts attributable to any noncontrolling interests exceeds 10 percent of such income of the registrant and its subsidiaries consolidated for the most recently completed fiscal year.

Note 1: A registrant that files its financial statements in accordance with or provides a reconciliation to U.S. Generally Accepted Accounting Principles shall make the prescribed tests using amounts determined under U.S. Generally Accepted Accounting Principles. A foreign private issuer that files its financial statements in accordance with IFRS as issued by the IASB shall make the prescribed tests using amounts determined under IFRS as issued by the IASB.

Computational note 1 to paragraph (3). For purposes of making the prescribed income test the following guidance should be applied:

1. When a loss exclusive of amounts attributable to any noncontrolling interests has been incurred by either the parent and its subsidiaries consolidated or the tested subsidiary, but not both, the equity in the income or loss of the tested subsidiary exclusive of amounts attributable to any noncontrolling interests should be excluded from such income of the registrant and its subsidiaries consolidated for purposes of the computation.

2.   If income of the registrant and its subsidiaries consolidated exclusive of amounts attributable to any noncontrolling interests for the most recent fiscal year is at least 10 percent lower than the average of the income for the last five fiscal years, such average income should be substituted for purposes of the computation. Any loss years should be omitted for purposes of computing average income.

Smaller reporting company: As used in this part, the term *smaller reporting company* means an issuer that is not an investment company, an asset-backed issuer, or a majority-owned subsidiary of a parent that is not a smaller reporting company and that:
1.   Had a public float of less than $ 250 million; or
2.   Had annual revenues of less than $100 million and either:
     i.   no public float; or
     ii. A public float of less than $700 million
3.   Whether an issuer is a smaller reporting company is determined on an annual basis.
     i.   For issuers that are required to file reports under section 13(a) or 15(d) of the Exchange Act:
          A.   Public float is measured as of the last business day of the issuer's most recently completed second fiscal quarter and computed by multiplying the aggregate worldwide number of shares of its voting and non-voting common equity held by non-affiliates by the price at which the common equity was last sold, or the average of the bid and asked prices of common equity, in the principal market for the common equity;
          B.   Annual revenues are as of the most recently completed fiscal year for which audited financial statements are available; and
          C.   An issuer must reflect the determination of whether it came within the definition of smaller reporting company in its quarterly report on Form 10-Q for the first fiscal quarter of the next year, indicating on the cover page of that filing, and in subsequent filings for that fiscal year, whether it is a smaller reporting company, except that, if a determination based on public float indicates that the issuer is newly eligible to be a smaller reporting company, the issuer may choose to reflect this determination beginning with its first quarterly report on Form 10-Q following the determination, rather than waiting until the first fiscal quarter of the next year.
     ii. For determinations based on an initial registration statement under the Securities Act or Exchange Act for shares of its common equity:
          A.   Public float is measured as of a date within 30 days of the date of the filing of the registration statement and computed by multiplying the aggregate worldwide number of shares of its voting and non-voting common equity held by non-affiliates before the registration plus, in the case of a Securities Act registration statement, the number of shares of its voting and non-voting common equity included in the registration statement by the estimated public offering price of the shares;
          B.   Annual revenues are as of the most recently completed fiscal year for which audited financial statements are available; and
          C.   The issuer must reflect the determination of whether it came within the definition of smaller reporting company in the registration statement and must appropriately indicate on the cover page of the filing, and subsequent filings for the fiscal year in which the filing is made, whether it is a smaller reporting

company. The issuer must re-determine its status at the end of its second fiscal quarter and then reflect any change in status as provided in paragraph (3)(i)(C) of this definition. In the case of a determination based on an initial Securities Act registration statement, an issuer that was not determined to be a smaller reporting company has the option to re-determine its status at the conclusion of the offering covered by the registration statement based on the actual offering price and number of shares sold.

iii. Once an issuer determines that it does not qualify for smaller reporting company status because it exceeded one or more of the current thresholds, it will remain unqualified unless when making its annual determination either:

A. It determines that its public float was less than $200 million; or

B. It determines that its public float and its annual revenues meet the requirements for subsequent qualification included in the following chart:

Prior Annual Revenues	Prior Public Float			
	None or less than $700 million		$700 million or more	
Less than $100 million	Neither threshold exceeded		**Public float**	Less than $560 million; and
			Revenues	Less than $100 million
$100 million or more	**Public Float**	None or less than $700 million; and	**Public Float**	Less than $560 million; and
	Revenues	Less than $80 million	**Revenues**	Less than $80 million

Instruction 1 to definition of "smaller reporting company": A registrant that qualifies as a smaller reporting company under the public float thresholds identified in paragraphs (1) and (3)(iii)(A) of this definition will qualify as a smaller reporting company regardless of its revenues.

Instruction 2 to definition of "smaller reporting company": A foreign private issuer is not eligible to use the requirements for smaller reporting companies unless it uses the forms and rules designated for domestic issuers and provides financial statements prepared in accordance with U.S. Generally Accepted Accounting Principles.

Subsidiary. A *subsidiary* of a specified person is an affiliate controlled by such person directly, or indirectly through one or more intermediaries. (See also *majority owned subsidiary, significant subsidiary, totally held subsidiary,* and *wholly owned subsidiary.*)

Sub-underwriter. The term sub-underwriter means a dealer that is participating as an underwriter in an offering by committing to purchase securities from a principal underwriter for the securities but is not itself in privity of contract with the issuer of the securities.

Succession. The term *succession* means the direct acquisition of the assets comprising a going business, whether by merger, consolidation, purchase, or other direct transfer. The term does not include the acquisition of control of a business unless followed by the direct acquisition of its assets. The terms *succeed* and *successor* have meanings correlative to the foregoing.

Totally held subsidiary. The term *totally held subsidiary* means a subsidiary (1) substantially all of whose outstanding securities are owned by its parent and/or the parent's other totally held subsidiaries, and (2) which is not indebted to any person other than its parent and/or the parent's other totally held subsidiaries in an amount which is material in relation to the particular subsidiary, excepting indebtedness incurred in the ordinary course of business which is not overdue and which matures within one year from the date of its creation, whether evidenced by securities or not.

Voting securities. The term *voting securities* means securities the holders of which are presently entitled to vote for the election of directors.

Well-known seasoned issuer. A *well-known seasoned issuer* is an issuer that, as of the most recent determination date determined pursuant to paragraph (2) of this definition:

1. i. Meets all the registrant requirements of General Instruction I.A. of Form S-3 or Form F-3 and either:

   A. As of a date within 60 days of the determination date, has a worldwide market value of its outstanding voting and non-voting common equity held by nonaffiliates of $700 million or more; or

   B. 1. As of a date within 60 days of the determination date, has issued in the last three years at least $1 billion aggregate principal amount of non-convertible securities, other than common equity, in primary offerings for cash, not exchange, registered under the Act; and

      2. Will register only non-convertible securities, other than common equity, and full and unconditional guarantees permitted pursuant to paragraph (1)(ii) of this definition unless, at the determination date, the issuer also is eligible to register a primary offering of its securities relying on General Instruction I.B.1. of Form S-3 or Form F-3.

      3. Provided that as to a parent issuer only, for purposes of calculating the aggregate principal amount of outstanding non-convertible securities under paragraph (1)(i)(B)(1) of this definition, the parent issuer may include the aggregate principal amount of non-convertible securities, other than common equity, of its majority-owned subsidiaries issued in registered primary offerings for cash, not exchange, that it has fully and unconditionally guaranteed, within the meaning of Rule 3-10 of Regulation S-X in the last three years; or

   ii. Is a majority-owned subsidiary of a parent that is a well-known seasoned issuer pursuant to paragraph (1)(i) of this definition and, as to the subsidiaries' securities that are being or may be offered on that parent's registration statement:

   A. The parent has provided a full and unconditional guarantee, as defined in Rule 3-10 of Regulation S-X, of the payment obligations on the subsidiary's securities and the securities are non-convertible securities, other than common equity;

   B. The securities are guarantees of:

      (1) Non-convertible securities, other than common equity, of its parent being registered; or

      (2) Non-convertible securities, other than common equity, of another majority-owned subsidiary being registered where there is a full and

unconditional guarantee, as defined in Rule 3-10 of Regulation S-X, of such non-convertible securities by the parent; or

    C. The securities of the majority-owned subsidiary meet the conditions of General Instruction I.B.2 of Form S-3 or Form F-3.

  iii. Is not an ineligible issuer as defined in this section.

  iv. Is not an asset-backed issuer as defined in Item 1101 of Regulation AB.

  v. Is not an investment company registered under the Investment Company Act of 1940 or a business development company as defined in section 2(a)(48) of the Investment Company Act of 1940.

2. For purposes of this definition, the determination date as to whether an issuer is a well-known seasoned issuer shall be the latest of:

  i. The time of filing of its most recent shelf registration statement; or

  ii. The time of its most recent amendment (by post-effective amendment, incorporated report filed pursuant to section 13 or 15(d) of the Securities Exchange Act of 1934, or form of prospectus) to a shelf registration statement for purposes of complying with section 10(a)(3) of the Act (or if such amendment has not been made within the time period required by section 10(a)(3) of the Act, the date on which such amendment is required); or

  iii. In the event that the issuer has not filed a shelf registration statement or amended a shelf registration statement for purposes of complying with section 10(a)(3) of the Act for sixteen months, the time of filing of the issuer's most recent annual report on Form 10-K or Form 20-F (or if such report has not been filed by its due date, such due date).

Wholly owned subsidiary. The term *wholly owned subsidiary* means a subsidiary substantially all of whose outstanding voting securities are owned by its parent and/or the parent's other wholly owned subsidiaries.

Written communication. Except as otherwise specifically provided or the context otherwise requires, a *written communication* is any communication that is written, printed, a radio or television broadcast, or a graphic communication as defined in this section.

Note to "written communication." A communication that is a radio or television broadcast is a written communication regardless of the means of transmission of the broadcast.

Rule 408 – Additional Information

a. In addition to the information expressly required to be included in a registration statement, there shall be added such further material information, if any, as may be necessary to make the required statements, in the light of the circumstances under which they are made, not misleading.

b. Notwithstanding paragraph (a) of this section, unless otherwise required to be included in the registration statement, the failure to include in a registration statement information included in a free writing prospectus will not, solely by virtue of inclusion of the information in a free writing prospectus (as defined in Rule 405), be considered an omission of material information required to be included in the registration statement.

Rule 409 – Information Unknown or Not Reasonably Available

Information required need be given only insofar as it is known or reasonably available to the registrant. If any required information is unknown and not reasonably available to the registrant, either because the obtaining thereof could involve unreasonable effort or expense, or because it rests peculiarly within the knowledge of another person not affiliated with the registrant, the information may be omitted, subject to the following conditions:

    a. The registrant shall give such information on the subject as it possesses or can acquire without unreasonable effort or expense, together with the sources thereof.

    b. The registrant shall include a statement either showing that unreasonable effort or expense would be involved or indicating the absence of any affiliation with the person within whose knowledge the information rests and stating the result of a request made to such person for the information.

Rule 412 – Modified or Superseded Documents

    a. Any statement contained in a document incorporated or deemed to be incorporated by reference or deemed to be part of a registration statement or the prospectus that is part of the registration statement shall be deemed to be modified or superseded for purposes of the registration statement or the prospectus that is part of the registration statement to the extent that a statement contained in the prospectus that is part of the registration statement or in any other subsequently filed document which also is or is deemed to be incorporated by reference or deemed to be part of the registration statement or prospectus that is part of the registration statement modifies or replaces such statement. Any statement contained in a document that is deemed to be incorporated by reference or deemed to be part of a registration statement or the prospectus that is part of the registration statement after the most recent effective date or after the date of the most recent prospectus that is part of the registration statement may modify or replace existing statements contained in the registration statement or the prospectus that is part of the registration statement.

    b. The modifying or superseding statement may, but need not, state that it has modified or superseded a prior statement or include any other information set forth in the document which is not so modified or superseded. The making of a modifying or superseding statement shall not be deemed an admission that the modified or superseded statement, when made, constituted an untrue statement of a material fact, an omission to state a material fact necessary to make a statement not misleading, or the employment of a manipulative, deceptive, or fraudulent device, contrivance, scheme, transaction, act, practice, course of business or artifice to defraud, as those terms are used in the Act, the Securities Exchange Act of 1934, the Investment Company Act of 1940, or the rules and regulations thereunder.

Rule 413 – Registration of Additional Securities and Additional Classes of Securities.

    a. Except as provided in section 24(f) of the Investment Company Act of 1940 and in paragraph (b) of this section, where a registration statement is already in effect, the

111

registration of additional securities shall only be effected through a separate registration statement relating to the additional securities.

b. Notwithstanding paragraph (a) of this section, the following additional securities or additional classes of securities may be added to an automatic shelf registration statement already in effect by filing a post-effective amendment to that automatic shelf registration statement:

1. Securities of a class different than those registered on the effective automatic shelf registration statement identified as provided in Rule 430B(a); or

2. Securities of a majority-owned subsidiary that are permitted to be included in an automatic shelf registration statement, provided that the subsidiary and the securities are identified as provided in Rule 430B and the subsidiary satisfies the signature requirements of an issuer in the post-effective amendment.

Rule 415 – Delayed or Continuous Offering and Sale of Securities

a. Securities may be registered for an offering to be made on a continuous or delayed basis in the future, provided, that:

1. The registration statement pertains only to:

    i. Securities which are to be offered or sold solely by or on behalf of a person or persons other than the registrant, a subsidiary of the registrant or a person of which the registrant is a subsidiary;

    ii. Securities which are to be offered and sold pursuant to a dividend or interest reinvestment plan or an employee benefit plan of the registrant;

    iii. Securities which are to be issued upon the exercise of outstanding options, warrants or rights;

    iv. Securities which are to be issued upon conversion of other outstanding securities;

    v. Securities which are pledged as collateral;

    vi. Securities which are registered on Form F-6;

    vii. Asset-backed securities, (as defined in Rule 1101(c) registered (or qualified to be registered) on Form SF-3 which are to be offered and sold on an immediate or delayed basis by or on behalf of the registrant;

    Instruction to paragraph (a)(1)(vii): The requirements of General Instruction I.B.1 of Form SF-3 must be met for any offerings of an asset-backed security (as defined in Rule 1101(c)) registered in reliance on this paragraph (a)(1)(vii).

    viii. Securities which are to be issued in connection with business combination transactions;

    ix. Securities, other than asset-backed securities, the offering of which will be commenced promptly, will be made on a continuous basis and may continue for a period in excess of 30 days from the date of initial effectiveness;

x.   Securities registered (or qualified to be registered) on Form S-3 or Form F-3 which are to be offered and sold on an immediate, continuous or delayed basis by or on behalf of the registrant, a majority owned subsidiary of the registrant or a person of which the registrant is a majority-owned subsidiary; or

xi. Shares of common stock which are to be offered and sold on a delayed or continuous basis by or on behalf of a registered closed-end management investment company or business development company that makes periodic repurchase offers pursuant to Rule 23c-3.

xii. Asset-backed securities (as defined in Rule 1101(c)) that are to be offered and sold on a continuous basis if the offering is commenced promptly and being conducted on the condition that the consideration paid for such securities will be promptly refunded to the purchaser unless:

A. All of the securities being offered are sold at a specified price within a specified time; and

B. The total amount due to the seller is received by him by a specified date.

2.   Securities in paragraph (a)(1)(viii) of this section and securities in paragraph (a)(1)(ix) of this section that are not registered on Form S-3 or Form F-3 may only be registered in an amount which, at the time the registration statement becomes effective, is reasonably expected to be offered and sold within two years from the initial effective date of the registration.

3.   The registrant furnishes the undertakings required by Item 512(a) of Regulation S-K except that a registrant that is an investment company filing on Form N-2 must furnish the undertakings required by Item 34.4 of Form N-2.

4.   In the case of a registration statement pertaining to an at the market offering of equity securities by or on behalf of the registrant, the offering must come within paragraph (a)(1)(x) of this section. As used in this paragraph, the term "at the market offering" means an offering of equity securities into an existing trading market for outstanding shares of the same class at other than a fixed price.

5.   Securities registered on an automatic shelf registration statement and securities described in paragraphs (a)(1)(vii), (ix), and (x) of this section may be offered and sold only if not more than three years have elapsed since the initial effective date of the registration statement under which they are being offered and sold, *provided, however,* that if a new registration statement has been filed pursuant to paragraph (a)(6) of this section:

i.   If the new registration statement is an automatic shelf registration statement, it shall be immediately effective pursuant to Rule 462(e); or

ii. If the new registration statement is not an automatic shelf registration statement:

A. Securities covered by the prior registration statement may continue to be offered and sold until the earlier of the effective date of the new registration statement or 180 days after the third anniversary of the initial effective date of the prior registration statement; and

B. A continuous offering of securities covered by the prior registration statement that commenced within three years of the initial effective date may continue until the effective date of the new registration statement if such offering is permitted under the new registration statement.

6.   Prior to the end of the three-year period described in paragraph (a)(5) of this section, an issuer may file a new registration statement covering securities described in such paragraph (a)(5) of this section, which may, if permitted, be an automatic shelf registration statement. The new registration statement and prospectus included therein must include all the information that would be required at that time in a prospectus relating to all offering(s) that it covers. Prior to the effective date of the new registration statement (including at the time of filing in the case of an automatic shelf registration statement), the issuer may include on such new registration statement any unsold securities covered by the earlier registration statement by identifying on the bottom of the facing page of the new registration statement or latest amendment thereto the amount of such unsold securities being included and any filing fee paid in connection with such unsold securities, which will continue to be applied to such unsold securities. The offering of securities on the earlier registration statement will be deemed terminated as of the date of effectiveness of the new registration statement.

b.   This section shall not apply to any registration statement pertaining to securities issued by a face-amount certificate company or redeemable securities issued by an open-end management company or unit investment trust under the Investment Company Act of 1940 or any registration statement filed by any foreign government or political subdivision thereof.

Rule 420 – Legibility of Prospectus

a.   The body of all printed prospectuses and all notes to financial statements and other tabular data included therein shall be in roman type at least as large and as legible as 10-point modern type.
However,
1.   to the extent necessary for convenient presentation, financial statements and other tabular data, including tabular data in notes, and
2.   prospectuses deemed to be omitting prospectuses under Rule 482 may be in roman type at least as large and as legible as 8-point modern type. All such type shall be leaded at least 2 points.

b.   Where a prospectus is distributed through an electronic medium, issuers may satisfy legibility requirements applicable to printed documents, such as paper size, type size and font, bold-face type, italics and red ink, by presenting all required information in a format readily communicated to investors, and where indicated, in a manner reasonably calculated to draw investor attention to specific information.

Rule 421 – Presentation of Information in Prospectuses

a.   The information required in a prospectus need not follow the order of the items or other requirements in the form. Such information shall not, however, be set forth in such fashion as to obscure any of the required information or any information necessary to keep the required information from being incomplete or misleading. Where an item requires information to be given in a prospectus in tabular form it shall be given in substantially the tabular form specified in the item.

b.   You must present the information in a prospectus in a clear, concise and understandable manner. You must prepare the prospectus using the following standards:

      1.   Present information in clear, concise sections, paragraphs, and sentences. Whenever possible, use short, explanatory sentences and bullet lists;

      2.   Use descriptive headings and subheadings;

      3.   Avoid frequent reliance on glossaries or defined terms as the primary means of explaining information in the prospectus. Define terms in a glossary or other section of the document only if the meaning is unclear from the context. Use a glossary only if it facilitates understanding of the disclosure; and

      4.   Avoid legal and highly technical business terminology.

Note to Rule 421(b): In drafting the disclosure to comply with this section, you should avoid the following:

      1.   Legalistic or overly complex presentations that make the substance of the disclosure difficult to understand;

      2.   Vague "boilerplate" explanations that are imprecise and readily subject to different interpretations;

      3.   Complex information copied directly from legal documents without any clear and concise explanation of the provision(s); and

      4.   Disclosure repeated in different sections of the document that increases the size of the document but does not enhance the quality of the information.

c.   All information required to be included in a prospectus shall be clearly understandable without the necessity of referring to the particular form or to the general rules and regulations. Except as to financial statements and information required in a tabular form, the information set forth in a prospectus may be expressed in condensed or summarized form. In lieu of repeating information in the form of notes to financial statements, references may be made to other parts of the prospectus where such information is set forth.

d. 1.   To enhance the readability of the prospectus, you must use plain English principles in the organization, language, and design of the front and back cover pages, the summary, and the risk factors section.

      2.   You must draft the language in these sections so that at a minimum it substantially complies with each of the following plain English writing principles:

           Short sentences; Definite, concrete, everyday words; Active voice; Tabular presentation or bullet lists for complex material, whenever possible; No legal jargon or highly technical business terms; and No multiple negatives.

      3.   In designing these sections or other sections of the prospectus, you may include pictures, logos, charts, graphs, or other design elements so long as the design is not misleading and the required information is clear. You are encouraged to use tables, schedules, charts and graphic illustrations of the results of operations, balance sheet, or other financial data that present the data in an understandable manner. Any presentation must be consistent with the financial statements and non-financial information in the prospectus. You must draw the graphs and charts to scale. Any information you provide must not be misleading.

Instruction to Rule 421: You should read Securities Act Release No. 33-7497 (January 28, 1998) for information on plain English principles.

Rule 424 – Filing of Prospectuses; Number of Copies

a.   Except as provided in paragraph (f) of this section, five copies of every form of prospectus sent or given to any person prior to the effective date of the registration statement which varies from the form or forms of prospectus included in the registration statement as filed pursuant to Rule 402(a) shall be filed as a part of the registration statement not later than the date such form of prospectus is first sent or given to any person: *Provided, however,* That only a form of prospectus that contains substantive changes from or additions to a prospectus previously filed with the Commission as part of a registration statement need be filed pursuant to this paragraph (a).

b.   Ten copies of each form of prospectus purporting to comply with section 10 of the Act, except for documents constituting a prospectus pursuant to Rule 428(a) or free writing prospectuses pursuant to Rule 164 and Rule 433, shall be filed with the Commission in the form in which it is used after the effectiveness of the registration statement and identified as required by paragraph (e) of this section; *provided, however,* that only a form of prospectus that contains substantive changes from or additions to a previously filed prospectus is required to be filed;

     Provided, further, that this paragraph (b) shall not apply in respect of a form of prospectus contained in a registration statement and relating solely to securities offered at competitive bidding, which prospectus is intended for use prior to the opening of bids. Ten copies of the form of prospectus shall be filed or transmitted for filing as follows:

     1.   A form of prospectus that discloses information previously omitted from the prospectus filed as part of an effective registration statement in reliance upon Rule 430A under the Securities Act shall be filed with the commission no later than the second business day following the earlier of the date of determination of the offering price or the date it is first used after effectiveness in connection with a public offering or sales, or transmitted by a means reasonably calculated to result in filing with the Commission by that date.

     2.   A form of prospectus that is used in connection with a primary offering of securities pursuant to Rule 415(a)(1)(x) or a primary offering of securities registered for issuance on a delayed basis pursuant to Rule 415(a)(1)(vii) or (viii) and that, in the case of Rule 415(a)(1)(viii) discloses the public offering price, description of securities or similar matters, and in the case of Rule 415(a)(1)(vii) and (x) discloses information previously omitted from the prospectus filed as part of an effective registration statement in reliance on Rule 430B, or, in the case of asset-backed securities, Rule 430D shall be filed with the Commission no later than the second business day following the earlier of the date of the determination of the offering price or the date it is first used after effectiveness in connection with a public offering or sales, or transmitted by a means reasonably calculated to result in filing with the Commission by that date.

     3.   A form of prospectus that reflects facts or events other than those covered in paragraphs (b)(1), (2) and (6) of this section that constitute a substantive change from or addition to the information set forth in the last form of prospectus filed with the Commission under this section or as part of a registration statement under the Securities Act shall be filed with the Commission no later than the fifth business day after the date it is first used after effectiveness in connection with

a public offering or sales, or transmitted by a means reasonably calculated to result in filing with the Commission by that date.

4.   A form of prospectus that discloses information, facts or events covered in both paragraphs (b) (1) and (3) shall be filed with the Commission no later than the second business day following the earlier of the date of the determination of the offering price or the date it is first used after effectiveness in connection with a public offering or sales, or transmitted by a means reasonably calculated to result in filing with the Commission by that date.

5.   A form of prospectus that discloses information, facts or events covered in both paragraphs (b) (2) and (3) shall be filed with the Commission no later than the second business day following the earlier of the date of the determination of the offering price or the date it is first used after effectiveness in connection with a public offering or sales, or transmitted by a means reasonably calculated to result in filing with the Commission by that date.

6.   A form of prospectus used in connection with an offering of securities under Canada's National Policy Statement No. 45 pursuant to Rule 415 under the Securities Act that is not made in the United States shall be filed with the Commission no later than the date it is first used in Canada, or transmitted by a means reasonably calculated to result in filing with the Commission by that date.

7.   A form of prospectus that identifies selling security holders and the amounts to be sold by them that was previously omitted from the registration statement and the prospectus in reliance upon Rule 430B shall be filed with the Commission no later than the second business day following the earlier of the date of sale or the date of first use or transmitted by a means reasonably calculated to result in filing with the Commission by that date.

8.   A form of prospectus otherwise required to be filed pursuant to paragraph (b) of this section that is not filed within the time frames specified in paragraph (b) of this section must be filed pursuant to this paragraph as soon as practicable after the discovery of such failure to file.

Note to paragraph (b) of Rule 424: A form of prospectus required to be filed pursuant to another paragraph of Rule 424(b) that is filed under Rule 424(b)(8) shall nonetheless be "required to be filed" under such other paragraph.

Instruction: Notwithstanding Rule 424 (b)(2) and (b)(5) above, a form of prospectus or prospectus supplement relating to an offering of asset-backed securities under Rule 415(a)(1)(vii) or Rule 415(a)(1)(xii) that is required to be filed pursuant to paragraph (b) of this section, shall be filed with the Commission no later than the second business day following the date it is first used after effectiveness in connection with a public offering or sales, or transmitted by a means reasonably calculated to result in filing with the Commission by that date.

c.   If a form of prospectus, other than one filed pursuant to paragraph (b)(1) or (b)(4) of this Rule, consists of a prospectus supplement attached to a form of prospectus that

1.   previously has been filed or

2.   was not required to be filed pursuant to paragraph (b) because it did no contain substantive changes from a prospectus that previously was filed, only the prospectus supplement need be filed under paragraph (b) of this rule, provided that the first page of each prospectus supplement includes a cross reference to the date(s) of the related prospectus and any prospectus supplements thereto that

together constitute the prospectus required to be delivered by Section 5(b) of the Securities Act with respect to the securities currently being offered or sold. The cross reference may be set forth in longhand, provided it is legible.

Note: Any prospectus supplement being filed separately that is smaller than a prospectus page should be attached to an 8-1/2" x 11" sheet of paper.

d.   Every prospectus consisting of a radio or television broadcast shall be reduced to writing. Five copies of every such prospectus shall be filed with the Commission in accordance with the requirements of this section.

e.   Each copy of a form of prospectus filed under this rule shall contain in the upper right corner of the cover page the paragraph of this rule, including the subparagraph if applicable, under which the filing is made, and the file number of the registration statement to which the prospectus relates. The information required by this paragraph may be set forth in longhand, provided it is legible.

f.   This rule shall not apply with respect to prospectuses of an investment company registered under the Investment Company Act of 1940 or a business development company.

g.   A form of prospectus filed pursuant to this section that operates to reflect the payment of filing fees for an offering or offerings pursuant to Rule 456(b) must include on its cover page the calculation of registration fee table reflecting the payment of such filing fees for the securities that are the subject of the payment.

h.   1.   Three copies of a form of prospectus relating to an offering of asset-backed securities pursuant to Rule 415(a)(1)(vii) or Rule 415(a)(1)(xii) disclosing information previously omitted from the prospectus filed as part of an effective registration statement in reliance on Rule 430D shall be filed with the Commission at least three business days before the date of the first sale in the offering, or if used earlier, the earlier of:
        i.   The applicable number of business days before the date of the first sale; or
        ii.   The second business day after first use.

      2.   Three copies of a prospectus supplement relating to an offering of asset-backed securities pursuant to Rule 415(a)(vii) or Rule 415(a)(1)(xii) that reflects any material change from the information contained in a prospectus filed in accordance with Rule 424(h)(1) shall be filed with the Commission at least forty-eight hours before the date and time of the first sale in the offering. The prospectus supplement must clearly delineate what material information has changed and how the information has changed from the prospectus filed in accordance with Rule 424(h)(1).

Instruction to paragraph (h): The filing requirements of this paragraph (h) do not apply if a filing is made solely to add fees pursuant to Rule 457 and for no other purpose.

Rule 430 – Prospectus for Use Prior to Effective Date

a.   A form of prospectus filed as a part of the registration statement shall be deemed to meet the requirements of section 10 of the Act for the purpose of section 5(b)(1) thereof prior to the effective date of the registration statement, provided such form of prospectus contains substantially the information required by the Act and the rules and regulations thereunder to be included in a prospectus meeting the requirements of section 10(a) of the Act for the securities being registered, or contains substantially that information except for the omission of information with respect to the offering price, underwriting discounts or commissions, discounts or commissions to dealers, amount of proceeds, conversion rates, call prices, or other matters dependent upon the offering price. Every such form of prospectus shall be deemed to have been filed as a part of the registration statement for the purpose of section 7 of the Act.

b.   A form of prospectus filed as part of a registration statement on Form N-1A, Form N-2, Form N-3, Form N-4, or Form N-6 shall be deemed to meet the requirements of Section 10 of the Act for the purpose of Section 5(b)(1) thereof prior to the effective date of the registration statement, *Provided* that:

1.   Such form of prospectus meets the requirements of paragraph (a) of this section; and

2.   Such registration statement contains a form of Statement of Additional Information that is made available to persons receiving such prospectus upon written or oral request, and without charge, unless the form of prospectus contains the information otherwise required to be disclosed in the form of Statement of Additional Information. Every such form of prospectus shall be deemed to have been filed as part of the registration statement for the purpose of section 7 of the Act.

Rule 430A – Prospectus in a Registration Statement at the Time of Effectiveness

a.   The form of prospectus filed as part of a registration statement that is declared effective may omit information with respect to the public offering price, underwriting syndicate (including any material relationships between the registrant and underwriters not named therein), underwriting discounts or commissions, discounts or commissions to dealers, amount of proceeds, conversion rates, call prices and other items dependent upon the offering price, delivery dates, and terms of the securities dependent upon the offering date; and such form of prospectus need not contain such information in order for the registration statement to meet the requirements of Section 7 of the Securities Act for the purposes of Section 5 thereof, *Provided* that:

1.   The securities to be registered are offered for cash;

2.   The registrant furnishes the undertakings required by Item 512(i) of Regulation S-K.

3.   The information omitted in reliance upon paragraph (a) from the form of prospectus filed as part of a registration statement that is declared effective is contained in a form of prospectus filed with the Commission pursuant to Rule 424(b) or Rule 497(h) under the Securities Act; except that if such form of prospectus is not so filed by the later of fifteen business days after the effective date of the registration statement or fifteen business days after the effectiveness

of a post-effective amendment thereto that contains a form of prospectus, or transmitted by a means reasonably calculated to result in filing with the Commission by that date, the information omitted in reliance upon paragraph (a) must be contained in an effective post-effective amendment to the registration statement.

Instruction to paragraph (a): A decrease in the volume of securities offered or change in the bona fide estimate of the maximum offering price range from that indicated in the form of prospectus filed as part of a registration statement that is declared effective may be disclosed in the form of prospectus filed with the Commission pursuant to Rule 424(b) or Rule 497(h) under the Securities Act so long as the decrease in the volume or change in the price range would not materially change the disclosure contained in the registration statement at effectiveness. Notwithstanding the foregoing, any increase or decrease in volume (if the total dollar value of securities offered would not exceed that which was registered) and any deviation from the low or high end of the range may be reflected in the form of prospectus filed with the Commission pursuant to Rule 424(b)(1) or Rule 497(h) if, in the aggregate, the changes in volume and price represent no more than a 20% change in the maximum aggregate offering price set forth in the "Calculation of Registration Fee" table in the effective registration statement.

b. The information omitted in reliance upon paragraph (a) from the form of prospectus filed as part of an effective registration statement, and contained in the form of prospectus filed with the Commission pursuant to Rule 424(b) or Rule 497(h) under the Securities Act, shall be deemed to be a part of the registration statement as of the time it was declared effective.

c. When used prior to determination of the offering price of the securities, a form of prospectus relating to the securities offered pursuant to a registration statement that is declared effective with information omitted from the form of prospectus filed as part of such effective registration statement in reliance upon this Rule 430A need not contain information omitted pursuant to paragraph (a), in order to meet the requirements of Section 10 of the Securities Act for the purpose of section 5(b)(1) thereof. This provision shall not limit the information required to be contained in a form of prospectus meeting the requirements of section 10(a) of the Act for the purposes of section 5(b)(2) thereof or exception (a) of Section 2(a)(10) thereof.

d. This rule shall not apply to registration statements for securities to be offered by competitive bidding.

e. In the case of a registration statement filed on Form N-1A, Form N-2, Form N-3, Form N-4, or Form N-6, the references to "form of prospectus" in paragraphs (a) and (b) of this section and the accompanying Note shall be deemed also to refer to the form of Statement of Additional Information filed as part of such a registration statement.

f. This section may apply to registration statements that are immediately effective pursuant to Rule 462(e) and (f).

Note: If information is omitted in reliance upon paragraph (a) from the form of prospectus filed as part of an effective registration statement, or effective post-effective amendment thereto, the registrant must ascertain promptly whether a form of prospectus transmitted for filing under Rule 424(b) of Rule 497(h) under the Securities Act actually was received for filing by the Commission and, in the event that it was not, promptly file such prospectus.

Rule 430B – Prospectus in a Registration Statement after Effective Date

a. A form of prospectus filed as part of a registration statement for offerings pursuant to Rule 415(a)(1)(x) may omit from the information required by the form to be in the prospectus information that is unknown or not reasonably available to the issuer pursuant to Rule 409. In addition, a form of prospectus filed as part of an automatic shelf registration statement for offerings pursuant to Rule 415(a), other than Rule 415(a)(1)(viii), also may omit information as to whether the offering is a primary offering or an offering on behalf of persons other than the issuer, or a combination thereof, the plan of distribution for the securities, a description of the securities registered other than an identification of the name or class of such securities, and the identification of other issuers. Each such form of prospectus shall be deemed to have been filed as part of the registration statement for the purpose of section 7 of the Act.

b. A form of prospectus filed as part of a registration statement for offerings pursuant to Rule 415(a)(1)(i) by an issuer eligible to use Form S-3 or Form F-3 for primary offerings pursuant to General Instruction I.B.1 of such forms, may omit the information specified in paragraph (a) of this section, and may also omit the identities of selling security holders and amounts of securities to be registered on their behalf if:

1. The registration statement is an automatic shelf registration statement as defined in Rule 405; or
2. All of the following conditions are satisfied:
   i. The initial offering transaction of the securities (or securities convertible into such securities) the resale of which are being registered on behalf of each of the selling security holders, was completed;
   ii. The securities (or securities convertible into such securities) were issued and outstanding prior to the original date of filing the registration statement covering the resale of the securities;
   iii. The registration statement refers to any unnamed selling security holders in a generic manner by identifying the initial offering transaction in which the securities were sold; and
   iv. The issuer is not and during the past three years neither the issuer nor any of its predecessors was:
      (A) A blank check company as defined in Rule 419(a)(2);
      (B) A shell company, other than a business combination related shell company, each as defined in Rule 405; or
      (C) An issuer in an offering of penny stock as defined in Rule 3a51-1 of the Securities Exchange Act of 1934.

c. A form of prospectus that is part of a registration statement that omits information in reliance upon paragraph (a) or (b) of this section meets the requirements of section 10 of the Act for the purpose of section 5(b)(1) thereof. This provision shall not limit the information required to be contained in a form of prospectus in order to meet the requirements of section 10(a) of the Act for the purposes of section 5(b)(2) thereof or exception (a) of section 2(a)(10) thereof.

d.   Information omitted from a form of prospectus that is part of an effective registration statement in reliance on paragraph (a) or (b) of this section may be included subsequently in the prospectus that is part of a registration statement by:

     1.   A post-effective amendment to the registration statement;

     2.   A prospectus filed pursuant to Rule 424(b); or

     3.   If the applicable form permits, including the information in the issuer's periodic or current reports filed pursuant to section 13 or 15(d) of the Securities Exchange Act of 1934 that are incorporated or deemed incorporated by reference into the prospectus that is part of the registration statement in accordance with applicable requirements, subject to the provisions of paragraph (h) of this section.

e.   Information omitted from a form of prospectus that is part of an effective registration statement in reliance on paragraph (a) or (b) of this section and contained in a form of prospectus required to be filed with the Commission pursuant to Rule 424(b), other than as provided in paragraph (f) of this section, shall be deemed part of and included in the registration statement as of the date such form of filed prospectus is first used after effectiveness.

f.   1.   Information omitted from a form of prospectus that is part of an effective registration statement in reliance on paragraph (a) or (b) of this section and is contained in a form of prospectus required to be filed with the Commission pursuant to Rule 424(b)(2), (b)(5), or (b)(7), shall be deemed to be part of and included in the registration statement on the earlier of the date such subsequent form of prospectus is first used or the date and time of the first contract of sale of securities in the offering to which such subsequent form of prospectus relates.

     2.   The date on which a form of prospectus is deemed to be part of and included in the registration statement pursuant to paragraph (f)(1) of this section shall be deemed, for purposes of liability under section 11 of the Act of the issuer and any underwriter at the time only, to be a new effective date of the part of such registration statement relating to the securities to which such form of prospectus relates, such part of the registration statement consisting of all information included in the registration statement and any prospectus relating to the offering of such securities (including information relating to the offering in a prospectus already included in the registration statement) as of such date and all information relating to the offering included in reports and materials incorporated by reference into such registration statement and prospectus as of such date, and in each case not modified or superseded pursuant to Rule 412. The offering of such securities at that time shall be deemed to be the initial bona fide offering thereof.

     3.   If a registration statement is amended to include or is deemed to include, through incorporation by reference or otherwise, except as otherwise provided in Rule 436, a report or opinion of any person made on such person's authority as an expert whose consent would be required under section 7 of the Act because of being named as having prepared or certified part of the registration statement, then for purposes of this section and for liability purposes under section 11 of

the Act, the part of the registration statement for which liability against such person is asserted shall be considered as having become effective with respect to such person as of the time the report or opinion is deemed to be part of the registration statement and a consent required pursuant to section 7 of the Act has been provided as contemplated by section 11 of the Act.

4. Except for an effective date resulting from the filing of a form of prospectus filed for purposes of including information required by section 10(a)(3) of the Act or pursuant to Item 512(a)(1)(ii) of Regulation S-K, the date a form of prospectus is deemed part of and included in the registration statement pursuant to this paragraph shall not be an effective date established pursuant to paragraph (f)(2) of this section as to:

   i. Any director (or person acting in such capacity) of the issuer;

   ii. Any person signing any report or document incorporated by reference into the registration statement, except for such a report or document incorporated by reference for purposes of including information required by section 10(a)(3) of the Act or pursuant to Item 512(a)(1)(ii) of Regulation S-K (such person except for such reports being deemed not to be a person who signed the registration statement within the meaning of section 11(a) of the Act).

5. The date a form of prospectus is deemed part of and included in the registration statement pursuant to paragraph (f)(2) of this section shall not be an effective date established pursuant to paragraph (f)(2) of this section as to:

   i. Any accountant with respect to financial statements or other financial information contained in the registration statement as of a prior effective date and for which the accountant previously provided a consent to be named as required by section 7 of the Act, unless the form of prospectus contains new audited financial statements or other financial information as to which the accountant is an expert and for which a new consent is required pursuant to section 7 of the Act or Rule 436; and

   ii. Any other person whose report or opinion as an expert or counsel has, with their consent, previously been included in the registration statement as of a prior effective date, unless the form of prospectus contains a new report or opinion for which a new consent is required pursuant to section 7 of the Act or Rule 436.

g. Notwithstanding paragraph (e) or (f) of this section or paragraph (a) of Rule 412, no statement made in a registration statement or prospectus that is part of the registration statement or made in a document incorporated or deemed incorporated by reference into the registration statement or prospectus that is part of the registration statement after the effective date of such registration statement or portion thereof in respect of an offering determined pursuant to this section will, as to a purchaser with a time of contract of sale prior to such effective date, supersede or modify any statement that was made in the registration statement or prospectus that was part of the registration statement or made in any such document immediately prior to such effective date.

h. Where a form of prospectus filed pursuant to Rule 424(b) relating to an offering does not include disclosure of omitted information regarding the terms of the offering, the securities, or the plan of distribution, or selling security holders for the securities that are the subject of the form of prospectus, because such omitted information has been included in periodic or current reports filed pursuant to section 13 or 15(d) of the Securities Exchange Act of 1934 incorporated or deemed incorporated by reference into the prospectus, the issuer shall file a form of prospectus identifying the periodic or current reports that are incorporated or deemed incorporated by reference into the prospectus that is part of the registration statement that contain such omitted information. Such form of prospectus shall be required to be filed, depending on the nature of the incorporated information, pursuant to Rule 424(b)(2), (b)(5), or (b)(7).

i.   Issuers relying on this section shall furnish the undertakings required by Item 512(a) of Regulation S-K.

Note to Rule 430B: The provisions of paragraph (b) of Rule 401 shall apply to any prospectus filed for purposes of including information required by section 10(a)(3) of the Act.

Rule 430C – Prospectus in a Registration Statement Pertaining to an Offering other than Pursuant to Rule 430A or Rule 430B after the Effective Date

a.   In offerings made other than in reliance on Rule 430B or Rule 430D and other than for prospectuses filed in reliance on Rule 430A, information contained in a form of prospectus required to be filed with the Commission pursuant to Rule 424(b) or Rule 497(b), (c), (d), or (e), shall be deemed to be part of and included in the registration statement on the date it is first used after effectiveness.

b.   Notwithstanding paragraph (a) of this section or paragraph (a) of Rule 412, no statement made in a registration statement or prospectus that is part of the registration statement or made in a document incorporated or deemed incorporated by reference into the registration statement or prospectus that is part of the registration statement will, as to a purchaser with a time of contract of sale prior to such first use, supersede or modify any statement that was made in the registration statement or prospectus that was part of the registration statement or made in any such document immediately prior to such date of first use.

c.   Nothing in this section shall affect the information required to be included in an issuer's registration statement and prospectus.

d.   Issuers subject to paragraph (a) of this section shall furnish the undertakings required by Item 512(a) of Regulation S-K, or Item 34.4 of Form N-2, as applicable.

Rule 431 – Summary Prospectuses

a.   A summary prospectus prepared and filed (except a summary prospectus filed by an open-end management investment company registered under the Investment Company Act of 1940) as part of a registration statement in accordance with this section shall be deemed to be a prospectus permitted under section 10(b) of the Act for the purposes of section 5(b)(1) of the Act if the form used for registration of the securities to be offered provides for the use of a summary prospectus and the following conditions are met:

1.   i.   The registrant is organized under the laws of the United States or any State or Territory or the District of Columbia and has its principal business operations in the United States or its territories; or
      ii.   The registrant is a foreign private issuer eligible to use Form F-2;
2.   The registrant has a class of securities registered pursuant to section 12(b) of the Securities Exchange Act of 1934 or has a class of equity securities registered pursuant to section 12(g) of that Act or is required to file reports pursuant to section 15(d) of that Act;
3.   The registrant:
      i.   Has been subject to the requirements of section 12 or 15(d) of the Securities Exchange Act of 1934 and has filed all the material required to be filed pursuant to sections 13, 14 or 15(d) of that Act for a period of at least thirty-six calendar months immediately preceding the filing of the registration statement; and
      ii.   has filed in a timely manner all reports required to be filed during the twelve calendar months and any portion of a month immediately preceding the filing of the registration statement and, if the registrant has used (during the twelve calendar months and any portion of a month immediately preceding the filing of the registration statement) Rule 12b-25(b) under the Securities Exchange Act of 1934 with respect to a report or portion of a report, that report or portion thereof has actually been filed within the time period prescribed by that Rule; and
4.   Neither the registrant nor any of its consolidated or unconsolidated subsidiaries has, since the end of its last fiscal year for which certified financial statements of the registrant and its consolidated subsidiaries were included in a report filed pursuant to section 13(a) or 15(d) of the Securities Exchange Act of 1934:
      i.   failed to pay any dividend or sinking fund installment on preferred stock; or
      ii.   defaulted on any installment or installments on indebtedness for borrowed money, or on any rental on one or more long term leases, which defaults in the aggregate are material to the financial position of the registrant and its consolidated and unconsolidated subsidiaries, taken as a whole.

b.   A summary prospectus shall contain the information specified in the instructions as to summary prospectuses in the form used for registration of the securities to be offered. Such prospectus may include any other information the substance of which is contained in the registration statement except as otherwise specifically provided in the instructions as to summary prospectuses in the form used for registration. It shall not include any information the substance of which is not contained in the registration statement except that a summary prospectus may contain any information specified in Rule 134(a). No reference need be made to inapplicable terms and negative answers to any item of the form may be omitted.

c.   All information included in a summary prospectus, other than the statement required by paragraph (e) of this section, may be expressed in such condensed or summarized form as may be appropriate in the light of the circumstances under which the prospectus is to be used. The information need not follow the numerical sequence of the items of the form used for registration. Every summary prospectus shall be dated approximately as of the date of its first use.

d. When used prior to the effective date of the registration statement, a summary prospectus shall be captioned a "Preliminary Summary Prospectus" and shall comply with the applicable requirements relating to a preliminary prospectus.

e. A statement to the following effect shall be prominently set forth in conspicuous print at the beginning or at the end of every summary prospectus:

> "Copies of a more complete prospectus may be obtained from" (Insert name(s), address(es) and telephone number(s)).

Copies of a summary prospectus filed with the Commission pursuant to paragraph (g) of this section may omit the names of persons from whom the complete prospectus may be obtained.

f. Any summary prospectus published in a newspaper, magazine or other periodical need only be set in type at least as large as 7 point modern type. Nothing in this rule shall prevent the use of reprints of a summary prospectus published in a newspaper, magazine, or other periodical, if such reprints are clearly legible.

g. Eight copies of every proposed summary prospectus shall be filed as a part of the registration statement, or as an amendment thereto, at least 5 days (exclusive of Saturdays, Sundays and holidays) prior to the use thereof, or prior to the release for publication by any newspaper, magazine or other person, whichever is earlier. The Commission may, however, in its discretion, authorize such use or publication prior to the expiration of the 5-day period upon a written request for such authorization. Within 7 days after the first use or publication thereof, 5 additional copies shall be filed in the exact form in which it was used or published.

Rule 433 – Conditions to Permissible Post-filing Free Writing Prospectuses

a. **Scope of section**. This section applies to any free writing prospectus with respect to securities of any issuer (except as set forth in Rule 164 that are the subject of a registration statement that has been filed under the Act). Such a free writing prospectus that satisfies the conditions of this section may include information the substance of which is not included in the registration statement. Such a free writing prospectus that satisfies the conditions of this section will be a prospectus permitted under section 10(b) of the Act for purposes of sections 2(a)(10), 5(b)(1), and 5(b)(2) of the Act and will, for purposes of considering it a prospectus, be deemed to be public, without regard to its method of use or distribution, because it is related to the public offering of securities that are the subject of a filed registration statement.

b. **Permitted use of free writing prospectus**. Subject to the conditions of this paragraph (b) and satisfaction of the conditions set forth in paragraphs (c) through (g) of this section, a free writing prospectus may be used under this section and Rule 164 in connection with a registered offering of securities:
    1. Eligibility and prospectus conditions for seasoned issuers and well-known seasoned issuers. Subject to the provisions of Rule 164(e), (f), and (g), the issuer

or any other offering participant may use a free writing prospectus in the following offerings after a registration statement relating to the offering has been filed that includes a prospectus that, other than by reason of this section or Rule 431, satisfies the requirements of section 10 of the Act:

    i.   Offerings of securities registered on Form S-3 pursuant to General Instruction I.B.1, I.B.2, I.C., or I.D. thereof or on Form SF-3;

    ii.   Offerings of securities registered on Form F-3 pursuant to General Instruction I.A.5, I.B.1, I.B.2, or I.C. thereof;

    iii. Any other offering not excluded from reliance on this section and Rule 164 of securities of a well-known seasoned issuer; and

    iv. Any other offering not excluded from reliance on this section and Rule 164 of securities of an issuer eligible to use Form S-3 or Form F-3 for primary offerings pursuant to General Instruction I.B.1 of such Forms.

2.   Eligibility and prospectus conditions for non-reporting and unseasoned issuers. If the issuer does not fall within the provisions of paragraph (b)(1) of this section, then, subject to the provisions of Rule 164(e), (f), and (g), any person participating in the offer or sale of the securities may use a free writing prospectus as follows:

    i.   If the free writing prospectus is or was prepared by or on behalf of or used or referred to by an issuer or any other offering participant, if consideration has been or will be given by the issuer or other offering participant for the dissemination (in any format) of any free writing prospectus (including any published article, publication, or advertisement), or if section 17(b) of the Act requires disclosure that consideration has been or will be given by the issuer or other offering participant for any activity described therein in connection with the free writing prospectus, then a registration statement relating to the offering must have been filed that includes a prospectus that, other than by reason of this section or Rule 431, satisfies the requirements of section 10 of the Act, including a price range where required by rule, and the free writing prospectus shall be accompanied or preceded by the most recent such prospectus; *provided, however*, that use of the free writing prospectus is not conditioned on providing the most recent such prospectus if a prior such prospectus has been provided and there is no material change from the prior prospectus reflected in the most recent prospectus; *provided, further* that after effectiveness and availability of a final prospectus meeting the requirements of section 10(a) of the Act, no such earlier prospectus may be provided in satisfaction of this condition, and such final prospectus must precede or accompany any free writing prospectus provided after such availability, whether or not an earlier prospectus had been previously provided.

Notes to paragraph (b)(2)(i) of Rule 433.

    1.   The condition that a free writing prospectus shall be accompanied or preceded by the most recent prospectus satisfying the requirements of section 10 of the Act would be satisfied if a free writing prospectus that is an electronic communication contained an active hyperlink to such most recent prospectus; and

    2.   A communication for which disclosure would be required under section 17(b) of the Act as a result of consideration given or to be given,

directly or indirectly, by or on behalf of an issuer or other offering participant is an offer by the issuer or such other offering participant as the case may be and is, if written, a free writing prospectus of the issuer or other offering participant.

    ii.   Where paragraph (b)(2)(i) of this section does not apply, a registration statement relating to the offering has been filed that includes a prospectus that, other than by reason of this section or Rule 431 satisfies the requirements of section 10 of the Act, including a price range where required by rule. For purposes of paragraph (f) of this section, the prospectus included in the registration statement relating to the offering that has been filed does not have to include a price range otherwise required by rule.

3.   Successors. A successor issuer will be considered to satisfy the applicable provisions of this paragraph (b) if:

    i.   Its predecessor and it, taken together, satisfy the conditions, provided that the succession was primarily for the purpose of changing the state or other jurisdiction of incorporation of the predecessor or forming a holding company and the assets and liabilities of the successor at the time of succession were substantially the same as those of the predecessor; or

    ii.   All predecessors met the conditions at the time of succession and the issuer has continued to do so since the succession.

c.   **Information in a free writing prospectus.**

1.   A free writing prospectus used in reliance on this section may include information the substance of which is not included in the registration statement but such information shall not conflict with:

    i.   Information contained in the filed registration statement, including any prospectus or prospectus supplement that is part of the registration statement (including pursuant to Rule 430B, Rule 430C or Rule 430D) and not superseded or modified; or

    ii.   Information contained in the issuer's periodic and current reports filed or furnished to the Commission pursuant to section 13 or 15(d) of the Securities Exchange Act of 1934 that are incorporated by reference into the registration statement and not superseded or modified.

2.   i.   A free writing prospectus used in reliance on this section shall contain substantially the following legend:

> The issuer has filed a registration statement (including a prospectus) with the SEC for the offering to which this communication relates. Before you invest, you should read the prospectus in that registration statement and other documents the issuer has filed with the SEC for more complete information about the issuer and this offering. You may get these documents for free by visiting EDGAR on the SEC Web site at www.sec.gov. Alternatively, the issuer, any underwriter or any dealer participating in the offering will arrange to send you the prospectus if you request it by calling toll-free 1-8[xx-xxx-xxxx].

    ii.   The legend also may provide an e-mail address at which the documents can be requested and may indicate that the documents also are available by accessing the issuer's Web site and provide the Internet address and the particular location of the documents on the Web site.

d. **Filing conditions.**
    1.   Except as provided in paragraphs (d)(3), (d)(4), (d)(5), (d)(6), (d)(7), (d)(8), and (f) of this section, the following shall be filed with the Commission under this section by a means reasonably calculated to result in filing no later than the date of first use. The free writing prospectus filed for purposes of this section will not be filed as part of the registration statement:
        i.   The issuer shall file:
          (A) Any issuer free writing prospectus, as defined in paragraph (h) of this section;
          (B) Any issuer information that is contained in a free writing prospectus prepared by or on behalf of or used by any other offering participant (but not information prepared by or on behalf of a person other than the issuer on the basis of or derived from that issuer information); and
          (C) A description of the final terms of the issuer's securities in the offering or of the offering contained in a free writing prospectus or portion thereof prepared by or on behalf of the issuer or any offering participant, after such terms have been established for all classes in the offering; and
        ii.   Any offering participant, other than the issuer, shall file any free writing prospectus that is used or referred to by such offering participant and distributed by or on behalf of such person in a manner reasonably designed to lead to its broad unrestricted dissemination.
    2.   Each free writing prospectus or issuer information contained in a free writing prospectus filed under this section shall identify in the filing the Commission file number for the related registration statement or, if that file number is unknown, a description sufficient to identify the related registration statement.
    3.   The condition to file a free writing prospectus under paragraph (d)(1) of this section shall not apply if the free writing prospectus does not contain substantive changes from or additions to a free writing prospectus previously filed with the Commission.
    4.   The condition to file issuer information contained in a free writing prospectus of an offering participant other than the issuer shall not apply if such information is included (including through incorporation by reference) in a prospectus or free writing prospectus previously filed that relates to the offering.
    5.   Notwithstanding the provisions of paragraph (d)(1) of this section:
        i.   To the extent a free writing prospectus or portion thereof otherwise required to be filed contains a description of terms of the issuer's securities in the offering or of the offering that does not reflect the final terms, such free writing prospectus or portion thereof is not required to be filed; and
        ii.   A free writing prospectus or portion thereof that contains only a description of the final terms of the issuer's securities in the offering or of the offerings shall be filed by the issuer within two days of the later of the date such final terms have been established for all classes of the offering and the date of first use.

6.   i.   Notwithstanding the provisions of paragraph (d) of this section, in an offering of asset-backed securities, a free writing prospectus or portion thereof required to be filed that contains only ABS informational and computational materials as defined in Item 1101(a) of Regulation AB, may be filed under this section within the timeframe permitted by Rule 426(b) and such filing will satisfy the filing conditions under this section.

      ii.   In the event that a free writing prospectus is used in reliance on this section and Rule 164 and the conditions of this section and Rule 164 (which may include the conditions of paragraph (d)(6)(i) of this section) are satisfied with respect thereto, then the use of that free writing prospectus shall not be conditioned on satisfaction of the provisions, including without limitation the filing conditions, of Rule 167 and Rule 426. In the event that ABS informational and computational materials are used in reliance on Rule 167 and Rule 426 and the conditions of those rules are satisfied with respect thereto, then the use of those materials shall not be conditioned on the satisfaction of the conditions of Rule 164 and this section.

7.   The condition to file a free writing prospectus or issuer information pursuant to this paragraph (d) for a free writing prospectus used at the same time as a communication in a business combination transaction subject to Rule 425 shall be satisfied if:

      i.   The free writing prospectus or issuer information is filed in accordance with the provisions of Rule 425, including the filing timeframe of Rule 425;

      ii.   The filed material pursuant to Rule 425 indicates on the cover page that it also is being filed pursuant to Rule 433; and

      iii. The filed material pursuant to Rule 425 contains the information specified in paragraph (c)(2) of this section.

8.   Notwithstanding any other provision of this paragraph (d):

      i.   A road show for an offering that is a written communication is a free writing prospectus, provided that, except as provided in paragraph (d)(8)(ii) of this section, a written communication that is a road show shall not be required to be filed; and

      ii.   In the case of a road show that is a written communication for an offering of common equity or convertible equity securities by an issuer that is, at the time of the filing of the registration statement for the offering, not required to file reports with the Commission pursuant to section 13 or section 15(d) of the Securities Exchange Act of 1934, such a road show is required to be filed pursuant to this section unless the issuer of the securities makes at least one version of a bona fide electronic road show available without restriction by means of graphic communication to any person, including any potential investor in the securities (and if there is more than one version of a road show for the offering that is a written communication, the version available without restriction is made available no later than the other versions).

Note to paragraph (d)(8): A communication that is provided or transmitted simultaneously with a road show and is provided or transmitted in a manner designed to make the communication available only as part of the road show and not separately is deemed to be part of the road show. Therefore, if the road show is not a written communication, such a simultaneous communication (even if it would otherwise be a graphic communication or other written communication) is also deemed not to be written. If the road show is written and not required to be filed, such a simultaneous communication is also not required to be filed. Otherwise, a written communication that is an offer contained in a separate file from a road show, whether or not the road show is a written communication, or otherwise transmitted separately from a road show, will be a free writing prospectus subject to any applicable filing conditions of paragraph (d) of this section.

e. **Treatment of information on, or hyperlinked from, an issuer's Web site.**
    1. An offer of an issuer's securities that is contained on an issuer's Web site or hyperlinked by the issuer from the issuer's Web site to a third party's Web site is a written offer of such securities by the issuer and, unless otherwise exempt or excluded from the requirements of section 5(b)(1) of the Act, the filing conditions of paragraph (d) of this section apply to such offer.
    2. Notwithstanding paragraph (e)(1) of this section, historical issuer information that is identified as such and located in a separate section of the issuer's Web site containing historical issuer information, that has not been incorporated by reference into or otherwise included in a prospectus of the issuer for the offering and that has not otherwise been used or referred to in connection with the offering, will not be considered a current offer of the issuer's securities and therefore will not be a free writing prospectus.

f. **Free writing prospectuses published or distributed by media.** Any written offer for which an issuer or any other offering participant or any person acting on its behalf provided, authorized, or approved information that is prepared and published or disseminated by a person unaffiliated with the issuer or any other offering participant that is in the business of publishing, radio or television broadcasting or otherwise disseminating written communications would be considered at the time of publication or dissemination to be a free writing prospectus prepared by or on behalf of the issuer or such other offering participant for purposes of this section subject to the following:
    1. The conditions of paragraph (b)(2)(i) of this section will not apply and the conditions of paragraphs (c)(2) and (d) of this section will be deemed to be satisfied if:
        i.   No payment is made or consideration given by or on behalf of the issuer or other offering participant for the written communication or its dissemination; and
        ii. The issuer or other offering participant in question files the written communication with the Commission, and includes in the filing the legend required by paragraph (c)(2) of this section, within four business days after the issuer or other offering participant becomes aware of the publication, radio or television broadcast, or other dissemination of the written communication.
    2. The filing obligation under paragraph (f)(1)(ii) of this section shall be subject to the following:
        i.   The issuer or other offering participant shall not be required to file a free writing prospectus if the substance of that free writing prospectus has previously been filed with the Commission;

        ii.   Any filing made pursuant to paragraph (f)(1)(ii) of this section may include information that the issuer or offering participant in question reasonably believes is necessary or appropriate to correct information included in the communication; and

        iii. In lieu of filing the actual written communication as published or disseminated as required by paragraph (f)(1)(ii) of this section, the issuer or offering participant in question may file a copy of the materials provided to the media, including transcripts of interviews or similar materials, provided the copy or transcripts contain all the information provided to the media.

3.   For purposes of this paragraph (f) of this section, an issuer that is in the business of publishing or radio or television broadcasting may rely on this paragraph (f) as to any publication or radio or television broadcast that is a free writing prospectus in respect of an offering of securities of the issuer if the issuer or an affiliate:

        i.   Is the publisher of a bona fide newspaper, magazine, or business or financial publication of general and regular circulation or bona fide broadcaster of news including business and financial news;

        ii.   Has established policies and procedures for the independence of the content of the publications or broadcasts from the offering activities of the issuer; and

        iii. Publishes or broadcasts the communication in the ordinary course.

g.   **Record retention.** Issuers and offering participants shall retain all free writing prospectuses they have used, and that have not been filed pursuant to paragraph (d) or (f) of this section, for three years following the initial bona fide offering of the securities in question.

Note to paragraph (g).

To the extent that the record retention requirements of Rule 17a-4 of the Securities Exchange Act of 1934 apply to free writing prospectuses required to be retained by a broker-dealer under this section, such free writing prospectuses are required to be retained in accordance with such requirements.

h.   **Definitions.** For purposes of this section:

1.   An issuer free writing prospectus means a free writing prospectus prepared by or on behalf of the issuer or used or referred to by the issuer and, in the case of an asset-backed issuer, prepared by or on behalf of a depositor, sponsor, or servicer (as defined in Item 1101 of Regulation AB) or affiliated depositor or used or referred to by any such person.

2.   Issuer information means material information about the issuer or its securities that has been provided by or on behalf of the issuer.

3.   A written communication or information is prepared or provided by or on behalf of a person if the person or an agent or representative of the person authorizes the communication or information or approves the communication or information before it is used. An offering participant other than the issuer shall not be an agent or representative of the issuer solely by virtue of its acting as an offering participant.

4.   A road show means an offer (other than a statutory prospectus or a portion of a statutory prospectus filed as part of a registration statement) that contains a

presentation regarding an offering by one or more members of the issuer's management (and in the case of an offering of asset-backed securities, management involved in the securitization or servicing function of one or more of the depositors, sponsors, or servicers (as such terms are defined in Item 1101 of Regulation AB) or an affiliated depositor) and includes discussion of one or more of the issuer, such management, and the securities being offered; and

5.   A bona fide electronic road show means a road show that is a written communication transmitted by graphic means that contains a presentation by one or more officers of an issuer or other persons in an issuer's management (and in the case of an offering of asset-backed securities, management involved in the securitization or servicing function of one or more of the depositors, sponsors, or servicers (as such terms are defined in Item 1101 of Regulation AB) or an affiliated depositor) and, if more than one road show that is a written communication is being used, includes discussion of the same general areas of information regarding the issuer, such management, and the securities being offered as such other issuer road show or shows for the same offering that are written communications.

Note to Rule 433.

This section does not affect the operation of the provisions of clause (a) of section 2(a)(10) of the Act providing an exception from the definition of "prospectus."

Rule 460 – Distribution of Preliminary Prospectus

a.   Pursuant to the statutory requirement that the Commission in ruling upon requests for acceleration of the effective date of a registration statement shall have due regard to the adequacy of the information respecting the issuer theretofore available to the public, the Commission may consider whether the persons making the offering have taken reasonable steps to make the information contained in the registration statement conveniently available to underwriters and dealers who it is reasonably anticipated will be invited to participate in the distribution of the security to be offered or sold.

b.

1.   As a minimum, reasonable steps to make the information conveniently available would involve the distribution, to each underwriter and dealer who it is reasonably anticipated will be invited to participate in the distribution of the security, a reasonable time in advance of the anticipated effective date of the registration statement, of as many copies of the proposed form of preliminary prospectus permitted by Rule 430 as appears to be reasonable to secure adequate distribution of the preliminary prospectus.

2.   In the case of a registration statement filed by a closed-end investment company on Form N-2, reasonable steps to make information conveniently available would involve distribution of a sufficient number of copies of the Statement of Additional Information required by Rule 430(b) as it appears to be reasonable to secure their adequate distribution either to each underwriter or dealer who it is reasonably anticipated will be invited to participate in the distribution of the security, or to the underwriter, dealer or other source named on the cover page of the preliminary prospectus as being the person investors should contact in order to obtain the Statement of Additional Information.

   c.   The granting of acceleration will not be conditioned upon

       1.   The distribution of a preliminary prospectus in any state where such distribution would be illegal; or

       2.   The distribution of a preliminary prospectus

           i.   in the case of a registration statement relating solely to securities to be offered at competitive bidding, provided the undertaking in Item 512(d)(1) of Regulation S-K is included in the registration statement and distribution of prospectuses pursuant to such undertaking is made prior to the publication or distribution of the invitation for bids, or

           ii.   In the case of a registration statement relating to a security issued by a face-amount certificate company or a redeemable security issued by an open-end management company or unit investment trust if any other security of the same class is currently being offered or sold, pursuant to an effective registration statement by the issuer or by or through an underwriter, or

           iii.   In the case of an offering of subscription rights unless it is contemplated that the distribution will be made through dealers and the underwriters intend to make the offering during the stockholders' subscription period, in which case copies of the preliminary prospectus must be distributed to dealers prior to the effective date of the registration statement in the same fashion as is required in the case of other offerings through underwriters, or

           iv.   In the case of a registration statement pertaining to a security to be offered pursuant to an exchange offer or transaction described in Rule 145.

Rule 461 – Acceleration of Effective Date

   a.   Requests for acceleration of the effective date of a registration statement shall be made by the registrant and the managing underwriters of the proposed issue, or, if there are no managing underwriters, by the principal underwriters of the proposed issue, and shall state the date upon which it is desired that the registration statement shall become effective. Such requests may be made in writing or orally, provided that, if an oral request is to be made, a letter indicating that fact and stating that the registrant and the managing or principal underwriters are aware of their obligations under the Act must accompany the registration statement for a pre-effective amendment thereto) at the time of filing with the Commission. Written requests may be sent to the Commission by facsimile transmission. If, by reason of the expected arrangement in connection with the offering, it is to be requested that the registration statement shall become effective at a particular hour of the day, the Commission must be advised to that effect not later than the second business day before the day which it is desired that the registration statement shall become effective. A person's request for acceleration will be considered confirmation of such person's awareness of the person's obligations under the Act. Not later than the time of filing the last amendment prior to the effective date of the registration statement, the registrant shall inform the Commission as to whether or not the amount of compensation to be allowed or paid to the underwriters and any other arrangements among the registrant, the underwriters and other broker dealers participating in the distribution, as described in the registration statement, have been reviewed to the extent required by the National Association of Securities Dealers, Inc. and such Association has issued a statement expressing no objections to the compensation and other arrangements.

b. Having due regard to the adequacy of information respecting the registrant theretofore available to the public, to the facility with which the nature of the securities to be registered, their relationship to the capital structure of the registrant issuer and the rights of holders thereof can be understood, and to the public interest and the protection of investors, as provided in section 8(a) of the Act, it is the general policy of the Commission, upon request, as provided in paragraph (a) of this section, to permit acceleration of the effective date of the registration statement as soon as possible after the filing of appropriate amendments, if any. In determining the date on which a registration statement shall become effective, the following are included in the situations in which the Commission considers that the statutory standards of section 8(a) may not be met and may refuse to accelerate the effective date:

1. Where there has not been a bona fide effort to make the prospectus reasonably concise, readable, and in compliance with the plain English requirements of Rule 421(d) of Regulation C in order to facilitate an understanding of the information in the prospectus.

2. Where the form of preliminary prospectus, which has been distributed by the issuer or underwriter, is found to be inaccurate or inadequate in any material respect, until the Commission has received satisfactory assurance that appropriate correcting material has been sent to all underwriters and dealers who received such preliminary prospectus or prospectuses in quantity sufficient for their information and the information of others to whom the inaccurate or inadequate material was sent.

3. Where the Commission is currently making an investigation of the issuer, a person controlling the issuer, or one of the underwriters, if any, of the securities to be offered, pursuant to any of the Acts administered by the Commission.

4. Where one or more of the underwriters, although firmly committed to purchase securities covered by the registration statement, is subject to and does not meet the financial responsibility requirements of Rule 15c3-1 under the Securities Exchange Act of 1934. For the purposes of this paragraph underwriters will be deemed to be firmly committed even though the obligation to purchase is subject to the usual conditions as to receipt of opinions of counsel, accountants, etc., the accuracy of warranties or representations, the happening of calamities or the occurrence of other events the determination of which is not expressed to be in the sole or absolute discretion of the underwriters.

5. Where there have been transactions in securities of the registrant by persons connected with or proposed to be connected with the offering which may have artificially affected or may artificially affect the market price of the security being offered.

6. Where the amount of compensation to be allowed or paid to the underwriters and any other arrangements among the registrant, the underwriters and other broker dealers participating in the distribution, as described in the registration statement, if required to be reviewed by the [Financial Industry Regulatory Authority (FINRA)], have been reviewed by [FINRA] and the [FINRA] has not

issued a statement expressing no objections to the compensation and other arrangements.

7. Where, in the case of a significant secondary offering at the market, the registrant, selling security holders and underwriters have not taken sufficient measures to insure compliance with Regulation M.

c. Insurance against liabilities arising under the Act, whether the cost of insurance is borne by the registrant, the insured or some other person, will not be considered a bar to acceleration, unless the registrant is a registered investment company or a business development company and the cost of such insurance is borne by other than an insured officer or director of the registrant. In the case of such a registrant, the Commission may refuse to accelerate the effective date of the registration statement when the registrant is organized or administered pursuant to any instrument (including a contract for insurance against liabilities arising under the Act) that protects or purports to protect any director or officer of the company against any liability to the company or its security holders to which he or she would otherwise be subject by reason of willful misfeasance, bad faith, gross negligence or reckless disregard of the duties involved in the conduct of his or her office.

Rule 462 – Immediate Effectiveness of Certain Registration Statements and Post-Effective Amendments

a. A registration statement on Form S-8 and a registration statement on Form S-3 or on Form F-3 for a dividend or interest reinvestment plan shall become effective upon filing with the Commission.

b. A registration statement and any post-effective amendment thereto shall become effective upon filing with the Commission if:
1. The registration statement is for registering additional securities of the same class(es) as were included in an earlier registration statement for the same offering and declared effective by the Commission;
2. The new registration statement is filed prior to the time confirmations are sent or given; and
3. The new registration statement registers additional securities in an amount and at a price that together represent no more than 20% of the maximum aggregate offering price set forth for each class of securities in the "Calculation of Registration Fee" table contained in such earlier registration statement.

c. If the prospectus contained in a post-effective amendment filed prior to the time confirmations are sent or given contains no substantive changes from or additions to the prospectus previously filed as part of the effective registration statement, other than price-related information omitted from the registration statement in reliance on Rule 430A of the Act, such post-effective amendment shall become effective upon filing with the Commission.

d. A post-effective amendment filed solely to add exhibits to a registration statement shall become effective upon filing with the Commission.

e.   An automatic shelf registration statement, including an automatic shelf registration statement filed in accordance with Rule 415(a)(6), and any post-effective amendment thereto, including a post-effective amendment filed to register additional classes of securities pursuant to Rule 413(b), shall become effective upon filing with the Commission.

f.   A post-effective amendment filed pursuant to paragraph (e) of this section for purposes of adding a new issuer and its securities as permitted by Rule 413(b) that satisfies the requirements of Form S-3 or Form F-3, as applicable, including the signatures required by Rule 402(e), and contains a prospectus satisfying the requirements of Rule 430B, shall become effective upon filing with the Commission.

Rule 473 – Delaying Amendments

a.   An amendment in the following form filed with a registration statement, or as an amendment to a registration statement which has not become effective, shall be deemed, for the purpose of section 8(a) of the Act, to be filed on such date or dates as may be necessary to delay the effective date of such registration statement
   1.   until the registrant shall file a further amendment which specifically states as provided in paragraph (b) of this section that such registration statement shall thereafter become effective in accordance with section 8(a) of the Act, or
   2.   until the registration statement shall become effective on such date as the Commission, acting pursuant to section 8(a), may determine:
       The registrant hereby amends this registration statement on such date or dates as may be necessary to delay its effective date until the registrant shall file a further amendment which specifically states that this registration statement shall thereafter become effective in accordance with section 8(a) of the Securities Act of 1933 or until the registration statement shall become effective on such date as the Commission acting pursuant to said section 8(a), may determine.

b.   An amendment which for the purpose of paragraph (a)(1) of this section specifically states that a registration statement shall thereafter become effective in accordance with section 8(a) of the Act, shall be in the following form:
       This registration statement shall hereafter become effective in accordance with the provisions of section 8(a) of the Securities Act of 1933.

c.   An amendment pursuant to paragraph (a) of this section which is filed with a registration statement shall be set forth on the facing page thereof following the calculation of the registration fee. Any such amendment filed after the filing of the registration statement, any amendment altering the proposed date of public sale of the securities being registered, or any amendment filed pursuant to paragraph (b) of this section may be made by telegram, letter or facsimile transmission. Each such telegraphic amendment shall be confirmed in writing within a reasonable time by the filing of a signed copy of the amendment. Such confirmation shall not be deemed an amendment.

d. No amendments pursuant to paragraph (a) of this section may be filed with a registration statement on Form F-7, F-8 or F-80; on Form F-9 or F-10 relating to an offering being made contemporaneously in the United States and the registrant's home jurisdiction; on Form S-8; on Form S-3 or F-3 relating to a dividend or interest reinvestment plan; or on Form S-4 complying with General Instruction G of that Form.

Regulation A

Rule 241 – Solicitations of interest

a.   **Solicitation of interest**. At any time before making a determination as to the exemption from registration under the Act under which an offering of securities will be conducted, an issuer or any person authorized to act on behalf of an issuer may communicate orally or in writing to determine whether there is any interest in a contemplated offering of securities exempt from registration under the Act. Such communications are deemed to be an offer of a security for sale for purposes of the antifraud provisions of the Federal securities laws. No solicitation or acceptance of money or other consideration, nor of any commitment, binding or otherwise, from any person is permitted until the issuer makes a determination as to the exemption to be relied on and the offering, meeting the requirements of the exemption, is commenced.

b.   **Conditions**. The communications must state that:
   1.   The issuer is considering an offering of securities exempt from registration under the Act, but has not determined a specific exemption from registration the issuer intends to rely on for the subsequent offer and sale of the securities;
   2.   No money or other consideration is being solicited, and if sent in response, will not be accepted;
   3.   No offer to buy the securities can be accepted and no part of the purchase price can be received until the issuer determines the exemption under which the offering is intended to be conducted and, where applicable, the filing, disclosure, or qualification requirements of such exemption are met; and
   4.   A person's indication of interest involves no obligation or commitment of any kind.

c.   **Indications of interest**. Any written communication under this section may include a means by which a person may indicate to the issuer that such person is interested in a potential offering. The issuer may require the name, address, telephone number, and/or email address in any response form included pursuant to this paragraph (c).

Rule 251 – Scope of Exemption

a.   **Tier 1 and Tier 2.** A public offer or sale of eligible securities, as defined in Rule 261, pursuant to Regulation A shall be exempt under section 3(b) from the registration requirements of the Securities Act of 1933 (the "Securities Act").
   1.   *Tier 1*. Offerings pursuant to Regulation A in which the sum of all cash and other consideration to be received for the securities being offered ("aggregate offering price") plus the gross proceeds for all securities sold pursuant to other offering statements within the 12 months before the start of and during the current offering of securities ("aggregate sales") does not exceed $20,000,000, including not more than $6,000,000 offered by all selling security holders that are affiliates of the issuer ("Tier 1 offerings").
   2.   *Tier 2*. Offerings pursuant to Regulation A in which the sum of the aggregate offering price and aggregate sales does not exceed $50,000,000, including not

more than $15,000,000 offered by all selling security holders that are affiliates of the issuer ("Tier 2 offerings").

3. *Additional limitation on secondary sales in first year.* The portion of the aggregate offering price attributable to the securities of selling security holders shall not exceed 30% of the aggregate offering price of a particular offering in:

    i.   The issuer's first offering pursuant to Regulation A; or
    ii. Any subsequent Regulation A offering that is qualified within one year of the qualification date of the issuer's first offering.

Note to paragraph (a). Where a mixture of cash and non-cash consideration is to be received, the aggregate offering price must be based on the price at which the securities are offered for cash. Any portion of the aggregate offering price or aggregate sales attributable to cash received in a foreign currency must be translated into United States currency at a currency exchange rate in effect on, or at a reasonable time before, the date of the sale of the securities. If securities are not offered for cash, the aggregate offering price or aggregate sales must be based on the value of the consideration as established by bona fide sales of that consideration made within a reasonable time, or, in the absence of sales, on the fair value as determined by an accepted standard. Valuations of non-cash consideration must be reasonable at the time made. If convertible securities or warrants are being offered and such securities are convertible, exercisable, or exchangeable within one year of the offering statement's qualification or at the discretion of the issuer, the underlying securities must also be qualified and the aggregate offering price must include the actual or maximum estimated conversion, exercise, or exchange price of such securities.

b. **Issuer**. The issuer of the securities:

    1. Is an entity organized under the laws of the United States or Canada, or any State, Province, Territory or possession thereof, or the District of Columbia, with its principal place of business in the United States or Canada;

    2. [Reserved];

    3. Is not a development stage company that either has no specific business plan or purpose, or has indicated that its business plan is to merge with or acquire an unidentified company or companies;

    4. Is not an investment company registered or required to be registered under the Investment Company Act of 1940 or a business development company as defined in section 2(a)(48) of the Investment Company Act of 1940;

    5. Is not issuing fractional undivided interests in oil or gas rights, or a similar interest in other mineral rights;

    6. Is not, and has not been, subject to any order of the Commission entered pursuant to Section 12(j) of the Exchange Act within five years before the filing of the offering statement;

    7. Has filed with the Commission all reports required to be filed, if any, pursuant to Rule 257 during the two years before the filing of the offering statement (or for such shorter period that the issuer was required to file such reports); and

    8. Is not disqualified under Rule 262.

c. **Integration with other offerings**. Offers or sales made in reliance on this Regulation A will not be integrated with:

    1. Prior offers or sales of securities; or

2. Subsequent offers or sales of securities that are:
    i.   Registered under the Securities Act, except as provided in Rule 255(e);
    ii. Exempt from registration under Rule 701;
    iii. Made pursuant to an employee benefit plan;
    iv. Exempt from registration under Regulation S
    v.   Made more than six months after the completion of the Regulation A offering; or
    vi. Exempt from registration under Section 4(a)(6) of the Securities Act.

Note to paragraph (c). If these safe harbors do not apply, whether subsequent offers and sales of securities will be integrated with the Regulation A offering will depend on the particular facts and circumstances.

d. **Offering conditions—**
    1. *Offers.*
        i. Except as allowed by Rule 255, no offer of securities may be made unless an offering statement has been filed with the Commission.
        ii. After the offering statement has been filed, but before it is qualified:
            A. Oral offers may be made;
            B. Written offers pursuant to Rule 254 may be made; and
            C. Solicitations of interest and other communications pursuant to Rule 255 may be made.
        iii. Offers may be made after the offering statement has been qualified, but any written offers must be accompanied with or preceded by the most recent offering circular filed with the Commission for such offering.
    2. *Sales.*
        i. No sale of securities may be made:
            A. Until the offering statement has been qualified;
            B. By issuers that are not currently required to file reports pursuant to Rule 257(b), until a Preliminary Offering Circular is delivered at least 48 hours before the sale to any person that before qualification of the offering statement had indicated an interest in purchasing securities in the offering, including those persons that responded to an issuer's solicitation of interest materials; and
            C. In a Tier 2 offering of securities that are not listed on a registered national securities exchange upon qualification, unless the purchaser is either an accredited investor (as defined in Rule 501 or the aggregate purchase price to be paid by the purchaser for the securities (including the actual or maximum estimated conversion, exercise, or exchange price for any underlying securities that have been qualified) is no more than ten percent (10%) of the greater of such purchaser's:
                (1) Annual income or net worth if a natural person (with annual income and net worth for such natural person purchasers determined as provided in Rule 501; or
                (2) Revenue or net assets for such purchaser's most recently completed fiscal year end if a non-natural person.

                Note to paragraph (d)(2)(i)(C). When securities underlying warrants or convertible securities are being qualified pursuant to Tier 2 of Regulation A one year or more after the qualification of an offering for which investment limitations previously applied, purchasers of the underlying securities for which investment limitations would apply at that later date may determine compliance with the ten percent (10%) investment limitation using the conversion, exercise, or exchange price to acquire the underlying securities at that later time without aggregating such price with the price of the overlying warrants or convertible securities.

     D. The issuer may rely on a representation of the purchaser when determining compliance with the ten percent (10%) investment limitation in this paragraph (d)(2)(i)(C), provided that the issuer does not know at the time of sale that any such representation is untrue.

  ii. In a transaction that represents a sale by the issuer or an underwriter, or a sale by a dealer within 90 calendar days after qualification of the offering statement, each underwriter or dealer selling in such transaction must deliver to each purchaser from it, not later than two business days following the completion of such sale, a copy of the Final Offering Circular, subject to the following provisions:

     A. If the sale was by the issuer and was not effected by or through an underwriter or dealer, the issuer is responsible for delivering the Final Offering Circular as if the issuer were an underwriter;

     B. For continuous or delayed offerings pursuant to paragraph (d)(3) of this section, the 90 calendar day period for dealers shall commence on the day of the first bona fide offering of securities under such offering statement;

     C. If the security is listed on a registered national securities exchange, no offering circular need be delivered by a dealer more than 25 calendar days after the later of the qualification date of the offering statement or the first date on which the security was bona fide offered to the public;

     D. No offering circular need be delivered by a dealer if the issuer is subject, immediately prior to the time of the filing of the offering statement, to the reporting requirements of Rule 257(b) (§ 230.257(b)); and

     E. The Final Offering Circular delivery requirements set forth in paragraph (d)(2)(ii) of this section may be satisfied by delivering a notice to the effect that the sale was made pursuant to a qualified offering statement that includes the uniform resource locator ("URL"), which, in the case of an electronic-only offering, must be an active hyperlink, where the Final Offering Circular, or the offering statement of which such Final Offering Circular is part, may be obtained on the Commission's Electronic Data Gathering, Analysis and Retrieval System ("EDGAR") and contact information sufficient to notify a purchaser where a request for a Final Offering Circular can be sent and received in response.

3. *Continuous or delayed offerings.*

  i. Continuous or delayed offerings may be made under this Regulation A, so long as the offering statement pertains only to:

A. Securities that are to be offered or sold solely by or on behalf of a person or persons other than the issuer, a subsidiary of the issuer, or a person of which the issuer is a subsidiary;

B. Securities that are to be offered and sold pursuant to a dividend or interest reinvestment plan or an employee benefit plan of the issuer;

C. Securities that are to be issued upon the exercise of outstanding options, warrants, or rights;

D. Securities that are to be issued upon conversion of other outstanding securities;

E. Securities that are pledged as collateral; or

F. Securities the offering of which will be commenced within two calendar days after the qualification date, will be made on a continuous basis, may continue for a period in excess of 30 calendar days from the date of initial qualification, and will be offered in an amount that, at the time the offering statement is qualified, is reasonably expected to be offered and sold within two years from the initial qualification date. These securities may be offered and sold only if not more than three years have elapsed since the initial qualification date of the offering statement under which they are being offered and sold; provided, however, that if a new offering statement has been filed pursuant to this paragraph (d)(3)(i)(F), securities covered by the prior offering statement may continue to be offered and sold until the earlier of the qualification date of the new offering statement or 180 calendar days after the third anniversary of the initial qualification date of the prior offering statement. Before the end of such three-year period, an issuer may file a new offering statement covering the securities. The new offering statement must include all the information that would be required at that time in an offering statement relating to all offerings that it covers. Before the qualification date of the new offering statement, the issuer may include as part of such new offering statement any unsold securities covered by the earlier offering statement by identifying on the cover page of the new offering circular, or the latest amendment, the amount of such unsold securities being included. The offering of securities on the earlier offering statement will be deemed terminated as of the date of qualification of the new offering statement. Securities may be sold pursuant to this paragraph (d)(3)(i)(F) only if the issuer is current in its annual and semiannual filings pursuant to Rule 257(b) at the time of such sale.

ii. At the market offerings, by or on behalf of the issuer or otherwise, are not permitted under this Regulation A. As used in this paragraph (d)(3)(ii), the term at the market offering means an offering of equity securities into an existing trading market for outstanding shares of the same class at other than a fixed price.

e. **Confidential treatment**. A request for confidential treatment may be made under Rule 406 for information required to be filed, and Rule 83 for information not required to be filed.

f.   **Electronic filing.** Documents filed or otherwise provided to the Commission pursuant to this Regulation A must be submitted in electronic format by means of EDGAR in accordance with the EDGAR rules set forth in Regulation S-T.

Rule 252 – Offering Statement

a.   **Documents to be included.** The offering statement consists of the contents required by Form 1-A and any other material information necessary to make the required statements, in light of the circumstances under which they are made, not misleading.

b.   **Paper, printing, language and pagination.** Except as otherwise specified in this rule, the requirements for offering statements are the same as those specified in Rule 403 for registration statements under the Act. No fee is payable to the Commission upon either the submission or filing of an offering statement on Form 1-A, or any amendment to an offering statement.

c.   **Signatures.** The issuer, its principal executive officer, principal financial officer, principal accounting officer, and a majority of the members of its board of directors or other governing body, must sign the offering statement in the manner prescribed by Form 1-A. If a signature is by a person on behalf of any other person, evidence of authority to sign must be filed, except where an executive officer signs for the issuer.

d.   **Non-public submission.** An issuer whose securities have not been previously sold pursuant to a qualified offering statement under this Regulation A or an effective registration statement under the Securities Act may submit a draft offering statement to the Commission for non-public review by the staff of the Commission before public filing, provided that the offering statement shall not be qualified less than 21 calendar days after the public filing with the Commission of:
1.   The initial non-public submission;
2.   All non-public amendments; and
3.   All non-public correspondence submitted by or on behalf of the issuer to the Commission staff regarding such submissions (subject to any separately approved confidential treatment request under Rule 251(e).

e.   **Qualification.** An offering statement and any amendment thereto can be qualified only at such date and time as the Commission may determine.

f.   **Amendments.**
1.   i.   Amendments to an offering statement must be signed and filed with the Commission in the same manner as the initial filing. Amendments to an offering statement must be filed under cover of Form 1-A and must be numbered consecutively in the order in which filed.
     ii. Every amendment that includes amended audited financial statements must include the consent of the certifying accountant to the use of such accountant's certification in connection with the amended financial statements in the offering statement or offering circular and to being named as having audited such financial statements.

iii. Amendments solely relating to Part III of Form 1-A must comply with the requirements of paragraph (f)(1)(i) of this section, except that such amendments may be limited to Part I of Form 1-A, an explanatory note, and all of the information required by Part III of Form 1-A.

2. Post-qualification amendments must be filed in the following circumstances for ongoing offerings:

i. At least every 12 months after the qualification date to include the financial statements that would be required by Form 1-A as of such date; or

ii. To reflect any facts or events arising after the qualification date of the offering statement (or the most recent post-qualification amendment thereof) which, individually or in the aggregate, represent a fundamental change in the information set forth in the offering statement.

Rule 253 – Offering Circular

a. **Contents**. An offering circular must include the information required by Form 1-A for offering circulars.

b. **Information that may be omitted**. Notwithstanding paragraph (a) of this section, a qualified offering circular may omit information with respect to the public offering price, underwriting syndicate (including any material relationships between the issuer or selling security holders and the unnamed underwriters, brokers or dealers), underwriting discounts or commissions, discounts or commissions to dealers, amount of proceeds, conversion rates, call prices and other items dependent upon the offering price, delivery dates, and terms of the securities dependent upon the offering date; provided, that the following conditions are met:

1. The securities to be qualified are offered for cash.

2. The outside front cover page of the offering circular includes a bona fide estimate of the range of the maximum offering price and the maximum number of shares or other units of securities to be offered or a bona fide estimate of the principal amount of debt securities offered, subject to the following conditions:

i. The range must not exceed $2 for offerings where the upper end of the range is $10 or less or 20% if the upper end of the price range is over $10; and

ii. The upper end of the range must be used in determining the aggregate offering price under Rule 251(a).

3. The offering statement does not relate to securities to be offered by competitive bidding.

4. The volume of securities (the number of equity securities or aggregate principal amount of debt securities) to be offered may not be omitted in reliance on this paragraph (b).

Note to paragraph (b). A decrease in the volume of securities offered or a change in the bona fide estimate of the offering price range from that indicated in the offering circular filed as part of a qualified offering statement may be disclosed in the offering circular filed with the Commission pursuant to Rule 253(g), so long as the decrease in the volume of securities offered or change in the price range would not materially change the disclosure contained in the offering statement at qualification. Notwithstanding the foregoing, any decrease in the volume of securities offered and any deviation from the low or high end of the price range may be reflected in the

145

offering circular supplement filed with the Commission pursuant to Rule 253(g)(1) or (3) if, in the aggregate, the decrease in volume and/or change in price represent no more than a 20% change from the maximum aggregate offering price calculable using the information in the qualified offering statement. In no circumstances may this paragraph be used to offer securities where the maximum aggregate offering price would result in the offering exceeding the limit set forth in Rule 251(a) or if the change would result in a Tier 1 offering becoming a Tier 2 offering. An offering circular supplement may not be used to increase the volume of securities being offered. Additional securities may only be offered pursuant to a new offering statement or post-qualification amendment qualified by the Commission.

c. **Filing of omitted information**. The information omitted from the offering circular in reliance upon paragraph (b) of this section must be contained in an offering circular filed with the Commission pursuant to paragraph (g) of this section; except that if such offering circular is not so filed by the later of 15 business days after the qualification date of the offering statement or 15 business days after the qualification of a post-qualification amendment thereto that contains an offering circular, the information omitted in reliance upon paragraph (b) of this section must be contained in a qualified post-qualification amendment to the offering statement.

d. **Presentation of information**.
   1.   Information in the offering circular must be presented in a clear, concise and understandable manner and in a type size that is easily readable. Repetition of information should be avoided; cross-referencing of information within the document is permitted.
   2.   Where an offering circular is distributed through an electronic medium, issuers may satisfy legibility requirements applicable to printed documents by presenting all required information in a format readily communicated to investors.

e. **Date**. An offering circular must be dated approximately as of the date it was filed with the Commission.

f. **Cover page legend**. The cover page of every offering circular must display the following statement highlighted by prominent type or in another manner:

> THE UNITED STATES SECURITIES AND EXCHANGE COMMISSION DOES NOT PASS UPON THE MERITS OF OR GIVE ITS APPROVAL TO ANY SECURITIES OFFERED OR THE TERMS OF THE OFFERING, NOR DOES IT PASS UPON THE ACCURACY OR COMPLETENESS OF ANY OFFERING CIRCULAR OR OTHER SOLICITATION MATERIALS. THESE SECURITIES ARE OFFERED PURSUANT TO AN EXEMPTION FROM REGISTRATION WITH THE COMMISSION; HOWEVER, THE COMMISSION HAS NOT MADE AN INDEPENDENT DETERMINATION THAT THE SECURITIES OFFERED ARE EXEMPT FROM REGISTRATION.

g. **Offering circular supplements.**

1. An offering circular that discloses information previously omitted from the offering circular in reliance upon Rule 253(b) must be filed with the Commission no later than two business days following the earlier of the date of determination of the offering price or the date such offering circular is first used after qualification in connection with a public offering or sale.

2. An offering circular that reflects information other than that covered in paragraph (g)(1) of this section that constitutes a substantive change from or addition to the information set forth in the last offering circular filed with the Commission must be filed with the Commission no later than five business days after the date it is first used after qualification in connection with a public offering or sale. If an offering circular filed pursuant to this paragraph (g)(2) consists of an offering circular supplement attached to an offering circular that previously had been filed or was not required to be filed pursuant to paragraph (g) of this section because it did not contain substantive changes from an offering circular that previously was filed, only the offering circular supplement need be filed under paragraph (g) of this section, provided that the cover page of the offering circular supplement identifies the date(s) of the related offering circular and any offering circular supplements thereto that together constitute the offering circular with respect to the securities currently being offered or sold.

3. An offering circular that discloses information, facts or events covered in both paragraphs (g)(1) and (2) of this section must be filed with the Commission no later than two business days following the earlier of the date of the determination of the offering price or the date it is first used after qualification in connection with a public offering or sale.

4. An offering circular required to be filed pursuant to paragraph (g) of this section that is not filed within the time frames specified in paragraphs (g)(1) through (3) of this section, as applicable, must be filed pursuant to this paragraph (g)(4) as soon as practicable after the discovery of such failure to file.

5. Each offering circular filed under this section must contain in the upper right corner of the cover page the paragraphs of paragraphs (g)(1) through (4) of this section under which the filing is made, and the file number of the offering statement to which the offering circular relates.

Rule 254 – Preliminary Offering Circular

After the filing of an offering statement, but before its qualification, written offers of securities may be made if they meet the following requirements:

a. **Outside front cover page.** The outside front cover page of the material bears the caption Preliminary Offering Circular, the date of issuance, and the following legend, which must be highlighted by prominent type or in another manner:

> AN OFFERING STATEMENT PURSUANT TO REGULATION A RELATING TO THESE SECURITIES HAS BEEN FILED WITH THE SECURITIES AND EXCHANGE COMMISSION. INFORMATION CONTAINED IN THIS PRELIMINARY OFFERING CIRCULAR IS SUBJECT TO COMPLETION OR AMENDMENT. THESE SECURITIES MAY NOT BE SOLD NOR MAY

OFFERS TO BUY BE ACCEPTED BEFORE THE OFFERING STATEMENT FILED WITH THE COMMISSION IS QUALIFIED. THIS PRELIMINARY OFFERING CIRCULAR SHALL NOT CONSTITUTE AN OFFER TO SELL OR THE SOLICITATION OF AN OFFER TO BUY NOR MAY THERE BE ANY SALES OF THESE SECURITIES IN ANY STATE IN WHICH SUCH OFFER, SOLICITATION OR SALE WOULD BE UNLAWFUL BEFORE REGISTRATION OR QUALIFICATION UNDER THE LAWS OF ANY SUCH STATE. WE MAY ELECT TO SATISFY OUR OBLIGATION TO DELIVER A FINAL OFFERING CIRCULAR BY SENDING YOU A NOTICE WITHIN TWO BUSINESS DAYS AFTER THE COMPLETION OF OUR SALE TO YOU THAT CONTAINS THE URL WHERE THE FINAL OFFERING CIRCULAR OR THE OFFERING STATEMENT IN WHICH SUCH FINAL OFFERING CIRCULAR WAS FILED MAY BE OBTAINED.

b.   **Other contents**. The Preliminary Offering Circular contains substantially the information required to be in an offering circular by Form 1-A, except that certain information may be omitted under Rule 253(b) subject to the conditions set forth in such rule.

c.   **Filing**. The Preliminary Offering Circular is filed as a part of the offering statement.

Rule 255 – Solicitations of interest and other communications

a.   **Solicitation of interest.** At any time before the qualification of an offering statement, including before the non-public submission or public filing of such offering statement, an issuer or any person authorized to act on behalf of an issuer may communicate orally or in writing to determine whether there is any interest in a contemplated securities offering. Such communications are deemed to be an offer of a security for sale for purposes of the antifraud provisions of the federal securities laws. No solicitation or acceptance of money or other consideration, nor of any commitment, binding or otherwise, from any person is permitted until qualification of the offering statement.

b.   **Conditions**. The communications must:
1.   State that no money or other consideration is being solicited, and if sent in response, will not be accepted;
2.   State that no offer to buy the securities can be accepted and no part of the purchase price can be received until the offering statement is qualified, and any such offer may be withdrawn or revoked, without obligation or commitment of any kind, at any time before notice of its acceptance given after the qualification date;
3.   State that a person's indication of interest involves no obligation or commitment of any kind; and
4.   After the public filing of the offering statement:
   i.   State from whom a copy of the most recent version of the Preliminary Offering Circular may be obtained, including a phone number and address of such person;

      ii.   Provide the URL where such Preliminary Offering Circular, or the offering statement in which such Preliminary Offering Circular was filed, may be obtained; or

      iii. Include a complete copy of the Preliminary Offering Circular.

c.   **Indications of interest.** Any written communication under this rule may include a means by which a person may indicate to the issuer that such person is interested in a potential offering. This issuer may require the name, address, telephone number, and/or e-mail address in any response form included pursuant to this paragraph (c).

d.   **Revised solicitations of interest.** If solicitation of interest materials are used after the public filing of the offering statement and such solicitation of interest materials contain information that is inaccurate or inadequate in any material respect, revised solicitation of interest materials must be redistributed in a substantially similar manner as such materials were originally distributed. Notwithstanding the foregoing in this paragraph (d), if the only information that is inaccurate or inadequate is contained in a Preliminary Offering Circular provided with the solicitation of interest materials pursuant to paragraphs (b)(4)(i) or (ii) of this section, no such redistribution is required in the following circumstances:

    1.   in the case of paragraph (b)(4)(i) of this section, the revised Preliminary Offering Circular will be provided to any persons making new inquiries and will be recirculated to any persons making any previous inquiries; or

    2.   in the case of paragraph (b)(4)(ii) of this section, the URL continues to link directly to the most recent Preliminary Offering Circular or to the offering statement in which such revised Preliminary Offering Circular was filed.

Rule 256 – Definition of "qualified purchaser"

For purposes of § 18(b)(3) of the Securities Act, a "qualified purchaser" means any person to whom securities are offered or sold pursuant to a Tier 2 offering of this Regulation A.

Rule 257 – Periodic and current reporting; exit report

a.   **Tier 1***: Exit report.* Each issuer that has filed an offering statement for a Tier 1 offering that has been qualified pursuant to this Regulation A must file an exit report on Form 1-Z not later than 30 calendar days after the termination or completion of the offering.

b.   **Tier 2***: Periodic and current reporting.* Each issuer that has filed an offering statement for a Tier 2 offering that has been qualified pursuant to this Regulation A must file with the Commission the following periodic and current reports:

    1.   *Annual reports.* An annual report on Form 1-K for the fiscal year in which the offering statement became qualified and for any fiscal year thereafter, unless the issuer's obligation to file such annual report is suspended under paragraph (d) of this section. Annual reports must be filed within the period specified in Form 1-K.

    2.   *Special financial report.*

      i.   A special financial report on Form 1-K or Form 1-SA if the offering statement did not contain the following:

> A.   audited financial statements for the issuer's most recent fiscal year (or for the life of the issuer if less than a full fiscal year) preceding the fiscal year in which the issuer's offering statement became qualified; or
>
> B.   unaudited financial statements covering the first six months of the issuer's current fiscal year if the offering statement was qualified during the last six months of that fiscal year.

ii.   The special financial report described in paragraph (b)(2)(i)(A) of this section must be filed under cover of Form 1-K within 120 calendar days after the qualification date of the offering statement and must include audited financial statements for such fiscal year or other period specified in that paragraph, as the case may be. The special financial report described in paragraph (b)(2)(i)(B) of this section must be filed under cover of Form 1-SA within 90 calendar days after the qualification date of the offering statement and must include the semiannual financial statements for the first six months of the issuer's fiscal year, which may be unaudited.

iii.   A special financial report must be signed in accordance with the requirements of the form on which it is filed.

3.   *Semiannual report.* A semiannual report on Form 1-SA within the period specified in Form 1-SA. Semiannual reports must cover the first six months of each fiscal year of the issuer, commencing with the first six months of the fiscal year immediately following the most recent fiscal year for which full financial statements were included in the offering statement, or, if the offering statement included financial statements for the first six months of the fiscal year following the most recent full fiscal year, for the first six months of the following fiscal year.

4.   *Current reports.* Current reports on Form 1-U with respect to the matters and within the period specified in that form, unless substantially the same information has been previously reported to the Commission by the issuer under cover of Form 1-K or Form 1-SA.

5.   *Reporting by successor issuers.* Where in connection with a succession by merger, consolidation, exchange of securities, acquisition of assets or otherwise, securities of any issuer that is not required to file reports pursuant to paragraph (b) of this section are issued to the holders of any class of securities of another issuer that is required to file such reports, the duty to file reports pursuant to paragraph (b) of this section shall be deemed to have been assumed by the issuer of the class of securities so issued.   The successor issuer must, after the consummation of the succession, file reports in accordance with paragraph (b) of this section, unless that issuer is exempt from filing such reports or the duty to file such reports is terminated or suspended under paragraph (d) of this section.

6.   *Exchange Act reporting requirements.* The duty to file reports under this rule shall be deemed to have been met if the issuer is subject to the reporting requirements of Section 13 or 15(d) of the Exchange Act and, as of each Form 1-K and Form 1-SA due date, has filed all reports required to be filed by Section 13 or 15(d) of the Exchange Act during the 12 months (or such shorter period that the registrant was required to file such reports) preceding such due date.

c. **Amendments**. All amendments to the reports described in paragraphs (a) and (b) of this section must be filed under cover of the form amended, marked with the letter A to designate the document as an amendment, e.g., "1-K/A," and in compliance with pertinent requirements applicable to such reports. Amendments filed pursuant to this paragraph (c) must set forth the complete text of each item as amended, but need not include any items that were not amended. Amendments must be numbered sequentially and be filed separately for each report amended. Amendments must be signed on behalf of the issuer by a duly authorized representative of the issuer. An amendment to any report required to include certifications as specified in the applicable form must include new certifications by the appropriate persons.

d. **Suspension of duty to file reports**.
   1. [Reserved].
   2. The duty to file reports under paragraph (b) of this section with respect to a class of securities held of record (as defined in Rule 12g5-1) by less than 300 persons, or less than 1,200 persons for a bank (as defined in Section 3(a)(6) of the Exchange Act), or a bank holding company (as defined in section 2 of the Bank Holding Company Act of 1956), shall be suspended for such class of securities immediately upon filing with the Commission an exit report on Form 1-Z if the issuer of such class has filed all reports due pursuant to this rule before the date of such Form 1-Z filing for the shorter of:
      i. The period since the issuer became subject to such reporting obligation; or
      ii. Its most recent three fiscal years and the portion of the current year preceding the date of filing Form 1-Z.
   3. For the purposes of paragraph (d)(2) of this section, the term class shall be construed to include all securities of an issuer that are of substantially similar character and the holders of which enjoy substantially similar rights and privileges. If the Form 1-Z is subsequently withdrawn or if it is denied because the issuer was ineligible to use the form, the issuer must, within 60 calendar days, file with the Commission all reports which would have been required if such exit report had not been filed. If the suspension resulted from the issuer's merger into, or consolidation with, another issuer or issuers, the notice must be filed by the successor issuer.
   4. The ability to suspend reporting, as described in paragraph (d)(2) of this section, is not available for any class of securities if:
      i. During that fiscal year a Tier 2 offering statement was qualified;
      ii. The issuer has not filed an annual report under this rule or the Exchange Act for the fiscal year in which a Tier 2 offering statement was qualified; or
      iii. Offers or sales of securities of that class are being made pursuant to a Tier 2 Regulation A offering.

e. **Termination of duty to file reports**. If the duty to file reports is deemed to have been met pursuant to paragraph (b)(6) of this section and such status ends because the issuer terminates or suspends its duty to file reports under the Exchange Act, the issuer's obligation to file reports under paragraph (b) of this section shall:
   1. Automatically terminate if the issuer is eligible to suspend its duty to file reports under paragraphs (d)(2) and (3) of this section; or

2.   Recommence with the report covering the most recent financial period after that included in any effective registration statement or filed Exchange Act report.

Rule 258 – Suspension of the exemption

a.   **Suspension**. The Commission may at any time enter an order temporarily suspending a Regulation A exemption if it has reason to believe that:

1.   No exemption is available or any of the terms, conditions or requirements of Regulation A have not been complied with;

2.   The offering statement, any sales or solicitation of interest material, or any report filed pursuant to Rule 257 contains any untrue statement of a material fact or omits to state a material fact necessary in order to make the statements made, in light of the circumstances under which they are made, not misleading;

3.   The offering is being made or would be made in violation of section 17 of the Securities Act;

4.   An event has occurred after the filing of the offering statement that would have rendered the exemption hereunder unavailable if it had occurred before such filing;

5.   Any person specified in Rule 262(a) has been indicted for any crime or offense of the character specified in Rule 262(a)(1), or any proceeding has been initiated for the purpose of enjoining any such person from engaging in or continuing any conduct or practice of the character specified in Rule 262(a)(2), or any proceeding has been initiated for the purposes of Rule 262(a)(3)-(8); or

6.   The issuer or any promoter, officer, director, or underwriter has failed to cooperate, or has obstructed or refused to permit the making of an investigation by the Commission in connection with any offering made or proposed to be made in reliance on Regulation A.

b.   **Notice and hearing**. Upon the entry of an order under paragraph (a) of this section, the Commission will promptly give notice to the issuer, any underwriter, and any selling security holder:

1.   That such order has been entered, together with a brief statement of the reasons for the entry of the order; and

2.   That the Commission, upon receipt of a written request within 30 calendar days after the entry of the order, will, within 20 calendar days after receiving the request, order a hearing at a place to be designated by the Commission.

c.   **Suspension order**. If no hearing is requested and none is ordered by the Commission, an order entered under paragraph (a) of this section shall become permanent on the 30th calendar day after its entry and shall remain in effect unless or until it is modified or vacated by the Commission. Where a hearing is requested or is ordered by the Commission, the Commission will, after notice of and opportunity for such hearing, either vacate the order or enter an order permanently suspending the exemption.

d.   **Permanent suspension**. The Commission may, at any time after notice of and opportunity for hearing, enter an order permanently suspending the exemption for any reason upon which it could have entered a temporary suspension order under paragraph

(a) of this section. Any such order shall remain in effect until vacated by the Commission.

e. **Notice procedures**. All notices required by this rule must be given by personal service, registered or certified mail to the addresses given by the issuer, any underwriter and any selling security holder in the offering statement.

Rule 259 – Withdrawal or abandonment of offering statements

a. **Withdrawal**. If none of the securities that are the subject of an offering statement has been sold and such offering statement is not the subject of a proceeding under Rule 258, the offering statement may be withdrawn with the Commission's consent. The application for withdrawal must state the reason the offering statement is to be withdrawn and must be signed by an authorized representative of the issuer. Any withdrawn document will remain in the Commission's files, as well as the related request for withdrawal.

b. **Abandonment**. When an offering statement, or a post-qualification amendment to such statement, has been on file with the Commission for nine months without amendment and has not become qualified, the Commission may, in its discretion, declare the offering statement or post-qualification amendment abandoned. If the offering statement has been amended, or if the post-qualification amendment has been amended, the nine-month period shall be computed from the date of the latest amendment .

Rule 260 – Insignificant deviations from a term, condition or requirement of Regulation A

a. **Failure to comply**. A failure to comply with a term, condition or requirement of Regulation A will not result in the loss of the exemption from the requirements of section 5 of the Securities Act for any offer or sale to a particular individual or entity, if the person relying on the exemption establishes that:
1. The failure to comply did not pertain to a term, condition or requirement directly intended to protect that particular individual or entity;
2. The failure to comply was insignificant with respect to the offering as a whole, provided that any failure to comply with Rule 251(a), (b), and (d)(1) and (3) shall be deemed to be significant to the offering as a whole; and
3. A good faith and reasonable attempt was made to comply with all applicable terms, conditions and requirements of Regulation A.

b. **Action by Commission**. A transaction made in reliance upon Regulation A must comply with all applicable terms, conditions and requirements of the regulation. Where an exemption is established only through reliance upon paragraph (a) of this section, the failure to comply shall nonetheless be actionable by the Commission under section 20 of the Securities Act.

c. **Suspension**. This provision provides no relief or protection from a proceeding under Rule 258.

Rule 261 – Definitions

As used in this Regulation A, all terms have the same meanings as in Rule 405 except that all references to registrant in those definitions shall refer to the issuer of the securities to be offered and sold under Regulation A. In addition, these terms have the following meanings:

a. **Affiliated issuer**. An affiliate (as defined in Rule 501) of the issuer that is issuing securities in the same offering.

b. **Business day**. Any day except Saturdays, Sundays or United States federal holidays.

c. **Eligible securities**. Equity securities, debt securities, and securities convertible or exchangeable to equity interests, including any guarantees of such securities, but not including asset-backed securities as such term is defined in Item 1101(c) of Reg. AB.

d. **Final order**. A written directive or declaratory statement issued by a federal or state agency described in Rule 262(a)(3) under applicable statutory authority that provides for notice and an opportunity for hearing, which constitutes a final disposition or action by that federal or state agency.

e. **Final offering circular**. The more recent of: the current offering circular contained in a qualified offering statement; and any offering circular filed pursuant to Rule 253(g). If, however, the issuer is relying on Rule 253(b), the Final Offering Circular is the most recent of the offering circular filed pursuant to Rule 253(g)(1) or (3) and any subsequent offering circular filed pursuant to Rule 253(g).

f. **Offering statement**. An offering statement prepared pursuant to Regulation A.

g. **Preliminary offering circular**. The offering circular described in Rule 254.

Rule 262 – Disqualification provisions

a. **Disqualification events**. No exemption under Regulation A shall be available for a sale of securities if the issuer; any predecessor of the issuer; any affiliated issuer; any director, executive officer, other officer participating in the offering, general partner or managing member of the issuer; any beneficial owner of 20 percent or more of the issuer's outstanding voting equity securities, calculated on the basis of voting power; any promoter connected with the issuer in any capacity at the time of filing, any offer after qualification, or such sale; any person that has been or will be paid (directly or indirectly) remuneration for solicitation of purchasers in connection with such sale of securities; any general partner or managing member of any such solicitor; or any director, executive officer or other officer participating in the offering of any such solicitor or general partner or managing member of such solicitor:

　　1. Has been convicted, within 10 years before the filing of the offering statement (or five years, in the case of issuers, their predecessors and affiliated issuers), of any felony or misdemeanor:

　　　　i.   In connection with the purchase or sale of any security;

　　　　ii. Involving the making of any false filing with the Commission; or

iii. Arising out of the conduct of the business of an underwriter, broker, dealer, municipal securities dealer, investment adviser or paid solicitor of purchasers of securities.

2. Is subject to any order, judgment or decree of any court of competent jurisdiction, entered within five years before the filing of the offering statement, that, at the time of such filing or such sale, restrains or enjoins such person from engaging or continuing to engage in any conduct or practice:

   i. In connection with the purchase or sale of any security;
   ii. Involving the making of any false filing with the Commission; or
   iii. Arising out of the conduct of the business of an underwriter, broker, dealer, municipal securities dealer, investment adviser or paid solicitor or purchasers of securities;

3. Is subject to a final order (as defined in Rule 261) of a state securities commission (or an agency or officer of a state performing like functions); a state authority that supervises or examines banks, savings associations, or credit unions; a state insurance commission (or an agency or officer of a state performing like functions); an appropriate federal banking agency; the U.S. Commodity Futures Trading Commission; or the National Credit Union Administration that:

   i. At the time of the filing of the offering statement, bars the person from:
      A. Association with an entity regulated by such commission, authority, agency, or officer;
      B. Engaging in the business of securities, insurance or banking; or
      C. Engaging in savings association or credit union activities; or
   ii. Constitutes a final order based on a violation of any law or regulation that prohibits fraudulent, manipulative, or deceptive conduct entered within ten years before such filing of the offering statement;

4. Is subject to an order of the Commission entered pursuant to section 15(b) or 15B(c) of the Securities Exchange Act of 1934 or section 203(e) or (f) of the Investment Advisers Act of 1940 that, at the time of the filing of the offering statement:

   i. Suspends or revokes such person's registration as a broker, dealer, municipal securities dealer or investment adviser;
   ii. Places limitations on the activities, functions or operations of such person; or
   iii. Bars such person from being associated with any entity or from participating in the offering of any penny stock;

5. Is subject to any order of the Commission entered within five years before the filing of the offering statement that, at the time of such filing, orders the person to cease and desist from committing or causing a violation or future violation of:

   i. Any scienter-based anti-fraud provision of the federal securities laws, including without limitation section 17(a)(1) of the Securities Act of 1933, section 10(b) of the Securities Exchange Act of 1934 and Rule 10b-5, section 15(c)(1) of the Securities Exchange Act of 1934 and section 206(1) of the Investment Advisers Act of 1940, or any other rule or regulation thereunder; or
   ii. Section 5 of the Securities Act of 1933.

6.   Is suspended or expelled from membership in, or suspended or barred from association with a member of, a registered national securities exchange or a registered national or affiliated securities association for any act or omission to act constituting conduct inconsistent with just and equitable principles of trade;

7.   Has filed (as a registrant or issuer), or was or was named as an underwriter in, any registration statement or offering statement filed with the Commission that, within five years before the filing of the offering statement, was the subject of a refusal order, stop order, or order suspending the Regulation A exemption, or is, at the time of such filing, the subject of an investigation or proceeding to determine whether a stop order or suspension order should be issued; or

8.   Is subject to a United States Postal Service false representation order entered within five years before the filing of the offering statement, or is, at the time of such filing, subject to a temporary restraining order or preliminary injunction with respect to conduct alleged by the United States Postal Service to constitute a scheme or device for obtaining money or property through the mail by means of false representations.

b.   **Transition, waivers, reasonable care exception**. Paragraph (a) of this section shall not apply:

1.   With respect to any order under Rule 262(a)(3) or (5) that occurred or was issued before June 19, 2015;

2.   Upon a showing of good cause and without prejudice to any other action by the Commission, if the Commission determines that it is not necessary under the circumstances that an exemption be denied;

3.   If, before the filing of the offering statement, the court or regulatory authority that entered the relevant order, judgment or decree advises in writing (whether contained in the relevant judgment, order or decree or separately to the Commission or its staff) that disqualification under paragraph (a) of this section should not arise as a consequence of such order, judgment or decree; or

4.   If the issuer establishes that it did not know and, in the exercise of reasonable care, could not have known that a disqualification existed under paragraph (a) of this section.

Note to paragraph (b)(4). An issuer will not be able to establish that it has exercised reasonable care unless it has made, in light of the circumstances, factual inquiry into whether any disqualifications exist. The nature and scope of the factual inquiry will vary based on the facts and circumstances concerning, among other things, the issuer and the other offering participants.

c.   **Affiliated issuers**. For purposes of paragraph (a) of this section, events relating to any affiliated issuer that occurred before the affiliation arose will be not considered disqualifying if the affiliated entity is not:

1.   In control of the issuer; or

2.   Under common control with the issuer by a third party that was in control of the affiliated entity at the time of such events.

d.   **Disclosure of prior "bad actor" events**. The issuer must include in the offering circular a description of any matters that would have triggered disqualification under paragraphs (a)(3) and (5) of this section but occurred before June 19, 2015. The failure to provide such information shall not prevent an issuer from relying on Regulation A if the issuer establishes that it did not know and, in the exercise of reasonable care, could not have known of the existence of the undisclosed matter or matters.

Rule 263 – Consent to service of process

a. If the issuer is not organized under the laws of any of the states or territories of the United States of America, it shall furnish to the Commission a written irrevocable consent and power of attorney on Form F-X at the time of filing the offering statement required by Rule 252.

b. Any change to the name or address of the agent for service of the issuer shall be communicated promptly to the Commission through amendment of the requisite form and referencing the file number of the relevant offering statement.

Regulation Crowdfunding: General Rules And Regulations

Subpart A – General

Rule 100 – Crowdfunding exemption and requirements

a. **Exemption**. An issuer may offer or sell securities in reliance on section 4(a)(6) of the Securities Act of 1933 (the "Securities Act"), provided that:

    1. The aggregate amount of securities sold to all investors by the issuer in reliance on section 4(a)(6) of the Securities Act during the 12-month period preceding the date of such offer or sale, including the securities offered in such transaction, shall not exceed $5,000,000;

    2. Where the purchaser is not an accredited investor (as defined in Rule 501), the aggregate amount of securities sold to such an investor across all issuers in reliance on section 4(a)(6) of the Securities Act during the 12-month period preceding the date of such transaction, including the securities sold to such investor in such transaction, shall not exceed:

        i. The greater of $2,200, or 5 percent of the greater of the investor's annual income or net worth, if either the investor's annual income or net worth is less than $124,000; or

        ii. Ten percent of the greater of the investor's annual income or net worth, not to exceed an amount sold of $124,000, if both the investor's annual income and net worth are equal to or more than $124,000;

    Instruction 1 to paragraph (a)(2). To determine the investment limit for a natural person, the person's annual income and net worth shall be calculated as those values are calculated for purposes of determining accredited investor status in accordance with Rule 501 of this chapter.

    Instruction 2 to paragraph (a)(2). A person's annual income and net worth may be calculated jointly with that person's spouse; however, when such a joint calculation is used, the aggregate investment of the investor spouses may not exceed the limit that would apply to an individual investor at that income or net worth level.

    Instruction 3 to paragraph (a)(2). An issuer offering and selling securities in reliance on section 4(a)(6) of the Securities Act may rely on the efforts of an intermediary required by Rule 303(b) to ensure that the aggregate amount of securities purchased by an investor in offerings pursuant to section 4(a)(6) of the Securities Act will not cause the investor to exceed the limit set forth in section 4(a)(6) of the Securities Act and Rule 100(a)(2), *provided that* the issuer does not know that the investor has exceeded the investor limits or would exceed the investor limits as a result of purchasing securities in the issuer's offering.

    3. The transaction is conducted through an intermediary that complies with the requirements in section 4A(a) of the Securities Act and the related requirements in this part, and the transaction is conducted exclusively through the intermediary's platform; and

    Instruction to paragraph (a)(3). An issuer shall not conduct an offering or concurrent offerings in reliance on section 4(a)(6) of the Securities Act of 1933 using more than one intermediary.

4.   The issuer complies with the requirements in section 4A(b) of the Securities Act and the related requirements in this part; *provided, however,* that the failure to comply with Rules 202, 203(a)(3) and 203(b) shall not prevent an issuer from relying on the exemption provided by section 4(a)(6) of the Securities Act.

b. **Applicability**. The crowdfunding exemption shall not apply to transactions involving the offer or sale of securities by any issuer that:

1.   Is not organized under, and subject to, the laws of a State or territory of the United States or the District of Columbia;

2.   Is subject to the requirement to file reports pursuant to section 13 or section 15(d) of the Securities Exchange Act of 1934 (the "Exchange Act");

3.   Is an investment company, as defined in section 3 of the Investment Company Act of 1940, or is excluded from the definition of investment company by section 3(b) or section 3(c) of that Act;

4.   Is not eligible to offer or sell securities in reliance on section 4(a)(6) of the Securities Act as a result of a disqualification as specified in Rule 503(a);

5.   Has sold securities in reliance on section 4(a)(6) of the Securities Act and has not filed with the Commission and provided to investors, to the extent required, the ongoing annual reports required by this part during the two years immediately preceding the filing of the required offering statement; or

Instruction to paragraph (b)(5). An issuer delinquent in its ongoing reports can again rely on section 4(a)(6) of the Securities Act once it has filed with the Commission and provided to investors both of the annual reports required during the two years immediately preceding the filing of the required offering statement.

6.   Has no specific business plan or has indicated that its business plan is to engage in a merger or acquisition with an unidentified company or companies.

***

c. **Issuer**. For purposes of Rule 201(r), calculating aggregate amounts offered and sold in Rule 100(a) and Rule 201(t), and determining whether an issuer has previously sold securities in Rule 201(t)(3), *issuer* includes all entities controlled by or under common control with the issuer and any predecessors of the issuer.

Instruction to paragraph (c). The term *control* means the possession, direct or indirect, of the power to direct or cause the direction of the management and policies of the entity, whether through the ownership of voting securities, by contract or otherwise.

d. **Investor**. For purposes of this part, investor means any investor or any potential investor, as the context requires. A crowdfunding vehicle Rule 3a-9 of this chapter) is not considered an investor for the purposes of this part.

Subpart B – Requirements for Issuers

Rule 201 – Disclosure requirements

An issuer offering or selling securities in reliance on section 4(a)(6) of the Securities Act and in accordance with section 4A of the Securities Act and this part, and any co-issuer jointly offering or selling securities with such an issuer in reliance on the same, must file with the Commission and provide to investors and the relevant intermediary the following information:

a. The name, legal status (including its form of organization, jurisdiction in which it is organized and date of organization), physical address and website of the issuer;

b. The names of the directors and officers (and any persons occupying a similar status or performing a similar function) of the issuer, all positions and offices with the issuer held by such persons, the period of time in which such persons served in the position or office and their business experience during the past three years, including:
    1. Each person's principal occupation and employment, including whether any officer is employed by another employer; and
    2. The name and principal business of any corporation or other organization in which such occupation and employment took place.
    Instruction to paragraph (b). For purposes of this paragraph (b), the term *officer* means a president, vice president, secretary, treasurer or principal financial officer, comptroller or principal accounting officer, and any person routinely performing similar functions.

c. The name of each person, as of the most recent practicable date but no earlier than 120 days prior to the date the offering statement or report is filed, who is a beneficial owner of 20 percent or more of the issuer's outstanding voting equity securities, calculated on the basis of voting power;

d. A description of the business of the issuer and the anticipated business plan of the issuer;

e. The current number of employees of the issuer;

f. A discussion of the material factors that make an investment in the issuer speculative or risky;

g. The target offering amount and the deadline to reach the target offering amount, including a statement that if the sum of the investment commitments does not equal or exceed the target offering amount at the offering deadline, no securities will be sold in the offering, investment commitments will be cancelled and committed funds will be returned;

h. Whether the issuer will accept investments in excess of the target offering amount and, if so, the maximum amount that the issuer will accept and how oversubscriptions will be allocated, such as on a pro-rata, first come-first served, or other basis;

i. A description of the purpose and intended use of the offering proceeds;
    Instruction to paragraph (i). An issuer must provide a reasonably detailed description of any intended use of proceeds, such that investors are provided with enough information to understand how the offering proceeds will be used. If an issuer has identified a range of possible uses, the issuer should identify and describe each probable use and the factors the issuer may consider in allocating proceeds among the potential uses. If the issuer will accept proceeds in excess of the target offering amount, the issuer

must describe the purpose, method for allocating oversubscriptions, and intended use of the excess proceeds with similar specificity.

j.   A description of the process to complete the transaction or cancel an investment commitment, including a statement that:
1.   Investors may cancel an investment commitment until 48 hours prior to the deadline identified in the issuer's offering materials;
2.   The intermediary will notify investors when the target offering amount has been met;
3.   If an issuer reaches the target offering amount prior to the deadline identified in its offering materials, it may close the offering early if it provides notice about the new offering deadline at least five business days prior to such new offering deadline (absent a material change that would require an extension of the offering and reconfirmation of the investment commitment); and
4.   If an investor does not cancel an investment commitment before the 48-hour period prior to the offering deadline, the funds will be released to the issuer upon closing of the offering and the investor will receive securities in exchange for his or her investment;

k.   A statement that if an investor does not reconfirm his or her investment commitment after a material change is made to the offering, the investor's investment commitment will be cancelled and the committed funds will be returned;

l.   The price to the public of the securities or the method for determining the price, provided that, prior to any sale of securities, each investor shall be provided in writing the final price and all required disclosures;

m.   A description of the ownership and capital structure of the issuer, including:
1.   The terms of the securities being offered and each other class of security of the issuer, including the number of securities being offered and/or outstanding, whether or not such securities have voting rights, any limitations on such voting rights, how the terms of the securities being offered may be modified and a summary of the differences between such securities and each other class of security of the issuer, and how the rights of the securities being offered may be materially limited, diluted or qualified by the rights of any other class of security of the issuer;
2.   A description of how the exercise of rights held by the principal shareholders of the issuer could affect the purchasers of the securities being offered;
3.   The name and ownership level of each person, as of the most recent practicable date but no earlier than 120 days prior to the date the offering statement or report is filed, who is the beneficial owner of 20 percent or more of the issuer's outstanding voting equity securities, calculated on the basis of voting power;
4.   How the securities being offered are being valued, and examples of methods for how such securities may be valued by the issuer in the future, including during subsequent corporate actions;
5.   The risks to purchasers of the securities relating to minority ownership in the issuer and the risks associated with corporate actions including additional

issuances of securities, issuer repurchases of securities, a sale of the issuer or of assets of the issuer or transactions with related parties; and

6.   A description of the restrictions on transfer of the securities, as set forth in 501;

n.   The name, SEC file number and Central Registration Depository (CRD) number (as applicable) of the intermediary through which the offering is being conducted;

o.   A description of the intermediary's financial interests in the issuer's transaction and in the issuer, including:

1.   The amount of compensation to be paid to the intermediary, whether as a dollar amount or a percentage of the offering amount, or a good faith estimate if the exact amount is not available at the time of the filing, for conducting the offering, including the amount of referral and any other fees associated with the offering, and

2.   Any other direct or indirect interest in the issuer held by the intermediary, or any arrangement for the intermediary to acquire such an interest;

p.   A description of the material terms of any indebtedness of the issuer, including the amount, interest rate, maturity date and any other material terms;

q.   A description of exempt offerings conducted within the past three years;
Instruction to paragraph (q). In providing a description of any prior exempt offerings, disclose:

1.   The date of the offering;
2.   The offering exemption relied upon;
3.   The type of securities offered; and
4.   The amount of securities sold and the use of proceeds;

r.   A description of any transaction since the beginning of the issuer's last fiscal year, or any currently proposed transaction, to which the issuer was or is to be a party and the amount involved exceeds five percent of the aggregate amount of capital raised by the issuer in reliance on section 4(a)(6) of the Securities Act during the preceding 12-month period, inclusive of the amount the issuer seeks to raise in the current offering under section 4(a)(6) of the Securities Act, in which any of the following persons had or is to have a direct or indirect material interest:

1.   Any director or officer of the issuer;
2.   Any person who is, as of the most recent practicable date but no earlier than 120 days prior to the date the offering statement or report is filed, the beneficial owner of 20 percent or more of the issuer's outstanding voting equity securities, calculated on the basis of voting power;
3.   If the issuer was incorporated or organized within the past three years, any promoter of the issuer; or
4.   Any member of the family of any of the foregoing persons, which includes a child, stepchild, grandchild, parent, stepparent, grandparent, spouse or spousal equivalent, sibling, mother-in-law, father-in-law, son-in-law, daughter-in-law, brother-in-law, or sister-in-law, and shall include adoptive relationships. The term *spousal equivalent* means a cohabitant occupying a relationship generally equivalent to that of a spouse.

Instruction 1 to paragraph (r). For each transaction identified, disclose the name of the specified person and state his or her relationship to the issuer, and the nature and, where practicable, the approximate amount of his or her interest in the transaction. The amount of such interest shall be computed without regard to the amount of the profit or loss involved in the transaction. Where it is not practicable to state the approximate amount of the interest, the approximate amount involved in the transaction shall be disclosed.

Instruction 2 to paragraph (r). For purposes of paragraph (r), a transaction includes, but is not limited to, any financial transaction, arrangement or relationship (including any indebtedness or guarantee of indebtedness) or any series of similar transactions, arrangements or relationships.

s.   A discussion of the issuer's financial condition, including, to the extent material, liquidity, capital resources and historical results of operations;

Instruction 1 to paragraph (s). The discussion must cover each period for which financial statements of the issuer are provided. An issuer also must include a discussion of any material changes or trends known to management in the financial condition and results of operations of the issuer subsequent to the period for which financial statements are provided.

Instruction 2 to paragraph (s). For issuers with no prior operating history, the discussion should focus on financial milestones and operational, liquidity and other challenges. For issuers with an operating history, the discussion should focus on whether historical results and cash flows are representative of what investors should expect in the future. Issuers should take into account the proceeds of the offering and any other known or pending sources of capital. Issuers also should discuss how the proceeds from the offering will affect the issuer's liquidity, whether receiving these funds and any other additional funds is necessary to the viability of the business, and how quickly the issuer anticipates using its available cash. In addition, issuers should describe the other available sources of capital to the business, such as lines of credit or required contributions by shareholders.

Instruction 3 to paragraph (s). References to the issuer in this paragraph and its instructions refer to the issuer and its predecessors, if any.

t.   For offerings that, together with all other amounts sold under section 4(a)(6) of the Securities Act within the preceding 12-month period, have, in the aggregate, the following target offering amounts:

1. $124,000 or less, the amount of total income, taxable income and total tax, or the equivalent line items, as reported on the federal income tax returns filed by the issuer for the most recently completed year (if any), which shall be certified by the principal executive officer of the issuer to reflect accurately the information reported on the issuer's federal income tax returns, and financial statements of the issuer, which shall be certified by the principal executive officer of the issuer to be true and complete in all material respects. If financial statements of the issuer are available that have either been reviewed or audited by a public accountant that is independent of the issuer, the issuer must provide those financial statements instead and need not include the information reported on the federal income tax returns or the certifications of the principal executive officer;

2.   More than $124,000, but not more than $618,000, financial statements of the

issuer reviewed by a public accountant that is independent of the issuer. If financial statements of the issuer are available that have been audited by a public accountant that is independent of the issuer, the issuer must provide those financial statements instead and need not include the reviewed financial statements; and

3.   More than $618,000, financial statements of the issuer audited by a public accountant that is independent of the issuer; *provided, however*, that for issuers that have not previously sold securities in reliance on section 4(a)(6) of the Securities Act, offerings that have a target offering amount of more than $618,000, but not more than $1,235,000, financial statements of the issuer reviewed by a public accountant that is independent of the issuer. If financial statements of the issuer are available that have been audited by a public accountant that is independent of the issuer, the issuer must provide those financial statements instead and need not include the reviewed financial statements.

Instruction 1 to paragraph (t). To determine the financial statements required under this paragraph (t), an issuer must aggregate amounts sold in reliance on section 4(a)(6) of the Securities Act within the preceding 12-month period and the offering amount in the offering for which disclosure is being provided. If the issuer will accept proceeds in excess of the target offering amount, the issuer must include the maximum offering amount that the issuer will accept in the calculation to determine the financial statements required under this paragraph (t).

Instruction 2 to paragraph (t). An issuer may voluntarily meet the requirements of this paragraph (t) for a higher aggregate target offering amount.

Instruction 3 to paragraph (t). The financial statements must be prepared in accordance with U.S. generally accepted accounting principles and include balance sheets, statements of comprehensive income, statements of cash flows, statements of changes in stockholders' equity and notes to the financial statements. If the financial statements are not audited, they must be labeled as "unaudited." The financial statements must cover the two most recently completed fiscal years or the period(s) since inception, if shorter.

Instruction 4 to paragraph (t). For an offering conducted in the first 120 days of a fiscal year, the financial statements provided may be for the two fiscal years prior to the issuer's most recently completed fiscal year; however, financial statements for the two most recently completed fiscal years must be provided if they are otherwise available. If more than 120 days have passed since the end of the issuer's most recently completed fiscal year, the financial statements provided must be for the issuer's two most recently completed fiscal years. If the 120th day falls on a Saturday, Sunday, or holiday, the next business day shall be considered the 120th day for purposes of determining the age of the financial statements.

Instruction 5 to paragraph (t). An issuer may elect to delay complying with any new or revised financial accounting standard that applies to companies that are not issuers (as defined under section 2(a) of the Sarbanes-Oxley Act of 2002 until the date that such companies are required to comply with such new or revised accounting standard. Issuers electing this accommodation must disclose it at the time the issuer files its offering statement and apply the election to all standards. Issuers electing not to use this accommodation must forgo this accommodation for all financial accounting standards and may not elect to rely on this accommodation in any future filings.

Instruction 6 to paragraph (t). An issuer required to provide information from a tax return under paragraph (t)(1) of this section before filing a tax return with the U.S. Internal Revenue Service for the most recently completed fiscal year may provide information from its tax return for the prior year (if any), provided that the issuer provides information from the tax return for the most recently completed fiscal year when it is filed with the U.S. Internal Revenue Service (if the tax return is filed during the offering period). An issuer that requested an extension from the U.S. Internal Revenue Service would not be required to provide information from the tax return until the date the return is filed, if filed during the offering period. If an issuer has not yet filed a tax return and is not required to file a tax return before the end of the offering period, then the tax return information does not need to be provided.

Instruction 7 to paragraph (t). An issuer providing financial statements that are not audited or reviewed and tax information as specified under paragraph (t)(1) of this section must have its principal executive officer provide the following certification:

I, [identify the certifying individual], certify that:

1.   the financial statements of [identify the issuer] included in this Form are true and complete in all material respects; and

2.   the tax return information of [identify the issuer] included in this Form reflects accurately the information reported on the tax return for [identify the issuer] filed for the fiscal year ended [date of most recent tax return].

[Signature and title].

Instruction 8 to paragraph (t). Financial statement reviews shall be conducted in accordance with the Statements on Standards for Accounting and Review Services issued by the Accounting and Review Services Committee of the American Institute of Certified Public Accountants. A signed review report must accompany the reviewed financial statements, and an issuer must notify the public accountant of the issuer's intended use of the review report in the offering. An issuer will not be in compliance with the requirement to provide reviewed financial statements if the review report includes modifications.

Instruction 9 to paragraph (t). Financial statement audits shall be conducted in accordance with either auditing standards issued by the American Institute of Certified Public Accountants (referred to as U.S. Generally Accepted Auditing Standards) or the standards of the Public Company Accounting Oversight Board. A signed audit report must accompany audited financial statements, and an issuer must notify the public accountant of the issuer's intended use of the audit report in the offering. An issuer will not be in compliance with the requirement to provide audited financial statements if the audit report includes a qualified opinion, an adverse opinion, or a disclaimer of opinion.

Instruction 10 to paragraph (t) To qualify as a public accountant that is independent of the issuer for purposes of this part, the accountant must satisfy the independence standards of either:

i.   Rule 2-01 of this chapter, or

ii.   The American Institute of Certified Public Accountants. The public accountant that audits or reviews the financial statements provided by an issuer must be:

      A. Duly registered and in good standing as a certified public accountant under the laws of the place of his or her residence or principal office; or

      B. In good standing and entitled to practice as a public accountant under the laws of his or her place of residence or principal office.

Instruction 11 to paragraph (t). Except as set forth in Rule 100(c), references to the issuer in this paragraph (t) and its instructions (2) through (10) refer to the issuer and its predecessors, if any.

u.   Any matters that would have triggered disqualification under Rule 503(a) but occurred before May 16, 2016. The failure to provide such disclosure shall not prevent an issuer from continuing to rely on the exemption provided by section 4(a)(6) of the Securities Act if the issuer establishes that it did not know and, in the exercise of reasonable care, could not have known of the existence of the undisclosed matter or matters;

Instruction to paragraph (u). An issuer will not be able to establish that it could not have known of a disqualification unless it has made factual inquiry into whether any disqualifications exist. The nature and scope of the factual inquiry will vary based on the facts and circumstances concerning, among other things, the issuer and the other offering participants.

v.   Updates regarding the progress of the issuer in meeting the target offering amount, to be provided in accordance with Rule 203;

w.   Where on the issuer's website investors will be able to find the issuer's annual report, and the date by which such report will be available on the issuer's website;

x.   Whether the issuer or any of its predecessors previously failed to comply with the ongoing reporting requirements of Rule 202; and

y.   Any material information necessary in order to make the statements made, in light of the circumstances under which they were made, not misleading.

z.   Any written communication or broadcast script provided in accordance with Rule 206 or, if within 30 days of the initial filing of the offering statement, Rule 241 of this chapter.

Instruction to Rule 201. If disclosure provided pursuant to any paragraph of this section also satisfies the requirements of one or more other paragraphs of this section, it is not necessary to repeat the disclosure. Instead of repeating information, an issuer may include a cross-reference to disclosure contained elsewhere in the offering statement or report, including to information in the financial statements.

***

Rule 202 – Ongoing reporting requirements

a.   An issuer that has offered and sold securities in reliance on section 4(a)(6) of the Securities Act and in accordance with section 4A of the Securities Act and this part must file with the Commission and post on the issuer's website an annual report along with the financial statements of the issuer certified by the principal executive officer of the issuer to be true and complete in all material respects and a description of the financial condition of the issuer as described in Rule 201(s). If, however, an issuer has available financial statements that have either been reviewed or audited by a public accountant that is independent of the issuer, those financial statements must be provided and the certification by the principal executive officer will not be required. The annual report also must include the disclosure required by paragraphs (a), (b), (c), (d), (e), (f), (m), (p), (q), (r), and (x) of Rule 201. The report must be filed in accordance with the requirements of Rule 203 and Form C and no later than 120 days after the end of the fiscal year covered by the report.

Instruction 1 to paragraph (a). Instructions (3), (8), (9), (10), and (11) to paragraph (t) of Rule 201 shall apply for purposes of this section.

Instruction 2 to paragraph (a). An issuer providing financial statements that are not audited or reviewed must have its principal executive officer provide the following certification:

> I, [identify the certifying individual], certify that the financial statements of [identify the issuer] included in this Form are true and complete in all material respects.
>
> [Signature and title].

b.   An issuer must continue to comply with the ongoing reporting requirements until one of the following occurs:

1.   The issuer is required to file reports under section 13(a) or section 15(d) of the Exchange Act;

2.   The issuer has filed, since its most recent sale of securities pursuant to this part, at least one annual report pursuant to this section and has fewer than 300 holders of record;

3.   The issuer has filed, since its most recent sale of securities pursuant to this part, the annual reports required pursuant to this section for at least the three most recent years and has total assets that do not exceed $10,000,000;

4.   The issuer or another party repurchases all of the securities issued in reliance on section 4(a)(6) of the Securities Act, including any payment in full of debt securities or any complete redemption of redeemable securities; or

5.   The issuer liquidates or dissolves its business in accordance with state law.

Rule 203 – Filing requirements and form.

a.   **Form C: Offering statement and amendments**.

1.   *Offering statement.* Except as allowed by Rule 206, an issuer offering or selling securities in reliance on section 4(a)(6) of the Securities Act and in accordance with section 4A of the Securities Act and this part, and any co-issuer jointly offering or selling securities with such an issuer in reliance on the same, must file with the Commission and provide to investors and the relevant intermediary

a Form C: Offering Statement (Form C) prior to the commencement of the offering of securities. An issuer that is both offering or selling securities with a co-issuer and separately offering or selling securities on its own must file with the Commission and provide to investors and the relevant intermediary a separate Form C for such offering. Every Form C must include the information required by Rule 201..

2. *Amendments to offering statement.* An issuer must file with the Commission and provide to investors and the relevant intermediary an amendment to the offering statement filed on Form C to disclose any material changes, additions or updates to information that it provides to investors through the intermediary's platform, for any offering that has not yet been completed or terminated. The amendment must be filed on Form C: Amendment (Form C/A) and if the amendment reflects material changes, additions or updates, the issuer shall check the box indicating that investors must reconfirm an investment commitment within five business days or the investor's commitment will be considered cancelled.

3. *Progress updates.* (i) An issuer must file with the Commission and provide to investors and the relevant intermediary a Form C: Progress Update (Form C-U) to disclose its progress in meeting the target offering amount no later than five business days after each of the dates when the issuer reaches 50 percent and 100 percent of the target offering amount.

    i.   If the issuer will accept proceeds in excess of the target offering amount, the issuer must file with the Commission and provide to investors and the relevant intermediary, no later than five business days after the offering deadline, a final Form C-U to disclose the total amount of securities sold in the offering.

    ii. The requirements of paragraphs (a)(3)(i) and (ii) of this section shall not apply to an issuer if the relevant intermediary makes publicly available on the intermediary's platform frequent updates regarding the progress of the issuer in meeting the target offering amount; however, the issuer must still file a Form C-U to disclose the total amount of securities sold in the offering no later than five business days after the offering deadline.

    Instruction to paragraph (a)(3). If multiple Forms C-U are triggered within the same five business day period, the issuer may consolidate such progress updates into one Form C-U, so long as the Form C-U discloses the most recent threshold that was met and the Form C-U is filed with the Commission and provided to investors and the relevant intermediary by the day on which the first progress update is due.

Instruction 1 to paragraph (a). An issuer would satisfy the requirement to provide to the relevant intermediary the information required by this paragraph (a) if it provides to the relevant intermediary a copy of the disclosures filed with the Commission.

Instruction 2 to paragraph (a). An issuer would satisfy the requirement to provide to investors the information required by this paragraph (a) if the issuer refers investors to the information on the intermediary's platform by means of a posting on the issuer's website or by e-mail.

b. **Form C: Annual report and termination of reporting**.

    1.   *Annual reports.* An issuer that has sold securities in reliance on section 4(a)(6) of the Securities Act and in accordance with section 4A of the Securities Act and

this part must file an annual report on Form C: Annual Report (Form C-AR) with the Commission no later than 120 days after the end of the fiscal year covered by the report. The annual report shall include the information required by Rule 202(a).

2. *Amendments to annual report.* An issuer must file with the Commission an amendment to the annual report filed on Form C: Annual Report (Form C-AR) to make a material change to the previously filed annual report as soon as practicable after discovery of the need for the material change. The amendment must be filed on Form C: Amendment to Annual Report (Form C-AR/A).

3. *Termination of reporting.* An issuer eligible to terminate its obligation to file annual reports with the Commission pursuant to Rule 202(b) must file with the Commission, within five business days from the date on which the issuer becomes eligible to terminate its reporting obligation, Form C: Termination of Reporting (Form C-TR) to advise investors that the issuer will cease reporting pursuant to this part.

Rule 204 – Advertising

a.

1. An issuer may not, directly or indirectly, advertise the terms of an offering made in reliance on section 4(a)(6) of the Securities Act, except for oral or written communications that meet the requirements of paragraph (b) of this section or of Rule 206.

Instruction to paragraph (a). For purposes of this paragraph (a), *issuer* includes persons acting on behalf of the issuer.

b. A notice may advertise any of the terms of an issuer's offering made in reliance on section 4(a)(6) of the Securities Act if it directs investors to the intermediary's platform and includes no more than the following information:

1. A statement that the issuer is conducting an offering pursuant to section 4(a)(6) of the Securities Act, the name of the intermediary through which the offering is being conducted, and information (including a link in any written communications) directing the potential investor to the intermediary's platform;

2. The terms of the offering; and

3. Factual information about the legal identity and business location of the issuer, limited to the name of the issuer of the security, the address, phone number and website of the issuer, the e-mail address of a representative of the issuer and a brief description of the business of the issuer.

c. Notwithstanding the prohibition on advertising any of the terms of the offering, an issuer, and persons acting on behalf of the issuer, may communicate with investors and potential investors about the terms of the offering through communication channels provided by the intermediary on the intermediary's platform, provided that an issuer identifies itself as the issuer in all communications. Persons acting on behalf of the issuer must identify their affiliation with the issuer in all communications on the intermediary's platform.

d. Notwithstanding the requirement that a notice advertising any of the terms of an issuer's offering made in reliance on section 4(a)(6) of the Securities Act (15 U.S.C. 77d(a)(6)) include no more than the information specified in paragraph (b) of this section, an issuer conducting an offering in reliance on Regulation Crowdfunding concurrently with another offering that discloses the terms of the Regulation Crowdfunding offering in the disclosure document for the other offering will not be deemed to have exceeded these disclosure limitations if the disclosure document for the other offering satisfies all the other requirements of this section. If the disclosure document for the other offering is filed on the Commission's Electronic Data Gathering and Retrieval System (EDGAR), the link required by paragraph (b)(1) may not be a live hyperlink.

Instruction to Rule 204. For purposes of this section, *terms of the offering* means the amount of securities offered, the nature of the securities, the price of the securities and the closing date of the offering the planned use of proceeds and the issuer's progress toward meeting its funding target.

Rule 205 – Promoter compensation

a. An issuer, or person acting on behalf of the issuer, shall be permitted to compensate or commit to compensate, directly or indirectly, any person to promote the issuer's offerings made in reliance on section 4(a)(6) of the Securities Act through communication channels provided by an intermediary on the intermediary's platform, but only if the issuer or person acting on behalf of the issuer, takes reasonable steps to ensure that the person promoting the offering clearly discloses the receipt, past or prospective, of such compensation with any such communication.

Instruction to paragraph (a). The disclosure required by this paragraph is required, with each communication, for persons engaging in promotional activities on behalf of the issuer through the communication channels provided by the intermediary, regardless of whether or not the compensation they receive is specifically for the promotional activities. This includes persons hired specifically to promote the offering as well as to persons who are otherwise employed by the issuer or who undertake promotional activities on behalf of the issuer.

b. Other than as set forth in paragraph (a) of this section, an issuer or person acting on behalf of the issuer shall not compensate or commit to compensate, directly or indirectly, any person to promote the issuer's offerings made in reliance on section 4(a)(6) of the Securities Act, unless such promotion is limited to notices permitted by, and in compliance with, Rule 204.

Rule 206 – Solicitations of interest and other communications

a. **Solicitation of interest**. At any time before the filing of an offering statement, an issuer may communicate orally or in writing to determine whether there is any interest in a contemplated securities offering. Such communications are deemed to be an offer of a security for sale for purposes of the antifraud provisions of the Federal securities laws. No solicitation or acceptance of money or other consideration, nor of any commitment, binding or otherwise, from any person is permitted until the offering statement is filed.

b. **Conditions.** The communications must:
   1. State that no money or other consideration is being solicited, and if sent in response, will not be accepted;
   2. State that no offer to buy the securities can be accepted and no part of the purchase price can be received until the offering statement is filed and only through an intermediary's platform; and
   3. State that a person's indication of interest involves no obligation or commitment of any kind.

c. **Indications of interest.** Any written communication under this section may include a means by which a person may indicate to the issuer that such person is interested in a potential offering. This issuer may require the name, address, telephone number, and/or email address in any response form included pursuant to this paragraph (c).

Subpart C – Requirements for Intermediaries

Rule 300 – Intermediaries

a. **Requirements.** A person acting as an intermediary in a transaction involving the offer or sale of securities in reliance on section 4(a)(6) of the Securities Act must:
   1. Be registered with the Commission as a broker under section 15(b) of the Exchange Act or as a funding portal in accordance with the requirements of Rule 400; and
   2. Be a member a national securities association registered under section 15A of the Exchange Act.

b. **Financial interests.** Any director, officer or partner of an intermediary, or any person occupying a similar status or performing a similar function, may not have a financial interest in an issuer that is offering or selling securities in reliance on section 4(a)(6) of the Securities Act through the intermediary's platform, or receive a financial interest in an issuer as compensation for the services provided to or for the benefit of the issuer in connection with the offer or sale of such securities. An intermediary may not have a financial interest in an issuer that is offering or selling securities in reliance on section 4(a)(6) of the Securities Act through the intermediary's platform unless:
   1. the intermediary receives the financial interest from the issuer as compensation for the services provided to, or for the benefit of, the issuer in connection with the offer or sale of the securities being offered or sold in reliance on section 4(a)(6) of the Securities Act through the intermediary's platform; and
   2. the financial interest consists of securities of the same class and having the same terms, conditions and rights as the securities being offered or sold in reliance on section 4(a)(6) of the Securities Act through the intermediary's platform. For purposes of this paragraph, a *financial interest in an issuer* means a direct or indirect ownership of, or economic interest in, any class of the issuer's securities.

c. **Definitions.** For purposes of this part:
   1. *Associated person of a funding portal* or *person associated with a funding portal* means any partner, officer, director or manager of a funding portal (or any person occupying a similar status or performing similar functions), any person directly

or indirectly controlling or controlled by such funding portal, or any employee of a funding portal, except that any person associated with a funding portal whose functions are solely clerical or ministerial shall not be included in the meaning of such term for purposes of section 15(b) of the Exchange Act (other than paragraphs (4) and (6) of section 15(b) of the Exchange Act).

2. *Funding portal* means a broker acting as an intermediary in a transaction involving the offer or sale of securities in reliance on section 4(a)(6) of the Securities Act, that does not:

   i. Offer investment advice or recommendations;

   ii. Solicit purchases, sales or offers to buy the securities displayed on its platform;

   iii. Compensate employees, agents, or other persons for such solicitation or based on the sale of securities displayed or referenced on its platform; or

   iv. Hold, manage, possess, or otherwise handle investor funds or securities.

3. *Intermediary* means a broker registered under section 15(b) of the Exchange Act or a funding portal registered under Rule 400 and includes, where relevant, an associated person of the registered broker or registered funding portal.

4. *Platform* means a program or application accessible via the Internet or other similar electronic communication medium through which a registered broker or a registered funding portal acts as an intermediary in a transaction involving the offer or sale of securities in reliance on section 4(a)(6) of the Securities Act.

   Instruction to paragraph (c)(4). An intermediary through which a crowdfunding transaction is conducted may engage in back office or other administrative functions other than on the intermediary's platform.

Rule 301 – Measures to reduce risk of fraud

An intermediary in a transaction involving the offer or sale of securities in reliance on section 4(a)(6) of the Securities Act must:

a. Have a reasonable basis for believing that an issuer seeking to offer and sell securities in reliance on section 4(a)(6) of the Securities Act through the intermediary's platform complies with the requirements in section 4A(b) of the Act and the related requirements in this part. In satisfying this requirement, an intermediary may rely on the representations of the issuer concerning compliance with these requirements unless the intermediary has reason to question the reliability of those representations;

b. Have a reasonable basis for believing that the issuer has established means to keep accurate records of the holders of the securities it would offer and sell through the intermediary's platform, provided that an intermediary may rely on the representations of the issuer concerning its means of recordkeeping unless the intermediary has reason to question the reliability of those representations. An intermediary will be deemed to have satisfied this requirement if the issuer has engaged the services of a transfer agent that is registered under Section 17A of the Exchange Act.

c. Deny access to its platform to an issuer if the intermediary:

   1. Has a reasonable basis for believing that the issuer or any of its officers, directors (or any person occupying a similar status or performing a similar function) or

beneficial owners of 20 percent or more of the issuer's outstanding voting equity securities, calculated on the basis of voting power, is subject to a disqualification under Rule 503. In satisfying this requirement, an intermediary must, at a minimum, conduct a background and securities enforcement regulatory history check on each issuer whose securities are to be offered by the intermediary and on each officer, director or beneficial owner of 20 percent or more of the issuer's outstanding voting equity securities, calculated on the basis of voting power.

2.   Has a reasonable basis for believing that the issuer or the offering presents the potential for fraud or otherwise raises concerns about investor protection. In satisfying this requirement, an intermediary must deny access if it reasonably believes that it is unable to adequately or effectively assess the risk of fraud of the issuer or its potential offering. In addition, if an intermediary becomes aware of information after it has granted access that causes it to reasonably believe that the issuer or the offering presents the potential for fraud or otherwise raises concerns about investor protection, the intermediary must promptly remove the offering from its platform, cancel the offering, and return (or, for funding portals, direct the return of) any funds that have been committed by investors in the offering.

***

Rule 302 – Account opening

a.   **Accounts and electronic delivery**.

     1.   No intermediary or associated person of an intermediary may accept an investment commitment in a transaction involving the offer or sale of securities in reliance on section 4(a)(6) of the Securities Act until the investor has opened an account with the intermediary and the intermediary has obtained from the investor consent to electronic delivery of materials.

     2.   An intermediary must provide all information that is required to be provided by the intermediary under subpart C of this part (Rules 300 through 305), including, but not limited to, educational materials, notices and confirmations, through electronic means. Unless otherwise indicated in the relevant rule of subpart C of this part, in satisfying this requirement, an intermediary must provide the information through an electronic message that contains the information, through an electronic message that includes a specific link to the information as posted on intermediary's platform, or through an electronic message that provides notice of what the information is and that it is located on the intermediary's platform or on the issuer's website. Electronic messages include, but are not limited to, e-mail, social media messages, instant messages or other electronic media messages.

b.   **Educational materials**.

     1.   In connection with establishing an account for an investor, an intermediary must deliver educational materials to such investor that explain in plain language and are otherwise designed to communicate effectively and accurately:

         i.   The process for the offer, purchase and issuance of securities through the intermediary and the risks associated with purchasing securities offered and sold in reliance on section 4(a)(6) of the Securities Act;

ii.   The types of securities offered and sold in reliance on section 4(a)(6) of the Securities Act available for purchase on the intermediary's platform and the risks associated with each type of security, including the risk of having limited voting power as a result of dilution;

iii.   The restrictions on the resale of a security offered and sold in reliance on section 4(a)(6) of the Securities Act;

iv.   The types of information that an issuer is required to provide under Rule 202, the frequency of the delivery of that information and the possibility that those obligations may terminate in the future;

v.   The limitations on the amounts an investor may invest pursuant to Rule 100(a)(2);

vi.   The limitations on an investor's right to cancel an investment commitment and the circumstances in which an investment commitment may be cancelled by the issuer;

vii.   The need for the investor to consider whether investing in a security offered and sold in reliance on section 4(a)(6) of the Securities Act is appropriate for that investor;

viii.   That following completion of an offering conducted through the intermediary, there may or may not be any ongoing relationship between the issuer and intermediary; and

ix.   That under certain circumstances an issuer may cease to publish annual reports and, therefore, an investor may not continually have current financial information about the issuer.

2.   An intermediary must make the most current version of its educational material available on its platform at all times and, if at any time, the intermediary makes a material revision to its educational materials, it must make the revised educational materials available to all investors before accepting any additional investment commitments or effecting any further transactions in securities offered and sold in reliance on section 4(a)(6) of the Securities Act.

c.   **Promoters**. In connection with establishing an account for an investor, an intermediary must inform the investor that any person who promotes an issuer's offering for compensation, whether past or prospective, or who is a founder or an employee of an issuer that engages in promotional activities on behalf of the issuer on the intermediary's platform, must clearly disclose in all communications on the intermediary's platform, respectively, the receipt of the compensation and that he or she is engaging in promotional activities on behalf of the issuer.

d.   **Compensation disclosure**. When establishing an account for an investor, an intermediary must clearly disclose the manner in which the intermediary is compensated in connection with offerings and sales of securities in reliance on section 4(a)(6) of the Securities Act.

Rule 303 – Requirements with respect to transactions

a.   **Issuer information**. An intermediary in a transaction involving the offer or sale of securities in reliance on section 4(a)(6) of the Securities Act must make available to the Commission and to investors any information required to be provided by the issuer of the securities under Rules 201 and 203(a).

1.   This information must be made publicly available on the intermediary's platform, in a manner that reasonably permits a person accessing the platform to save, download, or otherwise store the information;

2.   This information must be made publicly available on the intermediary's platform for a minimum of 21 days before any securities are sold in the offering, during which time the intermediary may accept investment commitments;

3.   This information, including any additional information provided by the issuer, must remain publicly available on the intermediary's platform until the offer and sale of securities in reliance on section 4(a)(6) of the Securities Act is completed or cancelled; and

4.   An intermediary may not require any person to establish an account with the intermediary to access this information.

b.   **Investor qualification.** Each time before accepting any investment commitment (including any additional investment commitment from the same person), an intermediary must:

1.   Have a reasonable basis for believing that the investor satisfies the investment limitations established by section 4(a)(6)(B) of the Act and this part. An intermediary may rely on an investor's representations concerning compliance with the investment limitation requirements concerning the investor's annual income, net worth, and the amount of the investor's other investments made pursuant to section 4(a)(6) of the Securities Act unless the intermediary has reason to question the reliability of the representation.

2.   Obtain from the investor:

     i.   A representation that the investor has reviewed the intermediary's educational materials delivered pursuant to Rule 302(b), understands that the entire amount of his or her investment may be lost, and is in a financial condition to bear the loss of the investment; and

     ii.   A questionnaire completed by the investor demonstrating the investor's understanding that:

        A.   There are restrictions on the investor's ability to cancel an investment commitment and obtain a return of his or her investment;

        B.   It may be difficult for the investor to resell securities acquired in reliance on section 4(a)(6) of the Securities Act; and

        C.   Investing in securities offered and sold in reliance on section 4(a)(6) of the Securities Act involves risk, and the investor should not invest any funds in an offering made in reliance on section 4(a)(6) of the Securities Act unless he or she can afford to lose the entire amount of his or her investment.

c.   **Communication channels.** An intermediary must provide on its platform communication channels by which persons can communicate with one another and with representatives of the issuer about offerings made available on the intermediary's platform, provided:

1.   If the intermediary is a funding portal, it does not participate in these communications other than to establish guidelines for communication and remove abusive or potentially fraudulent communications;

2. The intermediary permits public access to view the discussions made in the communication channels;

3. The intermediary restricts posting of comments in the communication channels to those persons who have opened an account with the intermediary on its platform; and

4. The intermediary requires that any person posting a comment in the communication channels clearly and prominently disclose with each posting whether he or she is a founder or an employee of an issuer engaging in promotional activities on behalf of the issuer, or is otherwise compensated, whether in the past or prospectively, to promote the issuer's offering.

d. **Notice of investment commitment.** An intermediary must promptly, upon receipt of an investment commitment from an investor, give or send to the investor a notification disclosing:

1. The dollar amount of the investment commitment;
2. The price of the securities, if known;
3. The name of the issuer; and
4. The date and time by which the investor may cancel the investment commitment.

e. **Maintenance and transmission of funds.**

1. An intermediary that is a registered broker must comply with the requirements of Rule 15c2-4.

2. An intermediary that is a funding portal must direct investors to transmit the money or other consideration directly to a qualified third party that has agreed in writing to hold the funds for the benefit of, and to promptly transmit or return the funds to, the persons entitled thereto in accordance with paragraph (e)(3) of this section. For purposes of this subpart C (Rules 300 through 305), a qualified third party means a:

   i. Registered broker or dealer that carries customer or broker or dealer accounts and holds funds or securities for those persons; or

   ii. Bank or credit union (where such credit union is insured by National Credit Union Administration) that has agreed in writing either to hold the funds in escrow for the persons who have the beneficial interests therein and to transmit or return such funds directly to the persons entitled thereto when so directed by the funding portal as described in paragraph (e)(3) of this section, or to maintain a bank or credit union account (or accounts) for the exclusive benefit of investors and the issuer.

3. A funding portal that is an intermediary in a transaction involving the offer or sale of securities in reliance on section 4(a)(6) of the Securities Act shall promptly direct the qualified third party to:

   i. Transmit funds from the qualified third party to the issuer when the aggregate amount of investment commitments from all investors is equal to or greater than the target amount of the offering and the cancellation period as set forth in Rule 304 has elapsed, *provided that* in no event may the funding portal direct this transmission of funds earlier than 21 days after the date on which the intermediary makes publicly available on its platform the information required to be provided by the issuer under Rules 201 and 203(a);

    ii. Return funds to an investor when an investment commitment has been cancelled in accordance with Rule 304 (including for failure to obtain effective reconfirmation as required under Rule 304(c)); and

    iii. Return funds to investors when an issuer does not complete the offering.

  f. **Confirmation of transaction**.

    1. An intermediary must, at or before the completion of a transaction in a security in reliance on section 4(a)(6) of the Securities Act, give or send to each investor a notification disclosing:

      i. The date of the transaction;

      ii. The type of security that the investor is purchasing;

      iii. The identity, price, and number of securities purchased by the investor, as well as the number of securities sold by the issuer in the transaction and the price(s) at which the securities were sold;

      iv. If a debt security, the interest rate and the yield to maturity calculated from the price paid and the maturity date;

      v. If a callable security, the first date that the security can be called by the issuer; and

      vi. The source, form and amount of any remuneration received or to be received by the intermediary in connection with the transaction, including any remuneration received or to be received by the intermediary from persons other than the issuer.

    2. An intermediary satisfying the requirements of paragraph (f)(1) of this section is exempt from the requirements of Rule 10b-10 of this chapter with respect to a transaction in a security offered and sold in reliance on section 4(a)(6) of the Securities Act .

Rule 304 – Completion of offerings, cancellations and reconfirmations

  a. **Generally**. An investor may cancel an investment commitment for any reason until 48 hours prior to the deadline identified in the issuer's offering materials. During the 48 hours prior to such deadline, an investment commitment may not be cancelled except as provided in paragraph (c) of this section.

  b. **Early completion of offering**. If an issuer reaches the target offering amount prior to the deadline identified in its offering materials pursuant to Rule 201(g), the issuer mayclose the offering on a date earlier than the deadline identified in its offering materials pursuant to Rule 201(g), *provided that:*

    1. The offering remains open for a minimum of 21 days pursuant to Rule 303(a);

    2. The intermediary provides notice to any potential investors, and gives or sends notice to investors that have made investment commitments in the offering, of:

      i. The new, anticipated deadline of the offering;

      ii. The right of investors to cancel investment commitments for any reason until 48 hours prior to the new offering deadline; and

      iii. Whether the issuer will continue to accept investment commitments during the 48-hour period prior to the new offering deadline.

3.   The new offering deadline is scheduled for and occurs at least five business days after the notice required in paragraph (b)(2) of this section is provided; and

4.   At the time of the new offering deadline, the issuer continues to meet or exceed the target offering amount.

c.   **Cancellations and reconfirmations based on material changes**.
1.   If there is a material change to the terms of an offering or to the information provided by the issuer, the intermediary must give or send to any investor who has made an investment commitment notice of the material change and that the investor's investment commitment will be cancelled unless the investor reconfirms his or her investment commitment within five business days of receipt of the notice. If the investor fails to reconfirm his or her investment within those five business days, the intermediary within five business days thereafter must:
   i.   Give or send the investor a notification disclosing that the commitment was cancelled, the reason for the cancellation and the refund amount that the investor is expected to receive; and
   ii.   Direct the refund of investor funds.
2.   If material changes to the offering or to the information provided by the issuer regarding the offering occur within five business days of the maximum number of days that an offering is to remain open, the offering must be extended to allow for a period of five business days for the investor to reconfirm his or her investment.

d.   **Return of funds if offering is not completed**. If an issuer does not complete an offering, an intermediary must within five business days:
1.   Give or send each investor a notification of the cancellation, disclosing the reason for the cancellation, and the refund amount that the investor is expected to receive;
2.   Direct the refund of investor funds; and
3.   Prevent investors from making investment commitments with respect to that offering on its platform.

Rule 305 – Payments to third parties

a.   **Prohibition on payments for personally identifiable information**. An intermediary may not compensate any person for providing the intermediary with the personally identifiable information of any investor or potential investor in securities offered and sold in reliance on section 4(a)(6) of the Securities Act .

b.   For purposes of this rule, personally identifiable information means information that can be used to distinguish or trace an individual's identity, either alone or when combined with other personal or identifying information that is linked or linkable to a specific individual.

***

Rule 501 – Restrictions on resales

    a.   Securities issued in a transaction exempt from registration pursuant to section 4(a)(6) of the Securities Act and in accordance with section 4A of the Securities Act and this part may not be transferred by any purchaser of such securities during the one-year period beginning when the securities were issued in a transaction exempt from registration pursuant to section 4(a)(6) of the Securities Act, unless such securities are transferred:

        1.   To the issuer of the securities;

        2.   To an accredited investor;

        3.   As part of an offering registered with the Commission; or

        4.   To a member of the family of the purchaser or the equivalent, to a trust controlled by the purchaser, to a trust created for the benefit of a member of the family of the purchaser or the equivalent, or in connection with the death or divorce of the purchaser or other similar circumstance.

    b.   For purposes of this Rule 501, the term *accredited investor* shall mean any person who comes within any of the categories set forth in Rule 501(a) of this chapter, or who the seller reasonably believes comes within any of such categories, at the time of the sale of the securities to that person.

    c.   For purposes of this section, the term *member of the family of the purchaser or the equivalent* includes a child, stepchild, grandchild, parent, stepparent, grandparent, spouse or spousal equivalent, sibling, mother-in-law, father-in-law, son-in-law, daughter-in-law, brother-in-law, or sister-in-law of the purchaser, and shall include adoptive relationships. For purposes of this paragraph (c), the term *spousal equivalent* means a cohabitant occupying a relationship generally equivalent to that of a spouse.

Rule 502 –Insignificant deviations from a term, condition or requirement of this part (Regulation Crowdfunding)

    a.   A failure to comply with a term, condition, or requirement of this part will not result in the loss of the exemption from the requirements of Section 5 of the Securities Act for any offer or sale to a particular individual or entity, if the issuer relying on the exemption shows:

        1.   The failure to comply was insignificant with respect to the offering as a whole;

        2.   The issuer made a good faith and reasonable attempt to comply with all applicable terms, conditions and requirements of this part; and

        3.   The issuer did not know of such failure where the failure to comply with a term, condition or requirement of this part was the result of the failure of the intermediary to comply with the requirements of section 4A(a) of the Securities Act and the related rules, or such failure by the intermediary occurred solely in offerings other than the issuer's offering.

    b.   Paragraph (a) of this section shall not preclude the Commission from bringing an enforcement action seeking any appropriate relief for an issuer's failure to comply with all applicable terms, conditions and requirements of this part.

Rule 503 – Disqualification provisions

a. **Disqualification events.** No exemption under section 4(a)(6) of the Securities Act shall be available for a sale of securities if the issuer; any predecessor of the issuer; any affiliated issuer; any director, officer, general partner or managing member of the issuer; any beneficial owner of 20 percent or more of the issuer's outstanding voting equity securities, calculated on the basis of voting power; any promoter connected with the issuer in any capacity at the time of filing, any offer after filing, or such sale; any person that has been or will be paid (directly or indirectly) remuneration for solicitation of purchasers in connection with such sale of securities; or any general partner, director, officer or managing member of any such solicitor:

1. Has been convicted, within 10 years before the filing of the offering statement or such sale (or five years, in the case of issuers, their predecessors and affiliated issuers), of any felony or misdemeanor:

    i. In connection with the purchase or sale of any security;

    ii. Involving the making of any false filing with the Commission; or

    iii. Arising out of the conduct of the business of an underwriter, broker, dealer, municipal securities dealer, investment adviser, funding portal or paid solicitor of purchasers of securities;

2. Is subject to any order, judgment or decree of any court of competent jurisdiction, entered within five years before the filing of the information required by section 4A(b) of the Securities Act or such sale that, at the time of such filing or sale, restrains or enjoins such person from engaging or continuing to engage in any conduct or practice:

    i. In connection with the purchase or sale of any security;

    ii. Involving the making of any false filing with the Commission; or

    iii. Arising out of the conduct of the business of an underwriter, broker, dealer, municipal securities dealer, investment adviser, funding portal or paid solicitor of purchasers of securities;

3. Is subject to a final order of a State securities commission (or an agency or officer of a State performing like functions); a State authority that supervises or examines banks, savings associations or credit unions; a State insurance commission (or an agency or officer of a state performing like functions); an appropriate Federal banking agency; the U.S. Commodity Futures Trading Commission; or the National Credit Union Administration that:

    i. At the time of the filing of the information required by section 4A(b) of the Securities Act or such sale, bars the person from:

        A. Association with an entity regulated by such commission, authority, agency or officer;

        B. Engaging in the business of securities, insurance or banking; or

        C. Engaging in savings association or credit union activities; or

    ii. Constitutes a final order based on a violation of any law or regulation that prohibits fraudulent, manipulative or deceptive conduct entered within ten years before such filing of the offering statement or such sale;

    Instruction to paragraph (a)(3). *Final order* shall mean a written directive or declaratory statement issued by a Federal or State agency, described in this paragraph (a)(3), under applicable statutory authority that provides for notice and an opportunity for hearing, which constitutes a final disposition or action by that Federal or State agency.

4.   Is subject to an order of the Commission entered pursuant to section 15(b) or 15B(c) of the Exchange Act or section 203(e) or (f) of the Investment Advisers Act of 1940 that, at the time of the filing of the information required by section 4A(b) of the Securities Act or such sale:

    i.   Suspends or revokes such person's registration as a broker, dealer, municipal securities dealer, investment adviser or funding portal;

    ii.   Places limitations on the activities, functions or operations of such person; or

    iii.   Bars such person from being associated with any entity or from participating in the offering of any penny stock;

5.   Is subject to any order of the Commission entered within five years before the filing of the information required by section 4A(b) of the Securities Act or such sale that, at the time of such filing or sale, orders the person to cease and desist from committing or causing a violation or future violation of:

    i.   Any scienter-based anti-fraud provision of the Federal securities laws, including without limitation section 17(a)(1) of the Securities Act, section 10(b) of the Exchange Act and Rule 10b-5, section 15(c)(1) of the Exchange Act and section 206(1) of the Investment Advisers Act of 1940 or any other rule or regulation thereunder; or

    ii.   Section 5 of the Securities Act (15 U.S.C. 77e);

6.   Is suspended or expelled from membership in, or suspended or barred from association with a member of, a registered national securities exchange or a registered national or affiliated securities association for any act or omission to act constituting conduct inconsistent with just and equitable principles of trade;

7.   Has filed (as a registrant or issuer), or was or was named as an underwriter in, any registration statement or Regulation A offering statement filed with the Commission that, within five years before the filing of the information required by section 4A(b) of the Securities Act or such sale, was the subject of a refusal order, stop order, or order suspending the Regulation A exemption, or is, at the time of such filing or sale, the subject of an investigation or proceeding to determine whether a stop order or suspension order should be issued; or

8.   Is subject to a United States Postal Service false representation order entered within five years before the filing of the information required by section 4A(b) of the Securities Act or such sale, or is, at the time of such filing or sale, subject to a temporary restraining order or preliminary injunction with respect to conduct alleged by the United States Postal Service to constitute a scheme or device for obtaining money or property through the mail by means of false representations.

Instruction to paragraph (a): With respect to any beneficial owner of 20 percent or more of the issuer's outstanding voting equity securities, calculated on the basis of voting power, the issuer is required to determine whether a disqualifying event has occurred only as of the time of filing of the offering statement and not from the time of such sale.

b.   **Transition, waivers, reasonable care exception.** Paragraph (a) of this section shall not apply:

1.   With respect to any conviction, order, judgment, decree, suspension, expulsion or bar that occurred or was issued before May 16, 2016;

2. Upon a showing of good cause and without prejudice to any other action by the Commission, if the Commission determines that it is not necessary under the circumstances that an exemption be denied;

3. If, before the filing of the information required by section 4A(b) of the Securities Act or such sale, the court or regulatory authority that entered the relevant order, judgment or decree advises in writing (whether contained in the relevant judgment, order or decree or separately to the Commission or its staff) that disqualification under paragraph (a) of this section should not arise as a consequence of such order, judgment or decree; or

4. If the issuer establishes that it did not know and, in the exercise of reasonable care, could not have known that a disqualification existed under paragraph (a) of this section.

Instruction to paragraph (b)(4). An issuer will not be able to establish that it has exercised reasonable care unless it has made, in light of the circumstances, factual inquiry into whether any disqualifications exist. The nature and scope of the factual inquiry will vary based on the facts and circumstances concerning, among other things, the issuer and the other offering participants.

c. **Affiliated issuers.** For purposes of paragraph (a) of this section, events relating to any affiliated issuer that occurred before the affiliation arose will be not considered disqualifying if the affiliated entity is not:

1. In control of the issuer; or

2. Under common control with the issuer by a third party that was in control of the affiliated entity at the time of such events.

d. **Intermediaries.** A person that is subject to a statutory disqualification as defined in section 3(a)(39) of the Exchange Act may not act as, or be an associated person of, an intermediary in a transaction involving the offer or sale of securities in reliance on section 4(a)(6) of the Securities Act unless so permitted pursuant to Commission rule or order.

Instruction to paragraph (d). Rule 17f-2 of this chapter generally requires the fingerprinting of every person who is a partner, director, officer or employee of a broker, subject to certain exceptions.

Rule 504 – Definition of "qualified purchaser"

For purposes of section 18(b)(3) of the Securities Act, a "qualified purchaser" means any person to whom securities are offered or sold pursuant to an offering under Regulation Crowdfunding.

Regulation D

Rule 500 – Use of Regulation D

Users of Regulation D should note the following:

a. Regulation D relates to transactions exempted from the registration requirements of section 5 of the Securities Act of 1933 (the Act). Such transactions are not exempt from the antifraud, civil liability, or other provisions of the federal securities laws. Issuers are reminded of their obligation to provide such further material information, if any, as may be necessary to make the information required under Regulation D, in light of the circumstances under which it is furnished, not misleading.

b. Nothing in Regulation D obviates the need to comply with any applicable state law relating to the offer and sale of securities. Regulation D is intended to be a basic element in a uniform system of federal-state limited offering exemptions consistent with the provisions of sections 18 and 19(c) of the Act. In those states that have adopted Regulation D, or any version of Regulation D, special attention should be directed to the applicable state laws and regulations, including those relating to registration of persons who receive remuneration in connection with the offer and sale of securities, to disqualification of issuers and other persons associated with offerings based on state administrative orders or judgments, and to requirements for filings of notices of sales.

c. Attempted compliance with any rule in Regulation D does not act as an exclusive election; the issuer can also claim the availability of any other applicable exemption. For instance, an issuer's failure to satisfy all the terms and conditions of rule 506(b) shall not raise any presumption that the exemption provided by section 4(a)(2) of the Act is not available.

d. Regulation D is available only to the issuer of the securities and not to any affiliate of that issuer or to any other person for resales of the issuer's securities. Regulation D provides an exemption only for the transactions in which the securities are offered or sold by the issuer, not for the securities themselves.

e. Regulation D may be used for business combinations that involve sales by virtue of rule 145(a) or otherwise.

f. In view of the objectives of Regulation D and the policies underlying the Act, Regulation D is not available to any issuer for any transaction or chain of transactions that, although in technical compliance with Regulation D, is part of a plan or scheme to evade the registration provisions of the Act. In such cases, registration under the Act is required.

g. Securities offered and sold outside the United States in accordance with Regulation S need not be registered under the Act. Regulation S may be relied upon for such offers and sales even if coincident offers and sales are made in accordance with Regulation D inside the United States. Thus, for example, persons who are offered and sold securities in accordance with Regulation S would not be counted in the calculation of the number of purchasers under Regulation D. Similarly, proceeds from such sales would not be included in the aggregate offering price. The provisions of this paragraph (g), however, do not apply if the issuer elects to rely solely on Regulation D for offers or sales to persons made outside the United States.

Rule 501 – Definitions and Terms Used in Regulation D

As used in Regulation D, the following terms shall have the meaning indicated:

a. **Accredited investor.** *Accredited investor* shall mean any person who comes within any of the following categories, or who the issuer reasonably believes comes within any of the following categories, at the time of the sale of the securities to that person:

1. Any bank as defined in section 3(a)(2) of the Act, or any savings and loan association or other institution as defined in section 3(a)(5)(A) of the Act whether acting in its individual or fiduciary capacity; any broker or dealer registered pursuant to section 15 of the Securities Exchange Act of 1934; any investment adviser registered pursuant to section 203 of the Investment Advisers Act of 1940 or registered pursuant to the laws of a state; any investment adviser relying on the exemption from registering with the Commission under section 203(l) or (m) of the Investment Advisers Act of 1940; any insurance company as defined in section 2(a)(13) of the Act; any investment company registered under the Investment Company Act of 1940 or a business development company as defined in section 2(a)(48) of that act; any Small Business Investment Company licensed by the U.S. Small Business Administration under section 301(c) or (d) of the Small Business Investment Act of 1958; any Rural Business Investment Company as defined in section 384A of the Consolidated Farm and Rural Development Act; any plan established and maintained by a state, its political subdivisions, or any agency or instrumentality of a state or its political subdivisions, for the benefit of its employees, if such plan has total assets in excess of $5,000,000; any employee benefit plan within the meaning of the Employee Retirement Income Security Act of 1974 if the investment decision is made by a plan fiduciary, as defined in section 3(21) of such act, which is either a bank, savings and loan association, insurance company, or registered investment adviser, or if the employee benefit plan has total assets in excess of $5,000,000 or, if a self-directed plan, with investment decisions made solely by persons that are accredited investors;

2. Any private business development company as defined in section 202(a)(22) of the Investment Advisers Act of 1940;

3. Any organization described in section 501(c)(3) of the Internal Revenue Code, corporation, Massachusetts or similar business trust, partnership, or limited liability company, not formed for the specific purpose of acquiring the securities offered, with total assets in excess of $5,000,000;

4. Any director, executive officer, or general partner of the issuer of the securities being offered or sold, or any director, executive officer, or general partner of a general partner of that issuer;

5. Any natural person whose individual net worth, or joint net worth with that person's spouse or spousal equivalent, at the time of his purchase exceeds $1,000,000;

   i. Except as provided in paragraph (a)(5)(ii) of this section, for purposes of calculating net worth under this paragraph (a)(5):

      A. The person's primary residence shall not be included as an asset;

      B. Indebtedness that is secured by the person's primary residence, up to the estimated fair market value of the primary residence at the time of the sale of securities, shall not be included as a liability (except that if the amount of such indebtedness outstanding at the time of sale of securities exceeds the amount outstanding 60 days before such time, other than as a result of the acquisition of the primary residence, the amount of such excess shall be included as a liability); and

C. Indebtedness that is secured by the person's primary residence in excess of the estimated fair market value of the primary residence at the time of the sale of securities shall be included as a liability;

Note 1 to paragraph (a)(5): For the purposes of calculating joint net worth in this paragraph (a)(5): joint net worth can be the aggregate net worth of the investor and spouse or spousal equivalent; assets need not be held jointly to be included in the calculation. Reliance on the joint net worth standard of this paragraph (a)(5) does not require that the securities be purchased jointly.

ii. Paragraph (a)(5)(i) of this section will not apply to any calculation of a person's net worth made in connection with a purchase of securities in accordance with a right to purchase such securities, provided that:

A. Such right was held by the person on July 20, 2010;

B. The person qualified as an accredited investor on the basis of net worth at the time the person acquired such right; and

C. The person held securities of the same issuer, other than such right, on July 20, 2010.

6. Any natural person who had an individual income in excess of $200,000 in each of the two most recent years or joint income with that person's spouse or spousal equivalent in excess of $300,000 in each of those years and has a reasonable expectation of reaching the same income level in the current year;

7. Any trust, with total assets in excess of $5,000,000, not formed for the specific purpose of acquiring the securities offered, whose purchase is directed by a sophisticated person as described in Rule 506(b)(2)(ii) and

8. Any entity in which all of the equity owners are accredited investors.

Note 1 to paragraph (a)(8): It is permissible to look through various forms of equity ownership to natural persons in determining the accredited investor status of entities under this paragraph (a)(8). If those natural persons are themselves accredited investors, and if all other equity owners of the entity seeking accredited investor status are accredited investors, then this paragraph (a)(8) may be available.

9. Any entity, of a type not listed in paragraphs (a)(1), (a)(2), (a)(3), (a)(7), or (a)(8), not formed for the specific purpose of acquiring the securities offered, owning investments in excess of $5,000,000;

Note 1 to paragraph (a)(9): For the purposes of this paragraph (a)(9), "investments" is defined in rule 2a51-1(b) under the Investment Company Act of 1940.

10. Any natural person holding in good standing one or more professional certifications or designations or credentials from an accredited educational institution that the Commission has designated as qualifying an individual for accredited investor status. In determining whether to designate a professional certification or designation or credential from an accredited educational

institution for purposes of this paragraph (a)(10), the Commission will consider, among others, the following attributes:

   i. The certification, designation, or credential arises out of an examination or series of examinations administered by a self-regulatory organization or other industry body or is issued by an accredited educational institution;

   ii. The examination or series of examinations is designed to reliably and validly demonstrate an individual's comprehension and sophistication in the areas of securities and investing;

   iii. Persons obtaining such certification, designation, or credential can reasonably be expected to have sufficient knowledge and experience in financial and business matters to evaluate the merits and risks of a prospective investment; and

   iv. An indication that an individual holds the certification or designation is either made publicly available by the relevant self-regulatory organization or other industry body or is otherwise independently verifiable;

Note 1 to paragraph (a)(10): The Commission will designate professional certifications or designations or credentials for purposes of this paragraph (a)(10), by order, after notice and an opportunity for public comment. The professional certifications or designations or credentials currently recognized by the Commission as satisfying the above criteria will be posted on the Commission's website.

11. Any natural person who is a "knowledgeable employee," as defined in rule 3c-5(a)(4) under the Investment Company Act of 1940, of the issuer of the securities being offered or sold where the issuer would be an investment company, as defined in section 3 of such act, but for the exclusion provided by either section 3(c)(1) or section 3(c)(7) of such act;

12. Any "family office," as defined in rule 202(a)(11)(G)-1 under the Investment Advisers Act of 1940:

   i. With assets under management in excess of $5,000,000,

   ii. That is not formed for the specific purpose of acquiring the securities offered, and

   iii. Whose prospective investment is directed by a person who has such knowledge and experience in financial and business matters that such family office is capable of evaluating the merits and risks of the prospective investment; and

13. Any "family client," as defined in rule 202(a)(11)(G)-1 under the Investment Advisers Act of 1940, of a family office meeting the requirements in paragraph (a)(12) of this section and whose prospective investment in the issuer is directed by such family office pursuant to paragraph (a)(12)(iii).

b. **Affiliate**. An *affiliate* of, or person *affiliated* with, a specified person shall mean a person that directly, or indirectly through one or more intermediaries, controls or is controlled by, or is under common control with, the person specified.

c. **Aggregate offering price**. *Aggregate offering price* shall mean the sum of all cash, services, property, notes, cancellation of debt, or other consideration to be received by an issuer for issuance of its securities. Where securities are being offered for both cash and non-cash consideration, the aggregate offering price shall be based on the price at which the securities are offered for cash. Any portion of the aggregate offering price attributable to cash received in a foreign currency shall be translated into United States currency at the currency exchange rate in effect at a reasonable time prior to or on the date of the sale of the securities. If securities are not offered for cash, the aggregate offering price shall be based on the value of the consideration as established by bona fide sales of that consideration made within a reasonable time, or, in the absence of sales, on the fair value as determined by an accepted standard. Such valuations of non-cash consideration must be reasonable at the time made.

d.   **Business combination**. *Business combination* shall mean any transaction of the type specified in paragraph (a) of Rule 145 under the Act and any transaction involving the acquisition by one issuer, in exchange for all or a part of its own or its parent's stock, of stock of another issuer if, immediately after the acquisition, the acquiring issuer has control of the other issuer (whether or not it had control before the acquisition).

e.   **Calculation of number of purchasers**. For purposes of calculating the number of purchasers under Rule 506(b) only, the following shall apply:
1.   The following purchasers shall be excluded:
    i.   Any relative, spouse or relative of the spouse of a purchaser who has the same primary residence as the purchaser;
    ii. Any trust or estate in which a purchaser and any of the persons related to him as specified in paragraph (e)(1)(i) or (e)(1)(iii) of this section collectively have more than 50 percent of the beneficial interest (excluding contingent interests);
    iii. Any corporation or other organization of which a purchaser and any of the persons related to him as specified in paragraph (e)(1)(i) or (e)(1)(ii) of this section collectively are beneficial owners of more than 50 percent of the equity securities (excluding directors' qualifying shares) or equity interests; and
    iv. Any accredited investor.
2.   A corporation, partnership or other entity shall be counted as one purchaser. If, however, that entity is organized for the specific purpose of acquiring the securities offered and is not an accredited investor under paragraph (a)(8) of this section, then each beneficial owner of equity securities or equity interests in the entity shall count as a separate purchaser for all provisions of Regulation D, except to the extent provided in paragraph (e)(1) of this section.
3.   A non-contributory employee benefit plan within the meaning of Title I of the Employee Retirement Income Security Act of 1974 shall be counted as one purchaser where the trustee makes all investment decisions for the plan.

f.   **Executive officer**. *Executive officer* shall mean the president, any vice president in charge of a principal business unit, division or function (such as sales, administration or finance), any other officer who performs a policy making function, or any other person who performs similar policy making functions for the issuer. Executive officers of subsidiaries may be deemed executive officers of the issuer if they perform such policy making functions for the issuer.

g. **Final order**. Final order shall mean a written directive or declaratory statement issued by a federal or state agency described in Rule 506(d)(1)(iii) under applicable statutory authority that provides for notice and an opportunity for hearing, , which constitutes a final disposition or action by that federal or state agency.

h. **Issuer**. The definition of the term *issuer* in section 2(a)(4) of the Act shall apply, except that in the case of a proceeding under the Federal Bankruptcy Code, the trustee or debtor in possession shall be considered the issuer in an offering under a plan or reorganization, if the securities are to be issued under the plan.

i. **Purchaser representative**. *Purchaser representative* shall mean any person who satisfies all of the following conditions or who the issuer reasonably believes satisfies all of the following conditions:

1. Is not an affiliate, director, officer or other employee of the issuer, or beneficial owner of 10 percent or more of any class of the equity securities or 10 percent or more of the equity interest in the issuer, except where the purchaser is:

    i. A relative of the purchaser representative by blood, marriage or adoption and not more remote than a first cousin;
    A trust or estate in which the purchaser representative and any persons related to him as specified in paragraph (h)(1)(i) or (h)1(iii) of this section collectively have more than 50 percent of the beneficial interest (excluding contingent interest) or of which the purchaser representative serves as trustee, executor, or in any similar capacity; or

    ii. A corporation or other organization of which the purchaser representative and any persons related to him as specified in paragraph (h)(1)(i) or (h)(1)(ii) of this section collectively are the beneficial owners of more than 50 percent of the equity securities (excluding directors' qualifying shares) or equity interests;

2. Has such knowledge and experience in financial and business matters that he is capable of evaluating, alone, or together with other purchaser representatives of the purchaser, or together with the purchaser, the merits and risks of the prospective investment;

3. Is acknowledged by the purchaser in writing, during the course of the transaction, to be his purchaser representative in connection with evaluating the merits and risks of the prospective investment; and

4. Discloses to the purchaser in writing a reasonable time prior to the sale of securities to that purchaser any material relationship between himself or his affiliates and the issuer or its affiliates that then exists, that is mutually understood to be contemplated, or that has existed at any time during the previous two years, and any compensation received or to be received as a result of such relationship.

j. **Spousal equivalent.** The term *spousal equivalent* shall mean a cohabitant occupying a relationship generally equivalent to that of a spouse.

Note 1 to Rule 501: A person acting as a purchaser representative should consider the applicability of the registration and antifraud provisions relating to brokers and dealers under the Securities Exchange Act of 1934 (*Exchange Act*) and relating to investment advisers under the Investment Advisers Act of 1940.

Note 2 to Rule 501: The acknowledgment required by paragraph [(i)](3) and the disclosure required by paragraph [(i)](4) of this section must be made with specific reference to each prospective investment. Advance blanket acknowledgment, such as for *all securities transactions* or *all private placements,* is not sufficient.

Note 3 to Rule 501: Disclosure of any material relationships between the purchaser representative or his affiliates and the issuer or its affiliates does not relieve the purchaser representative of his obligation to act in the interest of the purchaser.

Rule 502 – General Conditions to Be Met

The following conditions shall be applicable to offers and sales made under Regulation D:

a. **Integration.** To determine whether offers and sales should be integrated, see Rule 152.

b. **Information Requirements-**
   1. When information must be furnished. If the issuer sells securities under Rule 506(b) to any purchaser that is not an accredited investor, the issuer shall furnish the information specified in paragraph (b)(2) of this section to such purchaser a reasonable time prior to sale. The issuer is not required to furnish the specified information to purchasers when it sells securities under Rule 504, or to any accredited investor.

      Note: When an issuer provides information to investors pursuant to paragraph (b)(1), it should consider providing such information to accredited investors as well, in view of the anti-fraud provisions of the federal securities laws.

   2. Type of information to be furnished.
      i. If the issuer is not subject to the reporting requirements of section 13 or 15(d) of the Exchange Act, at a reasonable time prior to the sale of securities the issuer shall furnish to the purchaser, to the extent material to an understanding of the issuer, its business and the securities being offered:
         A. Non-financial statement information. If the issuer is eligible to use Regulation A, the same kind of information as would be required in Part II of Form 1-A. If the issuer is not eligible to use Regulation A, the same kind of information as required in Part I of a registration statement filed under the Securities Act on the form that the issuer would be entitled to use.
         B. Financial statement information.
            1. Offerings up to $20,000,000. The financial statement information required by paragraph (b) of Part F/S of Form 1-A. Such financial statement information must be prepared in accordance with generally accepted accounting principles in the United States (US GAAP). If the issuer is a foreign private issuer, such financial statements must be prepared in accordance with either US GAAP or International Financial Reporting Standards (IFRS) as issued by the International Accounting Standards Board (IASB). If the financial statements comply with

IFRS, such compliance must be explicitly and unreservedly stated in the notes to the financial statements and if the financial statements are audited, the auditor's report must include an opinion on whether the financial statements comply with IFRS as issued by the IASB.

2. Offerings over $20,000,000. The financial statement information required by paragraph (c) of Part F/S of Form 1-A (referenced in § 239.90 of this chapter). If the issuer is a foreign private issuer, such financial statements must be prepared in accordance with either US GAAP or IFRS as issued by the IASB. If the financial statements comply with IFRS, such compliance must be explicitly and unreservedly stated in the notes to the financial statements and the auditor's report must include an opinion on whether the financial statements comply with IFRS as issued by the IASB.

C. If the issuer is a foreign private issuer eligible to use Form 20-F, the issuer shall disclose the same kind of information required to be included in a registration statement filed under the Act on the form that the issuer would be entitled to use. The financial statements need be certified only to the extent required by paragraph (b)2(i) (B) (*1*), (*2*) or (*3*) of this section, as appropriate.

ii. If the issuer is subject to the reporting requirements of section 13 or 15(d) of the Exchange Act, at a reasonable time prior to the sale of securities the issuer shall furnish to the purchaser the information specified in paragraph (b)2(ii)(A) or (B) of this section, and in either event the information specified in paragraph (b)(2)(ii)(C) of this section:

A. The issuer's annual report to shareholders for the most recent fiscal year, if such annual report meets the requirements of Rule 14a-3 or Rule14c-3 under the Exchange Act, the definitive proxy statement filed in connection with that annual report, and, if requested by the purchaser in writing, a copy of the issuer's most recent Form 10-K under the Exchange Act.

B. The information contained in an annual report on Form 10-K under the Exchange Act or in a registration statement on Form S-1 or S-11 under the Act or on Form 10 under the Exchange Act, whichever filing is the most recent required to be filed.

C. The information contained in any reports or documents required to be filed by the issuer under sections 13(a), 14(a), 14(c), and 15(d) of the Exchange Act since the distribution or filing of the report or registration statement specified in paragraphs (b)2(ii) (A) or (B), and a brief description of the securities being offered, the use of the proceeds from the offering, and any material changes in the issuer's affairs that are not disclosed in the documents furnished.

D. If the issuer is a foreign private issuer, the issuer may provide in lieu of the information specified in paragraph (b)2(ii) (A) or (B) of this section, the information contained in its most recent filing on Form 20-F or Form F-1.

iii. Exhibits required to be filed with the Commission as part of a registration statement or report, other than an annual report to shareholders or parts of that report incorporated by reference in a Form 10-K report, need not be furnished to each purchaser that is not an accredited investor if the contents of material exhibits are identified and such exhibits are made available to a purchaser, upon his written request, a reasonable time prior to his purchase.

iv. At a reasonable time prior to the sale of securities to any purchaser that is not an accredited investor in a transaction under Rule 506(b), the issuer shall furnish to the purchaser a brief description in writing of any material written information concerning the offering that has been provided by the issuer to any accredited investor but not previously delivered to such unaccredited purchaser. The issuer shall furnish any portion or all of this information to the purchaser, upon his written request a reasonable time prior to his purchase.

v. The issuer shall also make available to each purchaser at a reasonable time prior to his purchase of securities in a transaction under Rule 506 the opportunity to ask questions and receive answers concerning the terms and conditions of the offering and to obtain any additional information which the issuer possesses or can acquire without unreasonable effort or expense that is necessary to verify the accuracy of information furnished under paragraph (b)2(i) or (ii) of this section.

vi. For business combinations or exchange offers, in addition to information required by Form S-4, the issuer shall provide to each purchaser at the time the plan is submitted to security holders, or, with an exchange, during the course of the transaction and prior to sale, written information about any terms or arrangements of the proposed transactions that are materially different from those for all other security holders. For purposes of this subsection, an issuer which is not subject to the reporting requirements of section 13 or 15(d) of the Exchange Act may satisfy the requirements of Part I.B. or C. of Form S-4 by compliance with paragraph (b)(2)(i) of this Rule 502.

vii. At a reasonable time prior to the sale of securities to any purchaser that is not an accredited investor in a transaction under Rule 506(b), the issuer shall advise the purchaser of the limitations on resale in the manner contained in paragraph (d)(2) of this section. Such disclosure may be contained in other materials required to be provided by this paragraph.

viii. At a reasonable time prior to the sale of securities to any purchaser that is not an accredited investor in a transaction under Rule 506(b), the issuer shall provide the purchaser with any written communication or broadcast script used under the authorization of Rule 241 within 30 days prior to such sale.

c. **Limitation on Manner of Offering.** Except as provided in Rule 504(b)(1) or Rule 506(c), neither the issuer nor any person acting on its behalf shall offer or sell the securities by any form of general solicitation or general advertising, including, but not limited to, the following:

1. Any advertisement, article, notice or other communication published in any newspaper, magazine, or similar media or broadcast over television or radio; and
2. Any seminar or meeting whose attendees have been invited by any general solicitation or general advertising;

   Provided, however, that publication by an issuer of a notice in accordance with Rule 135c or filing with the Commission by an issuer of a notice of sales on Form D in which the issuer has made a good faith and reasonable attempt to comply with the requirements of such form, shall not be deemed to constitute general solicitation or general advertising for purposes of this section; *Provided further,* that, if the requirements of Rule 135e are satisfied, providing any journalist with access to press conferences held outside of the United States, to meetings with issuer or selling security holder representatives conducted outside of the United States, or to written press-related materials released outside the United States, at or in which a present or proposed offering of securities is discussed, will not be deemed to constitute general solicitation or general advertising for purposes of this section.

d. **Limitations on Resale.** Except as provided in Rule 504(b)(1), securities acquired in a transaction under Regulation D shall have the status of securities acquired in a transaction under section 4(a)(2) of the Act and cannot be resold without registration under the Act or an exemption therefrom. The issuer shall exercise reasonable care to assure that the purchasers of the securities are not underwriters within the meaning of section 2(a)(11) of the Act, which reasonable care may be demonstrated by the following:
   1. Reasonable inquiry to determine if the purchaser is acquiring the securities for himself or for other persons;
   2. Written disclosure to each purchaser prior to sale that the securities have not been registered under the Act and, therefore, cannot be resold unless they are registered under the Act or unless an exemption from registration is available; and
   3. Placement of a legend on the certificate or other document that evidences the securities stating that the securities have not been registered under the Act and setting forth or referring to the restrictions on transferability and sale of the securities.

   While taking these actions will establish the requisite reasonable care, it is not the exclusive method to demonstrate such care. Other actions by the issuer may satisfy this provision. In addition, Rule 502(b)2(vii) requires the delivery of written disclosure of the limitations on resale to investors in certain instances.

Rule 503 – Filing of Notice of Sales

a. **When notice of sales on Form D is required and permitted to be filed.**
   1. An issuer offering or selling securities in reliance on Rule 504or Rule 506 must file with the Commission a notice of sales containing the information required by Form D for each new offering of securities no later than 15 calendar days after the first sale of securities in the offering, unless the end of that period falls on a Saturday, Sunday or holiday, in which case the due date would be the first business day following.

2. An issuer may file an amendment to a previously filed notice of sales on Form D at any time.

3. An issuer must file an amendment to a previously filed notice of sales on Form D for an offering:

    i.   To correct a material mistake of fact or error in the previously filed notice of sales on Form D, as soon as practicable after discovery of the mistake or error;

    ii. To reflect a change in the information provided in the previously filed notice of sales on Form D, as soon as practicable after the change, except that no amendment is required to reflect a change that occurs after the offering terminates or a change that occurs solely in the following information:

         A. The address or relationship to the issuer of a related person identified in response to Item 3 of the notice of sales on Form D;

         B. An issuer's revenues or aggregate net asset value;

         C. The minimum investment amount, if the change is an increase, or if the change, together with all other changes in that amount since the previously filed notice of sales on Form D, does not result in a decrease of more than 10%;

         D. Any address or state(s) of solicitation shown in response to Item 12 of the notice of sales on Form D;

         E. The total offering amount, if the change is a decrease, or if the change, together with all other changes in that amount since the previously filed notice of sales on Form D, does not result in an increase of more than 10%;

         F. The amount of securities sold in the offering or the amount remaining to be sold;

         G. The number of non-accredited investors who have invested in the offering, as long as the change does not increase the number to more than 35;

         H. The total number of investors who have invested in the offering; or

         I. The amount of sales commissions, finders' fees or use of proceeds for payments to executive officers, directors or promoters, if the change is a decrease, or if the change, together with all other changes in that amount since the previously filed notice of sales on Form D, does not result in an increase of more than 10%; and

    iii. Annually, on or before the first anniversary of the filing of the notice of sales on Form D or the filing of the most recent amendment to the notice of sales on Form D, if the offering is continuing at that time.

4. An issuer that files an amendment to a previously filed notice of sales on Form D must provide current information in response to all requirements of the notice of sales on Form D regardless of why the amendment is filed.

b. **How notice of sales on Form D must be filed and signed.**

    1. A notice of sales on Form D must be filed with the Commission in electronic format by means of the Commission's Electronic Data Gathering, Analysis,

and Retrieval System (EDGAR) in accordance with EDGAR rules set forth in Regulation S-T.

2.   Every notice of sales on Form D must be signed by a person duly authorized by the issuer.

Rule 504 – Exemption for Limited Offers and Sales of Securities Not Exceeding $10,000,000

a.   **Exemption.** Offers and sales of securities that satisfy the conditions in paragraph (b) of this Rule 504 by an issuer that is not:

1.   subject to the reporting requirements of section 13 or 15(d) of the Exchange Act,:

2.   an investment company; or

3.   a development stage company that either has no specific business plan or purpose or has indicated that its business plan is to engage in a merger or acquisition with an unidentified company or companies, or other entity or person, shall be exempt from the provision of section 5 of the Act under section 3(b) of the Act.

b.   **Conditions to be Met.**

1.   General conditions. To qualify for exemption under this Rule 504, offers and sales must satisfy the terms and conditions of Rule 501 and Rule 502 (a), (c) and (d), except that the provisions of Rule 502 (c) and (d) will not apply to offers and sales of securities under this Rule 504 that are made:

   i.   Exclusively in one or more states that provide for the registration of the securities, and require the public filing and delivery to investors of a substantive disclosure document before sale, and are made in accordance with those state provisions;

   ii.   In one or more states that have no provision for the registration of the securities or the public filing or delivery of a disclosure document before sale, if the securities have been registered in at least one state that provides for such registration, public filing and delivery before sale, offers and sales are made in that state in accordance with such provisions, and the disclosure document is delivered before sale to all purchasers (including those in the states that have no such procedure); or

   iii. Exclusively according to state law exemptions from registration that permit general solicitation and general advertising so long as sales are made only to "accredited investors" as defined in Rule 501(a).

2.   The aggregate offering price for an offering of securities under this Rule 504, as defined in Rule 501(c), shall not exceed $10,000,000, less the aggregate offering price for all securities sold within the 12 months before the start of and during the offering of securities under this Rule 504 or in violation of section 5(a) of the Securities Act.

Instruction to paragraph (b)(2): If a transaction under Rule 504 fails to meet the limitation on the aggregate offering price, it does not affect the availability of this Rule 504 for the other transactions considered in applying such limitation. For example, if an issuer sold $10,000,000 of its securities on June 1, 2021 under this Rule 504 and an additional $500,000 of its securities on December 1, 2021, this Rule 504 would not be available for the later sale, but would still be applicable to the January 1, 2021 sale.

3.   **Disqualifications**. No exemption under this section shall be available for the securities of any issuer if such issuer would be subject to disqualification under Rule 506(d) on or after January 20, 2017; provided that disclosure of prior "bad actor" events shall be required in accordance with Rule 506(e).

Instruction to paragraph (b)(3): For purposes of disclosure of prior "bad actor" events pursuant to Rule 506(e), an issuer shall furnish to each purchaser, a reasonable time prior to sale, a description in writing of any matters that would have triggered disqualification under this paragraph (b)(3) but occurred before January 20, 2017.

Rule 505 – [Removed and Reserved]

Rule 506 – Exemption for Limited Offers and Sales Without Regard to Dollar Amount of Offering

a.   **Exemption.** Offers and sales of securities by an issuer that satisfy the conditions in paragraph (b) or (c) of this Rule 506 shall be deemed to be transactions not involving any public offering within the meaning of section 4(a)(2) of the Act.

b.   **Conditions to be met in offerings subject to limitation on manner of offering-**

1.   General conditions. To qualify for an exemption under this section, offers and sales must satisfy all the terms and conditions of Rule 501 and Rule 502.

2.   Specific Conditions-

    i.   Limitation on number of purchasers. There are no more than, or the issuer reasonably believes that there are no more than, 35 purchasers of securities from the issuer in offerings under this section in any 90-calendar-day period. **Note to paragraph (b)(2)(i)**: See Rule 501(e) for the calculation of the number of purchasers and Rule 502(a) for what may or may not constitute an offering under paragraph (b) of this section.

    ii.   Nature of purchasers. Each purchaser who is not an accredited investor either alone or with his purchaser representative(s) has such knowledge and experience in financial and business matters that he is capable of evaluating the merits and risks of the prospective investment, or the issuer reasonably believes immediately prior to making any sale that such purchaser comes within this description.

c.   **Conditions to be met in offerings not subject to limitation on manner of offering**

1.   General conditions. To qualify for exemption under this section, sales must satisfy all the terms and conditions of Rules 501 and 502(a) and (d).

2.   Specific conditions

    i.   Nature of purchasers. All purchasers of securities sold in any offering under paragraph (c) of this section are accredited investors.

    ii.   Verification of accredited investor status. The issuer shall take reasonable steps to verify that purchasers of securities sold in any offering under paragraph (c) of this section are accredited investors. The issuer shall be deemed to take reasonable steps to verify if the issuer uses, at its option, one of the following non-exclusive and non-mandatory methods of verifying that a natural person who purchases securities in such offering is an accredited investor; provided, however, that the issuer does not have knowledge that such person is not an accredited investor:

    A. In regard to whether the purchaser is an accredited investor on the basis of income, reviewing any Internal Revenue Service form that reports the purchaser's income for the two most recent years (including, but not limited to, Form W-2, Form 1099, Schedule K-1 to Form 1065, and Form 1040) and obtaining a written representation from the purchaser that he or she has a reasonable expectation of reaching the income level necessary to qualify as an accredited investor during the current year;

    B. In regard to whether the purchaser is an accredited investor on the basis of net worth, reviewing one or more of the following types of documentation dated within the prior three months and obtaining a written representation from the purchaser that all liabilities necessary to make a determination of net worth have been disclosed:

        1. With respect to assets: bank statements, brokerage statements and other statements of securities holdings, certificates of deposit, tax assessments, and appraisal reports issued by independent third parties; and

        2. With respect to liabilities: a consumer report from at least one of the nationwide consumer reporting agencies;

    C. Obtaining a written confirmation from one of the following persons or entities that such person or entity has taken reasonable steps to verify that the purchaser is an accredited investor within the prior three months and has determined that such purchaser is an accredited investor:

        1. A registered broker-dealer;

        2. An investment adviser registered with the Securities and Exchange Commission;

        3. A licensed attorney who is in good standing under the laws of the jurisdictions in which he or she is admitted to practice law; or

        4. A certified public accountant who is duly registered and in good standing under the laws of the place of his or her residence or principal office;

    D. In regard to any person who purchased securities in an issuer's Rule 506(b) offering as an accredited investor prior to September 23, 2013 and continues to hold such securities, for the same issuer's Rule 506(c) offering, obtaining a certification by such person at the time of sale that he or she qualifies as an accredited investor; or

    E. In regard to any person that the issuer previously took reasonable steps to verify as an accredited investor in accordance with this paragraph (c)(2)(ii), so long as the issuer is not aware of information to the contrary, obtaining a written representation from such person at the time of sale that he or she qualifies as an accredited investor. A written representation under this method of verification will satisfy the issuer's obligation to verify the person's accredited investor status for a period of five years from the date the person was previously verified as an accredited investor

Instructions to paragraph (c)(2)(ii):

1. The issuer is not required to use any of these methods in verifying the accredited investor status of natural persons who are purchasers. These methods are examples of the types of non-exclusive and non-mandatory methods that satisfy the verification requirement in Rule 506(c)(2)(ii).

2. In the case of a person who qualifies as an accredited investor based on joint income with that person's spouse, the issuer would be deemed to satisfy the verification requirement in Rule 506(c)(2)(ii)(A) by reviewing copies of Internal Revenue Service forms that report income for the two most recent years in regard to, and obtaining written representations from, both the person and the spouse.

3. In the case of a person who qualifies as an accredited investor based on joint net worth with that person's spouse, the issuer would be deemed to satisfy the verification requirement in Rule 506(c)(2)(ii)(B) by reviewing such documentation in regard to, and obtaining written representations from, both the person and the spouse.

d. **"Bad Actor" disqualification.**

1. No exemption under this section shall be available for a sale of securities if the issuer; any predecessor of the issuer; any affiliated issuer; any director, executive officer, other officer participating in the offering, general partner or managing member of the issuer; any beneficial owner of 20% or more of the issuer's outstanding voting equity securities, calculated on the basis of voting power; any promoter connected with the issuer in any capacity at the time of such sale; any investment manager of an issuer that is a pooled investment fund; any person that has been or will be paid (directly or indirectly) remuneration for solicitation of purchasers in connection with such sale of securities; any general partner or managing member of any such investment manager or solicitor; or any director, executive officer or other officer participating in the offering of any such investment manager or solicitor or general partner or managing member of such investment manager or solicitor:

   i. Has been convicted, within ten years before such sale (or five years, in the case of issuers, their predecessors and affiliated issuers), of any felony or misdemeanor:

      A. In connection with the purchase or sale of any security;

      B. Involving the making of any false filing with the Commission; or

      C. Arising out of the conduct of the business of an underwriter, broker, dealer, municipal securities dealer, investment adviser or paid solicitor of purchasers of securities;

   ii. Is subject to any order, judgment or decree of any court of competent jurisdiction, entered within five years before such sale, that, at the time of such sale, restrains or enjoins such person from engaging or continuing to engage in any conduct or practice:

    A.   In connection with the purchase or sale of any security;

    B.   Involving the making of any false filing with the Commission; or

    C.   Arising out of the conduct of the business of an underwriter, broker, dealer, municipal securities dealer, investment adviser or paid solicitor of purchasers of securities;

iii.   Is subject to a final order of a state securities commission (or an agency or officer of a state performing like functions); a state authority that supervises or examines banks, savings associations, or credit unions; a state insurance commission (or an agency or officer of a state performing like functions); an appropriate federal banking agency; the U.S. Commodity Futures Trading Commission; or the National Credit Union Administration that:

    A.   At the time of such sale, bars the person from:

        1.   Association with an entity regulated by such commission, authority, agency, or officer;

        2.   Engaging in the business of securities, insurance or banking; or

        3.   Engaging in savings association or credit union activities; or

    B.   Constitutes a final order based on a violation of any law or regulation that prohibits fraudulent, manipulative, or deceptive conduct entered within ten years before such sale;

iv.   Is subject to an order of the Commission entered pursuant to section 15(b) or 15B(c) of the Securities Exchange Act of 1934) or section 203(e) or (f) of the Investment Advisers Act of 1940) that, at the time of such sale:

    A.   Suspends or revokes such person's registration as a broker, dealer, municipal securities dealer or investment adviser;

    B.   Places limitations on the activities, functions or operations of such person; or

    C.   Bars such person from being associated with any entity or from participating in the offering of any penny stock;

v.   Is subject to any order of the Commission entered within five years before such sale that, at the time of such sale, orders the person to cease and desist from committing or causing a violation or future violation of:

    A.   Any scienter-based anti-fraud provision of the federal securities laws, including without limitation section 17(a)(1) of the Securities Act of 1933, section 10(b) of the Securities Exchange Act of 1934 and Rule 10b-5, section 15(c)(1) of the Securities Exchange Act of 1934 and section 206(1) of the Investment Advisers Act of 1940, or any other rule or regulation thereunder; or

    B.   Section 5 of the Securities Act of 1933.

vi.   Is suspended or expelled from membership in, or suspended or barred from association with a member of, a registered national securities exchange or a registered national or affiliated securities association for any act or omission to act constituting conduct inconsistent with just and equitable principles of trade;

vii.   Has filed (as a registrant or issuer), or was or was named as an underwriter in, any registration statement or Regulation A offering statement filed with the Commission that, within five years before such sale, was the subject of a refusal order, stop order, or order suspending the Regulation A exemption, or is, at the time of such sale, the subject of an investigation or proceeding to determine whether a stop order or suspension order should be issued; or

viii.   Is subject to a United States Postal Service false representation order entered within five years before such sale, or is, at the time of such sale, subject to a temporary restraining order or preliminary injunction with respect to conduct alleged by the United States Postal Service to constitute a scheme or device for obtaining money or property through the mail by means of false representations.

2.   Paragraph (d)(1) of this section shall not apply:

i.   With respect to any conviction, order, judgment, decree, suspension, expulsion or bar that occurred or was issued before September 23, 2013;

ii.   Upon a showing of good cause and without prejudice to any other action by the Commission, if the Commission determines that it is not necessary under the circumstances that an exemption be denied;

iii.   If, before the relevant sale, the court or regulatory authority that entered the relevant order, judgment or decree advises in writing (whether contained in the relevant judgment, order or decree or separately to the Commission or its staff) that disqualification under paragraph (d)(1) of this section should not arise as a consequence of such order, judgment or decree; or

iv.   If the issuer establishes that it did not know and, in the exercise of reasonable care, could not have known that a disqualification existed under paragraph (d)(1) of this section.

Instruction to paragraph (d)(2)(iv). An issuer will not be able to establish that it has exercised reasonable care unless it has made, in light of the circumstances, factual inquiry into whether any disqualifications exist. The nature and scope of the factual inquiry will vary based on the facts and circumstances concerning, among other things, the issuer and the other offering participants.

3.   For purposes of paragraph (d)(1) of this section, events relating to any affiliated issuer that occurred before the affiliation arose will be not considered disqualifying if the affiliated entity is not:

i.   In control of the issuer; or

ii.   Under common control with the issuer by a third party that was in control of the affiliated entity at the time of such events.

e.   **Disclosure of prior "bad actor" events**. The issuer shall furnish to each purchaser, a reasonable time prior to sale, a description in writing of any matters that would have triggered disqualification under paragraph (d)(1) of this section but occurred before September 23, 2013. The failure to furnish such information timely shall not prevent an issuer from relying on this section if the issuer establishes that it did not know and, in the exercise of reasonable care, could not have known of the existence of the undisclosed matter or matters.

Instruction to paragraph (e). An issuer will not be able to establish that it has exercised reasonable care unless it has made, in light of the circumstances, factual inquiry into whether any disqualifications exist. The nature and scope of the factual inquiry will vary based on the facts and circumstances concerning, among other things, the issuer and the other offering participants.

Rule 507 – Disqualifying Provision Relating to Exemptions Under Rules 504 & 506

a. No exemption under Rule 504 or Rule 506 shall be available for an issuer if such issuer, any of its predecessors or affiliates have been subject to any order, judgment, or decree of any court of competent jurisdiction temporarily, preliminary or permanently enjoining such person for failure to comply with Rule 503.

b. Paragraph (a) of this section shall not apply if the Commission determines, upon a showing of good cause, that it is not necessary under the circumstances that the exemption be denied.

Rule 508 – Insignificant Deviations from a Term, Condition or Requirement of Reg. D

a. A failure to comply with a term, condition or requirement of Rule 504 or Rule 506 will not result in the loss of the exemption from the requirements of section 5 of the Act for any offer or sale to a particular individual or entity, if the person relying on the exemption shows:
   1. The failure to comply did not pertain to a term, condition or requirement directly intended to protect that particular individual or entity; and
   2. The failure to comply was insignificant with respect to the offering as a whole, provided that any failure to comply with paragraph (c) of Rule 502, paragraph (b)(2) of Rule 504 and paragraph (b)(2)(i) of Rule 506 shall be deemed to be significant to the offering as a whole; and
   3. A good faith and reasonable attempt was made to comply with all applicable terms, conditions and requirements of Rule 504 or Rule 506.

b. A transaction made in reliance on Rule 504 or Rule 506 shall comply with all applicable terms, conditions and requirements of Regulation D. Where an exemption is established only through reliance upon paragraph (a) of this section, the failure to comply shall nonetheless be actionable by the Commission under section 20 of the Act.

Regulation S

Rule 901 – General Statement

For the purposes only of section 5 of the Act, the terms **offer, offer to sell, sell, sale,** and **offer to buy** shall be deemed to include offers and sales that occur within the United States and shall be deemed not to include offers and sales that occur outside the United States.

Rule 902 – Definitions

As used in Regulation S, the following terms shall have the meanings indicated.

- a. **Debt securities.** *Debt securities* of an issuer is defined to mean any security other than an equity security as defined in Rule 405, as well as the following:
  1. Non-participatory preferred stock, which is defined as non-convertible capital stock, the holders of which are entitled to a preference in payment of dividends and in distribution of assets on liquidation, dissolution, or winding up of the issuer, but are not entitled to participate in residual earnings or assets of the issuer; and
  2. Asset-backed securities, which are securities of a type that either:
     - i. Represent an ownership interest in a pool of discrete assets, or certificates of interest or participation in such assets (including any rights designed to assure servicing, or the receipt or timeliness of receipt by holders of such assets, or certificates of interest or participation in such assets, of amounts payable thereunder), provided that the assets are not generated or originated between the issuer of the security and its affiliates; or
     - ii. Are secured by one or more assets or certificates of interest or participation in such assets, and the securities, by their terms, provide for payments of principal and interest (if any) in relation to payments or reasonable projections of payments on assets meeting the requirements of paragraph (a)(2)(i) of this section, or certificates of interest or participations in assets meeting such requirements.
     - iii. For purposes of paragraph (a)(2) of this section, the term "assets" means securities, installment sales, accounts receivable, notes, leases or other contracts, or other assets that by their terms convert into cash over a finite period of time.

- b. **Designated offshore securities market.** *Designated offshore securities market* means:
  1. The Eurobond market, as regulated by the International Securities Market Association; the Alberta Stock Exchange; the Amsterdam Stock Exchange; the Australian Stock Exchange Limited; the Bermuda Stock Exchange; the Bourse de Bruxelles; the Copenhagen Stock Exchange; the European Association of Securities Dealers Automated Quotation; the Frankfurt Stock Exchange; the Helsinki Stock Exchange; The Stock Exchange of Hong Kong Limited; the Irish Stock Exchange; the Istanbul Stock Exchange; the Johannesburg Stock Exchange; the London Stock Exchange; the Bourse de Luxembourg; the

Mexico Stock Exchange; the Borsa Valori di Milan; the Montreal Stock Exchange; the Oslo Stock Exchange; the Bourse de Paris; the Stock Exchange of Singapore Ltd.; the Stockholm Stock Exchange; the Tokyo Stock Exchange; the Toronto Stock Exchange; the Vancouver Stock Exchange; the Warsaw Stock Exchange and the Zurich Stock Exchange; and

2.   Any foreign securities exchange or non-exchange market designated by the Commission. Attributes to be considered in determining whether to designate an offshore securities market, among others, include:

    i.   Organization under foreign law;

    ii.   Association with a generally recognized community of brokers, dealers, banks, or other professional intermediaries with an established operating history;

    iii.   Oversight by a governmental or self-regulatory body;

    iv.   Oversight standards set by an existing body of law;

    v.   Reporting of securities transactions on a regular basis to a governmental or self-regulatory body;

    vi.   A system for exchange of price quotations through common communications media; and

    vii.   An organized clearance and settlement system.

c.   **Directed selling efforts**.

1.   *Directed selling efforts* means any activity undertaken for the purpose of, or that could reasonably be expected to have the effect of, conditioning the market in the United States for any of the securities being offered in reliance on this Regulation S. Such activity includes placing an advertisement in a publication "with a general circulation in the United States" that refers to the offering of securities being made in reliance upon this Regulation S.

2.   Publication "with a general circulation in the United States":

    i.   Is defined as any publication that is printed primarily for distribution in the United States, or has had, during the preceding twelve months, an average circulation in the United States of 15,000 or more copies per issue; and

    ii.   Will encompass only the U.S. edition of any publication printing a separate U.S. edition if the publication, without considering its U.S. edition, would not constitute a publication with a general circulation in the United States.

3.   The following are not "directed selling efforts":

    i.   Placing an advertisement required to be published under U.S. or foreign law, or under rules or regulations of a U.S. or foreign regulatory or self-regulatory authority, provided the advertisement contains no more information than legally required and includes a statement to the effect that the securities have not been registered under the Act and may not be offered or sold in the United States (or to a U.S. person, if the advertisement relates to an offering under Category 2 or 3 (paragraph (b)(2) or (b)(3)) in Rule 903) absent registration or an applicable exemption from the registration requirements;

    ii.   Contact with persons excluded from the definition of "U.S. person" pursuant to paragraph (k)(2)(vi) of this section or persons holding accounts excluded from the definition of "U.S. person" pursuant to paragraph (k)(2)(i) of this section, solely in their capacities as holders of such accounts;

iii. A tombstone advertisement in any publication with a general circulation in the United States, provided:

    A. The publication has less than 20% of its circulation, calculated by aggregating the circulation of its U.S. and comparable non-U.S. editions, in the United States;

    B. Such advertisement contains a legend to the effect that the securities have not been registered under the Act and may not be offered or sold in the United States (or to a U.S. person, if the advertisement relates to an offering under Category 2 or 3 (paragraph (b)(2) or (b)(3)) in Rule 903) absent registration or an applicable exemption from the registration requirements; and

    C. Such advertisement contains no more information than:

        1. The issuer's name;

        2. The amount and title of the securities being sold;

        3. A brief indication of the issuer's general type of business;

        4. The price of the securities;

        5. The yield of the securities, if debt securities with a fixed (non-contingent) interest provision;

        6. The name and address of the person placing the advertisement, and whether such person is participating in the distribution;

        7. The names of the managing underwriters;

        8. The dates, if any, upon which the sales commenced and concluded;

        9. Whether the securities are offered or were offered by rights issued to security holders and, if so, the class of securities that are entitled or were entitled to subscribe, the subscription ratio, the record date, the dates (if any) upon which the rights were issued and expired, and the subscription price; and

       10. Any legend required by law or any foreign or U.S. regulatory or self- regulatory authority;

iv. Bona fide visits to real estate, plants or other facilities located in the United States and tours thereof conducted for a prospective investor by an issuer, a distributor, any of their respective affiliates or a person acting on behalf of any of the foregoing;

v. Distribution in the United States of a foreign broker-dealer's quotations by a third-party system that distributes such quotations primarily in foreign countries if:

    A. Securities transactions cannot be executed between foreign broker-dealers and persons in the United States through the system; and

    B. The issuer, distributors, their respective affiliates, persons acting on behalf of any of the foregoing, foreign broker-dealers and other participants in the system do not initiate contacts with U.S. persons or persons within the United States, beyond those contacts exempted under Rule 15a-6 under the Exchange Act.

vi.   Publication by an issuer of a notice in accordance with Rule 135 or Rule 135c;

vii. Providing any journalist with access to press conferences held outside of the United States, to meetings with the issuer or selling security holder representatives conducted outside the United States, or to written press-related materials released outside the United States, at or in which a present or proposed offering of securities is discussed, if the requirements of Rule 135e are satisfied; and

viii. Publication or distribution of a research report by a broker or dealer in accordance with Rule 138(c) or Rule 139(b).

d.   **Distributor.** *Distributor* means any underwriter, dealer, or other person who participates, pursuant to a contractual arrangement, in the distribution of the securities offered or sold in reliance on this Regulation S (Rule 901 through Rule 905, and Preliminary Notes).

e.   **Domestic issuer/Foreign issuer.** *Domestic issuer* means any issuer other than a "foreign government" or "foreign private issuer" (both as defined in Rule 405). *Foreign issuer* means any issuer other than a *domestic issuer*.

f.   **Distribution compliance period.** *Distribution compliance period* means a period that begins when the securities were first offered to persons other than distributors in reliance upon this Regulation S (Rule 901 through Rule 905, and Preliminary Notes) or the date of closing of the offering, whichever is later, and continues until the end of the period of time specified in the relevant provision of Rule 903, except that:

1.   All offers and sales by a distributor of an unsold allotment or subscription shall be deemed to be made during the distribution compliance period;

2.   In a continuous offering, the distribution compliance period shall commence upon completion of the distribution, as determined and certified by the managing underwriter or person performing similar functions;

3.   In a continuous offering of non-convertible debt securities offered and sold in identifiable tranches, the distribution compliance period for securities in a tranche shall commence upon completion of the distribution of such tranche, as determined and certified by the managing underwriter or person performing similar functions; and

4.   That in a continuous offering of securities to be acquired upon the exercise of warrants, the distribution compliance period shall commence upon completion of the distribution of the warrants, as determined and certified by the managing underwriter or person performing similar functions, if requirements of Rule 903(b)(5) are satisfied.

g.   **Offering restrictions.** *Offering restrictions* means:

1.   Each distributor agrees in writing:

i.   That all offers and sales of the securities prior to the expiration of the distribution compliance period specified in Category 2 or 3 (paragraph (b)(2) or (b)(3)) in Rule 903, as applicable, shall be made only in accordance with the provisions of Rule 903 or Rule 904; pursuant to registration of the securities under the Act; or pursuant to an available exemption from the registration requirements of the Act; and

    ii.   For offers and sales of equity securities of domestic issuers, not to engage in hedging transactions with regard to such securities prior to the expiration of the distribution compliance period specified in Category 2 or 3 (para (b)(2) or (b)(3)) in Rule 903, as applicable, unless in compliance with the Act; and

2.   All offering materials and documents (other than press releases) used in connection with offers and sales of the securities prior to the expiration of the distribution compliance period specified in Category 2 or 3 (paragraph (b)(2) or (b)(3)) in Rule 903, as applicable, shall include statements to the effect that the securities have not been registered under the Act and may not be offered or sold in the United States or to U.S. persons (other than distributors) unless the securities are registered under the Act, or an exemption from the registration requirements of the Act is available. For offers and sales of equity securities of domestic issuers, such offering materials and documents also must state that hedging transactions involving those securities may not be conducted unless in compliance with the Act. Such statements shall appear:

    i.   On the cover or inside cover page of any prospectus or offering circular used in connection with the offer or sale of the securities;

    ii.   In the underwriting section of any prospectus or offering circular used in connection with the offer or sale of the securities; and

    iii.   In any advertisement made or issued by the issuer, any distributor, any of their respective affiliates, or any person acting on behalf of any of the foregoing. Such statements may appear in summary form on prospectus cover pages and in advertisements.

h. **Offshore transaction.**

    1.   An offer or sale of securities is made in an *offshore transaction* if:

        i.   The offer is not made to a person in the United States; and

        ii.   Either:

            A.   At the time the buy order is originated, the buyer is outside the United States, or the seller and any person acting on its behalf reasonably believe that the buyer is outside the United States; or

            B.   For purposes of:

                1.   Rule 903, the transaction is executed in, on or through a physical trading floor of an established foreign securities exchange that is located outside the United States; or

                2.   Rule 904, the transaction is executed in, on or through the facilities of a designated offshore securities market described in paragraph (b) of this section, and neither the seller nor any person acting on its behalf knows that the transaction has been pre-arranged with a buyer in the United States.

    2.   Notwithstanding paragraph (h)(1) of this section, offers and sales of securities specifically targeted at identifiable groups of U.S. citizens abroad, such as members of the U.S. armed forces serving overseas, shall not be deemed to be made in "offshore transactions."

3. Notwithstanding paragraph (h)(1) of this section, offers and sales of securities to persons excluded from the definition of "U.S. person" pursuant to paragraph (k)(2)(vi) of this section or persons holding accounts excluded from the definition of "U.S. person" pursuant to paragraph (k)(2)(i) of this section, solely in their capacities as holders of such accounts, shall be deemed to be made in "offshore transactions."

4. Notwithstanding paragraph (h)(1) of this section, publication or distribution of a research report in accordance with Rule 138(c) or Rule 139(b) by a broker or dealer at or around the time of an offering in reliance on Regulation S will not cause the transaction to fail to be an offshore transaction as defined in this section.

i. **Reporting issuer.** *Reporting issuer* means an issuer other than an investment company registered or required to register under the 1940 Act that:
    1. Has a class of securities registered pursuant to Section 12(b) or 12(g) of the Exchange Act or is required to file reports pursuant to Section 15(d) of the Exchange Act; and
    2. Has filed all the material required to be filed pursuant to Section 13(a) or 15(d) of the Exchange Act for a period of at least twelve months immediately preceding the offer or sale of securities made in reliance upon this Regulation S (or for such shorter period that the issuer was required to file such material).

j. **Substantial U.S. market interest.**
    1. *Substantial U.S. market interest* with respect to a class of an issuer's equity securities means:
        i. The securities exchanges and inter-dealer quotation systems in the United States in the aggregate constituted the single largest market for such class of securities in the shorter of the issuer's prior fiscal year or the period since the issuer's incorporation; or
        ii. 20 percent or more of all trading in such class of securities took place in, on or through the facilities of securities exchanges and inter-dealer quotation systems in the United States and less than 55 percent of such trading took place in, on or through the facilities of securities markets of a single foreign country in the shorter of the issuer's prior fiscal year or the period since the issuer's incorporation.
    2. *Substantial U.S. market interest* with respect to an issuer's debt securities means:
        i. Its debt securities, in the aggregate, are held of record (as that term is defined in Rule 12g5-1 under the Exchange Act and used for purposes of paragraph (j)(2) of this section) by 300 or more U.S. persons;
        ii. $1 billion or more of: The principal amount outstanding of its debt securities, the greater of liquidation preference or par value of its securities described in Rule 902(a)(1), and the principal amount or principal balance of its securities described in Rule 902(a)(2), in the aggregate, is held of record by U.S. persons; and
        iii. 20 percent or more of: The principal amount outstanding of its debt securities, the greater of liquidation preference or par value of its securities described in Rule 902(a)(1), and the principal amount or

principal balance of its securities described in Rule 902(a)(1), in the aggregate, is held of record by U.S. persons.

3. Notwithstanding paragraph (j)(2) of this section, substantial U.S. market interest with respect to an issuer's debt securities is calculated without reference to securities that qualify for the exemption provided by Section 3(a)(3) of the Act.

k. **U.S. person**.

1. *U.S. person* means:

   i. Any natural person resident in the United States;
   ii. Any partnership or corporation organized or incorporated under the laws of the United States;
   iii. Any estate of which any executor or administrator is a U.S. person;
   iv. Any trust of which any trustee is a U.S. person;
   v. Any agency or branch of a foreign entity located in the United States;
   vi. Any non-discretionary account or similar account (other than an estate or trust) held by a dealer or other fiduciary for the benefit or account of a U.S. person;
   vii. Any discretionary account or similar account (other than an estate or trust) held by a dealer or other fiduciary organized, incorporated, or (if an individual) resident in the United States; and
   viii. Any partnership or corporation if:
      A. Organized or incorporated under the laws of any foreign jurisdiction; and
      B. Formed by a U.S. person principally for the purpose of investing in securities not registered under the Act, unless it is organized or incorporated, and owned, by accredited investors (as defined in Rule 501(a)) who are not natural persons, estates or trusts.

2. The following are not *U.S. persons*:

   i. Any discretionary account or similar account (other than an estate or trust) held for the benefit or account of a non-U.S. person by a dealer or other professional fiduciary organized, incorporated, or (if an individual) resident in the United States;
   ii. Any estate of which any professional fiduciary acting as executor or administrator is a U.S. person if:
      A. An executor or administrator of the estate who is not a U.S. person has sole or shared investment discretion with respect to the assets of the estate; and
      B. The estate is governed by foreign law;
   iii. Any trust of which any professional fiduciary acting as trustee is a U.S. person, if a trustee who is not a U.S. person has sole or shared investment discretion with respect to the trust assets, and no beneficiary of the trust (and no settlor if the trust is revocable) is a U.S. person;
   iv. An employee benefit plan established and administered in accordance with the law of a country other than the United States and customary practices and documentation of such country;
   v. Any agency or branch of a U.S. person located outside the United States if:
      A. The agency or branch operates for valid business reasons; and

  B. The agency or branch is engaged in the business of insurance or banking and is subject to substantive insurance or banking regulation, respectively, in the jurisdiction where located; and

 vi. The International Monetary Fund, the International Bank for Reconstruction and Development, the Inter-American Development Bank, the Asian Development Bank, the African Development Bank, the United Nations, and their agencies, affiliates and pension plans, and any other similar international organizations, their agencies, affiliates and pension plans.

l. **United States.** *United States* means the United States of America, its territories and possessions, any State of the United States, and the District of Columbia

Rule 903 – Offers or Sales of Securities by the Issuer, a Distributor, Any of their Respective Affiliates, or Any Person Acting on Behalf of Any of the Foregoing; Conditions Relating to Specific Securities

a. An offer or sale of securities by the issuer, a distributor, any of their respective affiliates, or any person acting on behalf of any of the foregoing, shall be deemed to occur outside the United States within the meaning of Rule 901 if:

1. The offer or sale is made in an offshore transaction;
2. No directed selling efforts are made in the United States by the issuer, a distributor, any of their respective affiliates, or any person acting on behalf of any of the foregoing; and
3. The conditions of paragraph (b) of this section, as applicable, are satisfied.

b. **Additional Conditions.**
1. **Category 1**. No conditions other than those set forth in paragraph (a) apply to securities in this category. Securities are eligible for this category if:
 i. The securities are issued by a foreign issuer that reasonably believes at the commencement of the offering that:
  A. There is no substantial U.S. market interest in the class of securities to be offered or sold (if equity securities are offered or sold);
  B. There is no substantial U.S. market interest in its debt securities (if debt securities are offered or sold);
  C. There is no substantial U.S. market interest in the securities to be purchased upon exercise (if warrants are offered or sold); and
  D. There is no substantial U.S. market interest in either the convertible securities or the underlying securities (if convertible securities are offered or sold);
 ii. The securities are offered and sold in an overseas directed offering, which means:
  A. An offering of securities of a foreign issuer that is directed into a single country other than the United States to the residents thereof and that is made in accordance with the local laws and customary practices and documentation of such country; or

B.   An offering of non-convertible debt securities of a domestic issuer that is directed into a single country other than the United States to the residents thereof and that is made in accordance with the local laws and customary practices and documentation of such country, provided that the principal and interest of the securities (or par value, as applicable) are denominated in a currency other than U.S. dollars and such securities are neither convertible into U.S. dollar-denominated securities nor linked to U.S. dollars (other than through related currency or interest rate swap transactions that are commercial in nature) in a manner that in effect converts the securities to U.S. dollar- denominated securities.

iii.   The securities are backed by the full faith and credit of a foreign government; or

iv.   The securities are offered and sold to employees of the issuer or its affiliates pursuant to an employee benefit plan established and administered in accordance with the law of a country other than the United States, and customary practices and documentation of such country, provided that:

A.   The securities are issued in compensatory circumstances for bona fide services rendered to the issuer or its affiliates in connection with their businesses and such services are not rendered in connection with the offer or sale of securities in a capital-raising transaction;

B.   Any interests in the plan are not transferable other than by will or the laws of descent or distribution;

C.   The issuer takes reasonable steps to preclude the offer and sale of interests in the plan or securities under the plan to U.S. residents other than employees on temporary assignment in the United States; and

D.   Documentation used in connection with any offer pursuant to the plan contains a statement that the securities have not been registered under the Act and may not be offered or sold in the United States unless registered or an exemption from registration is available.

2.   **Category 2**. The following conditions apply to securities that are not eligible for Category 1 (paragraph (b)(1)) of this section and that are equity securities of a reporting foreign issuer, or debt securities of a reporting issuer or of a non-reporting foreign issuer.

i.   Offering restrictions are implemented;

ii.   The offer or sale, if made prior to the expiration of a 40-day distribution compliance period, is not made to a U.S. person or for the account or benefit of a U.S. person (other than a distributor); and

iii.   Each distributor selling securities to a distributor, a dealer, as defined in section 2(a)(12) of the Act, or a person receiving a selling concession, fee or other remuneration in respect of the securities sold, prior to the expiration of a 40-day distribution compliance period, sends a confirmation or other notice to the purchaser stating that the purchaser is subject to the same restrictions on offers and sales that apply to a distributor.

3.   **Category 3**. The following conditions apply to securities that are not eligible for Category 1 or 2 (paragraph (b)(1) or (b)(2)) of this section:
   i.   Offering restrictions are implemented;
   ii. In the case of debt securities:
        A. The offer or sale, if made prior to the expiration of a 40-day distribution compliance period, is not made to a U.S. person or for the account or benefit of a U.S. person (other than a distributor); and
        B. The securities are represented upon issuance by a temporary global security which is not exchangeable for definitive securities until the expiration of the 40-day distribution compliance period and, for persons other than distributors, until certification of beneficial ownership of the securities by a non-U.S. person or a U.S. person who purchased securities in a transaction that did not require registration under the Act;
   iii. In the case of equity securities:
        A. The offer or sale, if made prior to the expiration of a one-year distribution compliance period (or a six-month distribution compliance period if the issuer is a reporting issuer), is not made to a U.S. person or for the account or benefit of a U.S. person (other than a distributor); and
        B. The offer or sale, if made prior to the expiration of a one-year distribution compliance period (or a six-month distribution compliance period if the issuer is a reporting issuer), is made pursuant to the following conditions:
            1. The purchaser of the securities (other than a distributor) certifies that it is not a U.S. person and is not acquiring the securities for the account or benefit of any U.S. person or is a U.S. person who purchased securities in a transaction that did not require registration under the Act;
            2. The purchaser of the securities agrees to resell such securities only in accordance with the provisions of this Regulation S, pursuant to registration under the Act, or pursuant to an available exemption from registration; and agrees not to engage in hedging transactions with regard to such securities unless in compliance with the Act;
            3. The securities of a domestic issuer contain a legend to the effect that transfer is prohibited except in accordance with the provisions of this Regulation S, pursuant to registration under the Act, or pursuant to an available exemption from registration; and that hedging transactions involving those securities may not be conducted unless in compliance with the Act;
            4. The issuer is required, either by contract or a provision in its bylaws, articles, charter or comparable document, to refuse to register any transfer of the securities not made in accordance with the provisions of this Regulation S, pursuant to registration under the Act, or pursuant to an available exemption from registration; *provided, however,* that if the securities are in bearer form or foreign law prevents the issuer of the securities

from refusing to register securities transfers, other reasonable procedures (such as a legend described in paragraph (b)(3)(iii)(B)(3) of this section) are implemented to prevent any transfer of the securities not made in accordance with the provisions of this Regulation S; and

    iv. Each distributor selling securities to a distributor, a dealer (as defined in section 2(a)(12) of the Act), or a person receiving a selling concession, fee or other remuneration, prior to the expiration of a 40-day distribution compliance period in the case of debt securities, or a one-year distribution compliance period (or a six-month distribution compliance period if the issuer is a reporting issuer) in the case of equity securities, sends a confirmation or other notice to the purchaser stating that the purchaser is subject to the same restrictions on offers and sales that apply to a distributor.

4.   **Guaranteed securities**. Notwithstanding paragraphs (b)(1) through (b)(3) of this section, in offerings of debt securities fully and unconditionally guaranteed as to principal and interest by the parent of the issuer of the debt securities, only the requirements of paragraph (b) of this section that are applicable to the offer and sale of the guarantee must be satisfied with respect to the offer and sale of the guaranteed debt securities.

5.   **Warrants**. An offer or sale of warrants under Category 2 or 3 (paragraph (b)(2) or (b)(3)) of this section also must comply with the following requirements:

    i. Each warrant must bear a legend stating that the warrant and the securities to be issued upon its exercise have not been registered under the Act and that the warrant may not be exercised by or on behalf of any U.S. person unless registered under the Act or an exemption from such registration is available;

    ii. Each person exercising a warrant is required to give:

        A. Written certification that it is not a U.S. person and the warrant is not being exercised on behalf of a U.S. person; or

        B. A written opinion of counsel to the effect that the warrant and the securities delivered upon exercise thereof have been registered under the Act or are exempt from registration thereunder; and

    iii. Procedures are implemented to ensure that the warrant may not be exercised within the United States, and that the securities may not be delivered within the United States upon exercise, other than in offerings deemed to meet the definition of "offshore transaction" pursuant to Rule 902(h), unless registered under the Act or an exemption from such registration is available.

Rule 904 – Offshore Resales

a. An offer or sale of securities by any person other than the issuer, a distributor, any of their respective affiliates (except any officer or director who is an affiliate solely by virtue of holding such position), or any person acting on behalf of any of the foregoing, shall be deemed to occur outside the United States within the meaning of Rule 901 if:

1. The offer or sale are made in an offshore transaction;
2. No directed selling efforts are made in the United States by the seller, an affiliate, or any person acting on their behalf; and
3. The conditions of paragraph (b) of this section, if applicable, are satisfied.

b. **Additional conditions**.
    1. Resales by dealers and persons receiving selling concessions. In the case of an offer or sale of securities prior to the expiration of the distribution compliance period specified in Category 2 or 3 (paragraph (b)(2) or (b)(3)) of Rule 903, as applicable, by a dealer, as defined in Section 2(a)(12) of the Act, or a person receiving a selling concession, fee or other remuneration in respect of the securities offered or sold:
        i.   Neither the seller nor any person acting on its behalf knows that the offeree or buyer of the securities is a U.S. person; and
        ii. If the seller or any person acting on the seller's behalf knows that the purchaser is a dealer, as defined in Section 2(a)(12) of the Act, or is a person receiving a selling concession, fee or other remuneration in respect of the securities sold, the seller or a person acting on the seller's behalf sends to the purchaser a confirmation or other notice stating that the securities may be offered and sold during the distribution compliance period only in accordance with the provisions of this Regulation S (Rule 901 through Rule 905, and Preliminary Notes); pursuant to registration of the securities under the Act; or pursuant to an available exemption from the registration requirements of the Act.
    2. Resales by certain affiliates. In the case of an offer or sale of securities by an officer or director of the issuer or a distributor, who is an affiliate of the issuer or distributor solely by virtue of holding such position, no selling concession, fee or other remuneration is paid in connection with such offer or sale other than the usual and customary broker's commission that would be received by a person executing such transaction as agent.

Rule 905 – Resale Limitations

Equity securities of domestic issuers acquired from the issuer, a distributor, or any of their respective affiliates in a transaction subject to the conditions of Rule 901 or Rule 903 are deemed to be "restricted securities" as defined in Rule 144. Resales of any of such restricted securities by the offshore purchaser must be made in accordance with this Regulation S, the registration requirements of the Act or an exemption therefrom. Any "restricted securities," as defined in Rule 144, that are equity securities of a domestic issuer will continue to be deemed to be restricted securities, notwithstanding that they were acquired in a resale transaction made pursuant to Rule 901 or Rule 904.

Regulation S-K

Item 101 – Description of Business

   a. **General development of business.** Describe the general development of the business of the registrant, its subsidiaries and any predecessor(s).

      1. In describing developments, only information material to an understanding of the general development of the business is required. Disclosure may include, but should not be limited to, the following topics:

         i.   Any material changes to a previously disclosed business strategy;

         ii. The nature and effects of any material bankruptcy, receivership, or any similar proceeding with respect to the registrant or any of its significant subsidiaries;

         iii. The nature and effects of any material reclassification, merger or consolidation of the registrant or any of its significant subsidiaries; and

         iv. The acquisition or disposition of any material amount of assets otherwise than in the ordinary course of business.

      2. Notwithstanding the provisions of Rule 411(b) or Rule 12b-23(a) of this chapter, as applicable, a registrant may only forgo providing a full discussion of the general development of its business for a filing other than an initial registration statement if it provides an update to the general development of its business, disclosing all of the material developments that have occurred since the most recent registration statement or report that includes a full discussion of the general development of its business. In addition, the registrant must incorporate by reference, and include one active hyperlink to one registration statement or report that includes, the full discussion of the general development of the registrant's business.

      3. Registrants, (i) filing a registration statement on Form S-1 under the Securities Act or on Form 10 under the Exchange Act, (ii) not subject to the reporting requirements of section 13(a) or 15(d) of the Exchange Act immediately prior to the filing of such registration statement, and (iii) that (including predecessors) have not received revenue from operations during each of the three fiscal years immediately prior to the filing of registration statement, shall provide the following information:

         A. if the registration statement is filed prior to the end of the registrant's second fiscal quarter, a description of the registrant's plan of operation for the remainder of the fiscal year; or

         B. if the registration statement is filed subsequent to the end of the registrant's second fiscal quarter, a description of the registrant's plan of operation for the remainder of the fiscal year and for the first six months of the next fiscal year. If such information is not available, the reasons for its not being available shall be stated. Disclosure relating to any plan shall include such matters as:

            1. In the case of a registration statement on Form S-1, a statement in narrative form indicating the registrant's opinion as to the period of time that the proceeds from the offering will satisfy cash requirements and whether in the next six months it will be necessary to raise additional funds to meet the expenditures required for

operating the business of the registrant; the specific reasons for such opinion shall be set forth and categories of expenditures and sources of cash resources shall be identified; however, amounts of expenditures and cash resources need not be provided; in addition, if the narrative statement is based on a cash budget, such budget shall be furnished to the Commission as supplemental information, but not as part of the registration statement;

2. An explanation of material product research and development to be performed during the period covered in the plan;

3. Any anticipated material acquisition of plant and equipment and the capacity thereof;

4. Any anticipated material changes in number of employees in the various departments such as research and development, production, sales or administration; and

5. Other material areas which may be peculiar to the registrant's business.

b. **[Reserved]**

c. **Description of business.**

1. Describe the business done and intended to be done by the registrant and its subsidiaries, focusing upon the registrant's dominant segment or each reportable segment about which financial information is presented in the financial statements. When describing each segment, only information material to an understanding of the business taken as a whole is required. Disclosure may include, but should not be limited to, the information specified in paragraphs (c)(1)(i) through (v) of this section..

   i. Revenue-generating activities, products and/or services, and any dependence on revenue-generating activities, key products, services, product families or customers, including governmental customers;

   ii. Status of development efforts for new or enhanced products, trends in market demand and competitive conditions;

   iii. Resources material to a registrant's business, such as:

      A. Sources and availability of raw materials; and

      B. The duration and effect of all patents, trademarks, licenses, franchises, and concessions held;

   iv. A description of any material portion of the business that may be subject to renegotiation of profits or termination of contracts or subcontracts at the election of the Government; and.

   v. The extent to which the business is or may be seasonal.

2. Discuss the information specified in paragraphs (c)(2)(i) and (ii) of this section with respect to, and to the extent material to an understanding of, the registrant's business taken as a whole, except that, if the information is material to a particular segment, you should additionally identify that segment.

   i. The material effects that compliance with government regulations, including environmental regulations, may have upon the capital expenditures, earnings and competitive position of the registrant and its subsidiaries, including the estimated capital expenditures for environmental control facilities for the current fiscal year and any other material subsequent period; and

 ii. A description of the registrant's human capital resources, including the number of persons employed by the registrant, and any human capital measures or objectives that the registrant focuses on in managing the business (such as, depending on the nature of the registrant's business and workforce, measures or objectives that address the development, attraction and retention of personnel).

d. **[Reserved]**

e. **Available information.** Disclose the information in paragraphs (e)(1), (e)(2) and (e)(3) of this section in any registration statement you file under the Securities Act, and disclose the information in paragraphs (e)(3) of this section if you are an accelerated filer (as defined in Rule 12b-2) filing an annual report on Form 10-K:

 1. Whether you file reports with the Securities and Exchange Commission. If you are a reporting company, identify the reports and other information you file with the SEC.

 2. State that the SEC maintains an Internet site that contains reports, proxy and information statements, and other information regarding issuers that file electronically with the SEC and state the address of that site (http://www.sec.gov).

 3. Disclose your Internet address, if you have one.

f. **Reports to security holders.** Disclose the following information in any registration statement you file under the Securities Act:

 1. If the SEC's proxy rules or regulations, or stock exchange requirements, do not require you to send an annual report to security holders or to holders of American depository receipts, describe briefly the nature and frequency of reports that you will give to security holders. Specify whether the reports that you give will contain financial information that has been examined and reported on, with an opinion expressed "by" an independent public or certified public accountant.

 2. For a foreign private issuer, if the report will not contain financial information prepared in accordance with U.S. generally accepted accounting principles, you must state whether the report will include a reconciliation of this information with U.S. generally accepted accounting principles.

g. **Enforceability of civil liabilities against foreign persons.** Disclose the following if you are a foreign private issuer filing a registration statement under the Securities Act:

 1. Whether or not investors may bring actions under the civil liability provisions of the U.S. federal securities laws against the foreign private issuer, any of its officers and directors who are residents of a foreign country, any underwriters or experts named in the registration statement that are residents of a foreign country, and whether investors may enforce these civil liability provisions when the assets of the issuer or these other persons are located outside of the United States. The disclosure must address the following matters:

  i. The investor's ability to effect service of process within the United States on the foreign private issuer or any person;

      ii.   The investor's ability to enforce judgments obtained in U.S. courts against foreign persons based upon the civil liability provisions of the U.S. federal securities laws;

      iii.   The investor's ability to enforce, in an appropriate foreign court, judgments of U.S. courts based upon the civil liability provisions of the U.S. federal securities laws; and

      iv.   The investor's ability to bring an original action in an appropriate foreign court to enforce liabilities against the foreign private issuer or any person based upon the U.S. federal securities laws.

2.   If you provide this disclosure based on an opinion of counsel, name counsel in the prospectus and file as an exhibit to the registration statement a signed consent of counsel to the use of its name and opinion.

h.   **Smaller reporting companies**. A smaller reporting company, as defined by Rule 10(f)(1), may satisfy its obligations under this Item by describing the development of its business pursuant to this paragraph (h). In describing developments under paragraphs (h)(1) through (3), information should be provided for the period of time that is material to an understanding of the general development of the business. Notwithstanding the provisions of Rule 411(b) or Rule 12b-23(a) of this chapter as applicable, a smaller reporting company may only forgo providing a full discussion of the general development of its business for a filing other than an initial registration statement if it provides an update to the general development of its business disclosing all of the material developments that have occurred since the most recent registration statement or report that includes a full discussion of the general development of its business. In addition, the smaller reporting company must incorporate by reference, and include one active hyperlink to one registration statement or report that includes, the full discussion of the general development of the registrant's business. If the smaller reporting company has not been in business for three years, provide the same information for predecessor(s) of the smaller reporting company if there are any. This business development description should include:

1.   Form and year of organization;

2.   Any bankruptcy, receivership or similar proceeding; and

3.   Any material reclassification, merger, consolidation, or purchase or sale of a significant amount of assets not in the ordinary course of business.

4.   Business of the smaller reporting company. Briefly describe the business and include, to the extent material to an understanding of the smaller reporting company:

      i.   Principal products or services and their markets;

      ii.   Distribution methods of the products or services;

      iii. Status of any publicly announced new product or service;

      iv. Competitive business conditions and the smaller reporting company's competitive position in the industry and methods of competition;

      v.   Sources and availability of raw materials and the names of principal suppliers;

      vi. Dependence on one or a few major customers;

      vii. Patents, trademarks, licenses, franchises, concessions, royalty agreements or labor contracts, including duration;

       viii. Need for any government approval of principal products or services. If government approval is necessary and the smaller reporting company has not yet received that approval, discuss the status of the approval within the government approval process;

       ix. Effect of existing or probable governmental regulations on the business;

       x. [Reserved];

       xi. Costs and effects of compliance with environmental laws (federal, state and local); and

       xii. Number of total employees and number of full-time employees.

5. Reports to security holders. Disclose the following in any registration statement you file under the Securities Act of 1933:

    i. If you are not required to deliver an annual report to security holders, whether you will voluntarily send an annual report and whether the report will include audited financial statements;

    ii. Whether you file reports with the Securities and Exchange Commission. If you are a reporting company, identify the reports and other information you file with the Commission; and

    iii. State that the Commission maintains an Internet site that contains reports, proxy and information statements, and other information regarding issuers that file electronically with the Commission and state the address of that site (http://www.sec.gov). Disclose your Internet address, if available..

6. Foreign issuers. Provide the information required by Item 101(g) of Regulation S-K.

Instructions to Item 101:

1. In determining what information about the industry segments is material to an understanding of the registrant's business taken as a whole and therefore required to be disclosed, pursuant to paragraph (c) of this Item, the registrant should take into account both quantitative and qualitative factors such as the significance of the matter to the registrant (e.g., whether a matter with a relatively minor impact on the registrant's business is represented by management to be important to its future profitability), the pervasiveness of the matter (e.g., whether it affects or may affect numerous items in the segment information), and the impact of the matter (e.g., whether it distorts the trends reflected in the segment information). Situations may arise when information should be disclosed about a segment, although the information in quantitative terms may not appear significant to the registrant's business taken as a whole.

2. Base the determination of whether information about segments is required for a particular year upon an evaluation of interperiod comparability. For instance, interperiod comparability would require a registrant to report segment information in the current period even if not material under the criteria for reportability of FASB ASC Topic 280, *Segment Reporting*, No. 131 if a segment has been significant in the immediately preceding period and the registrant expects it to be significant in the future.

3. The Commission, upon written request of the registrant and where consistent with the protection of investors, may permit the omission of any of the information required by this Item or the furnishing in substitution thereof of appropriate information of comparable character.

Item 102 – Description of Property

To the extent material, disclose the location and general character of the registrant's principal physical properties. In addition, identify the segment(s), as reported in the financial statements, that use the properties described. If any such property is not held in fee or is held subject to an encumbrance that is material to the registrant, so state and describe briefly how held.

Instruction 1 to Item 102: This item requires information that will reasonably inform investors as to the suitability, adequacy, productive capacity, and extent of utilization of the principal physical properties of the registrant and its subsidiaries, to the extent the described properties are material. A registrant should engage in a comprehensive consideration of the materiality of its properties. If appropriate, descriptions may be provided on a collective basis; detailed descriptions of the physical characteristics of individual properties or legal descriptions by metes and bounds are not required and shall not be given.

Instruction 2 to Item 102: In determining materiality under this Item, the registrant should take into account both quantitative and qualitative factors. See Instruction 1 to Item 101 of Regulation S-K.

Instruction 3 to Item 102. In the case of an extractive enterprise, material information shall be given as to production, reserves, locations, development and the nature of the registrant's interest. If individual properties are of major significance to an industry segment:

A. More detailed information concerning these matters shall be furnished; and
B. Appropriate maps shall be used to disclose location data of significant properties except in cases for which numerous maps would be required.

Instruction 4 to Item 102.

A. If reserve estimates are referred to in the document, the staff of the Office of Engineering, Division of Corporation Finance of the Commission, shall be consulted. That Office may request that a copy of the full report of the engineer or other expert who estimated the reserves be furnished as supplemental information and not as part of the filing. See Rule 418 of Regulation C and Rule 12b-4 of Regulation 12B with respect to the submission to, and return by, the Commission of supplemental information.
B. If the estimates of reserves, or any estimated valuation thereof, are represented as being based on estimates prepared or reviewed by independent consultants, those independent consultants shall be named in the document.

Instruction 5 to Item 102. Estimates of oil or gas reserves other than proved or, in the case of other extractive reserves, estimates other than proved or probable reserves, and any estimated values of such reserves shall not be disclosed in any document publicly filed with the Commission, unless such information is required to be disclosed in the document by foreign or state law; *provided, however*, that where such estimates previously have been provided to a person (or any of its affiliates) that is offering to acquire, merge or consolidate with the registrant or otherwise to acquire the registrant's securities, such estimates may be included in documents relating to such acquisition.

Instruction 6 to Item 102. The definitions in Rule 4-10(a) of Regulation S-X shall apply to this Item with respect to oil and gas operations.

Item 103 – Legal Proceedings

a. Describe briefly any material pending legal proceedings, other than ordinary routine litigation incidental to the business, to which the registrant or any of its subsidiaries is a party or of which any of their property is the subject. Include the name of the court or agency in which the proceedings are pending, the date instituted, the principal parties thereto, a description of the factual basis alleged to underlie the proceedings and the relief sought. Include similar information as to any such proceedings known to be contemplated by governmental authorities. Information may be provided by hyperlink or cross-reference to legal proceedings disclosure elsewhere in the document, such as in Management's Discussion & Analysis (MD&A), Risk Factors and notes to the financial statements.

b. No information need be given under this section for proceedings:

1. That involve negligence or other claims or actions if the business ordinarily results in such claims or actions, unless the claim or action departs from the normal kind of such claims or actions; or

2. That involve primarily a claim for damages if the amount involved, exclusive of interest and costs, does not exceed 10 percent of the current assets of the registrant and its subsidiaries on a consolidated basis. However, if any proceeding presents in large degree the same legal or factual issues as other proceedings pending or known to be contemplated, the amount involved in such other proceedings shall be included in computing such percentage.

c. Notwithstanding paragraph (b) of this section, disclosure under this section shall include, but shall not be limited to:

1. Any material bankruptcy, receivership, or similar proceeding with respect to the registrant or any of its significant subsidiaries;

2. Any material proceedings to which any director, officer or affiliate of the registrant, any owner of record or beneficially of more than five percent of any class of voting securities of the registrant, or any associate of any such director, officer, affiliate of the registrant, or security holder is a party adverse to the registrant or any of its subsidiaries or has a material interest adverse to the registrant or any of its subsidiaries;

3. Administrative or judicial proceedings (including proceedings which present in large degree the same issues) arising under any Federal, State, or local provisions that have been enacted or adopted regulating the discharge of materials into the environment or primarily for the purpose of protecting the environment. Such proceedings shall not be deemed "ordinary routine litigation incidental to the business" and shall be described if:

i. Such proceeding is material to the business or financial condition of the registrant;

ii. Such proceeding involves primarily a claim for damages, or involves potential monetary sanctions, capital expenditures, deferred charges or charges to income and the amount involved, exclusive of interest and costs, exceeds 10 percent of the current assets of the registrant and its subsidiaries on a consolidated basis; or

iii. A governmental authority is a party to such proceeding and such proceeding involves potential monetary sanctions, unless the registrant reasonably believes that such proceeding will result in no monetary sanctions, or in monetary sanctions, exclusive of interest and costs, of less than $300,000 or, at the election of the registrant, such other threshold that

      A. the registrant determines is reasonably designed to result in disclosure of any such proceeding that is material to the business or financial condition is disclosed,

      B. the registrant discloses (including any change thereto) in each annual and quarterly report, and

      C. does not exceed the lesser of $1 million or one percent of the current assets of the registrant and its subsidiaries on a consolidated basis; provided, however, that such proceedings that are similar in nature may be grouped and described generically.

Item 104 – Mine Safety Disclosure

a. A registrant that is the operator, or that has a subsidiary that is an operator, of a coal or other mine shall provide the information specified below for the time period covered by the report:

    1. For each coal or other mine of which the registrant or a subsidiary of the registrant is an operator, identify the mine and disclose:

        i. The total number of violations of mandatory health or safety standards that could significantly and substantially contribute to the cause and effect of a coal or other mine safety or health hazard under section 104 of the Federal Mine Safety and Health Act of 1977 for which the operator received a citation from the Mine Safety and Health Administration.

        ii. The total number of orders issued under section 104(b) of such Act.

        iii. The total number of citations and orders for unwarrantable failure of the mine operator to comply with mandatory health or safety standards under section 104(d) of such Act.

        iv. The total number of flagrant violations under section 110(b)(2) of such Act.

        v. The total number of imminent danger orders issued under section 107(a) of such Act.

        vi. The total dollar value of proposed assessments from the Mine Safety and Health Administration under such Act

        Instruction to Item 104(a)(1)(vi): Registrants must provide the total dollar value of assessments proposed by MSHA relating to any type of violation during the period covered by the report, regardless of whether the registrant has challenged or appealed the assessment.

        vii. The total number of mining-related fatalities.

        Instruction to Item 104(a)(1)(vii): Registrants must report all fatalities occurring at a coal or other mine during the period covered by the report unless the fatality has been determined by MSHA to be unrelated to mining activity.

    2. A list of coal or other mines, of which the registrant or a subsidiary of the registrant is an operator, that receive written notice from the Mine Safety and Health Administration of:

        i. A pattern of violations of mandatory health or safety standards that are of such nature as could have significantly and substantially contributed to

Regulation S-K   **Item 105**

the cause and effect of coal or other mine health or safety hazards under section 104(e) of such Act; or

    ii. The potential to have such a pattern.

3. Any pending legal action before the Federal Mine Safety and Health Review Commission involving such coal or other mine.

    Instruction to Item 104(a)(3): The registrant must report the total number of legal actions that were pending before the Federal Mine Safety and Health Review Commission as of the last day of the time period covered by the report, as well as the aggregate number of legal actions instituted and the aggregate number of legal actions resolved during the reporting period. With respect to the total number of legal actions that were pending before the Federal Mine Safety and Health Review Commission as of the last day of the time period covered by the report, the registrant must also report the number of such legal actions that are (a) contests of citations and orders referenced in Subpart B of 29 CFR Part 2700; (b) contests of proposed penalties referenced in Subpart C of 29 CFR Part 2700; (c) complaints for compensation referenced in Subpart D of 29 CFR Part 2700; (d) complaints of discharge, discrimination or interference referenced in Subpart E of 29 CFR Part 2700; (e) applications for temporary relief referenced in Subpart F of 29 CFR Part 2700; and (f) appeals of judges' decisions or orders to the Federal Mine Safety and Health Review Commission referenced in Subpart H of 29 CFR Part 2700.

b. **Definitions**. For purposes of this Item:

1. The term *coal or other mine* means a coal or other mine, as defined in section 3 of the Federal Mine Safety and Health Act of 1977, that is subject to the provisions of such Act.
2. The term *operator* has the meaning given the term in section 3 of the Federal Mine Safety and Health Act of 1977.
3. The term *subsidiary* has the meaning given the term in Exchange Act Rule 12b-2.

Instructions to Item 104:

1. The registrant must provide the information required by this Item as specified by § 601(b)(95) of this chapter. In addition, the registrant must provide a statement, in an appropriately captioned section of the periodic report, that the information concerning mine safety violations or other regulatory matters required by Section 1503(a) of the Dodd-Frank Wall Street Reform and Consumer Protection Act and this Item is included in exhibit 95 to the periodic report.
2. When the disclosure required by this item is included in an exhibit to an annual report on Form 10-K, the information is to be provided for the registrant's fiscal year.

Item 105 – Risk factors

a. Where appropriate, provide under the caption "Risk Factors" a discussion of the material factors that make an investment in the registrant or offering speculative or risky. This discussion must be organized logically with relevant headings and each risk factor should be set forth under a subcaption that adequately describes the risk. The presentation of risks that could apply generically to any registrant or any offering is discouraged, but to the extent generic risk factors are presented, disclose them at the end of the risk factor section under the caption "General Risk Factors."

223

b. Concisely explain how each risk affects the registrant or the securities being offered. If the discussion is longer than 15 pages, include in the forepart of the prospectus or annual report, as applicable, a series of concise, bulleted or numbered statements that is no more than two pages summarizing the principal factors that make an investment in the registrant or offering speculative or risky. If the risk factor discussion is included in a registration statement, it must immediately follow the summary section required by Item 503 of Regulation S-K. If you do not include a summary section, the risk factor section must immediately follow the cover page of the prospectus or the pricing information section that immediately follows the cover page. Pricing information means price and price-related information that you may omit from the prospectus in an effective registration statement based on Rule 430A. The registrant must furnish this information in plain English. See Rule 421(d) of Regulation C of this chapter. .

Item 201 – Market Price of and Dividends on the Registrant's Common Equity and Related Stockholder Matters

a. **Market information.**
    1.
        i.   Identify the principal United States market(s) and the corresponding trading symbol(s) for each class of the registrant's common equity. In the case of foreign registrants, also identify the principal foreign public trading market(s), if any, and the corresponding trading symbol(s) for each class of the registrant's common equity.
        ii. If the principal United States market for such common equity is not an exchange, indicate, as applicable, that any over-the-counter market quotations reflect inter-dealer prices, without retail mark-up, mark-down or commission and may not necessarily represent actual transactions.
        iii. Where there is no established public trading market for a class of common equity, furnish a statement to that effect and, if applicable, state the range of high and low bid information for each full quarterly period within the two most recent fiscal years and anysubsequent interim period for which financial statements are included, or are required to be included by 17 CFR 210.3-01 through 210.3-20 (Article 3 of Regulation S-X), indicating the source of such quotations. Reference to quotations shall be qualified by appropriate explanation. For purposes of this Item the existence of limited or sporadic quotations should not of itself be deemed to constitute an "established public trading market."
        iv. Where a foreign registrant has identified a principal established foreign trading market for its common equity pursuant to paragraph (a)(1) of this Item, also provide market price information comparable, to the extent practicable, to that required for the principal United States market, including the source of such information. Such prices shall be stated in the currency in which they are quoted. The registrant may translate such prices into United States currency at the currency exchange rate in effect on the date the price disclosed was reported on the foreign exchange. If the primary United States market for the registrant's common equity trades using American Depositary Receipts, the United States prices disclosed shall be on that basis.

v.   If the information called for by this Item is being presented in a registration statement filed pursuant to the Securities Act or a proxy or information statement filed pursuant to the Exchange Act, the document also shall include price information as of the latest practicable date, and, in the case of securities to be issued in connection with an acquisition, business combination or other reorganization, as of the date immediately prior to the public announcement of such transaction.

2.   If the information called for by this paragraph (a) is being presented in a registration statement on Form S-1 under the Securities Act or on Form 10 under the Exchange Act relating to a class of common equity for which at the time of filing there is no established United States public trading market, indicate the amount(s) of common equity (i) that is subject to outstanding options or warrants to purchase, or securities convertible into, common equity of the registrant; (ii) that could be sold pursuant to Rule 144 under the Securities Act or that the registrant has agreed to register under the Securities Act for sale by security holders; or (iii) that is being, or has been publicly proposed to be, publicly offered by the registrant (unless such common equity is being offered pursuant to an employee benefit plan or dividend reinvestment plan), the offering of which could have a material effect on the market price of the registrant's common equity.

b.   **Holders.**

1.   Set forth the approximate number of holders of each class of common equity of the registrant as of the latest practicable date.

2.   If the information called for by this paragraph (b) is being presented in a registration statement filed pursuant to the Securities Act or a proxy statement or information statement filed pursuant to the Exchange Act that relates to an acquisition, business combination or other reorganization, indicate the effect of such transaction on the amount and percentage of present holdings of the registrant's common equity owned beneficially by (i) any person (including any group as that term is used in section 13(d)(3) of the Exchange Act) who is known to the registrant to be the beneficial owner of more than five percent of any class of the registrant's common equity and (ii) each director and nominee and (iii) all directors and officers as a group, and the registrant's present commitments to such persons with respect to the issuance of shares of any class of its common equity.

c.   **Dividends**

1.   State the frequency and amount of any cash dividends declared on each class of its common equity by the registrant for the two most recent fiscal years and any subsequent interim period for which financial statements are required to be presented by Article 3 of Regulation S-X. Where there are restrictions (including, where appropriate, restrictions on the ability of registrant's subsidiaries to transfer funds to the registrant in the form of cash dividends, loans or advances) that currently materially limit the registrant's ability to pay such dividends or that the registrant reasonably believes are likely to limit materially the future payment of dividends on the common equity so state and either (i) describe briefly (where appropriate quantify) such restrictions, or (ii) cross

reference to the specific discussion of such restrictions in the Management's Discussion and Analysis of financial condition and operating results prescribed by Item 303 of Regulation S-K and the description of such restrictions required by Regulation S-X in the registrant's financial statements.

2.   Where registrants have a record of paying no cash dividends although earnings indicate an ability to do so, they are encouraged to consider the question of their intention to pay cash dividends in the foreseeable future and, if no such intention exists, to make a statement of that fact in the filing. Registrants which have a history of paying cash dividends also are encouraged to indicate whether they currently expect that comparable cash dividends will continue to be paid in the future and, if not, the nature of the change in the amount or rate of cash dividend payments.

d.   **Securities authorized for issuance under equity compensation plans.**

1.   In the following tabular format, provide the information specified in paragraph (d)(2) of this Item as of the end of the most recently completed fiscal year with respect to compensation plans (including individual compensation arrangements) under which equity securities of the registrant are authorized for issuance, aggregated as follows:

    i.   All compensation plans previously approved by security holders; and
    ii. All compensation plans not previously approved by security holders.

Equity Compensation Plan Information			
Plan category	Number of securities to be issued upon exercise of outstanding options, warrants and rights	Weighted-average exercise price of outstanding options, warrants and rights	Number of securities remaining available for future issuance under equity compensation plans (excluding securities reflected in column (a))
	(a)	(b)	(c)
Equity compensation plans approved by security holders			
Equity compensation plans not approved by security holders			
Total			

2.   The table shall include the following information as of the end of the most recently completed fiscal year for each category of equity compensation plan described in paragraph (d)(1) of this Item:

    i.   The number of securities to be issued upon the exercise of outstanding options, warrants and rights (column (a));
    ii. The weighted-average exercise price of the outstanding options, warrants and rights disclosed pursuant to paragraph (d)(2)(i) of this Item (column (b)); and

      iii.   Other than securities to be issued upon the exercise of the outstanding options, warrants and rights disclosed in paragraph (d)(2)(i) of this Item, the number of securities remaining available for future issuance under the plan (column (c)).

3.   For each compensation plan under which equity securities of the registrant are authorized for issuance that was adopted without the approval of security holders, describe briefly, in narrative form, the material features of the plan.

Instructions to Item 201(d):

1.   Disclosure shall be provided with respect to any compensation plan and individual compensation arrangement of the registrant (or parent, subsidiary or affiliate of the registrant) under which equity securities of the registrant are authorized for issuance to employees or non-employees (such as directors, consultants, advisors, vendors, customers, suppliers or lenders) in exchange for consideration in the form of goods or services as described in FASB ASC Topic 718, *Compensation-Stock-Based Compensation*, and FASC ASC Subtopic 505-50, *Equity—Equity-Based Payments to Non-Employers*. No disclosure is required with respect to:

      i.   Any plan, contract or arrangement for the issuance of warrants or rights to all security holders of the registrant as such on a pro rata basis (such as a stock rights offering) or

      ii.   Any employee benefit plan that is intended to meet the qualification requirements of Section 401(a) of the Internal Revenue Code.

2.   For purposes of this paragraph, an "individual compensation arrangement" includes, but is not limited to, the following: a written compensation contract within the meaning of "employee benefit plan" under Rule 405 under the Securities Act and a plan (whether or not set forth in any formal document) applicable to one person as provided under Item 402(a)(6)(ii) of Regulation S-K.

3.   If more than one class of equity security is issued under its equity compensation plans, a registrant should aggregate plan information for each class of security.

4.   A registrant may aggregate information regarding individual compensation arrangements with the plan information required under paragraph (d)(1)(i) and (ii) of this Item, as applicable.

5.   A registrant may aggregate information regarding a compensation plan assumed in connection with a merger, consolidation or other acquisition transaction pursuant to which the registrant may make subsequent grants or awards of its equity securities with the plan information required under paragraph (d)(1)(i) and (ii) of this Item, as applicable. A registrant shall disclose on an aggregated basis in a footnote to the table the information required under paragraph (d)(2)(i) and (ii) of this Item with respect to any individual options, warrants or rights assumed in connection with a merger, consolidation or other acquisition transaction.

6.   To the extent that the number of securities remaining available for future issuance disclosed in column (c) includes securities available for future issuance under any compensation plan or individual compensation arrangement other than upon the exercise of an option, warrant or right, disclose the number of securities and type of plan separately for each such plan in a footnote to the table.

7.   If the description of an equity compensation plan set forth in a registrant's financial statements contains the disclosure required by paragraph (d)(3) of this Item, a cross-reference to such description will satisfy the requirements of paragraph (d)(3) of this Item.

8. If an equity compensation plan contains a formula for calculating the number of securities available for issuance under the plan, including, without limitation, a formula that automatically increases the number of securities available for issuance by a percentage of the number of outstanding securities of the registrant, a description of this formula shall be disclosed in a footnote to the table.

9. Except where it is part of a document that is incorporated by reference into a prospectus, the information required by this paragraph need not be provided in any registration statement filed under the Securities Act.

e. **Performance graph.**

1. Provide a line graph comparing the yearly percentage change in the registrant's cumulative total shareholder return on a class of common stock registered under section 12 of the Exchange Act (as measured by dividing the sum of the cumulative amount of dividends for the measurement period, assuming dividend reinvestment, and the difference between the registrant's share price at the end and the beginning of the measurement period; by the share price at the beginning of the measurement period) with:

     i. The cumulative total return of a broad equity market index assuming reinvestment of dividends, that includes companies whose equity securities are traded on the same exchange or are of comparable market capitalization; *provided, however,* that if the registrant is a company within the Standard & Poor's 500 Stock Index, the registrant must use that index; and

     ii. The cumulative total return, assuming reinvestment of dividends, of:

         A. A published industry or line-of-business index;

         B. Peer issuer(s) selected in good faith. If the registrant does not select its peer issuer(s) on an industry or line-of-business basis, the registrant shall disclose the basis for its selection; or

         C. Issuer(s) with similar market capitalization(s), but only if the registrant does not use a published industry or line-of-business index and does not believe it can reasonably identify a peer group. If the registrant uses this alternative, the graph shall be accompanied by a statement of the reasons for this selection.

2. For purposes of paragraph (e)(1) of this Item, the term "measurement period" shall be the period beginning at the "measurement point" established by the market close on the last trading day before the beginning of the registrant's fifth preceding fiscal year, through and including the end of the registrant's last completed fiscal year. If the class of securities has been registered under section 12 of the Exchange Act for a shorter period of time, the period covered by the comparison may correspond to that time period.

3. For purposes of paragraph (e)(1)(ii)(A) of this Item, the term "published industry or line-of-business index" means any index that is prepared by a party other than the registrant or an affiliate and is accessible to the registrant's security holders; *provided, however*, that registrants may use an index prepared by the registrant or affiliate if such index is widely recognized and used.

4. If the registrant selects a different index from an index used for the immediately preceding fiscal year, explain the reason(s) for this change and also compare the

registrant's total return with that of both the newly selected index and the index used in the immediately preceding fiscal year.

Instructions to Item 201(e):

1. In preparing the required graphic comparisons, the registrant should:
   a. Use, to the extent feasible, comparable methods of presentation and assumptions for the total return calculations required by paragraph (e)(1) of this Item; *provided, however*, that if the registrant constructs its own peer group index under paragraph (e)(1)(ii)(B), the same methodology must be used in calculating both the registrant's total return and that on the peer group index; and
   b. Assume the reinvestment of dividends into additional shares of the same class of equity securities at the frequency with which dividends are paid on such securities during the applicable fiscal year.

2. In constructing the graph:
   a. The closing price at the measurement point must be converted into a fixed investment, stated in dollars, in the registrant's stock (or in the stocks represented by a given index) with cumulative returns for each subsequent fiscal year measured as a change from that investment; and
   b. Each fiscal year should be plotted with points showing the cumulative total return as of that point. The value of the investment as of each point plotted on a given return line is the number of shares held at that point multiplied by the then-prevailing share price.

3. The registrant is required to present information for the registrant's last five fiscal years, and may choose to graph a longer period; but the measurement point, however, shall remain the same.

4. Registrants may include comparisons using performance measures in addition to total return, such as return on average common shareholders' equity.

5. If the registrant uses a peer issuer(s) comparison or comparison with issuer(s) with similar market capitalizations, the identity of those issuers must be disclosed and the returns of each component issuer of the group must be weighted according to the respective issuer's stock market capitalization at the beginning of each period for which a return is indicated.

6. A registrant that qualifies as a "smaller reporting company," as defined by Item 10(f)(1), is not required to provide the information required by paragraph (e) of this Item.

7. The information required by paragraph (e) of this Item need not be provided in any filings other than an annual report to security holders required by Exchange Act Rule 14a-3 or Exchange Act Rule 14c-3 that precedes or accompanies a registrant's proxy or information statement relating to an annual meeting of security holders at which directors are to be elected (or special meeting or written consents in lieu of such meeting). Such information will not be deemed to be incorporated by reference into any filing under the Securities Act or the Exchange Act, except to the extent that the registrant specifically incorporates it by reference.

8. The information required by paragraph (e) of this Item shall not be deemed to be "soliciting material" or to be "filed" with the Commission or subject to Regulation 14A or 14C, other than as provided in this item, or to the liabilities of section 18 of the Exchange Act, except to the extent that the registrant specifically requests

that such information be treated as soliciting material or specifically incorporates it by reference into a filing under the Securities Act or the Exchange Act.

Instructions to Item 201:

1. [Reserved].
2. Bid information reported pursuant to this Item shall be adjusted to give retroactive effect to material changes resulting from stock dividends, stock splits and reverse stock splits.
3. The computation of the approximate number of holders of registrant's common equity may be based upon the number of record holders or also may include individual participants in security position listings. See Rule 17Ad-8 under the Exchange Act. The method of computation that is chosen shall be indicated.
4. If the registrant is a foreign issuer, describe briefly
    A. Any governmental laws, decrees or regulations in the country in which the registrant is organized that restrict the export or import of capital, including, but not limited to, foreign exchange controls, or that affect the remittance of dividends or other payments to nonresident holders of the registrant's common equity; and
    B. All taxes, including withholding provisions, to which United States common equity holders are subject under existing laws and regulations of the foreign country in which the registrant is organized. Include a brief description of pertinent provisions of any reciprocal tax treaty between such foreign country and the United States regarding withholding. If there is no such treaty, so state.
5. If the registrant is a foreign private issuer whose common equity of the class being registered is wholly or partially in bearer form, the response to this Item shall so indicate together with as much information as the registrant is able to provide with respect to security holdings in the United States. If the securities being registered trade in the United States in the form of American Depositary Receipts or similar certificates, the response to this Item shall so indicate together with the name of the depositary issuing such receipts and the number of shares or other units of the underlying security representing the trading units in such receipts.

Item 202 – Description of Registrant's Securities

a. **Capital stock.** If capital stock is to be registered, state the title of the class and describe such of the matters listed in paragraphs (a)(1) through (5) as are relevant. A complete legal description of the securities need not be given.
    1. Outline briefly: (i) dividend rights; (ii) terms of conversion; (iii) sinking fund provisions; (iv) redemption provisions; (v) voting rights, including any provisions specifying the vote required by security holders to take action; (vi) any classification of the Board of Directors, and the impact of such classification where cumulative voting is permitted or required; (vii) liquidation rights; (viii) preemption rights; and (ix) liability to further calls or to assessment by the registrant and for liabilities of the registrant imposed on its stockholders under state statutes (e.g., to laborers, servants or employees of the registrant), unless such disclosure would be immaterial because the financial resources of the registrant or other factors make it improbable that liability under such state statues would be imposed; (x) any restriction on alienability of the securities to be registered; and (xi) any provision discriminating against any existing or prospective holder of such securities as a result of such security holder owning a substantial amount of securities.

2.   If the rights of holders of such stock may be modified otherwise than by a vote of a majority or more of the shares outstanding, voting as a class, so state and explain briefly.

3.   If preferred stock is to be registered, describe briefly any restriction on the repurchase or redemption of shares by the registrant while there is any arrearage in the payment of dividends or sinking fund installments. If there is no such restriction, so state.

4.   If the rights evidenced by, or amounts payable with respect to, the shares to be registered are, or may be, materially limited or qualified by the rights of any other authorized class of securities, include the information regarding such other securities as will enable investors to understand such limitations or qualifications. No information need be given, however, as to any class of securities all of which will be retired, provided appropriate steps to ensure such retirement will be completed prior to or upon delivery by the registrant of the shares.

5.   Describe briefly or cross-reference to a description in another part of the document, any provision of the registrant's charter or by-laws that would have an effect of delaying, deferring or preventing a change in control of the registrant and that would operate only with respect to an extraordinary corporate transaction involving the registrant (or any of its subsidiaries), such as a merger, reorganization, tender offer, sale or transfer of substantially all of its assets, or liquidation. Provisions and arrangements required by law or imposed by governmental or judicial authority need not be described or discussed pursuant to this paragraph (a)(5). Provisions or arrangements adopted by the registrant to effect, or further, compliance with laws or governmental or judicial mandate are not subject to the immediately preceding sentence where such compliance did not require the specific provisions or arrangements adopted.

b.   **Debt securities.** If debt securities are to be registered, state the title of such securities, the principal amount being offered, and, if a series, the total amount authorized and the total amount outstanding as of the most recent practicable date; and describe such of the matter listed in paragraphs (b)(1) through (10) as are relevant. A complete legal description of the securities need not be given. For purposes solely of this Item, debt securities that differ from one another only as to the interest rate or maturity shall be regarded as securities of the same class. Outline briefly:

1.   Provisions with respect to maturity, interest, conversion, redemption, amortization, sinking fund, or retirement;

2.   Provisions with respect to the kind and priority of any lien securing the securities, together with a brief identification of the principal properties subject to such lien;

3.   Provisions with respect to the subordination of the rights of holders of the securities to other security holders or creditors of the registrant; where debt securities are designated as subordinated in accordance with Instruction 1 to this Item, set forth the aggregate amount of outstanding indebtedness as of the most recent practicable date that by the terms of such debt securities would be senior to such subordinated debt and describe briefly any limitation on the issuance of such additional senior indebtedness or state that there is no such limitation;

4.   Provisions restricting the declaration of dividends or requiring the maintenance of any asset ratio or the creation or maintenance of reserves;

5.   Provisions restricting the incurrence of additional debt or the issuance of additional securities; in the case of secured debt, whether the securities being registered are to be issued on the basis of unbonded bondable property, the deposit of cash or otherwise; as of the most recent practicable date, the approximate amount of unbonded bondable property available as a basis for the issuance of bonds; provisions permitting the withdrawal of cash deposited as a basis for the issuance of bonds; and provisions permitting the release or substitution of assets securing the issue; *Provided, however,* That provisions permitting the release of assets upon the deposit of equivalent funds or the pledge of equivalent property, the release of property no longer required in the business, obsolete property, or property taken by eminent domain or the application of insurance moneys, and other similar provisions need not be described;

6.   The general type of event that constitutes a default and whether or not any periodic evidence is required to be furnished as to the absence of default or as to compliance with the terms of the indenture;

7.   Provisions relating to modification of the terms of the security or the rights of security holders;

8.   If the rights evidenced by the securities to be registered are, or may be, materially limited or qualified by the rights of any other authorized class of securities, the information regarding such other securities as will enable investors to understand the rights evidenced by the securities; to the extent not otherwise disclosed pursuant to this Item; no information need be given, however, as to any class of securities all of which will be retired, provided appropriate steps to ensure such retirement will be completed prior to or upon delivery by the registrant of the securities;

9.   If debt securities are to be offered at a price such that they will be deemed to be offered at an "original issue discount" as defined in paragraph (a) of section 1273 of the Internal Revenue Code, or if a debt security is sold in a package with another security and the allocation of the offering price between the two securities may have the effect of offering the debt security at such an original issue discount, the tax effects thereof pursuant to sections 1271-1278;

10.   The name of the trustee(s) and the nature of any material relationship with the registrant or with any of its affiliates; the percentage of securities of the class necessary to require the trustee to take action; and what indemnification the trustee may require before proceeding to enforce the lien.

c.   **Warrants and rights.** If the securities described are to be offered pursuant to warrants or rights state:
1.   The amount of securities called for by such warrants or rights;
2.   The period during which and the price at which the warrants or rights are exercisable;
3.   The amount of warrants or rights outstanding;
4.   Provisions for changes to or adjustments in the exercise price; and
5.   Any other material terms of such rights on warrants.

d. **Other securities.** If securities other than capital stock, debt, warrants or rights are to be registered, include a brief description (comparable to that required in paragraphs (a), (b) and (c) of Item 202) of the rights evidenced thereby.

e. **Market information for securities other than common equity.** If securities other than common equity are to be registered and there is an established public trading market for such securities (as that term is used in Item 201 of Regulation S-K) provide market information with respect to such securities comparable to that required by paragraph (a) of Item 201 of Regulation S-K.

f. **American Depositary Receipts.** If Depositary Shares represented by American Depositary Receipts are being registered, furnish the following information:
   1. The name of the depositary and the address of its principal executive office.
   2. State the title of the American Depositary Receipts and identify the deposited security. Describe briefly the terms of deposit, including the provisions, if any, with respect to:
      i. The amount of deposited securities represented by one unit of American Depositary Receipts;
      ii. The procedure for voting, if any, the deposited securities;
      iii. The collection and distribution of dividends;
      iv. The transmission of notices, reports and proxy soliciting material;
      v. The sale or exercise of rights;
      vi. The deposit or sale of securities resulting from dividends, splits or plans of reorganization;
      vii. Amendment, extension or termination of the deposit;
      viii. Rights of holders of receipts to inspect the transfer books of the depositary and the list of holders of receipts;
      ix. Restrictions upon the right to deposit or withdraw the underlying securities;
      x. Limitation upon the liability of the depositary.
   3. Describe all fees and charges which may be imposed directly or indirectly against the holder of the American Depositary Receipts, indicating the type of service, the amount of fee or charges and to whom paid.

Instructions to Item 202:
1. Wherever the title of securities is required to be stated, there shall be given such information as will indicate the type and general character of the securities, including the following:
   A. In the case of shares, the par or stated value, if any; the rate of dividends, if fixed, and whether cumulative or non-cumulative; a brief indication of the preference, if any; and if convertible or redeemable, a statement to that effect;
   B. In the case of debt, the rate of interest; the date of maturity or, if the issue matures serially, a brief indication of the serial maturities, such as "maturing serially from 1955 to 1960"; if the payment of principal or interest is contingent, an appropriate indication of such contingency; a brief indication of the priority of the issue; and, if convertible or callable, a statement to that effect; or
   C. In the case of any other kind of security, appropriate information of comparable character.
2. If the registrant is a foreign registrant, include (to the extent not disclosed in the document pursuant to Item 201 of Regulation S-K or otherwise) in the description of the securities:

    A. A brief description of any limitations on the right of nonresident or foreign owners to hold or vote such securities imposed by foreign law or by the charter or other constituent document of the registrant, or if no such limitations are applicable, so state;

    B. A brief description of any governmental laws, decrees or regulations in the country in which the registrant is organized affecting the remittance of dividends, interest and other payments to nonresident holders of the securities being registered;

    C. A brief outline of all taxes, including withholding provisions, to which United States security holders are subject under existing laws and regulations of the foreign country in which the registrant is organized; and

    D. A brief description of pertinent provisions of any reciprocal tax treaty between such foreign country and the United States regarding withholding or, if there is no such treaty, so state.

3. Section 305(a)(2) of the Trust Indenture Act of 1939 ("Trust Indenture Act"), shall not be deemed to require the inclusion in a registration statement, prospectus, or annual report on Form 10-K of any information not required by this Item or Item 601(b)(4)(vi) of this chapter.

4. Where convertible securities or stock purchase warrants are being registered that are subject to redemption or call, the description of the conversion terms of the securities or material terms of the warrants shall disclose:

    A. Whether the right to convert or purchase the securities will be forfeited unless it is exercised before the date specified in a notice of the redemption or call;

    B. The expiration or termination date of the warrants;

    C. The kinds, frequency and timing of notice of the redemption or call, including the cities or newspapers in which notice will be published (where the securities provide for a class of newspapers or group of cities in which the publication may be made at the discretion of the registrant, the registrant should describe such provision); and

    D. In the case of bearer securities, that investors are responsible for making arrangements to prevent loss of the right to convert or purchase in the event of redemption of call, for example, by reading the newspapers in which the notice of redemption or call may be published.

5. The response to paragraph (f) shall include information with respect to fees and charges in connection with (A) the deposit or substitution of the underlying securities; (B) receipt and distribution of dividends; (C) the sale or exercise of rights; (D) the withdrawal of the underlying security; and (E) the transferring, splitting or grouping of receipts. Information with respect to the right to collect the fees and charges against dividends received and deposited securities shall be included in response to this item.

Note to Item 202: If the securities being described have been accepted for listing on an exchange, the exchange may be identified. The document should not, however, convey the impression that the registrant may apply successfully for listing of the securities on an exchange or that, in the case of an underwritten offering, the underwriters may request the registrant to apply for such listing, unless there is reasonable assurance that the securities to be offered will be acceptable to a securities exchange for listing.

Item 302 – Supplementary Financial Information

    a. **Disclosure of material quarterly changes.** When there are one or more retrospective changes to the statements of comprehensive income for any of the quarters within the two most recent fiscal years or any subsequent interim period for which financial statements are included or are required to be included by Article 3 of Regulation S-X that individually or in the aggregate are material, provide an explanation of the reasons for such material changes and disclose, for each affected quarterly period and the fourth quarter in the affected year, summarized financial information related to the statements of comprehensive income as specified Rule 1-02(bb)(1)(ii) of Regulation S-X and earnings per share reflecting such changes.

1.   If the financial statements to which this information relates have been reported on by an accountant, appropriate professional standards and procedures, as enumerated in Auditing Standards issued by the Public Company Accounting Oversight Board ("PCAOB"), shall be followed by the reporting accountant with regard to the disclosure required by this paragraph (a).

2.   This paragraph (a) applies to any registrant, except a foreign private issuer, that has securities registered pursuant to sections 12(b) (other than mutual life insurance companies) or 12(g) of the Exchange Act after the registrant's initial registration of securities under these sections.

3.   A registrant that qualifies as a smaller reporting company, as defined by Item 10(f)(1), is not required to provide the information required by this section.

b.   **Information about oil and gas producing activities.** Registrants engaged in oil and gas producing activities shall present the information about oil and gas producing activities (as those activities are defined in Regulation S-X, Rule 4-10(a)) specified in paragraphs 9-34 of Statement of Financial Accounting Standards ("SFAS") No. 69, "Disclosures about Oil and Gas Producing Activities." If such oil and gas producing activities are regarded as significant under one or more of the tests set forth in paragraph 8 of SFAS No. 69.

Instructions to Paragraph (b):

1.   (a) FASB ASC Subtopic disclosures that relate to annual periods shall be presented for each annual period for which a statement of comprehensive income (as defined in Rule 1-02 of Regulation S-X) is required, (b) SFAS No. 69 disclosures required as of the end of an annual period shall be presented as of the date of each audited balance sheet required, and (c) FASB ASC Subtopic 932-235 disclosures required as of the beginning of an annual period shall be presented as of the beginning of each annual period for which a statement of comprehensive income (as defined in Rule 1-02 of Regulation S-X) is required.

2.   This paragraph, together with Rule 4-10 of Regulation S-X, prescribes financial reporting standards for the preparation of accounts by persons engaged, in whole or in part, in the production of crude oil or natural gas in the United States, pursuant to Section 503 of the Energy Policy and Conservation Act of 1975 ("EPCA") and Section 11(c) of the Energy Supply and Environmental Coordination Act of 1974 ("ESECA") as amended by Section 506 of EPCA. The application of the paragraph to those oil and gas producing operations of companies regulated for ratemaking purposes on an individual-company-cost-of-service basis may, however, give appropriate recognition to differences arising because of the effect of the ratemaking process.

3.   Any person exempted by the Department of Energy from any record-keeping or reporting requirements pursuant to Section 11(c) of ESECA, as amended, is similarly exempted from the related provisions of this paragraph in the preparation of accounts pursuant to EPCA. This exemption does not affect the applicability of this paragraph to filings pursuant to the federal securities laws.

Item 303 – Management's discussion and analysis of financial condition and results of operations

    a.   **Objective.** The objective of the discussion and analysis is to provide material information relevant to an assessment of the financial condition and results of operations of the registrant including an evaluation of the amounts and certainty of cash flows from operations and from outside sources. The discussion and analysis must focus specifically on material events and uncertainties known to management that are reasonably likely to cause reported financial information not to be necessarily indicative of future operating results or of future financial condition. This includes descriptions and amounts of matters that have had a material impact on reported operations, as well as matters that are reasonably likely based on management's assessment to have a material impact on future operations. The discussion and analysis must be of the financial statements and other statistical data that the registrant believes will enhance a reader's understanding of the registrant's financial condition, cash flows and other changes in financial condition and results of operations. A discussion and analysis that meets the requirements of this paragraph (a) is expected to better allow investors to view the registrant from management's perspective.

    b.   **Full fiscal years**. The discussion of financial condition, changes in financial condition and results of operations must provide information as specified in paragraphs (b)(1) through (3) of this section and such other information that the registrant believes to be necessary to an understanding of its financial condition, changes in financial condition and results of operations. Where the financial statements reflect material changes from period-to-period in one or more line items, including where material changes within a line item offset one another, describe the underlying reasons for these material changes in quantitative and qualitative terms. Where in the registrant's judgment a discussion of segment information and/or of other subdivisions (e.g., geographic areas, product lines) of the registrant's business would be necessary to an understanding of such business, the discussion must focus on each relevant reportable segment and/or other subdivision of the business and on the registrant as a whole.

        1.   *Liquidity and capital resources.* Analyze the registrant's ability to generate and obtain adequate amounts of cash to meet its requirements and its plans for cash in the short-term (i.e., the next 12 months from the most recent fiscal period end required to be presented) and separately in the long-term (i.e., beyond the next 12 months). The discussion should analyze material cash requirements from known contractual and other obligations. Such disclosures must specify the type of obligation and the relevant time period for the related cash requirements. As part of this analysis, provide the information in paragraphs (b)(1)(i) and (ii) of this section.

            i.   *Liquidity.* Identify any known trends or any known demands, commitments, events or uncertainties that will result in or that are reasonably likely to result in the registrant's liquidity increasing or decreasing in any material way. If a material deficiency is identified, indicate the course of action that the registrant has taken or proposes to take to remedy the deficiency. Also identify and separately describe internal and external sources of liquidity, and briefly discuss any material unused sources of liquid assets.

ii. *Capital resources.*
   A. Describe the registrant's material cash requirements, including commitments for capital expenditures, as of the end of the latest fiscal period, the anticipated source of funds needed to satisfy such cash requirements and the general purpose of such requirements.
   B. Describe any known material trends, favorable or unfavorable, in the registrant's capital resources. Indicate any reasonably likely material changes in the mix and relative cost of such resources. The discussion must consider changes among equity, debt, and any off-balance sheet financing arrangements.

2. *Results of operations.*
   i. Describe any unusual or infrequent events or transactions or any significant economic changes that materially affected the amount of reported income from continuing operations and, in each case, indicate the extent to which income was so affected. In addition, describe any other significant components of revenues or expenses that, in the registrant's judgment, should be described in order to understand the registrant's results of operations.
   ii. Describe any known trends or uncertainties that have had or that the registrant reasonably expects will have a material favorable or unfavorable impact on net sales or revenues or income from continuing operations. If the registrant knows of events that will cause a material change in the relationship between costs and revenues (such as known or reasonably likely future increases in costs of labor or materials or price increases or inventory adjustments), the change in the relationship must be disclosed.
   iii. If the statement of comprehensive income presents material changes from period to period in net sales or revenue, if applicable, describe the extent to which such changes are attributable to changes in prices or to changes in the volume or amount of goods or services being sold or to the introduction of new products or services.

3. *Critical accounting estimates.* Critical accounting estimates are those estimates made in accordance with generally accepted accounting principles that involve a significant level of estimation uncertainty and have had or are reasonably likely to have a material impact on the financial condition or results of operations of the registrant. Provide qualitative and quantitative information necessary to understand the estimation uncertainty and the impact the critical accounting estimate has had or is reasonably likely to have on financial condition or results of operations to the extent the information is material and reasonably available. This information should include why each critical accounting estimate is subject to uncertainty and, to the extent the information is material and reasonably available, how much each estimate and/or assumption has changed over a relevant period, and the sensitivity of the reported amount to the methods, assumptions and estimates underlying its calculation.

Instructions to paragraph (b):
1. Generally, the discussion must cover the periods covered by the financial statements included in the filing and the registrant may use any presentation that in the registrant's judgment enhances a reader's understanding. A smaller

reporting company's discussion must cover the two-year period required in Article 8 of Regulation S-X) and may use any presentation that in the registrant's judgment enhances a reader's understanding. For registrants providing financial statements covering three years in a filing, discussion about the earliest of the three years may be omitted if such discussion was already included in the registrant's prior filings on EDGAR that required disclosure in compliance with Item 303 of Regulation S-K, provided that registrants electing not to include a discussion of the earliest year must include a statement that identifies the location in the prior filing where the omitted discussion may be found. An emerging growth company, as defined in Rule 405 of the Securities Act) or Rule 12b-2 of the Exchange Act, may provide the discussion required in paragraph (b) of this section for its two most recent fiscal years if, pursuant to Section 7(a) of the Securities Act of 1933, it provides audited financial statements for two years in a Securities Act registration statement for the initial public offering of the emerging growth company's common equity securities.

2.   If the reasons underlying a material change in one line item in the financial statements also relate to other line items, no repetition of such reasons in the discussion is required and a line-by-line analysis of the financial statements as a whole is neither required nor generally appropriate. Registrants need not recite the amounts of changes from period to period if they are readily computable from the financial statements. The discussion must not merely repeat numerical data contained in the financial statements.

3.   Provide the analysis in a format that facilitates easy understanding and that supplements, and does not duplicate, disclosure already provided in the filing. For critical accounting estimates, this disclosure must supplement, but not duplicate, the description of accounting policies or other disclosures in the notes to the financial statements.

4.   For the liquidity and capital resources disclosure, discussion of material cash requirements from known contractual obligations may include, for example, lease obligations, purchase obligations, or other liabilities reflected on the registrant's balance sheet. Except where it is otherwise clear from the discussion, the registrant must discuss those balance sheet conditions or income or cash flow items which the registrant believes may be indicators of its liquidity condition .

5.   Where financial statements presented or incorporated by reference in the registration statement are required by Rule 4-08(e)(3) of Regulation S-X to include disclosure of restrictions on the ability of both consolidated and unconsolidated subsidiaries to transfer funds to the registrant in the form of cash dividends, loans or advances, the discussion of liquidity must include a discussion of the nature and extent of such restrictions and the impact such restrictions have had or are reasonably likely to have on the ability of the parent company to meet its cash obligations.

6.   Any forward-looking information supplied is expressly covered by the safe harbor rule for projections. See Rule 175 under the Securities Act , Rule 3b-6 under the Exchange Act and Securities Act Release No. 6084 (June 25, 1979) .

7.   All references to the registrant in the discussion and in this section mean the registrant and its subsidiaries consolidated.

8.   Discussion of commitments or obligations, including contingent obligations, arising from arrangements with unconsolidated entities or persons that have or

are reasonably likely to have a material current or future effect on a registrant's financial condition, changes in financial condition, revenues or expenses, results of operations, liquidity, cash requirements or capital resources must be provided even when the arrangement results in no obligations being reported in the registrant's consolidated balance sheets. Such off-balance sheet arrangements may include: guarantees; retained or contingent interests in assets transferred; contractual arrangements that support the credit, liquidity or market risk for transferred assets; obligations that arise or could arise from variable interests held in an unconsolidated entity; or obligations related to derivative instruments that are both indexed to and classified in a registrant's own equity under U.S. GAAP.

9. If the registrant is a foreign private issuer, briefly discuss any pertinent governmental economic, fiscal, monetary, or political policies or factors that have materially affected or could materially affect, directly or indirectly, its operations or investments by United States nationals. The discussion must also consider the impact of hyperinflation if hyperinflation has occurred in any of the periods for which audited financial statements or unaudited interim financial statements are filed. See § 210.3-20(c) of this chapter (Rule 3-20(c) of Regulation S-X) for a discussion of cumulative inflation rates that may trigger the requirement in this instruction 9 to this paragraph (b).

10. If the registrant is a foreign private issuer, the discussion must focus on the primary financial statements presented in the registration statement or report. The foreign private issuer must refer to the reconciliation to United States generally accepted accounting principles and discuss any aspects of the difference between foreign and United States generally accepted accounting principles, not discussed in the reconciliation, that the registrant believes are necessary for an understanding of the financial statements as a whole, if applicable.

11. The term *statement of comprehensive income* is as defined in § 210.1-02 of this chapter (Rule 1-02 of Regulation S-X).

c. Interim periods. If interim period financial statements are included or are required to be included by Article 3 of Regulation S-X, a management's discussion and analysis of the financial condition and results of operations must be provided so as to enable the reader to assess material changes in financial condition and results of operations between the periods specified in paragraphs (c)(1) and (2) of this section. The discussion and analysis must include a discussion of material changes in those items specifically listed in paragraph (b) of this section.

1. *Material changes in financial condition.* Discuss any material changes in financial condition from the end of the preceding fiscal year to the date of the most recent interim balance sheet provided. If the interim financial statements include an interim balance sheet as of the corresponding interim date of the preceding fiscal year, any material changes in financial condition from that date to the date of the most recent interim balance sheet provided also must be discussed. If discussions of changes from both the end and the corresponding interim date of the preceding fiscal year are required, the discussions may be combined at the discretion of the registrant.

2.   *Material changes in results of operations.*
    i.   Discuss any material changes in the registrant's results of operations with respect to either the most recent quarter for which a statement of comprehensive income is provided and the corresponding quarter for the preceding fiscal year or, in the alternative, the most recent quarter for which a statement of comprehensive income is provided and the immediately preceding sequential quarter. If the latter immediately preceding sequential quarter is discussed, then provide in summary form the financial information for that immediately preceding sequential quarter that is subject of the discussion or identify the registrant's prior filings on EDGAR that present such information. If there is a change in the form of presentation from period to period that forms the basis of comparison from previous periods provided pursuant to this paragraph, the registrant must discuss the reasons for changing the basis of comparison and provide both comparisons in the first filing in which the change is made.

Instructions to paragraph (c).

1.   If interim financial statements are presented together with financial statements for full fiscal years, the discussion of the interim financial information must be prepared pursuant to this paragraph (c) and the discussion of the full fiscal year's information must be prepared pursuant to paragraph (b) of this Item. Such discussions may be combined. Instructions 2, 3, 4, 6, 8, and 11 to paragraph (b) of this section apply to this paragraph (c).

2.   The registrant's discussion of material changes in results of operations must identify any significant elements of the registrant's income or loss from continuing operations which do not arise from or are not necessarily representative of the registrant's ongoing business.

Item 304 – Changes In and Disagreements With Accountants on Accounting and Financial Disclosure

a.
1.   If during the registrant's two most recent fiscal years or any subsequent interim period, an independent accountant who was previously engaged as the principal accountant to audit the registrant's financial statements, or an independent accountant who was previously engaged to audit a significant subsidiary and on whom the principal accountant expressed reliance in its report, has resigned (or indicated it has declined to stand for re-election after the completion of the current audit) or was dismissed, then the registrant shall:
    i.   State whether the former accountant resigned, declined to stand for re-election or was dismissed and the date thereof.
    ii.   State whether the principal accountant's report on the financial statements for either of the past two years contained an adverse opinion or a disclaimer of opinion, or was qualified or modified as to uncertainty, audit scope, or accounting principles; and also describe the nature of each such adverse opinion, disclaimer of opinion, modification, or qualification.
    iii. State whether the decision to change accountants was recommended or approved by:

     A. Any audit or similar committee of the board of directors, if the issuer has such a committee; or

     B. The board of directors, if the issuer has no such committee.

iv. State whether during the registrant's two most recent fiscal years and any subsequent interim period preceding such resignation, declination or dismissal there were any disagreements with the former accountant on any matter of accounting principles or practices, financial statement disclosure, or auditing scope or procedure, which disagreement(s), if not resolved to the satisfaction of the former accountant, would have caused it to make reference to the subject matter of the disagreement(s) in connection with its report. Also, (A) describe each such disagreement; (B) state whether any audit or similar committee of the board of directors, or the board of directors, discussed the subject matter of each of such disagreements with the former accountant; and (C) state whether the registrant has authorized the former accountant to respond fully to the inquiries of the successor accountant concerning the subject matter of each of such disagreements and, if not, describe the nature of any limitation thereon and the reason therefore. The disagreements required to be reported in response to this Item include both those resolved to the former accountant's satisfaction and those not resolved to the former accountant's satisfaction.

     Disagreements contemplated by this Item are those that occur at the decision-making level, i.e., between personnel of the registrant responsible for presentation of its financial statements and personnel of the accounting firm responsible for rendering its report.

v. Provide the information required by paragraph (a)(1)(iv) of this Item for each of the kinds of events (even though the registrant and the former accountant did not express a difference of opinion regarding the event) listed in paragraphs (a)(1)(v) (A) through (D) of this section, that occurred within the registrant's two most recent fiscal years and any subsequent interim period preceding the former accountant's resignation, declination to stand for re-election, or dismissal ("reportable events"). If the event led to a disagreement or difference of opinion, then the event should be reported as a disagreement under paragraph (a)(1)(iv) and need not be repeated under this paragraph.

     A. The accountant's having advised the registrant that the internal controls necessary for the registrant to develop reliable financial statements do not exist;

     B. The accountant's having advised the registrant that information has come to the accountant's attention that has led it to no longer be able to rely on management's representations, or that has made it unwilling to be associated with the financial statements prepared by management;

     C.

         1. The accountant's having advised the registrant of the need to expand significantly the scope of its audit, or that information has come to the accountant's attention during the time period covered by Item 304(a)(1)(iv), that if further investigated may:

          i. Materially impact the fairness or reliability of either: a previously issued audit report or the underlying financial statements; or the financial statements issued or to be issued covering the fiscal period(s) subsequent to the date of the most recent financial statements covered by an audit report (including information that may prevent it from rendering an unqualified audit report on those financial statements), or

          ii. Cause it to be unwilling to rely on management's representations or be associated with the registrant's financial statements, and

     2. Due to the accountant's resignation (due to audit scope limitations or otherwise) or dismissal, or for any other reason, the accountant did not so expand the scope of its audit or conduct such further investigation; or

   D.

     1. The accountant's having advised the registrant that information has come to the accountant's attention that it has concluded materially impacts the fairness or reliability of either (i) a previously issued audit report or the underlying financial statements, or (ii) the financial statements issued or to be issued covering the fiscal period(s) subsequent to the date of the most recent financial statements covered by an audit report (including information that, unless resolved to the accountant's satisfaction, would prevent it from rendering an unqualified audit report on those financial statements), and

     2. Due to the accountant's resignation, dismissal or declination to stand for re-election, or for any other reason, the issue has not been resolved to the accountant's satisfaction prior to its resignation, dismissal or declination to stand for re-election.

2. If during the registrant's two most recent fiscal years or any subsequent interim period, a new independent accountant has been engaged as either the principal accountant to audit the registrant's financial statements, or as an independent accountant to audit a significant subsidiary and on whom the principal accountant is expected to express reliance in its report, then the registrant shall identify the newly engaged accountant and indicate the date of such accountant's engagement. In addition, if during the registrant's two most recent fiscal years, and any subsequent interim period prior to engaging that accountant, the registrant (or someone on its behalf) consulted the newly engaged accountant regarding:

     i. Either: the application of accounting principles to a specified transaction, either completed or proposed; or the type of audit opinion that might be rendered on the registrant's financial statements, and either a written report was provided to the registrant or oral advice was provided that the new accountant concluded was an important factor considered by the registrant in reaching a decision as to the accounting, auditing or financial reporting issue; or

     ii. Any matter that was either the subject of a disagreement (as defined in paragraph (a)(1)(iv) and the related instructions to this item) or a reportable event (as described in paragraph (a)(1)(v)), then the registrant shall

  A. So state and identify the issues that were the subjects of those consultations;

  B. Briefly describe the views of the newly engaged accountant as expressed orally or in writing to the registrant on each such issue and, if written views were received by the registrant, file them as an exhibit to the report or registration statement requiring compliance with this Item 304(a);

  C. State whether the former accountant was consulted by the registrant regarding any such issues, and if so, provide a summary of the former accountant's views; and

  D. Request the newly engaged accountant to review the disclosure required by this Item 304(a) before it is filed with the Commission and provide the new accountant the opportunity to furnish the registrant with a letter addressed to the Commission containing any new information, clarification of the registrant's expression of its views, or the respects in which it does not agree with the statements made by the registrant in response to Item 304(a). The registrant shall file any such letter as an exhibit to the report or registration statement containing the disclosure required by this Item.

3. The registrant shall provide the former accountant with a copy of the disclosures it is making in response to this Item 304(a) that the former accountant shall receive no later than the day that the disclosures are filed with the Commission. The registrant shall request the former accountant to furnish the registrant with a letter addressed to the Commission stating whether it agrees with the statements made by the registrant in response to this Item 304(a) and, if not, stating the respects in which it does not agree. The registrant shall file the former accountant's letter as an exhibit to the report on registration statement containing this disclosure. If the former accountant's letter is unavailable at the time of filing such report or registration statement, then the registrant shall request the former accountant to provide the letter as promptly as possible so that the registrant can file the letter with the Commission within ten business days after the filing of the report or registration statement. Notwithstanding the ten business day period, the registrant shall file the letter by amendment within two business days of receipt; if the letter is received on a Saturday, Sunday or holiday on which the Commission is not open for business, then the two business day period shall begin to run on and shall include the first business day thereafter. The former accountant may provide the registrant with an interim letter highlighting specific areas of concern and indicating that a more detailed letter will be forthcoming within the ten business day period noted above. If not filed with the report or registration statement containing the registrant's disclosure under this Item 304(a), then the interim letter, if any, shall be filed by the registrant by amendment within two business days of receipt.

    b.   If:

        1.   In connection with a change in accountants subject to paragraph (a) of this Item 304, there was any disagreement of the type described in paragraph (a)(1)(iv) or any reportable event as described in paragraph (a)(1)(v) of this Item;

        2.   During the fiscal year in which the change in accountants took place or during the subsequent fiscal year, there have been any transactions or events similar to those which involved such disagreement or reportable event; and

        3.   Such transactions or events were material and were accounted for or disclosed in a manner different from that which the former accountants apparently would have concluded was required, the registrant shall state the existence and nature of the disagreement or reportable event and also state the effect on the financial statements if the method had been followed which the former accountants apparently would have concluded was required.

            These disclosures need not be made if the method asserted by the former accountants ceases to be generally accepted because of authoritative standards or interpretations subsequently issued.

Instructions to Item 304:

1.   The disclosure called for by paragraph (a) of this Item need not be provided if it has been previously reported as that term is defined in Rule 12b-2 under the Exchange Act; the disclosure called for by paragraph (a) must be *provided, however*, notwithstanding prior disclosure, if required pursuant to Item 9 of Schedule 14A. The disclosure called for by paragraph (b) of this section must be furnished, where required, notwithstanding any prior disclosure about accountant changes or disagreements.

2.   When disclosure is required by paragraph (a) of this section in an annual report to security holders pursuant to Rule 14a-3 or Rule 14c-3, or in a proxy or information statement filed pursuant to the requirements of Schedule 14A or 14C , in lieu of a letter pursuant to paragraph (a)(2)(D) or (a)(3), prior to filing such materials with or furnishing such materials to the Commission, the registrant shall furnish the disclosure required by paragraph (a) of this section to any former accountant engaged by the registrant during the period set forth in paragraph (a) of this section and to the newly engaged accountant. If any such accountant believes that the statements made in response to paragraph (a) of this section are incorrect or incomplete, it may present its views in a brief statement, ordinarily expected not to exceed 200 words, to be included in the annual report or proxy or information statement. This statement shall be submitted to the registrant within ten business days of the date the accountant receives the registrant's disclosure. Further, unless the written views of the newly engaged accountant required to be filed as an exhibit by paragraph 304(a)(2)(B) have been previously filed with the Commission the registrant shall file a Form 8-K concurrently with the annual report or proxy or information statement for the purpose of filing the written views as exhibits thereto.

3.   The information required by Item 304(a) need not be provided for a company being acquired by the registrant that is not subject to the filing requirements of either section 13(a) or 15(d) of the Exchange Act, or, because of section 12(i) of the Exchange Act, has not furnished an annual report to security holders pursuant to Rule 14a-3 or Rule 14c-3 for its latest fiscal year.

4.   The term "disagreements" as used in this Item shall be interpreted broadly, to include any difference of opinion concerning any matter of accounting principles or practices, financial statement disclosure, or auditing scope or procedure which (if not resolved to the satisfaction of the former accountant) would have caused it to make reference to the subject

matter of the disagreement in connection with its report. It is not necessary for there to have been an argument to have had a disagreement, merely a difference of opinion. For purposes of this Item, however, the term disagreements does not include initial differences of opinion based on incomplete facts or preliminary information that were later resolved to the former accountant's satisfaction by, and providing the registrant and the accountant do not continue to have a difference of opinion upon, obtaining additional relevant facts or information.

5. In determining whether any disagreement or reportable event has occurred, an oral communication from the engagement partner or another person responsible for rendering the accounting firm's opinion (or their designee) will generally suffice as the accountant advising the registrant of a reportable event or as a statement of a disagreement at the "decision-making level" within the accounting firm and require disclosure under this Item.

Item 305 – Quantitative and Qualitative Disclosures about Market Risk

  a. **Quantitative information about market risk.**

    1. Registrants shall provide, in their reporting currency, quantitative information about market risk as of the end of the latest fiscal year, in accordance with one of the following three disclosure alternatives. In preparing this quantitative information, registrants shall categorize market risk sensitive instruments into instruments entered into for trading purposes and instruments entered into for purposes other than trading purposes. Within both the trading and other than trading portfolios, separate quantitative information shall be presented, to the extent material, for each market risk exposure category (i.e., interest rate risk, foreign currency exchange rate risk, commodity price risk, and other relevant market risks, such as equity price risk). A registrant may use one of the three alternatives set forth in this section for all of the required quantitative disclosures about market risk. A registrant also may choose, from among the three alternatives, one disclosure alternative for market risk sensitive instruments entered into for trading purposes and another disclosure alternative for market risk sensitive instruments entered into for other than trading purposes. Alternatively, a registrant may choose any disclosure alternative, from among the three alternatives, for each risk exposure category within the trading and other than trading portfolios. The three disclosure alternatives are:

      i. A.

        1. Tabular presentation of information related to market risk sensitive instruments; such information shall include fair values of the market risk sensitive instruments and contract terms sufficient to determine future cash flows from those instruments, categorized by expected maturity dates.

        2. Tabular information relating to contract terms shall allow readers of the table to determine expected cash flows from the market risk sensitive instruments for each of the next five years. Comparable tabular information for any remaining years shall be displayed as an aggregate amount.

        3. Within each risk exposure category, the market risk sensitive instruments shall be grouped based on common characteristics. Within the foreign currency exchange rate risk category, the market risk sensitive instruments shall be grouped by functional

currency and within the commodity price risk category, the market risk sensitive instruments shall be grouped by type of commodity.

    4.   See the Appendix to this Item for a suggested format for presentation of this information; and

B.   Registrants shall provide a description of the contents of the table and any related assumptions necessary to understand the disclosures required under paragraph (a)(1)(i)(A) of this Item 305; or

ii.

A.   Sensitivity analysis disclosures that express the potential loss in future earnings, fair values, or cash flows of market risk sensitive instruments resulting from one or more selected hypothetical changes in interest rates, foreign currency exchange rates, commodity prices, and other relevant market rates or prices over a selected period of time. The magnitude of selected hypothetical changes in rates or prices may differ among and within market risk exposure categories; and

B.   Registrants shall provide a description of the model, assumptions, and parameters, which are necessary to understand the disclosures required under paragraph (a)(1)(ii)(A) of this Item 305; or

iii.

A.   Value at risk disclosures that express the potential loss in future earnings, fair values, or cash flows of market risk sensitive instruments over a selected period of time, with a selected likelihood of occurrence, from changes in interest rates, foreign currency exchange rates, commodity prices, and other relevant market rates or prices;

B.

    1.   For each category for which value at risk disclosures are required under paragraph (a)(1)(iii)(A) of this Item 305, provide either:

        i.   The average, high and low amounts, or the distribution of the value at risk amounts for the reporting period; or

        ii.   The average, high and low amounts, or the distribution of actual changes in fair values, earnings, or cash flows from the market risk sensitive instruments occurring during the reporting period; or

        iii.   The percentage or number of times the actual changes in fair values, earnings, or cash flows from the market risk sensitive instruments exceeded the value at risk amounts during the reporting period;

    2.   Information required under paragraph (a)(1)(iii)(B)(1) of this Item 305 is not required for the first fiscal year end in which a registrant must present Item 305 information; and

C.   Registrants shall provide a description of the model, assumptions, and parameters, which are necessary to understand the disclosures required under paragraphs (a)(1)(iii)(A) and (B) of this Item 305.

2.   Registrants shall discuss material limitations that cause the information required under paragraph (a)(1) of this Item 305 not to reflect fully the net market risk

exposures of the entity. This discussion shall include summarized descriptions of instruments, positions, and transactions omitted from the quantitative market risk disclosure information or the features of instruments, positions, and transactions that are included, but not reflected fully in the quantitative market risk disclosure information.

3.   Registrants shall present summarized market risk information for the preceding fiscal year. In addition, registrants shall discuss the reasons for material quantitative changes in market risk exposures between the current and preceding fiscal years. Information required by this paragraph (a)(3), however, is not required if disclosure is not required under paragraph (a)(1) of this Item 305 for the current fiscal year. Information required by this paragraph (a)(3) is not required for the first fiscal year end in which a registrant must present Item 305 information.

4.   If registrants change disclosure alternatives or key model characteristics, assumptions, and parameters used in providing quantitative information about market risk (e.g., changing from tabular presentation to value at risk, changing the scope of instruments included in the model, or changing the definition of loss from fair values to earnings), and if the effects of any such change is material, the registrant shall:

    i.   Explain the reasons for the change; and

    ii. Either provide summarized comparable information, under the new disclosure method, for the year preceding the current year or, in addition to providing disclosure for the current year under the new method, provide disclosures for the current year and preceding fiscal year under the method used in the preceding year.

Instructions to Paragraph 305(a):

1.   Under paragraph 305(a)(1):

    A. For each market risk exposure category within the trading and other than trading portfolios, registrants may report the average, high, and low sensitivity analysis or value at risk amounts for the reporting period, as an alternative to reporting year-end amounts.

    B. In determining the average, high, and low amounts for the fiscal year under instruction 1.A. of the Instructions to Paragraph 305(a), registrants should use sensitivity analysis or value at risk amounts relating to at least four equal time periods throughout the reporting period (e.g., four quarter-end amounts, 12 month-end amounts, or 52 week-end amounts).

    C. Functional currency means functional currency as defined by generally accepted accounting principles (see, e.g., FASB, Statement of Financial Accounting Standards No. 52, "Foreign Currency Translation", ("FAS 52") paragraph 20 (December 1981)).

    D. Registrants using the sensitivity analysis and value at risk disclosure alternatives are encouraged, but not required, to provide quantitative amounts that reflect the aggregate market risk inherent in the trading and other than trading portfolios.

2.   Under paragraph 305(a)(1)(i):

    A. Examples of contract terms sufficient to determine future cash flows from market risk sensitive instruments include, but are not limited to:

      i.   Debt instruments–principal amounts and weighted average effective interest rates;

      ii.   Forwards and futures–contract amounts and weighted average settlement prices;

      iii.   Options–contract amounts and weighted average strike prices;

      iv.   Swaps–notional amounts, weighted average pay rates or prices, and weighted average receive rates or prices; and

      v.   Complex instruments–likely to be a combination of the contract terms presented in 2.A.i. through iv. of this Instruction;

B. When grouping based on common characteristics, instruments should be categorized, at a minimum, by the following characteristics, when material:

      i.   Fixed rate or variable rate assets or liabilities;

      ii.   Long or short forwards and futures;

      iii.   Written or purchased put or call options with similar strike prices;

      iv.   Receive fixed and pay variable swaps, receive variable and pay fixed swaps, and receive variable and pay variable swaps;

      v.   The currency in which the instruments' cash flows are denominated;

      vi.   Financial instruments for which foreign currency transaction gains and losses are reported in the same manner as translation adjustments under generally accepted accounting principles (see, e.g., FAS 52 paragraph 20 (December 1981)); and

      vii. Derivatives used to manage risks inherent in anticipated transactions;

C. Registrants may aggregate information regarding functional currencies that are economically related, managed together for internal risk management purposes, and have statistical correlations of greater than 75% over each of the past three years;

D. Market risk sensitive instruments that are exposed to rate or price changes in more than one market risk exposure category should be presented within the tabular information for each of the risk exposure categories to which those instruments are exposed;

E. If a currency swap (see, e.g., FAS 52 Appendix E for a definition of currency swap) eliminates all foreign currency exposures in the cash flows of a foreign currency denominated debt instrument, neither the currency swap nor the foreign currency denominated debt instrument are required to be disclosed in the foreign currency risk exposure category. However, both the currency swap and the foreign currency denominated debt instrument should be disclosed in the interest rate risk exposure category; and

F. The contents of the table and related assumptions that should be described include, but are not limited to:

      i.   The different amounts reported in the table for various categories of the market risk sensitive instruments (e.g., principal amounts for debt, notional amounts for swaps, and contract amounts for options and futures);

      ii.   The different types of reported market rates or prices (e.g., contractual rates or prices, spot rates or prices, forward rates or prices); and

      iii.   Key prepayment or reinvestment assumptions relating to the timing of reported amounts.

3. Under paragraph 305(a)(1)(ii):
    A. Registrants should select hypothetical changes in market rates or prices that are expected to reflect reasonably possible near-term changes in those rates and prices. In this regard, absent economic justification for the selection of a different amount, registrants should use changes that are not less than 10 percent of end of period market rates or prices;
    B. For purposes of instruction 3.A. of the Instructions to Paragraph 305(a), the term reasonably possible has the same meaning as defined by generally accepted accounting principles (see, e.g., FASB, Statement of Financial Accounting Standards No. 5, "Accounting for Contingencies," ("FAS 5") paragraph 3 (March 1975));
    C. For purposes of instruction 3.A. of the Instructions to Paragraph 305(a), the term near term means a period of time going forward up to one year from the date of the financial statements (see generally AICPA, Statement of Position 94-6, "Disclosure of Certain Significant Risks and Uncertainties," ("SOP 94-6") at paragraph 7 (December 30, 1994));
    D. Market risk sensitive instruments that are exposed to rate or price changes in more than one market risk exposure category should be included in the sensitivity analysis disclosures for each market risk category to which those instruments are exposed;
    E. Registrants with multiple foreign currency exchange rate exposures should prepare foreign currency sensitivity analysis disclosures that measure the aggregate sensitivity to changes in all foreign currency exchange rate exposures, including the effects of changes in both transactional currency/functional currency exchange rate exposures and functional currency/reporting currency exchange rate exposures. For example, assume a French division of a registrant presenting its financial statements in U.S. dollars ($US) invests in a deutschmark(DM)-denominated debt security. In these circumstances, the $US is the reporting currency and the DM is the transactional currency. In addition, assume this division determines that the French franc (FF) is its functional currency according to FAS 52. In preparing the foreign currency sensitivity analysis disclosures, this registrant should report the aggregate potential loss from hypothetical changes in both the DM/FF exchange rate exposure and the FF/$US exchange rate exposure; and
    F. Model, assumptions, and parameters that should be described include, but are not limited to, how loss is defined by the model (e.g., loss in earnings, fair values, or cash flows), a general description of the modeling technique (e.g., duration modeling, modeling that measures the change in net present values arising from selected hypothetical changes in market rates or prices, and a description as to how optionality is addressed by the model), the types of instruments covered by the model (e.g., derivative financial instruments, other financial instruments, derivative commodity instruments, and whether other instruments are included voluntarily, such as certain commodity instruments and positions, cash flows from anticipated transactions, and certain financial instruments excluded under instruction 3.C.ii. of the General Instructions to Paragraphs 305(a) and 305(b)), and other relevant information about the model's assumptions and parameters, (e.g., the magnitude and timing of selected hypothetical changes in market rates or prices used, the method by

which discount rates are determined, and key prepayment or reinvestment assumptions).

4. Under paragraph 305(a)(1)(iii):

   A. The confidence intervals selected should reflect reasonably possible near-term changes in market rates and prices. In this regard, absent economic justification for the selection of different confidence intervals, registrants should use intervals that are 95 percent or higher;

   B. For purposes of instruction 4.A. of the Instructions to Paragraph 305(a), the term reasonably possible has the same meaning as defined by generally accepted accounting principles (see, e.g., FAS 5, paragraph 3 (March 1975));

   C. For purposes of instruction 4.A. of the Instructions to Paragraphs 305(a), the term near term means a period of time going forward up to one year from the date of the financial statements (see generally SOP 94-6, at paragraph 7 (December 30, 1994));

   D. Registrants with multiple foreign currency exchange rate exposures should prepare foreign currency value at risk analysis disclosures that measure the aggregate sensitivity to changes in all foreign currency exchange rate exposures, including the aggregate effects of changes in both transactional currency/functional currency exchange rate exposures and functional currency/reporting currency exchange rate exposures. For example, assume a French division of a registrant presenting its financial statements in U.S. dollars ($US) invests in a deutschmark (DM)-denominated debt security. In these circumstances, the $US is the reporting currency and the DM is the transactional currency. In addition, assume this division determines that the French franc (FF) is its functional currency according to FAS 52. In preparing the foreign currency value at risk disclosures, this registrant should report the aggregate potential loss from hypothetical changes in both the DM/FF exchange rate exposure and the FF/$US exchange rate exposure; and

   E. Model, assumptions, and parameters that should be described include, but are not limited to, how loss is defined by the model (e.g., loss in earnings, fair values, or cash flows), the type of model used (e.g., variance/covariance, historical simulation, or Monte Carlo simulation and a description as to how optionality is addressed by the model), the types of instruments covered by the model (e.g., derivative financial instruments, other financial instruments, derivative commodity instruments, and whether other instruments are included voluntarily, such as certain commodity instruments and positions, cash flows from anticipated transactions, and certain financial instruments excluded under instruction 3.C.ii. of the General Instructions to Paragraphs 305(a) and 305(b)), and other relevant information about the model's assumptions and parameters, (e.g., holding periods, confidence intervals, and, when appropriate, the methods used for aggregating value at risk amounts across market risk exposure categories, such as by assuming perfect positive correlation, independence, or actual observed correlation).

5. Under paragraph 305(a)(2), limitations that should be considered include, but are not limited to:

   A. The exclusion of certain market risk sensitive instruments, positions, and transactions from the disclosures required under paragraph 305(a)(1) (e.g., derivative commodity instruments not permitted by contract or business custom to be settled in cash or with another financial instrument, commodity positions, cash flows from anticipated transactions, and certain financial instruments excluded under instruction 3.C.ii. of the General Instructions to Paragraphs 305(a) and 305(b)). Failure to include such instruments, positions, and transactions in preparing the disclosures under paragraph 305(a)(1) may be a limitation because the resulting disclosures may not fully reflect the net market risk of a registrant; and

    B.   The ability of disclosures required under paragraph 305(a)(1) to reflect fully the market risk that may be inherent in instruments with leverage, option, or prepayment features (e.g., options, including written options, structured notes, collateralized mortgage obligations, leveraged swaps, and options embedded in swaps).

b.   **Qualitative information about market risk.**
    1.   To the extent material, describe:
        i.   The registrant's primary market risk exposures;
        ii.   How those exposures are managed. Such descriptions shall include, but not be limited to, a discussion of the objectives, general strategies, and instruments, if any, used to manage those exposures; and
        iii.   Changes in either the registrant's primary market risk exposures or how those exposures are managed, when compared to what was in effect during the most recently completed fiscal year and what is known or expected to be in effect in future reporting periods.
    2.   Qualitative information about market risk shall be presented separately for market risk sensitive instruments entered into for trading purposes and those entered into for purposes other than trading.

Instructions to Paragraph 305(b):
1.   For purposes of disclosure under paragraph 305(b), primary market risk exposures means:
    A.   The following categories of market risk: interest rate risk, foreign currency exchange rate risk, commodity price risk, and other relevant market rate or price risks (e.g., equity price risk); and
    B.   Within each of these categories, the particular markets that present the primary risk of loss to the registrant. For example, if a registrant has a material exposure to foreign currency exchange rate risk and, within this category of market risk, is most vulnerable to changes in dollar/yen, dollar/pound, and dollar/peso exchange rates, the registrant should disclose those exposures. Similarly, if a registrant has a material exposure to interest rate risk and, within this category of market risk, is most vulnerable to changes in short-term U.S. prime interest rates, it should disclose the existence of that exposure.
2.   For purposes of disclosure under paragraph 305(b), registrants should describe primary market risk exposures that exist as of the end of the latest fiscal year, and how those exposures are managed.

Instructions to Paragraphs 305(a) and 305(b):
1.   The disclosures called for by paragraphs 305(a) and 305(b) are intended to clarify the registrant's exposures to market risk associated with activities in derivative financial instruments, other financial instruments, and derivative commodity instruments.

2. In preparing the disclosures under paragraphs 305(a) and 305(b), registrants are required to include derivative financial instruments, other financial instruments, and derivative commodity instruments.

3. For purposes of paragraphs 305(a) and 305(b), derivative financial instruments, other financial instruments, and derivative commodity instruments (collectively referred to as "market risk sensitive instruments") are defined as follows:

A. Derivative financial instruments has the same meaning as defined by generally accepted accounting principles (see, e.g., FASB, Statement of Financial Accounting Standards No. 119, "Disclosure about Derivative Financial Instruments and Fair Value of Financial Instruments," ("FAS 119") paragraphs 5-7 (October 1994)), and includes futures, forwards, swaps, options, and other financial instruments with similar characteristics;

B. Other financial instruments means all financial instruments as defined by generally accepted accounting principles for which fair value disclosures are required (see, e.g., FASB, Statement of Financial Accounting Standards No. 107, "Disclosures about Fair Value of Financial Instruments," ("FAS 107") paragraphs 3 and 8 (December 1991)), except for derivative financial instruments, as defined above;

C.

   i.   Other financial instruments include, but are not limited to, trade accounts receivable, investments, loans, structured notes, mortgage-backed securities, trade accounts payable, indexed debt instruments, interest-only and principal-only obligations, deposits, and other debt obligations;

   ii. Other financial instruments exclude employers' and plans' obligations for pension and other post-retirement benefits, substantively extinguished debt, insurance contracts, lease contracts, warranty obligations and rights, unconditional purchase obligations, investments accounted for under the equity method, noncontrolling interests in consolidated enterprises, and equity instruments issued by the registrant and classified in stockholders' equity in the statement of financial position (see, e.g., FAS 107, paragraph 8 (December 1991)). For purposes of this item, trade accounts receivable and trade accounts payable need not be considered other financial instruments when their carrying amounts approximate fair value; and

D. Derivative commodity instruments include, to the extent such instruments are not derivative financial instruments, commodity futures, commodity forwards, commodity swaps, commodity options, and other commodity instruments with similar characteristics that are permitted by contract or business custom to be settled in cash or with another financial instrument. For purposes of this paragraph, settlement in cash includes settlement in cash of the net change in value of the derivative commodity instrument (e.g., net cash settlement based on changes in the price of the underlying commodity).

4.

A. In addition to providing required disclosures for the market risk sensitive instruments defined in instruction 2. of the General Instructions to Paragraphs 305(a) and 305(b), registrants are encouraged to include other market risk sensitive instruments, positions, and transactions within the disclosures required under paragraphs 305(a) and 305(b). Such instruments, positions, and transactions might include commodity positions, derivative commodity instruments that are not permitted by contract or business custom to be settled in cash or with another financial instrument, cash flows from anticipated transactions, and certain financial instruments excluded under instruction 3.C.ii. of the General Instructions to Paragraphs 305(a) and 305(b).

B. Registrants that voluntarily include other market risk sensitive instruments, positions and transactions within their quantitative disclosures about market risk under the sensitivity analysis or value at risk disclosure alternatives are not required to provide separate market risk disclosures for any voluntarily selected instruments, positions, or transactions. Instead, registrants selecting the sensitivity analysis and value at risk disclosure alternatives are permitted to present comprehensive market risk disclosures, which reflect the combined market risk exposures inherent in both the required and any voluntarily selected instruments, position, or transactions. Registrants that choose the tabular presentation disclosure alternative should present voluntarily selected instruments, positions, or transactions in a manner consistent with the requirements in Item 305(a) for market risk sensitive instruments.

C. If a registrant elects to include voluntarily a particular type of instrument, position, or transaction in their quantitative disclosures about market risk, that registrant should include all, rather than some, of those instruments, positions, or transactions within those disclosures. For example, if a registrant holds in inventory a particular type of commodity position and elects to include that commodity position within their market risk disclosures, the registrant should include the entire commodity position, rather than only a portion thereof, in their quantitative disclosures about market risk.

5.

A. Under paragraphs 305(a) and 305(b), a materiality assessment should be made for each market risk exposure category within the trading and other than trading portfolios.

B. For purposes of making the materiality assessment under instruction 5.A. of the General Instructions to Paragraphs 305(a) and 305(b), registrants should evaluate both:

    i. The materiality of the fair values of derivative financial instruments, other financial instruments, and derivative commodity instruments outstanding as of the end of the latest fiscal year; and

    ii. The materiality of potential, near-term losses in future earnings, fair values, and/or cash flows from reasonably possible near-term changes in market rates or prices.

    iii. If either paragraphs B.i. or B.ii. in this instruction of the General Instructions to Paragraphs 305(a) and 305(b) are material, the registrant should disclose quantitative and qualitative information about market risk, if such market risk for the particular market risk exposure category is material.

C. For purposes of instruction 5.B.i. of the General Instructions to Paragraphs 305(a) and 305(b), registrants generally should not net fair values, except to the extent allowed under generally accepted accounting principles (see, e.g.,

FASB Interpretation No. 39, "Offsetting of Amounts Related to Certain Contracts" (March 1992)). For example, under this instruction, the fair value of assets generally should not be netted with the fair value of liabilities.

D. For purposes of instruction 5.B.ii. of the General Instructions to Paragraphs 305(a) and 305(b), registrants should consider, among other things, the magnitude of:

    i. Past market movements;

    ii. Reasonably possible, near-term market movements; and

    iii. Potential losses that may arise from leverage, option, and multiplier features.

E. For purposes of instructions 5.B.ii and 5.D.ii of the General Instructions to Paragraphs 305(a) and 305(b), the term near term means a period of time going forward up to one year from the date of the financial statements (see generally SOP 94-6, at paragraph 7 (December 30, 1994)).

F. For the purpose of instructions 5.B.ii. and 5.D.ii. of the General Instructions to Paragraphs 305(a) and 305(b), the term reasonably possible has the same meaning as defined by generally accepted accounting principles (see, e.g., FAS 5, paragraph 3 (March 1975)).

6. For purposes of paragraphs 305(a) and 305(b), registrants should present the information outside of, and not incorporate the information into, the financial statements (including the footnotes to the financial statements). In addition, registrants are encouraged to provide the required information in one location. However, alternative presentation, such as inclusion of all or part of the information in Management's Discussion and Analysis, may be used at the discretion of the registrant. If information is disclosed in more than one location, registrants should provide cross-references to the locations of the related disclosures.

7. For purposes of the instructions to paragraphs 305(a) and 305(b), trading purposes has the same meaning as defined by generally accepted accounting principles (see, e.g., FAS 119, paragraph 9a (October 1994)). In addition, anticipated transactions means transactions (other than transactions involving existing assets or liabilities or transactions necessitated by existing firm commitments) an enterprise expects, but is not obligated, to carry out in the normal course of business (see, e.g., FASB, Statement of Financial Accounting Standards No. 80, "Accounting for Futures Contracts," para 9 (Aug. 1984)).

c. **Interim periods.** If interim period financial statements are included or are required to be included by Article 3 of Regulation S-X, discussion and analysis shall be provided so as to enable the reader to assess the sources and effects of material changes in information that would be provided under Item 305 of Regulation S-K from the end of the preceding fiscal year to the date of the most recent interim balance sheet.

Instructions to Paragraph 305(c):

1. Information required under paragraph (c) of this Item 305 is not required until after the first fiscal year end in which this Item 305 is applicable.

d. **Safe Harbor.**

1. The safe harbor provided in Section 27A of the Securities Act of 1933 and Section 21E of the Securities Exchange Act of 1934 ("statutory safe harbors")

shall apply, with respect to all types of issuers and transactions, to information provided pursuant to paragraphs (a), (b), and (c) of this Item 305, provided that the disclosure is made by: an issuer; a person acting on behalf of the issuer; an outside reviewer retained by the issuer making a statement on behalf of the issuer; or an underwriter, with respect to information provided by the issuer or information derived from information provided by the issuer.

2.   For purposes of paragraph (d) of this Item 305 only:

      i. All information required by paragraphs (a), (b)(1)(i), (b)(1)(iii), and (c) of this Item 305 is considered forward looking statements for purposes of the statutory safe harbors, except for historical facts such as the terms of particular contracts and the number of market risk sensitive instruments held during or at the end of the reporting period; and

     ii. With respect to paragraph (a) of this Item 305, the meaningful cautionary statements prong of the statutory safe harbors will be satisfied if a registrant satisfies all requirements of that same paragraph (a) of this Item 305.

e.   **Smaller Reporting Companies.** A smaller reporting company, as in 10(f)(1), is not required to provide the information required by this Item.

Instructions to Paragraphs 305(a) through 305(e):

1.   Bank registrants, thrift registrants, and non-bank and non-thrift registrants with market capitalizations on January 28, 1997 in excess of $2.5 billion should provide Item 305 disclosures in filings with the Commission that include annual financial statements for fiscal years ending after June 15, 1997. Non-bank and non-thrift registrants with market capitalizations on January 28, 1997 of $2.5 billion or less should provide Item 305 disclosures in filings with the Commission that include financial statements for fiscal years ending after June 15, 1998.

2.

    A. For purposes of instruction 1. of the General Instructions to Paragraphs 305(a), 305(b), 305(c), 305(d), and 305(e), bank registrants and thrift registrants include any registrant which has control over a depository institution.

    B. For purposes of instruction 2.A. of the General Instructions to Paragraphs 305(a), 305(b), 305(c), 305(d), and 305(e), a registrant has control over a depository institution if:

      i. The registrant directly or indirectly or acting through one or more other persons owns, controls, or has power to vote 25% or more of any class of voting securities of the depository institution;

     ii. The registrant controls in any manner the election of a majority of the directors or trustees of the depository institution; or

    iii. The Federal Reserve Board or Office of Thrift Supervision determines, after notice and opportunity for hearing, that the registrant directly or indirectly exercises a controlling influence over the management or policies of the depository institution.

    C. For purposes of instruction 2.B. of the General Instructions to Paragraphs 305(a), 305(b), 305(c), 305(d), and 305(e), a depository institution means any of the following:

      i. An insured depository institution as defined in section 3(c)(2) of the Federal Deposit Insurance Act;

ii. An institution organized under the laws of the United States, any State of the United States, the District of Columbia, any territory of the United States, Puerto Rico, Guam, American Somoa, or the Virgin Islands, which both accepts demand deposits or deposits that the depositor may withdraw by check or similar means for payment to third parties or others and is engaged in the business of making commercial loans.

D. For purposes of instruction 1. of the General Instructions to Paragraphs 305(a), 305(b), 305(c), 305(d) and 305(e), market capitalization is the aggregate market value of common equity as set forth in General Instruction I.B.1. of Form S-3; *provided however*, that common equity held by affiliates is included in the calculation of market capitalization; and *provided further* that instead of using the 60 day period prior to filing referenced in General Instruction I.B.1. of Form S-3, the measurement date is January 28, 1997.

Appendix to Item 305–Tabular Disclosures

The tables set forth below are illustrative of the format that might be used when a registrant elects to present the information required by paragraph (a)(1)(i)(A) of Item 305 regarding terms and information about derivative financial instruments, other financial instruments, and derivative commodity instruments. These examples are for illustrative purposes only. Registrants are not required to display the information in the specific format illustrated below. Alternative methods of display are permissible as long as the disclosure requirements of the section are satisfied. Furthermore, these examples were designed primarily to illustrate possible formats for presentation of the information required by the disclosure item and do not purport to illustrate the broad range of derivative financial instruments, other financial instruments, and derivative commodity instruments utilized by registrants.

Interest Rate Sensitivity

The table below provides information about the Company's derivative financial instruments and other financial instruments that are sensitive to changes in interest rates, including interest rate swaps and debt obligations. For debt obligations, the table presents principal cash flows and related weighted average interest rates by expected maturity dates. For interest rate swaps, the table presents notional amounts and weighted average interest rates by expected (contractual) maturity dates. Notional amounts are used to calculate the contractual payments to be exchanged under the contract. Weighted average variable rates are based on implied forward rates in the yield curve at the reporting date. The information is presented in U.S. dollar equivalents, which is the Company's reporting currency. The instrument's actual cash flows are denominated in both U.S. dollars ($US) and German deutschmarks (DM), as indicated in parentheses.

December 31, 19X1								
	Expected maturity date							
	19X2	**19X3**	**19X4**	**19X5**	**19X6**	**There-after**	**Total**	**Fair value**
Liabilities	(US$ Equivalent in millions)							
Long-term Debt:								
Fixed Rate ($US)	$XXX	$XXX	$XXX	$XXX	$XXX	$XXX	$XXX	$XXX
Ave interest rate	X.X%	X.X%	X.X%	X.X%	X.X%	X.X%	X.X%	
Fixed Rate (DM)	XXX	XXX	XXX	XXX	XXX	XXX	XXX	XXX
Ave interest rate	X.X%	X.X%	X.X%	X.X%	X.X%	X.X%	X.X%	
Variable Rate ($US)	XXX	XXX	XXX	XXX	XXX	XXX	XXX	XXX
Ave interest rate	X.X%	X.X%	X.X%	X.X%	X.X%	X.X%	X.X%	
Interest Rate Derivatives	(In millions)							
Interest Rate Swaps								
Variable to Fixed ($US)	$XXX	$XXX	$XXX	$XXX	$XXX	$XXX	$XXX	$XXX
Average pay rate	X.X%	X.X%	X.X%	X.X%	X.X%	X.X%	X.X%	
Ave receive rate	X.X%	X.X%	X.X%	X.X%	X.X%	X.X%	X.X%	
Fixed to Variable ($US)	XXX	XXX	XXX	XXX	XXX	XXX	XXX	XXX
Average pay rate	X.X%	X.X%	X.X%	X.X%	X.X%	X.X%	X.X%	
Ave receive rate	X.X%	X.X%	X.X%	X.X%	X.X%	X.X%	X.X%	

Exchange Rate Sensitivity

The table below provides information about the Company's derivative financial instruments, other financial instruments, and firmly committed sales transactions by functional currency and presents such information in U.S. dollar equivalents. The table summarizes information on instruments and transactions that are sensitive to foreign currency exchange rates, including foreign currency forward exchange agreements, deutschmark (DM)-denominated debt obligations, and firmly committed DM sales transactions. For debt obligations, the table presents principal cash flows and related weighted average interest rates by expected maturity dates. For firmly committed DM-sales transactions, sales amounts are presented by the expected transaction date, which are not expected to exceed two years. For foreign currency forward exchange agreements, the table presents the notional amounts and weighted average exchange rates by expected (contractual) maturity dates. These notional amounts generally are used to calculate the contractual payments to be exchanged under the contract.

December 31, 19X1								
	Expected maturity date							
	19X2	**19X3**	**19X4**	**19X5**	**19X6**	**There-after**	**Total**	**Fair value**
On-Balance Sheet Financial Instruments	**(US$ Equivalent in millions)**							
$US Functional Currency:								
Liabilities								
Long-Term Debt:								
Fixed Rate (DM)	$XXX	$XXX	$XXX	$XXX	$XXX	$XXX	$XXX	$XXX
Avg interest rate	X.X	X.X	X.X	X.X	X.X	X.X	X.X	....
Anticipated Transactions and Related Derivatives	**Expected maturity or transaction date** **(US$ Equivalent in millions)**							
$US Functional Currency:								
Firmly committed Sales Contracts (DM)	$XXX	$XXX	....	....	....	....	$XXX	$XXX
Forward Exchange Agmts (Receive $US/Pay DM):								
Contract Amount	XXX	XXX	....	....	....	....	XXX	XXX
Avg Contractual Exchange Rate	X.X	X.X	....	....	....	....	X.X	....

Commodity Price Sensitivity

The table below provides information about the Company's corn inventory and futures contracts that are sensitive to changes in commodity prices, specifically corn prices. For inventory, the table presents the carrying amount and fair value at December 31, 19x1. For the futures contracts the table presents the notional amounts in bushels, the weighted average contract prices, and the total dollar contract amount by expected maturity dates, the latest of which occurs one year from the reporting date. Contract amounts are used to calculate the contractual payments and quantity of corn to be exchanged under the futures contracts.

December 31, 19X1		
	Carrying amount	Fair Value
	(In millions)	
On Balance Sheet Commodity Position and Related Derivatives Corn Inventory	$XXX	$XXX
	Expected maturity 1992	Fair value
Related Derivatives Futures Contracts (Short):		
Contract Volumes (100,000 bushels)...............	XXX	....
Weighted Average Price (Per 100,000 bushels).............	$X.XX	....
Contract Amount ($US in millions)...............	$XXX	$XXX

Item 401 – Directors, Executive Officers, Promoters and Control Persons

a. **Identification of directors**. List the names and ages of all directors of the registrant and all persons nominated or chosen to become directors; indicate all positions and offices with the registrant held by each such person; state his term of office as director and any period(s) during which he has served as such; describe briefly any arrangement or understanding between him and any other person(s) (naming such person(s)) pursuant to which he was or is to be selected as a director or nominee.

Instructions to Paragraph 401(a):

1. Do not include arrangements or understandings with directors or officers of the registrant acting solely in their capacities as such.

2. No nominee or person chosen to become a director who has not consented to act as such shall be named in response to this Item. In this regard, with respect to proxy statements, see Rule 14a-4(d) under the Exchange Act.

3. If the information called for by this paragraph (a) is being presented in a proxy or information statement, no information need be given respecting any director whose term of office as a director will not continue after the meeting to which the statement relates.

4. With regard to proxy statements in connection with action to be taken concerning the election of directors, if fewer nominees are named than the number fixed by or pursuant to the governing instruments, state the reasons for this procedure and that the proxies cannot be voted for a greater number of persons than the number of nominees named.

5. With regard to proxy statements in connection with action to be taken concerning the election of directors, if the solicitation is made by persons other than management, information shall be given as to nominees of the persons making the solicitation. In all other instances, information shall be given as to directors and persons nominated for election or chosen by management to become directors.

b. **Identification of executive officers**. List the names and ages of all executive officers of the registrant and all persons chosen to become executive officers; indicate all positions and offices with the registrant held by each such person; state his term of office as officer and the period during which he has served as such and describe briefly any arrangement or understanding between him and any other person(s) (naming such person) pursuant to which he was or is to be selected as an officer.
    Instructions to Paragraph 401(b):
    1. Do not include arrangements or understandings with directors or officers of the registrant acting solely in their capacities as such.
    2. No person chosen to become an executive officer who has not consented to act as such shall be named in response to this Item.

c. **Identification of certain significant employees.** Where the registrant employs persons such as production managers, sales managers, or research scientists who are not executive officers but who make or are expected to make significant contributions to the business of the registrant, such persons shall be identified and their background disclosed to the same extent as in the case of executive officers. Such disclosure need not be made if the registrant was subject to section 13(a) or 15(d) of the Exchange Act or was exempt from section 13(a) by section 12(g)(2)(G) of such Act immediately prior to the filing of the registration statement, report, or statement to which this Item is applicable.

d. **Family relationships.** State the nature of any family relationship between any director, executive officer, or person nominated or chosen by the registrant to become a director or executive officer.
    Instruction to Paragraph 401(d):
    The term "family relationship" means any relationship by blood, marriage, or adoption, not more remote than first cousin.

e. **Business experience–**
    1. Background. Briefly describe the business experience during the past five years of each director, executive officer, person nominated or chosen to become a director or executive officer, and each person named in answer to paragraph (c) of Item 401, including: each person's principal occupations and employment during the past five years; the name and principal business of any corporation or other organization in which such occupations and employment were carried on; and whether such corporation or organization is a parent, subsidiary or other

affiliate of the registrant. In addition, for each director or person nominated or chosen to become a director, briefly discuss the specific experience, qualifications, attributes or skills that led to the conclusion that the person should serve as a director for the registrant at the time that the disclosure is made, in light of the registrant's business and structure. If material, this disclosure should cover more than the past five years, including information about the person's particular areas of expertise or other relevant qualifications. When an executive officer or person named in response to paragraph (c) of Item 401 has been employed by the registrant or a subsidiary of the registrant for less than five years, a brief explanation shall be included as to the nature of the responsibility undertaken by the individual in prior positions to provide adequate disclosure of his prior business experience. What is required is information relating to the level of his professional competence, which may include, depending upon the circumstances, such specific information as the size of the operation supervised.

2.   Directorships. Indicate any other directorships held, including any other directorships held during the past five years, by each director or person nominated or chosen to become a director in any company with a class of securities registered pursuant to section 12 of the Exchange Act or subject to the requirements of section 15(d) of such Act or any company registered as an investment company under the Investment Company Act of 1940, naming such company.

Instruction to Paragraph 401(e):

For the purposes of paragraph (e)(2), where the other directorships of each director or person nominated or chosen to become a director include directorships of two or more registered investment companies that are part of a "fund complex" as that term is defined in Item 22(a) of Schedule 14A under the Exchange Act, the registrant may, rather than listing each such investment company, identify the fund complex and provide the number of investment company directorships held by the director or nominee in such fund complex.

f.   **Involvement in certain legal proceedings.** Describe any of the following events that occurred during the past ten years and that are material to an evaluation of the ability or integrity of any director, person nominated to become a director or executive officer of the registrant:

1.   A petition under the Federal bankruptcy laws or any state insolvency law was filed by or against, or a receiver, fiscal agent or similar officer was appointed by a court for the business or property of such person, or any partnership in which he was a general partner at or within two years before the time of such filing, or any corporation or business association of which he was an executive officer at or within two years before the time of such filing;

2.   Such person was convicted in a criminal proceeding or is a named subject of a pending criminal proceeding (excluding traffic violations and other minor offenses);

3.   Such person was the subject of any order, judgment, or decree, not subsequently reversed, suspended or vacated, of any court of competent jurisdiction, permanently or temporarily enjoining him from, or otherwise limiting, the following activities:

i. Acting as a futures commission merchant, introducing broker, commodity trading advisor, commodity pool operator, floor broker, leverage transaction merchant, any other person regulated by the Commodity Futures Trading Commission, or an associated person of any of the foregoing, or as an investment adviser, underwriter, broker or dealer in securities, or as an affiliated person, director or employee of any investment company, bank, savings and loan association or insurance company, or engaging in or continuing any conduct or practice in connection with such activity;

ii. Engaging in any type of business practice; or

iii. Engaging in any activity in connection with the purchase or sale of any security or commodity or in connection with any violation of Federal or State securities laws or Federal commodities laws;

4. Such person was the subject of any order, judgment or decree, not subsequently reversed, suspended or vacated, of any Federal or State authority barring, suspending or otherwise limiting for more than 60 days the right of such person to engage in any activity described in paragraph (f)(3)(i) of this section, or to be associated with persons engaged in any such activity;

5. Such person was found by a court of competent jurisdiction in a civil action or by the Commission to have violated any Federal or State securities law, and the judgment in such civil action or finding by the Commission has not been subsequently reversed, suspended, or vacated;

6. Such person was found by a court of competent jurisdiction in a civil action or by the Commodity Futures Trading Commission to have violated any Federal commodities law, and the judgment in such civil action or finding by the Commodity Futures Trading Commission has not been subsequently reversed, suspended or vacated;

7. Such person was the subject of, or a party to, any Federal or State judicial or administrative order, judgment, decree, or finding, not subsequently reversed, suspended or vacated, relating to an alleged violation of:

i. Any Federal or State securities or commodities law or regulation; or

ii. Any law or regulation respecting financial institutions or insurance companies including, but not limited to, a temporary or permanent injunction, order of disgorgement or restitution, civil money penalty or temporary or permanent cease-and-desist order, or removal or prohibition order; or

iii. Any law or regulation prohibiting mail or wire fraud or fraud in connection with any business entity; or

8. Such person was the subject of, or a party to, any sanction or order, not subsequently reversed, suspended or vacated, of any self-regulatory organization (as defined in Section 3(a)(26) of the Exchange Act), any registered entity (as defined in Section 1(a)(29) of the Commodity Exchange Act), or any equivalent exchange, association, entity or organization that has disciplinary authority over its members or persons associated with a member.

Instructions to Paragraph 401(f):

1. For purposes of computing the ten-year period referred to in this paragraph, the date of a reportable event shall be deemed the date on which the final order, judgment or decree was entered, or the date on which any rights of appeal from

preliminary orders, judgments, or decrees have lapsed. With respect to bankruptcy petitions, the computation date shall be the date of filing for uncontested petitions or the date upon which approval of a contested petition became final.

2. If any event specified in this paragraph (f) has occurred and information in regard thereto is omitted on the grounds that it is not material, the registrant may furnish to the Commission, at time of filing (or at the time preliminary materials are filed, or ten days before definitive materials are filed in preliminary filing is not required, pursuant to Rule 14a-6 or 14c-5 under the Exchange Act), as supplemental information and not as part of the registration statement, report, or proxy or information statement, materials to which the omission relates, a description of the event and a statement of the reasons for the omission of information in regard thereto.

3. The registrant is permitted to explain any mitigating circumstances associated with events reported pursuant to this paragraph.

4. If the information called for by this paragraph (f) is being presented in a proxy or information statement, no information need be given respecting any director whose term of office as a director will not continue after the meeting to which the statement relates.

5. This paragraph (f)(7) shall not apply to any settlement of a civil proceeding among private litigants.

g. **Promoters and control persons.**

1. Registrants, which have not been subject to the reporting requirements of section 13(a) or 15(d) of the Exchange Act for the twelve months immediately prior to the filing of the registration statement, report, or statement to which this Item is applicable, and which had a promoter at any time during the past five fiscal years, shall describe with respect to any promoter, any of the events enumerated in paragraphs (f)(1) through (f)(6) of this Item that occurred during the past five years and that are material to a voting or investment decision.

2. Registrants, which have not been subject to the reporting requirements of section 13(a) or 15(d) of the Exchange Act for the twelve months immediately prior to the filing of the registration statement, report, or statement to which this Item is applicable, shall describe with respect to any control person, any of the events enumerated in paragraphs (f)(1) through (f)(6) of this section that occurred during the past five years and that are material to a voting or investment decision.

Instructions to Paragraph 401(g):

1. Instructions 1 through 3 to paragraph (f) shall apply to this paragraph (g).

2. Paragraph (g) shall not apply to any subsidiary of a registrant which has been reporting pursuant to section 13(a) or 15(d) of the Exchange Act for the twelve months immediately prior to the filing of the registration statement, report or statement.

Instruction to Item 401.

The information regarding executive officers called for by this Item need not be furnished in proxy or information statements prepared in accordance with Schedule 14A or Schedule 14C under the Exchange Act if you are relying on General Instruction G of Form 10-K under the Exchange Act, such information is furnished in a separate section captioned "Information about our Executive Officers," and is included in Part I of your annual report on Form 10-K.

Item 402 – Executive compensation

a   **General**

1.   Treatment of foreign private issuers. A foreign private issuer will be deemed to comply with this Item if it provides the information required by Items 6.B, 6.E.2, and 6.F of Form 20-F, with more detailed information provided if otherwise made publicly available or required to be disclosed by the issuer's home jurisdiction or a market in which its securities are listed or traded, or paragraph (19) of General Instruction B of Form 40-F, as applicable. A foreign private issuer that elects to provide domestic Item 402 disclosure must provide the disclosure required by Item 402(w) in its annual report or registration statement, as applicable.

2.   All compensation covered. This Item requires clear, concise and understandable disclosure of all plan and non-plan compensation awarded to, earned by, or paid to the named executive officers designated under paragraph (a)(3) of this Item, and directors covered by paragraph (k) of this Item, by any person for all services rendered in all capacities to the registrant and its subsidiaries, unless otherwise specifically excluded from disclosure in this Item. All such compensation shall be reported pursuant to this Item, even if also called for by another requirement, including transactions between the registrant and a third party where a purpose of the transaction is to furnish compensation to any such named executive officer or director. No amount reported as compensation for one fiscal year need be reported in the same manner as compensation for a subsequent fiscal year; amounts reported as compensation for one fiscal year may be required to be reported in a different manner pursuant to this Item.

3.   Persons covered. Disclosure shall be provided pursuant to this Item for each of the following (the "named executive officers"):

   i.   All individuals serving as the registrant's principal executive officer or acting in a similar capacity during the last completed fiscal year ("PEO"), regardless of compensation level;

   ii. All individuals serving as the registrant's principal financial officer or acting in a similar capacity during the last completed fiscal year ("PFO"), regardless of compensation level;

   iii. The registrant's three most highly compensated executive officers other than the PEO and PFO who were serving as executive officers at the end of the last completed fiscal year; and

   iv. Up to two additional individuals for whom disclosure would have been provided pursuant to paragraph (a)(3)(iii) of this Item but for the fact that the individual was not serving as an executive officer of the registrant at the end of the last completed fiscal year.

Instructions to Item 402(a)(3).

1.   Determination of most highly compensated executive officers. The determination as to which executive officers are most highly compensated shall be made by reference to total compensation for the last completed fiscal year (as required to be disclosed pursuant to paragraph (c)(2)(x) of this Item) reduced by the amount required to be disclosed pursuant to paragraph (c)(2)(viii) of this Item, *provided, however,* that no disclosure need be

provided for any executive officer, other than the PEO and PFO, whose total compensation, as so reduced, does not exceed $100,000.

2.   Inclusion of executive officer of subsidiary. It may be appropriate for a registrant to include as named executive officers one or more executive officers or other employees of subsidiaries in the disclosure required by this Item. See Rule 3b-7 under the Exchange Act.

3.   Exclusion of executive officer due to overseas compensation. It may be appropriate in limited circumstances for a registrant not to include in the disclosure required by this Item an individual, other than its PEO or PFO, who is one of the registrant's most highly compensated executive officers due to the payment of amounts of cash compensation relating to overseas assignments attributed predominantly to such assignments.

4.   Information for full fiscal year. If the PEO or PFO served in that capacity during any part of a fiscal year with respect to which information is required, information should be provided as to all of his or her compensation for the full fiscal year. If a named executive officer (other than the PEO or PFO) served as an executive officer of the registrant (whether or not in the same position) during any part of the fiscal year with respect to which information is required, information shall be provided as to all compensation of that individual for the full fiscal year.

5.   Omission of table or column. A table or column may be omitted if there has been no compensation awarded to, earned by, or paid to any of the named executive officers or directors required to be reported in that table or column in any fiscal year covered by that table.

6.   Definitions. For purposes of this Item:

     i.   The term *stock* means instruments such as common stock, restricted stock, restricted stock units, phantom stock, phantom stock units, common stock equivalent units or any similar instruments that do not have option-like features, and the term *option* means instruments such as stock options, stock appreciation rights and similar instruments with option-like features. The term *stock appreciation rights* ("SARs") refers to SARs payable in cash or stock, including SARs payable in cash or stock at the election of the registrant or a named executive officer. The term *equity* is used to refer generally to stock and/or options.

     ii. The term *plan* includes, but is not limited to, the following: Any plan, contract, authorization or arrangement, whether or not set forth in any formal document, pursuant to which cash, securities, similar instruments, or any other property may be received. A plan may be applicable to one person. Except with respect to the disclosure required by paragraph (t) of this Item, registrants may omit information regarding group life, health, hospitalization, or medical reimbursement plans that do not discriminate in scope, terms or operation, in favor of executive officers or directors of the registrant and that are available generally to all salaried employees.

     iii. The term *incentive plan* means any plan providing compensation intended to serve as incentive for performance to occur over a specified period, whether such performance is measured by reference to financial performance of the registrant or an affiliate, the registrant's stock price, or any other performance measure. An *equity incentive plan* is an incentive plan or portion of an incentive plan under which awards are granted that fall within the scope of FASB ASC Topic 718, *Compensation-Stock Compensation.* A *non-equity incentive plan* is an incentive plan or portion of an incentive plan that is not an equity incentive plan. The term *incentive plan award* means an award provided under an incentive plan.

    iv.   The terms *date of grant* or *grant date* refer to the grant date determined for financial statement reporting purposes pursuant to FASB ASC Topic 718.

    v.   *Closing market price* is defined as the price at which the registrant's security was last sold in the principal United States market for such security as of the date for which the closing market price is determined.

b. **Compensation discussion and analysis.**

    1.   Discuss the compensation awarded to, earned by, or paid to the named executive officers. The discussion shall explain all material elements of the registrant's compensation of the named executive officers. The discussion shall describe the following:

       i.   The objectives of the registrant's compensation programs;

       ii.   What the compensation program is designed to reward;

       iii. Each element of compensation;

       iv.   Why the registrant chooses to pay each element;

       v.   How the registrant determines the amount (and, where applicable, the formula) for each element to pay; and

       vi.   How each compensation element and the registrant's decisions regarding that element fit into the registrant's overall compensation objectives and affect decisions regarding other elements.

       vii. Whether and, if so, how the registrant has considered the results of the most recent shareholder advisory vote on executive compensation required by section 14A of the Exchange Act or Rule 14a-20 of this chapter in determining compensation policies and decisions and, if so, how that consideration has affected the registrant's executive compensation decisions and policies.

    2.   While the material information to be disclosed under Compensation Discussion and Analysis will vary depending upon the facts and circumstances, examples of such information may include, in a given case, among other things, the following:

       i.   The policies for allocating between long-term and currently paid out compensation;

       ii.   The policies for allocating between cash and non-cash compensation, and among different forms of non-cash compensation;

       iii. For long-term compensation, the basis for allocating compensation to each different form of award (such as relationship of the award to the achievement of the registrant's long-term goals, management's exposure to downside equity performance risk, correlation between cost to registrant and expected benefits to the registrant);

       iv.   How the determination is made as to when awards are granted, including awards of equity-based compensation such as options;

v.   What specific items of corporate performance are taken into account in setting compensation policies and making compensation decisions;

vi.   How specific forms of compensation are structured and implemented to reflect these items of the registrant's performance, including whether discretion can be or has been exercised (either to award compensation absent attainment of the relevant performance goal(s) or to reduce or increase the size of any award or payout), identifying any particular exercise of discretion, and stating whether it applied to one or more specified named executive officers or to all compensation subject to the relevant performance goal(s);

vii.   How specific forms of compensation are structured and implemented to reflect the named executive officer's individual performance and/or individual contribution to these items of the registrant's performance, describing the elements of individual performance and/or contribution that are taken into account;

viii.   Registrant policies and decisions regarding the adjustment or recovery of awards or payments if the relevant registrant performance measures upon which they are based are restated or otherwise adjusted in a manner that would reduce the size of an award or payment;

ix.   The factors considered in decisions to increase or decrease compensation materially;

x.   How compensation or amounts realizable from prior compensation are considered in setting other elements of compensation (e.g., how gains from prior option or stock awards are considered in setting retirement benefits);

xi.   With respect to any contract, agreement, plan or arrangement, whether written or unwritten, that provides for payment(s) at, following, or in connection with any termination or change-in-control, the basis for selecting particular events as triggering payment (e.g., the rationale for providing a single trigger for payment in the event of a change-in-control);

xii.   The impact of the accounting and tax treatments of the particular form of compensation;

xiii.   The registrant's equity or other security ownership requirements or guidelines (specifying applicable amounts and forms of ownership), and any registrant policies regarding hedging the economic risk of such ownership;

xiv.   Whether the registrant engaged in any benchmarking of total compensation, or any material element of compensation, identifying the benchmark and, if applicable, its components (including component companies); and

xv.   The role of executive officers in determining executive compensation.

Instructions to Item 402(b).

1.   The purpose of the Compensation Discussion and Analysis is to provide to investors material information that is necessary to an understanding of the registrant's compensation policies and decisions regarding the named executive officers.

2.   The Compensation Discussion and Analysis should be of the information contained in the tables and otherwise disclosed pursuant to this Item. The Compensation Discussion and Analysis should also cover actions regarding executive compensation that were taken after the registrant's last fiscal year's end. Actions that should be addressed might include, as examples only, the adoption or implementation of new or modified programs and policies or specific decisions that were made or steps that were taken that could affect a fair understanding of the named executive officer's compensation for the last fiscal year. Moreover, in some situations it may be necessary to discuss prior years in order to give context to the disclosure provided.

3.   The Compensation Discussion and Analysis should focus on the material principles underlying the registrant's executive compensation policies and decisions and the most important factors relevant to analysis of those policies and decisions. The Compensation Discussion and Analysis shall reflect the individual circumstances of the registrant and shall avoid boilerplate language and repetition of the more detailed information set forth in the tables and narrative disclosures that follow.

4.   Registrants are not required to disclose target levels with respect to specific quantitative or qualitative performance-related factors considered by the compensation committee or the board of directors, or any other factors or criteria involving confidential trade secrets or confidential commercial or financial information, the disclosure of which would result in competitive harm for the registrant. The standard to use when determining whether disclosure would cause competitive harm for the registrant is the same standard that would apply when a registrant requests confidential treatment of confidential trade secrets or confidential commercial or financial information pursuant to Securities Act Rule 406 and Exchange Act Rule 24b-2, each of which incorporates the criteria for non-disclosure when relying upon Exemption 4 of the Freedom of Information Act and Rule 80(b)(4) thereunder. A registrant is not required to seek confidential treatment under the procedures in Securities Act Rule 406 and Exchange Act Rule 24b-2 if it determines that the disclosure would cause competitive harm in reliance on this instruction; however, in that case, the registrant must discuss how difficult it will be for the executive or how likely it will be for the registrant to achieve the undisclosed target levels or other factors.

5.   Disclosure of target levels that are non-GAAP financial measures will not be subject to Regulation G and Item 10(e); however, disclosure must be provided as to how the number is calculated from the registrant's audited financial statements.

c.   **Summary compensation table**.

     1.   General. Provide the information specified in paragraph (c)(2) of this Item, concerning the compensation of the named executive officers for each of the registrant's last three completed fiscal years, in a Summary Compensation Table in the tabular format specified below.

SUMMARY COMPENSATION TABLE

Name and Principal Position	Year	Salary ($)	Bonus ($)	Stock Awards ($)	Option Awards ($)	Non-Equity Incentive Plan Compen- sation ($)	Change in Pension Value and Nonqualified Deferred Compensation Earnings ($)	All Other Compen- sation ($)	Total ($)
(a)	(b)	(c)	(d)	(e)	(f)	(g)	(h)	(i)	(j)
PEO									
PFO									
A									
B									
C									

2. The Table shall include:

i. The name and principal position of the named executive officer (column (a));

ii. The fiscal year covered (column (b));

iii. The dollar value of base salary (cash and non-cash) earned by the named executive officer during the fiscal year covered (column (c));

iv. The dollar value of bonus (cash and non-cash) earned by the named executive officer during the fiscal year covered (column (d));

Instructions to Item 402(c)(2)(iii) and (iv).

1. If the amount of salary or bonus earned in a given fiscal year is not calculable through the latest practicable date, a footnote shall be included disclosing that the amount of salary or bonus is not calculable through the latest practicable date and providing the date that the amount of salary or bonus is expected to be determined, and such amount must then be disclosed in a filing under Item 5.02(f) of Form 8-K.

2. Registrants shall include in the salary column (column (c)) or bonus column (column (d)) any amount of salary or bonus forgone at the election of a named executive officer under which stock, equity-based or other forms of non-cash compensation instead have been received by the named executive officer. However, the receipt of any such form of non-cash compensation instead of salary or bonus must be disclosed in a footnote added to the salary or bonus column and, where applicable, referring to the Grants of Plan-Based Awards Table (required by paragraph (d) of this Item) where the stock, option or non-equity incentive plan award elected by the named executive officer is reported.

v. For awards of stock, the aggregate grant date fair value computed in accordance with FASB ASC Topic 718 (column (e));

vi. For awards of options, with or without tandem SARs (including awards that subsequently have been transferred), the aggregate grant date fair value computed in accordance with FASB ASC Topic 718 (column (f));

Instruction 1 to Item 402(c)(2)(v) and (vi).
For awards reported in columns (e) and (f), include a footnote disclosing all assumptions made in the valuation by reference to a discussion of those assumptions in the registrant's financial statements, footnotes to the financial statements, or discussion in the Management's Discussion and Analysis. The sections so referenced are deemed part of the disclosure provided pursuant to this Item.

Instruction 2 to Item 402(c)(2)(v) and (vi).
If at any time during the last completed fiscal year, the registrant has adjusted or amended the exercise price of options or SARs previously awarded to a named executive officer, whether through amendment, cancellation or replacement grants, or any other means ("repriced"), or otherwise has materially modified such awards, the registrant shall include, as awards required to be reported in column (f), the incremental fair value, computed as of the repricing or modification date in accordance with FASB ASC Topic 718, with respect to that repriced or modified award.

Instruction 3 to Item 402(c)(2)(v) and (vi). For any awards that are subject to performance conditions, report the value at the grant date based upon the probable outcome of such conditions. This amount should be consistent with the estimate of aggregate compensation cost to be recognized over the service period determined as of the grant date under FASB ASC Topic 718, excluding the effect of estimated forfeitures. In a footnote to the table, disclose the value of the award at the grant date assuming that the highest level of performance conditions will be achieved if an amount less than the maximum was included in the table. .

vii.   The dollar value of all earnings for services performed during the fiscal year pursuant to awards under non-equity incentive plans as defined in paragraph (a)(6)(iii) of this Item, and all earnings on any outstanding awards (column (g));

Instructions to Item 402(c)(2)(vii).

1.   If the relevant performance measure is satisfied during the fiscal year (including for a single year in a plan with a multi-year performance measure), the earnings are reportable for that fiscal year, even if not payable until a later date, and are not reportable again in the fiscal year when amounts are paid to the named executive officer.

2.   All earnings on non-equity incentive plan compensation must be identified and quantified in a footnote to column (g), whether the earnings were paid during the fiscal year, payable during the period but deferred at the election of the named executive officer, or payable by their terms at a later date.

viii.   The sum of the amounts specified in paragraphs (c)(2)(viii)(A) and (B) of this Item (column (h)) as follows:

A.   The aggregate change in the actuarial present value of the named executive officer's accumulated benefit under all defined benefit and actuarial pension plans (including supplemental plans) from the pension plan measurement date used for financial statement reporting purposes with respect to the registrant's audited financial statements for the prior completed fiscal year to the pension plan measurement date used for financial statement reporting purposes with respect to the registrant's audited financial statements for the covered fiscal year; and

B. Above-market or preferential earnings on compensation that is deferred on a basis that is not tax-qualified, including such earnings on nonqualified defined contribution plans;

Instructions to Item 402(c)(2)(viii).

1. The disclosure required pursuant to paragraph (c)(2)(viii)(A) of this Item applies to each plan that provides for the payment of retirement benefits, or benefits that will be paid primarily following retirement, including but not limited to tax-qualified defined benefit plans and supplemental executive retirement plans, but excluding tax-qualified defined contribution plans and nonqualified defined contribution plans. For purposes of this disclosure, the registrant should use the same amounts required to be disclosed pursuant to paragraph (h)(2)(iv) of this Item for the covered fiscal year and the amounts that were or would have been required to be reported for the executive officer pursuant to paragraph (h)(2)(iv) of this Item for the prior completed fiscal year.

2. Regarding paragraph (c)(2)(viii)(B) of this Item, interest on deferred compensation is above-market only if the rate of interest exceeds 120% of the applicable federal long-term rate, with compounding (as prescribed under section 1274(d) of the Internal Revenue Code) at the rate that corresponds most closely to the rate under the registrant's plan at the time the interest rate or formula is set. In the event of a discretionary reset of the interest rate, the requisite calculation must be made on the basis of the interest rate at the time of such reset, rather than when originally established. Only the above-market portion of the interest must be included. If the applicable interest rates vary depending upon conditions such as a minimum period of continued service, the reported amount should be calculated assuming satisfaction of all conditions to receiving interest at the highest rate. Dividends (and dividend equivalents) on deferred compensation denominated in the registrant's stock ("deferred stock") are preferential only if earned at a rate higher than dividends on the registrant's common stock. Only the preferential portion of the dividends or equivalents must be included. Footnote or narrative disclosure may be provided explaining the registrant's criteria for determining any portion considered to be above-market.

3. The registrant shall identify and quantify by footnote the separate amounts attributable to each of paragraphs (c)(2)(viii)(A) and (B) of this Item. Where such amount pursuant to paragraph (c)(2)(viii)(A) is negative, it should be disclosed by footnote but should not be reflected in the sum reported in column (h).

ix. All other compensation for the covered fiscal year that the registrant could not properly report in any other column of the Summary Compensation Table (column (i)). Each compensation item that is not properly reportable in columns (c) - (h), regardless of the amount of the compensation item, must be included in column (i). Such compensation must include, but is not limited to:

A. Perquisites and other personal benefits, or property, unless the aggregate amount of such compensation is less than $10,000;

B. All "gross-ups" or other amounts reimbursed during the fiscal year for the payment of taxes;

C. For any security of the registrant or its subsidiaries purchased from the registrant or its subsidiaries (through deferral of salary or bonus, or otherwise) at a discount from the market price of such security at the date of purchase, unless that discount is available generally, either to all security holders or to all salaried employees of the registrant, the compensation cost, if any, computed in accordance with FASB ASC Topic 718;

D. The amount paid or accrued to any named executive officer pursuant to a plan or arrangement in connection with:

1. Any termination, including without limitation through retirement, resignation, severance or constructive termination (including a change in responsibilities) of such executive officer's employment with the registrant and its subsidiaries; or

2. A change in control of the registrant;

E. Registrant contributions or other allocations to vested and unvested defined contribution plans;

F. The dollar value of any insurance premiums paid by, or on behalf of, the registrant during the covered fiscal year with respect to life insurance for the benefit of a named executive officer; and

G. The dollar value of any dividends or other earnings paid on stock or option awards, when those amounts were not factored into the grant date fair value required to be reported for the stock or option award in column (e) or (f); and

Instructions to Item 402(c)(2)(ix).

1. Non-equity incentive plan awards and earnings and earnings on stock and options, except as specified in paragraph (c)(2)(ix)(G) of this Item, are required to be reported elsewhere as provided in this Item and are not reportable as All Other Compensation in column (i).

2. Benefits paid pursuant to defined benefit and actuarial plans are not reportable as All Other Compensation in column (i) unless accelerated pursuant to a change in control; information concerning these plans is reportable pursuant to paragraphs (c)(2)(viii)(A) and (h) of this Item.

3. Any item reported for a named executive officer pursuant to paragraph (c)(2)(ix) of this Item that is not a perquisite or personal benefit and whose value exceeds $10,000 must be identified and quantified in a footnote to column (i). This requirement applies only to compensation for the last fiscal year. All items of compensation are required to be included in the Summary Compensation Table without regard to whether such items are required to be identified other than as specifically noted in this Item.

4.   Perquisites and personal benefits may be excluded as long as the total value of all perquisites and personal benefits for a named executive officer is less than $10,000. If the total value of all perquisites and personal benefits is $10,000 or more for any named executive officer, then each perquisite or personal benefit, regardless of its amount, must be identified by type. If perquisites and personal benefits are required to be reported for a named executive officer pursuant to this rule, then each perquisite or personal benefit that exceeds the greater of $25,000 or 10% of the total amount of perquisites and personal benefits for that officer must be quantified and disclosed in a footnote. The requirements for identification and quantification apply only to compensation for the last fiscal year. Perquisites and other personal benefits shall be valued on the basis of the aggregate incremental cost to the registrant. With respect to the perquisite or other personal benefit for which footnote quantification is required, the registrant shall describe in the footnote its methodology for computing the aggregate incremental cost. Reimbursements of taxes owed with respect to perquisites or other personal benefits must be included in column (i) and are subject to separate quantification and identification as tax reimbursements (paragraph (c)(2)(ix)(B) of this Item) even if the associated perquisites or other personal benefits are not required to be included because the total amount of all perquisites or personal benefits for an individual named executive officer is less than $10,000 or are required to be identified but are not required to be separately quantified.

5.   For purposes of paragraph (c)(2)(ix)(D) of this Item, an accrued amount is an amount for which payment has become due.

x.   The dollar value of total compensation for the covered fiscal year (column (j)). With respect to each named executive officer, disclose the sum of all amounts reported in columns (c) through (i).

Instructions to Item 402(c).

1.   Information with respect to fiscal years prior to the last completed fiscal year will not be required if the registrant was not a reporting company pursuant to section 13(a) or 15(d) of the Exchange Act at any time during that year, except that the registrant will be required to provide information for any such year if that information previously was required to be provided in response to a Commission filing requirement.

2.   All compensation values reported in the Summary Compensation Table must be reported in dollars and rounded to the nearest dollar. Reported compensation values must be reported numerically, providing a single numerical value for each grid in the table. Where compensation was paid to or received by a named executive officer in a different currency, a footnote must be provided to identify that currency and describe the rate and methodology used to convert the payment amounts to dollars.

3.   If a named executive officer is also a director who receives compensation for his or her services as a director, reflect that compensation in the Summary Compensation Table and provide a footnote identifying and itemizing such

compensation and amounts. Use the categories in the Director Compensation Table required pursuant to paragraph (k) of this Item.

4. Any amounts deferred, whether pursuant to a plan established under section 401(k) of the Internal Revenue Code), or otherwise, shall be included in the appropriate column for the fiscal year in which earned.

5. Reduce the amount reported in the applicable Summary Compensation Table column for the fiscal year in which the amount recovered initially was reported as compensation by any amounts recovered pursuant to a registrant's compensation recovery policy required by the listing standards adopted pursuant to Rule 10D-1, and identify such amounts by footnote.

d. **Grants of plan-based awards table**.
1. Provide the information specified in paragraph (d)(2) of this Item, concerning each grant of an award made to a named executive officer in the last completed fiscal year under any plan, including awards that subsequently have been transferred, in the following tabular format:

GRANTS OF PLAN-BASED AWARDS

Name	Grant Date	Estimated Future Payouts Under Non-Equity Incentive Plan Awards			Estimated Future Payouts Under Equity Incentive Plan Awards			All Other Stock Awards: Number of Shares of Stock or Units (#)	All Other Option Awards: Number of Securities Under-lying Options (#)	Exercise or Base Price of Option Awards ($/Sh)	Grant Date Fair Value of Stock and Option Awards
		Thresh-old ($)	Target ($)	Maximum ($)	Thresh-old (#)	Target (#)	Maximum (#)				
(a)	(b)	(c)	(d)	(e)	(f)	(g)	(h)	(i)	(j)	(k)	(l)
PEO											
PFO											
A											
B											
C											

2. The Table shall include:
   i. The name of the named executive officer (column (a));
   ii. The grant date for equity-based awards reported in the table (column (b)). If such grant date is different than the date on which the compensation committee (or a committee of the board of directors performing a similar function or the full board of directors) takes action or is deemed to take action to grant such awards, a separate, adjoining column shall be added between columns (b) and (c) showing such date;

iii.   The dollar value of the estimated future payout upon satisfaction of the conditions in question under non-equity incentive plan awards granted in the fiscal year, or the applicable range of estimated payouts denominated in dollars (threshold, target and maximum amount) (columns (c) thru (e));

iv.   The number of shares of stock, or the number of shares underlying options to be paid out or vested upon satisfaction of the conditions in question under equity incentive plan awards granted in the fiscal year, or the applicable range of estimated payouts denominated in the number of shares of stock, or the number of shares underlying options under the award (threshold, target and maximum amount) (columns (f) through (h));

v.   The number of shares of stock granted in the fiscal year that are not required to be disclosed in columns (f) through (h) (column (i));

vi.   The number of securities underlying options granted in the fiscal year that are not required to be disclosed in columns (f) through (h) (column (j)); and

vii.   The per-share exercise or base price of the options granted in the fiscal year (column (k)). If such exercise or base price is less than the closing market price of the underlying security on the date of the grant, a separate, adjoining column showing the closing market price on the date of the grant shall be added after column (k).

viii.   The grant date fair value of each equity award computed in accordance with FASB ASC Topic 718 (column (*l*)). If at any time during the last completed fiscal year, the registrant has adjusted or amended the exercise or base price of options, SARs or similar option-like instruments previously awarded to a named executive officer, whether through amendment, cancellation or replacement grants, or any other means ("repriced"), or otherwise has materially modified such awards, the incremental fair value, computed as of the repricing or modification date in accordance with FASB ASC Topic 718, with respect to that repriced or modified award, shall be reported.

Instructions to Item 402(d).

1.   Disclosure on a separate line shall be provided in the Table for each grant of an award made to a named executive officer during the fiscal year. If grants of awards were made to a named executive officer during the fiscal year under more than one plan, identify the particular plan under which each such grant was made.

2.   For grants of incentive plan awards, provide the information called for by columns (c), (d) and (e), or (f), (g) and (h), as applicable. For columns (c) and (f), threshold refers to the minimum amount payable for a certain level of performance under the plan. For columns (d) and (g), target refers to the amount payable if the specified performance target(s) are reached. For columns (e) and (h), maximum refers to the maximum payout possible under the plan. If the award provides only for a single estimated payout, that amount must be reported as the target in columns (d) and (g). In columns (d) and (g), registrants must provide a representative amount based on the previous fiscal year's performance if the target amount is not determinable.

3.   In determining if the exercise or base price of an option is less than the closing market price of the underlying security on the date of the grant, the registrant may use either the closing market price as specified in paragraph (a)(6)(v) of this Item, or if no market exists, any other formula prescribed for the security. Whenever the

exercise or base price reported in column (k) is not the closing market price, describe the methodology for determining the exercise or base price either by a footnote or accompanying textual narrative.

4. A tandem grant of two instruments, only one of which is granted under an incentive plan, such as an option granted in tandem with a performance share, need be reported only in column (i) or (j), as applicable. For example, an option granted in tandem with a performance share would be reported only as an option grant in column (j), with the tandem feature noted either by a footnote or accompanying textual narrative.

5. Disclose the dollar amount of consideration, if any, paid by the executive officer for the award in a footnote to the appropriate column.

6. If non-equity incentive plan awards are denominated in units or other rights, a separate, adjoining column between columns (b) and (c) shall be added quantifying the units or other rights awarded.

7. Options, SARs and similar option-like instruments granted in connection with a repricing transaction or other material modification shall be reported in this Table. However, the disclosure required by this Table does not apply to any repricing that occurs through a pre-existing formula or mechanism in the plan or award that results in the periodic adjustment of the option or SAR exercise or base price, an antidilution provision in a plan or award, or a recapitalization or similar transaction equally affecting all holders of the class of securities underlying the options or SARs.

8. For any equity awards that are subject to performance conditions, report in column (l) the value at the grant date based upon the probable outcome of such conditions. This amount should be consistent with the estimate of aggregate compensation cost to be recognized over the service period determined as of the grant date under FASB ASC Topic 718, excluding the effect of estimated forfeitures.

e. **Narrative disclosure to summary compensation table and grants of plan-based awards table.**

1. Provide a narrative description of any material factors necessary to an understanding of the information disclosed in the tables required by paragraphs (c) and (d) of this Item. Examples of such factors may include, in given cases, among other things:

   i. The material terms of each named executive officer's employment agreement or arrangement, whether written or unwritten;

   ii. If at any time during the last fiscal year, any outstanding option or other equity-based award was repriced or otherwise materially modified (such as by extension of exercise periods, the change of vesting or forfeiture conditions, the change or elimination of applicable performance criteria, or the change of the bases upon which returns are determined), a description of each such repricing or other material modification;

   iii. The material terms of any award reported in response to paragraph (d) of this Item, including a general description of the formula or criteria to be applied in determining the amounts payable, and the vesting schedule. For example, state where applicable that dividends will be paid on stock, and if so, the applicable dividend rate and whether that rate is preferential. Describe any performance-based conditions, and any other material conditions, that are applicable to the award. For purposes of the Table required by paragraph (d) of this Item and the narrative disclosure required by paragraph (e) of this Item, performance-based conditions include both performance conditions and market conditions, as those terms are defined in FASB ASC Topic 718; and

iv. An explanation of the amount of salary and bonus in proportion to total compensation.

Instructions to Item 402(e)(1).

1. The disclosure required by paragraph (e)(1)(ii) of this Item would not apply to any repricing that occurs through a pre-existing formula or mechanism in the plan or award that results in the periodic adjustment of the option or SAR exercise or base price, an antidilution provision in a plan or award, or a recapitalization or similar transaction equally affecting all holders of the class of securities underlying the options or SARs.

2. Instructions 4 and 5 to Item 402(b) apply regarding disclosure pursuant to paragraph (e)(1) of target levels with respect to specific quantitative or qualitative performance-related factors considered by the compensation committee or the board of directors, or any other factors or criteria involving confidential trade secrets or confidential commercial or financial information, the disclosure of which would result in competitive harm for the registrant.

3. Reserved.

f. **Outstanding equity awards at fiscal year-end table**.

1. Provide the information specified in paragraph (f)(2) of this Item, concerning unexercised options; stock that has not vested; and equity incentive plan awards for each named executive officer outstanding as of the end of the registrant's last completed fiscal year in the following tabular format:

OUTSTANDING EQUITY AWARDS AT FISCAL YEAR-END

Name	Option Awards					Stock Awards			
Name	Number of Securities Underlying Unexercised Options (#) Exercisable	Number of Securities Underlying Unexercised Options (#) Unexercisable	Equity Incentive Plan Awards: Number of Securities Underlying Unexercised Unearned Options (#)	Option Exercise Price ($)	Option Expiration Date	Number of Shares or Units of Stock That Have Not Vested (#)	Market Value of Shares or Units of Stock That Have Not Vested ($)	Equity Incentive Plan Awards: Number of Unearned Shares, Units or Other Rights That Have Not Vested (#)	Equity Incentive Plan Awards: Market or Payout Value of Unearned Shares, Units or Other Rights That Have Not Vested ($)
(a)	(b)	(c)	(d)	(e)	(f)	(g)	(h)	(i)	(j)
PEO									
PFO									
A									
B									
C									

2. The Table shall include:
    i.   The name of the named executive officer (column (a));
    ii.   On an award-by-award basis, the number of securities underlying unexercised options, including awards that have been transferred other than for value, that are exercisable and that are not reported in column (d) (column (b));
    iii. On an award-by-award basis, the number of securities underlying unexercised options, including awards that have been transferred other than for value, that are unexercisable and that are not reported in column (d) (column (c));
    iv.   On an award-by-award basis, the total number of shares underlying unexercised options awarded under any equity incentive plan that have not been earned (column (d));
    v.   For each instrument reported in columns (b), (c) and (d), as applicable, the exercise or base price (column (e));
    vi.   For each instrument reported in columns (b), (c) and (d), as applicable, the expiration date (column (f));
    vii. The total number of shares of stock that have not vested and that are not reported in column (i) (column (g));
    viii. The aggregate market value of shares of stock that have not vested and that are not reported in column (j) (column (h));
    ix.   The total number of shares of stock, units or other rights awarded under any equity incentive plan that have not vested and that have not been

earned, and, if applicable the number of shares underlying any such unit or right (column (i)); and

x. The aggregate market or payout value of shares of stock, units or other rights awarded under any equity incentive plan that have not vested and that have not been earned (column (j)).

Instructions to Item 402(f)(2).

1. Identify by footnote any award that has been transferred other than for value, disclosing the nature of the transfer.

2. The vesting dates of options, shares of stock and equity incentive plan awards held at fiscal-year end must be disclosed by footnote to the applicable column where the outstanding award is reported.

3. Compute the market value of stock reported in column (h) and equity incentive plan awards of stock reported in column (j) by multiplying the closing market price of the registrant's stock at the end of the last completed fiscal year by the number of shares or units of stock or the amount of equity incentive plan awards, respectively. The number of shares or units reported in columns (d) or (i), and the payout value reported in column (j), shall be based on achieving threshold performance goals, except that if the previous fiscal year's performance has exceeded the threshold, the disclosure shall be based on the next higher performance measure (target or maximum) that exceeds the previous fiscal year's performance. If the award provides only for a single estimated payout, that amount should be reported. If the target amount is not determinable, registrants must provide a representative amount based on the previous fiscal year's performance.

4. Multiple awards may be aggregated where the expiration date and the exercise and/or base price of the instruments is identical. A single award consisting of a combination of options, SARs and/or similar option-like instruments shall be reported as separate awards with respect to each tranche with a different exercise and/or base price or expiration date.

5. Options or stock awarded under an equity incentive plan are reported in columns (d) or (i) and (j), respectively, until the relevant performance condition has been satisfied. Once the relevant performance condition has been satisfied, even if the option or stock award is subject to forfeiture conditions, options are reported in column (b) or (c), as appropriate, until they are exercised or expire, or stock is reported in columns (g) and (h) until it vests.

g. **Option exercises and stock vested table.**

1. Provide the information specified in paragraph (g)(2) of this Item, concerning each exercise of stock options, SARs and similar instruments, and each vesting of stock, including restricted stock, restricted stock units and similar instruments, during the last completed fiscal year for each of the named executive officers on an aggregated basis in the following tabular format:

OPTION EXERCISES AND STOCK VESTED

	Option Awards		Stock Awards	
Name	Number of Shares Acquired on Exercise (#)	Value Realized on Exercise ($)	Number of Shares Acquired on Vesting (#)	Value Realized on Vesting ($)
(a)	(b)	(c)	(d)	(e)
PEO				
PFO				
A				
B				
C				

2.   The Table shall include:
      i.   The name of the executive officer (column (a));
      ii.   The number of securities for which the options were exercised (column (b));
      iii.   The aggregate dollar value realized upon exercise of options, or upon the transfer of an award for value (column (c));
      iv.   The number of shares of stock that have vested (column (d)); and
      v.   The aggregate dollar value realized upon vesting of stock, or upon the transfer of an award for value (column (e)).

Instruction to Item 402(g)(2).

Report in column (c) the aggregate dollar amount realized by the named executive officer upon exercise of the options or upon the transfer of such instruments for value. Compute the dollar amount realized upon exercise by determining the difference between the market price of the underlying securities at exercise and the exercise or base price of the options. Do not include the value of any related payment or other consideration provided (or to be provided) by the registrant to or on behalf of a named executive officer, whether in payment of the exercise price or related taxes. (Any such payment or other consideration provided by the registrant is required to be disclosed in accordance with paragraph (c)(2)(ix) of this Item.) Report in column (e) the aggregate dollar amount realized by the named executive officer upon the vesting of stock or the transfer of such instruments for value. Compute the aggregate dollar amount realized upon vesting by multiplying the number of shares of stock or units by the market value of the underlying shares on the vesting date. For any amount realized upon exercise or vesting for which receipt has been deferred, provide a footnote quantifying the amount and disclosing the terms of the deferral.

h. **Pension benefits**.
   1.   Provide the information specified in paragraph (h)(2) of this Item with respect to each plan that provides for payments or other benefits at, following, or in connection with retirement, in the following tabular format:

PENSION BENEFITS

Name	Plan Name	Number of Years Credited Service (#)	Present Value of Accumulated Benefit ($)	Payments During Last Fiscal Year ($)
(a)	(b)	(c)	(d)	(e)
PEO				
PFO				
A				
B				
C				

   2.   The Table shall include:
      i.   The name of the executive officer (column (a));
      ii.   The name of the plan (column (b));
      iii. The number of years of service credited to the named executive officer under the plan, computed as of the same pension plan measurement date used for financial statement reporting purposes with respect to the registrant's audited financial statements for the last completed fiscal year (column (c));
      iv. The actuarial present value of the named executive officer's accumulated benefit under the plan, computed as of the same pension plan measurement date used for financial statement reporting purposes with respect to the registrant's audited financial statements for the last completed fiscal year (column (d)); and
      v.   The dollar amount of any payments and benefits paid to the named executive officer during the registrant's last completed fiscal year (column (e)).

Instructions to Item 402(h)(2).
   1.   The disclosure required pursuant to this Table applies to each plan that provides for specified retirement payments and benefits, or payments and benefits that will be provided primarily following retirement, including but not limited to tax-qualified defined benefit plans and supplemental executive retirement plans, but excluding tax-qualified defined contribution plans and nonqualified defined contribution plans. Provide a separate row for each such plan in which the named executive officer participates.

2. For purposes of the amount(s) reported in column (d), the registrant must use the same assumptions used for financial reporting purposes under generally accepted accounting principles, except that retirement age shall be assumed to be the normal retirement age as defined in the plan, or if not so defined, the earliest time at which a participant may retire under the plan without any benefit reduction due to age. The registrant must disclose in the accompanying textual narrative the valuation method and all material assumptions applied in quantifying the present value of the current accrued benefit. A benefit specified in the plan document or the executive's contract itself is not an assumption. Registrants may satisfy all or part of this disclosure by reference to a discussion of those assumptions in the registrant's financial statements, footnotes to the financial statements, or discussion in the Management's Discussion and Analysis. The sections so referenced are deemed part of the disclosure provided pursuant to this Item.

3. For purposes of allocating the current accrued benefit between tax qualified defined benefit plans and related supplemental plans, apply the limitations applicable to tax qualified defined benefit plans established by the Internal Revenue Code and the regulations thereunder that applied as of the pension plan measurement date.

4. If a named executive officer's number of years of credited service with respect to any plan is different from the named executive officer's number of actual years of service with the registrant, provide footnote disclosure quantifying the difference and any resulting benefit augmentation.

3. Provide a succinct narrative description of any material factors necessary to an understanding of each plan covered by the tabular disclosure required by this paragraph. While material factors will vary depending upon the facts, examples of such factors may include, in given cases, among other things:

i. The material terms and conditions of payments and benefits available under the plan, including the plan's normal retirement payment and benefit formula and eligibility standards, and the effect of the form of benefit elected on the amount of annual benefits. For this purpose, normal retirement means retirement at the normal retirement age as defined in the plan, or if not so defined, the earliest time at which a participant may retire under the plan without any benefit reduction due to age;

ii. If any named executive officer is currently eligible for early retirement under any plan, identify that named executive officer and the plan, and describe the plan's early retirement payment and benefit formula and eligibility standards. For this purpose, early retirement means retirement at the early retirement age as defined in the plan, or otherwise available to the executive under the plan;

iii. The specific elements of compensation (e.g., salary, bonus, etc.) included in applying the payment and benefit formula, identifying each such element;

iv. With respect to named executive officers' participation in multiple plans, the different purposes for each plan; and

v. Registrant policies with regard to such matters as granting extra years of credited service.

i. **Nonqualified defined contribution and other nonqualified deferred compensation plans**.

1. Provide the information specified in paragraph (i)(2) of this Item with respect to each defined contribution or other plan that provides for the deferral of compensation on a basis that is not tax-qualified in the following tabular format:

NONQUALIFIED DEFERRED COMPENSATION

Name	Executive Contributions in Last FY ($)	Registrant Contributions in Last FY ($)	Aggregate Earnings in Last FY ($)	Aggregate Withdrawals/ Distributions ($)	Aggregate Balance at Last FYE ($)
(a)	(b)	(c)	(d)	(e)	(f)
PFO					
PEO					
A					
B					
C					

2. The Table shall include:
    i.   The name of the executive officer (column (a));
    ii.   The dollar amount of aggregate executive contributions during the registrant's last fiscal year (column (b));
    iii. The dollar amount of aggregate registrant contributions during the registrant's last fiscal year (column (c));
    iv.   The dollar amount of aggregate interest or other earnings accrued during the registrant's last fiscal year (column (d));
    v.   The aggregate dollar amount of all withdrawals by and distributions to the executive during the registrant's last fiscal year (column (e)); and
    vi.   The dollar amount of total balance of the executive's account as of the end of the registrant's last fiscal year (column (f)).

    Instruction to Item 402(i)(2).
    Provide a footnote quantifying the extent to which amounts reported in the contributions and earnings columns are reported as compensation in the last completed fiscal year in the registrant's Summary Compensation Table and amounts reported in the aggregate balance at last fiscal year end (column (f)) previously were reported as compensation to the named executive officer in the registrant's Summary Compensation Table for previous years.

3. Provide a succinct narrative description of any material factors necessary to an understanding of each plan covered by tabular disclosure required by this paragraph. While material factors will vary depending upon the facts, examples of such factors may include, in given cases, among other things:
    i.   The type(s) of compensation permitted to be deferred, and any limitations (by percentage of compensation or otherwise) on the extent to which deferral is permitted;

      ii. The measures for calculating interest or other plan earnings (including whether such measure(s) are selected by the executive or the registrant and the frequency and manner in which selections may be changed), quantifying interest rates and other earnings measures applicable during the registrant's last fiscal year; and

      iii. Material terms with respect to payouts, withdrawals and other distributions.

j. **Potential payments upon termination or change-in-control.** Regarding each contract, agreement, plan or arrangement, whether written or unwritten, that provides for payment(s) to a named executive officer at, following, or in connection with any termination, including without limitation resignation, severance, retirement or a constructive termination of a named executive officer, or a change in control of the registrant or a change in the named executive officer's responsibilities, with respect to each named executive officer:

1. Describe and explain the specific circumstances that would trigger payment(s) or the provision of other benefits, including perquisites and health care benefits;

2. Describe and quantify the estimated payments and benefits that would be provided in each covered circumstance, whether they would or could be lump sum, or annual, disclosing the duration, and by whom they would be provided;

3. Describe and explain how the appropriate payment and benefit levels are determined under the various circumstances that trigger payments or provision of benefits;

4. Describe and explain any material conditions or obligations applicable to the receipt of payments or benefits, including but not limited to non-compete, non-solicitation, non-disparagement or confidentiality agreements, including the duration of such agreements and provisions regarding waiver of breach of such agreements; and

5. Describe any other material factors regarding each such contract, agreement, plan or arrangement.

Instructions to Item 402(j).

1. The registrant must provide quantitative disclosure under these requirements, applying the assumptions that the triggering event took place on the last business day of the registrant's last completed fiscal year, and the price per share of the registrant's securities is the closing market price as of that date. In the event that uncertainties exist as to the provision of payments and benefits or the amounts involved, the registrant is required to make a reasonable estimate (or a reasonable estimated range of amounts) applicable to the payment or benefit and disclose material assumptions underlying such estimates or estimated ranges in its disclosure. In such event, the disclosure would require forward-looking information as appropriate.

2. Perquisites and other personal benefits or property may be excluded only if the aggregate amount of such compensation will be less than $10,000. Individual perquisites and personal benefits shall be identified and quantified as required by Instruction 4 to paragraph (c)(2)(ix) of this Item. For purposes of quantifying health care benefits, the registrant must use the assumptions used for financial reporting purposes under generally accepted accounting principles.

3. To the extent that the form and amount of any payment or benefit that would be provided in connection with any triggering event is fully disclosed pursuant to paragraph (h) or (i) of this Item, reference may be made to that disclosure. However, to the extent that the form or amount of any such payment or benefit would be enhanced or its vesting or other provisions accelerated in connection with any triggering event, such enhancement or acceleration must be disclosed pursuant to this paragraph.

4. Where a triggering event has actually occurred for a named executive officer and that individual was not serving as a named executive officer of the registrant at the end of the last completed fiscal year, the disclosure required by this paragraph for that named executive officer shall apply only to that triggering event.

5. The registrant need not provide information with respect to contracts, agreements, plans or arrangements to the extent they do not discriminate in scope, terms or operation, in favor of executive officers of the registrant and that are available generally to all salaried employees.

k. **Compensation of directors**.

1. Provide the information specified in paragraph (k)(2) of this Item, concerning the compensation of the directors for the registrant's last completed fiscal year, in the following tabular format:

DIRECTOR COMPENSATION

Name	Fees Earned or Paid in Cash ($)	Stock Awards ($)	Option Awards ($)	Non-Equity Incentive Plan Compensation ($)	Change in Pension Value and Nonqualified Deferred Compensation Earnings	All Other Compensation ($)	Total ($)
(a)	(b)	(c)	(d)	(e)	(f)	(g)	(h)
A							
B							
C							
D							
E							

2. The Table shall include:

i. The name of each director unless such director is also a named executive officer under paragraph (a) of this Item and his or her compensation for service as a director is fully reflected in the Summary Compensation Table pursuant to paragraph (c) of this Item and otherwise as required pursuant to paragraphs (d) through (j) of this Item (column (a));

ii.   The aggregate dollar amount of all fees earned or paid in cash for services as a director, including annual retainer fees, committee and/or chairmanship fees, and meeting fees (column (b));

iii.   For awards of stock, the aggregate grant date fair value computed in accordance with FASB ASC Topic 718 (column (c));

iv.   For awards of options, with or without tandem SARs (including awards that subsequently have been transferred), the aggregate grant date fair value computed in accordance with FASB ASC Topic 718 (column (d))

Instruction to Item 402(k)(2)(iii) and (iv).

For each director, disclose by footnote to the appropriate column: the grant date fair value of each equity award computed in accordance with FASB ASC Topic 718; for each option, SAR or similar option like instrument for which the registrant has adjusted or amended the exercise or base price during the last completed fiscal year, whether through amendment, cancellation or replacement grants, or any other means ("repriced"), or otherwise has materially modified such awards, the incremental fair value, computed as of the repricing or modification date in accordance with FASB ASC Topic 718; and the aggregate number of stock awards and the aggregate number of option awards outstanding at fiscal year end. However, the disclosure required by this Instruction does not apply to any repricing that occurs through a pre-existing formula or mechanism in the plan or award that results in the periodic adjustment of the option or SAR exercise or base price, an antidilution provision in a plan or award, or a recapitalization or similar transaction equally affecting all holders of the class of securities underlying the options or SARs.

v.   The dollar value of all earnings for services performed during the fiscal year pursuant to non-equity incentive plans as defined in paragraph (a)(6)(iii) of this Item, and all earnings on any outstanding awards (column (e));

vi.   The sum of the amounts specified in paragraphs (k)(2)(vi)(A) and (B) of this Item (column (f)) as follows:

A.   The aggregate change in the actuarial present value of the director's accumulated benefit under all defined benefit and actuarial pension plans (including supplemental plans) from the pension plan measurement date used for financial statement reporting purposes with respect to the registrant's audited financial statements for the prior completed fiscal year to the pension plan measurement date used for financial statement reporting purposes with respect to the registrant's audited financial statements for the covered fiscal year; and

B.   Above-market or preferential earnings on compensation that is deferred on a basis that is not tax-qualified, including such earnings on nonqualified defined contribution plans;

vii.   All other compensation for the covered fiscal year that the registrant could not properly report in any other column of the Director Compensation Table (column (g)). Each compensation item that is not properly reportable in columns (b)-(f), regardless of the amount of the compensation item, must be included in column (g). Such compensation must include, but is not limited to:

A.   Perquisites and other personal benefits, or property, unless the aggregate amount of such compensation is less than $10,000;

B.   All "gross-ups" or other amounts reimbursed during the fiscal year for the payment of taxes;

C.   For any security of the registrant or its subsidiaries purchased from the registrant or its subsidiaries (through deferral of salary or bonus, or otherwise) at a discount from the market price of such security at the date of purchase, unless that discount is available generally, either to all security holders or to all salaried employees of the registrant, the compensation cost, if any, computed in accordance with FASB ASC Topic 718;

D.   The amount paid or accrued to any director pursuant to a plan or arrangement in connection with:

   1.   The resignation, retirement or any other termination of such director; or

   2.   A change in control of the registrant;

E.   Registrant contributions or other allocations to vested and unvested defined contribution plans;

F.   Consulting fees earned from, or paid or payable by the registrant and/or its subsidiaries (including joint ventures)

G.   The annual costs of payments and promises of payments pursuant to director legacy programs and similar charitable award programs;

H.   The dollar value of any insurance premiums paid by, or on behalf of, the registrant during the covered fiscal year with respect to life insurance for the benefit of a director; and

I.   The dollar value of any dividends or other earnings paid on stock or option awards, when those amounts were not factored into the grant date fair value required to be reported for the stock or option award in column (c) or (d); and

Instructions to Item 402(k)(2)(vii).

1.   Programs in which registrants agree to make donations to one or more charitable institutions in a director's name, payable by the registrant currently or upon a designated event, such as the retirement or death of the director, are charitable awards programs or director legacy programs for purposes of the disclosure required by paragraph (k)(2)(vii)(G) of this Item. Provide footnote disclosure of the total dollar amount payable under the program and other material terms of each such program for which tabular disclosure is provided.

2.   Any item reported for a director pursuant to paragraph (k)(2)(vii) of this Item that is not a perquisite or personal benefit and whose value exceeds $10,000 must be identified and quantified in a footnote to column (g). All items of compensation are required to be included in the Director Compensation Table without regard to whether such items are required to be identified other than as specifically noted in this Item.

3. Perquisites and personal benefits may be excluded as long as the total value of all perquisites and personal benefits for a director is less than $10,000. If the total value of all perquisites and personal benefits is $10,000 or more for any director, then each perquisite or personal benefit, regardless of its amount, must be identified by type. If perquisites and personal benefits are required to be reported for a director pursuant to this rule, then each perquisite or personal benefit that exceeds the greater of $25,000 or 10% of the total amount of perquisites and personal benefits for that director must be quantified and disclosed in a footnote. Perquisites and other personal benefits shall be valued on the basis of the aggregate incremental cost to the registrant. With respect to the perquisite or other personal benefit for which footnote quantification is required, the registrant shall describe in the footnote its methodology for computing the aggregate incremental cost. Reimbursements of taxes owed with respect to perquisites or other personal benefits must be included in column (g) and are subject to separate quantification and identification as tax reimbursements (paragraph (k)(2)(vii)(B) of this Item) even if the associated perquisites or other personal benefits are not required to be included because the total amount of all perquisites or personal benefits for an individual director is less than $10,000 or are required to be identified but are not required to be separately quantified.

viii. The dollar value of total compensation for the covered fiscal year (column (h)). With respect to each director, disclose the sum of all amounts reported in columns (b) through (g).

Instruction to Item 402(k)(2).

Two or more directors may be grouped in a single row in the Table if all elements of their compensation are identical. The names of the directors for whom disclosure is presented on a group basis should be clear from the Table.

3. Narrative to director compensation table.

Provide a narrative description of any material factors necessary to an understanding of the director compensation disclosed in this Table. While material factors will vary depending upon the facts, examples of such factors may include, in given cases, among other things:

i. A description of standard compensation arrangements (such as fees for retainer, committee service, service as chairman of the board or a committee, and meeting attendance); and

ii. Whether any director has a different compensation arrangement, identifying that director and describing the terms of that arrangement.

Instruction to Item 402(k).

In addition to the Instruction to paragraphs (k)(2)(iii) and (iv) and the Instructions to paragraph (k)(2)(vii) of this Item, the following apply equally to paragraph (k) of this Item: Instructions 2 and 4 to paragraph (c) of this Item; Instructions to paragraphs (c)(2)(iii) and (iv) of this Item; Instructions to paragraphs (c)(2)(v) and (vi) of this Item; Instructions to paragraph (c)(2)(vii) of this Item; Instructions to paragraph (c)(2)(viii) of this Item; and Instructions 1 and 5 to paragraph (c)(2)(ix) of this Item. These Instructions apply to the columns in the Director Compensation Table that are analogous to the columns in the Summary Compensation Table to which they refer and to disclosures under paragraph (k) of this Item that correspond to analogous disclosures provided for in paragraph (c) of this Item to which they refer.

l.   **Smaller reporting companies and emerging growth companies**. A registrant that qualifies as a "smaller reporting company," as defined by Item 10(f), or is an "emerging growth company," as defined in Rule 405 of the Securities Act or Rule 12b-2 of the Exchange Act, may provide the scaled disclosure in paragraphs (m) through (r) instead of paragraphs (a) through (k), (s), and (u) of this Item.

***

s.   **Narrative disclosure of the registrant's compensation policies and practices as they relate to the registrant's risk management**. To the extent that risks arising from the registrant's compensation policies and practices for its employees are reasonably likely to have a material adverse effect on the registrant, discuss the registrant's policies and practices of compensating its employees, including non-executive officers, as they relate to risk management practices and risk-taking incentives. While the situations requiring disclosure will vary depending on the particular registrant and compensation policies and practices, situations that may trigger disclosure include, among others, compensation policies and practices: at a business unit of the company that carries a significant portion of the registrant's risk profile; at a business unit with compensation structured significantly differently than other units within the registrant; at a business unit that is significantly more profitable than others within the registrant; at a business unit where compensation expense is a significant percentage of the unit's revenues; and that vary significantly from the overall risk and reward structure of the registrant, such as when bonuses are awarded upon accomplishment of a task, while the income and risk to the registrant from the task extend over a significantly longer period of time. The purpose of this paragraph (s) is to provide investors material information concerning how the registrant compensates and incentivizes its employees that may create risks that are reasonably likely to have a material adverse effect on the registrant. While the information to be disclosed pursuant to this paragraph (s) will vary depending upon the nature of the registrant's business and the compensation approach, the following are examples of the issues that the registrant may need to address for the business units or employees discussed:

1.   The general design philosophy of the registrant's compensation policies and practices for employees whose behavior would be most affected by the incentives established by the policies and practices, as such policies and practices relate to or affect risk taking by employees on behalf of the registrant, and the manner of their implementation;

2.   The registrant's risk assessment or incentive considerations, if any, in structuring its compensation policies and practices or in awarding and paying compensation;

3.   How the registrant's compensation policies and practices relate to the realization of risks resulting from the actions of employees in both the short term and the long term, such as through policies requiring claw backs or imposing holding periods;

4.   The registrant's policies regarding adjustments to its compensation policies and practices to address changes in its risk profile;

5. Material adjustments the registrant has made to its compensation policies and practices as a result of changes in its risk profile; and

6. The extent to which the registrant monitors its compensation policies and practices to determine whether its risk management objectives are being met with respect to incentivizing its employees.

t. **Golden Parachute Compensation.**

1. In connection with any proxy or consent solicitation material providing the disclosure required by section 14A(b)(1) of the Exchange Act or any proxy or consent solicitation that includes disclosure under Item 14 of Schedule 14A pursuant to Note A of Schedule 14A (excluding any proxy or consent solicitation of an "emerging growth company," as defined in Rule 405 of the Securities Act or Rule 12b-2 of the Exchange Act, with respect to each named executive officer of the acquiring company and the target company, provide the information specified in paragraphs (t)(2) and (3) of this section regarding any agreement or understanding, whether written or unwritten, between such named executive officer and the acquiring company or target company, concerning any type of compensation, whether present, deferred or contingent, that is based on or otherwise relates to an acquisition, merger, consolidation, sale or other disposition of all or substantially all assets of the issuer, as follows:

Golden Parachute Compensation

Name	Cash ($)	Equity ($)	Pension/NQDC ($)	Perquisites/ Benefits ($)	Tax Reimburs ement ($)	Other ($)	Total ($)
(a)	(b)	(c)	(d)	(e)	(f)	(g)	(h)
PEO							
PFO							
A							
B							
C							

2. The table shall include, for each named executive officer:

i.   The name of the named executive officer (column (a));

ii. The aggregate dollar value of any cash severance payments, including but not limited to payments of base salary, bonus, and pro-rated non-equity incentive compensation plan payments (column (b));

iii. The aggregate dollar value of:

A. Stock awards for which vesting would be accelerated;

B. In-the-money option awards for which vesting would be accelerated; and

C. Payments in cancellation of stock and option awards (column (c));

iv. The aggregate dollar value of pension and nonqualified deferred compensation benefit enhancements (column (d));

v.   The aggregate dollar value of perquisites and other personal benefits or property, and health care and welfare benefits (column (e));

vi. The aggregate dollar value of any tax reimbursements (column (f));

vii. The aggregate dollar value of any other compensation that is based on or otherwise relates to the transaction not properly reported in columns (b) through (f) (column (g)); and

viii. The aggregate dollar value of the sum of all amounts reported in columns (b) through (g) (column (h)).

Instructions to Item 402(t)(2).

1.   If this disclosure is included in a proxy or consent solicitation seeking approval of an acquisition, merger, consolidation, or proposed sale or other disposition of all or substantially all the assets of the registrant, or in a proxy or consent solicitation that includes disclosure under Item 14 of Schedule 14A pursuant to Note A of Schedule 14A, the disclosure provided by this table shall be quantified assuming that the triggering event took place on the latest practicable date, and that the price per share of the registrant's securities shall be determined as follows: if the shareholders are to receive a fixed dollar amount, the price per share shall be that fixed dollar amount, and if such value is not a fixed dollar amount, the price per share shall be the average closing market price of the registrant's securities over the first five business days following the first public announcement of the transaction. Compute the dollar value of in-the-money option awards for which vesting would be accelerated by determining the difference between this price and the exercise or base price of the options. Include only compensation that is based on or otherwise relates to the subject transaction. Apply Instruction 1 to Item 402(t) with respect to those executive officers for whom disclosure was required in the issuer's most recent filing with the Commission under the Securities Act or Exchange Act that required disclosure pursuant to Item 402(c).

2.   If this disclosure is included in a proxy solicitation for the annual meeting at which directors are elected for purposes of subjecting the disclosed agreements or understandings to a shareholder vote under section 14A(a)(1) of the Exchange Act, the disclosure provided by this table shall be quantified assuming that the triggering event took place on the last business day of the registrant's last completed fiscal year, and the price per share of the registrant's securities is the closing market price as of that date. Compute the dollar value of in-the-money option awards for which vesting would be accelerated by determining the difference between this price and the exercise or base price of the options.

3.   In the event that uncertainties exist as to the provision of payments and benefits or the amounts involved, the registrant is required to make a reasonable estimate applicable to the payment or benefit and disclose material assumptions underlying such estimates in its disclosure. In such event, the disclosure would require forward-looking information as appropriate.

4.   For each of columns (b) through (g), include a footnote quantifying each separate form of compensation included in the aggregate total reported. Include the value of all perquisites and other personal benefits or property.

Individual perquisites and personal benefits shall be identified and quantified as required by Instruction 4 to Item 402(c)(2)(ix) of this section. For purposes of quantifying health care benefits, the registrant must use the assumptions used for financial reporting purposes under generally accepted accounting principles.

5. For each of columns (b) through (h), include a footnote quantifying the amount payable attributable to a double-trigger arrangement (i.e., amounts triggered by a change-in-control for which payment is conditioned upon the executive officer's termination without cause or resignation for good reason within a limited time period following the change-in-control), specifying the time-frame in which such termination or resignation must occur in order for the amount to become payable, and the amount payable attributable to a single-trigger arrangement (i.e., amounts triggered by a change-in-control for which payment is not conditioned upon such a termination or resignation of the executive officer).

6. A registrant conducting a shareholder advisory vote pursuant to Rule 14a-21(c) of this chapter to cover new arrangements and understandings, and/or revised terms of agreements and understandings that were previously subject to a shareholder advisory vote pursuant to 14a-21(a) of this chapter, shall provide two separate tables. One table shall disclose all golden parachute compensation, including both the arrangements and amounts previously disclosed and subject to a shareholder advisory vote under section 14A(a)(1) of the Exchange Act and Rule 14a-21(a) of this chapter and the new arrangements and understandings and/or revised terms of agreements and understandings that were previously subject to a shareholder advisory vote. The second table shall disclose only the new arrangements and/or revised terms subject to the separate shareholder vote under section 14A(b)(2) of the Exchange Act and Rule 14a-21(c) of this chapter.

7. In cases where this Item 402(t)(2) requires disclosure of arrangements between an acquiring company and the named executive officers of the soliciting target company, the registrant shall clarify whether these agreements are included in the separate shareholder advisory vote pursuant to Rule 14a-21(c) of this chapter by providing a separate table of all agreements and understandings subject to the shareholder advisory vote required by section 14A(b)(2) of the Exchange Act and Rule 14a-21(c) of this chapter, if different from the full scope of golden parachute compensation subject to Item 402(t) disclosure.

3. Provide a succinct narrative description of any material factors necessary to an understanding of each such contract, agreement, plan or arrangement and the payments quantified in the tabular disclosure required by this paragraph. Such factors shall include, but not be limited to a description of:

i. The specific circumstances that would trigger payment(s);

ii. Whether the payments would or could be lump sum, or annual, disclosing the duration, and by whom they would be provided; and 139

iii. Any material conditions or obligations applicable to the receipt of payment or benefits, including but not limited to non-compete, non-solicitation, non-disparagement or confidentiality agreements, including the duration of such agreements and provisions regarding waiver or breach of such agreements.

Instructions to Item 402(t).

1. A registrant that does not qualify as a "smaller reporting company," as defined by Rule 10(f)(1) of this chapter, must provide the information required by this Item 402(t) with respect to the individuals covered by Items 402(a)(3)(i), (ii) and (iii) of this section. A registrant that qualifies as a "smaller reporting company," as defined by Rule 10(f)(1) of this chapter, must provide the information required by this Item 402(t) with respect to the individuals covered by Items 402(m)(2)(i) and (ii) of this section.

2. The obligation to provide the information in this Item 402(t) shall not apply to agreements and understandings described in paragraph (t)(1) of this section with senior management of foreign private issuers, as defined in Rule 3b-4 of this chapter.

u. **Pay ratio disclosure**.
    1. Disclose:
        i   The median of the annual total compensation of all employees of the registrant, excep the PEO of the registrant;
        ii. The annual total compensation of the PEO of the registrant; and
        iii. The ratio of the amount in paragraph (u)(1)(i) of this Item to the amount in paragraph (u)(1)(ii) of this Item. For purposes of the ratio required by this paragraph (u)(1)(iii), the amount n paragraph (u)(1)(i) of this Item shall equal one, or, alternatively, the ratio may be expressed narratively as the multiple that the amount in paragraph (u)(1)(ii) of this Item bears to the amount in paragraph (u)(1)(i) of this Item.
    2. For purposes of this paragraph (u),
        i.   *Total compensation* for the median of annual total compensation of all employees of the registrant and the PEO of the registrant shall be determined in accordance with paragraph (c)(2)(x) of this Item 402. In determining the total compensation, all references to "named executive officer" in this Item 402 and the instructions thereto may be deemed to refer instead, as applicable, to "employee" and, for non-salaried employees, references to "base salary" and "salary" in this Item 402 and the instructions thereto may be deemed to refer instead, as applicable, to "wages plus overtime";
        ii. *Annual total compensation* means total compensation for the registrant's last completed fiscal year; and
        iii. *Registrant* means the registrant and its consolidated subsidiaries.
    3. For purposes of this paragraph (u), *employee* or *employee of the registrant* means an individual employed by the registrant or any of its consolidated subsidiaries, whether as a full-time, part-time, seasonal, or temporary worker, as of a date chosen by the registrant within the last three months of the registrant's last completed fiscal year. The definition of employee or employee of the registrant does not include those workers who are employed, and whose compensation is determined, by an unaffiliated third party but who provide services to the registrant or its consolidated subsidiaries as independent contractors or "leased" workers;

293

4. For purposes of this paragraph (u), an employee located in a jurisdiction outside the United States (a "non-U.S. employee") may be exempt from the definition of employee or employee of the registrant under either of the following conditions:

    i. The employee is employed in a foreign jurisdiction in which the laws or regulations governing data privacy are such that, despite its reasonable efforts to obtain or process the information necessary for compliance with this paragraph (u), the registrant is unable to do so without violating such data privacy laws or regulations. The registrant's reasonable efforts shall include, at a minimum, using or seeking an exemption or other relief under any governing data privacy laws or regulations. If the registrant chooses to exclude any employees using this exemption, it shall list the excluded jurisdictions, identify the specific data privacy law or regulation, explain how complying with this paragraph (u) violates such data privacy law or regulation (including the efforts made by the registrant to use or seek an exemption or other relief under such law or regulation), and provide the approximate number of employees exempted from each jurisdiction based on this exemption. In addition, if a registrant excludes any non-U.S. employees in a particular jurisdiction under this exemption, it must exclude all non-U.S. employees in that jurisdiction. Further, the registrant shall obtain a legal opinion from counsel that opines on the inability of the registrant to obtain or process the information necessary for compliance with this paragraph (u) without violating the jurisdiction's laws or regulations governing data privacy, including the registrant's inability to obtain an exemption or other relief under any governing laws or regulations. The registrant shall file the legal opinion as an exhibit to the filing in which the pay ratio disclosure is included.

    ii. The registrant's non-U.S. employees account for 5% or less of the registrant's total employees. In that circumstance, if the registrant chooses to exclude any non-U.S. employees under this exemption, it must exclude all non-U.S. employees. Additionally, if a registrant's non-U.S. employees exceed 5% of the registrant's total U.S. and non-U.S. employees, it may exclude up to 5% of its total employees who are non-U.S. employees; *provided, however,* if a registrant excludes any non-U.S. employees in a particular jurisdiction, it must exclude all non-U.S. employees in that jurisdiction. If more than 5% of a registrant's employees are located in any one non-U.S. jurisdiction, the registrant may not exclude any employees in that jurisdiction under this exemption.

        A. In calculating the number of non-U.S. employees that may be excluded under this Item 402(u)(4)(ii) ("*de minimis*" exemption), a registrant shall count against the total any non-U.S. employee exempted under the data privacy law exemption under Item 402(u)(4)(i) ("data privacy" exemption). A registrant may exclude any non-U.S. employee from a jurisdiction that meets the data privacy exemption, even if the number of excluded employees exceeds 5% of the registrant's total employees. If, however, the number of employees excluded under the data privacy exemption equals or exceeds 5% of the registrant's total employees, the registrant may not use the *de minimis* exemption. Additionally, if the number of employees excluded under the data privacy exemption is less than 5% of the registrant's total employees, the registrant may use the *de minimis* exemption to exclude no more than the number of non-U.S. employees that, combined with the data privacy exemption, does not exceed 5% of the registrant's total employees.

B. If a registrant excludes non-U.S. employees under the *de minimis* exemption, it must disclose the jurisdiction or jurisdictions from which those employees are being excluded, the approximate number of employees excluded from each jurisdiction under the *de minimis* exemption, the total number of its U.S. and non-U.S. employees irrespective of any exemption (data privacy or *de minimis*), and the total number of its U.S. and non-U.S. employees used for its *de minimis* calculation.

Instruction 1 to Item 402(u). Disclosing the date chosen for identifying the median employee. A registrant shall disclose the date within the last three months of its last completed fiscal year that it selected pursuant to paragraph (u)(3) of this Item to identify its median employee. If the registrant changes the date it uses to identify the median employee from the prior year, the registrant shall disclose this change and provide a brief explanation about the reason or reasons for the change.

Instruction 2 to Item 402(u). Identifying the median employee. A registrant is required to identify its median employee only once every three years and calculate total compensation for that employee each year; provided that, during a registrant's last completed fiscal year there has been no change in its employee population or employee compensation arrangements that it reasonably believes would result in a significant change to its pay ratio disclosure. If there have been no changes that the registrant reasonably believes would significantly affect its pay ratio disclosure, the registrant shall disclose that it is using the same median employee in its pay ratio calculation and describe briefly the basis for its reasonable belief. For example, the registrant could disclose that there has been no change in its employee population or employee compensation arrangements that it believes would significantly impact the pay ratio disclosure. If there has been a change in the registrant's employee population or employee compensation arrangements that the registrant reasonably believes would result in a significant change in its pay ratio disclosure, the registrant shall re-identify the median employee for that fiscal year. If it is no longer appropriate for the registrant to use the median employee identified in year one as the median employee in years two or three because of a change in the original median employee's circumstances that the registrant reasonably believes would result in a significant change in its pay ratio disclosure, the registrant may use another employee whose compensation is substantially similar to the original median employee based on the compensation measure used to select the original median employee.

Instruction 3 to Item 402(u). Updating for the last completed fiscal year. Pay ratio information (i.e., the disclosure called for by paragraph (u)(1) of this Item) with respect to the registrant's last completed fiscal year is not required to be disclosed until the filing of its annual report on Form 10-K for that last completed fiscal year or, if later, the filing of a definitive proxy or information statement relating to its next annual meeting of shareholders (or written consents in lieu of such a meeting) following the end of such fiscal year; provided that, the required pay ratio information must, in any event, be filed as provided in General Instruction G(3) of Form 10-K not later than 120 days after the end of such fiscal year.

Instruction 4 to Item 402(u). Methodology and use of estimates.

1. Registrants may use reasonable estimates both in the methodology used to identify the median employee and in calculating the annual total compensation or any elements of total compensation for employees other than the PEO.

2. In determining the employees from which the median employee is identified, a registrant may use its employee population or statistical sampling and/or other reasonable methods.

3. A registrant may identify the median employee using annual total compensation or any other compensation measure that is consistently applied to all employees included in the calculation, such as information derived from the registrant's tax and/or payroll records. In using a compensation measure other than annual total compensation to identify the median employee, if that measure is recorded on a basis other than the registrant's fiscal year (such as information derived from tax and/or payroll records), the registrant may use the same annual period that is used to derive those amounts. Where a compensation measure other than annual total compensation is used to identify the median employee, the registrant must disclose the compensation measure used.

4. In identifying the median employee, whether using annual total compensation or any other compensation measure that is consistently applied to all employees included in the calculation, the registrant may make cost-of-living adjustments to the compensation of employees in jurisdictions other than the jurisdiction in which the PEO resides so that the compensation is adjusted to the cost of living in the jurisdiction in which the PEO resides. If the registrant uses a cost-of-living adjustment to identify the median employee, and the median employee identified is an employee in a jurisdiction other than the jurisdiction in which the PEO resides, the registrant must use the same cost-of-living adjustment in calculating the median employee's annual total compensation and disclose the median employee's jurisdiction. The registrant also shall briefly describe the cost-of-living adjustments it used to identify the median employee and briefly describe the cost-of-living adjustments it used to calculate the median employee's annual total compensation, including the measure used as the basis for the cost-of-living adjustment. A registrant electing to present the pay ratio in this manner also shall disclose the median employee's annual total compensation and pay ratio without the cost-of-living adjustment. To calculate this pay ratio, the registrant will need to identify the median employee without using any cost-of-living adjustments.

5. The registrant shall briefly describe the methodology it used to identify the median employee. It shall also briefly describe any material assumptions, adjustments (including any cost-of-living adjustments), or estimates it used to identify the median employee or to determine total compensation or any elements of total compensation, which shall be consistently applied. The registrant shall clearly identify any estimates used. The required descriptions should be a brief overview; it is not necessary for the registrant to provide technical analyses or formulas. If a registrant changes its methodology or its material assumptions, adjustments, or estimates from those used in its pay ratio disclosure for the prior fiscal year, and if the effects of any such change are significant, the registrant shall briefly describe the change and the reasons for the change. Registrants must also disclose if they

changed from using the cost-of-living adjustment to not using that adjustment and if they changed from not using the cost-of-living adjustment to using it.

6. Registrants may, at their discretion, include personal benefits that aggregate less than $10,000 and compensation under non-discriminatory benefit plans in calculating the annual total compensation of the median employee as long as these items are also included in calculating the PEO's annual total compensation. The registrant shall also explain any difference between the PEO's annual total compensation used in the pay ratio disclosure and the total compensation amounts reflected in the Summary Compensation Table, if material.

Instruction 5 to Item 402(u). Permitted annualizing adjustments. A registrant may annualize the total compensation for all permanent employees (full-time or part-time) that were employed by the registrant for less than the full fiscal year (such as newly hired employees or permanent employees on an unpaid leave of absence during the period). A registrant may not annualize the total compensation for employees in temporary or seasonal positions. A registrant may not make a full-time equivalent adjustment for any employee.

Instruction 6 to Item 402(u). PEO compensation not available. A registrant that is relying on Instruction 1 to Item 402(c)(2)(iii) and (iv) in connection with the salary or bonus of the PEO for the last completed fiscal year, shall disclose that the pay ratio required by paragraph (u) of this Item is not calculable until the PEO salary or bonus, as applicable, is determined and shall disclose the date that the PEO's actual total compensation is expected to be determined. The disclosure required by paragraph (u) of this Item shall then be disclosed in the filing under Item 5.02(f) of Form 8-K that discloses the PEO's salary or bonus in accordance with Instruction 1 to Item 402(c)(2)(iii) and (iv).

Instruction 7 to Item 402(u). Transition periods for registrants.

1. Upon becoming subject to the requirements of Section 13(a) or 15(d) of the Exchange Act, a registrant shall comply with paragraph (u) of this Item with respect to compensation for the first fiscal year following the year in which it became subject to such requirements, but not for any fiscal year commencing before January 1, 2017. The registrant may omit the disclosure required by paragraph (u) of this Item from any filing until the filing of its annual report on Form 10-K for such fiscal year or, if later, the filing of a proxy or information statement relating to its next annual meeting of shareholders (or written consents in lieu of such a meeting) following the end of such year; provided that, such disclosure shall, in any event, be filed as provided in General Instruction G(3) of Form 10-K not later than 120 days after the end of such fiscal year.

2. A registrant may omit any employees that became its employees as the result of the business combination or acquisition of a business for the fiscal year in which the transaction becomes effective, but the registrant must disclose the approximate number of employees it is omitting. Those employees shall be included in the total employee count for the triennial calculations of the median employee in the year following the transaction for purposes of evaluating whether a significant change had occurred. The registrant shall identify the acquired business excluded for the fiscal year in which the business combination or acquisition becomes effective.

3. A registrant shall comply with paragraph (u) of this Item with respect to compensation or the first fiscal year commencing on or after the date the registrant

ceases to be a smaller reporting company, but not for any fiscal year commencing before January 1, 2017.

Instruction 8 to Item 402(u). Emerging growth companies. A registrant is not required to comply with paragraph (u) of this Item if it is an emerging growth company as defined in Section 2(a)(19) of the Securities Act or Section 3(a)(80) of the Exchange Act. A registrant shall comply with paragraph (u) of this Item with respect to compensation for the first fiscal year commencing on or after the date the registrant ceases to be an emerging growth company, but not for any fiscal year commencing before Jan. 1, 2017.

Instruction 9 to Item 402(u). Additional information. Registrants may present additional information, including additional ratios, to supplement the required ratio, but are not required to do so. Any additional information shall be clearly identified, not misleading, and not presented with greater prominence than the required ratio.

Instruction 10 to Item 402(u). Multiple PEOs during the year. A registrant with more than one non-concurrent PEO serving during its fiscal year may calculate the annual total compensation for its PEO in either of the following manners:

1. The registrant may calculate the compensation provided to each person who served as PEO during the year for the time he or she served as PEO and combine those figures; or

2. The registrant may look to the PEO serving in that position on the date it selects to identify the median employee and annualize that PEO's compensation.

Regardless of the alternative selected, the registrant shall disclose which option it chose and how it calculated its PEO's annual total compensation.

Instruction 11 to Item 402(u). Employees' personally identifiable information. Registrants are not required to, and should not, disclose any personally identifiable information about that employee other than his or her compensation. Registrants may choose to generally identify an employee's position to put the employee's compensation in context, but registrants are not required to provide this information and should not do so if providing the information could identify any specific individual.

v. **Pay versus performance.** In connection with any proxy or information statement for which the rules of the Commission require executive compensation disclosure pursuant to this section (excluding any proxy or information statement of an "emerging growth company," as defined in Rule 405 of this chapter or Rule 12b-2 of this chapter):

1. Provide the information specified in paragraph (v)(2) of this section for each of the registrant's last five completed fiscal years in the following tabular format:

PAY VERSUS PERFORMANCE

Year (a)	Summary Compensation on Table Total for PEO (b)	Compensation Actually Paid to PEO (c)	Average Summary Compensation Table Total for Non-PEO Named Executive Officers (d)	Average Compensation Actually Paid to Non-PEO Named Executive Officers (e)	Value of Initial Fixed $100 Investment Based On		Net Income (h)	[Company-Selected Measure] (i)
					Total Shareholder Return (f)	Peer Group Total Share-holder Return (g)		

2.   The table required by paragraph (v)(1) of this section must include:

    i.   The fiscal year covered (column (a)).

    ii.   The PEO's (as defined in paragraph (a)(3) of this section) total compensation for the covered fiscal year as reported in the Summary Compensation Table pursuant to paragraph (c)(2)(x) of this section, or paragraph (n)(2)(x) of this section for smaller reporting companies (column (b)), and the average total compensation reported for the remaining named executive officers collectively reported pursuant to such applicable paragraph (column (d)). If more than one person served as the registrant's PEO during the covered fiscal year, provide the total compensation, as reported in accordance with the immediately preceding sentence, for each person who served as the PEO during that period separately in an additional column (b) for each such person.

    iii.   The executive compensation actually paid to the PEO (column (c)) and the average executive compensation actually paid to the remaining named executive officers collectively (column (e)). If more than one person served as the registrant's PEO during the covered fiscal year, provide the compensation actually paid to each person who served as PEO during that period separately in an additional column (c) for each such person. For purposes of columns (c) and (e) of the table required by paragraph (v)(1) of this section, executive compensation actually paid must be the total compensation for the covered fiscal year for each named executive officer as provided in paragraph (c)(2)(x) of this section, or paragraph (n)(2)(x) of this section for smaller reporting companies, adjusted to:

      A.   Deduct the aggregate change in the actuarial present value of the named executive officer's accumulated benefit under all defined benefit and actuarial pension plans reported in the Summary Compensation Table in accordance with paragraph (c)(2)(viii)(A) of this section;

      B.   1.   Add, for all defined benefit and actuarial pension plans reported in the Summary Compensation Table in accordance with paragraph (c)(2)(viii)(A) of this section, the aggregate of:

          i.   Service cost, calculated as the actuarial present value of each named executive officer's benefit under all such plans attributable to services rendered during the covered fiscal year; and

          ii.   Prior service cost, calculated as the entire cost of benefits granted (or credit for benefits reduced) in a plan amendment (or initiation) during the covered fiscal year that are attributed by the benefit formula to services rendered in periods prior to the amendment.

        2.   "Service cost" and "prior service cost" must be calculated using the same methodology as used for the registrant's financial statements under generally accepted accounting principles.

      C.   1.   Deduct the amounts reported in the Summary Compensation Table pursuant to paragraphs (c)(2)(v) and (vi) of this section and then include an amount calculated as follows for all stock awards, and all option awards, with or without tandem SARs (as defined in paragraph (a)(6)(i) of this section) (including awards that subsequently have been transferred):

 i. Add the fair value as of the end of the covered fiscal year of all awards granted during the covered fiscal year that are outstanding and unvested as of the end of the covered fiscal year;

 ii. Add the amount equal to the change as of the end of the covered fiscal year (from the end of the prior fiscal year) in fair value (whether positive or negative) of any awards granted in any prior fiscal year that are outstanding and unvested as of the end of the covered fiscal year;

 iii. Add, for awards that are granted and vest in the same year, the fair value as of the vesting date;

 iv. Add the amount equal to the change as of the vesting date (from the end of the prior fiscal year) in fair value (whether positive or negative) of any awards granted in any prior fiscal year for which all applicable vesting conditions were satisfied at the end of or during the covered fiscal year;

 v. Subtract, for any awards granted in any prior fiscal year that fail to meet the applicable vesting conditions during the covered fiscal year, the amount equal to the fair value at the end of the prior fiscal year; and

 vi. Add the dollar value of any dividends or other earnings paid on stock or option awards in the covered fiscal year prior to the vesting date that are not otherwise included in the total compensation for the covered fiscal year.

2. If at any time during the last completed fiscal year, the registrant has adjusted or amended the exercise price of options or SARs held by a named executive officer, whether through amendment, cancellation or replacement grants, or any other means, or otherwise has materially modified such awards, the changes in fair value included pursuant to this paragraph (v)(2)(iii)(C) must take into account the excess fair value, if any, of any such modified award over the fair value of the original award as of the date of such modification.

3. Fair value amounts must be computed in a manner consistent with the fair value methodology used to account for share-based payments in the registrant's financial statements under generally accepted accounting principles. For any awards that are subject to performance conditions, calculate the change in fair value as of the end of the covered fiscal year based upon the probable outcome of such conditions as of the last day of the fiscal year.

iv. For purposes of columns (f) and (g) of the table required by paragraph (v)(1) of this section, for each fiscal year disclose the cumulative total shareholder return of the registrant (column (f)) and peer group cumulative total shareholder return (column (g)) calculated, except as set forth below, in the same manner as under Item 201(e) of Regulation S-K. For purposes of calculating the cumulative total shareholder return of the registrant and peer group cumulative total shareholder return, the term "measurement period" must be the period beginning at the "measurement point" established by the market close on the last trading day before the registrant's earliest fiscal year in the table, through and including the end of the fiscal year for which cumulative total shareholder return of the registrant or peer group cumulative total shareholder return is being calculated. The closing price at the measurement point must be converted into a fixed investment of one hundred dollars, stated in dollars, in the registrant's stock (or in the stocks represented by the peer group). For each fiscal year, the amount included in the table must be the value of such fixed investment based on the cumulative total shareholder return as of the end of that year. The same methodology must be used in calculating both the registrant's total shareholder return and that of the peer group. For purposes of determining the total shareholder return of the registrant's peer group, the registrant must use the same index or issuers used by it for purposes of Item 201(e)(1)(ii) of this chapter or, if applicable, the companies it uses as a peer group for purposes of its disclosures under paragraph (b) of this section. If the peer group is not a published industry or line-of-business index, the identity of the issuers composing the group must be disclosed in a footnote. The returns of each component issuer of the group must be weighted according to the respective issuers' stock market capitalization at the beginning of each period for which a return is indicated. If the registrant selects or otherwise uses a different peer group from the peer group used by it for the immediately preceding fiscal year, explain, in a footnote, the reason(s) for this change and compare the registrant's cumulative total return with that of both the newly selected peer group and the peer group used in the immediately preceding fiscal year.

v. The registrant's net income for each fiscal year (column (h)).

vi. An amount for each fiscal year attributable to an additional financial performance measure included in the Tabular List provided pursuant to paragraph (v)(6) of this section, designated as the Company-Selected Measure, which in the registrant's assessment represents the most important financial performance measure (that is not otherwise required to be disclosed in the table) used by the registrant to link compensation actually paid to the registrant's named executive officers, for the most recently completed fiscal year, to company performance (column (i)). For purposes of this paragraph (v) of this section, "financial performance measures" means measures that are determined and presented in accordance with the accounting principles used in preparing the issuer's financial statements, any measures that are derived wholly or in part from such measures, and stock price and total shareholder return. A financial performance measure need not be presented within the registrant's financial statements or otherwise included in a filing with the Commission to be a Company-Selected Measure. Disclosure of any

Company-Selected Measure, or any additional measure that the registrant elects to provide, that is not a financial measure under generally accepted accounting principles will not be subject to Rules 100 through 102 of this chapter (Regulation G) and Item 10(e) of this chapter; however, disclosure must be provided as to how the number is calculated from the registrant's audited financial statements

3. For each amount disclosed in columns (c) and (e) of the table required by paragraph (v)(1) of this section, disclose in footnotes to the table each of the amounts deducted and added pursuant to paragraph (v)(2)(iii) of this section, the name of each named executive officer included as a PEO or in the calculation of the average remaining named executive officer compensation, and the fiscal years in which such persons are included. For disclosure of the executive compensation actually paid to named executive officers other than the PEO, provide the amounts required under this paragraph as averages.

4. For the value of equity awards added pursuant to paragraph (v)(2)(iii)(C) of this section, disclose in a footnote to the table required by paragraph (v)(1) of this section any assumption made in the valuation that differs materially from those disclosed as of the grant date of such equity awards.

5. In proxy or information statements in which disclosure is required pursuant to this Item, use the information provided in the table required by paragraph (v)(1) of this section to provide a clear description (graphically, narratively, or a combination of the two) of the relationships:

    i. Between:
        A. The executive compensation actually paid by the registrant to the PEO (column (c)) and the average of the executive compensation actually paid to the named executive officers other than the PEO (column (e)) included in the Summary Compensation Table; and
        B. The cumulative total shareholder return of the registrant (column (f)), across the registrant's last five completed fiscal years;

    ii. Between:
        A. The executive compensation actually paid by the registrant to the PEO (column (c)) and the average of the executive compensation actually paid to the named executive officers other than the PEO (column (e)) included in the Summary Compensation Table; and
        B. Net income of the registrant (column (h)), across the registrant's last five completed fiscal years; and

    iii. Between:
        A. The executive compensation actually paid by the registrant to the PEO (column (c)) and the average of the executive compensation actually paid to the named executive officers other than the PEO (column (e)) included in the Summary Compensation Table; and
        B. The Company-Selected Measure (column (i)), across the registrant's last five completed fiscal years.

    iv. The description provided in response to paragraph (v)(5)(i) of this section must also include a comparison of the cumulative total shareholder return of the registrant (column (f)) and cumulative total shareholder return of the registrant's peer group (column (g)) over the same period. If a registrant elects to provide any additional measures in the table, each additional measure must be accompanied by a clear description of the relationship between:

    A.   The executive compensation actually paid by the registrant to the PEO (column (c)) and the average of the executive compensation actually paid to the named executive officers other than the PEO (column (e)) included in the Summary Compensation Table; and

    B.   That additional measure, across the registrant's last five completed fiscal years.

6.   Subject to paragraph (v)(6)(iii) of this section, provide a tabular list of at least three, and up to seven, financial performance measures, which in the registrant's assessment represent the most important financial performance measures used by the registrant to link compensation actually paid to the registrant's named executive officers, for the most recently completed fiscal year, to company performance ("Tabular List").

    i.   The registrant may provide the Tabular List disclosure either as one tabular list, as two separate tabular lists (one for the PEO, and one for all named executive officers other than the PEO), or as separate tabular lists for the PEO and each named executive officer other than the PEO. If the registrant elects to provide multiple tabular lists in accordance with the immediately preceding sentence, each tabular list must include at least three, and up to seven, financial performance measures, which in the registrant's assessment represent the most important financial performance measures used by the registrant to link compensation actually paid to that, or those, particular named executive officer, or officers, for the most recently completed fiscal year, to company performance.

    ii.   If fewer than three financial performance measures were used by the registrant to link compensation actually paid to the registrant's named executive officers, for the most recently completed fiscal year, to company performance, the Tabular List must include all such measures that were used, if any.

    iii.   A registrant may include non-financial performance measures (i.e., performance measures other than those that fall within the definition of financial performance measures) used by the registrant to link compensation actually paid to the registrant's named executive officers, for the most recently completed fiscal year, to company performance in the Tabular List, if it determines that such measures are among its three to seven most important performance measures, and it has disclosed its most important three (or fewer, if the registrant only uses fewer) financial performance measures, in accordance with this paragraph (v)(6).

    iv.   The Tabular List may include a maximum of seven performance measures, regardless of whether the registrant elects to include non-financial performance measures in the Tabular List.

7.   The disclosure provided pursuant to this paragraph (v), including, but not limited to, any disclosure provided pursuant to paragraphs (v)(3) and (6) of this section, must appear with, and in the same format as, the rest of the disclosure required to be provided pursuant to this section and, in addition, must be provided in an

Interactive Data File in accordance with Item 405 of this chapter and the EDGAR Filer Manual.

8.   A registrant that qualifies as a "smaller reporting company," as defined by Item 10(f)(1) of this chapter, may provide the information required by this paragraph (v) for three years, instead of five years. A smaller reporting company may provide the disclosure required by this paragraph (v) for only two fiscal years in the first filing in which it provides this disclosure, and is not required to provide the disclosure required by paragraph (v)(2)(iv) or (v)(5) of this section with respect to the total shareholder return of any peer group, or the Company-Selected Measure disclosure required by paragraph (v)(2)(vi) of this section, or the Tabular List provided pursuant to paragraph (v)(6) of this section. For purposes of paragraph (v)(2)(iii) of this section with respect to smaller reporting companies, executive compensation actually paid must be the total compensation for the covered fiscal year for each named executive officer as provided in paragraph (n)(2)(x) of this section, adjusted to deduct the amounts reported in the Summary Compensation Table pursuant to paragraphs (n)(2)(v) and (vi) of this section, and to add in their place the fair value of the amounts added in paragraph (v)(2)(iii)(C) of this section. Disclose in a footnote to the table required pursuant to paragraph (v)(1) of this section for the PEO and average remaining named executive officer compensation the amounts deducted from, and added to, the Summary Compensation Table pursuant to this instruction, the name of each named executive officer included as a PEO or in the calculation of the average remaining named executive officer compensation, and the fiscal years in which they are included. A smaller reporting company is required to comply with paragraph (v)(7) of this section in the third filing in which it provides the disclosure required by this paragraph (v).

Instructions to paragraph (v).

1.   Transitional relief. A registrant may provide the disclosure required by this paragraph (v) for three years, instead of five years, in the first filing in which it provides this disclosure, and may provide disclosure for an additional year in each of the two subsequent annual filings in which this disclosure is required.

2.   New registrants. Information for fiscal years prior to the last completed fiscal year will not be required if the registrant was not required to report pursuant to Section 13(a) or 15(d) of the Exchange Act at any time during that year.3.   Incorporation by reference. The information required by paragraph (v) of this section will not be deemed to be incorporated by reference into any filing under the Securities Act or the Exchange Act, except to the extent that the registrant specifically incorporates it by reference.

w.   **Disclosure of a registrant's action to recover erroneously awarded compensation**.

1.   If at any time during or after the last completed fiscal year the registrant was required to prepare an accounting restatement that required recovery of erroneously awarded compensation pursuant to the registrant's compensation recovery policy required by the listing standards adopted pursuant to Rule 10D-1, or there was an outstanding balance as of the end of the last completed fiscal year of erroneously awarded compensation to be recovered from the application of the policy to a prior restatement, the registrant must provide the following information:

    i.   For each restatement:
- A. The date on which the registrant was required to prepare an accounting restatement;
- B. The aggregate dollar amount of erroneously awarded compensation attributable to such accounting restatement, including an analysis of how the amount was calculated;
- C. If the financial reporting measure as defined in Rule 10D-1(d) related to a stock price or total shareholder return metric, the estimates that were used in determining the erroneously awarded compensation attributable to such accounting restatement and an explanation of the methodology used for such estimates;
- D. The aggregate dollar amount of erroneously awarded compensation that remains outstanding at the end of the last completed fiscal year; and
- E. If the aggregate dollar amount of erroneously awarded compensation has not yet been determined, disclose this fact, explain the reason(s) and disclose the information required in paragraphs (w)(1)(i)(B) through (D) of this section in the next filing that is required to include disclosure pursuant to Item 402 of Regulation S-K;

    ii. If recovery would be impracticable pursuant to Rule 10D-1(b)(1)(iv), for each current and former named executive officer and for all other current and former executive officers as a group, disclose the amount of recovery forgone and a brief description of the reason the listed registrant decided in each case not to pursue recovery; and

    iii. For each current and former named executive officer from whom, as of the end of the last completed fiscal year, erroneously awarded compensation had been outstanding for 180 days or longer since the date the registrant determined the amount the individual owed, disclose the dollar amount of outstanding erroneously awarded compensation due from each such individual.

2. If at any time during or after its last completed fiscal year the registrant was required to prepare an accounting restatement, and the registrant concluded that recovery of erroneously awarded compensation was not required pursuant to the registrant's compensation recovery policy required by the listing standards adopted pursuant to Rule 10D-1, briefly explain why application of the recovery policy resulted in this conclusion.

3. The information must appear with, and in the same format as, the rest of the disclosure required to be provided pursuant to this Item 402. The information is required only in proxy or information statements that call for Item 402 disclosure and the registrant's annual report on Form 10-K, and will not be deemed to be incorporated by reference into any filing under the Securities Act, except to the extent that the listed registrant specifically incorporates it by reference.

4. The disclosure must be provided in an Interactive Data File in accordance with Rule 405 of Regulation S-T and the EDGAR Filer Manual.

    x.   **Disclosure of the registrant's policies and practices related to the grant of certain equity awards close in time to the release of material nonpublic information.**

        1.   Discuss the registrant's policies and practices on the timing of awards of options in relation to the disclosure of material nonpublic information by the registrant, including how the board determines when to grant such awards (for example, whether such awards are granted on a predetermined schedule); whether the board or compensation committee takes material nonpublic information into account when determining the timing and terms of such an award, and, if so, how the board or compensation committee takes material nonpublic information into account when determining the timing and terms of such an award; and whether the registrant has timed the disclosure of material nonpublic information for the purpose of affecting the value of executive compensation.

        2.

            i.   If, during the last completed fiscal year, the registrant awarded options to a named executive officer in the period beginning four business days before the filing of a periodic report on Form 10-Q or Form 10-K, or the filing or furnishing of a current report on Form 8-K that discloses material nonpublic information (other than a current report on Form 8-K disclosing a material new option award grant under Item 5.02(e) of that form), and ending one business day after the filing or furnishing of such report provide the information specified in paragraph (x)(2)(ii) of this section, concerning each such award for each of the named executive officers in the following tabular format:

Table 13 to paragraph (x)(2)(i)

Name (a)	Grant date (b)	Number of securities underlying the award (c)	Exercise price of the award ($/Sh) (d)	Grant date fair value of the award (e)	Percentage change in the closing market price of the securities underlying the award between the trading day ending immediately prior to the disclosure of material nonpublic information and the trading day beginning immediately following the disclosure of material nonpublic information (f)
PEO					
PFO					
A					
B					
C					

            ii.   The Table shall include:

                A.   The name of the named executive officer (column (a));

                B.   On an award-by-award basis, the grant date of the option award reported in the table (column (b));

                C.   On an award-by-award basis, the number of securities underlying the options, (column (c));

D. On an award-by-award basis, the per-share exercise price of the options (column (d));

E. On an award-by-award basis, the grant date fair value of each award computed using the same methodology as used for the registrant's financial statements under generally accepted accounting principles (column (e)).

F. For each instrument reported in column (b), disclose the percentage change in the market price of the underlying securities between the closing market price of the security one trading day prior to and the trading day beginning immediately following the disclosure of material nonpublic information (column (f)).

Instruction to paragraph (x)(2). A registrant that is a smaller reporting company or emerging growth company may limit the disclosures in the table to its PEO, the two most highly compensated executive officers other than the PEO who were serving as executive officers at the end of the last completed fiscal year, and up to two additional individuals who would have been the most highly compensated but for the fact that the individual was not serving as an executive officer at the end of the last completed fiscal year.

3. The disclosure provided pursuant to this paragraph (x) must be provided in an Interactive Data File as required by Rule 405 of Regulation S-T in accordance with the EDGAR Filer Manual.

Instruction to Item 402. Specify the applicable fiscal year in the title to each table required under this Item which calls for disclosure as of or for a completed fiscal year.

Item 403 – Security Ownership of Certain Beneficial Owners and Management

a. **Security ownership of certain beneficial owners.** Furnish the following information, as of the most recent practicable date, substantially in the tabular form indicated, with respect to any person (including any ``group'' as that term is used in section 13(d)(3) of the Exchange Act) who is known to the registrant to be the beneficial owner of more than five percent of any class of the registrant's voting securities. The address given in column (2) may be a business, mailing or residence address. Show in column (3) the total number of shares beneficially owned and in column (4) the percentage of class so owned. Of the number of shares shown in column (3), indicate by footnote or otherwise the amount known to be shares with respect to which such listed beneficial owner has the right to acquire beneficial ownership, as specified in Rule 13d-3(d)(1) under the Exchange Act.

(1) Title of Class	(2) Name and Address of Beneficial Owner	(3) Amount and Nature of Beneficial Ownership	(4) Percent of Class

b. **Security ownership of management.** Furnish the following information, as of the most recent practicable date, in substantially the tabular form indicated, as to each class of equity securities of the registrant or any of its parents or subsidiaries, including directors' qualifying shares, beneficially owned by all directors and nominees, naming them, each of the named executive officers as defined in Item 402(a)(3), and directors and executive officers of the registrant as a group, without naming them. Show in column (3) the total number of shares beneficially owned and in column (4) the percent of the class so owned. Of the number of shares shown in column (3), indicate, by footnote or otherwise, the amount of shares that are pledged as security and the amount of shares with respect to which such persons have the right to acquire beneficial ownership as specified in 13d-3(d)(1) of this chapter.

(1) Title of Class	(2) Name and Address of Beneficial Owner	(3) Amount and Nature of Beneficial Ownership	(4) Percent of Class

c.   **Changes in control.** Describe any arrangements, known to the registrant, including any pledge by any person of securities of the registrant or any of its parents, the operation of which may at a subsequent date result in a change in control of the registrant.

Instructions to Item 403:

1.   The percentages are to be calculated on the basis of the amount of outstanding securities, excluding securities held by or for the account of the registrant or its subsidiaries, plus securities deemed outstanding pursuant to Rule 13d-3(d)(1) under the Exchange Act. For purposes of paragraph (b), if the percentage of shares beneficially owned by any director or nominee, or by all directors and officers of the registrant as a group, does not exceed one percent of the class so owned, the registrant may, in lieu of furnishing a precise percentage, indicate this fact by means of an asterisk and explanatory footnote or other similar means.

2.   For the purposes of this Item, beneficial ownership shall be determined in accordance with Rule 13d-3 under the Exchange Act. Include such additional subcolumns or other appropriate explanation of column (3) necessary to reflect amounts as to which the beneficial owner has (A) sole voting power, (B) shared voting power, (C) sole investment power, or (D) shared investment power.

3.   The registrant shall be deemed to know the contents of any statements filed with the Commission pursuant to section 13(d) or 13(g) of the Exchange Act. When applicable, a registrant may rely upon information set forth in such statements unless the registrant knows or has reason to believe that such information is not complete or accurate or that a statement or amendment should have been filed and was not.

4.   For purposes of furnishing information pursuant to paragraph (a) of this Item, the registrant may indicate the source and date of such information.

5.   Where more than one beneficial owner is known to be listed for the same securities, appropriate disclosure should be made to avoid confusion. For purposes of paragraph (b), in computing the aggregate number of shares owned by directors and officers of the registrant as a group, the same shares shall not be counted more than once.

6.   Paragraph (c) of this Item does not require a description of ordinary default provisions contained in the charter, trust indentures or other governing instruments relating to securities of the registrant.

7.   Where the holder(s) of voting securities reported pursuant to paragraph (a) hold more than five percent of any class of voting securities of the registrant pursuant to any voting trust or similar agreement, state the title of such securities, the amount held or to be held pursuant to the trust or agreement (if not clear from the table) and the duration of the agreement. Give the names and addresses of the voting trustees and outline briefly their voting rights and other powers under the trust or agreement.

Item 404 – Transactions with related persons, promoters and certain control persons.

a. **Transactions with related persons**. Describe any transaction, since the beginning of the registrant's last fiscal year, or any currently proposed transaction, in which the registrant was or is to be a participant and the amount involved exceeds $120,000, and in which any related person had or will have a direct or indirect material interest. Disclose the following information regarding the transaction:

1. The name of the related person and the basis on which the person is a related person.

2. The related person's interest in the transaction with the registrant, including the related person's position(s) or relationship(s) with, or ownership in, a firm, corporation, or other entity that is a party to, or has an interest in, the transaction.

3. The approximate dollar value of the amount involved in the transaction.

4. The approximate dollar value of the amount of the related person's interest in the transaction, which shall be computed without regard to the amount of profit or loss.

5. In the case of indebtedness, disclosure of the amount involved in the transaction shall include the largest aggregate amount of principal outstanding during the period for which disclosure is provided, the amount thereof outstanding as of the latest practicable date, the amount of principal paid during the periods for which disclosure is provided, the amount of interest paid during the period for which disclosure is provided, and the rate or amount of interest payable on the indebtedness.

6. Any other information regarding the transaction or the related person in the context of the transaction that is material to investors in light of the circumstances of the particular transaction.

Instructions to Item 404(a).

1. For the purposes of paragraph (a) of this Item, the term related person means:

   a. Any person who was in any of the following categories at any time during the specified period for which disclosure under paragraph (a) of this Item is required:

      i. Any director or executive officer of the registrant;

      ii. Any nominee for director, when the information called for by paragraph (a) of this Item is being presented in a proxy or information statement relating to the election of that nominee for director; or

      iii. Any immediate family member of a director or executive officer of the registrant, or of any nominee for director when the information called for by paragraph (a) of this Item is being presented in a proxy or information statement relating to the election of that nominee for director, which means any child, stepchild, parent, stepparent, spouse, sibling, mother-in-law, father-in-law, son-in-law, daughter-in-law, brother-in-law, or sister-in-law of such director, executive officer or nominee for director, and any person (other than a tenant or employee) sharing the household of such director, executive officer or nominee for director; and

   b. Any person who was in any of the following categories when a transaction in which such person had a direct or indirect material interest occurred or existed:

      i. A security holder covered by Item 403(a); or

309

       ii.   Any immediate family member of any such security holder, which means any child, stepchild, parent, stepparent, spouse, sibling, mother-in-law, father-in-law, son-in-law, daughter-in-law, brother-in-law, or sister-in-law of such security holder, and any person (other than a tenant or employee) sharing the household of such security holder.

2.   For purposes of paragraph (a) of this Item, a transaction includes, but is not limited to, any financial transaction, arrangement or relationship (including any indebtedness or guarantee of indebtedness) or any series of similar transactions, arrangements or relationships.

3.   The amount involved in the transaction shall be computed by determining the dollar value of the amount involved in the transaction in question, which shall include:

    a.   In the case of any lease or other transaction providing for periodic payments or installments, the aggregate amount of all periodic payments or installments due on or after the beginning of the registrant's last fiscal year, including any required or optional payments due during or at the conclusion of the lease or other transaction providing for periodic payments or installments; and

    b.   In the case of indebtedness, the largest aggregate amount of all indebtedness outstanding at any time since the beginning of the registrant's last fiscal year and all amounts of interest payable on it during the last fiscal year.

4.   In the case of a transaction involving indebtedness:

    a.   The following items of indebtedness may be excluded from the calculation of the amount of indebtedness and need not be disclosed: amounts due from the related person for purchases of goods and services subject to usual trade terms, for ordinary business travel and expense payments and for other transactions in the ordinary course of business;

    b.   Disclosure need not be provided of any indebtedness transaction for the related persons specified in Instruction 1.b. to paragraph (a) of this Item; and

    c.   If the lender is a bank, savings and loan association, or broker-dealer extending credit under Federal Reserve Regulation T and the loans are not disclosed as nonaccrual, past due, restructured or potential problems (see Item III.C.1. and 2. of Industry Guide 3, Statistical Disclosure by Bank Holding Companies), disclosure under paragraph (a) of this Item may consist of a statement, if such is the case, that the loans to such persons:

       i.   Were made in the ordinary course of business;

       ii.   Were made on substantially the same terms, including interest rates and collateral, as those prevailing at the time for comparable loans with persons not related to the lender; and

       iii.   Did not involve more than the normal risk of collectibility or present other unfavorable features.

5.   a.   Disclosure of an employment relationship or transaction involving an executive officer and any related compensation solely resulting from that employment relationship or transaction need not be provided pursuant to paragraph (a) of this Item if:

       i.   The compensation arising from the relationship or transaction is reported pursuant to Item 402;

        ii.   The executive officer is not an immediate family member (as specified in Instruction 1 to paragraph (a) of this Item) and such compensation would have been reported under Item 402 as compensation earned for services to the registrant if the executive officer was a named executive officer as that term is defined in Item 402(a)(3), and such compensation had been approved, or recommended to the board of directors of the registrant for approval, by the compensation committee of the board of directors (or group of independent directors performing a similar function) of the registrant; or

        iii. The transaction involves the recovery of erroneously awarded compensation computed as provided in Rule 10D-1(b)(1)(iii) and the applicable listing standards for the registrant's securities, that is disclosed pursuant to Item 402(w).

    b.   Disclosure of compensation to a director need not be provided pursuant to paragraph (a) of this Item if the compensation is reported pursuant to Item 402(k).

6.   A person who has a position or relationship with a firm, corporation, or other entity that engages in a transaction with the registrant shall not be deemed to have an indirect material interest within the meaning of paragraph (a) of this Item where:

    a.   The interest arises only:

        i.   From such person's position as a director of another corporation or organization that is a party to the transaction; or

        ii.   From the direct or indirect ownership by such person and all other persons specified in Instruction 1 to paragraph (a) of this Item, in the aggregate, of less than a ten percent equity interest in another person (other than a partnership) which is a party to the transaction; or iii. From both such position and ownership; or

    b.   The interest arises only from such person's position as a limited partner in a partnership in which the person and all other persons specified in Instruction 1 to paragraph (a) of this Item, have an interest of less than ten percent, and the person is not a general partner of and does not hold another position in the partnership.

7.   Disclosure need not be provided pursuant to paragraph (a) of this Item if:

    a.   The transaction is one where the rates or charges involved in the transaction are determined by competitive bids, or the transaction involves the rendering of services as a common or contract carrier, or public utility, at rates or charges fixed in conformity with law or governmental authority;

    b.   The transaction involves services as a bank depositary of funds, transfer agent, registrar, trustee under a trust indenture, or similar services; or

    c.   The interest of the related person arises solely from the ownership of a class of equity securities of the registrant and all holders of that class of equity securities of the registrant received the same benefit on a pro rata basis.

b. **Review, approval or ratification of transactions with related persons.**

    1.   Describe the registrant's policies and procedures for the review, approval, or ratification of any transaction required to be reported under paragraph (a) of this Item. While the material features of such policies and procedures will vary

depending on the particular circumstances, examples of such features may include, in given cases, among other things:

 i. The types of transactions that are covered by such policies and procedures;

 ii. The standards to be applied pursuant to such policies and procedures;

 iii. The persons or groups of persons on the board of directors or otherwise who are responsible for applying such policies and procedures; and

 iv. A statement of whether such policies and procedures are in writing and, if not, how such policies and procedures are evidenced.

2. Identify any transaction required to be reported under paragraph (a) of this Item since the beginning of the registrant's last fiscal year where such policies and procedures did not require review, approval or ratification or where such policies and procedures were not followed.

Instruction to Item 404(b).

Disclosure need not be provided pursuant to this paragraph regarding any transaction that occurred at a time before the related person became one of the enumerated persons in Instruction 1.a.i., ii., or iii. to Item 404(a) if such transaction did not continue after the related person became one of the enumerated persons in Instruction 1.a.i., ii., or iii. to Item 404(a).

c. **Promoters and certain control persons**.

1. Registrants that are filing a registration statement on Form S-1 under the Securities Act or on Form 10 under the Exchange Act and that had a promoter at any time during the past five fiscal years shall:

 i. State the names of the promoter(s), the nature and amount of anything of value (including money, property, contracts, options or rights of any kind) received or to be received by each promoter, directly or indirectly, from the registrant and the nature and amount of any assets, services or other consideration therefore received or to be received by the registrant; and

 ii. As to any assets acquired or to be acquired by the registrant from a promoter, state the amount at which the assets were acquired or are to be acquired and the principle followed or to be followed in determining such amount, and identify the persons making the determination and their relationship, if any, with the registrant or any promoter. If the assets were acquired by the promoter within two years prior to their transfer to the registrant, also state the cost thereof to the promoter.

2. Registrants shall provide the disclosure required by paragraphs (c)(1)(i) and (c)(1)(ii) of this Item as to any person who acquired control of a registrant that is a shell company, or any person that is part of a group, consisting of two or more persons that agree to act together for the purpose of acquiring, holding, voting or disposing of equity securities of a registrant, that acquired control of a registrant that is a shell company. For purposes of this Item, shell company has the same meaning as in Rule 405 under the Securities Act and Rule 12b-2 under the Exchange Act.

d. **Smaller reporting companies**. A registrant that qualifies as a "smaller reporting company," as defined by Rule 10(f)(1), must provide the following information in order to comply with this Item:

1. The information required by paragraph (a) of this Item for the period specified there for a transaction in which the amount involved exceeds the lesser of $120,000 or one percent of the average of the smaller reporting company's total assets at year end for the last two completed fiscal years;
2. The information required by paragraph (c) of this Item; and
3. A list of all parents of the smaller reporting company showing the basis of control and as to each parent, the percentage of voting securities owned or other basis of control by its immediate parent, if any.

Instruction to Item 404(d)

1. Include information for any material underwriting discounts and commissions upon the sale of securities by the smaller reporting company where any of the persons specified in paragraph (a) of this Item was or is to be a principal underwriter or is a controlling person or member of a firm that was or is to be a principal underwriter.
2. For smaller reporting companies information shall be given for the period specified in paragraph (a) of this Item and, in addition, for the fiscal year preceding the small reporting company's last fiscal year.

Instructions to Item 404.

1. If the information called for by this Item is being presented in a registration statement filed pursuant to the Securities Act or the Exchange Act, information shall be given for the periods specified in the Item and, in addition, for the two fiscal years preceding the registrant's last fiscal year, unless the information is being incorporated by reference into a registration statement on Form S-4, in which case, information shall be given for the periods specified in the Item.
2. A foreign private issuer will be deemed to comply with this Item if it provides the information required by Item 7.B. of Form 20-F with more detailed information provided if otherwise made publicly available or required to be disclosed by the issuer's home jurisdiction or a market in which its securities are listed or traded.

Item 405 – Compliance with Section 16(a) of the Exchange Act

a. **Reporting obligation.** Every registrant having a class of equity securities registered pursuant to Section 12 of the Exchange Act and every closed-end investment company registered under the Investment Company Act of 1940 must:
1. Under the caption "Delinquent Section 16(a) Reports," identify each person who, at any time during the fiscal year, was a director, officer, beneficial owner of more than ten percentof any class of equity securities of the registrant registered pursuant to Section 12 of the Exchange Act, or any other person subject to Section 16 of the Exchange Act with respect to the registrant because of the requirements of Section 30 of the Investment Company Act ("reporting person") that failed to file on a timely basis reports required by Section 16(a) of the Exchange Act during the most recent fiscal year or prior fiscal years.
2. For each such person, set forth the number of late reports, the number of transactions that were not reported on a timely basis, and any known failure to file a required form. A known failure to file would include, but not be limited to, a failure to file a Form 3, which is required of all reporting persons, and a failure to file a Form 5 in the absence of the written representation referred to in

313

paragraph (b)(3) of this section, unless the registrant otherwise knows that no Form 5 is required.

Instruction 1 to Item 405(a). If no disclosure is required, registrants are encouraged to exclude the caption "Delinquent Section 16(a) Reports."

Instruction 2 to Item 405(a). The registrant is only required to disclose a failure to file timely once. For example, if in the most recently concluded fiscal year a reporting person filed a Form 4 disclosing a transaction that took place in the prior fiscal year, and should have been reported in that year, the registrant should disclose that late filing and transaction pursuant to this Item 405 with respect to the most recently concluded fiscal year, but not in material filed with respect to subsequent years.

b. **Scope of the Inquiry.** In determining whether disclosure is required pursuant to paragraph (a) of this section, the registrant may rely only on the following:

1. A review of Forms 3 and 4 and amendments thereto filed electronically with the Commission during the registrant's most recent fiscal year;

2. A review of Forms 5 and amendments thereto filed electronically with the Commission with respect to the registrant's most recent fiscal year; and

3. Any written representation from the reporting person that no Form 5 is required. The registrant must maintain the representation in its records for two years, making a copy available to the Commission or its staff upon request.

Item 406 – Code of Ethics

a. Disclose whether the registrant has adopted a code of ethics that applies to the registrant's principal executive officer, principal financial officer, principal accounting officer or controller, or persons performing similar functions. If the registrant has not adopted such a code of ethics, explain why it has not done so.

b. For purposes of this Item 406, the term *code of ethics* means written standards that are reasonably designed to deter wrongdoing and to promote:

1. Honest and ethical conduct, including the ethical handling of actual or apparent conflicts of interest between personal and professional relationships;

2. Full, fair, accurate, timely, and understandable disclosure in reports and documents that a registrant files with, or submits to, the Commission and in other public communications made by the registrant;

3. Compliance with applicable governmental laws, rules and regulations;

4. The prompt internal reporting of violations of the code to an appropriate person or persons identified in the code; and

5. Accountability for adherence to the code.

c. The registrant must:

1. File with the Commission a copy of its code of ethics that applies to the registrant's principal executive officer, principal financial officer, principal accounting officer or controller, or persons performing similar functions, as an exhibit to its annual report;

2. Post the text of such code of ethics on its Internet website and disclose, in its annual report, its Internet address and the fact that it has posted such code of ethics on its Internet Web site; or

3.   Undertake in its annual report filed with the Commission to provide to any person without charge, upon request, a copy of such code of ethics and explain the manner in which such request may be made.

d.   If the registrant intends to satisfy the disclosure requirement under Item 5.05 of Form 8-K regarding an amendment to, or a waiver from, a provision of its code of ethics that applies to the registrant's principal executive officer, principal financial officer, principal accounting officer or controller, or persons performing similar functions and that relates to any element of the code of ethics definition enumerated in paragraph (b) of this Item by posting such information on its Internet website, disclose the registrant's Internet address and such intention.

Instructions to Item 406:
1. A registrant may have separate codes of ethics for different types of officers. Furthermore, a code of ethics within the meaning of paragraph (b) of this Item may be a portion of a broader document that addresses additional topics or that applies to more persons than those specified in paragraph (a). In satisfying the requirements of paragraph (c), a registrant need only file, post or provide the portions of a broader document that constitutes a code of ethics as defined in paragraph (b) and that apply to the persons specified in paragraph (a).
2. If a registrant elects to satisfy paragraph (c) of this Item by posting its code of ethics on its website pursuant to paragraph (c)(2), the code of ethics must remain accessible on its Web site for as long as the registrant remains subject to the requirements of this Item and chooses to comply with this Item by posting its code on its Web site pursuant to paragraph (c)(2).
3. A registrant that is an Asset-Backed Issuer (as defined in Rule 13a-14(g) and 15d-14(g) under the Exchange Act) is not required to disclose the information required by this Item.

Item 407 – Corporate governance.

a.   **Director independence**. Identify each director and, when the disclosure called for by this paragraph is being presented in a proxy or information statement relating to the election of directors, each nominee for director, that is independent under the independence standards applicable to the registrant under paragraph (a)(1) of this Item. In addition, if such independence standards contain independence requirements for committees of the board of directors, identify each director that is a member of the compensation, nominating or audit committee that is not independent under such committee independence standards. If the registrant does not have a separately designated audit, nominating or compensation committee or committee performing similar functions, the registrant must provide the disclosure of directors that are not independent with respect to all members of the board of directors applying such committee independence standards.

1.   In determining whether or not the director or nominee for director is independent for the purposes of paragraph (a) of this Item, the registrant shall use the applicable definition of independence, as follows:

i.   If the registrant is a listed issuer whose securities are listed on a national securities exchange or in an inter-dealer quotation system which has requirements that a majority of the board of directors be independent, the registrant's definition of independence that it uses for determining if a majority of the board of directors is independent in compliance with the listing standards applicable to the registrant. When determining whether the members of a committee of the board of directors are independent, the registrant's definition of independence that it uses for determining if the members of that specific committee are independent in compliance with the independence standards applicable for the members of the specific committee in the listing standards of the national securities exchange or inter-dealer quotation system that the registrant uses for determining if a majority of the board of directors are independent. If the registrant does not have independence standards for a committee, the independence standards for that specific committee in the listing standards of the national securities exchange or inter-dealer quotation system that the registrant uses for determining if a majority of the board of directors are independent.

ii. If the registrant is not a listed issuer, a definition of independence of a national securities exchange or of an inter-dealer quotation system which has requirements that a majority of the board of directors be independent, and state which definition is used. Whatever such definition the registrant chooses, it must use the same definition with respect to all directors and nominees for director. When determining whether the members of a specific committee of the board of directors are independent, if the national securities exchange or national securities association whose standards are used has independence standards for the members of a specific committee, use those committee specific standards.

iii. If the information called for by paragraph (a) of this Item is being presented in a registration statement on Form S-1 under the Securities Act or on a Form 10 under the Exchange Act where the registrant has applied for listing with a national securities exchange or in an inter-dealer quotation system which has requirements that a majority of the board of directors be independent, the definition of independence that the registrant uses for determining if a majority of the board of directors is independent, and the definition of independence that the registrant uses for determining if members of the specific committee of the board of directors are independent, that is in compliance with the independence listing standards of the national securities exchange or inter-dealer quotation system on which it has applied for listing, or if the registrant has not adopted such definitions, the independence standards for determining if the majority of the board of directors is independent and if members of the committee of the board of directors are independent of that national securities exchange or inter-dealer quotation system.

2.   If the registrant uses its own definitions for determining whether its directors and nominees for director, and members of specific committees of the board of directors, are independent, disclose whether these definitions are available to security holders on the registrant's Web site. If so, provide the registrant's Web site address. If not, include a copy of these policies in an appendix to the registrant's proxy statement or information statement that is provided to security holders at least once every three fiscal years or if the policies have been materially amended since the beginning of the registrant's last fiscal year. If a current copy of the policies is not available to security holders on the registrant's Web site, and is not included as an appendix to the registrant's proxy statement

or information statement, identify the most recent fiscal year in which the policies were so included in satisfaction of this requirement.

3.   For each director and nominee for director that is identified as independent, describe, by specific category or type, any transactions, relationships or arrangements not disclosed pursuant to Item 404(a), or for investment companies, Item 22(b) of Schedule 14A, that were considered by the board of directors under the applicable independence definitions in determining that the director is independent.

Instructions to Item 407(a).

1.   If the registrant is a listed issuer whose securities are listed on a national securities exchange or in an inter-dealer quotation system which has requirements that a majority of the board of directors be independent, and also has exemptions to those requirements (for independence of a majority of the board of directors or committee member independence) upon which the registrant relied, disclose the exemption relied upon and explain the basis for the registrant's conclusion that such exemption is applicable. The same disclosure should be provided if the registrant is not a listed issuer and the national securities exchange or inter-dealer quotation system selected by the registrant has exemptions that are applicable to the registrant. Any national securities exchange or inter-dealer quotation system which has requirements that at least 50 percent of the members of a small business issuer's board of directors must be independent shall be considered a national securities exchange or inter-dealer quotation system which has requirements that a majority of the board of directors be independent for the purposes of the disclosure required by paragraph (a) of this Item.

2.   Registrants shall provide the disclosure required by paragraph (a) of this Item for any person who served as a director during any part of the last completed fiscal year, except that no information called for by paragraph (a) of this Item need be given in a registration statement filed at a time when the registrant is not subject to the reporting requirements of section 13(a) or 15(d) of the Exchange Act respecting any director who is no longer a director at the time of effectiveness of the registration statement.

3.   The description of the specific categories or types of transactions, relationships or arrangements required by paragraph (a)(3) of this Item must be provided in such detail as is necessary to fully describe the nature of the transactions, relationships or arrangements.

b.   **Board meetings and committees; annual meeting attendance.**

1.   State the total number of meetings of the board of directors (including regularly scheduled and special meetings) which were held during the last full fiscal year. Name each incumbent director who during the last full fiscal year attended fewer than 75 percent of the aggregate of:

    i.   The total number of meetings of the board of directors (held during the period for which he has been a director); and

    ii. The total number of meetings held by all committees of the board on which he served (during the periods that he served).

2.   Describe the registrant's policy, if any, with regard to board members' attendance at annual meetings of security holders and state the number of board members who attended the prior year's annual meeting.

           Instruction to Item 407(b)(2).

           In lieu of providing the information required by paragraph (b)(2) of this Item in the proxy statement, the registrant may instead provide the registrant's Web site address where such information appears.

3.   State whether or not the registrant has standing audit, nominating and compensation committees of the board of directors, or committees performing similar functions. If the registrant has such committees, however designated, identify each committee member, state the number of committee meetings held by each such committee during the last fiscal year and describe briefly the functions performed by each such committee. Such disclosure need not be provided to the extent it is duplicative of disclosure provided in accordance with paragraph (c), (d) or (e) of this Item.

c.   **Nominating committee.**

    1.   If the registrant does not have a standing nominating committee or committee performing similar functions, state the basis for the view of the board of directors that it is appropriate for the registrant not to have such a committee and identify each director who participates in the consideration of director nominees.

    2.   Provide the following information regarding the registrant's director nomination process:

        i.   State whether or not the nominating committee has a charter. If the nominating committee has a charter, provide the disclosure required by Instruction 2 to this Item regarding the nominating committee charter;

        ii.   If the nominating committee has a policy with regard to the consideration of any director candidates recommended by security holders, provide a description of the material elements of that policy, which shall include, but need not be limited to, a statement as to whether the committee will consider director candidates recommended by security holders;

        iii. If the nominating committee does not have a policy with regard to the consideration of any director candidates recommended by security holders, state that fact and state the basis for the view of the board of directors that it is appropriate for the registrant not to have such a policy;

        iv. If the nominating committee will consider candidates recommended by security holders, describe the procedures to be followed by security holders in submitting such recommendations;

        v.   Describe any specific minimum qualifications that the nominating committee believes must be met by a nominating committee-recommended nominee for a position on the registrant's board of directors, and describe any specific qualities or skills that the nominating committee believes are necessary for one or more of the registrant's directors to possess;

        vi. Describe the nominating committee's process for identifying and evaluating nominees for director, including nominees recommended by security holders, and any differences in the manner in which the nominating committee evaluates nominees for director based on whether the nominee is recommended by a security holder, and whether, and if so how, the nominating committee (or the board) considers diversity in identifying nominees for director. If the nominating committee (or the board) has a policy with regard to the consideration of diversity in identifying director nominees, describe how this policy is implemented, as well as how the nominating committee (or the board) assesses the effectiveness of its policy;

vii. With regard to each nominee approved by the nominating committee for inclusion on the registrant's proxy card (other than nominees who are executive officers or who are directors standing for re-election), state which one or more of the following categories of persons or entities recommended that nominee: security holder, non-management director, chief executive officer, other executive officer, third-party search firm, or other specified source. With regard to each such nominee approved by a nominating committee of an investment company, state which one or more of the following additional categories of persons or entities recommended that nominee: security holder, director, chief executive officer, other executive officer, or employee of the investment company's investment adviser, principal underwriter, or any affiliated person of the investment adviser or principal underwriter;

viii. If the registrant pays a fee to any third party or parties to identify or evaluate or assist in identifying or evaluating potential nominees, disclose the function performed by each such third party; and

ix. If the registrant's nominating committee received, by a date not later than the 120th calendar day before the date of the registrant's proxy statement released to security holders in connection with the previous year's annual meeting, a recommended nominee from a security holder that beneficially owned more than 5% of the registrant's voting common stock for at least one year as of the date the recommendation was made, or from a group of security holders that beneficially owned, in the aggregate, more than 5% of the registrant's voting common stock, with each of the securities used to calculate that ownership held for at least one year as of the date the recommendation was made, identify the candidate and the security holder or security holder group that recommended the candidate and disclose whether the nominating committee chose to nominate the candidate, provided, however, that no such identification or disclosure is required without the written consent of both the security holder or security holder group and the candidate to be so identified.

Instructions to Item 407(c)(2)(ix).

1. For purposes of paragraph (c)(2)(ix) of this Item, the percentage of securities held by a nominating security holder may be determined using information set forth in the registrant's most recent quarterly or annual report, and any current report subsequent thereto, filed with the Commission pursuant to the Exchange Act (or, in the case of a registrant that is an investment company registered under the Investment Company Act of 1940, the registrant's most recent report on Form N-CSR, unless the party relying on such report knows or has reason to believe that the information contained therein is inaccurate.

2. For purposes of the registrant's obligation to provide the disclosure specified in paragraph (c)(2)(ix) of this Item, where the date of the

annual meeting has been changed by more than 30 days from the date of the previous year's meeting, the obligation under that Item will arise where the registrant receives the security holder recommendation a reasonable time before the registrant begins to print and mail its proxy materials.

3. For purposes of paragraph (c)(2)(ix) of this Item, the percentage of securities held by a recommending security holder, as well as the holding period of those securities, may be determined by the registrant if the security holder is the registered holder of the securities. If the security holder is not the registered owner of the securities, he or she can submit one of the following to the registrant to evidence the required ownership percentage and holding period:

    a. A written statement from the "record" holder of the securities (usually a broker or bank) verifying that, at the time the security holder made the recommendation, he or she had held the required securities for at least one year; or

    b. If the security holder has filed a Schedule 13D, Schedule 13G, Form 3, Form 4, and/or Form 5, or amendments to those documents or updated forms, reflecting ownership of the securities as of or before the date of the recommendation, a copy of the schedule and/or form, and any subsequent amendments reporting a change in ownership level, as well as a written statement that the security holder continuously held the securities for the one-year period as of the date of the recommendation.

4. For purposes of the registrant's obligation to provide the disclosure specified in paragraph (c)(2)(ix) of this Item, the security holder or group must have provided to the registrant, at the time of the recommendation, the written consent of all parties to be identified and, where the security holder or group members are not registered holders, proof that the security holder or group satisfied the required ownership percentage and holding period as of the date of the recommendation.

Instruction to Item 407(c)(2).

For purposes of paragraph (c)(2) of this Item, the term nominating committee refers not only to nominating committees and committees performing similar functions, but also to groups of directors fulfilling the role of a nominating committee, including the entire board of directors.

3. Describe any material changes to the procedures by which security holders may recommend nominees to the registrant's board of directors, where those changes were implemented after the registrant last provided disclosure in response to the requirements of paragraph (c)(2)(iv) of this Item, or paragraph (c)(3) of this Item.

Instructions to Item 407(c)(3).

1. The disclosure required in paragraph (c)(3) of this Item need only be provided in a registrant's quarterly or annual reports.

2. For purposes of paragraph (c)(3) of this Item, adoption of procedures by which security holders may recommend nominees to the registrant's board of directors, where the registrant's most recent disclosure in response to the

requirements of paragraph (c)(2)(iv) of this Item, or paragraph (c)(3) of this Item, indicated that the registrant did not have in place such procedures, will constitute a material change.

d. **Audit committee.**

1. State whether or not the audit committee has a charter. If the audit committee has a charter, provide the disclosure required by Instruction 2 to this Item regarding the audit committee charter.

2. If a listed issuer's board of directors determines, in accordance with the listing standards applicable to the issuer, to appoint a director to the audit committee who is not independent (apart from the requirements in Rule 10A-3 of this chapter), including as a result of exceptional or limited or similar circumstances, disclose the nature of the relationship that makes that individual not independent and the reasons for the board of directors' determination.

3.   i. The audit committee must state whether:

        A. The audit committee has reviewed and discussed the audited financial statements with management;

        B. The audit committee has discussed with the independent auditors the matters required to be discussed by the applicable requirements of the Public Company Accounting Oversight Board and the Commission;

        C. The audit committee has received the written disclosures and the letter from the independent accountant required by applicable requirements of the Public Company Accounting Oversight Board regarding the independent accountant's communications with the audit committee concerning independence, and has discussed with the independent accountant the independent accountant's independence; and

        D. Based on the review and discussions referred to in paragraphs (d)(3)(i)(A) through (d)(3)(i)(C) of this Item, the audit committee recommended to the board of directors that the audited financial statements be included in the company's annual report on Form 10-K (or, for closed-end investment companies registered under the Investment Company Act of 1940, the annual report to shareholders required by section 30(e) of the Investment Company Act of 1940 and Rule 30d-1 thereunder for the last fiscal year for filing with the Commission.

   ii. The name of each member of the company's audit committee (or, in the absence of an audit committee, the board committee performing equivalent functions or the entire board of directors) must appear below the disclosure required by paragraph (d)(3)(i) of this Item.

4.   i. If the registrant meets the following requirements, provide the disclosure in paragraph (d)(4)(ii) of this Item:

        A. The registrant is a listed issuer, as defined in Rule 10A-3 of this chapter;

        B. The registrant is filing either an annual report on Form 10-K or a proxy statement or information statement pursuant to the Exchange

Act if action is to be taken with respect to the election of directors; and

    C.   The registrant is neither:

        1.   A subsidiary of another listed issuer that is relying on the exemption in Rule10A-3(c)(2) of this chapter; nor

        2.   Relying on any of the exemptions in Rule 10A-3(c)(4) through (c)(7) of this chapter.

    ii.

        A.   State whether or not the registrant has a separately-designated standing audit committee established in accordance with section 3(a)(58)(A) of the Exchange Act, or a committee performing similar functions. If the registrant has such a committee, however designated, identify each committee member. If the entire board of directors is acting as the registrant's audit committee as specified in section 3(a)(58)(B) of the Exchange Act, so state.

        B.   If applicable, provide the disclosure required by Rule 10A-3(d) of this chapter regarding an exemption from the listing standards for audit committees.

  5.   Audit committee financial expert.

    i.   A.   Disclose that the registrant's board of directors has determined that the registrant either:

        1.   Has at least one audit committee financial expert serving on its audit committee; or

        2.   Does not have an audit committee financial expert serving on its audit committee.

        B.   If the registrant provides the disclosure required by paragraph (d)(5)(i)(A)(1) of this Item, it must disclose the name of the audit committee financial expert and whether that person is independent, as independence for audit committee members is defined in the listing standards applicable to the listed issuer.

        C.   If the registrant provides the disclosure required by paragraph (d)(5)(i)(A)(2) of this Item, it must explain why it does not have an audit committee financial expert.

Instruction to Item 407(d)(5)(i).

If the registrant's board of directors has determined that the registrant has more than one audit committee financial expert serving on its audit committee, the registrant may, but is not required to, disclose the names of those additional persons. A registrant choosing to identify such persons must indicate whether they are independent pursuant to paragraph (d)(5)(i)(B) of this Item.

    ii.   For purposes of this Item, an audit committee financial expert means a person who has the following attributes:

        A.   An understanding of generally accepted accounting principles and financial statements;

        B.   The ability to assess the general application of such principles in connection with the accounting for estimates, accruals & reserves;

        C.   Experience preparing, auditing, analyzing or evaluating financial statements that present a breadth and level of complexity of accounting issues that are generally comparable to the breadth and complexity of issues that can reasonably be expected to be raised by the registrant's financial statements, or experience actively supervising one or more persons engaged in such activities;

    D. An understanding of internal control over financial reporting; and

    E. An understanding of audit committee functions.

iii. A person shall have acquired such attributes through:

    A. Education and experience as a principal financial officer, principal accounting officer, controller, public accountant or auditor or experience in one or more positions that involve the performance of similar functions;

    B. Experience actively supervising a principal financial officer, principal accounting officer, controller, public accountant, auditor or person performing similar functions;

    C. Experience overseeing or assessing the performance of companies or public accountants with respect to the preparation, auditing or evaluation of financial statements; or

    D. Other relevant experience.

iv. Safe harbor.

    A. A person who is determined to be an audit committee financial expert will not be deemed an expert for any purpose, including without limitation for purposes of section 11 of the Securities Act, as a result of being designated or identified as an audit committee financial expert pursuant to this Item 407.

    B. The designation or identification of a person as an audit committee financial expert pursuant to this Item 407 does not impose on such person any duties, obligations or liability that are greater than the duties, obligations and liability imposed on such person as a member of the audit committee and board of directors in the absence of such designation or identification.

    C. The designation or identification of a person as an audit committee financial expert pursuant to this Item does not affect the duties, obligations or liability of any other member of the audit committee or board of directors.

Instructions to Item 407(d)(5).

1. The disclosure under paragraph (d)(5) of this Item is required only in a registrant's annual report. The registrant need not provide the disclosure required by paragraph (d)(5) of this Item in a proxy or information statement unless that registrant is electing to incorporate this information by reference from the proxy or information statement into its annual report pursuant to General Instruction G(3) to Form 10-K.

2. If a person qualifies as an audit committee financial expert by means of having held a position described in paragraph (d)(5)(iii)(D) of this Item, the registrant shall provide a brief listing of that person's relevant experience. Such disclosure may be made by reference to disclosures required under Item 401(e).

3. In the case of a foreign private issuer with a two-tier board of directors, for purposes of paragraph (d)(5) of this Item, the term board of directors means

the supervisory or non-management board. In the case of a foreign private issuer meeting the requirements of Rule 10A-3(c)(3) of this chapter, for purposes of paragraph (d)(5) of this Item, the term board of directors means the issuer's board of auditors (or similar body) or statutory auditors, as applicable. Also, in the case of a foreign private issuer, the term generally accepted accounting principles in paragraph (d)(5)(ii)(A) of this Item means the body of generally accepted accounting principles used by that issuer in its primary financial statements filed with the Commission.

4. A registrant that is an Asset-Backed Issuer is not required to disclose the information required by paragraph (d)(5) of this Item.

Instructions to Item 407(d).

1. The information required by paragraphs (d)(1)-(3) of this Item shall not be deemed to be "soliciting material," or to be "filed" with the Commission or subject to Regulation 14A or 14C, other than as provided in this Item, or to the liabilities of section 18 of the Exchange Act, except to the extent that the registrant specifically requests that the information be treated as soliciting material or specifically incorporates it by reference into a document filed under the Securities Act or the Exchange Act. Such information will not be deemed to be incorporated by reference into any filing under the Securities Act or the Exchange Act, except to the extent that the registrant specifically incorporates it by reference.

2. The disclosure required by paragraphs (d)(1)-(3) of this Item need only be provided one time during any fiscal year.

3. The disclosure required by paragraph (d)(3) of this Item need not be provided in any filings other than a registrant's proxy or information statement relating to an annual meeting of security holders at which directors are to be elected (or special meeting or written consents in lieu of such meeting).

e. **Compensation committee.**

1. If the registrant does not have a standing compensation committee or committee performing similar functions, state the basis for the view of the board of directors that it is appropriate for the registrant not to have such a committee and identify each director who participates in the consideration of executive officer and director compensation.

2. State whether or not the compensation committee has a charter. If the compensation committee has a charter, provide the disclosure required by Instruction 2 to this Item regarding the compensation committee charter.

3. Provide a narrative description of the registrant's processes and procedures for the consideration and determination of executive and director compensation, including:

    i.   A.   The scope of authority of the compensation committee (or persons performing the equivalent functions); and

            B.   The extent to which the compensation committee (or persons performing the equivalent functions) may delegate any authority described in paragraph (e)(3)(i)(A) of this Item to other persons, specifying what authority may be so delegated and to whom;

    ii.   Any role of executive officers in determining or recommending the amount or form of executive and director compensation; and

iii. Any role of compensation consultants in determining or recommending the amount or form of executive and director compensation (other than any role limited_to consulting on any broad-based plan that does not discriminate in scope, terms, or operation, in favor of executive officers or directors of the registrant, and that is available generally to all salaried employees; or providing information that either is not customized for a particular registrant or that is customized based on parameters that are not developed by the compensation consultant, and about which the compensation consultant does not provide advice) during the registrant's last completed fiscal year, identifying such consultants, stating whether such consultants were engaged directly by the compensation committee (or persons performing the equivalent functions) or any other person, describing the nature and scope of their assignment, and the material elements of the instructions or directions given to the consultants with respect to the performance of their duties under the engagement:

A. If such compensation consultant was engaged by the compensation committee (or persons performing the equivalent functions) to provide advice or recommendations on the amount or form of executive and director compensation (other than any role limited_to consulting on any broad-based plan that does not discriminate in scope, terms, or operation, in favor of executive officers or directors of the registrant, and that is available generally to all salaried employees; or providing information that either is not customized for a particular registrant or that is customized based on parameters that are not developed by the compensation consultant, and about which the compensation consultant does not provide advice) and the compensation consultant or its affiliates also provided additional services to the registrant or its affiliates in an amount in excess of $120,000 during the registrant's last completed fiscal year, then disclose the aggregate fees for determining or recommending the amount or form of executive and director compensation and the aggregate fees for such additional services. Disclose whether the decision to engage the compensation consultant or its affiliates for these other services was made, or recommended, by management, and whether the compensation committee or the board approved such other services of the compensation consultant or its affiliates.

B. If the compensation committee (or persons performing the equivalent functions) has not engaged a compensation consultant, but management has engaged a compensation consultant to provide advice or recommendations on the amount or form of executive and director compensation (other than any role limited_to consulting on any broad-based plan that does not discriminate in scope, terms, or operation, in favor of executive officers or directors of the registrant, and that is available generally to all salaried employees; or providing information that either is not customized for a particular registrant or that is customized based on parameters that are not developed by the compensation consultant, and about which the compensation consultant does not provide advice) and such compensation consultant or its affiliates has provided additional services to the registrant in an amount in excess of $120,000 during the registrant's last completed fiscal year, then disclose the aggregate fees for determining or recommending the amount or form of executive and director compensation and the aggregate fees for any additional services provided by the compensation consultant or its affiliates.

iv. With regard to any compensation consultant identified in response to Item 407(e)(3)(iii) whose work has raised any conflict of interest, disclose the nature of the conflict and how the conflict is being addressed.

Instruction to Item 407(e)(3)(iv)

For purposes of this paragraph (e)(3)(iv), the factors listed in Rule 10C-1(b)(4)(i) through (vi) of this chapter are among the factors that should be considered in determining whether a conflict of interest exists.

4. Under the caption "Compensation Committee Interlocks and Insider Participation":

i. Identify each person who served as a member of the compensation committee of the registrant's board of directors (or board committee performing equivalent functions) during the last completed fiscal year, indicating each committee member who:

A. Was, during the fiscal year, an officer or employee of the registrant;

B. Was formerly an officer of the registrant; or

C. Had any relationship requiring disclosure by the registrant under any paragraph of Item 404. In this event, the disclosure required by Item 404 shall accompany such identification.

ii. If the registrant has no compensation committee (or other board committee performing equivalent functions), the registrant shall identify each officer and employee of the registrant, and any former officer of the registrant, who, during the last completed fiscal year, participated in deliberations of the registrant's board of directors concerning executive officer compensation.

iii. Describe any of the following relationships that existed during the last completed fiscal year:

A. An executive officer of the registrant served as a member of the compensation committee (or other board committee performing equivalent functions or, in the absence of any such committee, the entire board of directors) of another entity, one of whose executive officers served on the compensation committee (or other board committee performing equivalent functions or, in the absence of any such committee, the entire board of directors) of the registrant;

B. An executive officer of the registrant served as a director of another entity, one of whose executive officers served on the compensation committee (or other board committee performing equivalent functions or, in the absence of any such committee, the entire board of directors) of the registrant; and

C. An executive officer of the registrant served as a member of the compensation committee (or other board committee performing equivalent functions or, in the absence of any such committee, the entire board of directors) of another entity, one of whose executive officers served as a director of the registrant.

iv. Disclosure required under paragraph (e)(4)(iii) of this Item regarding a compensation committee member or other director of the registrant who also served as an executive officer of another entity shall be accompanied by the disclosure called for by Item 404 with respect to that person.

Instruction to Item 407(e)(4).

For purposes of paragraph (e)(4) of this Item, the term entity shall not include an entity exempt from tax under section 501(c)(3) of the Internal Revenue Code.

5. Under the caption "Compensation Committee Report:"

    i. The compensation committee (or other board committee performing equivalent functions or, in the absence of any such committee, the entire board of directors) must state whether:

        A. The compensation committee has reviewed and discussed the Compensation Discussion and Analysis required by Item 402(b) with management; and

        B. Based on the review and discussions referred to in paragraph (e)(5)(i)(A) of this Item, the compensation committee recommended to the board of directors that the Compensation Discussion and Analysis be included in the registrant's annual report on Form 10-K, proxy statement on Schedule 14A or information statement on Schedule 14C.

    ii. The name of each member of the registrant's compensation committee (or other board committee performing equivalent functions or, in the absence of any such committee, the entire board of directors) must appear below the disclosure required by paragraph (e)(5)(i) of this Item.

Instructions to Item 407(e)(5).

1. The information required by paragraph (e)(5) of this Item shall not be deemed to be "soliciting material," or to be "filed" with the Commission or subject to Regulation 14A or 14C, other than as provided in this Item, or to the liabilities of section 18 of the Exchange Act, except to the extent that the registrant specifically requests that the information be treated as soliciting material or specifically incorporates it by reference into a document filed under the Securities Act or the Exchange Act.

2. The disclosure required by paragraph (e)(5) of this Item need not be provided in any filings other than an annual report on Form 10-K, a proxy statement on Schedule 14A or an information statement on Schedule 14C. Such information will not be deemed to be incorporated by reference into any filing under the Securities Act or the Exchange Act, except to the extent that the registrant specifically incorporates it by reference. If the registrant elects to incorporate this information by reference from the proxy or information statement into its annual report on Form 10-K pursuant to General Instruction G(3) to Form 10-K, the disclosure required by paragraph (e)(5) of this Item will be deemed furnished in the annual report on Form 10-K and will not be deemed incorporated by reference into any filing under the Securities Act or the Exchange Act as a result as a result of furnishing the disclosure in this manner.

3.   The disclosure required by paragraph (e)(5) of this Item need only be provided one time during any fiscal year.

f.   **Shareholder communications.**
1.   State whether or not the registrant's board of directors provides a process for security holders to send communications to the board of directors and, if the registrant does not have such a process for security holders to send communications to the board of directors, state the basis for the view of the board of directors that it is appropriate for the registrant not to have such a process.
2.   If the registrant has a process for security holders to send communications to the board of directors:
   i.   Describe the manner in which security holders can send communications to the board and, if applicable, to specified individual directors; and
   ii.   If all security holder communications are not sent directly to board members, describe the registrant's process for determining which communications will be relayed to board members.

Instructions to Item 407(f).
1.   In lieu of providing the information required by paragraph (f)(2) of this Item in the proxy statement, the registrant may instead provide the registrant's Web site address where such information appears.
2.   For purposes of the disclosure required by paragraph (f)(2)(ii) of this Item, a registrant's process for collecting and organizing security holder communications, as well as similar or related activities, need not be disclosed provided that the registrant's process is approved by a majority of the independent directors or, in the case of a registrant that is an investment company, a majority of the directors who are not "interested persons" of the investment company as defined in section 2(a)(19) of the Investment Company Act of 1940.
3.   For purposes of this paragraph, communications from an officer or director of the registrant will not be viewed as "security holder communications." Communications from an employee or agent of the registrant will be viewed as "security holder communications" for purposes of this paragraph only if those communications are made solely in such employee's or agent's capacity as a security holder.
4.   For purposes of this paragraph, security holder proposals submitted pursuant to Rule 14a-8 of this chapter, and communications made in connection with such proposals, will not be viewed as "security holder communications."

g.   **Smaller reporting companies and emerging growth companies.**
1.   A registrant that qualifies as a "smaller reporting company," as defined by § 229.10(f)(1), is not required to provide:
   i.   The disclosure required in paragraph (d)(5) of this Item in its first annual report filed pursuant to Section 13(a) or 15(d) of the Exchange Act following the effective date of its first registration statement filed under the Securities Act or Exchange Act; and
   ii.   The disclosure required by paragraphs (e)(4) and (e)(5) of this Item.
2.   A registrant that qualifies as an "emerging growth company," as defined in Rule 405 of the Securities Act or Rule 12b-2 of the Exchange Act, is not required to provide the disclosure required by paragraph (e)(5) of this Item.

h. **Board leadership structure and role in risk oversight.** Briefly describe the leadership structure of the registrant's board, such as whether the same person serves as both principal executive officer and chairman of the board, or whether two individuals serve in those positions, and, in the case of a registrant that is an investment company, whether the chairman of the board is an "interested person" of the registrant as defined in section 2(a)(19) of the Investment Company Act. If one person serves as both principal executive officer and chairman of the board, or if the chairman of the board of a registrant that is an investment company is an "interested person" of the registrant, disclose whether the registrant has a lead independent director and what specific role the lead independent director plays in the leadership of the board. This disclosure should indicate why the registrant has determined that its leadership structure is appropriate given the specific characteristics or circumstances of the registrant. In addition, disclose the extent of the board's role in the risk oversight of the registrant, such as how the board administers its oversight function, and the effect that this has on the board's leadership structure.

Instructions to Item 407.

1. For purposes of this Item:
    a. Listed issuer means a listed issuer as defined in Rule 10A-3 of this chapter;
    b. National securities exchange means a national securities exchange registered pursuant to section 6(a) of the Exchange Act;
    c. Inter-dealer quotation system means an automated inter-dealer quotation system of a national securities association registered pursuant to section 15A(a) of the Exchange Act; and
    d. National securities association means a national securities association registered pursuant to section 15A(a) of the Exchange Act that has been approved by the Commission (as that definition may be modified or supplemented).

2. With respect to paragraphs (c)(2)(i), (d)(1) and (e)(2) of this Item, disclose whether a current copy of the applicable committee charter is available to security holders on the registrant's Web site, and if so, provide the registrant's Web site address. If a current copy of the charter is not available to security holders on the registrant's Web site, include a copy of the charter in an appendix to the registrant's proxy or information statement that is provided to security holders at least once every three fiscal years, or if the charter has been materially amended since the beginning of the registrant's last fiscal year. If a current copy of the charter is not available to security holders on the registrant's Web site, and is not included as an appendix to the registrant's proxy or information statement, identify in which of the prior fiscal years the charter was so included in satisfaction of this requirement.

Item 408 – Insider trading arrangements and policies.

a.
    1. Disclose whether, during the registrant's last fiscal quarter (the registrant's fourth fiscal quarter in the case of an annual report), any director or officer (as defined in Rule 16a-1(f) of this chapter) adopted or terminated:
        i. Any contract, instruction or written plan for the purchase or sale of securities of the registrant intended to satisfy the affirmative defenseconditions of Rule 10b5-1(c) (Rule 10b5-1(c) of this chapter) (a "Rule 10b5-1 trading arrangement"); and/or

            ii.   Any "non-Rule 10b5-1 trading arrangement" as defined in paragraph (c) of this section.

    2.   Identify whether the trading arrangement is intended to satisfy the affirmative defense of Rule 10b5-1(c), and provide a description of the material terms, other than terms with respect to the price at which the individual executing the Rule 10b5-1 trading arrangement or non-Rule 10b5-1 trading arrangement is authorized to trade, such as:

        A.   The name and title of the director or officer;

        B.   The date on which the director or officer adopted or terminated the trading arrangement;

        C.   The duration of the trading arrangement; and

        D.   The aggregate number of securities to be purchased or sold pursuant to the trading arrangement.

    3.   The disclosure provided pursuant to paragraphs (a)(1) and (2) of this section must be provided in an Interactive Data File as required by Rule 405 of Regulation S-T in accordance with the EDGAR Filer Manual.

b. 1.   Disclose whether the registrant has adopted insider trading policies and procedures governing the purchase, sale, and/or other dispositions of the registrant's securities by directors, officers and employees, or the registrant itself, that are reasonably designed to promote compliance with insider trading laws, rules and regulations, and any listing standards applicable to the registrant. If the registrant has not adopted such policies and procedures, explain why it has not done so.

    2.   If the registrant has adopted insider trading policies and procedures, the registrant must file such policies and procedures as an exhibit. If all of the registrant's insider trading policies and procedures are included in its code of ethics (as defined in Item 406(b)) and the code of ethics is filed as an exhibit pursuant to Item 406(c)(1), that would satisfy the exhibit requirement of this paragraph.

    3.   The disclosure provided pursuant to paragraph (b)(1) of this section must be provided in an Interactive Data File as required by Rule 405 in accordance with the EDGAR Filer Manual.

c. For purposes of this Item 408, a director or officer (as defined in Rule 16a-1(f) of this chapter) (each a "covered person") has entered into a non-Rule 10b5-1 trading arrangement where:

    1.   The covered person asserts that at a time when they were not aware of material nonpublic information about the security or the issuer of the security they had adopted a written arrangement for trading the securities; and

    2.   The trading arrangement:

        i.   Specified the amount of securities to be purchased or sold and the price at which and the date on which the securities were to be purchased or sold;

        ii.   Included a written formula or algorithm, or computer program, for determining the amount of securities to be purchased or sold and the price at which and the date on which the securities were to be purchased or sold; or

         iiii. Did not permit the covered person to exercise any subsequent influence over how, when, or whether to effect purchases or sales; provided, in addition, that any other person who, pursuant to the trading arrangement, did exercise such influence must not have been aware of material nonpublic information when doing so.

d.   1.   Disclose whether, during the registrant's last fiscal quarter (the registrant's fourth fiscal quarter in the case of an annual report), the registrant adopted or terminated any Rule 10b5-1 trading arrangement as that term is defined in paragraph (a)(1)(i) of this section. In addition, provide a description of the material terms of the Rule 10b5-1 trading arrangement (other than terms with respect to the price at which the party executing the Rule 10b5-1 trading arrangement is authorized to trade), such as:

       i.   The date on which the registrant adopted or terminated the Rule 10b5-1 trading arrangement;

       ii.   The duration of the Rule 10b5-1 trading arrangement; and

       iii.   The aggregate number of securities to be purchased or sold pursuant to the Rule 10b5-1 trading arrangement.

Note 1 to paragraph (d)(1): If the disclosure provided pursuant to Item 703 of this chapter contains disclosure that would satisfy the requirements of paragraph (d)(1) of this section, a cross-reference to that disclosure will also satisfy the requirements of paragraph (d)(1) of this section.

   2.   The disclosure provided pursuant to paragraph (d)(1) must be provided in an Interactive Data File as required by § 232.405 of this chapter (Rule 405 of Regulation S-T) in accordance with the EDGAR Filer Manual.

Item 501 – Forepart of Registration Statement and Outside Front Cover Page of Prospectus

The registrant must furnish the following information in plain English. See Rule 421(d) of Regulation C under the Securities Act.

a.   **Front cover page of the registration statement.** Where appropriate, include the delaying amendment legend from Rule 473 of Regulation C under the Securities Act.

b.   **Outside front cover page of the prospectus.** Limit the outside cover page to one page. If the following information applies to your offering, disclose it on the outside cover page of the prospectus.

   1.   Name. The registrant's name. A foreign registrant must give the English translation of its name.

   Instruction to Paragraph 501(b)(1)

   If your name is the same as that of a company that is well known, include information to eliminate any possible confusion with the other company. If your name indicates a line of business in which you are not engaged or in which you are engaged only to a limited extent, include information to eliminate any misleading inference as to your business.

   2.   Title and amount of securities. The title and amount of securities offered. Separately state the amount of securities offered by selling security holders, if

any. If the underwriter has any arrangement with the issuer, such as an over-allotment option, under which the underwriter may purchase additional shares in connection with the offering, indicate that this arrangement exists and state the amount of additional shares that the underwriter may purchase under the arrangement. Give a brief description of the securities except where the information is clear from the title of the security. For example, you are not required to describe common stock that has full voting, dividend and liquidation rights usually associated with common stock.

3. Offering price of the securities. Where you offer securities for cash, the price to the public of the securities, the underwriter's discounts and commissions, the net proceeds you receive, and any selling shareholder's net proceeds. Show this information on both a per share or unit basis and for the total amount of the offering. If you make the offering on a minimum/maximum basis, show this information based on the total minimum and total maximum amount of the offering. You may present the information in a table, term sheet format, or other clear presentation. You may present the information in any format that fits the design of the cover page so long as the information can be easily read and is not misleading:

Instruction to Paragraph 501(b)(3):

1. If a preliminary prospectus is circulated and you are not subject to the reporting requirements of Section 13(a) or 15(d) of the Exchange Act, provide, as applicable:
    A. A bona fide estimate of the range of the maximum offering price and the maximum number of securities offered; or
    B. A bona fide estimate of the principal amount of the debt securities offered.
2. If it is impracticable to state the price to the public, explain the method by which the price is to be determined. Instead of explaining the method on the outside front cover page of the prospectus, you may state that the offering price will be determined by a particular method or formula that is described in the prospectus and include a cross-reference to the location of such disclosure in the prospectus, including the page number. Highlight the cross-reference by prominent type or in another manner. If the securities are to be offered at the market price, or if the offering price is to be determined by a formula related to the market price, indicate the market and market price of the securities as of the latest practicable date.
3. If you file a registration statement on Form S-8, you are not required to comply with this paragraph (b)(3).
4. Market for the securities. The national securities exchange(s) where the securities being offered are listed. If the securities being offered are not listed on a national securities exchange, the principal United States market(s) where the registrant, through the engagement of a registered broker-dealer, has actively sought and achieved quotation. In each case, also disclose the corresponding trading symbol(s) for the securities on such market(s);
5. Risk factors. A cross-reference to the risk factors section, including the page number where it appears in the prospectus. Highlight this cross-reference by prominent type or in another manner;

6.   State legend. Any legend or statement required by the law of any state in which the securities are to be offered. You may combine this with any legend required by the SEC, if appropriate;

7.   Commission legend. A legend that indicates that neither the Securities and Exchange Commission nor any state securities commission has approved or disapproved of the securities or passed upon the accuracy or adequacy of the disclosures in the prospectus and that any contrary representation is a criminal offense. You may use one of the following or other clear, plain language:

Example A: Neither the Securities and Exchange Commission nor any state securities commission has approved or disapproved of these securities or passed upon the adequacy or accuracy of this prospectus. Any representation to the contrary is a criminal offense.

Example B: Neither the Securities and Exchange Commission nor any state securities commission has approved or disapproved of these securities or determined if this prospectus is truthful or complete. Any representation to the contrary is a criminal offense.

8.   Underwriting.

1.   Name(s) of the lead or managing underwriter(s) and an identification of the nature of the underwriting arrangements;

2.   If the offering is not made on a firm commitment basis, a brief description of the underwriting arrangements. You may use any clear, concise, and accurate description of the underwriting arrangements. You may use the following descriptions of underwriting arrangements where appropriate:

Example A: Best efforts offering. The underwriters are not required to sell any specific number or dollar amount of securities but will use their best efforts to sell the securities offered.

Example B: Best efforts, minimum-maximum offering. The underwriters must sell the minimum number of securities offered (insert number) if any are sold. The underwriters are required to use only their best efforts to sell the maximum number of securities offered (insert number).

3.   If you offer the securities on a best efforts or best efforts minimum/maximum basis, the date the offering will end, any minimum purchase requirements, and any arrangements to place the funds in an escrow, trust, or similar account. If you have not made any of these arrangements, state this fact and describe the effect on investors;

9.   Date of prospectus. The date of the prospectus;

10. Prospectus "Subject to Completion" legend.

i.   If you use the prospectus before the effective date of the registration statement or if you use Rule 430A to omit pricing information and the prospectus is used before you determine the public offering price, include a prominent statement that:

A.   The information in the prospectus will be amended or completed;

B.   A registration statement relating to these securities has been filed with the Securities and Exchange Commission;

           C.   The securities may not be sold until the registration statement becomes effective; and

           D.   The prospectus is not an offer to sell the securities, and it is not soliciting an offer to buy the securities, in any state where offers or sales are not permitted.

        ii.   The legend may be in the following or other clear, plain language: The information in this prospectus is not complete and may be changed. We may not sell these securities until the registration statement filed with the Securities and Exchange Commission is effective. This prospectus is not an offer to sell these securities and it is not soliciting an offer to buy these securities in any state where the offer or sale is not permitted.

        iii. Registrants may exclude the statement in paragraph (b)(10)(i)(D) of this Item if the offering is not prohibited by state law.

    11. If you use Rule 430A under the Securities Act to omit pricing information and the prospectus is used before you determine the public offering price, the information and legend in paragraph (b)(10) of this section.

Item 502 – Inside Front and Outside Back Cover Pages of Prospectus

The registrant must furnish this information in plain English. See Rule 421(d) of Regulation C.

    a.   **Table of contents.** On either the inside front or outside back cover page of the prospectus, provide a reasonably detailed table of contents. It must show the page number of the various sections or subdivisions of the prospectus. Include a specific listing of the risk factors section required by Item 105 of this Regulation S-K. You must include the table of contents immediately following the cover page in any prospectus you deliver electronically.

    b.   **Dealer prospectus delivery obligation.** On the outside back cover page of the prospectus, advise dealers of their prospectus delivery obligation, including the expiration date specified by Section 4[a](3) of the Securities Act and Rule 174 under such Act. If you do not know the expiration date on the effective date of the registration statement, include the expiration date in the copy of the prospectus you file under Rule 424(b) under the Securities Act. You do not have to include this information if dealers are not required to deliver a prospectus under Rule 174 under the Securities Act or Section 24(d) of the Investment Company Act. You may use the following or other clear, plain language:

       Dealer Prospectus Delivery Obligation

       Until (insert date), all dealers that effect transactions in these securities, whether or not participating in this offering, may be required to deliver a prospectus. This is in addition to the dealers' obligation to deliver a prospectus when acting as underwriters and with respect to their unsold allotments or subscriptions.

Item 503 – Prospectus Summary

The registrant must furnish this information in plain English. See Rule 421(d) of Regulation C of this chapter.

a. **Prospectus summary.** Provide a summary of the information in the prospectus where the length or complexity of the prospectus makes a summary useful. The summary should be brief. The summary should not contain, and is not required to contain, all of the detailed information in the prospectus. If you provide summary business or financial information, even if you do not caption it as a summary, you still must provide that information in plain English.

Instruction to Paragraph 503(a):
The summary should not merely repeat the text of the prospectus but should provide a brief overview of the key aspects of the offering. Carefully consider and identify those aspects of the offering that are the most significant and determine how best to highlight those points in clear, plain language.

b. **Address and telephone number.** Include, either on the cover page or in the summary section of the prospectus, the complete mailing address and telephone number of your principal executive offices.

c. [**Reserved**]

Item 504 – Use of Proceeds

State the principal purposes for which the net proceeds to the registrant from the securities to be offered are intended to be used and the approximate amount intended to be used for each such purpose. Where registrant has no current specific plan for the proceeds, or a significant portion thereof, the registrant shall so state and discuss the principal reasons for the offering.

Instructions to Item 504:
1. Where less than all the securities to be offered may be sold and more than one use is listed for the proceeds, indicate the order of priority of such purposes and discuss the registrant's plans if substantially less than the maximum proceeds are obtained. Such discussion need not be included if underwriting arrangements with respect to such securities are such that, if any securities are sold to the public, it reasonably can be expected that the actual proceeds will not be substantially less than the aggregate proceeds to the registrant shown pursuant to Item 501 of Regulation S-K.
2. Details of proposed expenditures need not be given; for example, there need be furnished only a brief outline of any program of construction or addition of equipment. Consideration should be given as to the need to include a discussion of certain matters addressed in the discussion and analysis of registrant's financial condition and results of operations, such as liquidity and capital expenditures.
3. If any material amounts of other funds are necessary to accomplish the specified purposes for which the proceeds are to be obtained, state the amounts and sources of such other funds needed for each such specified purpose and the sources thereof.
4. If any material part of the proceeds is to be used to discharge indebtedness, set forth the interest rate and maturity of such indebtedness. If the indebtedness to be discharged was incurred within one year, describe the use of the proceeds of such indebtedness other than short-term borrowings used for working capital.
5. If any material amount of the proceeds is to be used to acquire assets, otherwise than in the ordinary course of business, describe briefly and state the cost of the assets and, where such assets are to be acquired from affiliates of the registrant or their associates, give the names

of the persons from whom they are to be acquired and set forth the principle followed in determining the cost to the registrant.

6.   Where the registrant indicates that the proceeds may, or will, be used to finance acquisitions of other businesses, the identity of such businesses, if known, or, if not known, the nature of the businesses to be sought, the status of any negotiations with respect to the acquisition, and a brief description of such business shall be included. Where, however, pro forma financial statements reflecting such acquisition are not required by Regulation S-X to be included, in the registration statement, the possible terms of any transaction, the identification of the parties thereto or the nature of the business sought need not be disclosed, to the extent that the registrant reasonably determines that public disclosure of such information would jeopardize the acquisition. Where Regulation S-X would require financial statements of the business to be acquired to be included, the description of the business to be acquired shall be more detailed.

7.   The registrant may reserve the right to change the use of proceeds, provided that such reservation is due to certain contingencies that are discussed specifically and the alternatives to such use in that event are indicated.

Item 505 – Determination of Offering Price

a.   **Common equity.** Where common equity is being registered for which there is no established public trading market for purposes of paragraph (a) of Item 201 of Regulation S-K or where there is a material disparity between the offering price of the common equity being registered and the market price of outstanding shares of the same class, describe the various factors considered in determining such offering price.

b.   **Warrants, rights and convertible securities.** Where warrants, rights or convertible securities exercisable for common equity for which there is no established public trading market for purposes of paragraph (a) of Item 201 of Regulation S-K are being registered, describe the various factors considered in determining their exercise or conversion price.

Item 506 – Dilution

Where common equity securities are being registered and there is substantial disparity between the public offering price and the effective cash cost to officers, directors, promoters and affiliated persons of common equity acquired by them in transactions during the past five years, or which they have the right to acquire, and the registrant is not subject to the reporting requirements of sections 13(a) or 15(d) of the Exchange Act immediately prior to filing of the registration statement, there shall be included a comparison of the public contribution under the proposed public offering and the effective cash contribution of such persons. In such cases, and in other instances where common equity securities are being registered by a registrant that has had losses in each of its last three fiscal years and there is a material dilution of the purchasers' equity interest, the following shall be disclosed: The net tangible book value per share before and after the distribution;

a.   The amount of the increase in such net tangible book value per share attributable to the cash payments made by purchasers of the shares being offered; and

b.   The amount of the immediate dilution from the public offering price which will be absorbed by such purchasers.

Item 507 – Selling Security Holders

If any of the securities to be registered are to be offered for the account of security holders, name each such security holder, indicate the nature of any position, office, or other material relationship which the selling security holder has had within the past three years with the registrant or any of its predecessors or affiliates, and state the amount of securities of the class owned by such security holder prior to the offering, the amount to be offered for the security holder's account, the amount and (if one percent or more) the percentage of the class to be owned by such security holder after completion of the offering.

Item 508 – Plan of Distribution

a. **Underwriters and underwriting obligation.** If the securities are to be offered through underwriters, name the principal underwriters, and state the respective amounts underwritten. Identify each such underwriter having a material relationship with the registrant and state the nature of the relationship. State briefly the nature of the obligation of the underwriter(s) to take the securities.

Instruction to Paragraph 508(a):
All that is required as to the nature of the underwriters' obligation is whether the underwriters are or will be committed to take and to pay for all of the securities if any are taken, or whether it is merely an agency or the type of *best efforts* arrangement under which the underwriters are required to take and to pay for only such securities as they may sell to the public. Conditions precedent to the underwriters' taking the securities, including *market-outs,* need not be described except in the case of an agency or *best efforts* arrangement.

b. **New underwriters.** Where securities being registered are those of a registrant that has not previously been required to file reports pursuant to section 13(a) or 15(d) of the Exchange Act, or where a prospectus is required to include reference on its cover page to material risks pursuant to Item 501 of Regulation S-K, and any one or more of the managing underwriter(s) (or where there are no managing underwriters, a majority of the principal underwriters) has been organized, reactivated, or first registered as a broker-dealer within the past three years, these facts concerning such underwriter(s) shall be disclosed in the prospectus together with, where applicable, the disclosures that the principal business function of such underwriter(s) will be to sell the securities to be registered, or that the promoters of the registrant have a material relationship with such underwriter(s). Sufficient details shall be given to allow full appreciation of such underwriter(s) experience and its relationship with the registrant, promoters and their controlling persons.

c. **Other distributions.** Outline briefly the plan of distribution of any securities to be registered that are to be offered otherwise than through underwriters.

1. If any securities are to be offered pursuant to a dividend or interest reinvestment plan the terms of which provide for the purchase of some securities on the market, state whether the registrant or the participant pays fees, commissions, and expenses incurred in connection with the plan. If the participant will pay such fees, commissions and expenses, state the anticipated cost to participants by transaction or other convenient reference.

2.   If the securities are to be offered through the selling efforts of brokers or dealers, describe the plan of distribution and the terms of any agreement, arrangement, or understanding entered into with broker(s) or dealer(s) prior to the effective date of the registration statement, including volume limitations on sales, parties to the agreement and the conditions under which the agreement may be terminated. If known, identify the broker(s) or dealer(s) which will participate in the offering and state the amount to be offered through each.

3.   If any of the securities being registered are to be offered otherwise than for cash, state briefly the general purposes of the distribution, the basis upon which the securities are to be offered, the amount of compensation and other expenses of distribution, and by whom they are to be borne. If the distribution is to be made pursuant to a plan of acquisition, reorganization, readjustment or succession, describe briefly the general effect of the plan and state when it became or is to become operative. As to any material amount of assets to be acquired under the plan, furnish information corresponding to that required by Instruction 5 of Item 504 of Regulation S-K.

d.   **Offerings on exchange.** If the securities are to be offered on an exchange, indicate the exchange. If the registered securities are to be offered in connection with the writing of exchange-traded call options, describe briefly such transactions.

e.   **Underwriters' compensation.** Provide a table that sets out the nature of the compensation and the amount of discounts and commissions to be paid to the underwriter for each security and in total. The table must show the separate amounts to be paid by the company and the selling shareholders. In addition, include in the table all other items considered by the Financial Industry Regulatory Authority ("FINRA") to be underwriting compensation for purposes of FINRA rules.

Instructions to paragraph 508(e):

1.   The term "commissions" is defined in paragraph (17) of Schedule A of the Securities Act. Show separately in the table the cash commissions paid by the registrant and selling security holders. Also show in the table commissions paid by other persons. Disclose any finder's fee or similar payments in the table.

2.   Disclose the offering expenses specified in Item 511 of Regulation S-K.

3.   If the underwriter has any arrangement with the issuer, such as an over- allotment option, under which the underwriter may purchase additional shares in connection with the offering, indicate that this arrangement exists and state the amount of additional shares that the underwriter may purchase under the arrangement. Where the underwriter has such an arrangement, present maximum- minimum information in a separate column to the table, based on the purchase of all or none of the shares subject to the arrangement. Describe the key terms of the arrangement in the narrative.

f.   **Underwriter's representative on board of directors.** Describe any arrangement whereby the underwriter has the right to designate or nominate a member or members of the board of directors of the registrant. The registrant shall disclose the identity of any director so designated or nominated, and indicate whether or not a person so designated or nominated, or allowed to be designated or nominated by the underwriter is or may be a director, officer, partner, employee or affiliate of the underwriter.

g. **Indemnification of underwriters.** If the underwriting agreement provides for indemnification by the registrant of the underwriters or their controlling persons against any liability arising under the Securities Act, furnish a brief description of such indemnification provisions.

h. **Dealers' compensation.** State briefly the discounts and commissions to be allowed or paid to dealers, including all cash, securities, contracts or other considerations to be received by any dealer in connection with the sale of the securities. If any dealers are to act in the capacity of sub-underwriters and are to be allowed or paid any additional discounts or commissions for acting in such capacity, a general statement to that effect will suffice without giving the additional amounts to be sold.

i. **Finders.** Identify any finder and, if applicable, describe the nature of any material relationship between such finder and the registrant, its officers, directors, principal stockholders, finders or promoters or the principal underwriter(s), or if there is a managing underwriter(s), the managing underwriter(s), (including, in each case, affiliates or associates thereof).

j. **Discretionary accounts.** If the registrant was not, immediately prior to the filing of the registration statement, subject to the requirements of sections 13(a) or 15(d) of the Exchange Act, identify any principal underwriter that intends to sell to any accounts over which it exercises discretionary authority and include an estimate of the amount of securities so intended to be sold. The response to this paragraph shall be contained in a pre-effective amendment which shall be circulated if the information is not available when the registration statement is filed.

k. **Passive market making.** If the underwriters or any selling group members intend to engage in passive market making transactions as permitted by Rule 103 of Regulation M, indicate such intention and briefly describe passive market making.

l. **Stabilization and other transactions.**
   1. Briefly describe any transaction that the underwriter intends to conduct during the offering that stabilizes, maintains, or otherwise affects the market price of the offered securities. Include information on stabilizing transactions, syndicate short covering transactions, penalty bids, or any other transaction that affects the offered security's price. Describe the nature of the transactions clearly and explain how the transactions affect the offered security's price. Identify the exchange or other market on which these transactions may occur. If true, disclose that the underwriter may discontinue these transactions at any time;
   2. If the stabilizing began before the effective date of the registration statement, disclose the amount of securities bought, the prices at which they were bought and the period within which they were bought. If you use Rule 430A of this chapter, the prospectus you file under Rule 424(b) of this chapter or include in a post-effective amendment must contain information on the stabilizing transactions that took place before the determination of the public offering price; and
   3. If you are making a warrants or rights offering of securities to existing security holders and any securities not purchased by existing security holders are to be

reoffered to the public, disclose in a supplement to the prospectus or in the prospectus used in connection with the reoffering:

    i. The amount of securities bought in stabilization activities during the offering period and the price or range of prices at which the securities were bought;

    ii. The amount of the offered securities subscribed for during the offering period;

    iii. The amount of the offered securities subscribed for by the underwriter during the offering period;

    iv. The amount of the offered securities sold during the offering period by the underwriter and the price or price ranges at which the securities were sold; and

    v. The amount of the offered securities that will be reoffered to the public and the public offering price.

Item 509 – Interests of Named Experts and Counsel

If (a) any expert named in the registration statement as having prepared or certified any part thereof (or is named as having prepared or certified a report or valuation for use in connection with the registration statement), or (b) counsel for the registrant, underwriters or selling security holders named in the prospectus as having given an opinion upon the validity of the securities being registered or upon other legal matters in connection with the registration or offering of such securities, was employed for such purpose on a contingent basis, or at the time of such preparation, certification or opinion or at any time thereafter, through the date of effectiveness of the registration statement or that part of the registration statement to which such preparation, certification or opinion relates, had, or is to receive in connection with the offering, a substantial interest, direct or indirect, in the registrant or any of its parents or subsidiaries or was connected with the registrant or any of its parents or subsidiaries as a promoter, managing underwriter (or any principal underwriter, if there are no managing underwriters) voting trustee, director, officer, or employee, furnish a brief statement of the nature of such contingent basis, interest, or connection.

Instructions to Item 509:

1. The interest of an expert (other than an accountant) or counsel will not be deemed substantial and need not be disclosed if the interest, including the fair market value of all securities of the registrant owned, received and to be received, or subject to options, warrants or rights received or to be received by the expert or counsel does not exceed $50,000. For the purpose of this Instruction, the term *expert* or counsel includes the firm, corporation, partnership or other entity, if any, by which such expert or counsel is employed or of which he is a member or of counsel to and all attorneys in the case of counsel, and all nonclerical personnel in the case of named experts, participating in such matter on behalf of such firm, corporation, partnership or entity.

2. Accountants, providing a report on the financial statements, presented or incorporated by reference in the registration statement, should note Rule 2-01 of Regulation S-X for the Commission's requirements regarding "Qualification of Accountants" which discusses disqualifying interests.

Item 510 – Disclosure of Commission Position on Indemnification for Securities Act Liabilities

In addition to the disclosure prescribed by Item 702 of Regulation S-K, if the undertaking required by paragraph (h) of Item 512 of Regulation S-K is not required to be included in the registration statement because acceleration of the effective date of the registration statement is not being requested, and if waivers have not been obtained comparable to those specified in paragraph (h), a brief description of the indemnification provisions relating to directors, officers and controlling persons of the registrant against liability arising under the Securities Act (including any provision of the underwriting agreement which relates to indemnification of the underwriter or its controlling persons by the registrant against such liabilities where a director, officer or controlling person of the registrant is such an underwriter or controlling person thereof or a member of any firm which is such an underwriter) shall be included in the prospectus, together with a statement in substantially the following form:

> Insofar as indemnification for liabilities arising under the Securities Act of 1933 may be permitted to directors, officers or persons controlling the registrant pursuant to the foregoing provisions, the registrant has been informed that in the opinion of the Securities and Exchange Commission such indemnification is against public policy as expressed in the Act and is therefore unenforceable.

Item 511 – Other Expenses of Issuance and Distribution

Furnish a reasonably itemized statement of all expenses in connection with the issuance and distribution of the securities to be registered, other than underwriting discounts and commissions. If any of the securities to be registered are to be offered for the account of security holders, indicate the portion of such expenses to be borne by such security holder.

Instruction to Item 511:

Insofar as practicable, registration fees, Federal taxes, States taxes and fees, trustees' and transfer agents' fees, costs of printing and engraving, and legal, accounting, and engineering fees shall be itemized separately. Include as a separate item any premium paid by the registrant or any selling security holder on any policy obtained in connection with the offering and sale of the securities being registered which insures or indemnifies directors or officers against any liabilities they may incur in connection with the registration, offering, or sale of such securities. The information may be given as subject to future contingencies. If the amounts of any items are not known, estimates, identified as such, shall be given.

Item 512 – Undertakings

Include each of the following undertakings that is applicable to the offering being registered.
Rule 415 Offering. Include the following if the securities are registered pursuant to Rule 415 under the Securities Act:

> The undersigned registrant hereby undertakes:
>
> 1. To file, during any period in which offers or sales are being made, a post-effective amendment to this registration statement:
>
>   i.   To include any prospectus required by section 10(a)(3) of the Securities Act of 1933;
>
>   ii. To reflect in the prospectus any facts or events arising after the effective date of the registration statement (or the most recent post-effective

amendment thereof) which, individually or in the aggregate, represent a fundamental change in the information set forth in the registration statement. Notwithstanding the foregoing, any increase or decrease in volume of securities offered (if the total dollar value of securities offered would not exceed that which was registered) and any deviation from the low or high end of the estimated maximum offering range may be reflected in the form of prospectus filed with the Commission pursuant to Rule 424(b) if, in the aggregate, the changes in volume and price represent no more than 20% change in the maximum aggregate offering price set forth in the "Calculation of Registration Fee" table in the effective registration statement.

iii.   To include any material information with respect to the plan of distribution not previously disclosed in the registration statement or any material change to such information in the registration statement; *Provided, however*, That:

        A.   Paragraphs (a)(1)(i) and (a)(1)(ii) of this section do not apply if the registration statement is on Form S-8, and the information required to be included in a post-effective amendment by those paragraphs is contained in reports filed with or furnished to the Commission by the registrant pursuant to section 13 or section 15(d) of the Securities Exchange Act of 1934 that are incorporated by reference in the registration statement; and

        B.   Paragraphs (a)(1)(i), (a)(1)(ii) and (a)(1)(iii) of this section do not apply if the registration statement is on Form S-1, Form S-3, Form SF-3 or Form F-3 and the information required to be included in a post-effective amendment by those paragraphs is contained in reports filed with or furnished to the Commission by the registrant pursuant to section 13 or section 15(d) of the Securities Exchange Act of 1934 that are incorporated by reference in the registration statement, or, as to a registration statement on Form S-3, Form SF-3 or Form F-3, is contained in a form of prospectus filed pursuant to Rule 424(b) of this chapter that is part of the registration statement. .

2.   That, for the purpose of determining any liability under the Securities Act of 1933, each such post-effective amendment shall be deemed to be a new registration statement relating to the securities offered therein, and the offering of such securities at that time shall be deemed to be the initial bona fide offering thereof.

3.   To remove from registration by means of a post-effective amendment any of the securities being registered which remain unsold at the termination of the offering.

4.   If the registrant is a foreign private issuer, to file a post-effective amendment to the registration statement to include any financial statements required by Item 8.A. of Form 20-F at the start of any delayed offering or throughout a continuous offering. Financial statements and information otherwise required by Section 10(a)(3) of the Act need not be furnished, *provided* that the registrant includes in the prospectus, by means of a post-effective amendment, financial statements required pursuant to this paragraph (a)(4) and other information necessary to

ensure that all other information in the prospectus is at least as current as the date of those financial statements. Notwithstanding the foregoing, with respect to registration statements on Form F-3, a post-effective amendment need not be filed to include financial statements and information required by Section 10(a)(3) of the Act or Item 8.A of Form 20-F of this chapter if such financial statements and information are contained in periodic reports filed with or furnished to the Commission by the registrant pursuant to section 13 or section 15(d) of the Securities Exchange Act of 1934 that are incorporated by reference in the Form F-3.

5.   That, for the purpose of determining liability under the Securities Act of 1933 to any purchaser:

    i.   If the registrant is relying on Rule 430B:

        (A) Each prospectus filed by the registrant pursuant to Rule 424(b)(3) shall be deemed to be part of the registration statement as of the date the filed prospectus was deemed part of and included in the registration statement; and

        (B) Each prospectus required to be filed pursuant to Rule 424(b)(2), (b)(5), or (b)(7) as part of a registration statement in reliance on Rule 430B relating to an offering made pursuant to Rule 415(a)(1)(i), (vii), or (x) for the purpose of providing the information required by section 10(a) of the Securities Act of 1933 shall be deemed to be part of and included in the registration statement as of the earlier of the date such form of prospectus is first used after effectiveness or the date of the first contract of sale of securities in the offering described in the prospectus. As provided in Rule 430B, for liability purposes of the issuer and any person that is at that date an underwriter, such date shall be deemed to be a new effective date of the registration statement relating to the securities in the registration statement to which that prospectus relates, and the offering of such securities at that time shall be deemed to be the initial bona fide offering thereof. *Provided, however,* that no statement made in a registration statement or prospectus that is part of the registration statement or made in a document incorporated or deemed incorporated by reference into the registration statement or prospectus that is part of the registration statement will, as to a purchaser with a time of contract of sale prior to such effective date, supersede or modify any statement that was made in the registration statement or prospectus that was part of the registration statement or made in any such document immediately prior to such effective date; or

    ii.   If the registrant is subject to Rule 430C, each prospectus filed pursuant to Rule 424(b) as part of a registration statement relating to an offering, other than registration statements relying on Rule 430B or other than prospectuses filed in reliance on Rule 430A, shall be deemed to be part of and included in the registration statement as of the date it is first used after effectiveness. *Provided, however,* that no statement made in a registration statement or prospectus that is part of the registration statement or made in a document incorporated or deemed incorporated by reference into the registration statement or prospectus that is part of the registration statement will, as to a purchaser with a time of contract of sale prior to such first use, supersede or modify any statement that was made in the registration statement or prospectus that was part of the registration statement or made in any such document immediately prior to such date of first use.

***

6.   That, for the purpose of determining liability of the registrant under the Securities Act of 1933 to any purchaser in the initial distribution of the securities: The undersigned registrant undertakes that in a primary offering of securities of the undersigned registrant pursuant to this registration statement, regardless of the underwriting method used to sell the securities to the purchaser, if the securities are offered or sold to such purchaser by means of any of the following communications, the undersigned registrant will be a seller to the purchaser and will be considered to offer or sell such securities to such purchaser:

i.   Any preliminary prospectus or prospectus of the undersigned registrant relating to the offering required to be filed pursuant to Rule 424;

ii.   Any free writing prospectus relating to the offering prepared by or on behalf of the undersigned registrant or used or referred to by the undersigned registrant;

iii.   The portion of any other free writing prospectus relating to the offering containing material information about the undersigned registrant or its securities provided by or on behalf of the undersigned registrant; and

iv.   Any other communication that is an offer in the offering made by the undersigned registrant to the purchaser.

***

i.   Include the following in a registration statement permitted by Rule 430A under the Securities Act of 1933:

The undersigned registrant hereby undertakes that:

1.   For purposes of determining any liability under the Securities Act of 1933, the information omitted from the form of prospectus filed as part of this registration statement in reliance upon Rule 430A and contained in a form of prospectus filed by the registrant pursuant to Rule 424(b) (1) or (4) or 497(h) under the Securities Act shall be deemed to be part of this registration statement as of the time it was declared effective.

2.   For the purpose of determining any liability under the Securities Act of 1933, each post-effective amendment that contains a form of prospectus shall be deemed to be a new registration statement relating to the securities offered therein, and the offering of such securities at that time shall be deemed to be the initial bona fide offering thereof.

Item 701 – Recent Sales of Unregistered Securities; Use of Proceeds from Registered Securities

Furnish the following information as to all securities of the registrant sold by the registrant within the past three years which were not registered under the Securities Act. Include sales of reacquired securities, as well as new issues, securities issued in exchange for property, services, or other securities, and new securities resulting from the modification of outstanding securities.

a.   **Securities sold.** Give the date of sale and the title and amount of securities sold.

b.   **Underwriters and other purchasers.** Give the names of the principal underwriters, if any. As to any such securities not publicly offered, name the persons or identify the class of persons to whom the securities were sold.

c.   **Consideration.** As to securities sold for cash, state the aggregate offering price and the aggregate underwriting discounts or commissions. As to any securities sold otherwise than for cash, state the nature of the transaction and the nature and aggregate amount of consideration received by the registrant.

d.   **Exemption from registration claimed.** Indicate the section of the Securities Act or the rule of the Commission under which exemption from registration was claimed and state briefly the facts relied upon to make the exemption available.

e.   **Terms of conversion or exercise.** If the information called for by this paragraph (e) is being presented on Form 8-K, Form 10-Q or Form 10-K under the Exchange Act, and where the securities sold by the registrant are convertible or exchangeable into equity securities, or are warrants or options representing equity securities, disclose the terms of conversion or exercise of the securities.

f.   **Use of Proceeds.** As required by Rule 463 of this chapter, following the effective date of the first registration statement filed under the Securities Act by an issuer, the issuer or successor issuer shall report the use of proceeds on its first periodic report filed pursuant to sections 13(a) and 15(d) of the Exchange Act after effectiveness of its Securities Act registration statement, and thereafter on each of its subsequent periodic reports filed pursuant to sections 13(a) and 15(d) of the Exchange Act through the later of disclosure of the application of all the offering proceeds, or disclosure of the termination of the offering. If a report of the use of proceeds is required with respect to the first effective registration statement of the predecessor issuer, the successor issuer shall provide such a report. The information provided pursuant to paragraphs (f)(2) through (f)(4) of this Item need only be provided with respect to the first periodic report filed pursuant to sections 13(a) and 15(d) of the Exchange Act after effectiveness of the registration statement filed under the Securities Act. Subsequent periodic reports filed pursuant to sections 13(a) and 15(d) of the Exchange Act need only provide the information required in paragraphs (f)(2) through (f)(4) of this Item if any of such required information has changed since the last periodic report filed. In disclosing the use of proceeds in the first periodic report filed pursuant to the Exchange Act, the issuer or successor issuer should include the following information:

1.   The effective date of the Securities Act registration statement for which the use of proceeds information is being disclosed and the Commission file number assigned to the registration statement;

2.   If the offering has commenced, the offering date, and if the offering has not commenced, an explanation why it has not;

3.   If the offering terminated before any securities were sold, an explanation for such termination; and

4.   If the offering did not terminate before any securities were sold, disclose:

    i.   Whether the offering has terminated and, if so, whether it terminated before the sale of all securities registered;

    ii.   The name(s) of the managing underwriter(s), if any;

    iii.   The title of each class of securities registered and, where a class of convertible securities is being registered, the title of any class of securities into which such securities may be converted;

    iv.   For each class of securities (other than a class of securities into which a class of convertible securities registered may be converted without additional payment to the issuer) the following information, provided for both the account of the issuer and the account(s) of any selling security holder(s): the amount registered, the aggregate price of the offering amount registered, the amount sold and the aggregate offering price of the amount sold to date;

    v.   From the effective date of the Securities Act registration statement to the ending date of the reporting period, the amount of expenses incurred for the issuer's account in connection with the issuance and distribution of the securities registered for underwriting discounts and commissions, finders' fees, expenses paid to or for underwriters, other expenses and total expenses. Indicate if a reasonable estimate for the amount of expenses incurred is provided instead of the actual amount of expense. Indicate whether such payments were:

        A.   Direct or indirect payments to directors, officers, general partners of the issuer or their associates; to persons owning ten (10) percent or more of any class of equity securities of the issuer; and to affiliates of the issuer; or

        B.   Direct or indirect payments to others;

    vi.   The net offering proceeds to the issuer after deducting the total expenses described in paragraph (f)(4)(v) of this Item;

    vii.   From the effective date of the Securities Act registration statement to the ending date of the reporting period, the amount of net offering proceeds to the issuer used for construction of plant, building and facilities; purchase and installation of machinery and equipment; purchases of real estate; acquisition of other business(es); repayment of indebtedness; working capital; temporary investments (which should be specified); and any other purposes for which at least five (5) percent of the issuer's total offering proceeds or $100,000 (whichever is less) has been used (which should be specified). Indicate if a reasonable estimate for the amount of net offering proceeds applied is provided instead of the actual amount of net offering proceeds used. Indicate whether such payments were:

        A.   Direct or indirect payments to directors, officers, general partners of the issuer or their associates; to persons owning ten (10) percent or more of any class of equity securities of the issuer; and to affiliates of the issuer; or

        B.   Direct or indirect payments to others; and

viii. If the use of proceeds in paragraph (f)(4)(vii) of this Item represents a material change in the use of proceeds described in the prospectus, the issuer should describe briefly the material change.

Instructions to 701:
1. Information required by this Item 701 need not be set forth as to notes, drafts, bills of exchange, or bankers' acceptances which mature not later than one year from the date of issuance.
2. If the sales were made in a series of transactions, the information may be given by such totals and periods as will reasonably convey the information required.

Item 702 – Indemnification of Directors and Officers

State the general effect of any statute, charter provisions, by-laws, contract or other arrangements under which any controlling persons, director or officer of the registrant is insured or indemnified in any manner against liability which he may incur in his capacity as such.

Item 703 – Purchases of equity securities by the issuer and affiliated purchasers

a. Disclose the specified information in narrative form with respect to the issuer's repurchases of equity securities disclosed pursuant to Item 601(b)(26) of Regulation S-K and refer to the particular repurchases in the table in Item 601(b)(26) of Regulation S-K that correspond to the different parts of the narrative, if applicable:
   1. The objectives or rationales for each repurchase plan or program and the process or criteria used to determine the amount of repurchases;
   2. The number of shares (or units) purchased other than through a publicly announced plan or program, and the nature of the transaction (e.g., whether the purchases were made in open-market transactions, tender offers, in satisfaction of the issuer's obligations upon exercise of outstanding put options issued by the issuer, or other transactions);
   3. For publicly announced repurchase plans or programs:
      i. The date each plan or program was announced;
      ii. The dollar amount (or share or unit amount) approved;
      iii. The expiration date (if any) of each plan or program;
      iv. Each plan or program that has expired during the period covered by the table in Item 601(b)(26) of Regulation S-K; and
      v. Each plan or program the issuer has determined to terminate prior to expiration, or under which the issuer does not intend to make further purchases.
   4. Any policies and procedures relating to purchases and sales of the issuer's securities by its officers and directors during a repurchase program, including any restrictions on such transactions.

b. The disclosure provided pursuant to paragraph (a) of this section must be provided in an Interactive Data File as required by Rule 405 of Regulation S-T in accordance with the EDGAR Filer Manual.

Regulation AB – Asset-Backed Securities

Item 1100 – General

a. **Application of Regulation AB.** Regulation AB is the source of various disclosure items and requirements for "asset-backed securities" filings under the Securities Act of 1933 and the Securities Exchange Act of 1934. Unless otherwise specified, definitions to be used in this Regulation AB, including the definition of "asset-backed security," are set forth in Item 1101.

b. **Presentation of historical delinquency and loss information.** Several Items in Regulation AB call for the presentation of historical information and data on delinquencies and loss information. In providing such information:

1. Present delinquency experience in 30 or 31 day increments, as applicable, beginning at least with assets that are 30 or 31 days delinquent, as applicable, through the point that assets are written off or charged off as uncollectable. At a minimum, present such information by number of accounts and dollar amount. Present statistical information in a tabular or graphical format, if such presentation will aid understanding.

2. Disclose the total amount of delinquent assets as a percentage of the aggregate asset pool.

3. Present loss and cumulative loss information, as applicable, regarding charge-offs, charge-off rate, gross losses, recoveries and net losses (with a description of how these terms are defined), the number and amount of assets experiencing a loss and the number and amount of assets with a recovery, the ratio of aggregate net losses to average portfolio balance and the average of net loss on all assets that have experienced a net loss.

4. Categorize all delinquency and loss information by pool asset type.

5. In a registration statement under the Securities Act or the Exchange Act or in a prospectus to be filed pursuant to Rule 230.424, describe how delinquencies, charge-offs and uncollectable accounts are defined or determined, addressing the effect of any grace period, re-aging, restructure, partial payments considered current or other practices on delinquency and loss experience.

6. Describe any other material information regarding delinquencies and losses particular to the pool asset type(s), such as repossession information, foreclosure information and real estate owned (REO) or similar information.

***

Item 1101 – Definitions

The following definitions apply to the terms used in Regulation AB, unless specified otherwise:

***

b. **Asset-backed issuer** means an issuer whose reporting obligation results from either the registration of an offering of asset-backed securities under the Securities Act, or the registration of a class of asset-backed securities under section 12 of the Exchange Act.

c.

1.   **Asset-backed security** means a security that is primarily serviced by the cash flows of a discrete pool of receivables or other financial assets, either fixed or revolving, that by their terms convert into cash within a finite time period, plus any rights or other assets designed to assure the servicing or timely distributions of proceeds to the security holders; provided that in the case of financial assets that are leases, those assets may convert to cash partially by the cash proceeds from the disposition of the physical property underlying such leases.

***

2.   The following additional conditions apply in order to be considered an asset-backed security:

    i.   Neither the depositor nor the issuing entity is an investment company under the Investment Company Act of 1940 nor will become an investment company as a result of the asset-backed securities transaction.

    ii.   The activities of the issuing entity for the asset-backed securities are limited to passively owning or holding the pool of assets, issuing the asset-backed securities supported or serviced by those assets, and other activities reasonably incidental thereto.

    iii. No non-performing assets are part of the asset pool as of the measurement date.

    iv.   Delinquent assets do not constitute 50% or more, as measured by dollar volume, of the asset pool as of the measurement date.

    v.   With respect to securities that are backed by leases, the portion of the securitized pool balance attributable to the residual value of the physical property underlying the leases, as determined in accordance with the transaction agreements for the securities, does not constitute:

        A.   For motor vehicle leases, 65% or more, as measured by dollar volume, of the securitized pool balance as of the measurement date.

        B.   For all other leases, 50% or more, as measured by dollar volume, of the securitized pool balance as of the measurement date.

3.   Notwithstanding the requirement in paragraph (c)(1) of this section that the asset pool be a discrete pool of assets, the following are considered to be a discrete pool of assets for purposes of being considered an asset-backed security:

    i.   Master trusts. The offering related to the securities contemplates adding additional assets to the pool that backs such securities in connection with future issuances of asset-backed securities backed by such pool. The offering related to the securities also may contemplate additions to the asset pool, to the extent consistent with paragraphs (c)(3)(ii) and (c)(3)(iii) of this section, in connection with maintaining minimum pool balances in accordance with the transaction agreements for master trusts with revolving periods or receivables or other financial assets that arise under revolving accounts.

    ii.   Prefunding periods. The offering related to the securities contemplates a prefunding account where a portion of the proceeds of that offering is to be used for the future acquisition of additional pool assets, if the duration of the prefunding period does not extend for more than one year from the date of issuance of the securities and the portion of the proceeds for such prefunding account does not involve in excess of:

    A. For master trusts, 25% of the aggregate principal balance of the total asset pool whose cash flows support the securities; and

    B. For other offerings, 25% of the proceeds of the offering.

iii. Revolving periods. The offering related to the securities contemplates a revolving period where cash flows from the pool assets may be used to acquire additional pool assets, provided, that, for securities backed by receivables or other financial assets that do not arise under revolving accounts, the revolving period does not extend for more than three years from the date of issuance of the securities and the additional pool assets are of the same general character as the original pool assets.

***

m. **Asset representations reviewer** means any person appointed to review the underlying assets for compliance with the representations and warranties on the underlying pool assets and is not affiliated with any sponsor, depositor, servicer, or trustee of the transaction, or any of their affiliates. The asset representations reviewer shall not be the party to determine whether noncompliance with representations or warranties constitutes a breach of any contractual provision. The asset representations reviewer also shall not be the same party or an affiliate of any party hired by the sponsor or underwriter to perform pre-closing due diligence work on the pool assets.

Item 1104 – Sponsors

Provide the following information about the sponsor:

a. State the sponsor's name and describe the sponsor's form of organization.

b. Describe the general character of the sponsor's business.

c. Describe the sponsor's securitization program and state how long the sponsor has been engaged in the securitization of assets. The description must include, to the extent material, a general discussion of the sponsor's experience in securitizing assets of any type as well as a more detailed discussion of the sponsor's experience in and overall procedures for originating or acquiring and securitizing assets of the type included in the current transaction. Include to the extent material information regarding the size, composition and growth of the sponsor's portfolio of assets of the type to be securitized and information or factors related to the sponsor that may be material to an analysis of the origination or performance of the pool assets, such as whether any prior securitizations organized by the sponsor have defaulted or experienced an early amortization triggering event.

d. Describe the sponsor's material roles and responsibilities in its securitization program, including whether the sponsor or an affiliate is responsible for originating, acquiring, pooling or servicing the pool assets, and the sponsor's participation in structuring the transaction.

e.   **Repurchases and replacements**.
1.   If the underlying transaction agreements provide a covenant to repurchase or replace an underlying asset for breach of a representation or warranty, provide in the body of the prospectus for the prior three years, the information required by Rule 15Ga-1(a) concerning all assets securitized by the sponsor that were the subject of a demand to repurchase or replace for breach of the representations and warranties concerning the pool assets for all asset-backed securities (as that term is defined in Section 3(a)(77) of the Securities Exchange Act of 1934) where the underlying transaction agreements included a covenant to repurchase or replace an underlying asset of the same asset class held by non-affiliates of the sponsor, except that:
     i.   For prospectuses to be filed pursuant to Rule 424 of this chapter prior to February 14, 2013, information may be limited to the prior year; and
     ii. for prospectuses to be filed pursuant to Rule 424 of this chapter on or after February 14, 2013 but prior to February 14, 2014, information may be limited to the prior two years.
2.   Include a reference to the most recent Form ABS-15G filed by the securitizer (as that term is defined in Section 15G(a) of the Securities Exchange Act of 1934 in response to Rule 15Ga-1) and disclose the CIK number of the securitizer.
3.   For prospectuses to be filed pursuant to Rule.424 of this chapter, the information presented shall not be more than 135 days old.

f.   If the sponsor is required to repurchase or replace any asset for breach of a representation and warranty pursuant to the transaction agreements, provide information regarding the sponsor's financial condition to the extent that there is a material risk that the effect on its ability to comply with the provisions in the transaction agreements relating to the repurchase obligations for those assets resulting from such financial condition could have a material impact on pool performance or performance of the asset-backed securities.

g.   Describe any interest that the sponsor, or any affiliate of the sponsor, has retained in the transaction, including the amount and nature of that interest. Disclose any hedge (security specific or portfolio) materially related to the credit risk of the securities that was entered into by the sponsor or, if known, by an affiliate of the sponsor to offset the risk position held.
     Instruction to Item 1104(g). The disclosure required under this item shall separately state the amount and nature of any interest or asset retained in compliance with law, including any amounts that are retained by parties other than the sponsor in order to satisfy such requirements.

***

Item 1111 – Pool Assets

Describe the pool assets, including the information required by this Item 1111. Present statistical information in tabular or graphical format, if such presentation will aid understanding. Present statistical information in appropriate distributional groups or incremental ranges in addition to presenting appropriate overall pool totals, averages and weighted averages, if such presentation will aid in the understanding of the data. In addition to presenting the number, amount and percentage of pool assets by distributional group or range, also provide statistical information for each group or range by variables, to the extent material, such as, average balance, weighted average coupon, average age and remaining term, average loan-to-value or similar ratio and weighted average standardized credit score or other applicable measure of obligor credit quality. These variables are just examples and should be tailored to the particular asset class backing the asset-backed securities. Consider providing minimums and maximums when presenting averages on an aggregate basis and within each group or range. In addition, provide historical data on the pool assets as appropriate (e.g., the lesser of three years or the time such assets have existed) to allow material evaluation of the pool data. In making any calculations regarding overall pool balances, disregard any funds set aside for a prefunding account.

a. **Information regarding pool asset types and selection criteria**. Provide the following information:
1. A brief description of the type or types of pool assets to be securitized.
2. A general description of the material terms of the pool assets.
3. A description of the solicitation, credit-granting or underwriting criteria used to originate or purchase the pool assets, including, to the extent known, any changes in such criteria and the extent to which such policies and criteria are or could be overridden.
4. The method and criteria by which the pool assets were selected for the transaction.
5. The cut-off date or similar date for establishing the composition of the asset pool, if applicable.
6. If legal or regulatory provisions (such as bankruptcy, consumer protection, predatory lending, privacy, property rights or foreclosure laws or regulations) may materially affect pool asset performance or payments or expected payments on the asset-backed securities, briefly identify these provisions and their effects on such items.
    Instruction to Item 1111(a)(6).
    Unless a material concentration of assets exists, it is not necessary to provide details of the laws in each jurisdiction. Even in that case, a legalistic description or recitation of the laws or regulations in a particular jurisdiction is not required.
7.
    i. The nature of a review of the assets performed by an issuer or sponsor (required by Rule 193), including whether the issuer of any asset-backed security engaged a third party for purposes of performing the review of the pool assets underlying an asset-backed security; and
    ii. The findings and conclusions of the review of the assets by the issuer, sponsor, or third party described in paragraph (a)(7)(i) of this section.
    Instruction to Item 1111(a)(7): The disclosure required under this item shall provide an understanding of how the review related to the disclosure regarding the assets. For example, if benchmarks or criteria different from that specified in the prospectus were used to evaluate the assets, these should be described, as well as the findings and conclusions. If the review is of a sample of assets in the pool, disclose the size of the sample and the criteria used to select the assets

sampled. If the issuer has engaged a third party for purposes of performing the review of assets, and attributes the findings and conclusions of the review to the third party in the disclosure required by this item, the issuer must provide the name of the third-party reviewer and comply with the requirements of Rule 436 of this chapter.

8.   If any assets in the pool deviate from the disclosed underwriting criteria or other criteria or benchmark used to evaluate the assets, or any assets in the sample or assets otherwise known to deviate if only a sample was reviewed, disclose how those assets deviate from the disclosed underwriting criteria or other criteria or benchmark used to evaluate the assets and include data on the amount and characteristics of those assets that did not meet the disclosed standards. Disclose which entity (*e.g.*, sponsor, originator, or underwriter) or entities determined that those assets should be included in the pool, despite not having met the disclosed underwriting standards or other criteria or benchmark used to evaluate the assets, and what factors were used to make the determination, such as compensating factors or a determination that the exception was not material. If compensating or other factors were used, provide data on the amount of assets in the pool or in the sample that are represented as meeting each such factor and the amount of assets that do not meet those factors. If multiple entities are involved in the decision to include assets despite not having met the disclosed underwriting standards, this should be described and each participating entity should be disclosed.

b.   **Pool characteristics.** Describe the material characteristics of the asset pool. Provide appropriate introductory and explanatory information to introduce the characteristics, the methodology used in determining or calculating the characteristics and any terms or abbreviations used. While the material characteristics will vary depending on the nature of the pool assets, such characteristics may include, among other things:

1.   Number of each type of pool assets.

2.   Asset size, such as original balance and outstanding balance as of a designated cut-off date.

3.   Interest rate or rate of return, including type of interest rate if the pool includes different types, such as fixed and floating rates.

4.   Capitalized or uncapitalized accrued interest.

5.   Age, maturity, remaining term, average life (based on different prepayment assumptions), current payment/prepayment speeds and pool factors, as applicable.

6.   Servicer distribution, if different servicers service different pool assets.

7.   If a loan or similar receivable:

   i.   Amortization period.

   ii.   Loan purpose (e.g., whether a purchase or refinance) and status, if applicable (e.g., repayment or deferment).

   iii.   Loan-to-value (LTV) ratios and debt service coverage ratios (DSCR), as applicable.

   iv.   Type and/or use of underlying property, product or collateral (e.g., occupancy type for residential mortgages or industry sector for commercial mortgages).

8.   If a receivable or other financial asset that arises under a revolving account, such as a credit card receivable:
   i.   Monthly payment rate.
   ii.   Maximum credit lines.
   iii.   Average account balance.
   iv.   Yield percentages.
   v.   Type of asset.
   vi.   Finance charges, fees and other income earned.
   vii.   Balance reductions granted for refunds, returns, fraudulent charges or other reasons.
   viii.   Percentage of full-balance and minimum payments made.

9.   If the asset pool includes commercial mortgages, the following information, to the extent material:
   i.   For all commercial mortgages:
      A.   The location and present use of each mortgaged property.
      B.   Net operating income and net cash flow information, as well as the components of net operating income and net cash flow, for each mortgaged property.
      C.   Current occupancy rates for each mortgaged property.
      D.   The identity, square feet occupied by and lease expiration dates for the three largest tenants at each mortgaged property.
      E.   The nature and amount of all other material mortgages, liens or encumbrances against such properties and their priority.
   ii.   For each commercial mortgage that represents, by dollar value, 10% or more of the asset pool, as measured as of the cut-off date:
      A.   Any proposed program for the renovation, improvement or development of such properties, including the estimated cost thereof and the method of financing to be used.
      B.   The general competitive conditions to which such properties are or may be subject.
      C.   Management of such properties.
      D.   Occupancy rate expressed as a percentage for each of the last 5 years.
      E.   Principal business, occupations and professions carried on in, or from the properties.
      F.   Number of tenants occupying 10% or more of the total rentable square footage of such properties and principal nature of business of such tenant, and the principal provisions of the leases with those tenants including, but not limited to: rental per annum, expiration date, and renewal options.
      G.   The average effective annual rental per square foot or unit for each of the last three years prior to the date of filing.
      H.   Schedule of the lease expirations for each of the ten years starting with the year in which the registration statement is filed (or the year in which the prospectus supplement is dated, as applicable), stating:
         1.   The number of tenants whose leases will expire.
         2.   The total area in square feet covered by such leases.
         3.   The annual rental represented by such leases.
         4.   The percentage of gross annual rental represented by such leases.

Instruction to Item 1111(b)(9).

What is required is information material to an investor's understanding of the asset-backed securities. Detailed descriptions of the physical characteristics of individual properties or legal descriptions by metes and bounds are not required.

10. Whether the pool asset is secured or unsecured, and if secured, the type(s) of collateral.

11. Standardized credit scores of obligors and other information regarding obligor credit quality.

12. Billing and payment procedures, including frequency of payment, payment options, fees, charges and origination or payment incentives.

13. Information about the origination channel and origination process for the pool assets, such as originator information (and how acquired) and the level of origination documentation required, as applicable.

14. Geographic distribution, such as by state or other material geographic region. If 10% or more of the pool assets are or will be located in any one state or other geographic region, describe any economic or other factors specific to such state or region that may materially impact the pool assets or pool asset cash flows.

Instruction to Item 1111(b)(14).

For most assets, such as credit card accounts, motor vehicle leases, trade receivables and student loans, the location of the asset is the underlying obligor's billing address. For assets involving real estate, such as mortgages, the location of the asset is where the physical property underlying the asset is located.

15. Other concentrations material to the asset type (e.g., school type for student loans). If material, provide information required by paragraph (b)(14) of this section regarding such concentrations, as applicable.

c. **Delinquency and loss information.** Provide delinquency and loss information for the asset pool, including statistical information regarding delinquencies and losses.

d. **Sources of pool cash flow.** If the cash flows from the pool assets that are to be used to support the asset-backed securities are to come from more than one source (such as separate cash flows from lease payments and from the sale of the residual asset at the termination of the lease), provide the following information:

1. Disclose the specific sources of funds that will be used to make the payments and distributions on the asset-backed securities, and, if applicable, provide information on the relative amount and percentage of funds that are to be derived from each source, including a description of any assumptions, data, models and methodology used to derive such amounts. If payments on different classes or different categories of payments on or related to the asset-backed securities (e.g., principal, interest or expenses) are to come from different or segregated cash flows from the pool assets or other sources, disclose the source of funds that will be used for such payments.

2. Residual value information. If the asset pool includes leases or other assets where a portion of the securitized pool balance is attributable to the residual value of the underlying physical property underlying the leases, disclose the following:

      i.   How the residual values used to structure the transaction were estimated, including an explanation of any material discount rates, models or assumptions used and who selected such rates, models or assumptions.

      ii. Any material procedures or requirements incorporated to preserve residual values during the term of the lease, such as lessee responsibilities, prohibitions on subletting, indemnification or required insurance or guarantees.

      iii. The procedures by which the residual values will be realized and by whom those procedures will be carried out, including information on the experience of such party, any affiliations with a party described in Item 1119(a) of this Regulation AB and the compensation arrangements with such party.

      iv. Whether the pool assets are open-end leases (e.g., where the lessee is required to cover the shortfall between the residual value of the leased property and the sale proceeds) or closed-end leases (e.g., where the lessor is responsible for such shortfalls), and where both types of leases are included in the asset pool, the percentage of each.

      v. To the extent material, any lessor obligations that are required under the leases, and the effect or potential effect on the asset-backed securities from failure by the lessor to perform its obligations.

      vi. Statistical information regarding estimated residual values for the pool assets.

      vii. Summary historical statistics on turn-in rates, if applicable, and residual value realization rates by the party responsible for such process over the past three years, or such longer period as is material to an evaluation of the pool assets.

      viii. The effect on security holders if not enough cash flow is received from the realization of the residual values, whether there are any provisions to address this contingency, and how any cash flow greater than that necessary to pay security holders will be allocated.

e. **Representations and warranties and modification provisions relating to the pool assets**. Provide the following information:

    1.   Representations and warranties. Summarize any representations and warranties made concerning the pool assets by the sponsor, transferor, originator or other party to the transaction, and describe briefly the remedies available if those representations and warranties are breached, such as repurchase obligations

    2.   Modification provisions. Describe any provisions in the transaction agreements governing the modification of the terms of any asset, including how such modification may affect the cash flows from the assets or to the securities..

f. **Claims on pool assets.** Describe any material direct or contingent claim that parties other than the holders of the asset-backed securities have on any pool assets. Also, describe any material cross-collateralization or cross-default provisions relating to the pool assets.

g. **Revolving periods, prefunding accounts and other changes to the asset pool**. If the transaction contemplates a prefunding or revolving period, provide the following information, as applicable. Provide similar information regarding any other circumstances where pool assets may be added, substituted or removed from the asset pool, such as in the event of additional issuances of asset-backed securities in a master trust or a breach of a pool asset representation or warranty:

1.   The term or duration of any prefunding or revolving period.

2.   For prefunding periods, the amount of proceeds to be deposited in the prefunding account.

3.   For revolving periods, the maximum amount of additional assets that may be acquired during the revolving period, if applicable.

4.   The percentage of the asset pool and any class or series of the asset-backed securities represented by the prefunding account or the revolving account, if applicable.

5.   Triggers or events that would trigger limits on or terminate the prefunding or revolving period and the effects of such triggers. In particular for a revolving period, describe the operation of the revolving period and the amortization period.

6.   When and how new pool assets may be acquired during the prefunding or revolving period, and if, when and how pool assets can be removed or substituted. Describe any limits on the amount, type or speed with which pool assets may be acquired, substituted or removed.

7.   The acquisition or underwriting criteria for additional pool assets to be acquired during the prefunding or revolving period, including a description of any differences from the criteria used to select the current asset pool.

8.   Which party has the authority to add, remove or substitute assets from the asset pool or determine if such pool assets meet the acquisition or underwriting criteria for additional pool assets. In addition, disclose whether or not there will be any independent verification of such person's exercise of authority or determinations.

9.   Any requirements to add or remove minimum amounts of pool assets and any effects of not meeting those requirements.

10.   If applicable, the procedures and standards for the temporary investment of funds in a prefunding or revolving account pending use (including the disposition of gains and losses on pending funds) and a description of the financial products or instruments eligible for such accounts.

11.   The circumstances under which funds in a prefunding or revolving account will be returned to investors or otherwise disposed of.

12.   A statement of whether, and if so, how, investors will be notified of changes to the asset pool.

***

Item 1120 – Ratings

Disclose whether the issuance or sale of any class of offered securities is conditioned on the assignment of a rating by one or more rating agencies, whether or not NRSROs. If so, identify each rating agency and the minimum rating that must be assigned. Describe any arrangements to have such rating monitored while the asset-backed securities are outstanding.

UNITED STATES SECURITIES AND EXCHANGE COMMISSION
Washington, D.C. 20549

FORM C
UNDER THE SECURITIES ACT OF 1933

(Mark one.)

- ☐ **Form C: Offering Statement**
- ☐ **Form C-U: Progress Update:** _____
- ☐ **Form C/A: Amendment to Offering Statement:** _____
  - ☐ **Check box if Amendment is material and investors must reconfirm within five business days.**
- ☐ **Form C-AR: Annual Report**
- ☐ **Form C-AR/A: Amendment to Annual Report**
- ☐ **Form C-TR: Termination of Reporting**

Name of issuer: _____

Legal status of issuer:

Form: _____

Jurisdiction of Incorporation/Organization: _____

Date of organization: _____

Physical address of issuer: _____

Website of issuer: _____

Name of intermediary through which the offering will be conducted: _____

CIK number of intermediary: _____

SEC file number of intermediary: _____

CRD number, if applicable, of intermediary: _____

Amount of compensation to be paid to the intermediary, whether as a dollar amount or a percentage of the offering amount, or a good faith estimate if the exact amount is not available at the time of the filing, for conducting the offering, including the amount of referral and any other fees associated with the offering:

_____

Any other direct or indirect interest in the issuer held by the intermediary, or any arrangement for the intermediary to acquire such an interest:

_____

Type of security offered: _____

Target number of securities to be offered: _____

Price (or method for determining price): _____

Target offering amount: _____

Oversubscriptions accepted: ◻ Yes ◻ No

  If yes, disclose how oversubscriptions will be allocated: ◻ Pro-rata basis, ◻ First-come, first-served basis, ◻ Other – provide a description: _____

Maximum offering amount (if different from target offering amount): _____

Deadline to reach the target offering amount: _____

NOTE: If the sum of the investment commitments does not equal or exceed the target offering amount at the offering deadline, no securities will be sold in the offering, investment commitments will be cancelled and committed funds will be returned.

Current number of employees: _____

Total Assets:	Most recent fiscal year-end:	Prior fiscal year-end:
Cash & Cash Equiv:	Most recent fiscal year-end:	Prior fiscal year-end:
Accounts Receivable:	Most recent fiscal year-end:	Prior fiscal year-end:
Short-term Debt:	Most recent fiscal year-end:	Prior fiscal year-end:
Long-term Debt:	Most recent fiscal year-end:	Prior fiscal year-end:
Revenues/Sales	Most recent fiscal year-end:	Prior fiscal year-end:
Cost of Goods Sold:	Most recent fiscal year-end:	Prior fiscal year-end:
Taxes Paid:	Most recent fiscal year-end:	Prior fiscal year-end:
Net Income:	Most recent fiscal year-end:	Prior fiscal year-end:

Using the list below, select the jurisdictions in which the issuer intends to offer the securities:

[List will include all U.S. jurisdictions, with an option to add and remove them individually, add all and remove all.]

GENERAL INSTRUCTIONS

I.   Eligibility Requirements for Use of Form C

This Form shall be used for the offering statement, and any related amendments and progress reports, required to be filed by any issuer offering or selling securities in reliance on the exemption in Securities Act Section 4(a)(6) and in accordance with Section 4A and Regulation Crowdfunding. The term "issuer" includes any co-issuer jointly offering or selling securities with an issuer in reliance on the exemption in Securities Act Section 4(a)(6) and in accordance with Securities Act Section 4A and Regulation Crowdfunding) This Form also shall be used for an annual report required pursuant to Rule 202 of Regulation Crowdfunding and for the termination of reporting required pursuant to Rule 203(b)(2) of Regulation Crowdfunding. Careful attention should be directed to the terms, conditions and requirements of the exemption.

II.   Preparation and Filing of Form C

Information on the cover page will be generated based on the information provided in XML format. Other than the cover page, this Form is not to be used as a blank form to be filled in, but only as a guide in the preparation of Form C. General information regarding the preparation, format and how to file this Form is contained in Regulation S-T.

III.   Information to be Included in the Form

Item 1. Offering Statement Disclosure Requirements

An issuer filing this Form for an offering in reliance on Section 4(a)(6) of the Securities Act and pursuant to Regulation Crowdfunding must file the Form prior to the commencement of the offering and include the information required by Rule 201 of Regulation Crowdfunding.

An issuer must include in the XML-based portion of this Form: the information required by paragraphs (a), (e), (g), (h), (l), (n), and (o) of Rule 201 of Regulation Crowdfunding; selected financial data for the prior two fiscal years (including total assets, cash and cash equivalents, accounts receivable, short-term debt, long-term debt, revenues/sales, cost of goods sold, taxes paid and net income); the jurisdictions in which the issuer intends to offer the securities; and any information required by Rule 203(a)(3) of Regulation Crowdfunding.

Other than the information required to be provided in XML format, an issuer may provide the required information in the optional Question and Answer format included herein or in any other format included on the intermediary's platform, by filing such information as an exhibit to this Form, including copies of screen shots of the relevant information, as appropriate and necessary.

If disclosure in response to any paragraph of Rule 201 of Regulation Crowdfunding or Rule 203(a)(3) is responsive to one or more other paragraphs of Rule 201 of Regulation Crowdfunding or to Rule 203(a)(3) of Regulation Crowdfunding, issuers are not required to make duplicate disclosures.

Item 2. Legends

(a)   An issuer filing this Form for an offering in reliance on Section 4(a)(6) of the Securities Act and pursuant to Regulation Crowdfunding must include the following legends:

A crowdfunding investment involves risk. You should not invest any funds in this offering unless you can afford to lose your entire investment.

In making an investment decision, investors must rely on their own examination of the issuer and the terms of the offering, including the merits and risks involved. These securities have not been recommended or approved by any federal or state securities commission or regulatory authority. Furthermore, these authorities have not passed upon the accuracy or adequacy of this document.

The U.S. Securities and Exchange Commission does not pass upon the merits of any securities offered or the terms of the offering, nor does it pass upon the accuracy or completeness of any offering document or literature.

These securities are offered under an exemption from registration; however, the U.S. Securities and Exchange Commission has not made an independent determination that these securities are exempt from registration.

(b)   An issuer filing this Form for an offering in reliance on Section 4(a)(6) of the Securities Act and pursuant to Regulation Crowdfunding must disclose in the offering statement that it will file a report with the Commission annually and post the report on its website, no later than 120 days after the end of each fiscal year covered by the report. The issuer must also disclose how an issuer may terminate its reporting obligations in the future in accordance with Rule 202(b) of Regulation Crowdfunding.

Item 3. Annual Report Disclosure Requirements

An issuer filing this Form for an annual report, as required by Regulation Crowdfunding, must file the Form no later than 120 days after the issuer's fiscal year end covered by the report and include the information required by Rule 201(a), (b), (c), (d), (e), (f), (m), (p), (q), (r), (s), (t), (x) and (y) of Regulation Crowdfunding. For purposes of paragraph (t), the issuer shall provide financial statements certified by the principal executive officer of the issuer to be true and complete in all material respects. If, however, the issuer has available financial statements prepared in accordance with U.S. generally accepted accounting principles (U.S. GAAP) that have been reviewed or audited by an independent certified public accountant, those financial statements must be provided and the principal executive officer certification will not be required.

An issuer must include in the XML-based portion of this Form: the information required by paragraphs (a), and (e) of Rule 201 of Regulation Crowdfunding; and selected financial data for the prior two fiscal years (including total assets, cash and cash equivalents, accounts receivable, short-term debt, long-term debt, revenues/sales, cost of goods sold, taxes paid and net income).

SIGNATURES

Pursuant to the requirements of Sections 4(a)(6) and 4A of the Securities Act of 1933 and Regulation Crowdfunding, the issuer certifies that it has reasonable grounds to believe that it meets all of the requirements for filing on Form C and has duly caused this Form to be signed on its behalf by the duly authorized undersigned.

_____
(Issuer)

By

_____
(Signature and Title)

Pursuant to the requirements of Sections 4(a)(6) and 4A of the Securities Act of 1933 and Regulation Crowdfunding, this Form C has been signed by the following persons in the capacities and on the dates indicated.

_____
(Signature)

_____
(Title)

_____
(Date)

Instructions.

Instructions.
1. The form shall be signed by the issuer, its principal executive officer or officers, its principal financial officer, its controller or principal accounting officer and at least a majority of the board of directors or persons performing similar functions. If there is a co-issuer, the form shall also be signed by the co-issuer, its principal executive officer or officers, its principal financial officer, its controller or principal accounting officer and at least a majority of the board of directors or persons performing similar functions.
2. The name of each person signing the form shall be typed or printed beneath the signature.

Intentional misstatements or omissions of facts constitute federal criminal violations. *See* 18 U.S.C. 1001.

OPTIONAL QUESTION & ANSWER FORMAT
FOR AN OFFERING STATEMENT

Respond to each question in each paragraph of this part. Set forth each question and any notes, but not any instructions thereto, in their entirety. If disclosure in response to any question is responsive to one or more other questions, it is not necessary to repeat the disclosure. If a question or series of questions is inapplicable or the response is available elsewhere in the Form, either State that it is inapplicable, include a cross-reference to the responsive disclosure, or omit the question or series of questions. The term "issuer" in these questions and answers includes any "co-issuer" jointly offering or selling securities with the issuer in reliance on the exemption in Securities Act Section 4(a)(6) and in accordance with Securities Act Section 4A and Regulation Crowdfunding. Any information provided with respect to the issuer should also be separately provided with respect to any co-issuer.

***

Be very careful and precise in answering all questions. Give full and complete answers so that they are not misleading under the circumstances involved. Do not discuss any future performance or other anticipated event unless you have a reasonable basis to believe that it will actually occur within the foreseeable future. If any answer requiring significant information is materially inaccurate, incomplete or misleading, the Company, its management and principal shareholders may be liable to investors based on that information.

THE COMPANY

1.   Name of issuer: _____

ELIGIBILITY

2.   ☐ Check this box to certify that all of the following statements are true for the issuer:

- Organized under, and subject to, the laws of a State or territory of the United States or the District of Columbia.
- Not subject to the requirement to file reports pursuant to Section 13 or Section 15(d) of the Securities Exchange Act of 1934.
- Not an investment company registered or required to be registered under the Investment Company Act of 1940.
- Not ineligible to rely on this exemption under Section 4(a)(6) of the Securities Act as a result of a disqualification specified in Rule 503(a) of Regulation Crowdfunding. (For more information about these disqualifications, see Question 30 of this Question and Answer format).
- Has filed with the Commission and provided to investors, to the extent required, the ongoing annual reports required by Regulation Crowdfunding during the two years immediately preceding the filing of this offering statement (or for such shorter period that the issuer was required to file such reports).
- Not a development stage company that (a) has no specific business plan or (b) has indicated that its business plan is to engage in a merger or acquisition with an unidentified company or companies.

INSTRUCTION TO QUESTION 2: If any of these statements is not true, then you are NOT eligible to rely on this exemption under Section 4(a)(6) of the Securities Act.

3.   Has the issuer or any of its predecessors previously failed to comply with the ongoing reporting requirements of Rule 202 of Regulation Crowdfunding? ☐ Yes ☐ No
Explain: _____

DIRECTORS OF THE COMPANY

4.   Provide the following information about each director (and any persons occupying a similar status or performing a similar function) of the issuer:

Name:_____Dates of Board Service: _____
     Principal Occupation: _____
     Employer:_____Dates of Service: _____
     Employer's principal business: _____

List all positions and offices with the issuer held and the period of time in which the director served in the position or office:

Position:_____Dates of Service: _____
Position:_____Dates of Service: _____

Business Experience: List the employers, titles and dates of positions held during past three years with an indication of job responsibilities:

Employer: _____
Employer's principal business: _____
Title:_____Dates of Service: _____
Responsibilities: _____

Employer: _____
Employer's principal business: _____
Title:_____Dates of Service: _____
Responsibilities: _____

OFFICERS OF THE COMPANY

5.   Provide the following information about each officer (and any persons occupying a similar status or performing a similar function) of the issuer:

Name: _____
Title:_____Dates of Service: _____
Responsibilities: _____

List any prior positions and offices with the issuer and the period of time in which the officer served in the position or office:

Position:_____Dates of Service: _____
Responsibilities: _____

Position:_____Dates of Service: _____
Responsibilities: _____

Business Experience: List any other employers, titles and dates of positions held during past three years with an indication of job responsibilities:

Employer: _____
Employer's principal business: _____
Title:_____Dates of Service: _____
Responsibilities: _____

Employer: _____
Employer's principal business: _____
Title:_____Dates of Service: _____
Responsibilities: _____

INSTRUCTION TO QUESTION 5: For purposes of this Question 5, the term officer means a president, vice president, secretary, treasurer or principal financial officer, comptroller or principal accounting officer, and any person routinely performing similar functions.

PRINCIPAL SECURITY HOLDERS

6.   Provide the name and ownership level of each person, as of the most recent practicable date, who is the beneficial owner of 20 percent or more of the issuer's outstanding voting equity securities, calculated on the basis of voting power.

Name of Holder	No. and Class of Securities Now Held	% of Voting Power Prior to Offering
		%
		%
		%

INSTRUCTION TO QUESTION 6: The above information must be provided as of a date that is no more than 120 days prior to the date of filing of this offering statement.

To calculate total voting power, include all securities for which the person directly or indirectly has or shares the voting power, which includes the power to vote or to direct the voting of such securities. If the person has the right to acquire voting power of such securities within 60 days, including through the exercise of any option, warrant or right, the conversion of a security, or other arrangement, or if securities are held by a member of the family, through corporations or partnerships, or otherwise in a manner that would allow a person to direct or control the voting of the securities (or share in such direction or control — as, for example, a co-trustee) they should be included as being "beneficially owned." You should include an explanation of these circumstances in a footnote to the "Number of and Class of Securities Now Held." To calculate outstanding voting equity securities, assume all outstanding options are exercised and all outstanding convertible securities converted.

BUSINESS AND ANTICIPATED BUSINESS PLAN

7.   Describe in detail the business of the issuer and the anticipated business plan of the issuer.

RISK FACTORS

A crowdfunding investment involves risk. You should not invest any funds in this offering unless you can afford to lose your entire investment.

In making an investment decision, investors must rely on their own examination of the issuer and the terms of the offering, including the merits and risks involved. These securities have not been recommended or approved by any federal or state securities commission or regulatory authority. Furthermore, these authorities have not passed upon the accuracy or adequacy of this document.

The U.S. Securities and Exchange Commission does not pass upon the merits of any securities offered or the terms of the offering, nor does it pass upon the accuracy or completeness of any offering document or literature.

These securities are offered under an exemption from registration; however, the U.S. Securities and Exchange Commission has not made an independent determination that these securities are exempt from registration.

8.   Discuss the material factors that make an investment in the issuer speculative or risky:

     (1)   _____

     (2)   _____

     (3)   _____

     (4)   _____

INSTRUCTION TO QUESTION 8: Avoid generalized statements and include only those factors that are unique to the issuer. Discussion should be tailored to the issuer's business and the offering and should not repeat the factors addressed in the legends set forth above. No specific number of risk factors is required to be identified. Add additional lines and number as appropriate.

THE OFFERING

9.   What is the purpose of this offering?

10.   How does the issuer intend to use the proceeds of this offering?

	If Target Offering Amount Sold	If Maximum
Total Proceeds	$	$
Less: Offering Expenses		
(A)		
(B)		
(C)		
Net Proceeds	$	$
Use of Net Proceeds		
(A)		
(B)		
(C)		
Total Use of Net Proceeds	$	$

INSTRUCTION TO QUESTION 10: An issuer must provide a reasonably detailed description of any intended use of proceeds, such that investors are provided with an adequate amount of information to understand how the offering proceeds will be used. If an issuer has identified a range of possible uses, the issuer should identify and describe each probable use and the factors the issuer may consider in allocating proceeds among the potential uses. If the issuer will accept proceeds in excess of the target offering amount, the issuer must describe the purpose, method for allocating oversubscriptions, and intended use of the excess proceeds with similar specificity.

11.   (a) Did the issuer make use of any written communication or broadcast script for testing the waters either (i) under the authorization of Rule 241 within 30 days of the initial filing of the offering statement, or (ii) under the authorization of Rule 206? If so, provide copies of the materials used.

        (b) How will the issuer complete the transaction and deliver securities to the investors?

12.   How can an investor cancel an investment commitment?

        NOTE: Investors may cancel an investment commitment until 48 hours prior to the deadline identified in these offering materials.

        The intermediary will notify investors when the target offering amount has been met.

        If the issuer reaches the target offering amount prior to the deadline identified in the offering materials, it may close the offering early if it provides notice about the new offering deadline at least five business days prior to such new offering deadline (absent a material change that would require an extension of the offering and reconfirmation of the investment commitment).

        If an investor does not cancel an investment commitment before the 48-hour period prior to the offering deadline, the funds will be released to the issuer upon closing of the offering and the investor will receive securities in exchange for his or her investment.

        If an investor does not reconfirm his or her investment commitment after a material change is made to the offering, the investor's investment commitment will be cancelled and the committed funds will be returned.

OWNERSHIP AND CAPITAL STRUCTURE

The Offering

13.   Describe the terms of the securities being offered.

14.   Do the securities offered have voting rights?   □ Yes □ No

15.   Are there any limitations on any voting or other rights identified above?

☐ Yes ☐ No   Explain: _____

16.   How may the terms of the securities being offered be modified?

Restrictions on Transfer of the Securities Being Offered

The securities being offered may not be transferred by any purchaser of such securities during the one- year period beginning when the securities were issued, unless such securities are transferred:

(1)   to the issuer;

(2)   to an accredited investor;

(3)   as part of an offering registered with the U.S. Securities and Exchange Commission; or

(4)   to a member of the family of the purchaser or the equivalent, to a trust controlled by the purchaser, to a trust created for the benefit of a member of the family of the purchaser or the equivalent, or in connection with the death or divorce of the purchaser or other similar circumstance.

NOTE: The term "accredited investor" means any person who comes within any of the categories set forth in Rule 501(a) of Regulation D, or who the seller reasonably believes comes within any of such categories, at the time of the sale of the securities to that person.

The term "member of the family of the purchaser or the equivalent" includes a child, stepchild, grandchild, parent, stepparent, grandparent, spouse or spousal equivalent, sibling, mother-in-law, father-in-law, son-in-law, daughter-in-law, brother-in-law, or sister-in-law of the purchaser, and includes adoptive relationships. The term "spousal equivalent" means a cohabitant occupying a relationship generally equivalent to that of a spouse.

Description of Issuer's Securities

17.   What other securities or classes of securities of the issuer are outstanding? Describe the material terms of any other outstanding securities or classes of securities of the issuer.

Class of Security	Securities (or Amount) Authorized	Securities (or Amount) Outstanding	Voting Rights	Other Rights
Preferred Stock (list each class in order of preference:				
			□ Yes □ No	□ Yes □ No Specify:
			□ Yes □ No	□ Yes □ No Specify:
Common Stock:			□ Yes □ No	□ Yes □ No Specify:
Debt Securities:			□ Yes □ No	□ Yes □ No Specify:
Other:			□ Yes □ No	□ Yes □ No Specify:
			□ Yes □ No	□ Yes □ No Specify:

Class of Security	Securities Reserved for Issuance upon Exercise or Conversion
Warrants:	
Options:	
Other Rights:	

18.   How may the rights of the securities being offered be materially limited, diluted or qualified by the rights of any other class of security identified above?

19.   Are there any differences not reflected above between the securities being offered and each other class of security of the issuer?   □ Yes   □ No
        Explain: _____

20.   How could the exercise of rights held by the principal shareholders identified in Question 6 above affect the purchasers of the securities being offered?

21.   How are the securities being offered being valued? Include examples of methods for how such securities may be valued by the issuer in the future, including during subsequent corporate actions.

22.   What are the risks to purchasers of the securities relating to minority ownership in the issuer?

23.   What are the risks to purchasers associated with corporate actions including:
    - additional issuances of securities,
    - issuer repurchases of securities,
    - a sale of the issuer or of assets of the issuer or
    - transactions with related parties?

24.   Describe the material terms of any indebtedness of the issuer:

Creditor(s)	Amount Outstanding	Interest Rate	Maturity Date	Other Material Terms
	$_____	_____%		
	$_____	_____%		

25.   What other exempt offerings has the issuer conducted within the past three years?

Date of Offering	Exemption Relied Upon	Securities Offered	Amount Sold	Use of Proceeds
			$_____	
			$_____	

26.   Was or is the issuer or any entities controlled by or under common control with the issuer a party to any transaction since the beginning of the issuer's last fiscal year, or any currently proposed transaction, where the amount involved exceeds five percent of the aggregate amount of capital raised by the issuer in reliance on Section 4(a)(6) of the Securities Act during the preceding 12- month period, including the amount the issuer seeks to raise in the current offering, in which any of the following persons had or is to have a direct or indirect material interest:

    (1)   any director or officer of the issuer;

    (2)   any person who is, as of the most recent practicable date, the beneficial owner of 20 percent or more of the issuer's outstanding voting equity securities, calculated on the basis of voting power;

    (3)   if the issuer was incorporated or organized within the past three years, any promoter of the issuer; or

    (4)   any immediate family member of any of the foregoing persons.

If yes, for each such transaction, disclose the following:

Specified Person	Relationship to Issuer	Nature of Interest in Transaction	Amount of Interest
			$_____
			$_____

INSTRUCTIONS TO QUESTION 26:

The term transaction includes, but is not limited to, any financial transaction, arrangement or relationship (including any indebtedness or guarantee of indebtedness) or any series of similar transactions, arrangements or relationships.

Beneficial ownership for purposes of paragraph (2) shall be determined as of a date that is no more than 120 days prior to the date of filing of this offering statement and using the same calculation described in Question 6 of this Question and Answer format.

The term "member of the family" includes any child, stepchild, grandchild, parent, stepparent, grandparent, spouse or spousal equivalent, sibling, mother-in-law, father-in-law, son-in-law, daughter-in-law, brother-in-law, or sister-in-law of the person, and includes adoptive relationships. The term "spousal equivalent" means a cohabitant occupying a relationship generally equivalent to that of a spouse.

Compute the amount of a related party's interest in any transaction without regard to the amount of the profit or loss involved in the transaction. Where it is not practicable to state the approximate amount of the interest, disclose the approximate amount involved in the transaction.

FINANCIAL CONDITION OF THE ISSUER

27.   Does the issuer have an operating history?   □ Yes □ No

28.   Describe the financial condition of the issuer, including, to the extent material, liquidity, capital resources and historical results of operations.

INSTRUCTIONS TO QUESTION 28:

The discussion must cover each year for which financial statements are provided. Include a discussion of any known material changes or trends in the financial condition and results of operations of the issuer during any time period subsequent to the period for which financial statements are provided.

For issuers with no prior operating history, the discussion should focus on financial milestones and operational, liquidity and other challenges.

For issuers with an operating history, the discussion should focus on whether historical results and cash flows are representative of what investors should expect in the future.

Take into account the proceeds of the offering and any other known or pending sources of capital. Discuss how the proceeds from the offering will affect liquidity, whether receiving these funds and any other additional funds is necessary to the viability of the business, and how quickly the issuer anticipates using its available cash. Describe the other available sources of capital to the business, such as lines of credit or required contributions by shareholders.

References to the issuer in this Question 28 and these instructions refer to the issuer and its predecessors, if any.

FINANCIAL INFORMATION

29.   Include the financial information specified below covering the two most recently completed fiscal years or the period(s) since inception, if shorter:

Aggregate Offering Amount (defined below)	Financial Information Required	Financial Statement Requirements

(a) $107,000 or less:	• The following information or their equivalent line items as reported on the federal income tax return filed by the issuer for the most recently completed year (if any):
	  o Total income
	  o Taxable income; and
	  o Total tax;
	certified by the principal executive officer of the issuer to reflect accurately the information reported on the issuer's federal income tax returns; and
	• Financial statements of the issuer and its predecessors, if any.
		Financial statements must be **certified** by the principal executive officer of the issuer as set forth below.
		
		If financial statements are available that have either been reviewed or audited by a public accountant that is independent of the issuer, the issuer must provide those financial statements instead along with a signed audit or review report and need not include the information reported on the federal income tax returns or the certification of the principal executive officer.

(b) More than $107,000, but not more than $535,000:	• Financial statements of the issuer and its predecessors, if any.	Financial statements must be **reviewed** by a public accountant that is independent of the issuer and must include a signed review report. If financial statements of the issuer are available that have been audited by a public accountant that is independent of the issuer, the issuer must provide those financial statements instead along with a signed audit report and need not include the reviewed financial statements.
(c) More than $535,000:	• Financial statements of the issuer and its predecessors, if any	If the issuer **has** previously sold securities in reliance on Regulation Crowdfunding:

		Financial statements must be **audited** by a public accountant that is independent of the issuer and must include a signed audit report.
		If the issuer **has not** previously sold securities in reliance on Regulation Crowdfunding and it is offering more than $535,000 but not more than $1,070,000:
		Financial statements must be **reviewed** by a public accountant that is independent of the issuer and must include a signed review report.
		If financial statements of the issuer are available that have been audited by a public accountant that is independent of the issuer, the issuer must provide those financial statements instead along with a signed audit report and need not include the reviewed financial statements.

INSTRUCTIONS TO QUESTION 29:

To determine the financial statements required, the Aggregate Offering Amount for purposes of this Question 29 means the aggregate amounts offered and sold by the issuer, all entities controlled by or under common control with the issuer, and all predecessors of the issuer in reliance on Section 4(a)(6) of the Securities Act within the preceding 12-month period plus the current maximum offering amount provided on the cover of this Form.

To determine whether the issuer has previously sold securities in reliance on Regulation Crowdfunding for purposes of paragraph (c) of this Question 29, "issuer" means the issuer, all entities controlled by or under common control with the issuer, and all predecessors of the issuer.

Financial statements must be prepared in accordance with U.S. generally accepted accounting principles and must include balance sheets, statements of comprehensive income, statements of cash flows, statements of changes in stockholders' equity and notes to the financial statements. If the financial statements are not audited, they shall be labeled as "unaudited."

Issuers offering securities and required to provide the information set forth in row (a) before filing a tax return for the most recently completed fiscal year may provide information from the tax return filed for the prior year (if any), provided that the issuer provides information from the tax return for the most recently completed fiscal year when it is filed, if filed during the offering period. An issuer that requested an extension of the time to file would not be required to provide information from the tax return until the date when the return is filed, if filed during the offering period.

A principal executive officer certifying financial statements as described above must provide the following certification**:

I, [identify the certifying individual], certify that:

(1)   the financial statements of [identify the issuer] included in this Form are true and complete in all material respects; and

(2)   the tax return information of [identify the issuer] included in this Form reflects accurately the information reported on the tax return for [identify the issuer] filed for the fiscal year ended [date of most recent tax return].

[Signature]
[Title]

** Intentional misstatements or omissions of facts constitute federal criminal violations. *See* 18 U.S.C. 1001.

To qualify as a public accountant that is independent of the issuer for purposes of this Question 29, the accountant must satisfy the independence standards of either:
(i)   Rule 2-01 of Regulation S-X or
(ii)   the AICPA.

The public accountant that audits or reviews the financial statements provided by an issuer must be (1) duly registered and in good standing as a certified public accountant under the laws of the place of his or her residence or principal office or (2) in good standing and entitled to practice as a public accountant under the laws of his or her place of residence or principal office.

An issuer will not be in compliance with the requirement to provide reviewed financial statement if the issuer received a review report that includes modifications. An issuer will not be in compliance with the requirement to provide audited financial statements if the issuer received a qualified opinion, an adverse opinion, or a disclaimer of opinion.

The issuer must notify the public accountant of the issuer's intended use of the public accountant's audit or review report in the offering.

For an offering conducted in the first 120 days of a fiscal year, the financial statements provided may be for the two fiscal years prior to the issuer's most recently completed fiscal year; however, financial statements for the two most recently completed fiscal years must be provided if they are otherwise available. If more than 120 days have passed since the end of the issuer's most recently completed fiscal year, the financial statements provided must be for the issuer's two most recently completed fiscal years. If the 120th day falls on a Saturday, Sunday, or holiday, the next business day shall be considered the 120th day for purposes of determining the age of the financial statements.

An issuer may elect to delay complying with any new or revised financial accounting standard until the date that a company that is not an issuer (as defined under section 2(a) of the Sarbanes-Oxley Act of 2002 is required to comply with such new or revised accounting standard, if such standard also applies to companies that are not issuers. Issuers electing such extension of time accommodation must disclose it at the time the issuer files its offering statement and apply the election to all standards. Issuers electing not to use this accommodation must forgo this accommodation for all financial accounting standards and may not elect to rely on this accommodation in any future filings.

30.   With respect to the issuer, any predecessor of the issuer, any affiliated issuer, any director, officer, general partner or managing member of the issuer, any beneficial owner of 20 percent or more of the issuer's outstanding voting equity securities, calculated in the same form as described in Question 6 of this Question and Answer format, any promoter connected with the issuer in any capacity at the time of such sale, any person that has been or will be paid (directly or indirectly) remuneration for solicitation of purchasers in connection with such sale of securities, or any general partner, director, officer or managing member of any such solicitor, prior to May 16, 2016:

     (1)   Has any such person been convicted, within 10 years (or five years, in the case of issuers, their predecessors and affiliated issuers) before the filing of this offering statement, of any felony or misdemeanor:

         (i)   in connection with the purchase or sale of any security? □ Yes □ No

         (ii)   involving the making of any false filing with the Commission? □ Yes □ No

         (iii)   arising out of the conduct of the business of an underwriter, broker, dealer, municipal securities dealer, investment adviser, funding portal or paid solicitor of purchasers of securities? □ Yes □ No

      If Yes to any of the above, explain: _____

     (2)   Is any such person subject to any order, judgment or decree of any court of competent jurisdiction, entered within five years before the filing of the information required by Section 4A(b) of the Securities Act that, at the time of filing of this offering statement, restrains or enjoins such person from engaging or continuing to engage in any conduct or practice:

         (i)   in connection with the purchase or sale of any security? □ Yes □ No;

         (ii)   involving the making of any false filing with the Commission? □ Yes □ No

         (iii)   arising out of the conduct of the business of an underwriter, broker, dealer, municipal securities dealer, investment adviser, funding portal or paid solicitor of purchasers of securities? □ Yes □ No

      If Yes to any of the above, explain: _____

     (3)   Is any such person subject to a final order of a state securities commission (or an agency or officer of a state performing like functions); a state authority that supervises or examines banks, savings associations or credit unions; a state insurance commission (or an agency or officer of a state performing like functions); an appropriate federal banking agency; the U.S. Commodity Futures Trading Commission; or the National Credit Union Administration that:

         (i)   at the time of the filing of this offering statement bars the person from:

        (A) association with an entity regulated by such commission, authority, agency or officer? □ Yes □ No

        (B) engaging in the business of securities, insurance or banking? □ Yes □ No

        (C) engaging in savings association or credit union activities? □ Yes □ No

    (ii) constitutes a final order based on a violation of any law or regulation that prohibits fraudulent, manipulative or deceptive conduct and for which the order was entered within the 10-year period ending on the date of the filing of this offering statement? □ Yes □ No

If Yes to any of the above, explain: _____

(4) Is any such person subject to an order of the Commission entered pursuant to Section 15(b) or 15B(c) of the Exchange Act or Section 203(e) or (f) of the Investment Advisers Act of 1940 that, at the time of the filing of this offering statement:

    (i) suspends or revokes such person's registration as a broker, dealer, municipal securities dealer, investment adviser or funding portal? □ Yes □ No

    (ii) places limitations on the activities, functions or operations of such person? □ Yes □ No

    (iii) bars such person from being associated with any entity or from participating in the offering of any penny stock? □ Yes □ No

If Yes to any of the above, explain: _____

(5) Is any such person subject to any order of the Commission entered within five years before the filing of this offering statement that, at the time of the filing of this offering statement, orders the person to cease and desist from committing or causing a violation or future violation of:

    (i) any scienter-based anti-fraud provision of the federal securities laws, including without limitation Section 17(a)(1) of the Securities Act, Section 10(b) of the Exchange Act, Section 15(c)(1) of the Exchange Act and Section 206(1) of the Investment Advisers Act of 1940 or any other rule or regulation thereunder? □ Yes □ No

    (ii) Section 5 of the Securities Act? □ Yes □ No

If Yes to either of the above, explain: _____

(6) Is any such person suspended or expelled from membership in, or suspended or barred from association with a member of, a registered national securities exchange or a registered national or affiliated securities association for any act or omission to act constituting conduct inconsistent with just and equitable principles of trade? □ Yes □ No

If Yes, explain: _____

(7) Has any such person filed (as a registrant or issuer), or was any such person or was any such person named as an underwriter in, any registration statement or Regulation A offering statement filed with the Commission that, within 5 years before the filing of this offering statement, was the subject of a refusal order,

stop order, or order suspending the Reg. A exemption, or is any such person, at the time of such filing, the subject of an investigation or proceeding to determine whether a stop order or suspension order should be issued? □ Yes □ No
If Yes, explain: _____

(8) Is any such person subject to a United States Postal Service false representation order entered within five years before the filing of the information required by Section 4A(b) of the Securities Act, or is any such person, at the time of filing of this offering statement, subject to a temporary restraining order or preliminary injunction with respect to conduct alleged by the United States Postal Service to constitute a scheme or device for obtaining money or property through the mail by means of false representations? □ Yes □ No
If Yes, explain: _____

If you would have answered "Yes" to any of these questions had the conviction, order, judgment, decree, suspension, expulsion or bar occurred or been issued after May 16, 2016, then you are NOT eligible to rely on this exemption under Section 4(a)(6) of the Securities Act.

INSTRUCTIONS TO QUESTION 30:

Final order means a written directive or declaratory statement issued by a federal or state agency, described in Rule 503(a)(3) of Regulation Crowdfunding, under applicable statutory authority that provides for notice and an opportunity for hearing, which constitutes a final disposition or action by that federal or state agency.

No matters are required to be disclosed with respect to events relating to any affiliated issuer that occurred before the affiliation arose if the affiliated entity is not (i) in control of the issuer or (ii) under common control with the issuer by a third party that was in control of the affiliated entity at the time of such events.

OTHER MATERIAL INFORMATION

31. In addition to the information expressly required to be included in this Form, include:
    (1) any other material information presented to investors; and
    (2) such further material information, if any, as may be necessary to make the required statements, in the light of the circumstances under which they are made, not misleading.

INSTRUCTIONS TO QUESTION 31:

If information is presented to investors in a format, media or other means not able to be reflected in text or portable document format, the issuer should include
    (a) a description of the material content of such information;
    (b) a description of the format in which such disclosure is presented; and
    (c) in the case of disclosure in video, audio or other dynamic media or format, a transcript or description of such disclosure.

ONGOING REPORTING

The issuer will file a report electronically with the Securities & Exchange Commission annually and post the report on its website, no later than:

_____

(120 days after the end of each fiscal year covered by the report).

Once posted, the annual report may be found on the issuer's website at:

_____

The issuer must continue to comply with the ongoing reporting requirements until:

(1) the issuer is required to file reports under Section 13(a) or Section 15(d) of the Exchange Act;

(2) the issuer has filed at least one annual report pursuant to Regulation Crowdfunding and has fewer than 300 holders of record and has total assets that do not exceed $10,000,000;

(3) the issuer has filed at least three annual reports pursuant to Regulation Crowdfunding;

(4) the issuer or another party repurchases all of the securities issued in reliance on Section 4(a)(6) of the Securities Act, including any payment in full of debt securities or any complete redemption of redeemable securities; or

(5) the issuer liquidates or dissolves its business in accordance with state law.

UNITED STATES SECURITIES AND EXCHANGE COMMISSION
Washington, D.C. 20549

FORM S-1

REGISTRATION STATEMENT UNDER THE SECURITIES ACT OF 1933

(Exact name of registrant as specified in its charter)

(State or other jurisdiction of incorporation or organization)

(Primary Standard Industrial Classification Code Number)

(I.R.S. Employer Identification Number)

(Address, including zip code, and telephone number, including area code, of registrant's principal executive offices)

(Name, address, including zip code, and telephone number, including area code, of agent for service)

(Approximate date of commencement of proposed sale to the public)

If any of the securities being registered on this Form are to be offered on a delayed or continuous basis pursuant to Rule 415 under the Securities Act of 1933 check the following box: ❑

If this Form is Filed to register additional securities for an offering pursuant to Rule 462(b) under the Securities Act, please check the following box and list the Securities Act registration statement number of the earlier effective registration statement for this same offering. ❑

If this Form is a post-effective amendment filed pursuant to Rule 462(c) under the Securities Act, check the following box and list the Securities Act registration statement number of the earlier effective registration statement for the same offering. ❑

If this Form is a post-effective amendment filed pursuant to Rule 462(d) under the Securities Act, check the following box and list the Securities Act registration statement number of the earlier effective registration statement for the same offering. ❑

Indicate by check mark whether the registrant is a large accelerated filer, an accelerated filer, a non-accelerated filer, a smaller reporting company, or an emerging growth company. See the definitions of "large accelerated filer," "accelerated filer," "smaller reporting company," and "emerging growth company" in Rule 12b-2 of the Exchange Act.

Large accelerated filer	❑	Accelerated filer	❑
Non-accelerated filer	❑	Smaller reporting company	❑
		Emerging growth company	❑

If an emerging growth company, indicate by check mark if the registrant has elected not to use the extended transition period for complying with any new or revised financial accounting standards provided pursuant to Section 7(a)(2)(B) of the Securities Act . ❏

CALCULATION OF REGISTRATION FEE

Title of Each Class of Securities to be Registered	Amount to be Registered	Proposed Maximum Offering Price Per Unit	Proposed Maximum Aggregate Offering Price	Amount of Registration Fee

Note: Specific details relating to the fee calculation shall be furnished in notes to the table, including references to provisions of Rule 457 relied upon, if the basis of the calculation is not otherwise evident from the information presented in the table. If the filing fee is calculated pursuant to Rule 457(o) under the Securities Act, only the title of the class of securities to be registered, the proposed maximum aggregate offering price for that class of securities and the amount of registration fee need to appear in the Calculation of Registration Fee table. Any difference between the dollar amount of securities registered for such offerings and the dollar amount of securities sold may be carried forward on a future registration statement pursuant to Rule 429 under the Securities Act.

GENERAL INSTRUCTIONS

I.   Eligibility Requirements for Use of Form S-1

This Form shall be used for the registration under the Securities Act of 1933 ("Securities Act") of securities of all registrants for which no other form is authorized or prescribed, except that this Form shall not be used for securities of foreign governments or political subdivisions thereof, or asset-backed securities, as defined in Rule 1101(c).

II.   Application of General Rules and Regulations

A.   Attention is directed to the General Rules and Regulations under the Securities Act, particularly those comprising Regulation C thereunder. That Regulation contains general requirements regarding the preparation and filing of the registration statement.

B.   Attention is directed to Regulation S-K for the requirements applicable to the content of the non-financial statement portions of registration statements under the Securities Act. Where this Form directs the registrant to furnish information required by Regulation S-K and the item of Regulation S-K so provides, information need only be furnished to the extent appropriate.

C.   A registration statement filed (or submitted for confidential review) under Section 6 of the Securities Act by an emerging growth company, defined in Section 2(a)(19) of the Securities Act, prior to an initial public offering may omit financial information for historical periods otherwise required by Regulation S-X as of the time of filing (or confidential submission) of the registration statement, provided that:

1. The omitted financial information relates to a historical period that the registrant reasonably believes will not be required to be included in this Form at the time of the contemplated offering; and

2. Prior to the registrant distributing a preliminary prospectus to investors, the registration statement is amended to include all financial information required by Regulation S-X at the date of the amendment.

III.   Exchange Offers

If any of the securities being registered are to be offered in exchange for securities of any other issuer, the prospectus shall also include the information which would be required by item 11 if the securities of such other issuer were registered on this Form. There shall also be included the information concerning such securities of such other issuer which would be called for by Item 9 if such securities were being registered. In connection with this instruction, reference is made to Rule 409.

IV.   Roll-up Transactions

If the securities to be registered on this Form will be issued in a roll-up transaction as defined in Item 901(c) of Regulation S-K, attention is directed to the requirements of Form S-4 applicable to roll-up transactions, including, but not limited to, General Instruction I.

V.   Registration of Additional Securities

With respect to the registration of additional securities for an offering pursuant to Rule 462(b) under the Securities Act, the registrant may file a registration statement consisting only of the following: the facing page; a statement that the contents of the earlier registration statement, identified by file number, are incorporated by reference; required opinions and consents; the signature page; and any price-related information omitted from the earlier registration statement in reliance on Rule 430A that the registrant chooses to include in the new registration statement. The information contained in such a Rule 462(b) registration statement shall be deemed to be a part of the earlier registration statement as of the date of effectiveness of the Rule 462(b) registration statement. Any opinion or consent required in the Rule 462(b) registration statement may be incorporated by reference from the earlier registration statement with respect to the offering, if: (i) such opinion or consent expressly provides for such incorporation; and (ii) such opinion relates to the securities registered pursuant to Rule 462(b). *See* Rule 439(b) under the Securities Act.

VI.   Offerings of Asset-Backed Securities.

The following applies if a registration statement on this Form S-1 is being used to register an offering of asset-backed securities. Terms used in this General Instruction VI. have the same meaning as in Item 1101 of Regulation AB.

A.   *Items that May be Omitted.*
Such registrants may omit the information called for by Item 11, Information with Respect to the Registrant.

B.   *Substitute Information to be Included.*
In addition to the Items that are otherwise required by this Form, the registrant must furnish in the prospectus the information required by Items 1102 through 1120 of Regulation AB.

C.   *Signatures.*
The registration statement must be signed by the depositor, the depositor's principal executive officer or officers, principal financial officer and controller or principal accounting officer, and by at least a majority of the depositor's board of directors or persons performing similar functions.

VII.   Eligibility to Use Incorporation by Reference

If a registrant meets the following requirements in paragraphs A-F immediately prior to the time of filing a registration statement on this Form, it may elect to provide information required by Items 3 through 11 of this Form in accordance with Item 11A and Item 12 of this Form. Notwithstanding the foregoing, in the financial statements, incorporating by reference or cross-referencing to information outside of the financial statements is not permitted unless otherwise specifically permitted or required by the Commission's rules or by U.S. Generally Accepted Accounting Principles or International Financial Reporting Standards as issued by the International Accounting Standards Board, whichever is applicable.

A.   The registrant is subject to the requirement to file reports pursuant to Section 13 or Section 15(d) of the Securities Exchange Act of 1934 ("Exchange Act").

B.   The registrant has filed all reports and other materials required to be filed by Sections 13(a), 14, or 15(d) of the Exchange Act during the preceding 12 months (or for such shorter period that the registrant was required to file such reports and materials).

C.   The registrant has filed an annual report required under Section 13(a) or Section 15(d) of the Exchange Act for its most recently completed fiscal year.

D.   The registrant is not:
1.   And during the past three years neither the registrant nor any of its predecessors was:
(a) A blank check company as defined in Rule 419(a)(2);
(b) A shell company, other than a business combination related shell company, each as defined in Rule 405; or
(c) A registrant for an offering of penny stock as defined in Rule 3a51-1 of the Exchange Act.
2.   Registering an offering that effectuates a business combination transaction as defined in Rule 165(f)(1).

E. If a registrant is a successor registrant it shall be deemed to have satisfied conditions A., B., C., and D.2 above if:

1. Its predecessor and it, taken together, do so, provided that the succession was primarily for the purpose of changing the state of incorporation of the predecessor or forming a holding company and that the assets and liabilities of the successor at the time of succession were substantially the same as those of the predecessor; or

2. All predecessors met the conditions at the time of succession and the registrant has continued to do so since the succession.

F. The registrant makes its periodic and current reports filed pursuant to Section 13 or Section 15(d) of the Exchange Act that are incorporated by reference pursuant to Item 11A or Item 12 of this Form readily available and accessible on a Web site maintained by or for the registrant and containing information about the registrant.

PART I—INFORMATION REQUIRED IN PROSPECTUS

Item 1. Forepart of the Registration Statement and Outside Front Cover Page of Prospectus.

Set forth in the forepart of the registration statement and on the outside front cover page of the prospectus the information required by Item 501 of Regulation S-K.

Item 2. Inside Front and Outside Back Cover Pages of Prospectus.

Set forth on the inside front cover page of the prospectus or, where permitted, on the outside back cover page, the information required by Item 502 of Regulation S-K.

Item 3. Summary Information and Risk Factors.

Furnish the information required by Items 105 and 503 of Regulation S-K.

Item 4. Use of Proceeds.

Furnish the information required by Item 504 of Regulation S-K.

Item 5. Determination of Offering Price.

Furnish the information required by Item 505 of Regulation S-K.

Item 6. Dilution.

Furnish the information required by Item 506 of Regulation S-K.

Item 7. Selling Security Holders.

Furnish the information required by Item 507 of Regulation S-K.

Item 8.   Plan of Distribution.

Furnish the information required by Item 508 of Regulation S-K.

Item 9.   Description of Securities to be Registered.

Furnish the information required by Item 202 of Regulation S-K.

Item 10.   Interests of Named Experts and Counsel.

Furnish the information required by Item 509 of Regulation S-K.

Item 11.   Information with Respect to the Registrant.

Furnish the following information with respect to the registrant:

(a)   Information required by Item 101 of Regulation S-K, description of business;

(b)   Information required by Item 102 of Regulation S-K, description of property;

(c)   Information required by Item 103 of Regulation S-K, legal proceedings;

(d)   Where common equity securities are being offered, information required by Item 201 of Regulation S-K, market price of and dividends on the registrant's common equity and related stockholder matters;

(e)   Financial statements meeting the requirements of Regulation S-X (Schedules required under Regulation S-X shall be filed as "Financial Statement Schedules" pursuant to Item 15, Exhibits and Financial Statement Schedules, of this Form), as well as any financial information required by Rule 3-05 and Article 11 of Regulation S-X;

(f)   [Reserved];

(g)   Information required by Item 302 of Regulation S-K, supplementary financial information;

(h)   Information required by Item 303 of Regulation S-K, management's discussion and analysis of financial condition and results of operations;

(i)   Information required by Item 304 of Regulation S-K, changes in and disagreements with accountants on accounting and financial disclosure;

(j)   Information required by Item 305 of Regulation S-K, quantitative and qualitative disclosures about market risk,

(k)   Information required by Item 401 of Regulation S-K, directors and executive officers;

(l)   Information required by Item 402 of Regulation S-K, executive compensation, and information required by paragraph (e)(4) of Item 407 of Regulation S-K, corporate governance;

(m)   Information required by Item 403 of Regulation S-K, security ownership of certain beneficial owners and management; and

(n)   Information required by Item 404 of Regulation S-K, transactions with related persons, promoters and certain control persons, and Item 407(a) of Regulation S-K, corporate governance.

Item 11A   Material Changes.

If the registrant elects to incorporate information by reference pursuant to General Instruction VII, describe any and all material changes in the registrant's affairs which have occurred since the end of the latest fiscal year for which audited financial statements were included in the latest Form 10-K and which have not been described in a Form 10-Q or Form 8-K filed under the Exchange Act.

Item 12.   Incorporation of Certain Information by Reference.

If the registrant elects to incorporate information by reference pursuant to General Instruction VII:

(a)   It must specifically incorporate by reference into the prospectus contained in the registration statement the following documents by means of a statement to that effect in the prospectus listing all such documents:

(1) The registrant's latest annual report on Form 10-K filed pursuant to Section 13(a) or Section 15(d) of the Exchange Act which contains financial statements for the registrant's latest fiscal year for which a Form 10-K was required to have been filed; and

(2) All other reports filed pursuant to Section 13(a) or 15(d) of the Exchange Act or proxy or information statements filed pursuant to Section 14 of the Exchange Act since the end of the fiscal year covered by the annual report referred to in paragraph (a)(1) above.

Note to Item 12(a). Attention is directed to Rule 439 regarding consent to use of material incorporated by reference.

(b)   In addition to the incorporation by reference permitted pursuant to paragraph (a) of this Item, a smaller reporting company, as defined in Rule 405, may elect to incorporate by reference information filed after the effective date of the registration statement. A smaller reporting company making this election must state in the prospectus contained in the registration statement that all documents subsequently filed by the registrant pursuant to Sections 13(a), 13(c), 14 or 15(d) of the Exchange Act, prior to the termination of the offering shall be deemed to be incorporated by reference into the prospectus.

(c)   (1)   The registrant must state:

(i)   That it will provide to each person, including any beneficial owner, to whom a prospectus is delivered, a copy of any or all of the reports or documents that have been incorporated by reference in the prospectus contained in the registration statement but not delivered with the prospectus;

(ii)   That it will provide these reports or documents upon written or oral request;

(iii) That it will provide these reports or documents at no cost to the requester;

(iv) The name, address, telephone number, and e-mail address, if any, to which the request for these reports or documents must be made; and

(v) The registrant's Web site address, including the uniform resource locator (URL) where the incorporated reports and other documents may be accessed.

Note to Item 12(c)(1). If the registrant sends any of the information that is incorporated by reference in the prospectus contained in the registration statement to security holders, it also must send any exhibits that are specifically incorporated by reference in that information.

(2) The registrant must:
(i) Identify the reports and other information that it files with the SEC; and
(ii) State that the SEC maintains an Internet site that contains reports, proxy and information statements, and other information regarding issuers that file electronically with the SEC and state the address of that site (http://www.sec.gov).

Item 12A.   Disclosure of Commission Position on Indemnification for Securities Act Liabilities.

Furnish the information required by Item 510 of Regulation S-K.

PART II—INFORMATION NOT REQUIRED IN PROSPECTUS

Item 13.   Other Expenses of Issuance and Distribution.

Furnish the information required by Item 511 of Regulation S-K.

Item 14.   Indemnification of Directors and Officers.

Furnish the information required by Item 702 of Regulation S-X.

Item 15.   Recent Sales of Unregistered Securities.

Furnish the information required by Item 701 of Regulation S-K.

Item 16.   Exhibits and Financial Statement Schedules.

(a) Subject to the rules regarding incorporation by reference, furnish the exhibits as required by Item 601 of Regulation S-K.
(b) Furnish the financial statement schedules required by Regulation S-X and Item ll(e) of this Form. These schedules shall be lettered or numbered in the manner described for exhibits in paragraph (a).

Item 17.   Undertakings.

Furnish the undertakings required by Item 512 of Regulation S-K.

SIGNATURES

Pursuant to the requirements of the Securities Act of 1933, the registrant has duly caused this registration statement to be signed on its behalf by the undersigned, thereunto duly authorized, in the City of _____, State of _____ _____, on _____, 20_____.

_____

(Registrant)

By   _____

(Signature and Title)

Pursuant to the requirements of the Securities Act of 1933, this registration statement has been signed by the following persons in the capacities and on the dates indicated.

_____

(Signature)

_____

(Title)

_____

(Date)

Instructions.

1. The registration statement shall be signed by the registrant, its principal executive officer or officers, its principal financial officer, its controller or principal accounting officer and by at least a majority of the board of directors or persons performing similar functions. If the registrant is a foreign person, the registration statement shall also be signed by its authorized representative in the United States. Where the registrant is a limited partnership, the registration statement shall be signed by a majority of the board of directors of any corporate general partner signing the registration statement.

2. The name of each person who signs the registration statement shall be typed or printed beneath his signature. Any person who occupies more than one of the specified positions shall indicate each capacity in which he signs the registration statement. Attention is directed to Rule 402 concerning manual signatures and to Item 601 of Regulation S-K concerning signatures pursuant to powers of attorney.

INSTRUCTIONS AS TO SUMMARY PROSPECTUSES

1. A summary prospectus used pursuant to Rule 431, shall at the time of its use contain much of the information specified below as is then included in the registration statement. All other information and documents contained in the registration statement may be omitted.

    (a) As to Item 1, the aggregate offering price to the public, the aggregate underwriting discounts and commissions and the offering price per unit to the public;

(b) As to Item 4, a brief statement of the principal purposes for which the proceeds are to be used;

(c) As to Item 7, a statement as to the amount of the offering, if any, to be made for the account of security holders;

(d) As to Item 8, the name of the managing underwriter or underwriters and a brief statement as to the nature of the underwriter's obligation to take the securities; if any securities to be registered are to be offered otherwise than through underwriters, a brief statement as to the manner of distribution; and, if securities are to be offered otherwise than for cash, a brief statement as to the general purposes of the distribution, the basis upon which the securities are to be offered, the amount of compensation and other expenses of distribution, and by whom they are to be borne;

(e) As to Item 9, a brief statement as to dividend rights, voting rights, conversion rights, interest, maturity;

(f) As to Item 11, a brief statement of the general character of the business done and intended to be done and a brief statement of the nature and present status of any material pending legal proceedings; and

(g) A tabular presentation of notes payable, long term debt, deferred credits, minority interests, if material, and the equity section of the latest balance sheet filed, as may be appropriate; and

(h) Subject to appropriate variation to conform to the nature of the registrant's business, provide summarized financial information defined by Rule 1-02(bb)(1)(i) and (ii) of Regulation S-X in comparative columnar form for the periods for which financial statements are required by Regulation S-X.

2. The summary prospectus shall not contain a summary or condensation of any other required financial information except as provided above.

3. Where securities being registered are to be offered in exchange for securities of any other issuer, the summary prospectus also shall contain that information as to Items 9 and 11 specified in paragraphs (e) and (f) above which would be required if the securities of such other issuer were registered on this Form.

4. The Commission may, upon the request of the registrant, and where consistent with the protection of investors, permit the omission of any of the information herein required or the furnishing in substitution therefor of appropriate information of comparable character. The Commission may also require the inclusion of other information in addition to, or in substitution for, the information herein required in any case where such information is necessary or appropriate for the protection of investors.

UNITED STATES SECURITIES AND EXCHANGE COMMISSION
Washington, D.C. 20549

FORM S-3

REGISTRATION STATEMENT UNDER THE SECURITIES ACT OF 1933

(Exact name of registrant as specified in its charter)

(State or other jurisdiction of incorporation or organization)

(I.R.S. Employer Identification Number)

(Address, including zip code, and telephone number, including area code,
of registrant's principal executive offices)

(Name, address, including zip code, and telephone number, including area code,
of agent for service)

(Approximate date of commencement of proposed sale to the public)

If the only securities being registered on this Form are being offered pursuant to dividend or interest reinvestment plans, please check the following box: ❏

If any of the securities being registered on this Form are to be offered on a delayed or continuous basis pursuant to Rule 415 under the Securities Act of 1933, other than securities offered only in connection with dividend or interest reinvestment plans, check the following box: ❏

If this Form is filed to register additional securities for an offering pursuant to Rule 462(b) under the Securities Act, please check the following box and list the Securities Act registration statement number of the earlier effective registration statement for the same offering. ❏

If this Form is a post-effective amendment filed pursuant to Rule 462(c) under the Securities Act, check the following box and list the Securities Act registration statement number of the earlier effective registration statement for the same offering. ❏

If this Form is a registration statement pursuant to General Instruction I.D. or a post-effective amendment thereto that shall become effective upon filing with the Commission pursuant to Rule 462(e) under the Securities Act, check the following box. ❏

If this Form is a post-effective amendment to a registration statement filed pursuant to General Instruction I.D. filed to register additional securities or additional classes of securities pursuant to Rule 413(b) under the Securities Act, check the following box. ❏

Indicate by check mark whether the registrant is a large accelerated filer, an accelerated filer, a non-accelerated filer, a smaller reporting company, or an emerging growth company. See the definitions of "large accelerated filer," "accelerated filer," "smaller reporting company," and "emerging growth company" in Rule 12b-2 of the Exchange Act.

Large accelerated filer   ❑   Accelerated filer   ❑
Non-accelerated filer   ❑   Smaller reporting company   ❑
                                       Emerging growth company   ❑

If an emerging growth company, indicate by check mark if the registrant has elected not to use the extended transition period for complying with any new or revised financial accounting standards provided pursuant to Section 7(a)(2)(B) of the Securities Act . ❑

CALCULATION OF REGISTRATION FEE

Title of Each Class to be Registered	Amount to be Registered	Proposed Maximum Offering Price Per Unit	Proposed Maximum Aggregate Offering Price	Amount of Registration Fee

Note:

1.   Specific details relating to the fee calculation shall be furnished in notes to the Fee Table, including references to provisions of Rule 457 relied upon, if the basis of the calculation is not otherwise evident from the information presented in the Fee Table.

2.   If the filing fee is calculated pursuant to Rule 457(o) under the Securities Act, only the title of the class of securities to be registered, the proposed maximum aggregate offering price for that class of securities, and the amount of registration fee need to appear in the Fee Table. Where two or more classes of securities are being registered pursuant to General Instruction II.D., however, the Fee Table need only specify the maximum aggregate offering price for all classes; the Fee Table need not specify by each class the proposed maximum aggregate offering price (see General Instruction II.D.).

3.   If the filing fee is calculated pursuant to Rule 457(r) under the Securities Act, the Fee Table must state that it registers an unspecified amount of securities of each identified class of securities and must provide that the issuer is relying on Rule 456(b) and Rule 457(r). If the Fee Table is amended in a post-effective amendment to the registration statement or in a prospectus filed in accordance with Rule 456(b)(1)(ii), the Fee Table must specify the aggregate offering price for all classes of securities in the referenced offering or offerings and the applicable registration fee.

4.   Any difference between the dollar amount of securities registered for such offerings and the dollar amount of securities sold may be carried forward on a future registration statement pursuant to Rule 457 under the Securities Act.

GENERAL INSTRUCTIONS

I.   **Eligibility Requirements for Use of Form S-3**

This instruction sets forth registrant requirements and transaction requirements for the use of Form S-3. Any registrant which meets the requirements of I.A. below ("Registrant Requirements") may use this Form for the registration of securities under the Securities Act of 1933 ("Securities Act") which are offered in any transaction specified in I.B. below ("Transaction Requirement") provided that the requirement applicable to the specified transaction are met. With respect to majority-owned subsidiaries, see Instruction I.C. below. With respect to well-known seasoned issuers and majority-owned subsidiaries of well-known seasoned issuers, see Instruction I.D.

A.   **Registrant Requirements**. Registrants must meet the following conditions in order to use this Form S-3 for registration under the Securities Act of securities offered in the transactions specified in I. B. below:

1.   The registrant is organized under the laws of the United States or any State or Territory or the District of Columbia and has its principal business operations in the United States or its territories.

2.   The registrant has a class of securities registered pursuant to Section 12(b) of the Securities Exchange Act of 1934 ("Exchange Act") or a class of equity securities registered pursuant to Section 12(g) of the Exchange Act or is required to file reports pursuant to Section 15(d) of the Exchange Act.

3.   The registrant: (a) has been subject to the requirements of Section 12 or 15(d) of the Exchange Act and has filed all the material required to be filed pursuant to Sections 13, 14 or 15(d) for a period of at least twelve calendar months immediately preceding the filing of the registration statement on this Form; and (b) has filed in a timely manner all reports required to be filed during the twelve calendar months and any portion of a month immediately preceding the filing of the registration statement, other than a report that is required solely pursuant to Item 1.01, 1.02, 1.04, 2.03, 2.04, 2.05, 2.06, 4.02(a) or 5.02(e) of Form 8-K. If the registrant has used (during the twelve calendar months and any portion of a month immediately preceding the filing of the registration statement) Rule 12b-25(b) under the Exchange Act with respect to a report or a portion of a report, that report or portion thereof has actually been filed within the time period prescribed by that rule.

4.   Neither the registrant nor any of its consolidated or unconsolidated subsidiaries have, since the end of the last fiscal year for which certified financial statements of the registrant and its consolidated subsidiaries were included in a report filed pursuant to Section 13(a) or 15(d) of the Exchange Act: (a) failed to pay any dividend or sinking fund installment on preferred stock; or (b) defaulted (i) on any installment or installments on indebtedness for borrowed money, or (ii) on any rental on one or more long term leases, which defaults in the aggregate are material to the financial position of the

registrant and its consolidated and unconsolidated subsidiaries, taken as a whole.

5.   A foreign issuer, other than a foreign government, which satisfies all of the above provisions of these registrant eligibility requirements except the provisions in I.A.1. relating to organization and principal business shall be deemed to have met these registrant eligibility requirements provided that such a foreign issuer files the same reports with the Commission under Section 13(a) or 15(d) of the Exchange Act as a domestic registrant pursuant to I.A.3. above.

6.   If the registrant is a successor registrant, it shall be deemed to have met conditions 1., 2., 3., and 5., above if: (a) its predecessor and it, taken together, do so, provided that the succession was primarily for the purpose of changing the state of incorporation of the predecessor or forming a holding company and that the assets and liabilities of the successor at the time of succession were substantially the same as those of the predecessor; or (b) if all predecessors met the conditions at the time of succession and the registrant has continued to do so since the succession.

7.   *Electronic filings:* In addition to satisfying the foregoing conditions, a registrant subject to the electronic filing requirements of Rule 101 of Regulation S-T shall have:
   a.   Filed with the Commission all required electronic filings, including electronic copies of documents submitted in paper pursuant to a hardship exemption as provided by Rule 201 or Rule 202(d) of Regulation S-T; and
   b.   Submitted electronically to the Commission and posted on its corporate Web site, if any, all Interactive Data Files required to be submitted and posted pursuant to Rule 405 of Regulation S-T during the 12 calendar months and any portion of a month immediately preceding the filing of the registration statement on this Form (or for such shorter period of time that the registrant was required to submit and post such files).

B.   **Transaction Requirements.** Security offerings meeting any of the following conditions and made by a registrant meeting the Registrant Requirements specified in I.A. above may be registered on this Form:

1.   *Primary Offerings by Certain Registrants.* Securities to be offered for cash by or on behalf of a registrant, or outstanding securities to be offered for cash for the account of any person other than the registrant, including securities acquired by standby underwriters in connection with the call or redemption by the registrant of warrants or a class of convertible securities; *provided* that the aggregate market value of the voting and non-voting common equity held by non-affiliates of the registrant is $75 million or more.
     Instruction paragraph (b)(1). For the purposes of this Form, "common equity" is as defined in Securities Act Rule 405. The aggregate market value of the registrant's outstanding voting and non-voting common equity shall be

computed by use of the price at which the common equity was last sold, or the average of the bid and asked prices of such common equity, in the principal market for such common equity as of a date within 60 days prior to the date of filing. See the definition of "affiliate" in Securities Act Rule 405, as of a date within 60 days prior to the date of filing. See the definition of "affiliate" in Securities Act Rule 405.

2. *Primary Offerings of Non-convertible Securities Other than Common Equity.* Non-convertible securities, other than common equity, to be offered for cash by or on behalf of a registrant, provided the registrant:

    i.   has issued (as of a date within 60 days prior to the filing of the registration statement) at least $1 billion in non-convertible securities, other than common equity, in primary offerings for cash, not exchange, registered under the Securities Act, over the prior three years; or

    ii. has outstanding (as of a date within 60 days prior to the filing of the registration statement) at least $750 million of non-convertible securities, other than common equity, issued in primary offerings for cash, not exchange, registered under the Securities Act; or

    iii. is a wholly-owned subsidiary of a well-known seasoned issuer; or

    iv. is a majority-owned operating partnership of a real estate investment trust that qualifies as a well-known seasoned issuer.

    Instruction. For purposes of paragraph (b)(2)(i) of this section, an insurance company, as defined in Section 2(a)(13) of the Securities Act of 1933, when using this Form S-3 to register offerings of securities subject to regulation under the insurance laws of any State or Territory of the United States or the District of Columbia ("insurance contracts"), may include purchase payments or premium payments for insurance contracts, including purchase payments or premium payments for variable insurance contracts (not including purchase payments or premium payments initially allocated to investment options that are not registered under the Securities Act of 1933, issued in offerings registered under the Securities Act over the prior three years. For purposes of paragraph (b)(ii) of this section, an insurance company, as defined in Section 2(a)(13) of the Securities Act of 1933, when using this Form S-3 to register offerings of insurance contracts, may include the contract value, as of the measurement date, of any outstanding insurance contracts, including variable insurance contracts (not including the value allocated as of the measurement date to investment options that are not registered under the Securities Act of 1933), issued in offerings registered under the Securities Act of 1933.

3. *Transactions Involving Secondary Offerings.* Outstanding securities to be offered for the account of any person other than the issuer, including securities acquired by standby underwriters in connection with the call or redemption by the issuer of warrants or a class of convertible securities, if securities of the same class are listed and registered on a national securities exchange or are quoted on the automated quotation system of a national securities association. (In addition, attention is directed to General Instruction C to Form S-8 for the registration of employee benefit plan securities for resale.)

4.   *Rights Offerings, Dividend or Interest Reinvestment Plans and Conversions or Warrants.* Securities to be offered (a) upon the exercise of outstanding rights granted by the issuer of the securities to be offered. If such rights are granted on a pro rata basis to all existing security holders of the class of securities to which the rights attach, or (b) pursuant to a dividend or interest reinvestment plan, or (c) upon the conversion of outstanding convertible securities or upon the exercise of outstanding transferable warrants issued by the issuer of the securities to be offered, or by an affiliate of such issuer: The issuer also must have provided, within the twelve calendar months immediately before the Form S-3 registration statement is filed, the information required by Items 401, 402, 403 and 407(c)(3), (d)(4), (d)(5) and (e)(4) of Regulation S-K to: all record holders of such rights, or to all participants in such plans, or to all record holders of such convertible securities or transferable warrants, respectively, material containing the information required by Rule 14a-3(b) under the Exchange Act and Items 401, 402 and 403 of Regulation S-K within the twelve calendar months immediately preceding the filing of the registration statement, except that the information required by Items 401, 402 and 403 of Regulation S-K need only be provided to holders of rights exercisable for common stock, holders of securities convertible into common stock, participants in plans which may invest in common stock, or in securities convertible into common stock or warrants exercisable for common stock, respectively.

5.   This Form shall not be used to register offerings of asset-backed securities, as defined in Rule 1101(c).

6.   *Limited Primary Offerings by Certain Other Registrants.* Securities to be offered for cash by or on behalf of a registrant; provided that:
     a.   the aggregate market value of securities sold by or on behalf of the registrant pursuant to this Instruction I.B.6. during the period of 12 calendar months immediately prior to, and including, the sale is no more than one-third of the aggregate market value of the voting and non-voting common equity held by non-affiliates of the registrant;
     b.   the registrant is not a shell company (as defined in Rule 405 of this chapter) and has not been a shell company for at least 12 calendar months previously and if it has been a shell company at any time previously, has filed current Form 10 information with the Commission at least 12 calendar months previously reflecting its status as an entity that is not a shell company; and
     c.   the registrant has at least one class of common equity securities listed and registered on a national securities exchange.

Instructions.
1.   "Common equity" is as defined in Securities Act Rule 405. For purposes of computing the aggregate market value of the registrant's outstanding voting and non-voting common equity pursuant to General Instruction I.B.6., registrants shall use the price at which the common equity was last sold, or the average of the bid and asked prices of such common equity, in the principal

market for such common equity as of a date within 60 days prior to the date of sale. See the definition of "affiliate" in Securities Act Rule 405.

2. For purposes of computing the aggregate market value of all securities sold by or on behalf of the registrant in offerings pursuant to General Instruction I.B.6. during any period of 12 calendar months, registrants shall aggregate the gross proceeds of such sales; provided, that, in the case of derivative securities convertible into or exercisable for shares of the registrant's common equity, registrants shall calculate the aggregate market value of any underlying equity shares in lieu of the market value of the derivative securities. The aggregate market value of the underlying equity shall be calculated by multiplying the maximum number of common equity shares into which the derivative securities are convertible or for which they are exercisable as of a date within 60 days prior to the date of sale, by the same per share market price of the registrant's equity used for purposes of calculating the aggregate market value of the registrant's outstanding voting and non-voting common equity pursuant to Instruction 1 to General Instruction I.B.6. If the derivative securities have been converted or exercised, the aggregate market value of the underlying equity shall be calculated by multiplying the actual number of shares into which the securities were converted or received upon exercise, by the market price of such shares on the date of conversion or exercise.

3. If the aggregate market value of the registrant's outstanding voting and nonvoting common equity computed pursuant to General Instruction I.B.6. equals or exceeds $75 million subsequent to the effective date of this registration statement, then the one-third limitation on sales specified in General Instruction I.B.6(a) shall not apply to additional sales made pursuant to this registration statement on or subsequent to such date and instead the registration statement shall be considered filed pursuant to General Instruction I.B.1.

4. The term "Form 10 information" means the information that is required by Form 10 or Form 20-F, as applicable to the registrant, to register under the Securities Exchange Act of 1934 each class of securities being registered using this form. A registrant may provide the Form 10 information in another Commission filing with respect to the registrant.

5. The date used in Instruction 2 to General Instruction I.B.6. shall be the same date used in Instruction 1 to General Instruction I.B.6.

6. A registrant's eligibility to register a primary offering on Form S-3 pursuant to General Instruction I.B.6. does not mean that the registrant meets the requirements of Form S-3 for purposes of any other rule or regulation of the Commission apart from Rule 415(a)(1)(x).

7. Registrants must set forth on the outside front cover of the prospectus the calculation of the aggregate market value of the registrant's outstanding voting and nonvoting common equity pursuant to General Instruction I.B.6. and the amount of all securities offered pursuant to General Instruction I.B.6. during the prior 12 calendar month period that ends on, and includes, the date of the prospectus.

8. For purposes of General Instruction I.B.6(c), a "national securities exchange" shall mean an exchange registered as such under Section 6(a) of the Securities Exchange Act of 1934.

C. **Majority-owned Subsidiaries.** If a registrant is a majority-owned subsidiary, security offerings may be registered on this Form if:

1. the registrant-subsidiary itself meets the Registrant Requirements and the applicable Transaction Requirement;

2. the parent of the registrant-subsidiary meets the Registrant Requirements and the conditions of Transaction Requirement B.2. (Primary Offerings of Non-Convertible Securities Other than Common Equity) are met;

3. the parent of the registrant-subsidiary meets the Registrant Requirements and the applicable Transaction Requirement, and provides a full and unconditional guarantee, as defined in Rule 3-10 of Regulation S-X, of the payment obligations on the securities being registered, and the securities being registered are non-convertible securities, other than common equity;

4. the parent of the registrant-subsidiary meets the Registrant Requirements and the applicable Transaction Requirement, and the securities of the registrant-subsidiary being registered are full and unconditional guarantees, as defined in Rule 3-10 of Regulation S-X, of the payment obligations on the parent's non-convertible securities, other than common equity, being registered; or

5. the parent of the registrant-subsidiary meets the Registrant Requirements and the applicable Transaction Requirement, and the securities of the registrant-subsidiary being registered are guarantees of the payment obligations on the non convertible securities, other than common equity, being registered by another majority-owned subsidiary of the parent where the parent provides a full and unconditional guarantee, as defined in Rule 3-10 of Regulation S-X, of such non-convertible securities.

Note to General Instruction I.C.: With regard to paragraphs I.C.3, I.C.4, and I.C.5 above, the guarantor is the issuer of a separate security consisting of the guarantee, which must be concurrently registered, but may be registered on the same registration statement as are the non-convertible guaranteed securities.

D. **Automatic Shelf Offerings by Well-known Seasoned Issuers.** Any registrant that is a well-known seasoned issuer as defined in Rule 405 at the most recent eligibility determination date specified in paragraph (2) of that definition may use this Form for registration under the Securities Act of securities offerings, other than pursuant to Rule 415(a)(1)(vii) or (viii), as follows:

1. The securities to be offered are:
   a. Any securities to be offered pursuant to Rule 415, Rule 430A, or Rule 430B by:
      i. A registrant that is a well-known seasoned issuer by reason of paragraph (1)(i)(A) of the definition in Rule 405; or
      ii. A registrant that is a well-known seasoned issuer only by reason of paragraph (1)(i)(B) of the definition in Rule 405 if the registrant also

is eligible to register a primary offering of its securities pursuant to Transaction Requirement I.B.1 of this Form;

b. Non-convertible securities, other than common equity, to be offered pursuant to Rule 415, Rule 430A, or Rule 430B by a registrant that is a well-known seasoned issuer only by reason of paragraph (1)(i)(B) of the definition in Rule 405 and does not fall within Transaction Requirement I.B.1 of this Form;

c. Securities of majority-owned subsidiaries of the parent registrant to be offered pursuant to Rule 415, Rule 430A, or Rule 430B if the parent registrant is a well-known seasoned issuer and the securities of the majority-owned subsidiary being registered meet the following requirements:

    i. Securities of a majority-owned subsidiary that is a well-known seasoned issuer at the time it becomes a registrant, other than by virtue of paragraph (1)(ii) of the definition of well-known seasoned issuer in Rule 405;

    ii. Securities of a majority-owned subsidiary that are non-convertible securities, other than common equity, and the parent registrant provides a full and unconditional guarantee, as defined in Rule 3-10 of Regulation S-X, of the payment obligations on the non-convertible securities;

    iii. Securities of a majority-owned subsidiary that are a guarantee of:

        (A) Non-convertible securities, other than common equity, of the parent registrant being registered;

        (B) Non-convertible securities, other than common equity, of another majority-owned subsidiary being registered and the parent registrant has provided a full and unconditional guarantee, as defined in Rule 3-10 of Regulation S-X, of the payment obligations on such non-convertible securities; or

    iv. Securities of a majority-owned subsidiary that meet the conditions of Transaction Requirement I.B.2. of this Form (Primary Offerings of Non-Convertible Securities Other than Common Equity).

d. Securities to be offered for the account of any person other than the issuer ("selling security holders"), provided that the registration statement and the prospectus are not required to separately identify the selling security holders or the securities to be sold by such persons until the filing of a prospectus, prospectus supplement, posteffective amendment to the registration statement, or periodic or current report under the Exchange Act that is incorporated by reference into the registration statement and prospectus, identifying the selling security holders and the amount of securities to be sold by each of them and, if included in a periodic or current report, a prospectus or prospectus supplement is filed, as required by Rule 430B, pursuant to Rule 424(b)(7).

2.   The registrant pays the registration fee pursuant to Rules 456(b) and 457(r) or in accordance with Rule 456(a).

3.   If the registrant is a majority-owned subsidiary, it is required to file and has filed reports pursuant to Section 13 or Section 15(d) of the Exchange Act and satisfies the requirements of the Form with regard to incorporation by reference or information about the majority-owned subsidiary is included in the registration statement (or a post-effective amendment to the registration statement).

4.   The registrant may register additional securities or classes of its or its majority-owned subsidiaries' securities on a post-effective amendment pursuant to Rule 413(b).

5.   An automatic shelf registration statement and post-effective amendment will become effective immediately pursuant to Rule 462(e) and (f) upon filing. All filings made on or in connection with automatic shelf registration statements on this Form become public upon filing with the Commission.

II.   **Application of General Rules and Regulations**

A.   Attention is directed to the General Rules and Regulations under the Securities Act, particularly Regulation C thereunder. That Regulation contains general requirements regarding the preparation and filing of registration statements.

B.   Attention is directed to Regulation S-K for the requirements applicable to the content of the non-financial statement portions of registration statements under the Securities Act. Where this Form directs the registrant to furnish information required by Regulation S-K and the item of Regulation S-K so provides, information need only be furnished to the extent appropriate. Notwithstanding Items 501 and 502 of Regulation S-K, no table of contents is required to be included in the prospectus or registration statement prepared on this Form. In addition to the information expressly required to be included in a registration statement on this Form S-3, registrants also may provide such other information as they deem appropriate.

C.   A "smaller reporting company," defined in Rule 405, that is eligible to use Form S-3 shall refer to the disclosure items in Regulation S-K with specific attention to the scaled disclosure provided for smaller reporting companies, if any. Smaller reporting companies may provide the financial information called for by Article 8 of Regulation S-X in lieu of the financial information called for by Item 11 in this form.

D.   Non-Automatic Shelf Registration Statements. Where two or more classes of securities being registered on this Form pursuant to General Instruction I.B.1. or I.B.2. are to be offered pursuant to Rule 415(a)(1)(x), and where this Form is not an automatic shelf registration statement, Rule 457(*o*) permits the registration fee to be calculated on the basis of the maximum offering price of all the securities listed in the Fee Table. In this event, while the Fee Table would list each of the classes of securities being registered and the aggregate proceeds to be raised, the Fee Table need not specify by each class information as to the amount to be registered, proposed maximum offering price per unit, and proposed maximum aggregate offering price.

E. Automatic Shelf Registration Statements. Where securities are being registered on this Form pursuant to General Instruction I.D., Rule 456(b) permits, but does not require, the registrant to pay the registration fee on a pay-as-you-go basis and Rule 457(r) permits, but does not require, the registration fee to be calculated on the basis of the aggregate offering price of the securities to be offered in an offering or offerings off the registration statement. If a registrant elects to pay all or a portion of the registration fee on a deferred basis, the Fee Table in the initial filing must identify the classes of securities being registered and provide that the registrant elects to rely on Rule 456(b) and Rule 457(r), but the Fee Table does not need to specify any other information. When the registrant amends the Fee Table in accordance with Rule 456(b)(1)(ii), the amended Fee Table must include either the dollar amount of securities being registered if paid in advance of or in connection with an offering or offerings or the aggregate offering price for all classes of securities referenced in the offerings and the applicable registration fee.

F. Information in Automatic and Non-Automatic Shelf Registration Statements. Where securities are being registered on this Form pursuant to General Instruction I.B.1, I.B.2, I.B.5, I.C., or I.D., information is only required to be furnished as of the date of initial effectiveness of the registration statement to the extent required by Rule 430A or Rule 430B. Required information about a specific transaction must be included in the prospectus in the registration statement by means of a prospectus that is deemed to be part of and included in the registration statement pursuant to Rule 430A or Rule 430B, a post-effective amendment to the registration statement, or a periodic or current report under the Exchange Act incorporated by reference into the registration statement and the prospectus and identified in a prospectus filed, as required by Rule 430B, pursuant to Rule 424(b).

G. Selling Security Holder Offerings. Where a registrant eligible to register primary offerings on this Form pursuant to General Instruction I.B.1 registers securities offerings on this Form pursuant to General Instruction I.B.1 or I.B.3 for the account of persons other than the registrant, if the offering of the securities, or securities convertible into such securities, that are being registered on behalf of the selling security holders was completed and the securities, or securities convertible into such securities, were issued and outstanding prior to the original date of filing the registration statement covering the resale of the securities, the registrant may, as permitted by Rule 430B(b), in lieu of identifying selling security holders prior to effectiveness of the resale registration statement, refer to unnamed selling security holders in a generic manner by identifying the initial transaction in which the securities were sold. Following effectiveness, the registrant must include in a prospectus filed pursuant to Rule 424(b)(7), a post-effective amendment to the registration statement, or an Exchange Act report incorporated by reference into the prospectus that is part of the registration statement (which Exchange Act report is identified in a prospectus filed, as required by Rule 430B, pursuant to Rule 424(b)(7)) the names of previously unidentified selling security holders and amounts of securities that they intend to sell. If this Form is being filed pursuant to General Instruction I.D. by a well-known seasoned issuer to register securities being offered for the account of persons other than the issuer, the registration statement and the prospectus included in the registration statement do not need to designate the securities that will be offered for the account of such persons, identify them, or identify the initial transaction in which the securities, or securities convertible into such securities, were sold until the registrant files a post-effective amendment to the registration statement, a prospectus pursuant to Rule 424(b), or an Exchange Act report (and prospectus filed, as required by Rule 430B, pursuant to Rule 424(b)(7)) containing information for the offering on behalf of such persons.

III. Dividend or Interest Reinvestment Plans: Filing and Effectiveness of Registration Statement; Requests for Confidential Treatment

A registration statement on this Form S-3 relating solely to securities offered pursuant to dividend or interest reinvestment plans will become effective automatically (Rule 462) upon filing (Rule 456). Post-effective amendments to such a registration statement on this Form shall become effective upon filing (Rule 464). All filings made on or in connection with this Form become public upon filing with the Commission. As a result, requests for confidential treatment made under Rule 406 must be processed with the Commission staff prior to the filing of such a registration statement. The number of copies of the registration statement and of each amendment required by Rules 402 and 472 shall be filed with the Commission: *provided, however,* That the number of additional copies referred to in Rule 402(b) may be reduced from ten to three and the number of additional copies referred to in Rule 472(a) may be reduced from eight to three, one of which shall be marked clearly and precisely to indicate changes.

IV. Registration of Additional Securities and Additional Classes of Securities

A. Registration of Additional Securities Pursuant to Rule 462(b). With respect to the registration of additional securities for an offering pursuant to Rule 462(b) under the Securities Act, the registrant may file a registration statement consisting only of the following: the facing page; a statement that the contents of the earlier registration statement, identified by file number, are incorporated by reference; required opinions and consents; the signature page; and any price-related information omitted from the earlier registration statement in reliance on Rule 430A that the registrant chooses to include in the new registration statement. The information contained in such a Rule 462(b) registration statement shall be deemed to be a part of the earlier registration statement as of the date of effectiveness of the Rule 462(b) registration statement. Any opinion or consent required in the Rule 462(b) registration statement may be incorporated by reference from the earlier registration statement with respect to the offering, if: (i) such opinion or consent expressly provides for such incorporation; and (ii) such opinion relates to the securities registered pursuant to Rule 462(b). *See* Rule 439(b) under the Securities Act.

B. Registration of Additional Securities or Classes of Securities or Additional Registrants After Effectiveness. A well-known seasoned issuer relying on General Instruction I.D. of this Form may register additional securities or classes of securities, pursuant to Rule 413(b) by filing a post-effective amendment to the effective registration statement. The well-known seasoned issuer may add majority-owned subsidiaries as additional registrants whose securities are eligible to be sold as part of the automatic shelf registration statement by filing a post-effective amendment identifying the additional registrants, and the registrant and the additional registrants and other persons required to sign the registration statement must sign the post-effective amendment. The post-effective amendment must consist of the facing page; any disclosure required by this Form that is necessary to update the registration statement to reflect the additional securities, additional classes of securities, or additional registrants; any required opinions and consents; and the signature page. Required information, consents, or opinions may be included in the prospectus and the registration statement through a post-effective amendment or may be provided through a document incorporated or deemed incorporated by reference into the registration statement and the prospectus that is part of the registration statement, or, as to the required information only, contained in a prospectus filed pursuant to Rule 424(b) that is deemed part of and included in the registration statement and prospectus that is part of the registration statement.

PART I – INFORMATION REQUIRED IN PROSPECTUS

Item 1.   Forepart of the Registration Statement and Outside Front Cover Pages of Prospectus.

Set forth in the forepart of the registration statement and on the outside front cover page of the prospectus the information required by Item 501 of Regulation S-K.

Item 2.   Inside Front and Outside Back Cover Pages of Prospectus.

Set forth on the inside front cover page of the prospectus or, where permitted, on the outside back cover page, the information required by Item 502 of Regulation S-K.

Item 3.   Summary Information and Risk Factors.

Furnish the information required by Items 105 and 503 of Regulation S-K.

Item 4.   Use of Proceeds.

Furnish the information required by Item 504 of Regulation S-K.

Item 5.   Determination of Offering Price.

Furnish the information required by Item 505 of Regulation S-K.

Item 6.   Dilution.

Furnish the information required by Item 506 of Regulation S-K.

Item 7.   Selling Security Holders.

Furnish the information required by Item 507 of Regulation S-K.

Item 8.   Plan of Distribution.

Furnish the information required by Item 508 of Regulation S-K.

Item 9.   Description of Securities to be Registered.

Furnish the information required by Item 202 of Regulation S-K, unless capital stock is to be registered and securities of the same class are registered pursuant to Section 12 of the Exchange Act.

Item 10.   Interests of Named Experts and Counsel.

Furnish the information required by Item 509 of Regulation S-K.

Item 11.   Material Changes.

a.   Describe any and all material changes in the registrant's affairs which have occurred since the end of the latest fiscal year for which certified financial statements were included in the latest annual report to security holders and which have not been described in a report on Form 10-Q or Form 8-K filed under the Exchange Act.

b.   Include in the prospectus, if not incorporated by reference therein from the reports filed under the Exchange Act specified in Item 12(a), a proxy or information statement filed pursuant to Section 14 of the Exchange Act, a prospectus previously filed pursuant to Rule 424(b) or (c) under the Securities Act or, where no prospectus is required to be filed pursuant to Rule 424(b), the prospectus included in the registration statement at effectiveness, or a Form 8-K filed during either of the two preceding years: (i) information required by Rule 3-05 and Article 11 of Regulation S-X; (ii) restated financial statements prepared in accordance with Regulation S-X if there has been a change in accounting principles or a correction in an error where such change or correction requires a material retroactive restatement of financial statements; (iii) restated financial statements prepared in accordance with Regulation S-X where a combination of entities under common control has been consummated subsequent to the most recent fiscal year and the transferred businesses, considered in the aggregate, are significant pursuant to Rule 11-01(b), or (iv) any financial information required because of a material disposition of assets outside the normal course of business.

Item 12.   Incorporation of Certain Information by Reference.

a.   The documents listed in (1) and (2) below shall be specifically incorporated by reference into the prospectus by means of a statement to that effect in the prospectus listing all such documents:

1.   the registrant's latest annual report on Form 10-K filed pursuant to Section 13(a) or 15(d) of the Exchange Act which contains financial statements for the registrant's latest fiscal year for which a Form 10-K were required to have been filed; and

2.   all other reports filed pursuant to Section 13(a) or 15(d) of the Exchange Act since the end of the fiscal year covered by the annual report referred to in (1) above; and

3.   if capital stock is to be registered and securities of the same class are registered under Section 12 of the Exchange Act, the description of such class of securities which is contained in a registration statement filed under the Exchange Act, including any amendment or reports filed for the purpose of updating such description.

b.   The prospectus shall also state that all documents subsequently filed by the registrant pursuant to Sections 13(a), 13(c), 14 or 15(d) of the Exchange Act, prior to the termination of the offering shall be deemed to be incorporated by reference into the prospectus.

Instruction. Attention is directed to Rule 439 regarding consent to use of material incorporated by reference.

c. 1. You must state
    (i)   that you will provide to each person, including any beneficial owner, to whom a prospectus is delivered, a copy of any or all of the information that has been incorporated by reference in the prospectus but not delivered with the prospectus;
    (ii) that you will provide this information upon written or oral request;
    (iii) that you will provide this information at no cost to the requester; and
    (iv) the name, address, and telephone number to which the request for this information must be made.

Note to Item 12(c)(1). If you send any of the information that is incorporated by reference in the prospectus to security holders, you also must send any exhibits that are specifically incorporated by reference in that information.

    2. You must
    (i)   identify the reports and other information that you file with the SEC; and
    (ii) State that the SEC maintains an Internet site that contains reports, proxy and information statements, and other information regarding issuers that file electronically with the SEC and state the address of that site (http://www.sec.gov). Disclose your Internet address, if available.

d. Any information required in the prospectus in response to Item 3 through Item 11 of this Form may be included in the prospectus through documents filed pursuant to Section 13(a), 14, or 15(d) of the Exchange Act that are incorporated or deemed incorporated by reference into the prospectus that is part of the registration statement. Notwithstanding the foregoing, in the financial statements, incorporating by reference or cross-referencing to information outside of the financial statements is not permitted unless otherwise specifically permitted or required by the Commission's rules or by U.S. Generally Accepted Accounting Principles or International Financial Reporting Standards as issued by the International Accounting Standards Board, whichever is applicable.

Item 13. Disclosure of Commission Position on Indemnification for Securities Act Liabilities.

Furnish the information required by Item 510 of Regulation S-K.

PART II – INFORMATION NOT REQUIRED IN PROSPECTUS

Item 14.   Other Expenses of Issuance and Distribution.

Furnish the information required by Item 511 of Regulation S-K.

Item 15.   Indemnification of Directors and Officers.

Furnish the information required by Item 702 of Regulation S-K.

Item 16.   Exhibits.

Subject to the rules regarding incorporation by reference, furnish the exhibits required by Item 601 of Regulation S-K.

Item 17.   Undertakings.

Furnish the undertakings required by Item 512 of Regulation S-K.

SIGNATURES

Pursuant to the requirements of the Securities Act of 1933, the registrant certifies that it has reasonable grounds to believe that it meets all of the requirements for filing on Form S-3 and has duly caused this registration statement to be signed on its behalf by the undersigned, thereunto duly authorized, in the City of _____, State of _____ _____, on _____

_____
(Registrant)

By _____
(Signature and Title)

Pursuant to the requirements of the Securities Act of 1933, this registration statement has been signed by the following persons in the capacities and on the dates indicated.

_____
(Signature)

_____
(Title)

_____
(Date)

Instructions

1. The registration statement shall be signed by the registrant, its principal executive officer or officers, its principal financial officer, its controller or principal accounting officer and by at least a majority of the board of directors or persons performing similar functions. If the registrant is a foreign person, the registration statement shall also be signed by its authorized representative in the United States. Where the registrant is a limited partnership, the registration statement shall be signed by a majority of the board of directors of any corporate general partner signing the registration statement.

2. The name of each person who signs the registration statement shall be typed or printed beneath his signature. Any person who occupies more than one of the specified positions shall indicate each capacity in which he signs the registration statement. Attention is directed to Rule 402 concerning manual signatures and to Item 601 of Regulation S-K concerning signatures pursuant to powers of attorney.

3. Where eligibility for use of the Form is based on the assignment of a security rating pursuant to Transaction Requirements B.2. or B.5., the registrant may sign the registration statement notwithstanding the fact that such security rating has not been assigned by the filing date, provided that the registrant reasonably believes, and so states, that the security rating requirement will be met by the time of sale.

Exchange Act – Statutes

Section 1 – Short Title

This Act may be cited as the "Securities Exchange Act of 1934."

Section 3

    a.   **Definitions**. When used in this title, unless the context otherwise requires–

        1.   The term "exchange" means any organization, association, or group of persons, whether incorporated or unincorporated, which constitutes, maintains, or provides a market place or facilities for bringing together purchasers and sellers of securities or for otherwise performing with respect to securities the functions commonly performed by a stock exchange as that term is generally understood, and includes the market place and the market facilities maintained by such exchange.

       10.   The term "security" means any note, stock, treasury stock, security future, bond, debenture, certificate of interest or participation in any profit-sharing agreement or in any oil, gas, or other mineral royalty or lease, any collateral-trust certificate, preorganization certificate or subscription, transferable share, investment contract, voting-trust certificate, certificate of deposit for a security, any put, call, straddle, option, or privilege on any security, certificate of deposit, or group or index of securities (including any interest therein or based on the value thereof), or any put, call, straddle, option, or privilege entered into on a national securities exchange relating to foreign currency, or in general, any instrument commonly known as a "security"; or any certificate of interest or participation in, temporary or interim certificate for, receipt for, or warrant or right to subscribe to or purchase, any of the foregoing; but shall not include currency or any note, draft, bill of exchange, or banker's acceptance which has a maturity at the time of issuance of not exceeding nine months, exclusive of days of grace, or any renewal thereof the maturity of which is likewise limited.

       14.   The terms "sale" and "sell" each include any contract to sell or otherwise dispose of. For security futures products, such term includes any contract, agreement, or transaction for future delivery.

       80.   The term 'emerging growth company' means an issuer that had total annual gross revenues of less than $1,000,000,000 (as such amount is indexed for inflation every 5 years by the Commission to reflect the change in the Consumer Price Index for All Urban Consumers published by the Bureau of Labor Statistics, setting the threshold to the nearest 1,000,000) during its most recently completed fiscal year. An issuer that is an emerging growth company as of the first day of that fiscal year shall continue to be deemed an emerging growth company until the earliest of—

           A.   the last day of the fiscal year of the issuer during which it had total annual gross revenues of $1,000,000,000 (as such amount is indexed for inflation every 5 years by the Commission to reflect the change in the Consumer Price Index for All Urban Consumers published by the Bureau of Labor Statistics, setting the threshold to the nearest 1,000,000) or more;

           B.   the last day of the fiscal year of the issuer following the fifth anniversary of the date of the first sale of common equity securities of the issuer pursuant to an effective registration statement under this title;

           C.   the date on which such issuer has, during the previous 3-year period, issued more than $1,000,000,000 in non-convertible debt; or

           D.   the date on which such issuer is deemed to be a 'large accelerated filer', as defined in Rule 12b–2 or any successor thereto.

80. The term 'funding portal' means any person acting as an intermediary in a transaction involving the offer or sale of securities for the account of others, solely pursuant to section 4(6) of the Securities Act of 1933, that does not—

    A. offer investment advice or recommendations;

    B. solicit purchases, sales, or offers to buy the securities offered or displayed on its website or portal;

    C. compensate employees, agents, or other persons for such solicitation or based on the sale of securities displayed or referenced on its website or portal;

    D. hold, manage, possess, or otherwise handle investor funds or securities; or

    E. engage in such other activities as the Commission, by rule, determines appropriate.

h. **Limited Exemption for Funding Portals.**

    1. In general. The Commission shall, by rule, exempt, conditionally or unconditionally, a registered funding portal from the requirement to register as a broker or dealer under section 15(a)(1), provided that such funding portal—

        A. remains subject to the examination, enforcement, and other rulemaking authority of the Commission;

        B. is a member of a national securities association registered under section 15A; and

        C. is subject to such other requirements under this title as the Commission determines appropriate under such rule.

    2. National Securities Association Membership. For purposes of sections 15(b)(8) and 15A, the term 'broker or dealer' includes a funding portal and the term 'registered broker or dealer' includes a registered funding portal, except to the extent that the Commission, by rule, determines otherwise, provided that a national securities association shall only examine for and enforce against a registered funding portal rules of such national securities association written specifically for registered funding portals.

Section 4C – Appearance and Practice Before the Commission

a. **Authority to Censure.** The Commission may censure any person, or deny, temporarily or permanently, to any person the privilege of appearing or practicing before the Commission in any way, if that person is found by the Commission, after notice and opportunity for hearing in the matter–

    1. not to possess the requisite qualifications to represent others;

    2. to be lacking in character or integrity, or to have engaged in unethical or improper professional conduct; or

    3. to have willfully violated, or willfully aided and abetted the violation of, any provision of the securities laws or the rules and regulations issued thereunder.

b. **Definition.** With respect to any registered public accounting firm or associated person, for purposes of this section, the term 'improper professional conduct' means–

    1. intentional or knowing conduct, including reckless conduct, that results in a violation of applicable professional standards; and

    2. negligent conduct in the form of–

A. a single instance of highly unreasonable conduct that results in a violation of applicable professional standards in circumstances in which the registered public accounting firm or associated person knows, or should know, that heightened scrutiny is warranted; or

B. repeated instances of unreasonable conduct, each resulting in a violation of applicable professional standards, that indicate a lack of competence to practice before the Commission

Section 4E – Deadline for Completing Enforcement Investigations and Compliance Examinations and Inspections

a. **Enforcement investigations.**

1. In general. Not later than 180 days after the date on which Commission staff provide a written Wells notification to any person, the Commission staff shall either file an action against such person or provide notice to the Director of the Division of Enforcement of its intent to not file an action.

2. Exceptions for certain complex actions. Notwithstanding paragraph (1), if the Director of the Division of Enforcement of the Commission or the Director's designee determines that a particular enforcement investigation is sufficiently complex such that a determination regarding the filing of an action against a person cannot be completed within the deadline specified in paragraph (1), the Director of the Division of Enforcement of the Commission or the Director's designee may, after providing notice to the Chairman of the Commission, extend such deadline as needed for one additional 180-day period. If after the additional 180-day period the Director of the Division of Enforcement of the Commission or the Director's designee determines that a particular enforcement investigation is sufficiently complex such that a determination regarding the filing of an action against a person cannot be completed within the additional 180-day period, the Director of the Division of Enforcement of the Commission or the Director's designee may, after providing notice to and receiving approval of the Commission, extend such deadline as needed for one or more additional successive 180-day periods.

b. **Compliance examinations and inspections.**

1. In general. Not later than 180 days after the date on which Commission staff completes the on-site portion of its compliance examination or inspection or receives all records requested from the entity being examined or inspected, whichever is later, Commission staff shall provide the entity being examined or inspected with written notification indicating either that the examination or inspection has concluded, has concluded without findings, or that the staff requests the entity undertake corrective action.

2. Exception for certain complex actions. Notwithstanding paragraph (1), if the head of any division or office within the Commission responsible for compliance examinations and inspections or his designee determines that a particular compliance examination or inspection is sufficiently complex such that a determination regarding concluding the examination or inspection, or regarding the staff requests the entity undertake corrective action, cannot be completed within the deadline specified in paragraph (1), the head of any

division or office within the Commission responsible for compliance examinations and inspections or his designee may, after providing notice to the Chairman of the Commission, extend such deadline as needed for one additional 180-day period.

Section 9 – Manipulation of Security Prices

a.   **Transactions relating to purchase or sale of security.** It shall be unlawful for any person, directly or indirectly, by the use of the mails or any means or instrumentality of interstate commerce, or of any facility of any national securities exchange, or for any member of a national securities exchange–

1.   For the purpose of creating a false or misleading appearance of active trading in any security other than a government security, or a false or misleading appearance with respect to the market for any such security, (A) to effect any transaction in such security which involves no change in the beneficial ownership thereof, or (B) to enter an order or orders for the purchase of such security with the knowledge that an order or orders of substantially the same size, at substantially the same time, and at substantially the same price, for the sale of any such security, has been or will be entered by or for the same or different parties, or (C) to enter any order or orders for the sale of any such security with the knowledge that an order or orders of substantially the same size, at substantially the same time, and at substantially the same price, for the purchase of such security, has been or will be entered by or for the same or different parties.

2.   To effect, alone or with 1 or more other persons, a series of transactions in any security other than a government security, or in connection with any security-based swap or security-based swap agreement with respect to such security creating actual or apparent active trading in such security, or raising or depressing the price of such security, for the purpose of inducing the purchase or sale of such security by others.

3.   If a dealer, broker, security-based swap dealer, major security-based swap participant, or other person selling or offering for sale or purchasing or offering to purchase the security, a security-based swap, or a security-based swap agreement with respect to such security, to induce the purchase or sale of any security other than a government security, any security-based swap, or any security-based swap agreement with respect to such security by the circulation or dissemination in the ordinary course of business of information to the effect that the price of any such security will or is likely to rise or fall because of market operations of any 1 or more persons conducted for the purpose of raising or depressing the price of such security.

4.   If a dealer, broker, security-based swap dealer, major security-based swap participant, or other person selling or offering for sale or purchasing or offering to purchase the security, a security-based swap, or security-based swap agreement with respect to such security, to make, regarding any security other than a government security, any security-based swap, or any security-based swap agreement with respect to such security, for the purpose of inducing the purchase or sale of such security, such security-based swap, or such security-based swap agreement any statement which was at the time and in the light of

413

the circumstances under which it was made, false or misleading with respect to any material fact, and which that person knew or had reasonable ground to believe was so false or misleading.

5.   For a consideration, received directly or indirectly from a broker, dealer, security-based swap dealer, major security-based swap participant, or other person selling or offering for sale or purchasing or offering to purchase the security, a security-based swap, or security-based swap agreement with respect to such security, to induce the purchase of any security other than a government security, any security-based swap, or any security-based swap agreement with respect to such security by the circulation or dissemination of information to the effect that the price of any such security will or is likely to rise or fall because of the market operations of any 1 or more persons conducted for the purpose of raising or depressing the price of such security.

6.   To effect either alone or with one or more other persons any series of transactions for the purchase and/or sale of any security other than a government security for the purpose of pegging, fixing, or stabilizing the price of such security in contravention of such rules and regulations as the Commission may prescribe as necessary or appropriate in the public interest or for the protection of investors.

b.   **Transactions relating to puts, calls, straddles, or options**. It shall be unlawful for any person to effect in contravention of such rules and regulations as the Commission may prescribe as necessary or appropriate in the public interest or for the protection of investors–

1.   any transaction in connection with any security whereby any party to such transaction acquires (A) any put, call, straddle, or other option or privilege of buying the security from or selling the security to another without being bound to do so; or (B) any security futures product on the security; or

2.   any transaction in connection with any security with relation to which he has, directly or indirectly, any interest in any (A) such put, call, straddle, option, or privilege; or (B) such security futures product; or

3.   any transaction in any security for the account of any person who he has reason to believe has, and who actually has, directly or indirectly, any interest in any (A) such put, call, straddle, option, or privilege; or (B) such security futures product with relation to such security.

c.   **Endorsement or guarantee of puts, calls, straddles, or options.** It shall be unlawful for any broker, dealer, or member of a national securities exchange directly or indirectly to endorse or guarantee the performance of any put, call, straddle, option, or privilege in relation to any security registered on a national securities exchange, in contravention of such rules and regulations as the Commission may prescribe as necessary or appropriate in the public interest or for the protection of investors.

d.   **Registered warrant, right, or convertible security not included in "put", "call", "straddle", or "option."** The terms "put", "call", "straddle", "option", or "privilege" as used in this section shall not include any registered warrant, right, or convertible security.

e. **Persons liable; suits at law or in equity.** Any person who willfully participates in any act or transaction in violation of subsection (a), (b) or (c) of this section, shall be liable to any person who shall purchase or sell any security at a price which was affected by such act or transaction, and the person so injured may sue in law or in equity in any court of competent jurisdiction to recover the damages sustained as a result of any such act or transaction. In any such suit the court may, in its discretion, require an undertaking for the payment of the costs of such suit, and assess reasonable costs, including reasonable attorneys' fees, against either party litigant. Every person who becomes liable to make any payment under this subsection may recover contribution as in cases of contract from any person who, if joined in the original suit, would have been liable to make the same payment. No action shall be maintained to enforce any liability created under this section, unless brought within one year after the discovery of the facts constituting the violation and within three years after such violation.

f. **Limitations on practices that affect market volatility.** It shall be unlawful for any person, by the use of the mails or any means or instrumentality of interstate commerce or of any facility of any national securities exchange, to use or employ any act or practice in connection with the purchase or sale of any equity security in contravention of such rules or regulations as the Commission may adopt, consistent with the public interest, the protection of investors, and the maintenance of fair and orderly markets–
   a. to prescribe means reasonably designed to prevent manipulation of price levels of the equity securities market or a substantial segment thereof; and
   b. to prohibit or constrain, during periods of extraordinary market volatility, any trading practice in connection with the purchase or sale of equity securities that the Commission determines (A) has previously contributed significantly to extraordinary levels of volatility that have threatened the maintenance of fair and orderly markets; and (B) is reasonably certain to engender such levels of volatility if not prohibited or constrained.

   In adopting rules under paragraph (2), the Commission shall, consistent with the purposes of this subsection, minimize the impact on the normal operations of the market and a natural person's freedom to buy or sell any equity security.

Section 10 – Manipulative and Deceptive Devices

It shall be unlawful for any person, directly or indirectly, by the use of any means or instrumentality of interstate commerce or of the mails, or of any facility of any national securities exchange–

a. 1. To effect a short sale, or to use or employ any stop-loss order in connection with the purchase or sale, of any other than a government security, in contravention of such rules and regulations as the Commission may prescribe as necessary or appropriate in the public interest or for the protection of investors.
   2. Paragraph (1) of this subsection shall not apply to security futures products.

b. To use or employ, in connection with the purchase or sale of any security registered on a national securities exchange or any security not so registered, or any securities-based swap agreement, any manipulative or deceptive device or contrivance in contravention

415

of such rules and regulations as the Commission may prescribe as necessary or appropriate in the public interest or for the protection of investors.

Section l0A – Audit Requirements

a. **In General**. Each audit required pursuant to this title of the financial statements of an issuer by a registered public accounting firm shall include, in accordance with generally accepted auditing standards, as may be modified or supplemented from time to time by the Commission–

1. procedures designed to provide reasonable assurance of detecting illegal acts that would have a direct and material effect on the determination of financial statement amounts;

2. procedures designed to identify related party transactions that are material to the financial statements or otherwise require disclosure therein; and

3. an evaluation of whether there is substantial doubt about the ability of the issuer to continue as a going concern during the ensuing fiscal year.

b. **Required Response to Audit Discoveries**

1. Investigation and report to management

   If, in the course of conducting an audit pursuant to this title to which subsection (a) of this section applies, the registered public accounting firm detects or otherwise becomes aware of information indicating that an illegal act (whether or not perceived to have a material effect on the financial statements of the issuer) has or may have occurred, the firm shall, in accordance with generally accepted auditing standards, as may be modified or supplemented from time to time by the Commission–

   A.
           i. determine whether it is likely that an illegal act has occurred; and

          ii. if so, determine and consider the possible effect of the illegal act on the financial statements of the issuer, including any contingent monetary effects, such as fines, penalties, and damages; and

   B. as soon as practicable, inform the appropriate level of the management of the issuer and assure that the audit committee of the issuer, or the board of directors of the issuer in the absence of such a committee, is adequately informed with respect to illegal acts that have been detected or have otherwise come to the attention of such firm in the course of the audit, unless the illegal act is clearly inconsequential.

2. Response to failure to take remedial action

   If, after determining that the audit committee of the board of directors of the issuer, or the board of directors of the issuer in the absence of an audit committee, is adequately informed with respect to illegal acts that have been detected or have otherwise come to the attention of the firm in the course of the audit of such firm, the registered public accounting firm concludes that–

   A. the illegal act has a material effect on the financial statements of the issuer;

   B. the senior management has not taken, and the board of directors has not caused senior management to take, timely and appropriate remedial actions with respect to the illegal act; and

C. the failure to take remedial action is reasonably expected to warrant departure from a standard report of the auditor, when made, or warrant resignation from the audit engagement;

the registered public accounting firm shall, as soon as practicable, directly report its conclusions to the board of directors.

3. Notice to Commission; response to failure to notify

An issuer whose board of directors receives a report under paragraph (2) shall inform the Commission by notice not later than 1 business day after the receipt of such report and shall furnish the registered public accounting firm making such report with a copy of the notice furnished to the Commission. If the registered public accounting firm fails to receive a copy of the notice before the expiration of the required 1-business-day period, the registered public accounting firm shall–

A. resign from the engagement; or

B. furnish to the Commission a copy of its report (or the documentation of any oral report given) not later than 1 business day following such failure to receive notice.

4. Report after resignation

If a registered public accounting firm resigns from an engagement under paragraph (3)(A), the firm shall, not later than 1 business day following the failure by the issuer to notify the Commission under paragraph (3), furnish to the Commission a copy of the report of the firm (or the documentation of any oral report given).

c. **Auditor Liability Limitation.** No registered public accounting firm shall be liable in a private action for any finding, conclusion, or statement expressed in a report made pursuant to paragraph (3) or (4) of subsection (b) of this section, including any rule promulgated pursuant thereto.

d. **Civil Penalties in Cease-and-Desist Proceedings.** If the Commission finds, after notice and opportunity for hearing in a proceeding instituted pursuant to section 21C, that a registered public accounting firm has willfully violated paragraph (3) or (4) of subsection (b) of this section, the Commission may, in addition to entering an order under section 21C, impose a civil penalty against the registered public accounting firm and any other person that the Commission finds was a cause of such violation. The determination to impose a civil penalty and the amount of the penalty shall be governed by the standards set forth in section 21B.

e. **Preservation of Existing Authority.** Except as provided in subsection (d) of this section, nothing in this section shall be held to limit or otherwise affect the authority of the Commission under this title.

f. **Definitions.** As used in this section, the term "illegal act" means an act or omission that violates any law, or any rule or regulation having the force of law. As used in this section, the term 'issuer' means an issuer (as defined in section 3), the securities of which are registered under section 12, or that is required to file reports pursuant to section 15(d), or that files or has filed a registration statement that has not yet become effective under the Securities Act of 1933, and that it has not withdrawn.

g. **Prohibited Activities.** Except as provided in subsection (h), it shall be unlawful for a registered public accounting firm (and any associated person of that firm, to the extent determined appropriate by the Commission) that performs for any issuer any audit required by this title or the rules of the Commission under this title or, beginning 180 days after the date of commencement of the operations of the Public Company Accounting Oversight Board established under section 101 of the Sarbanes-Oxley Act of 2002 (in this section referred to as the 'Board'), the rules of the Board, to provide to that issuer, contemporaneously with the audit, any non-audit service, including–

1. bookkeeping or other services related to the accounting records or financial statements of the audit client;
2. financial information systems design and implementation;
3. appraisal or valuation services, fairness opinions, or contribution-in-kind reports;
4. actuarial services;
5. internal audit outsourcing services;
6. management functions or human resources;
7. broker or dealer, investment adviser, or investment banking services;
8. legal services and expert services unrelated to the audit; and
9. any other service that the Board determines, by regulation, is impermissible.

h. **Preapproval Required for Non-Audit Services.** A registered public accounting firm may engage in any non-audit service, including tax services, that is not described in any of paragraphs (1) through (9) of subsection (g) for an audit client, only if the activity is approved in advance by the audit committee of the issuer, in accordance with subsection (i).

i. **Preapproval Requirements**
1. In general
   A. Audit committee action
      All auditing services (which may entail providing comfort letters in connection with securities underwritings or statutory audits required for insurance companies for purposes of State law) and non-audit services, other than as provided in subparagraph (B), provided to an issuer by the auditor of the issuer shall be preapproved by the audit committee of the issuer.
   B. De minimis exception
      The preapproval requirement under subparagraph (A) is waived with respect to the provision of non-audit services for an issuer, if–
      i. the aggregate amount of all such non-audit services provided to the issuer constitutes not more than 5 percent of the total amount of revenues paid by the issuer to its auditor during the fiscal year in which the nonaudit services are provided;
      ii. such services were not recognized by the issuer at the time of the engagement to be non-audit services; and

       iii. such services are promptly brought to the attention of the audit committee of the issuer and approved prior to the completion of the audit by the audit committee or by 1 or more members of the audit committee who are members of the board of directors to whom authority to grant such approvals has been delegated by the audit committee.

  2. Disclosure to investors

Approval by an audit committee of an issuer under this subsection of a non-audit service to be performed by the auditor of the issuer shall be disclosed to investors in periodic reports required by section 13(a).

  3. Delegation authority

The audit committee of an issuer may delegate to 1 or more designated members of the audit committee who are independent directors of the board of directors, the authority to grant preapprovals required by this subsection. The decisions of any member to whom authority is delegated under this paragraph to preapprove an activity under this subsection shall be presented to the full audit committee at each of its scheduled meetings.

  4. Approval of audit services for other purposes

In carrying out its duties under subsection (m)(2), if the audit committee of an issuer approves an audit service within the scope of the engagement of the auditor, such audit service shall be deemed to have been preapproved for purposes of this subsection.

j. **Audit Partner Rotation.** It shall be unlawful for a registered public accounting firm to provide audit services to an issuer if the lead (or coordinating) audit partner (having primary responsibility for the audit), or the audit partner responsible for reviewing the audit, has performed audit services for that issuer in each of the 5 previous fiscal years of that issuer.

k. **Reports to Audit Committees.** Each registered public accounting firm that performs for any issuer any audit required by this title shall timely report to the audit committee of the issuer–

  1. all critical accounting policies and practices to be used;

  2. all alternative treatments of financial information within generally accepted accounting principles that have been discussed with management officials of the issuer, ramifications of the use of such alternative disclosures and treatments, and the treatment preferred by the registered public accounting firm; and

  3. other material written communications between the registered public accounting firm and the management of the issuer, such as any management letter or schedule of unadjusted differences.

l. **Conflicts of Interest.** It shall be unlawful for a registered public accounting firm to perform for an issuer any audit service required by this title, if a chief executive officer, controller, chief financial officer, chief accounting officer, or any person serving in an equivalent position for the issuer, was employed by that registered independent public accounting firm and participated in any capacity in the audit of that issuer during the 1-year period preceding the date of the initiation of the audit.

m. **Standards Relating to Audit Committees**
1.   Commission rules
   - A.   In general
     Effective not later than 270 days after the date of enactment of this subsection, the Commission shall, by rule, direct the national securities exchanges and national securities associations to prohibit the listing of any security of an issuer that is not in compliance with the requirements of any portion of paragraphs (2) through (6).
   - B.   Opportunity to cure defects
     The rules of the Commission under subparagraph (A) shall provide for appropriate procedures for an issuer to have an opportunity to cure any defects that would be the basis for a prohibition under subparagraph (A), before the imposition of such prohibition.
2.   Responsibilities relating to registered public accounting firms
   The audit committee of each issuer, in its capacity as a committee of the board of directors, shall be directly responsible for the appointment, compensation, and oversight of the work of any registered public accounting firm employed by that issuer (including resolution of disagreements between management and the auditor regarding financial reporting) for the purpose of preparing or issuing an audit report or related work, and each such registered public accounting firm shall report directly to the audit committee.
3.   Independence
   - A.   In general
     Each member of the audit committee of the issuer shall be a member of the board of directors of the issuer, and shall otherwise be independent.
   - B.   Criteria
     In order to be considered to be independent for purposes of this paragraph, a member of an audit committee of an issuer may not, other than in his or her capacity as a member of the audit committee, the board of directors, or any other board committee–
     - i.   accept any consulting, advisory, or other compensatory fee from the issuer; or
     - ii.   be an affiliated person of the issuer or any subsidiary thereof.
   - C.   Exemption authority
     The Commission may exempt from the requirements of subparagraph (B) a particular relationship with respect to audit committee members, as the Commission determines appropriate in light of the circumstances.
4.   Complaints
   Each audit committee shall establish procedures for–
   - A.   the receipt, retention, and treatment of complaints received by the issuer regarding accounting, internal accounting controls, or auditing matters; and
   - B.   the confidential, anonymous submission by employees of the issuer of concerns regarding questionable accounting or auditing matters.
5.   Authority to engage advisers
   Each audit committee shall have the authority to engage independent counsel and other advisers, as it determines necessary to carry out its duties.

6.   Funding
Each issuer shall provide for appropriate funding, as determined by the audit committee, in its capacity as a committee of the board of directors, for payment of compensation–

A.   to the registered public accounting firm employed by the issuer for the purpose of rendering or issuing an audit report; and

B.   to any advisers employed by the audit committee under paragraph (5).

Section 10C – Compensation Committees

a.   **Independence of compensation committees**

1.   Listing standards. The Commission shall, by rule, direct the national securities exchanges and national securities associations to prohibit the listing of any equity security of an issuer, other than an issuer that is a controlled company, limited partnership, company in bankruptcy proceedings, open-ended management investment company that is registered under the Investment Company Act of 1940, or a foreign private issuer that provides annual disclosures to shareholders of the reasons that the foreign private issuer does not have an independent compensation committee, that does not comply with the requirements of this subsection.

2.   Independence of compensation committees. The rules of the Commission under paragraph (1) shall require that each member of the compensation committee of the board of directors of an issuer be—

A.   a member of the board of directors of the issuer; and

B.   independent.

3.   Independence. The rules of the Commission under paragraph (1) shall require that, in determining the definition of the term 'independence' for purposes of paragraph (2), the national securities exchanges and the national securities associations shall consider relevant factors, including—

A.   the source of compensation of a member of the board of directors of an issuer, including any consulting, advisory, or other compensatory fee paid by the issuer to such member of the board of directors; and

B.   whether a member of the board of directors of an issuer is affiliated with the issuer, a subsidiary of the issuer, or an affiliate of a subsidiary of the issuer.

4.   Exemption authority. The rules of the Commission under paragraph (1) shall permit a national securities exchange or a national securities association to exempt a particular relationship from the requirements of paragraph (2), with respect to the members of a compensation committee, as the national securities exchange or national securities association determines is appropriate, taking into consideration the size of an issuer and any other relevant factors.

b.   **Independence of compensation consultants and other compensation committee advisers.**

1.   In general. The compensation committee of an issuer may only select a compensation consultant, legal counsel, or other adviser to the compensation committee after taking into consideration the factors identified by the Commission under paragraph (2).

2.   Rules. The Commission shall identify factors that affect the independence of a compensation consultant, legal counsel, or other adviser to a compensation committee of an issuer. Such factors shall be competitively neutral among categories of consultants, legal counsel, or other advisers and preserve the ability of compensation committees to retain the services of members of any such category, and shall include—

    A.   the provision of other services to the issuer by the person that employs the compensation consultant, legal counsel, or other adviser;

    B.   the amount of fees received from the issuer by the person that employs the compensation consultant, legal counsel, or other adviser, as a percentage of the total revenue of the person that employs the compensation consultant, legal counsel, or other adviser;

    C.   the policies and procedures of the person that employs the compensation consultant, legal counsel, or other adviser that are designed to prevent conflicts of interest;

    D.   any business or personal relationship of the compensation consultant, legal counsel, or other adviser with a member of the compensation committee; and

    E.   any stock of the issuer owned by the compensation consultant, legal counsel, or other adviser.

c.   **Compensation committee authority relating to compensation consultants.**

    1.   Authority to retain compensation consultant.

        A.   In general. The compensation committee of an issuer, in its capacity as a committee of the board of directors, may, in its sole discretion, retain or obtain the advice of a compensation consultant.

        B.   Direct responsibility of compensation committee. The compensation committee of an issuer shall be directly responsible for the appointment, compensation, and oversight of the work of a compensation consultant.

        C.   Rule of construction. This paragraph may not be construed—

            i.   to require the compensation committee to implement or act consistently with the advice or recommendations of the compensation consultant; or

            ii.   to affect the ability or obligation of a compensation committee to exercise its own judgment in fulfillment of the duties of the compensation committee.

    2.   Disclosure. In any proxy or consent solicitation material for an annual meeting of the shareholders (or a special meeting in lieu of the annual meeting) occurring on or after the date that is 1 year after the date of enactment of this section, each issuer shall disclose in the proxy or consent material, in accordance with regulations of the Commission, whether—

        A.   the compensation committee of the issuer retained or obtained the advice of a compensation consultant; and

        B.   the work of the compensation consultant has raised any conflict of interest and, if so, the nature of the conflict and how the conflict is being addressed.

d. **Authority to engage independent legal counsel and other advisers.**
 1. In general. The compensation committee of an issuer, in its capacity as a committee of the board of directors, may, in its sole discretion, retain and obtain the advice of independent legal counsel and other advisers.
 2. Direct responsibility of compensation committee. The compensation committee of an issuer shall be directly responsible for the appointment, compensation, and oversight of the work of independent legal counsel and other advisers.
 3. Rule of construction. This subsection may not be construed—
    A. to require a compensation committee to implement or act consistently with the advice or recommendations of independent legal counsel or other advisers under this subsection; or
    B. to affect the ability or obligation of a compensation committee to exercise its own judgment in fulfillment of the duties of the compensation committee.

e. **Compensation of compensation consultants, independent legal counsel, and other advisers.** Each issuer shall provide for appropriate funding, as determined by the compensation committee in its capacity as a committee of the board of directors, for payment of reasonable compensation—
 1. to a compensation consultant; and
 2. to independent legal counsel or any other adviser to the compensation committee.

f. **Commission rules.**
 1. In general. Not later than 360 days after the date of enactment of this section, the Commission shall, by rule, direct the national securities exchanges and national securities associations to prohibit the listing of any security of an issuer that is not in compliance with the requirements of this section.
 2. Opportunity to cure defects. The rules of the Commission under paragraph (1) shall provide for appropriate procedures for an issuer to have a reasonable opportunity to cure any defects that would be the basis for the prohibition under paragraph (1), before the imposition of such prohibition.
 3. Exemption authority.
    A. In general. The rules of the Commission under paragraph (1) shall permit a national securities exchange or a national securities association to exempt a category of issuers from the requirements under this section, as the national securities exchange or the national securities association determines is appropriate.
    B. Considerations. In determining appropriate exemptions under subparagraph (A), the national securities exchange or the national securities association shall take into account the potential impact of the requirements of this section on smaller reporting issuers.

g. **Controlled company exemption.**
 1. In general. This section shall not apply to any controlled company.
 2. Definition. For purposes of this section, the term 'controlled company' means an issuer—

    A.   that is listed on a national securities exchange or by a national securities association; and

    B.   that holds an election for the board of directors of the issuer in which more than 50 percent of the voting power is held by an individual, a group, or another issuer.

Section 10D – Recovery of Erroneously Awarded Compensation Policy

a.   **Listing standards.** The Commission shall, by rule, direct the national securities exchanges and national securities associations to prohibit the listing of any security of an issuer that does not comply with the requirements of this section.

b.   **Recovery of funds.** The rules of the Commission under subsection (a) shall require each issuer to develop and implement a policy providing—

    1.   for disclosure of the policy of the issuer on incentive-based compensation that is based on financial information required to be reported under the securities laws; and

    2.   that, in the event that the issuer is required to prepare an accounting restatement due to the material noncompliance of the issuer with any financial reporting requirement under the securities laws, the issuer will recover from any current or former executive officer of the issuer who received incentive-based compensation (including stock options awarded as compensation) during the 3-year period preceding the date on which the issuer is required to prepare an accounting restatement, based on the erroneous data, in excess of what would have been paid to the executive officer under the accounting restatement.

Section 12 – Registration Requirements for Securities

a.   **General requirement of registration.** It shall be unlawful for any member, broker, or dealer to effect any transaction in any security (other than an exempted security) on a national securities exchange unless a registration is effective as to such security for such exchange in accordance with the provisions of this title and the rules and regulations thereunder. The provisions of this subsection shall not apply in respect of a security futures product traded on a national securities exchange.

b.   **Procedure for registration; information.** A security may be registered on a national securities exchange by the issuer filing an application with the exchange (and filing with the Commission such duplicate originals thereof as the Commission may require), which application shall contain–

    1.   Such information, in such detail, as to the issuer and any person directly or indirectly controlling or controlled by, or under direct or indirect common control with, the issuer, and any guarantor of the security as to principal or interest or both, as the Commission may by rules and regulations require, as necessary or appropriate in the public interest or for the protection of investors, in respect of the following:

    A.   the organization, financial structure, and nature of the business;

    B.   the terms, position, rights, and privileges of the different classes of securities outstanding;

C.   the terms on which their securities are to be, and during the preceding three years have been, offered to the public or otherwise;

D.   the directors, officers, and underwriters, and each security holder of record holding more than 10 per centum of any class of any equity security of the issuer (other than an exempted security), their remuneration and their interests in the securities of, and their material contracts with, the issuer and any person directly or indirectly controlling or controlled by, or under direct or indirect common control with, the issuer;

E.   remuneration to others than directors and officers exceeding $20,000 per annum;

F.   bonus and profit-sharing arrangements;

G.   management and service contracts;

H.   options existing or to be created in respect of their securities; (I) material contracts, not made in the ordinary course of business, which are to be executed in whole or in part at or after the filing of the application or which were made not more than two years before such filing, and every material patent or contract for a material patent right shall be deemed a material contract;

I.   material contracts, not made in the ordinary course of business, which are to be executed in whole or in part at or after the filing of the application or which were made not more than two years before such filing, and every material patent or contract for a material patent right shall be deemed a material contract;

J.   balance sheets for not more than the three preceding fiscal years, certified if required by the rules and regulations of the Commission by a registered public accounting firm;

K.   profit and loss statements for not more than the three preceding fiscal years, certified if required by the rules and regulations of the Commission by a registered public accounting firm; and

L.   any further financial statements which the Commission may deem necessary or appropriate for the protection of investors.

2.   Such copies of articles of incorporation, bylaws, trust indentures, or corresponding documents by whatever name known, underwriting arrangements, and other similar documents of, and voting trust agreements with respect to, the issuer and any person directly or indirectly controlling or controlled by, or under direct or indirect common control with, the issuer as the Commission may require as necessary or appropriate for the proper protection of investors and to insure fair dealing in the security.

3.   Such copies of material contracts, referred to in paragraph (1)(I) above, as the Commission may require as necessary or appropriate for the proper protection of investors and to insure fair dealing in the security.

g.   **Registration of securities by issuer; exemptions**

1.   Every issuer which is engaged in interstate commerce, or in a business affecting interstate commerce, or whose securities are traded by use of the mails or any means or instrumentality of interstate commerce shall–

> A. within 120 days after the last day of its first fiscal year on which the issuer has total assets exceeding $10,000,000 and a class of equity security (other than an exempted security) held of record by either
>> i. 2,000 persons, or
>> ii. 500 persons who are not accredited investors (as such term is defined by the Commission) and
>
> B. in the case of an issuer that is a bank or a bank holding company, as such term is defined in section 2 of the Bank Holding Company Act of 1956, not later than 120 days after the last day of its first fiscal year ended after the effective date of this subsection, on which the issuer has total assets exceeding $10,000,000 and a class of equity security (other than an exempted security) held of record by 2,000 or more persons,

register such security by filing with the Commission a registration statement (and such copies thereof as the Commission may require) with respect to such security containing such information and documents as the Commission may specify comparable to that which is required in an application to register a security pursuant to subsection (b) of this section. Each such registration statement shall become effective sixty days after filing with the Commission or within such shorter period as the Commission may direct. Until such registration statement becomes effective it shall not be deemed filed for the purposes of section 18. Any issuer may register any class of equity security not required to be registered by filing a registration statement pursuant to the provisions of this paragraph. The Commission is authorized to extend the date upon which any issuer or class of issuers is required to register a security pursuant to the provisions of this paragraph.

4. Registration of any class of security pursuant to this subsection shall be terminated ninety days, or such shorter period as the Commission may determine, after the issuer files a certification with the Commission that the number of holders of record of such class of security is reduced to less than 300 persons, or, in the case of a bank or a bank holding company, as such term is defined in section 2 of the Bank Holding Company Act of 1956, 1,200 persons. The Commission shall after notice and opportunity for hearing deny termination of registration if it finds that the certification is untrue. Termination of registration shall be deferred pending final determination on the question of denial.

5. For the purposes of this subsection the term "class" shall include all securities of an issuer which are of substantially similar character and the holders of which enjoy substantially similar rights and privileges. The Commission may for the purpose of this subsection define by rules and regulations the terms "total assets" and "held of record" as it deems necessary or appropriate in the public interest or for the protection of investors in order to prevent circumvention of the provisions of this subsection. For purposes of this subsection, a security futures product shall not be considered a class of equity security of the issuer of the securities underlying the security futures product. For purposes of determining whether an issuer is required to register a security with the Commission pursuant to paragraph (1), the definition of 'held of record' shall not include securities held by persons who received the securities pursuant to an employee compensa-

tion plan in transactions exempted from the registration requirements of section 5 of the Securities Act of 1933.

j. **Denial, suspension, or revocation of registration; notice and hearing.** The Commission is authorized, by order, as it deems necessary or appropriate for the protection of investors to deny, to suspend the effective date of, to suspend for a period not exceeding twelve months, or to revoke the registration of a security, if the Commission finds, on the record after notice and opportunity for hearing, that the issuer, of such security has failed to comply with any provision of this title or the rules and regulations thereunder. No member of a national securities exchange, broker, or dealer shall make use of the mails or any means or instrumentality of interstate commerce to effect any transaction in, or to induce the purchase or sale of, any security the registration of which has been and is suspended or revoked pursuant to the preceding sentence.

k. **Trading suspensions; emergency authority**
    1. Trading suspensions
        If in its opinion the public interest and the protection of investors so require, the Commission is authorized by order–
        A. summarily to suspend trading in any security (other than an exempted security) for a period not exceeding 10 business days, and
        B. summarily to suspend all trading on any national securities exchange or otherwise, in securities other than exempted securities, for a period not exceeding 90 calendar days.
        The action described in subparagraph (B) shall not take effect unless the Commission notifies the President of its decision and the President notifies the Commission that the President does not disapprove of such decision. If the actions described in subparagraph (A) or (B) involve a security futures product, the Commission shall consult with and consider the views of the Commodity Futures Trading Commission.

Section 13 – Periodical and Other Reports

a. **Reports by Issuer of Security; Contents.** Every issuer of a security registered pursuant to section 12 shall file with the Commission, in accordance with such rules and regulations as the Commission may prescribe as necessary or appropriate for the proper protection of investors and to insure fair dealing in the security–
    1. such information and documents (and such copies thereof) as the Commission shall require to keep reasonably current the information and documents required to be included in or filed with an application or registration statement filed pursuant to section 12, except that the Commission may not require the filing of any material contract wholly executed before July 1, 1962.
    2. such annual reports (and such copies thereof), certified if required by the rules and regulations of the Commission by independent public accountants, and such quarterly reports (and such copies thereof), as the Commission may prescribe.
    Every issuer of a security registered on a national securities exchange shall also file a duplicate original of such information, documents, and reports with the exchange. In

any registration statement, periodic report, or other reports to be filed with the Commission, an emerging growth company need not present selected financial data in accordance with Regulation S-K Item 301 for any period prior to the earliest audited period presented in connection with its first registration statement that became effective under this Act or the Securities Act of 1933 and, with respect to any such statement or reports, an emerging growth company may not be required to comply with any new or revised financial accounting standard until such date that a company that is not an issuer (as defined under section 2(a) of the Sarbanes-Oxley Act) is required to comply with such new or revised accounting standard, if such standard applies to companies that are not issuers.

b. **Form of Report; Books, Records, and Internal Accounting; Directives**
   1. The Commission may prescribe, in regard to reports made pursuant to this title, the form or forms in which the required information shall be set forth, the items or details to be shown in the balance sheet and the earning statement, and the methods to be followed in the preparation of reports, in the appraisal or valuation of assets and liabilities, in the determination of depreciation and depletion, in the differentiation of recurring and nonrecurring income, in the differentiation of investment and operating income, and in the preparation, where the Commission deems it necessary or desirable, of separate and/or consolidated balance sheets or income accounts of any person directly or indirectly controlling or controlled by the issuer, or any person under direct or indirect common control with the issuer; but in the case of the reports of any person whose methods of accounting are prescribed under the provisions of any law of the United States, or any rule or regulation thereunder, the rules and regulations of the Commission with respect to reports shall not be inconsistent with the requirements imposed by such law or rule or regulation in respect of the same subject matter (except that such rules and regulations of the Commission may be inconsistent with such requirements to the extent that the Commission determines that the public interest or the protection of investors so requires).
   2. Every issuer which has a class of securities registered pursuant to section 12 and every issuer which is required to file reports pursuant to section 15(d) shall–
      A. make and keep books, records, and accounts, which, in reasonable detail, accurately and fairly reflect the transactions and dispositions of the assets of the issuer;
      B. devise and maintain a system of internal accounting controls sufficient to provide reasonable assurances that–
         i. transactions are executed in accordance with management's general or specific authorization;
         ii. transactions are recorded as necessary (I) to permit preparation of financial statements in conformity with generally accepted accounting principles or any other criteria applicable to such statements, and (II) to maintain accountability for assets;
         iii. access to assets is permitted only in accordance with management's general or specific authorization; and
         iv. the recorded accountability for assets is compared with the existing assets at reasonable intervals and appropriate action is taken with respect to any differences; and

       C.   notwithstanding any other provision of law, pay the allocable share of such issuer of a reasonable annual accounting support fee or fees, determined in accordance with section 109 of the Sarbanes-Oxley Act of 2002.

3.   A.   With respect to matters concerning the national security of the United States, no duty or liability under paragraph (2) of this subsection shall be imposed upon any person acting in cooperation with the head of any Federal department or agency responsible for such matters if such act in cooperation with such head of a department or agency was done upon the specific, written directive of the head of such department or agency pursuant to Presidential authority to issue such directives. Each directive issued under this paragraph shall set forth the specific facts and circumstances with respect to which the provisions of this paragraph are to be invoked. Each such directive shall, unless renewed in writing, expire one year after the date of issuance.

       B.   Each head of a Federal department or agency of the United States who issues a directive pursuant to this paragraph shall maintain a complete file of all such directives and shall, on October 1 of each year, transmit a summary of matters covered by such directives in force at any time during the previous year to the Permanent Select Committee on Intelligence of the House of Representatives and the Select Committee on Intelligence of the Senate.

4.   No criminal liability shall be imposed for failing to comply with the requirements of paragraph (2) of this subsection except as provided in paragraph (5) of this subsection.

5.   No person shall knowingly circumvent or knowingly fail to implement a system of internal accounting controls or knowingly falsify any book, record, or account described in paragraph (2).

6.   Where an issuer which has a class of securities registered pursuant to section 12 of this title or an issuer which is required to file reports pursuant to section 15(d) holds 50 per centum or less of the voting power with respect to a domestic or foreign firm, the provisions of paragraph (2) require only that the issuer proceed in good faith to use its influence, to the extent reasonable under the issuer's circumstances, to cause such domestic or foreign firm to devise and maintain a system of internal accounting controls consistent with paragraph (2). Such circumstances include the relative degree of the issuer's ownership of the domestic or foreign firm and the laws and practices governing the business operations of the country in which such firm is located. An issuer which demonstrates good faith efforts to use such influence shall be conclusively presumed to have complied with the requirements of paragraph (2).

7.   For the purpose of paragraph (2) of this subsection, the terms "reasonable assurances" and "reasonable detail" mean such level of detail and degree of assurance as would satisfy prudent officials in the conduct of their own affairs.

c.   **Alternative Reports**. If in the judgment of the Commission any report required under subsection (a) of this section is inapplicable to any specified class or classes of issuers, the Commission shall require in lieu thereof the submission of such reports of comparable character as it may deem applicable to such class or classes of issuers.

i. **Accuracy of Financial Reports.** Each financial report that contains financial statements, and that is required to be prepared in accordance with (or reconciled to) generally accepted accounting principles under this title and filed with the Commission shall reflect all material correcting adjustments that have been identified by a registered public accounting firm in accordance with generally accepted accounting principles and the rules and regulations of the Commission.

j. **Off-Balance Sheet Transactions.** Not later than 180 days after the date of enactment of the Sarbanes-Oxley Act of 2002 [enacted July 30, 2002], the Commission shall issue final rules providing that each annual and quarterly financial report required to be filed with the Commission shall disclose all material off-balance sheet transactions, arrangements, obligations (including contingent obligations), and other relationships of the issuer with unconsolidated entities or other persons, that may have a material current or future effect on financial condition, changes in financial condition, results of operations, liquidity, capital expenditures, capital resources, or significant components of revenues or expenses.

k. **Prohibition on Personal Loans to Executives**
    A. In general
        It shall be unlawful for any issuer (as defined in section 2 of the Sarbanes-Oxley Act of 2002), directly or indirectly, including through any subsidiary, to extend or maintain credit, to arrange for the extension of credit, or to renew an extension of credit, in the form of a personal loan to or for any director or executive officer (or equivalent thereof) of that issuer. An extension of credit maintained by the issuer on the date of enactment of this subsection shall not be subject to the provisions of this subsection, provided that there is no material modification to any term of any such extension of credit or any renewal of any such extension of credit on or after that date of enactment.
    B. Limitation
        Paragraph (1) does not preclude any home improvement and manufactured home loans (as that term is defined in section 5 of the Home Owners' Loan Act), consumer credit (as defined in section 103 of the Truth in Lending Act), or any extension of credit under an open end credit plan (as defined in section 103 of the Truth in Lending Act), or a charge card (as defined in section 127(c)(4)(e) of the Truth in Lending Act), or any extension of credit by a broker or dealer registered under section 15 of this title to an employee of that broker or dealer to buy, trade, or carry securities, that is permitted under rules or regulations of the Board of Governors of the Federal Reserve System pursuant to section 7 of this title (other than an extension of credit that would be used to purchase the stock of that issuer), that is–
        i.   made or provided in the ordinary course of the consumer credit business of such issuer;
        ii. of a type that is generally made available by such issuer to the public; and
        iii. made by such issuer on market terms, or terms that are no more favorable than those offered by the issuer to the general public for such extensions of credit.

C.   Rule of construction for certain loans
Paragraph (1) does not apply to any loan made or maintained by an insured depository institution (as defined in section 3 of the Federal Deposit Insurance Act), if the loan is subject to the insider lending restrictions of section 22(h) of the Federal Reserve Act.

l.   **Real Time Issuer Disclosures.** Each issuer reporting under section 13(a) or 15(d) shall disclose to the public on a rapid and current basis such additional information concerning material changes in the financial condition or operations of the issuer, in plain English, which may include trend and qualitative information and graphic presentations, as the Commission determines, by rule, is necessary or useful for the protection of investors and in the public interest

Section 14 – Proxies

a.   **Solicitation of proxies in violation of rules and regulations.** It shall be unlawful for any person, by the use of the mails or by any means or instrumentality of interstate commerce or of any facility of a national securities exchange or otherwise, in contravention of such rules and regulations as the Commission may prescribe as necessary or appropriate in the public interest or for the protection of investors, to solicit or to permit the use of his name to solicit any proxy or consent or authorization in respect of any security (other than an exempted security) registered pursuant to section 12.

e.   **Untrue statement of material fact or omission of fact with respect to tender offer.** It shall be unlawful for any person to make any untrue statement of a material fact or omit to state any material fact necessary in order to make the statements made, in the light of the circumstances under which they are made, not misleading, or to engage in any fraudulent, deceptive, or manipulative acts or practices, in connection with any tender offer or request or invitation for tenders, or any solicitation of security holders in opposition to or in favor of any such offer, request, or invitation. The Commission shall, for the purposes of this subsection, by rules and regulations define, and prescribe means reasonably designed to prevent, such acts and practices as are fraudulent, deceptive, or manipulative.

Section 14A – Shareholder Approval of Executive Compensation

a.   **Separate resolution required.**
1.   In general. Not less frequently than once every 3 years, a proxy or consent or authorization for an annual or other meeting of the shareholders for which the proxy solicitation rules of the Commission require compensation disclosure shall include a separate resolution subject to shareholder vote to approve the compensation of executives, as disclosed pursuant to section Item 402 of Regulation S-K, or any successor thereto.
2.   Frequency of vote. Not less frequently than once every 6 years, a proxy or consent or authorization for an annual or other meeting of the shareholders for which the proxy solicitation rules of the Commission require compensation disclosure shall include a separate resolution subject to shareholder vote to

    determine whether votes on the resolutions required under paragraph (1) will occur every 1, 2, or 3 years.

3.   Effective date. The proxy or consent or authorization for the first annual or other meeting of the shareholders occurring after the end of the 6-month period beginning on the date of enactment of this section shall include—

    A.   the resolution described in paragraph (1); and

    B.   a separate resolution subject to shareholder vote to determine whether votes on the resolutions required under paragraph (1) will occur every 1, 2, or 3 years.

b.   **Shareholder approval of golden parachute compensation.**

1.   Disclosure. In any proxy or consent solicitation material (the solicitation of which is subject to the rules of the Commission pursuant to subsection (a)) for a meeting of the shareholders occurring after the end of the 6-month period beginning on the date of enactment of this section, at which shareholders are asked to approve an acquisition, merger, consolidation, or proposed sale or other disposition of all or substantially all the assets of an issuer, the person making such solicitation shall disclose in the proxy or consent solicitation material, in a clear and simple form in accordance with regulations to be promulgated by the Commission, any agreements or understandings that such person has with any named executive officers of such issuer (or of the acquiring issuer, if such issuer is not the acquiring issuer) concerning any type of compensation (whether present, deferred, or contingent) that is based on or otherwise relates to the acquisition, merger, consolidation, sale, or other disposition of all or substantially all of the assets of the issuer and the aggregate total of all such compensation that may (and the conditions upon which it may) be paid or become payable to or on behalf of such executive officer.

2.   Shareholder approval. Any proxy or consent or authorization relating to the proxy or consent solicitation material containing the disclosure required by paragraph (1) shall include a separate resolution subject to shareholder vote to approve such agreements or understandings and compensation as disclosed, unless such agreements or understandings have been subject to a shareholder vote under subsection (a).

c.   **Rule of construction.** The shareholder vote referred to in subsections (a) and (b) shall not be binding on the issuer or the board of directors of an issuer, and may not be construed—

1.   as overruling a decision by such issuer or board of directors;

2.   to create or imply any change to the fiduciary duties of such issuer or board of directors;

3.   to create or imply any additional fiduciary duties for such issuer or board of directors; or

4.   to restrict or limit the ability of shareholders to make proposals for inclusion in proxy materials related to executive compensation.

d.   **Disclosure of votes.** Every institutional investment manager subject to section 13(f) shall report at least annually how it voted on any shareholder vote pursuant to subsections (a) and (b), unless such vote is otherwise required to be reported publicly by rule or regulation of the Commission.

e.   **Exemption.** The Commission may, by rule or order, exempt an issuer or class of issuers from the requirement under subsection (a) or (b). In determining whether to make an exemption under this subsection, the Commission shall take into account, among other considerations, whether the requirements under subsections (a) and (b) disproportionately burdens small issuers.

Section 14B – Corporate Governance

Not later than 180 days after the date of enactment of this subsection, the Commission shall issue rules that require an issuer to disclose in the annual proxy sent to investors the reasons why the issuer has chosen—

1.   the same person to serve as chairman of the board of directors and chief executive officer (or in equivalent positions); or
2.   different individuals to serve as chairman of the board of directors and chief executive officer (or in equivalent positions of the issuer).

Section 15 – Registration and Regulation of Brokers and Dealers

c.   **Use of manipulative or deceptive devices; contravention of rules and regulations**
4.   If the Commission finds, after notice and opportunity for a hearing, that any person subject to the provisions of section 12, 13, 14, or subsection (d) of this section or any rule or regulation thereunder has failed to comply with any such provision, rule, or regulation in any material respect, the Commission may publish its findings and issue an order requiring such person, and any person who was a cause of the failure to comply due to an act or omission the person knew or should have known would contribute to the failure to comply, to comply, or to take steps to effect compliance, with such provision or such rule or regulation thereunder upon such terms and conditions and within such time as the Commission may specify in such order.

d.   **Filing of supplementary and periodic information.**
1.   In general. Each issuer which has filed a registration statement containing an undertaking which is or becomes operative under this subsection as in effect prior to August 20, 1964, and each issuer which shall after such date file a registration statement which has become effective pursuant to the Securities Act of 1933, as amended, shall file with the Commission, in accordance with such rules and regulations as the Commission may prescribe as necessary or appropriate in the public interest or for the protection of investors, such supplementary and periodic information, documents, and reports as may be required pursuant to section 13 in respect of a security registered pursuant to section 12. The duty to file under this subsection shall be automatically suspended if and so long as any issue of securities of such issuer is registered pursuant to section 12. The duty to file under this subsection shall also be automatically suspended as to any fiscal year, other than the fiscal year within

which such registration statement became effective, if, at the beginning of such fiscal year, the securities of each class, other than any class of asset-backed securities, to which the registration statement relates are held of record by less than 300 persons, or, in the case of bank or a bank holding company, as such term is defined in section 2 of the Bank Holding Company Act of 1956, 1,200 persons. For the purposes of this subsection, the term "class" shall be construed to include all securities of an issuer which are of substantially similar character and the holders of which enjoy substantially similar rights and privileges. The Commission may, for the purpose of this subsection, define by rules and regulations the term "held of record" as it deems necessary or appropriate in the public interest or for the protection of investors in order to prevent circumvention of the provisions of this subsection. Nothing in this subsection shall apply to securities issued by a foreign government or political subdivision thereof.

2.   Asset-backed securities.

    A.   Suspension of duty to file. The Commission may, by rule or regulation, provide for the suspension or termination of the duty to file under this subsection for any class of asset-backed security, on such terms and conditions and for such period or periods as the Commission deems necessary or appropriate in the public interest or for the protection of investors.

    B.   Classification of issuers. The Commission may, for purposes of this subsection, classify issuers and prescribe requirements appropriate for each class of issuers of asset-backed securities.

Section 15D – Securities Analysts And Research Reports

a.   **Analyst protections**

The Commission, or upon the authorization and direction of the Commission, a registered securities association or national securities exchange, shall have adopted, not later than 1 year after the date of enactment of this section [enacted July 30, 2002], rules reasonably designed to address conflicts of interest that can arise when securities analysts recommend equity securities in research reports and public appearances, in order to improve the objectivity of research and provide investors with more useful and reliable information, including rules designed--

1.   to foster greater public confidence in securities research, and to protect the objectivity and independence of securities analysts, by--

    A.   restricting the prepublication clearance or approval of research reports by persons employed by the broker or dealer who are engaged in investment banking activities, or persons not directly responsible for investment research, other than legal or compliance staff;

    B.   limiting the supervision and compensatory evaluation of securities analysts to officials employed by the broker or dealer who are not engaged in investment banking activities; and

    C.   requiring that a broker or dealer and persons employed by a broker or dealer who are involved with investment banking activities may not, directly or indirectly, retaliate against or threaten to retaliate against any securities analyst employed by that broker or dealer or its affiliates as a result of an adverse, negative, or otherwise unfavorable research report that may adversely affect the present or prospective investment banking relationship of the broker or dealer with the issuer that is the subject of the research report, except that such rules may not limit the authority of a broker or dealer to discipline a securities analyst for causes other than such research report in accordance with the policies and procedures of the firm;

2. to define periods during which brokers or dealers who have participated, or are to participate, in a public offering of securities as underwriters or dealers should not publish or otherwise distribute research reports relating to such securities or to the issuer of such securities;

3. to establish structural and institutional safeguards within registered brokers or dealers to assure that securities analysts are separated by appropriate informational partitions within the firm from the review, pressure, or oversight of those whose involvement in investment banking activities might potentially bias their judgment or supervision; and

4. to address such other issues as the Commission, or such association or exchange, determines appropriate.

b. **Disclosure**

The Commission, or upon the authorization and direction of the Commission, a registered securities association or national securities exchange, shall have adopted, not later than 1 year after the date of enactment of this section [enacted July 30, 2002], rules reasonably designed to require each securities analyst to disclose in public appearances, and each registered broker or dealer to disclose in each research report, as applicable, conflicts of interest that are known or should have been known by the securities analyst or the broker or dealer, to exist at the time of the appearance or the date of distribution of the report, including--

1. the extent to which the securities analyst has debt or equity investments in the issuer that is the subject of the appearance or research report;

2. whether any compensation has been received by the registered broker or dealer, or any affiliate thereof, including the securities analyst, from the issuer that is the subject of the appearance or research report, subject to such exemptions as the Commission may determine appropriate and necessary to prevent disclosure by virtue of this paragraph of material non-public information regarding specific potential future investment banking transactions of such issuer, as is appropriate in the public interest and consistent with the protection of investors;

3. whether an issuer, the securities of which are recommended in the appearance or research report, currently is, or during the 1-year period preceding the date of the appearance or date of distribution of the report has been, a client of the registered broker or dealer, and if so, stating the types of services provided to the issuer;

4. whether the securities analyst received compensation with respect to a research report, based upon (among any other factors) the investment banking revenues (either generally or specifically earned from the issuer being analyzed) of the registered broker or dealer; and

5. such other disclosures of conflicts of interest that are material to investors, research analysts, or the broker or dealer as the Commission, or such association or exchange, determines appropriate.

c. **Limitation.** Notwithstanding subsection (a) or any other provision of law, neither the Commission nor any national securities association registered under section 15A may adopt or maintain any rule or regulation in connection with an initial public offering of the common equity of an emerging growth company—

1. restricting, based on functional role, which associated persons of a broker, dealer, or member of a national securities association, may arrange for communications between a securities analyst and a potential investor; or

2. restricting a securities analyst from participating in any communications with the management of an emerging growth company that is also attended by any other associated person of a broker, dealer, or member of a national securities association whose functional role is other than as a securities analyst

d. **Definitions**
In this section—

1. the term 'securities analyst' means any associated person of a registered broker or dealer that is principally responsible for, and any associated person who reports directly or indirectly to a securities analyst in connection with, the preparation of the substance of a research report, whether or not any such person has the job title of 'securities analyst'; and

2. the term 'research report' means a written or electronic communication that includes an analysis of equity securities of individual companies or industries, and that provides information reasonably sufficient upon which to base an investment decision.

Section 15E – Registration of Nationally Recognized Statistical Rating Organizations

a. **Registration Procedures**

1. Application for registration.

    A. *In general.* A credit rating agency that elects to be treated as a nationally recognized statistical rating organization for purposes of this title (in this section referred to as the "applicant"), shall furnish to the Commission an application for registration, in such form as the Commission shall require, by rule or regulation issued in accordance with subsection (n), and containing the information described in subparagraph (B).

    B. *Required information.* An application for registration under this section shall contain information regarding--

        i.   credit ratings performance measurement statistics over short-term, mid-term, and long-term periods (as applicable) of the applicant;

        ii.   the procedures and methodologies that the applicant uses in determining credit ratings;

        iii. policies or procedures adopted and implemented by the applicant to prevent the misuse, in violation of this title (or the rules and regulations hereunder), of material, nonpublic information;

        iv.   the organizational structure of the applicant;

        v.   whether or not the applicant has in effect a code of ethics, and if not, the reasons therefor;

        vi.   any conflict of interest relating to the issuance of credit ratings by the applicant;

vii. the categories described in any of clauses (i) through (v) of section 3(a)(62)(B) with respect to which the applicant intends to apply for registration under this section;

viii. on a confidential basis, a list of the 20 largest issuers and subscribers that use the credit rating services of the applicant, by amount of net revenues received therefrom in the fiscal year immediately preceding the date of submission of the application;

ix. on a confidential basis, as to each applicable category of obligor described in any of clauses (i) through (v) of section 3(a)(62)(B), written certifications described in subparagraph (C), except as provided in subparagraph (D); and

x. any other information and documents concerning the applicant and any person associated with such applicant as the Commission, by rule, may prescribe as necessary or appropriate in the public interest or for the protection of investors.

C. *Written certifications.* Written certifications required by subparagraph (B)(ix)--

i. shall be provided from not fewer than 10 qualified institutional buyers, none of which is affiliated with the applicant;

ii. may address more than one category of obligors described in any of clauses (i) through (v) of section 3(a)(62)(B);

iii. shall include not fewer than 2 certifications for each such category of obligor; and

iv. shall state that the qualified institutional buyer—

I. meets the definition of a qualified institutional buyer under section 3(a)(64); and

II. has used the credit ratings of the applicant for at least the 3 years immediately preceding the date of the certification in the subject category or categories of obligors.

D. *Exemption from certification requirement.* A written certification under subparagraph (B)(ix) is not required with respect to any credit rating agency which has received, or been the subject of, a no-action letter from the staff of the Commission prior to August 2, 2006, stating that such staff would not recommend enforcement action against any broker or dealer that considers credit ratings issued by such credit rating agency to be ratings from a nationally recognized statistical rating organization.

E. *Limitation on liability of qualified institutional buyers.* No qualified institutional buyer shall be liable in any private right of action for any opinion or statement expressed in a certification made pursuant to subparagraph (B)(ix).

2. Review of application.

A. *Initial determination.* Not later than 90 days after the date on which the application for registration is furnished to the Commission under paragraph (1) (or within such longer period as to which the applicant consents) the Commission shall--

i. by order, grant such registration for ratings in the subject category or categories of obligors, as described in clauses (i) through (v) of section 3(a)(62)(B); or

ii. institute proceedings to determine whether registration should be denied.

B. *Conduct of proceedings.*

  i. Content. Proceedings referred to in subparagraph (A)(ii) shall--

  I. include notice of the grounds for denial under consideration and an opportunity for hearing; and

  II. be concluded not later than 120 days after the date on which the application for registration is furnished to the Commission under paragraph (1).

  ii. Determination. At the conclusion of such proceedings, the Commission, by order, shall grant or deny such application for registration.

  iii. Extension authorized. The Commission may extend the time for conclusion of such proceedings for not longer than 90 days, if it finds good cause for such extension and publishes its reasons for so finding, or for such longer period as to which the applicant consents.

C. *Grounds for decision.* The Commission shall grant registration under this subsection--

  i. if the Commission finds that the requirements of this section are satisfied; and

  ii. unless the Commission finds (in which case the Commission shall deny such registration) that--

  I. the applicant does not have adequate financial and managerial resources to consistently produce credit ratings with integrity and to materially comply with the procedures and methodologies disclosed under paragraph (1)(B) and with subsections (g), (h), (i), and (j); or

  II. if the applicant were so registered, its registration would be subject to suspension or revocation under subsection (d).

3. Public availability of information. Subject to section 24, the Commission shall, by rule, require a nationally recognized statistical rating organization, upon the granting of registration under this section, to make the information and documents submitted to the Commission in its completed application for registration, or in any amendment submitted under paragraph (1) or (2) of subsection (b), publicly available on its website, or through another comparable, readily accessible means, except as provided in clauses (viii) and (ix) of paragraph (1)(B).

b. **Update of registration.**

1. Update. Each nationally recognized statistical rating organization shall promptly amend its application for registration under this section if any information or document provided therein becomes materially inaccurate, except that a nationally recognized statistical rating organization is not required to amend--

A. the information required to be filed under subsection (a)(1)(B)(i) by furnishing information under this paragraph, but shall amend such information in the annual submission of the organization under paragraph (2) of this subsection; or

B. the certifications required to be provided under subsection (a)(1)(B)(ix) by filing information under this paragraph.

2. Certification. Not later than 90 days after the end of each calendar year, each nationally recognized statistical rating organization shall file with the Commission an amendment to its registration, in such form as the Commission, by rule, may prescribe as necessary or appropriate in the public interest or for the protection of investors--

A. certifying that the information and documents in the application for registration of such nationally recognized statistical rating organization (other than the certifications required under subsection (a)(1)(B)(ix)) continue to be accurate; and

B. listing any material change that occurred to such information or documents during the previous calendar year.

c. **Accountability for ratings procedures.**

1. Authority. The Commission shall have exclusive authority to enforce the provisions of this section in accordance with this title with respect to any nationally recognized statistical rating organization, if such nationally recognized statistical rating organization issues credit ratings in material contravention of those procedures relating to such nationally recognized statistical rating organization, including procedures relating to the prevention of misuse of nonpublic information and conflicts of interest, that such nationally recognized statistical rating organization--

A. includes in its application for registration under subsection (a)(1)(B)(ii); or

B. makes and disseminates in reports pursuant to section 17(a) or the rules and regulations thereunder.

2. Limitation. The rules and regulations that the Commission may prescribe pursuant to this title, as they apply to nationally recognized statistical rating organizations, shall be narrowly tailored to meet the requirements of this title applicable to nationally recognized statistical rating organizations. Notwithstanding any other provision of this section, or any other provision of law, neither the Commission nor any State (or political subdivision thereof) may regulate the substance of credit ratings or the procedures and methodologies by which any nationally recognized statistical rating organization determines credit ratings. Nothing in this paragraph may be construed to afford a defense against any action or proceeding brought by the Commission to enforce the antifraud provisions of the securities laws.

3. Internal controls over processes for determining credit ratings.

A. In general. Each nationally recognized statistical rating organization shall establish, maintain, enforce, and document an effective internal control structure governing the implementation of and adherence to policies, procedures, and methodologies for determining credit ratings, taking into consideration such factors as the Commission may prescribe, by rule.

B. Attestation requirement. The Commission shall prescribe rules requiring each nationally recognized statistical rating organization to submit to the Commission an annual internal controls report, which shall contain—

i. a description of the responsibility of the management of the nationally recognized statistical rating organization in establishing and maintaining an effective internal control structure under subparagraph (A);

ii.   an assessment of the effectiveness of the internal control structure of the nationally recognized statistical rating organization; and

iii.   the attestation of the chief executive officer, or equivalent individual, of the nationally recognized statistical rating organization.

d. **Censure, denial, or suspension of registration; notice and hearing**.

1.   In general. The Commission, by order, shall censure, place limitations on the activities, functions, or operations of, suspend for a period not exceeding 12 months, or revoke the registration of any nationally recognized statistical rating organization, or with respect to any person who is associated with, who is seeking to become associated with, or, at the time of the alleged misconduct, who was associated or was seeking to become associated with a nationally recognized statistical rating organization, the Commission, by order, shall censure, place limitations on the activities or functions of such person, suspend for a period not exceeding 1 year, or bar such person from being associated with a nationally recognized statistical rating organization, if the Commission finds, on the record after notice and opportunity for hearing, that such censure, placing of limitations, suspension, bar, or revocation is necessary for the protection of investors and in the public interest and that such nationally recognized statistical rating organization, or any person associated with such an organization, whether prior to or subsequent to becoming so associated--

A.   has committed or omitted any act, or is subject to an order or finding, enumerated in any time thereafter, of subparagraph (A), (D), (E), (H), or (G) of section 15(b)(4), has been convicted of any offense specified in section 15(b)(4)(B), or is enjoined from any action, conduct, or practice specified in subparagraph (C) of section 15(b)(4), during the 10-year period preceding the date of commencement of the proceedings under this subsection, or at any time thereafter;

B.   has been convicted during the 10-year period preceding the date on which an application for registration is furnished to the Commission under this section, or at any time thereafter of –

i.   any crime that is punishable by imprisonment for 1 or more years, and that is not described in section 15(b)(4)(B); or

ii.   a substantially equivalent crime by a foreign court of competent jurisdiction;

C.   is subject to any order of the Commission barring or suspending the right of the person to be associated with a nationally recognized statistical rating organization;

D.   fails to file the certifications required under subsection (b)(2);

E.   fails to maintain adequate financial and managerial resources to consistently produce credit ratings with integrity;

F.   has failed reasonably to supervise, with a view to preventing a violation of the securities laws, an individual who commits such a violation, if the individual is subject to the supervision of that person.

2.   Suspension or revocation for particular class of securities.

    A. In general. The Commission may temporarily suspend or permanently revoke the registration of a nationally recognized statistical rating organization with respect to a particular class or subclass of securities, if the Commission finds, on the record after notice and opportunity for hearing, that the nationally recognized statistical rating organization does not have adequate financial and managerial resources to consistently produce credit ratings with integrity.

    B. Considerations. In making any determination under subparagraph (A), the Commission shall consider—

        i. whether the nationally recognized statistical rating organization has failed over a sustained period of time, as determined by the Commission, to produce ratings that are accurate for that class or subclass of securities; and

        ii. such other factors as the Commission may determine.

e. **Termination of registration.**

    1. Voluntary withdrawal. A nationally recognized statistical rating organization may, upon such terms and conditions as the Commission may establish as necessary in the public interest or for the protection of investors, withdraw from registration by furnishing a written notice of withdrawal to the Commission.

    2. Commission authority. In addition to any other authority of the Commission under this title, if the Commission finds that a nationally recognized statistical rating organization is no longer in existence or has ceased to do business as a credit rating agency, the Commission, by order, shall cancel the registration under this section of such nationally recognized statistical rating organization.

f. **Representations.**

    1. Ban on representations of sponsorship by united states or agency thereof. It shall be unlawful for any nationally recognized statistical rating organization to represent or imply in any manner whatsoever that such nationally recognized statistical rating organization has been designated, sponsored, recommended, or approved, or that the abilities or qualifications thereof have in any respect been passed upon, by the United States or any agency, officer, or employee thereof.Ban on representation as NRSRO of unregistered credit rating agencies. It shall be unlawful for any credit rating agency that is not registered under this section as a nationally recognized statistical rating organization to state that such credit rating agency is a nationally recognized statistical rating organization registered under this title.

    2. Statement of registration under Securities Exchange Act of 1934 provisions. No provision of paragraph (1) shall be construed to prohibit a statement that a nationally recognized statistical rating organization is a nationally recognized statistical rating organization under this title, if such statement is true in fact and if the effect of such registration is not misrepresented.

g. **Prevention of misuse of nonpublic information.**

    1. Organization policies and procedures. Each nationally recognized statistical rating organization shall establish, maintain, and enforce written policies and

        procedures reasonably designed, taking into consideration the nature of the business of such nationally recognized statistical rating organization, to prevent the misuse in violation of this title, or the rules or regulations hereunder, of material, nonpublic information by such nationally recognized statistical rating organization or any person associated with such nationally recognized statistical rating organization.

2.   Commission authority. The Commission shall issue final rules in accordance with subsection (n) to require specific policies or procedures that are reasonably designed to prevent misuse in violation of this title (or the rules or regulations hereunder) of material, nonpublic information.

h.   **Management of conflicts of interest.**

    1.   Organization policies and procedures. Each nationally recognized statistical rating organization shall establish, maintain, and enforce written policies and procedures reasonably designed, taking into consideration the nature of the business of such nationally recognized statistical rating organization and affiliated persons and affiliated companies thereof, to address and manage any conflicts of interest that can arise from such business.

    2.   Commission authority. The Commission shall issue final rules in accordance with subsection (n) to prohibit, or require the management and disclosure of, any conflicts of interest relating to the issuance of credit ratings by a nationally recognized statistical rating organization, including, without limitation, conflicts of interest relating to--

       A. the manner in which a nationally recognized statistical rating organization is compensated by the obligor, or any affiliate of the obligor, for issuing credit ratings or providing related services;

       B. the provision of consulting, advisory, or other services by a nationally recognized statistical rating organization, or any person associated with such nationally recognized statistical rating organization, to the obligor, or any affiliate of the obligor;

       C. business relationships, ownership interests, or any other financial or personal interests between a nationally recognized statistical rating organization, or any person associated with such nationally recognized statistical rating organization, and the obligor, or any affiliate of the obligor; any affiliation of a nationally recognized statistical rating organization, or any person associated with such nationally recognized statistical rating organization, with any person that underwrites the securities or money market instruments that are the subject of a credit rating; and

       E. any other potential conflict of interest, as the Commission deems necessary or appropriate in the public interest or for the protection of investors.

    3.   Separation of ratings from sales and marketing.

       A. Rules required. The Commission shall issuerules to prevent the sales and marketing considerationsof a nationally recognized statistical rating organization from influencing the production of ratings by the nationally recognized statistical rating organization.

       B. Contents of rules. The rules issued under subparagraph (A) shall provide for—

      i.   exceptions for small nationally recognized statistical rating organizations with respect to which the Commission determines that the separation of the production of ratings and sales and marketing activities is not appropriate; and

      ii.   suspension or revocation of the registration of a nationally recognized statistical rating organization, if the Commission finds, on the record, after notice and opportunity for a hearing, that—

          I.   the nationally recognized statistical rating organization has committed a violation of a rule issued under this subsection; and

          II. the violation of a rule issued under this subsection affected a rating.

4.   Look-back requirement.

    A. Review by the nationally recognized statistical rating organization. Each nationally recognized statistical rating organization shall establish, maintain, and enforce policies and procedures reasonably designed to ensure that, in any case in which an employee of a person subject to a credit rating of the nationally recognized statistical rating organization or the issuer, underwriter, or sponsor of a security or money market instrument subject to a credit rating of the nationally recognized statistical rating organization was employed by the nationally recognized statistical rating organization and participated in any capacity in determining credit ratings for the person or the securities or money market instruments during the 1-year period preceding the date an action was taken with respect to the credit rating, the nationally recognized statistical rating organization shall—

      i.   conduct a review to determine whether any conflicts of interest of the employee influenced the credit rating; and

      ii. take action to revise the rating if appropriate, in accordance with such rules as the Commission shall prescribe.

    B. Review by Commission.

      i.   In general. The Commission shall conduct periodic reviews of the policies described in subparagraph (A) and the implementation of the policies at each nationally recognized statistical rating organization to ensure they are reasonably designed and implemented to most effectively eliminate conflicts of interest.

      ii. Timing of reviews. The Commission shall review the code of ethics and conflict of interest policy of each nationally recognized statistical rating organization—

          I.   not less frequently than annually; and

          II. whenever such policies are materially modified or amended.

5.   Report to Commission on certain employment transitions.

    A. Report required. Each nationally recognized statistical rating organization shall report to the Commission any case such organization knows or can reasonably be expected to know where a person associated with such organization within the previous 5 years obtains employment with any obligor, issuer, underwriter, or sponsor of a security or money market instrument for which the organization issued a credit rating during the 12-month period prior to such employment, if such employee—

      ii. was a senior officer of such organization;

        iii. participated in any capacity in determining credit ratings for such obligor, issuer, underwriter, or sponsor; or

        iv. supervised an employee described in clause (ii).

    B. Public disclosure. Upon receiving such a report, the Commission shall make such information publicly available.

i. **Prohibited conduct.**

    1. Prohibited acts and practices. The Commission shall issue final rules in accordance with subsection (n) to prohibit any act or practice relating to the issuance of credit ratings by a nationally recognized statistical rating organization that the Commission determines to be unfair, coercive, or abusive, including any act or practice relating to—

        A. conditioning or threatening to condition the issuance of a credit rating on the purchase by the obligor or an affiliate thereof of other services or products, including pre-credit rating assessment products, of the nationally recognized statistical rating organization or any person associated with such nationally recognized statistical rating organization;

        B. lowering or threatening to lower a credit rating on, or refusing to rate, securities or money market instruments issued by an asset pool or as part of any asset-backed or mortgage-backed securities transaction, unless a portion of the assets within such pool or part of such transaction, as applicable, also is rated by the nationally recognized statistical rating organization; or

        C. modifying or threatening to modify a credit rating or otherwise departing from its adopted systematic procedures and methodologies in determining credit ratings, based on whether the obligor, or an affiliate of the obligor, purchases or will purchase the credit rating or any other service or product of the nationally recognized statistical rating organization or any person associated with such organization.

    2. Rule of construction. Nothing in paragraph (1), or in any rules or regulations adopted thereunder, may be construed to modify, impair, or supersede the operation of any of the antitrust laws (as defined in the first section of the Clayton Act, except that such term includes section 5 of the Federal Trade Commission Act, to the extent that such section 5 applies to unfair methods of competition).

m. **Accountability.**

    1. In general. The enforcement and penalty provisions of this title shall apply to statements made by a credit rating agency in the same manner and to the same extent as such provisions apply to statements made by a registered public accounting firm or a securities analyst under the securities laws, and such statements shall not be deemed forward-looking statements for the purposes of section 21E.

    2. Rulemaking. The Commission shall issue such rules as may be necessary to carry out this subsection.

o. **NRSROs subject to Commission authority.**

    1. In general. No provision of the laws of any State or political subdivision thereof requiring the registration, licensing, or qualification as a credit rating agency or

a nationally recognized statistical rating organization shall apply to any nationally recognized statistical rating organization or person employed by or working under the control of a nationally recognized statistical rating organization.

2. Limitation. Nothing in this subsection prohibits the securities commission (or any agency or office performing like functions) of any State from investigating and bringing an enforcement action with respect to fraud or deceit against any nationally recognized statistical rating organization or person associated with a nationally recognized statistical rating organization.

q. **Transparency of rating performance.**

1. Rulemaking required. The Commission shall, by rule, require that each nationally recognized statistical rating organization publicly disclose information on the initial credit ratings determined by the nationally recognized statistical rating organization for each type of obligor, security, and money market instrument, and any subsequent changes to such credit ratings, for the purpose of allowing users of credit ratings to evaluate the accuracy of ratings and compare the performance of ratings by different nationally recognized statistical rating organizations.

2. Content. The rules of the Commission under this subsection shall require, at a minimum, disclosures that—

   A. are comparable among nationally recognized statistical rating organizations, to allow users of credit ratings to compare the performance of credit ratings across nationally recognized statistical rating organizations;

   B. are clear and informative for investors having a wide range of sophistication who use or might use credit ratings;

   C. include performance information over a range of years and for a variety of types of credit ratings, including for credit ratings withdrawn by the nationally recognized statistical rating organization;

   D. are published and made freely available by the nationally recognized statistical rating organization, on an easily accessible portion of its website, and in writing, when requested;

   E. are appropriate to the business model of a nationally recognized statistical rating organization; and

   F. each nationally recognized statistical rating organization include an attestation with any credit rating it issues affirming that no part of the rating was influenced by any other business activities, that the rating was based solely on the merits of the instruments being rated, and that such rating was an independent evaluation of the risks and merits of the instrument.

r. **Credit rating methodologies.** The Commission shall prescribe rules, for the protection of investors and in the public interest, with respect to the procedures and methodologies, including qualitative and quantitative data and models, used by nationally recognized statistical rating organizations that require each nationally recognized statistical rating organization—

1. to ensure that credit ratings are determined using procedures and methodologies, including qualitative and quantitative data and models, that are—

      A.   approved by the board of the nationally recognized statistical rating organization, a body performing a function similar to that of a board; and

      B.   in accordance with the policies and procedures of the nationally recognized statistical rating organization for the development and modification of credit rating procedures and methodologies;

2.   to ensure that when material changes to credit rating procedures and methodologies (including changes to qualitative and quantitative data and models) are made, that—

      A.   the changes are applied consistently to all credit ratings to which the changed procedures and methodologies apply;

      B.   to the extent that changes are made to credit rating surveillance procedures and methodologies, the changes are applied to then-current credit ratings by the nationally recognized statistical rating organization within a reasonable time period determined by the Commission, by rule; and

      C.   the nationally recognized statistical rating organization publicly discloses the reason for the change; and

3.   to notify users of credit ratings—

      A.   of the version of a procedure or methodology, including the qualitative methodology or quantitative inputs, used with respect to a particular credit rating;

      B.   when a material change is made to a procedure or methodology, including to a qualitative model or quantitative inputs;

      C.   when a significant error is identified in a procedure or methodology, including a qualitative or quantitative model, that may result in credit rating actions; and

      D.   of the likelihood of a material change described in subparagraph (B) resulting in a change in current credit ratings.

s.   **Transparency of credit rating methodologies and information reviewed.**

1.   Form for disclosures. The Commission shall require, by rule, each nationally recognized statistical rating organization to prescribe a form to accompany the publication of each credit rating that discloses—

      A.   information relating to—

          i.   the assumptions underlying the credit rating procedures and methodologies;

          ii.   the data that was relied on to determine the credit rating; and

          iii.   if applicable, how the nationally recognized statistical rating organization used servicer or remittance reports, and with what frequency, to conduct surveillance of the credit rating; and

      B.   information that can be used by investors and other users of credit ratings to better understand credit ratings in each class of credit rating issued by the nationally recognized statistical rating organization.

2.   Format. The form developed under paragraph (1) shall—

      A.   be easy to use and helpful for users of credit ratings to understand the information contained in the report;

      B.   require the nationally recognized statistical rating organization to provide the content described in paragraph (3)(B) in a manner that is directly comparable across types of securities; and

      C. be made readily available to users of credit ratings, in electronic or paper form, as the Commission may, by rule, determine.

3.   Content of form.

      A. Qualitiative content.   Each nationally recognized statistical rating organization shall disclose on the form developed under paragraph (1)—

           i.   the credit ratings produced by the nationally recognized statistical rating organization;

          ii. the main assumptions and principles used in constructing procedures and methodologies, including qualitative methodologies and quantitative inputs and assumptions about the correlation of defaults across underlying assets used in rating structured products;

        iii. the potential limitations of the credit ratings, and the types of risks excluded from the credit ratings that the nationally recognized statistical rating organization does not comment on, including liquidity, market, and other risks;

        iv. information on the uncertainty of the credit rating, including—

              I.   information on the reliability, accuracy, and quality of the data relied on in determining the credit rating; and

             II. a statement relating to the extent to which data essential to the determination of the credit rating were reliable or limited, including—

                  aa. any limits on the scope of historical data; and

                  bb. any limits in accessibility to certain documents or other types of information that would have better informed the credit rating;

          v.   whether and to what extent third party due diligence services have been used by the nationally recognized statistical rating organization, a description of the information that such third party reviewed in conducting due diligence services, and a description of the findings or conclusions of such third party;

          vi. a description of the data about any obligor, issuer, security, or money market instrument that were relied upon for the purpose of determining the credit rating;

        vii. a statement containing an overall assessment of the quality of information available and considered in producing a rating for an obligor, security, or money market instrument, in relation to the quality of information available to the nationally recognized statistical rating organization in rating similar issuances;

       viii. information relating to conflicts of interest of the nationally recognized statistical rating organization; and

        ix. such additional information as the Commission may require.

      B. Quantitative context. Each nationally recognized statistical rating organization shall disclose on the form developed under this subsection—

           i.   an explanation or measure of the potential volatility of the credit rating, including—

              I.   any factors that might lead to a change in the credit ratings; and

             II. the magnitude of the change that a user can expect under different market conditions;

        ii. information on the content of the rating, including—
            I. the historical performance of the rating; and
            II. the expected probability of default and the expected loss in the event of default;
       iii. information on the sensitivity of the rating to assumptions made by the nationally recognized statistical rating organization, including—
            I. 5 assumptions made in the ratings process that, without accounting for any other factor, would have the greatest impact on a rating if the assumptions were proven false or inaccurate; and
            II. an analysis, using specific examples, of how each of the 5 assumptions identified under subclause (I) impacts a rating;
       iv. such additional information as may be required by the Commission.

4.   Due diligence services for asset-backed securities.

    A. Findings. The issuer or underwriter of any asset-backed security shall make publicly available the findings and conclusions of any third-party due diligence report obtained by the issuer or underwriter.

    B. Certification required. In any case in which third-party due diligence services are employed by a nationally recognized statistical rating organization, an issuer, or an underwriter, the person providing the due diligence services shall provide to any nationally recognized statistical rating organization that produces a rating to which such services relate, written certification, as provided in subparagraph (C).

    C. Format and content. The Commission shall establish the appropriate format and content for the written certifications required under subparagraph (B), to ensure that providers of due diligence services have conducted a thorough review of data, documentation, and other relevant information necessary for a nationally recognized statistical rating organization to provide an accurate rating.

    D. Disclosure of certification. The Commission shall adopt rules requiring a nationally recognized statistical rating organization, at the time at which the nationally recognized statistical rating organization produces a rating, to disclose the certification described in subparagraph (B) to the public in a manner that allows the public to determine the adequacy and level of due diligence services provided by a third party.

t. **Corporate governance, organization, and management of conflicts of interest.**

  1.   Board of directors. Each nationally recognized statistical rating organization shall have a board of directors.

  2.   Independent directors.

    A. In general. At least 1/2 of the board of directors, but not fewer than 2 of the members thereof, shall be independent of the nationally recognized statistical rating agency. A portion of the independent directors shall include users of ratings from a nationally recognized statistical rating organization.

    B. Independence determination. In order to be considered independent for purposes of this subsection, a member of the board of directors of a nationally recognized statistical rating organization—
       i. may not, other than in his or her capacity as a member of the board of directors or any committee thereof—

I.   accept any consulting, advisory, or other compensatory fee from the nationally recognized statistical rating organization; or

II. be a person associated with the nationally recognized statistical rating organization or with any affiliated company thereof; and

ii. shall be disqualified from any deliberation involving a specific rating in which the independent board member has a financial interest in the outcome of the rating.

C.   Compensation and term. The compensation of the independent members of the board of directors of a nationally recognized statistical rating organization shall not be linked to the business performance of the nationally recognized statistical rating organization, and shall be arranged so as to ensure the independence of their judgment. The term of office of the independent directors shall be for a pre-agreed fixed period, not to exceed 5 years, and shall not be renewable.

3.   Duties of board of directors. In addition to the overall responsibilities of the board of directors, the board shall oversee—

A.   the establishment, maintenance, and enforcement of policies and procedures for determining credit ratings;

B.   the establishment, maintenance, and enforcement of policies and procedures to address, manage, and disclose any conflicts of interest;

C.   the effectiveness of the internal control system with respect to policies and procedures for determining credit ratings; and

D.   the compensation and promotion policies and practices of the nationally recognized statistical rating organization.

4.   Treatment of NRSRO subsidiaries. If a nationally recognized statistical rating organization is a subsidiary of a parent entity, the board of the directors of the parent entity may satisfy the requirements of this subsection by assigning to a committee of such board of directors the duties under paragraph (3), if—

A.   at least 1/2 of the members of the committee (including the chairperson of the committee) are independent, as defined in this section; and

B.   at least 1 member of the committee is a user of ratings from a nationally recognized statistical rating organization.

5.   Exception authority. If the Commission finds that compliance with the provisions of this subsection present an unreasonable burden on a small nationally recognized statistical rating organization, the Commission may permit the nationally recognized statistical rating organization to delegate such responsibilities to a committee that includes at least one individual who is a user of ratings of a nationally recognized statistical rating organization.

u.   **Duty to report tips alleging material violations of law.**

1.   Duty to report. Each nationally recognized statistical rating organization shall refer to the appropriate law enforcement or regulatory authorities any information that the nationally recognized statistical rating organization receives from a third party and finds credible that alleges that an issuer of securities rated by the nationally recognized statistical rating organization has committed or is committing a material violation of law that has not been adjudicated by a Federal or State court.

2.   Rule of construction. Nothing in paragraph (1) may be construed to require a nationally recognized statistical rating organization to verify the accuracy of the information described in paragraph (1).

v.   **Information from sources other than the issuer.**
In producing a credit rating, a nationally recognized statistical rating organization shall consider information about an issuer that the nationally recognized statistical rating organization has, or receives from a source other than the issuer or underwriter, that the nationally recognized statistical rating organization finds credible and potentially significant to a rating decision.

Section 15G – Credit Risk Retention

a.   **Definitions.** In this section—
     1.   the term 'Federal banking agencies' means the Office of the Comptroller of the Currency, the Board of Governors of the Federal Reserve System, and the Federal Deposit Insurance Corporation;
     2.   the term 'insured depository institution' has the same meaning as in section 3(c) of the Federal Deposit Insurance Act;
     3.   the term 'securitizer' means—
         A.   an issuer of an asset-backed security; or
         B.   a person who organizes and initiates an asset-backed securities transaction by selling or transferring assets, either directly or indirectly, including through an affiliate, to the issuer; and
     4.   the term 'originator' means a person who—
         A.   through the extension of credit or otherwise, creates a financial asset that collateralizes an asset-backed security; and
         B.   sells an asset directly or indirectly to a securitizer.

b.   **Regulations required.**
     1.   In general. Not later than 270 days after the date of enactment of this section, the Federal banking agencies and the Commission shall jointly prescribe regulations to require any securitizer to retain an economic interest in a portion of the credit risk for any asset that the securitizer, through the issuance of an asset-backed security, transfers, sells, or conveys to a third party.
     2.   Residential mortgages. Not later than 270 days after the date of the enactment of this section, the Federal banking agencies, the Commission, the Secretary of Housing and Urban Development, and the Federal Housing Finance Agency, shall jointly prescribe regulations to require any securitizer to retain an economic interest in a portion of the credit risk for any residential mortgage asset that the securitizer, through the issuance of an asset-backed security, transfers, sells, or conveys to a third party.

c.   **Standards for regulations.**
     1.   Standards. The regulations prescribed under subsection (b) shall—
         A.   prohibit a securitizer from directly or indirectly hedging or otherwise transferring the credit risk that the securitizer is required to retain with respect to an asset;

B. require a securitizer to retain—
    i. not less than 5 percent of the credit risk for any asset—
        I. that is not a qualified residential mortgage that is transferred, sold, or conveyed through the issuance of an asset-backed security by the securitizer; or
        II. that is a qualified residential mortgage that is transferred, sold, or conveyed through the issuance of an asset-backed security by the securitizer, if 1 or more of the assets that collateralize the asset-backed security are not qualified residential mortgages; or
    ii. less than 5 percent of the credit risk for an asset that is not a qualified residential mortgage that is transferred, sold, or conveyed through the issuance of an asset-backed security by the securitizer, if the originator of the asset meets the underwriting standards prescribed under paragraph (2)(B);

C. specify—
    i. the permissible forms of risk retention for purposes of this section;
    ii. the minimum duration of the risk retention required under this section; and
    iii. that a securitizer is not required to retain any part of the credit risk for an asset that is transferred, sold or conveyed through the issuance of an asset-backed security by the securitizer, if all of the assets that collateralize the asset-backed security are qualified residential mortgages;

D. apply, regardless of whether the securitizer is an insured depository institution;

E. with respect to a commercial mortgage, specify the permissible types, forms, and amounts of risk retention that would meet the requirements of subparagraph (B), which in the determination of the Federal banking agencies and the Commission may include—
    i. retention of a specified amount or percentage of the total credit risk of the asset;
    ii. retention of the first-loss position by a third-party purchaser that specifically negotiates for the purchase of such first loss position, holds adequate financial resources to back losses, provides due diligence on all individual assets in the pool before the issuance of the asset-backed securities, and meets the same standards for risk retention as the Federal banking agencies and the Commission require of the securitizer;
    iii. a determination by the Federal banking agencies and the Commission that the underwriting standards and controls for the asset are adequate; and
    iv. provision of adequate representations and warranties and related enforcement mechanisms; and

F. establish appropriate standards for retention of an economic interest with respect to collateralized debt obligations, securities collateralized by collateralized debt obligations, and similar instruments collateralized by other asset-backed securities; and

G. provide for—
    i. a total or partial exemption of any securitization, as may be appropriate in the public interest and for the protection of investors;
    ii. a total or partial exemption for the securitization of an asset issued or guaranteed by the United States, or an agency of the United States, as the Federal banking agencies and the Commission jointly determine appropriate in the public interest and for the protection of investors, except that, for purposes of this clause, the Federal National Mortgage Association and the Federal Home Loan Mortgage Corporation are not agencies of the United States;
    iii. a total or partial exemption for any asset-backed security that is a security issued or guaranteed by any State of the United States, or by any political subdivision of a State or territory, or by any public instrumentality of a State or territory that is exempt from the registration requirements of the Securities Act of 1933 by reason of section 3(a)(2) of that Act, or a security defined as a qualified scholarship funding bond in section 150(d)(2) of the Internal Revenue Code of 1986, as may be appropriate in the public interest and for the protection of investors; and
    iv. the allocation of risk retention obligations between a securitizer and an originator in the case of a securitizer that purchases assets from an originator, as the Federal banking agencies and the Commission jointly determine appropriate.

2. Asset classes.
    A. Asset classes. The regulations prescribed under subsection (b) shall establish asset classes with separate rules for securitizers of different classes of assets, including residential mortgages, commercial mortgages, commercial loans, auto loans, and any other class of assets that the Federal banking agencies and the Commission deem appropriate.
    B. Contents. For each asset class established under subparagraph (A), the regulations prescribed under subsection (b) shall include underwriting standards established by the Federal banking agencies that specify the terms, conditions, and characteristics of a loan within the asset class that indicate a low credit risk with respect to the loan.

d. **Originators.** In determining how to allocate risk retention obligations between a securitizer and an originator under subsection (c)(1)(E)(iv), the Federal banking agencies and the Commission shall—
1. reduce the percentage of risk retention obligations required of the securitizer by the percentage of risk retention obligations required of the originator; and
2. consider—
    A. whether the assets sold to the securitizer have terms, conditions, and characteristics that reflect low credit risk;
    B. whether the form or volume of transactions in securitization markets creates incentives for imprudent origination of the type of loan or asset to be sold to the securitizer; and

C. the potential impact of the risk retention obligations on the access of consumers and businesses to credit on reasonable terms, which may not include the transfer of credit risk to a third party.

e. **Exemptions, exceptions, and adjustments.**
1. In general. The Federal banking agencies and the Commission may jointly adopt or issue exemptions, exceptions, or adjustments to the rules issued under this section, including exemptions, exceptions, or adjustments for classes of institutions or assets relating to the risk retention requirement and the prohibition on hedging under subsection (c)(1).
2. Applicable standards. Any exemption, exception, or adjustment adopted or issued by the Federal banking agencies and the Commission under this paragraph shall—
    A. help ensure high quality underwriting standards for the securitizers and originators of assets that are securitized or available for securitization; and
    B. encourage appropriate risk management practices by the securitizers and originators of assets, improve the access of consumers and businesses to credit on reasonable terms, or otherwise be in the public interest and for the protection of investors.

Section 16 – Directors, Officers, and Principal Stockholders

a. **Disclosures required**
1. Directors, officers, and principal stockholders required to file. Every person who is directly or indirectly the beneficial owner of more than 10 percent of any class of any equity security (other than an exempted security) which is registered pursuant to section 12, or who is a director or an officer of the issuer of such security, shall file the statements required by this subsection with the Commission.
2. Time of filing.
    A. at the time of the registration of such security on a national securities exchange or by the effective date of a registration statement filed pursuant to section 12(g);
    B. within 10 days after he or she becomes such beneficial owner, director, or officer, or within such shorter time as the Commission may establish by rule;
    C. if there has been a change in such ownership, or if such person shall have purchased or sold a security-based swap agreement involving such equity security, before the end of the second business day following the day on which the subject transaction has been executed, or at such other time as the Commission shall establish, by rule, in any case in which the Commission determines that such 2-day period is not feasible.
3. Contents of statements. A statement filed--
    A. under subparagraph (A) or (B) of paragraph (2) shall contain a statement of the amount of all equity securities of such issuer of which the filing person is the beneficial owner; and
    B. under subparagraph (C) of such paragraph shall indicate ownership by the filing person at the date of filing, any such changes in such ownership, and

> such purchases and sales of the security-based swap agreements as have occurred since the most recent such filing under such subparagraph.

4.   Electronic filing and availability. Beginning not later than 1 year after the date of enactment of the Sarbanes-Oxley Act of 2002 –

   A.   a statement filed under subparagraph (C) of paragraph (2) shall be filed electronically;

   B.   the Commission shall provide each such statement on a publicly accessible Internet site not later than the end of the business day following that filing; and

   C.   the issuer (if the issuer maintains a corporate website) shall provide that statement on that corporate website, not later than the end of the business day following that filing.

b.   For the purpose of preventing the unfair use of information which may have been obtained by such beneficial owner, director, or officer by reason of his relationship to the issuer, any profit realized by him from any purchase and sale, or any sale and purchase, of any equity security of such issuer (other than an exempted security) within any period of less than six months, unless such security was acquired in good faith in connection with a debt previously contracted, shall inure to and be recoverable by the issuer, irrespective of any intention on the part of such beneficial owner, director, or officer in entering into such transaction of holding the security purchased or of not repurchasing the security sold for a period exceeding six months. Suit to recover such profit may be instituted at law or in equity in any court of competent jurisdiction by the issuer, or by the owner of any security of the issuer in the name and in behalf of the issuer if the issuer shall fail or refuse to bring such suit within sixty days after request or shall fail diligently to prosecute the same thereafter; but no such suit shall be brought more than two years after the date such profit was realized. This subsection shall not be construed to cover any transaction where such beneficial owner was not such both at the time of the purchase and sale, or the sale and purchase, of the security involved, or any transaction or transactions which the Commission by rules and regulations may exempt as not comprehended within the purpose of this subsection.

Section 18 – Liability for Misleading Statements

a.   **Persons liable; persons entitled to recover; defense of good faith; suit at law or in equity; costs, etc.** Any person who shall make or cause to be made any statement in any application, report, or document filed pursuant to this title or any rule or regulation thereunder or any undertaking contained in a registration statement as provided in subsection (d) of section 15, which statement was at the time and in the light of the circumstances under which it was made false or misleading with respect to any material fact, shall be liable to any person (not knowing that such statement was false or misleading) who, in reliance upon such statement, shall have purchased or sold a security at a price which was affected by such statement, for damages caused by such reliance, unless the person sued shall prove that he acted in good faith and had no knowledge that such statement was false or misleading. A person seeking to enforce such liability may sue at law or in equity in any court of competent jurisdiction. In any such suit the court may, in its discretion, require an undertaking for the payment of the costs of such suit, and assess reasonable costs, including reasonable attorneys' fees, against either party litigant.

b.   **Contribution.** Every person who becomes liable to make payment under this section may recover contribution as in cases of contract from any person who, if joined in the original suit, would have been liable to make the same payment.

c.   **Period of limitations**. No action shall be maintained to enforce any liability created under this section unless brought within one year after the discovery of the facts constituting the cause of action and within three years after such cause of action accrued.

Section 20 – Liabilities of Controlling Persons and Persons Who Aid and Abet Violations

a.   **Joint and several liability; good faith defense.** Every person who, directly or indirectly, controls any person liable under any provision of this title or of any rule or regulation thereunder shall also be liable jointly and severally with and to the same extent as such controlled person to any person to whom such controlled person is liable, unless the controlling person acted in good faith and did not directly or indirectly induce the act or acts constituting the violation or cause of action.

b.   **Unlawful activity through or by means of any other person.** It shall be unlawful for any person, directly or indirectly, to do any act or thing which it would be unlawful for such person to do under the provisions of this title or any rule or regulation thereunder through or by means of any other person.

c.   **Hindering, delaying, or obstructing the making or filing of any document, report, or information.** It shall be unlawful for any director or officer of, or any owner of any securities issued by, any issuer required to file any document, report, or information under this title or any rule or regulation thereunder without just cause to hinder, delay, or obstruct the making or filing of any such document, report, or information.

d.   **Liability for trading in securities while in possession of material nonpublic information.** Wherever communicating, or purchasing or selling a security while in possession of, material nonpublic information would violate, or result in liability to any purchaser or seller of the security under any provisions of this title, or any rule or regulation thereunder, such conduct in connection with a purchase or sale of a put, call, straddle, option, privilege or security-based swap agreement (as defined in section 3(a)78 of the Securities Exchange Act of 1934) with respect to such security or with respect to a group or index of securities including such security, shall also violate and result in comparable liability to any purchaser or seller of that security under such provision, rule, or regulation.

e.   **Prosecution of persons who aid and abet violations.** For purposes of any action brought by the Commission under paragraph (1) or (3) of section 21(d), any person that knowingly or recklessly provides substantial assistance to another person in violation of a provision of this title, or of any rule or regulation issued under this title, shall be deemed to be in violation of such provision to the same extent as the person to whom such assistance is provided.

Section 20A – Liability to Contemporaneous Traders for Insider Trading

a. **Private rights of action based on contemporaneous trading.** Any person who violates any provision of this title or the rules or regulations thereunder by purchasing or selling a security while in possession of material, nonpublic information shall be liable in an action in any court of competent jurisdiction to any person who, contemporaneously with the purchase or sale of securities that is the subject of such violation, has purchased (where such violation is based on a sale of securities) or sold (where such violation is based on a purchase of securities) securities of the same class.

b. **Limitations on liability**
   1. Contemporaneous trading actions limited to profit gained or loss avoided
      The total amount of damages imposed under subsection (a) of this section shall not exceed the profit gained or loss avoided in the transaction or transactions that are the subject of the violation.
   2. Offsetting disgorgements against liability
      The total amount of damages imposed against any person under subsection (a) of this section shall be diminished by the amounts, if any, that such person may be required to disgorge, pursuant to a court order obtained at the instance of the Commission, in a proceeding brought under section 21(d) relating to the same transaction or transactions.
   3. Controlling person liability
      No person shall be liable under this section solely by reason of employing another person who is liable under this section, but the liability of a controlling person under this section shall be subject to section 20(a).
   4. Statute of limitations
      No action may be brought under this section more than 5 years after the date of the last transaction that is the subject of the violation.

c. **Joint and several liability for communicating.** Any person who violates any provision of this title or the rules or regulations thereunder by communicating material, nonpublic information shall be jointly and severally liable under subsection (a) of this section with, and to the same extent as, any person or persons liable under subsection (a) of this section to whom the communication was directed.

d. **Authority not to restrict other express or implied rights of action.** Nothing in this section shall be construed to limit or condition the right of any person to bring an action to enforce a requirement of this title or the availability of any cause of action implied from a provision of this title.

e. **Provisions not to affect public prosecutions.** This section shall not be construed to bar or limit in any manner any action by the Commission or the Attorney General under any other provision of this title, nor shall it bar or limit in any manner any action to recover penalties, or to seek any other order regarding penalties.

Section 21 – Investigations and Actions

a. **Authority and discretion of Commission to investigate violations**

1. The Commission may, in its discretion, make such investigations as it deems necessary to determine whether any person has violated, is violating, or is about to violate any provision of this title, the rules or regulations thereunder, the rules of a national securities exchange or registered securities association of which such person is a member or a person associated with a member, the rules of a registered clearing agency in which such person is a participant, the rules of the Public Company Accounting Oversight Board, of which such person is a registered public accounting firm, a person associated with such a firm, or, as to any act, practice, or omission to act, while associated with such firm, a person formerly associated with such a firm, or the rules of the Municipal Securities Rulemaking Board, and may require or permit any person to file with it a statement in writing, under oath or otherwise as the Commission shall determine, as to all the facts and circumstances concerning the matter to be investigated. The Commission is authorized in its discretion, to publish information concerning any such violations, and to investigate any facts, conditions, practices, or matters which it may deem necessary or proper to aid in the enforcement of such provisions, in the prescribing of rules and regulations under this title, or in securing information to serve as a basis for recommending further legislation concerning the matters to which this title relates.

2. On request from a foreign securities authority, the Commission may provide assistance in accordance with this paragraph if the requesting authority states that the requesting authority is conducting an investigation which it deems necessary to determine whether any person has violated, is violating, or is about to violate any laws or rules relating to securities matters that the requesting authority administers or enforces. The Commission may, in its discretion, conduct such investigation as the Commission deems necessary to collect information and evidence pertinent to the request for assistance. Such assistance may be provided without regard to whether the facts stated in the request would also constitute a violation of the laws of the United States. In deciding whether to provide such assistance, the Commission shall consider whether (A) the requesting authority has agreed to provide reciprocal assistance in securities matters to the Commission; and (B) compliance with the request would prejudice the public interest of the United States.

b. **Attendance of witnesses; production of records.** For the purpose of any such investigation, or any other proceeding under this title, any member of the Commission or any officer designated by it is empowered to administer oaths and affirmations, subpoena witnesses, compel their attendance, take evidence, and require the production of any books, papers, correspondence, memoranda, or other records which the Commission deems relevant or material to the inquiry. Such attendance of witnesses and the production of any such records may be required from any place in the United States or any State at any designated place of hearing.

c. **Judicial enforcement of investigative power of Commission; refusal to obey subpoena; criminal sanctions.** In case of contumacy by, or refusal to obey a subpoena issued to, any person, the Commission may invoke the aid of any court of the United States within the jurisdiction of which such investigation or proceeding is carried on, or where such person resides or carries on business, in requiring the attendance and testimony of witnesses and the production of books, papers, correspondence, memoranda, and other records. And such court may issue an order requiring such person to appear before the Commission or member or officer designated by the Commission, there to produce records, if so ordered, or to give testimony touching the matter under investigation or in question; and any failure to obey such order of the court may be punished by such court as a contempt thereof. All process in any such case may be served in the judicial district whereof such person is an inhabitant or wherever he may be found. Any person who shall, without just cause, fail or refuse to attend and testify or to answer any lawful inquiry or to produce books, papers, correspondence, memoranda, and other records, if in his power so to do, in obedience to the subpoena of the Commission, shall be guilty of a misdemeanor and, upon conviction, shall be subject to a fine of not more than $1,000 or to imprisonment for a term of not more than one year, or both.

d. **Injunction proceedings; authority of court to prohibit persons from serving as officers and directors; money penalties in civil actions**
   1. Whenever it shall appear to the Commission that any person is engaged or is about to engage in acts or practices constituting a violation of any provision of this title, the rules or regulations thereunder, the rules of a national securities exchange or registered securities association of which such person is a member or a person associated with a member, the rules of a registered clearing agency in which such person is a participant, the rules of the Public Company Accounting Oversight Board, of which such person is a registered public accounting firm or a person associated with such a firm, or the rules of the Municipal Securities Rulemaking Board, it may in its discretion bring an action in the proper district court of the United States, the United States District Court for the District of Columbia, or the United States courts of any territory or other place subject to the jurisdiction of the United States, to enjoin such acts or practices, and upon a proper showing a permanent or temporary injunction or restraining order shall be granted without bond. The Commission may transmit such evidence as may be available concerning such acts or practices as may constitute a violation of any provision of this title or the rules or regulations thereunder to the Attorney General, who may, in his discretion, institute the necessary criminal proceedings under this title.
   2. Authority of court to prohibit persons from serving as officers and directors
   In any proceeding under paragraph (1) of this subsection, the court may prohibit, conditionally or unconditionally, and permanently or for such period of time as it shall determine, any person who violated section 10(b) or the rules or regulations thereunder from acting as an officer or director of any issuer that has a class of securities registered pursuant to section 12 or that is required to file reports pursuant to section 15(d) if the person's conduct demonstrates unfitness to serve as an officer or director of any such issuer.
   3. Civil money penalties and authority to seek disgorgement

A.   Authority of Commission

Whenever it shall appear to the Commission that any person has violated any provision of this title, the rules or regulations thereunder, or a cease-and-desist order entered by the Commission pursuant to section 21C, other than by committing a violation subject to a penalty pursuant to section 21A, the Commission may bring an action in a United States district court to seek, and the court shall have jurisdiction to

i.   impose, upon a proper showing, a civil penalty to be paid by the person who committed such violation; and

ii.   require disgorgement under paragraph (7) of any unjust enrichment by the person who received such unjust enrichment as a result of such violation.

B.   Amount of penalty

i.   First tier

The amount of a civil penalty imposed under subparagraph (A)(i) shall be determined by the court in light of the facts and circumstances. For each violation, the amount of the penalty shall not exceed the greater of (I) $5,000 for a natural person or $50,000 for any other person, or (II) the gross amount of pecuniary gain to such defendant as a result of the violation..

ii.   Second tier

Notwithstanding clause (i), the amount of a civil penalty imposed under subparagraph (A)(i) for each such violation shall not exceed the greater of (I) $50,000 for a natural person or $250,000 for any other person, or (II) the gross amount of pecuniary gain to such defendant as a result of the violation, if the violation described in subparagraph (A) involved fraud, deceit, manipulation, or deliberate or reckless disregard of a regulatory requirement.

iii.   Third tier

Notwithstanding clauses (i) and (ii), the amount of a civil penalty imposed under subparagraph (A)(i) for each violation described in that subparagraph shall not exceed the greater of (I) $100,000 for a natural person or $500,000 for any other person, or (II) the gross amount of pecuniary gain to such defendant as a result of the violation, if—

(aa) the violation described in subparagraph (A) involved fraud, deceit, manipulation, or deliberate or reckless disregard of a regulatory requirement; and

(bb) such violation directly or indirectly resulted in substantial losses or created a significant risk of substantial losses to other persons.

C.   Procedures for collection

i.   Payment of penalty to treasury

A penalty imposed under this section shall be payable into the Treasury of the United States, except as otherwise provided in section 308 of the Sarbanes-Oxley Act of 2002 and section 21F of the Securities Exchange Act of 1934.

ii.   Collection of penalties

459

If a person upon whom such a penalty is imposed shall fail to pay such penalty within the time prescribed in the court's order, the Commission may refer the matter to the Attorney General who shall recover such penalty by action in the appropriate United States district court.

    iii. Remedy not exclusive

The actions authorized by this paragraph may be brought in addition to any other action that the Commission or the Attorney General is entitled to bring.

    iv. Jurisdiction and venue

For purposes of section 27, actions under this paragraph shall be actions to enforce a liability or a duty created by this title.

D.   Special provisions relating to a violation of a cease-and-desist order

In an action to enforce a cease-and-desist order entered by the Commission pursuant to section 21C, each separate violation of such order shall be a separate offense, except that in the case of a violation through a continuing failure to comply with the order, each day of the failure to comply shall be deemed a separate offense.

4.   Prohibition of attorneys' fees paid from Commission disgorgement funds

Except as otherwise ordered by the court upon motion by the Commission, or, in the case of an administrative action, as otherwise ordered by the Commission, funds disgorged under paragraph (7) as the result of an action brought by the Commission in Federal court, or as a result of any Commission administrative action, shall not be distributed as payment for attorneys' fees or expenses incurred by private parties seeking distribution of the disgorged funds.

5.   Equitable Relief

In any action or proceeding brought or instituted by the Commission under any provision of the securities laws, the Commission may seek, and any Federal court may grant, any equitable relief that may be appropriate or necessary for the benefit of investors.

6.   Authority of a court to prohibit persons from participating in an offering of penny stock

A.   In general

In any proceeding under paragraph (1) against any person participating in, or, at the time of the alleged misconduct who was participating in, an offering of penny stock, the court may prohibit that person from participating in an offering of penny stock, conditionally or unconditionally, and permanently or for such period of time as the court shall determine.

B.   Definition

For purposes of this paragraph, the term 'person participating in an offering of penny stock' includes any person engaging in activities with a broker, dealer, or issuer for purposes of issuing, trading, or inducing or attempting to induce the purchase or sale of, any penny stock. The Commission may, by rule or regulation, define such term to include other activities, and may, by rule, regulation, or order, exempt any person or class of persons, in whole or in part, conditionally or unconditionally, from inclusion in such term.

7. Disgorgement. In any action or proceeding brought by the Commission under any provision of the securities laws, the Commission may seek, and any Federal court may order, disgorgement.

8. Limitation Periods.

    A. Disgorgement

    The Commission may bring a claim for disgorgement under paragraph (7)

        i. not later than 5 years after the latest date of the violation that gives rise to the action or proceeding in which the Commission seeks the claim occurs; or

        ii. not later than 10 years after the latest date of the violation that gives rise to the action or proceeding in which the Commission seeks the claim if the violation involves conduct that violates

            I. section 10(b);

            II. section 17(a)(1) of the Securities Act of 1933;

            III. section 206(1) of the Investment Advisers Act of 1940; or

            IV. any other provision of the securities laws for which scienter must be established.

    B. Equitable Remedies.

    The Commission may seek a claim for any equitable remedy, including for an injunction or for a bar, suspension, or cease and desist order, not later than 10 years after the latest date on which a violation that gives rise to the claim occurs.

    C. Calculation.

    For the purposes of calculating any limitations period under this paragraph with respect to an action or claim, any time in which the person against which the action or claim, as applicable, is brought is outside of the United States shall not count towards the accrual of that period.

9. Rule of Construction.

Nothing in paragraph (7) may be construed as altering any right that any private party may have to maintain a suit for a violation of this Act.

e. **Mandamus.** Upon application of the Commission the district courts of the United States and the United States courts of any territory or other place subject to the jurisdiction of the United States shall have jurisdiction to issue writs of mandamus, injunctions, and orders commanding (1) any person to comply with the provisions of this title, the rules, regulations, and orders thereunder, the rules of a national securities exchange or registered securities association of which such person is a member or person associated with a member, the rules of a registered clearing agency in which such person is a participant, the rules of the Public Company Accounting Oversight Board, of which such person is a registered public accounting firm or a person associated with such a firm, the rules of the Municipal Securities Rulemaking Board, or any undertaking contained in a registration statement as provided in subsection (d) of section 15, (2) any national securities exchange or registered securities association to enforce compliance by its members and persons associated with its members with the provisions of this title, the rules, regulations, and orders thereunder, and the rules of such exchange or association, or (3) any registered clearing agency to enforce compliance by its participants with the provisions of the rules of such clearing agency.

f. **Rules of self-regulatory organizations**. Notwithstanding any other provision of this title, the Commission shall not bring any action pursuant to subsection (d) or (e) of this section against any person for violation of, or to command compliance with, the rules of a self- regulatory organization or the Public Company Accounting Oversight Board unless it appears to the Commission that (1) such self- regulatory organization or the Public Company Accounting Oversight Board is unable or unwilling to take appropriate action against such person in the public interest and for the protection of investors, or (2) such action is otherwise necessary or appropriate in the public interest or for the protection of investors.

g. **Consolidation of actions; consent of Commission.** Notwithstanding the provisions of section 1407(a) of Title 28, or any other provision of law, no action for equitable relief instituted by the Commission pursuant to the securities laws shall be consolidated or coordinated with other actions not brought by the Commission, even though such other actions may involve common questions of fact, unless such consolidation is consented to by the Commission.

h. **Access to records**
    1. The Right to Financial Privacy Act of 1978 shall apply with respect to the Commission, except as otherwise provided in this subsection
    2. Notwithstanding section 1105 or 1107 of the Rights to Financial Privacy Act of 1978, the Commission may have access to and obtain copies of, or the information contained in financial records of a customer from a financial institution without prior notice to the customer upon an ex parte showing to an appropriate United States district court that the Commission seeks such financial records pursuant to a subpoena issued in conformity with the requirements of section 19(b) of the Securities Act of 1933, section 21(b) of the Securities Exchange Act of 1934, section 42(b) of the Investment Company Act of 1940, or section 209(b) of the Investment Advisers Act of 1940, and that the Commission has reason to believe that–
        A. delay in obtaining access to such financial records, or the required notice, will result in–
            i. flight from prosecution;
            ii. destruction of or tampering with evidence;
            iii. transfer of assets or records outside the territorial limits of the United States;
            iv. improper conversion of investor assets; or
            v. impeding the ability of the Commission to identify or trace the source or disposition of funds involved in any securities transaction;
        B. such financial records are necessary to identify or trace the record or beneficial ownership interest in any security;
        C. the acts, practices or course of conduct under investigation involve–
            i. the dissemination of materially false or misleading information concerning any security, issuer, or market, or the failure to make disclosures required under the securities laws, which remain uncorrected; or
            ii. a financial loss to investors or other persons protected under the securities laws which remains substantially uncompensated; or

D.   the acts, practices or course of conduct under investigation–
    i.   involve significant financial speculation in securities; or
    ii.   endanger the stability of any financial or investment intermediary.

3.   Any application under paragraph (2) for a delay in notice shall be made with reasonable specificity.

4.
A.   Upon a showing described in paragraph (2), the presiding judge or magistrate shall enter an ex parte order granting the requested delay for a period not to exceed ninety days and an order prohibiting the financial institution involved from disclosing that records have been obtained or that a request for records has been made.

B.   Extensions of the period of delay of notice provided in subparagraph (A) of up to ninety days each may be granted by the court upon application, but only in accordance with this subsection or section 1109(a), (b)(1), or (b)(2) of the Right to Financial Privacy Act of 1978.

C.   Upon expiration of the period of delay of notification ordered under subparagraph (A) or (B), the customer shall be served with or mailed a copy of the subpoena insofar as it applies to the customer together with the following notice which shall describe with reasonable specificity the nature of the investigation for which the Commission sought the financial records:

> Records or information concerning your transactions which are held by the financial institution named in the attached subpoena were supplied to the Securities and Exchange Commission on (date). Notification was withheld pursuant to a determination by the (title of court so ordering) under section 21(h) of the Securities Exchange Act of 1934 that (state reason). The purpose of the investigation or official proceeding was (state purpose).

5.   Upon application by the Commission, all proceedings pursuant to paragraphs (2) and (4) shall be held in camera and the records thereof sealed until expiration of the period of delay or such other date as the presiding judge or magistrate judge may permit.

6.   The Commission shall compile an annual tabulation of the occasions on which the Commission used each separate subparagraph or clause of paragraph (2) of this subsection or the provisions of the Right to Financial Privacy Act of 1978 to obtain access to financial records of a customer and include it in its annual report to the Congress. Section 1121(b) of the Right to Financial Privacy Act of 1978 shall not apply with respect to the Commission.

7.
A.   Following the expiration of the period of delay of notification ordered by the court pursuant to paragraph (4) of this subsection, the customer may, upon motion, reopen the proceeding in the district court which issued the order. If the presiding judge or magistrate judge finds that the movant is the customer to whom the records obtained by the Commission pertain, and that the Commission has obtained financial records or information contained therein in violation of this subsection, other than paragraph (1), it may order that the customer be granted civil penalties against the Commission in an amount equal to the sum of–

       i. $100 without regard to the volume of records involved;

      ii.   any out-of-pocket damages sustained by the customer as a direct result of the disclosure; and

     iii.   if the violation is found to have been willful, intentional, and without good faith, such punitive damages as the court may allow, together with the costs of the action and reasonable attorney's fees as determined by the court.

B.   Upon a finding that the Commission has obtained financial records or information contained therein in violation of this subsection, other than paragraph (1), the court, in its discretion, may also or in the alternative issue injunctive relief to require the Commission to comply with this subsection with respect to any subpoena which the Commission issues in the future for financial records of such customer for purposes of the same investigation.

C.   Whenever the court determines that the Commission has failed to comply with this subsection, other than paragraph (1), and the court finds that the circumstances raise questions of whether an officer or employee of the Commission acted in a willful and intentional manner and without good faith with respect to the violation, the Office of Personnel Management shall promptly initiate a proceeding to determine whether disciplinary action is warranted against the agent or employee who was primarily responsible for the violation. After investigating and considering the evidence submitted, the Office of Personnel Management shall submit its findings and recommendations to the Commission and shall send copies of the findings and recommendations to the officer or employee or his representative. The Commission shall take the corrective action that the Office of Personnel Management recommends.

8.   The relief described in paragraphs (7) and (10) shall be the only remedies or sanctions available to a customer for a violation of this subsection, other than paragraph (1), and nothing herein or in the Right to Financial Privacy Act of 1978 shall be deemed to prohibit the use in any investigation or proceeding of financial records, or the information contained therein, obtained by a subpoena issued by the Commission. In the case of an unsuccessful action under paragraph (7), the court shall award the costs of the action and attorney's fees to the Commission if the presiding judge or magistrate judge finds that the customer's claims were made in bad faith.

9.

A.   The Commission may transfer financial records or the information contained therein to any government authority if the Commission proceeds as a transferring agency in accordance with section 1112 of the Right to Financial Privacy Act of 1978, except that the customer notice required under section 1112(b) or (c) of such Act may be delayed upon a showing by the Commission, in accordance with the procedure set forth in paragraphs (4) and (5), that one or more of subparagraphs (A) through (D) of paragraph (2) apply.

B.   The Commission may, without notice to the customer pursuant to section 1112 or the Right to Financial Privacy Act of 1978, transfer financial records or the information contained therein to a State securities agency or to the Department of Justice. Financial records or information transferred by the Commission to the Department of Justice or to a State securities agency pursuant to the provisions of this subparagraph may be disclosed or used only in an administrative, civil, or criminal action or investigation by the Department of Justice or the State securities agency which arises out of or relates to the acts, practices, or courses of conduct investigated by the Commission, except that if the Department of Justice or the State securities agency determines that the information should be disclosed or used for any other purpose, it may do so if it notifies the customer, except as otherwise provided in the Right to Financial Privacy Act of 1978, within 30 days of its determination, or complies with the requirements of section 1109 of such Act regarding delay of notice.

10. Any government authority violating paragraph (9) shall be subject to the procedures and penalties applicable to the Commission under paragraph (7)(A) with respect to a violation by the Commission in obtaining financial records.

11. Notwithstanding the provisions of this subsection, the Commission may obtain financial records from a financial institution or transfer such records in accordance with provisions of the Right to Financial Privacy Act of 1978.

12. Nothing in this subsection shall enlarge or restrict any rights of a financial institution to challenge requests for records made by the Commission under existing law. Nothing in this subsection shall entitle a customer to assert any rights of a financial institution.

13. Unless the context otherwise requires, all terms defined in the Right to Financial Privacy Act of 1978 which are common to this subsection shall have the same meaning as in such Act.

i. **Information to CFTC.** The Commission shall provide the Commodity Futures Trading Commission with notice of the commencement of any proceeding and a copy of any order entered by the Commission against any broker or dealer registered pursuant to section 15(b)(11), any exchange registered pursuant to section 6(g), or any national securities association registered pursuant to section 15A(k).

Section 21A – Civil Penalties for Insider Trading

a. **Authority to impose civil penalties**
   1. Judicial actions by Commission authorized
      Whenever it shall appear to the Commission that any person has violated any provision of this title or the rules or regulations thereunder by purchasing or selling a security or security-based swap agreement while in possession of material, nonpublic information in, or has violated any such provision by communicating such information in connection with, a transaction on or through the facilities of a national securities exchange or from or through a broker or dealer, and which is not part of a public offering by an issuer of securities other than standardized options or security futures products, the Commission—
      A. may bring an action in a United States district court to seek, and the court shall have jurisdiction to impose, a civil penalty to be paid by the person who committed such violation; and

B.   may, subject to subsection (b)(1) of this section, bring an action in a United States district court to seek, and the court shall have jurisdiction to impose, a civil penalty to be paid by a person who, at the time of the violation, directly or indirectly controlled the person who committed such violation.

2.   Amount of penalty for person who committed violation

The amount of the penalty which may be imposed on the person who committed such violation shall be determined by the court in light of the facts and circumstances, but shall not exceed three times the profit gained or loss avoided as a result of such unlawful purchase, sale, or communication.

3.   Amount of penalty for controlling person

The amount of the penalty which may be imposed on any person who, at the time of the violation, directly or indirectly controlled the person who committed such violation, shall be determined by the court in light of the facts and circumstances, but shall not exceed the greater of $1,000,000, or three times the amount of the profit gained or loss avoided as a result of such controlled person's violation. If such controlled person's violation was a violation by communication, the profit gained or loss avoided as a result of the violation shall, for purposes of this paragraph only, be deemed to be limited to the profit gained or loss avoided by the person or persons to whom the controlled person directed such communication.

b.   **Limitations on liability**

1.   Liability of controlling persons

No controlling person shall be subject to a penalty under subsection (a)(1)(B) of this section unless the Commission establishes that–

A.   such controlling person knew or recklessly disregarded the fact that such controlled person was likely to engage in the act or acts constituting the violation and failed to take appropriate steps to prevent such act or acts before they occurred; or

B.   such controlling person knowingly or recklessly failed to establish, maintain, or enforce any policy or procedure required under section 15(f) or section 204A of the Investment Advisers Act of 1940 and such failure substantially contributed to or permitted the occurrence of the act or acts constituting the violation.

2.   Additional restrictions on liability

No person shall be subject to a penalty under subsection (a) of this section solely by reason of employing another person who is subject to a penalty under such subsection, unless such employing person is liable as a controlling person under paragraph (1) of this subsection. Section 20(a) shall not apply to actions under subsection (a) of this section.

c.   **Authority of Commission.** The Commission, by such rules, regulations, and orders as it considers necessary or appropriate in the public interest or for the protection of investors, may exempt, in whole or in part, either unconditionally or upon specific terms and conditions, any person or transaction or class of persons or transactions from this section.

d. **Procedures for collection**
  1. Payment of penalty to Treasury
      A penalty imposed under this section shall be payable into the Treasury of the United States, except as otherwise provided in section 308 of the Sarbanes-Oxley Act of 2002 and section 21F of this title.
  2. Collection of penalties
      If a person upon whom such a penalty is imposed shall fail to pay such penalty within the time prescribed in the court's order, the Commission may refer the matter to the Attorney General who shall recover such penalty by action in the appropriate United States district court.
  3. Remedy not exclusive
      The actions authorized by this section may be brought in addition to any other actions that the Commission or the Attorney General are entitled to bring.
  4. Jurisdiction and venue
      For purposes of section 27, actions under this section shall be actions to enforce a liability or a duty created by this title.
  5. Statute of limitations
      No action may be brought under this section more than 5 years after the date of the purchase or sale. This section shall not be construed to bar or limit in any manner any action by the Commission or the Attorney General under any other provision of this title, nor shall it bar or limit in any manner any action to recover penalties, or to seek any other order regarding penalties, imposed in an action commenced within 5 years of such transaction.

e. **Definition.** For purposes of this section, "profit gained" or "loss avoided" is the difference between the purchase or sale price of the security and the value of that security as measured by the trading price of the security a reasonable period after public dissemination of the nonpublic information.

f. **Limitation.** The authority of the Commission under this section with respect to security- based swap agreements shall be subject to the restrictions and limitations of section 3A(b).

g. **Duty of members and employees of Congress.**
  1. In general. Subject to the rule of construction under section 10 of the STOCK Act and solely for purposes of the insider trading prohibitions arising under this Act, including section 10(b) and Rule 10b–5 thereunder, each Member of Congress or employee of Congress owes a duty arising from a relationship of trust and confidence to the Congress, the United States Government, and the citizens of the United States with respect to material, nonpublic information derived from such person's position as a Member of Congress or employee of Congress or gained from the performance of such person's official responsibilities.
  2. Definitions. In this subsection
      A. the term 'Member of Congress' means a member of the Senate or House of Representatives, a Delegate to the House of Representatives, and the Resident Commissioner from Puerto Rico; and
      B. the term 'employee of Congress' means

        i. any individual (other than a Member of Congress), whose compensation is disbursed by the Secretary of the Senate or the Chief Administrative Officer of the House of Representatives; and

        ii. any other officer or employee of the legislative branch (as defined in section 109(11) of the Ethics in Government Act of 1978).

3. Rule of construction. Nothing in this subsection shall be construed to impair or limit the construction of the existing antifraud provisions of the securities laws or the authority of the Commission under those provisions.

h. **Duty of other federal officials.**

1. In general. Subject to the rule of construction under section 10 of the STOCK Act and solely for purposes of the insider trading prohibitions arising under this Act, including section 10(b), and Rule 10b–5 thereunder, each executive branch employee, each judicial officer, and each judicial employee owes a duty arising from a relationship of trust and confidence to the United States Government and the citizens of the United States with respect to material, nonpublic information derived from such person's position as an executive branch employee, judicial officer, or judicial employee or gained from the performance of such person's official responsibilities.

2. Definitions. In this subsection

    A. the term 'executive branch employee'

        i. has the meaning given the term 'employee' under section 2105 of title 5, United States Code;

        ii. includes—

           I. the President;

           II. the Vice President; and

           III. an employee of the United States Postal Service or the Postal Regulatory Commission;

    B. the term 'judicial employee' has the meaning given that term in section 109(8) of the Ethics in Government Act of 1978; and

    C. the term 'judicial officer' has the meaning given that term under section 109(10) of the Ethics in Government Act of 1978.

3. Rule of construction. Nothing in this subsection shall be construed to impair or limit the construction of the existing antifraud provisions of the securities laws or the authority of the Commission under those provisions.

i. **Participation in Initial Public Offerings.** An individual described in section 101(f) of the Ethics in Government Act of 1978 may not purchase securities that are the subject of an initial public offering (within the meaning given such term in section 12(f)(1)(G)(i)) in any manner other than is available to members of the public generally.

Section 21B – Civil Remedies In Administrative Proceedings

a. **Commission authority to assess money penalties.**

1. In general. In any proceeding instituted pursuant to sections 15(b)(4), 15(b)(6), 15D, 15B, 15C, or 17A against any person, the Commission or the appropriate regulatory agency may impose a civil penalty if it finds, on the record after notice

and opportunity for hearing, that such penalty is in the public interest and that such person–

A. has willfully violated any provision of the Securities Act of 1933, the Investment Company Act of 1940, the Investment Advisers Act of 1940, or this title, or the rules or regulations thereunder, or the rules of the Municipal Securities Rulemaking Board;

B. has willfully aided, abetted, counseled, commanded, induced, or procured such a violation by any other person;

C. has willfully made or caused to be made in any application for registration or report required to be filed with the Commission or with any other appropriate regulatory agency under this title, or in any proceeding before the Commission with respect to registration, any statement which was, at the time and in the light of the circumstances under which it was made, false or misleading with respect to any material fact, or has omitted to state in any such application or report any material fact which is required to be stated therein; or

D. has failed reasonably to supervise, within the meaning of section 15(b)(4)(E), with a view to preventing violations of the provisions of such statutes, rules and regulations, another person who commits such a violation, if such other person is subject to his supervision.

2. Cease and desist proceedings. In any proceeding instituted under section 21C against any person, the Commission may impose a civil penalty, if the Commission finds, on the record after notice and opportunity for hearing, that such person—

A. is violating or has violated any provision of this title, or any rule or regulation issued under this title; or

B. is or was a cause of the violation of any provision of this title, or any rule or regulation issued under this title.

b. **Maximum amount of penalty**

1. First tier

The maximum amount of penalty for each act or omission described in subsection (a) of this section shall be $5,000 for a natural person or $50,000 for any other person.

2. Second tier

Notwithstanding paragraph (1), the maximum amount of penalty for each such act or omission shall be $50,000 for a natural person or $250,000 for any other person if the act or omission described in subsection (a) of this section involved fraud, deceit, manipulation, or deliberate or reckless disregard of a regulatory requirement.

3. Third tier

Notwithstanding paragraphs (1) and (2), the maximum amount of penalty for each such act or omission shall be $100,000 for a natural person or $500,000 for any other person if–

A. the act or omission described in subsection (a) of this section involved fraud, deceit, manipulation, or deliberate or reckless disregard of a regulatory requirement; and

B.   such act or omission directly or indirectly resulted in substantial losses or created a significant risk of substantial losses to other persons or resulted in substantial pecuniary gain to the person who committed the act or omission.

c.   **Determination of public interest.** In considering under this section whether a penalty is in the public interest, the Commission or the appropriate regulatory agency may consider–

1.   whether the act or omission for which such penalty is assessed involved fraud, deceit, manipulation, or deliberate or reckless disregard of a regulatory requirement;

2.   the harm to other persons resulting either directly or indirectly from such act or omission;

3.   the extent to which any person was unjustly enriched, taking into account any restitution made to persons injured by such behavior;

4.   whether such person previously has been found by the Commission, another appropriate regulatory agency, or a self-regulatory organization to have violated the Federal securities laws, State securities laws, or the rules of a self-regulatory organization, has been enjoined by a court of competent jurisdiction from violations of such laws or rules, or has been convicted by a court of competent jurisdiction of violations of such laws or of any felony or misdemeanor described in section 15(b)(4)(B);

5.   the need to deter such person and other persons from committing such acts or omissions; and

6.   such other matters as justice may require.

d.   **Evidence concerning ability to pay.** In any proceeding in which the Commission or the appropriate regulatory agency may impose a penalty under this section, a respondent may present evidence of the respondent's ability to pay such penalty. The Commission or the appropriate regulatory agency may, in its discretion, consider such evidence in determining whether such penalty is in the public interest. Such evidence may relate to the extent of such person's ability to continue in business and the collectability of a penalty, taking into account any other claims of the United States or third parties upon such person's assets and the amount of such person's assets.

e.   **Authority to enter order requiring accounting and disgorgement.** In any proceeding in which the Commission or the appropriate regulatory agency may impose a penalty under this section, the Commission or the appropriate regulatory agency may enter an order requiring accounting and disgorgement, including reasonable interest. The Commission is authorized to adopt rules, regulations, and orders concerning payments to investors, rates of interest, periods of accrual, and such other matters as it deems appropriate to implement this subsection.

f.   **Security-based swaps.**

1.   Clearing agency. Any clearing agency that knowingly or recklessly evades or participates in or facilitates an evasion of the requirements of section 3C shall be liable for a civil money penalty in twice the amount otherwise available for a violation of section 3C.

2.   Security-based swap dealer or major security-based swap participant. Any security-based swap dealer or major security-based swap participant that knowingly or recklessly evades or participates in or facilitates an evasion of the requirements of section 3C shall be liable for a civil money penalty in twice the amount otherwise available for a violation of section 3C.

Section 21C – Cease-and-Desist Proceedings

a.   **Authority of Commission.** If the Commission finds, after notice and opportunity for hearing, that any person is violating, has violated, or is about to violate any provision of this title, or any rule or regulation thereunder, the Commission may publish its findings and enter an order requiring such person, and any other person that is, was, or would be a cause of the violation, due to an act or omission the person knew or should have known would contribute to such violation, to cease and desist from committing or causing such violation and any future violation of the same provision, rule, or regulation. Such order may, in addition to requiring a person to cease and desist from committing or causing a violation, require such person to comply, or to take steps to effect compliance, with such provision, rule, or regulation, upon such terms and conditions and within such time as the Commission may specify in such order. Any such order may, as the Commission deems appropriate, require future compliance or steps to effect future compliance, either permanently or for such period of time as the Commission may specify, with such provision, rule, or regulation with respect to any security, any issuer, or any other person.

b.   **Hearing.** The notice instituting proceedings pursuant to subsection (a) of this section shall fix a hearing date not earlier than 30 days nor later than 60 days after service of the notice unless an earlier or a later date is set by the Commission with the consent of any respondent so served.

c.   **Temporary order**
    1.   In general
         Whenever the Commission determines that the alleged violation or threatened violation specified in the notice instituting proceedings pursuant to subsection (a) of this section, or the continuation thereof, is likely to result in significant dissipation or conversion of assets, significant harm to investors, or substantial harm to the public interest, including, but not limited to, losses to the Securities Investor Protection Corporation, prior to the completion of the proceedings, the Commission may enter a temporary order requiring the respondent to cease and desist from the violation or threatened violation and to take such action to prevent the violation or threatened violation and to prevent dissipation or conversion of assets, significant harm to investors, or substantial harm to the public interest as the Commission deems appropriate pending completion of such proceedings. Such an order shall be entered only after notice and opportunity for a hearing, unless the Commission determines that notice and hearing prior to entry would be impracticable or contrary to the public interest. A temporary order shall become effective upon service upon the respondent and, unless set aside, limited, or suspended by the Commission or a court of compe-

tent jurisdiction, shall remain effective and enforceable pending the completion of the proceedings.

2.   Applicability

Paragraph (1) subsection shall apply only to a respondent that acts, or, at the time of the alleged misconduct acted, as a broker, dealer, investment adviser, investment company, municipal securities dealer, government securities broker, government securities dealer, registered public accounting firm (as defined in section 2 of the Sarbanes-Oxley Act of 2002), or transfer agent, or is, or was at the time of the alleged misconduct, an associated person of, or a person seeking to become associated with, any of the foregoing.

3.   Temporary freeze

A.   In general

i.   Issuance of temporary order

Whenever, during the course of a lawful investigation involving possible violations of the Federal securities laws by an issuer of publicly traded securities or any of its directors, officers, partners, controlling persons, agents, or employees, it shall appear to the Commission that it is likely that the issuer will make extraordinary payments (whether compensation or otherwise) to any of the foregoing persons, the Commission may petition a Federal district court for a temporary order requiring the issuer to escrow, subject to court supervision, those payments in an interest-bearing account for 45 days.

ii.   Standard

A temporary order shall be entered under clause (i), only after notice and opportunity for a hearing, unless the court determines that notice and hearing prior to entry of the order would be impracticable or contrary to the public interest.

iii.   Effective period

A temporary order issued under clause (i) shall–

I.   become effective immediately;

II.   be served upon the parties subject to it; and

III.   unless set aside, limited or suspended by a court of competent jurisdiction, shall remain effective and enforceable for 45 days.

iv.   Extensions authorized

The effective period of an order under this subparagraph may be extended by the court upon good cause shown for not longer than 45 additional days, provided that the combined period of the order shall not exceed 90 days.

B.   Process on Determination of violations

i.   Violations charged

If the issuer or other person described in subparagraph (A) is charged with any violation of the Federal securities laws before the expiration of the effective period of a temporary order under subparagraph (A) (including any applicable extension period), the order shall remain in effect, subject to court approval, until the conclusion of any legal proceedings related thereto, and the affected issuer or other person, shall have the right to petition the court for review of the order.

    ii. Violations not charged

If the issuer or other person described in subparagraph (A) is not charged with any violation of the Federal securities laws before the expiration of the effective period of a temporary order under subparagraph (A) (including any applicable extension period), the escrow shall terminate at the expiration of the 45-day effective period (or the expiration of any extension period, as applicable), and the disputed payments (with accrued interest) shall be returned to the issuer or other affected person.

d.   **Review of temporary orders**

   1. Commission review

At any time after the respondent has been served with a temporary cease and-desist order pursuant to subsection (c) of this section, the respondent may apply to the Commission to have the order set aside, limited, or suspended. If the respondent has been served with a temporary cease-and-desist order entered without a prior Commission hearing, the respondent may, within 10 days after the date on which the order was served, request a hearing on such application and the Commission shall hold a hearing and render a decision on such application at the earliest possible time.

   2. Judicial review. Within–

     A.   10 days after the date the respondent was served with a temporary cease-and-desist order entered with a prior Commission hearing, or

     B.   10 days after the Commission renders a decision on an application and hearing under paragraph (1), with respect to any temporary cease-and desist order entered without a prior Commission hearing,

the respondent may apply to the United States district court for the district in which the respondent resides or has its principal place of business, or for the District of Columbia, for an order setting aside, limiting, or suspending the effectiveness or enforcement of the order, and the court shall have jurisdiction to enter such an order. A respondent served with a temporary cease-and-desist order entered without a prior Commission hearing may not apply to the court except after hearing and decision by the Commission on the respondent's application under paragraph (1) of this subsection.

   3. No automatic stay of temporary order

The commencement of proceedings under paragraph (2) of this subsection shall not, unless specifically ordered by the court, operate as a stay of the Commission's order.

   4. Exclusive review

Section 25 shall not apply to a temporary order entered pursuant to this section.

e.   **Authority to enter order requiring accounting and disgorgement.** In any cease-and-desist proceeding under subsection (a), the Commission may enter an order requiring accounting and disgorgement, including reasonable interest. The Commission is authorized to adopt rules, regulations, and orders concerning payments to investors, rates of interest, periods of accrual, and such other matters as it deems appropriate to implement this subsection.

f.   **Authority of the Commission to prohibit persons from serving as officers or directors.** In any cease-and-desist proceeding under subsection (a), the Commission may issue an order to prohibit, conditionally or unconditionally, and permanently or for such period of time as it shall determine, any person who has violated section 10(b) or the rules or regulations thereunder, from acting as an officer or director of any issuer that has a class of securities registered pursuant to section 12, or that is required to file reports pursuant to section 15(d), if the conduct of that person demonstrates unfitness to serve as an officer or director of any such issuer.

Section 21D – Private Securities Litigation

a.   **Private class actions**
1.   In general
The provisions of this subsection shall apply in each private action arising under this title that is brought as a plaintiff class action pursuant to the Federal Rules of Civil Procedure.
2.   Certification filed with complaint
A.   In general
Each plaintiff seeking to serve as a representative party on behalf of a class shall provide a sworn certification, which shall be personally signed by such plaintiff and filed with the complaint, that–
i.   states that the plaintiff has reviewed the complaint and authorized its filing;
ii.   states that the plaintiff did not purchase the security that is the subject of the complaint at the direction of plaintiff's counsel or in order to participate in any private action arising under this title;
iii.   states that the plaintiff is willing to serve as a representative party on behalf of a class, including providing testimony at deposition and trial, if necessary;
iv.   sets forth all of the transactions of the plaintiff in the security that is the subject of the complaint during the class period specified in the complaint;
v.   identifies any other action under this title, filed during the 3-year period preceding the date on which the certification is signed by the plaintiff, in which the plaintiff has sought to serve as a representative party on behalf of a class; and
vi.   states that the plaintiff will not accept any payment for serving as a representative party on behalf of a class beyond the plaintiff's pro rata share of any recovery, except as ordered or approved by the court in accordance with paragraph (4).
B.   Nonwaiver of attorney-client privilege
The certification filed pursuant to subparagraph (A) shall not be construed to be a waiver of the attorney-client privilege.
3.   Appointment of lead plaintiff
A.   Early notice to class members

i. In general

Not later than 20 days after the date on which the complaint is filed, the plaintiff or plaintiffs shall cause to be published, in a widely circulated national business-oriented publication or wire service, a notice advising members of the purported plaintiff class–

I. of the pendency of the action, the claims asserted therein, and the purported class period; and

II. that, not later than 60 days after the date on which the notice is published, any member of the purported class may move the court to serve as lead plaintiff of the purported class.

ii. Multiple actions

If more than one action on behalf of a class asserting substantially the same claim or claims arising under this title is filed, only the plaintiff or plaintiffs in the first filed action shall be required to cause notice to be published in accordance with clause (i).

iii. Additional notices may be required under Federal rules

Notice required under clause (i) shall be in addition to any notice required pursuant to the Federal Rules of Civil Procedure.

B. Appointment of lead plaintiff

i. In general

Not later than 90 days after the date on which a notice is published under subparagraph (A)(i), the court shall consider any motion made by a purported class member in response to the notice, including any motion by a class member who is not individually named as a plaintiff in the complaint or complaints, and shall appoint as lead plaintiff the member or members of the purported plaintiff class that the court determines to be most capable of adequately representing the interests of class members (hereafter in this paragraph referred to as the "most adequate plaintiff") in accordance with this subparagraph.

ii. Consolidated actions

If more than one action on behalf of a class asserting substantially the same claim or claims arising under this title has been filed, and any party has sought to consolidate those actions for pretrial purposes or for trial, the court shall not make the determination required by clause (i) until after the decision on the motion to consolidate is rendered. As soon as practicable after such decision is rendered, the court shall appoint the most adequate plaintiff as lead plaintiff for the consolidated actions in accordance with this paragraph.

iii. Rebuttable presumption

I. In general

Subject to subclause (II), for purposes of clause (i), the court shall adopt a presumption that the most adequate plaintiff in any private action arising under this title is the person or group of persons that-

(aa) has either filed the complaint or made a motion in response to a notice under subparagraph (A)(i);

          (bb) in the determination of the court, has the largest financial interest in the relief sought by the class; and

          (cc) otherwise satisfies the requirements of Rule 23 of the Federal Rules of Civil Procedure.

     II. Rebuttal evidence

     The presumption described in subclause (I) may be rebutted only upon proof by a member of the purported plaintiff class that the presumptively most adequate plaintiff–

          (aa) will not fairly and adequately protect the interests of the class; or

          (bb) is subject to unique defenses that render such plaintiff incapable of adequately representing the class.

  iv. Discovery

     For purposes of this subparagraph, discovery relating to whether a member or members of the purported plaintiff class is the most adequate plaintiff may be conducted by a plaintiff only if the plaintiff first demonstrates a reasonable basis for a finding that the presumptively most adequate plaintiff is incapable of adequately representing the class.

  v. Selection of lead counsel

     The most adequate plaintiff shall, subject to the approval of the court, select and retain counsel to represent the class.

  vi. Restrictions on professional plaintiffs

     Except as the court may otherwise permit, consistent with the purposes of this section, a person may be a lead plaintiff, or an officer, director, or fiduciary of a lead plaintiff, in no more than 5 securities class actions brought as plaintiff class actions pursuant to the Federal Rules of Civil Procedure during any 3-year period.

4. Recovery by plaintiffs

The share of any final judgment or of any settlement that is awarded to a representative party serving on behalf of a class shall be equal, on a per share basis, to the portion of the final judgment or settlement awarded to all other members of the class. Nothing in this paragraph shall be construed to limit the award of reasonable costs and expenses (including lost wages) directly relating to the representation of the class to any representative party serving on behalf of a class.

5. Restrictions on settlements under seal

The terms and provisions of any settlement agreement of a class action shall not be filed under seal, except that on motion of any party to the settlement, the court may order filing under seal for those portions of a settlement agreement as to which good cause is shown for such filing under seal. For purposes of this paragraph, good cause shall exist only if publication of a term or provision of a settlement agreement would cause direct and substantial harm to any party.

6. Restrictions on payment of attorneys' fees and expenses

Total attorneys' fees and expenses awarded by the court to counsel for the plaintiff class shall not exceed a reasonable percentage of the amount of any damages and prejudgment interest actually paid to the class.

7.   Disclosure of settlement terms to class members
     Any proposed or final settlement agreement that is published or otherwise
     disseminated to the class shall include each of the following statements, along
     with a cover page summarizing the information contained in such statements:
     A.   Statement of plaintiff recovery
          The amount of the settlement proposed to be distributed to the parties to
          the action, determined in the aggregate and on an average per share basis.
     B.   Statement of potential outcome of case
          i.   Agreement on amount of damages
                If the settling parties agree on the average amount of damages per
                share that would be recoverable if the plaintiff prevailed on each
                claim alleged under this title, a statement concerning the average
                amount of such potential damages per share.
          ii.   Disagreement on amount of damages
                If the parties do not agree on the average amount of damages per
                share that would be recoverable if the plaintiff prevailed on each
                claim alleged under this title, a statement from each settling party
                concerning the issue or issues on which the parties disagree.
          iii. Inadmissibility for certain purposes
                A statement made in accordance with clause (i) or (ii) concerning the
                amount of damages shall not be admissible in any Federal or State
                judicial action or administrative proceeding, other than an action or
                proceeding arising out of such statement.
     C.   Statement of attorneys' fees or costs sought
          If any of the settling parties or their counsel intend to apply to the court
          for an award of attorneys' fees or costs from any fund established as part
          of the settlement, a statement indicating which parties or counsel intend
          to make such an application, the amount of fees and costs that will be
          sought (including the amount of such fees and costs determined on an
          average per share basis), and a brief explanation supporting the fees and
          costs sought. Such information shall be clearly summarized on the cover
          page of any notice to a party of any proposed or final settlement
          agreement.
     D.   Identification of lawyers' representatives
          The name, telephone number, and address of one or more representatives
          of counsel for the plaintiff class who will be reasonably available to
          answer questions from class members concerning any matter contained in
          any notice of settlement published or otherwise disseminated to the class.
     E.   Reasons for settlement
          A brief statement explaining the reasons why the parties are proposing
          the settlement.
     F.   Other information
          Such other information as may be required by the court.
8.   Security for payment of costs in class actions
     In any private action arising under this title that is certified as a class action
     pursuant to the Federal Rules of Civil Procedure, the court may require an
     undertaking from the attorneys for the plaintiff class, the plaintiff class, or both,
     or from the attorneys for the defendant, the defendant, or both, in such

proportions and at such times as the court determines are just and equitable, for the payment of fees and expenses that may be awarded under this subsection.

9.   Attorney conflict of interest

If a plaintiff class is represented by an attorney who directly owns or otherwise has a beneficial interest in the securities that are the subject of the litigation, the court shall make a determination of whether such ownership or other interest constitutes a conflict of interest sufficient to disqualify the attorney from representing the plaintiff class.

b.   **Requirements for securities fraud actions**

1.   Misleading statements and omissions

In any private action arising under this title in which the plaintiff alleges that the defendant–

A.   made an untrue statement of a material fact; or

B.   omitted to state a material fact necessary in order to make the statements made, in the light of the circumstances in which they were made, not misleading;

the complaint shall specify each statement alleged to have been misleading, the reason or reasons why the statement is misleading, and, if an allegation regarding the statement or omission is made on information and belief, the complaint shall state with particularity all facts on which that belief is formed.

2.   Required state of mind

A.   In general. Except as provided subparagraph (B), in any private action arising under this title in which the plaintiff may recover money damages only on proof that the defendant acted with a particular state of mind, the complaint shall, with respect to each act or omission alleged to violate this title, state with particularity facts giving rise to a strong inference that the defendant acted with the required state of mind.

B.   Exception. In the case of an action for money damages brought against a credit rating agency or a controlling person under this title, it shall be sufficient, for purposes of pleading any required state of mind in relation to such action, that the complaint state with particularity facts giving rise to a strong inference that the credit rating agency knowingly or recklessly failed—

i.   to conduct a reasonable investigation of the rated security with respect to the factual elements relied upon by its own methodology for evaluating credit risk; or

ii.   to obtain reasonable verification of such factual elements (which verification may be based on a sampling technique that does not amount to an audit) from other sources that the credit rating agency considered to be competent and that were independent of the issuer and underwriter.

3.   Motion to dismiss; stay of discovery

A.   Dismissal for failure to meet pleading requirements

In any private action arising under this title, the court shall, on the motion of any defendant, dismiss the complaint if the requirements of paragraphs (1) and (2) are not met.

      B.   Stay of discovery

In any private action arising under this title, all discovery and other proceedings shall be stayed during the pendency of any motion to dismiss, unless the court finds upon the motion of any party that particularized discovery is necessary to preserve evidence or to prevent undue prejudice to that party.

      C.   Preservation of evidence

        i.   In general

During the pendency of any stay of discovery pursuant to this paragraph, unless otherwise ordered by the court, any party to the action with actual notice of the allegations contained in the complaint shall treat all documents, data compilations (including electronically recorded or stored data), and tangible objects that are in the custody or control of such person and that are relevant to the allegations, as if they were the subject of a continuing request for production of documents from an opposing party under the Federal Rules of Civil Procedure.

        ii.   Sanction for willful violation

A party aggrieved by the willful failure of an opposing party to comply with clause (i) may apply to the court for an order awarding appropriate sanctions.

      D.   Circumvention of stay of discovery

Upon a proper showing, a court may stay discovery proceedings in any private action in a State court, as necessary in aid of its jurisdiction, or to protect or effectuate its judgments, in an action subject to a stay of discovery pursuant to this paragraph.

   4.   Loss causation

In any private action arising under this title, the plaintiff shall have the burden of proving that the act or omission of the defendant alleged to violate this title caused the loss for which the plaintiff seeks to recover damages.

c. **Sanctions for abusive litigation**

   1.   Mandatory review by court

In any private action arising under this title, upon final adjudication of the action, the court shall include in the record specific findings regarding compliance by each party and each attorney representing any party with each requirement of Rule 11(b) of the Federal Rules of Civil Procedure as to any complaint, responsive pleading, or dispositive motion.

   2.   Mandatory sanctions

If the court makes a finding under paragraph (1) that a party or attorney violated any requirement of Rule 11(b) of the Federal Rules of Civil Procedure as to any complaint, responsive pleading, or dispositive motion, the court shall impose sanctions on such party or attorney in accordance with Rule 11 of the Federal Rules of Civil Procedure. Prior to making a finding that any party or attorney has violated Rule 11 of the Federal Rules of Civil Procedure, the court shall give such party or attorney notice and an opportunity to respond.

   3.   Presumption in favor of attorneys' fees and costs

A.   In general

Subject to subparagraphs (B) and (C), for purposes of paragraph (2), the court shall adopt a presumption that the appropriate sanction–

i.   for failure of any responsive pleading or dispositive motion to comply with any requirement of Rule 11(b) of the Federal Rules of Civil Procedure is an award to the opposing party of the reasonable attorneys' fees and other expenses incurred as a direct result of the violation; and

ii.   for substantial failure of any complaint to comply with any requirement of Rule 11(b) of the Federal Rules of Civil Procedure is an award to the opposing party of the reasonable attorneys' fees and other expenses incurred in the action.

B.   Rebuttal evidence

The presumption described in subparagraph (A) may be rebutted only upon proof by the party or attorney against whom sanctions are to be imposed that–

i.   the award of attorneys' fees and other expenses will impose an unreasonable burden on that party or attorney and would be unjust, and the failure to make such an award would not impose a greater burden on the party in whose favor sanctions are to be imposed; or

ii.   the violation of Rule 11(b) of the Federal Rules of Civil Procedure was de minimis.

C.   Sanctions

If the party or attorney against whom sanctions are to be imposed meets its burden under subparagraph (B), the court shall award the sanctions that the court deems appropriate pursuant to Rule 11 of the Federal Rules of Civil Procedure.

d.   **Defendant's right to written interrogatories**. In any private action arising under this title in which the plaintiff may recover money damages, the court shall, when requested by a defendant, submit to the jury a written interrogatory on the issue of each such defendant's state of mind at the time the alleged violation occurred.

e.   **Limitation on damages**

1.   In general

Except as provided in paragraph (2), in any private action arising under this title in which the plaintiff seeks to establish damages by reference to the market price of a security, the award of damages to the plaintiff shall not exceed the difference between the purchase or sale price paid or received, as appropriate, by the plaintiff for the subject security and the mean trading price of that security during the 90-day period beginning on the date on which the information correcting the misstatement or omission that is the basis for the action is disseminated to the market.

2.   Exception

In any private action arising under this title in which the plaintiff seeks to establish damages by reference to the market price of a security, if the plaintiff sells or repurchases the subject security prior to the expiration of the 90-day period described in paragraph (1), the plaintiff's damages shall not exceed the difference between the purchase or sale price paid or received, as appropriate, by the plaintiff for the security and the mean trading price of the security during the period beginning immediately after dissemination of information correcting the misstatement or omission and ending on the date on which the plaintiff sells or repurchases the security.

3. Definition

For purposes of this subsection, the "mean trading price" of a security shall be an average of the daily trading price of that security, determined as of the close of the market each day during the 90-day period referred to in paragraph (1).

f. **Proportionate liability**

1. Applicability

Nothing in this subsection shall be construed to create, affect, or in any manner modify, the standard for liability associated with any action arising under the securities laws.

2. Liability for damages

A. Joint and several liability

Any covered person against whom a final judgment is entered in a private action shall be liable for damages jointly and severally only if the trier of fact specifically determines that such covered person knowingly committed a violation of the securities laws.

B. Proportionate liability

i. In general

Except as provided in subparagraph (A), a covered person against whom a final judgment is entered in a private action shall be liable solely for the portion of the judgment that corresponds to the percentage of responsibility of that covered person, as determined under paragraph (3).

ii. Recovery by and costs of covered person

In any case in which a contractual relationship permits, a covered person that prevails in any private action may recover the attorney's fees and costs of that covered person in connection with the action.

3. Determination of responsibility

A. In general

In any private action, the court shall instruct the jury to answer special interrogatories, or if there is no jury, shall make findings, with respect to each covered person and each of the other persons claimed by any of the parties to have caused or contributed to the loss incurred by the plaintiff, including persons who have entered into settlements with the plaintiff or plaintiffs, concerning–

i. whether such person violated the securities laws;

ii. the percentage of responsibility of such person, measured as a percentage of the total fault of all persons who caused or contributed to the loss incurred by the plaintiff; and

iii. whether such person knowingly committed a violation of the securities laws.

B. Contents of special interrogatories or findings

The responses to interrogatories, or findings, as appropriate, under subparagraph (A) shall specify the total amount of damages that the plaintiff is entitled to recover and the percentage of responsibility of each covered person found to have caused or contributed to the loss incurred by the plaintiff or plaintiffs.

C. Factors for consideration

In determining the percentage of responsibility under this paragraph, the trier of fact shall consider–

 i. the nature of the conduct of each covered person found to have caused or contributed to the loss incurred by the plaintiff or plaintiffs; and

 ii. the nature and extent of the causal relationship between the conduct of each such person and the damages incurred by the plaintiff or plaintiffs.

4. Uncollectible share

A. In general

Notwithstanding paragraph (2)(B), upon motion made not later than 6 months after a final judgment is entered in any private action, the court determines that all or part of the share of the judgment of the covered person is not collectible against that covered person, and is also not collectible against a covered person described in paragraph (2)(A), each covered person described in paragraph (2)(B) shall be liable for the uncollectible share as follows:

 i. Percentage of net worth

Each covered person shall be jointly and severally liable for the uncollectible share if the plaintiff establishes that–

  I. the plaintiff is an individual whose recoverable damages under the final judgment are equal to more than 10 percent of the net worth of the plaintiff; and

  II. the net worth of the plaintiff is equal to less than $200,000.

 ii. Other plaintiffs

With respect to any plaintiff not described in subclauses (I) and (II) of clause (i), each covered person shall be liable for the uncollectible share in proportion to the percentage of responsibility of that covered person, except that the total liability of a covered person under this clause may not exceed 50 percent of the proportionate share of that covered person, as determined under paragraph (3)(B).

 iii. Net worth

For purposes of this subparagraph, net worth shall be determined as of the date immediately preceding the date of the purchase or sale (as applicable) by the plaintiff of the security that is the subject of the action, and shall be equal to the fair market value of assets, minus liabilities, including the net value of the investments of the plaintiff in real and personal property (including personal residences).

B. Overall limit

In no case shall the total payments required pursuant to subparagraph (A) exceed the amount of the uncollectible share.

C. Covered persons subject to contribution

A covered person against whom judgment is not collectible shall be subject to contribution and to any continuing liability to the plaintiff on the judgment.

5. Right of contribution

To the extent that a covered person is required to make an additional payment pursuant to paragraph (4), that covered person may recover contribution–

A. from the covered person originally liable to make the payment;

B. from any covered person liable jointly and severally pursuant to paragraph (2)(A);

C. from any covered person held proportionately liable pursuant to this paragraph who is liable to make the same payment and has paid less than his or her proportionate share of that payment; or

D. from any other person responsible for the conduct giving rise to the payment that would have been liable to make the same payment.

6. Nondisclosure to jury

The standard for allocation of damages under paragraphs (2) and (3) and the procedure for reallocation of uncollectible shares under paragraph (4) shall not be disclosed to members of the jury.

7. Settlement discharge

A. In general

A covered person who settles any private action at any time before final verdict or judgment shall be discharged from all claims for contribution brought by other persons. Upon entry of the settlement by the court, the court shall enter a bar order constituting the final discharge of all obligations to the plaintiff of the settling covered person arising out of the action. The order shall bar all future claims for contribution arising out of the action–

i. by any person against the settling covered person; and

ii. by the settling covered person against any person, other than a person whose liability has been extinguished by the settlement of the settling covered person.

B. Reduction

If a covered person enters into a settlement with the plaintiff prior to final verdict or judgment, the verdict or judgment shall be reduced by the greater of–

i. an amount that corresponds to the percentage of responsibility of that covered person; or

ii. the amount paid to the plaintiff by that covered person.

8. Contribution

A covered person who becomes jointly and severally liable for damages in any private action may recover contribution from any other person who, if joined in the original action, would have been liable for the same damages. A claim for contribution shall be determined based on the percentage of responsibility of the claimant and of each person against whom a claim for contribution is made.

9. Statute of limitations for contribution

In any private action determining liability, an action for contribution shall be brought not later than 6 months after the entry of a final, nonappealable judgment in the action, except that an action for contribution brought by a covered person who was required to make an additional payment pursuant to paragraph (4) may be brought not later than 6 months after the date on which such payment was made.

10. Definitions

For purposes of this subsection–

    A. a covered person "knowingly commits a violation of the securities laws"–

        i. with respect to an action that is based on an untrue statement of material fact or omission of a material fact necessary to make the statement not misleading, if–

            I. that covered person makes an untrue statement of a material fact, with actual knowledge that the representation is false, or omits to state a fact necessary in order to make the statement made not misleading, with actual knowledge that, as a result of the omission, one of the material representations of the covered person is false; and

            II. persons are likely to reasonably rely on that misrepresentation or omission; and

        ii. with respect to an action that is based on any conduct that is not described in clause (i), if that covered person engages in that conduct with actual knowledge of the facts and circumstances that make the conduct of that covered person a violation of the securities laws;

    B. reckless conduct by a covered person shall not be construed to constitute a knowing commission of a violation of the securities laws by that covered person;

    C. the term "covered person" means–

        i. a defendant in any private action arising under this title; or

        ii. a defendant in any private action arising under section 11 of the Securities Act of 1933, who is an outside director of the issuer of the securities that are the subject of the action; and

    D. the term "outside director" shall have the meaning given such term by rule or regulation of the Commission.

Section 21E – Application of Safe Harbor for Forward-Looking Statements

a. **Applicability**

This section shall apply only to a forward-looking statement made by–

1. an issuer that, at the time that the statement is made, is subject to the reporting requirements of section 13(a) or section 15(d);

2. a person acting on behalf of such issuer;

3. an outside reviewer retained by such issuer making a statement on behalf of such issuer; or

4. an underwriter, with respect to information provided by such issuer or information derived from information provided by such issuer.

b. **Exclusions**. Except to the extent otherwise specifically provided by rule, regulation, or order of the Commission, this section shall not apply to a forward looking statement—

1.   that is made with respect to the business or operations of the issuer, if the issuer–

    A.   during the 3-year period preceding the date on which the statement was first made–

       i.   was convicted of any felony or misdemeanor described in clauses (i) through (iv) of section 15(b)(4)(B); or

       ii.   has been made the subject of a judicial or administrative decree or order arising out of a governmental action that–

          I.   prohibits future violations of the antifraud provisions of the securities laws;

          II.   requires that the issuer cease and desist from violating the antifraud provisions of the securities laws; or

          III.   determines that the issuer violated the antifraud provisions of the securities laws;

    B.   makes the forward-looking statement in connection with an offering of securities by a blank check company;

    C.   issues penny stock;

    D.   makes the forward-looking statement in connection with a rollup transaction; or

    E.   makes the forward-looking statement in connection with a going private transaction; or

2.   that is–

    A.   included in a financial statement prepared in accordance with generally accepted accounting principles;

    B.   contained in a registration statement of, or otherwise issued by, an investment company;

    C.   made in connection with a tender offer;

    D.   made in connection with an initial public offering;

    E.   made in connection with an offering by, or relating to the operations of, a partnership, limited liability company, or a direct participation investment program; or

    F.   made in a disclosure of beneficial ownership in a report required to be filed with the Commission pursuant to section 13(d).

c. **Safe harbor**

    1.   In general

    Except as provided in subsection (b) of this section, in any private action arising under this title that is based on an untrue statement of a material fact or omission of a material fact necessary to make the statement not misleading, a person referred to in subsection (a) of this section shall not be liable with respect to any forward-looking statement, whether written or oral, if and to the extent that–

    A.   the forward-looking statement is—

       i.   identified as a forward-looking statement, and is accompanied by meaningful cautionary statements identifying important factors that could cause actual results to differ materially from those in the forward looking statement; or

       ii.   immaterial; or

    B.   the plaintiff fails to prove that the forward-looking statement–

          i.   if made by a natural person, was made with actual knowledge by that person that the statement was false or misleading; or

          ii.   if made by a business entity, was–

             I.   made by or with the approval of an executive officer of that entity; and

             II. made or approved by such officer with actual knowledge by that officer that the statement was false or misleading.

2.   Oral forward-looking statements

In the case of an oral forward-looking statement made by an issuer that is subject to the reporting requirements of section 13(a) or section 15(d), or by a person acting on behalf of such issuer, the requirement set forth in paragraph (1)(A) shall be deemed to be satisfied–

A.   if the oral forward-looking statement is accompanied by a cautionary statement–

    i.   that the particular oral statement is a forward-looking statement; and

    ii.   that the actual results might differ materially from those projected in the forward-looking statement; and

B.   if—

    i.   the oral forward-looking statement is accompanied by an oral statement that additional information concerning factors that could cause actual results to materially differ from those in the forward-looking statement is contained in a readily available written document, or portion thereof;

    ii.   the accompanying oral statement referred to in clause (i) identifies the document, or portion thereof, that contains the additional information about those factors relating to the forward-looking statement; and

    iii. the information contained in that written document is a cautionary statement that satisfies the standard established in paragraph (1)(A).

3.   Availability

Any document filed with the Commission or generally disseminated shall be deemed to be readily available for purposes of paragraph (2).

4.   Effect on other safe harbors

The exemption provided for in paragraph (1) shall be in addition to any exemption that the Commission may establish by rule or regulation under subsection (g) of this section.

d.   **Duty to update.** Nothing in this section shall impose upon any person a duty to update a forward-looking statement.

e.   **Dispositive motion.** On any motion to dismiss based upon subsection (c)(1) of this section, the court shall consider any statement cited in the complaint and any cautionary statement accompanying the forward-looking statement, which are not subject to material dispute, cited by the defendant.

f.   **Stay pending decision on motion.** In any private action arising under this title, the court shall stay discovery (other than discovery that is specifically directed to the applicability of the exemption provided for in this section) during the pendency of any motion by a defendant for summary judgment that is based on the grounds that–

1. the statement or omission upon which the complaint is based is a forward-looking statement within the meaning of this section; and

2. the exemption provided for in this section precludes a claim for relief.

g. **Exemption authority.** In addition to the exemptions provided for in this section, the Commission may, by rule or regulation, provide exemptions from or under any provision of this title, including with respect to liability that is based on a statement or that is based on projections or other forward-looking information, if and to the extent that any such exemption is consistent with the public interest and the protection of investors, as determined by the Commission.

h. **Effect on other authority of Commission.** Nothing in this section limits, either expressly or by implication, the authority of the Commission to exercise similar authority or to adopt similar rules and regulations with respect to forward-looking statements under any other statute under which the Commission exercises rulemaking authority.

i. **Definitions.** For purposes of this section, the following definitions shall apply:

1. Forward-looking statement

    The term "forward-looking statement" means—

    A. a statement containing a projection of revenues, income (including income loss), earnings (including earnings loss) per share, capital expenditures, dividends, capital structure, or other financial items;

    B. a statement of the plans and objectives of management for future operations, including plans or objectives relating to the products or services of the issuer;

    C. a statement of future economic performance, including any such statement contained in a discussion and analysis of financial condition by the management or in the results of operations included pursuant to the rules and regulations of the Commission;

    D. any statement of the assumptions underlying or relating to any statement described in subparagraph (A), (B), or (C);

    E. any report issued by an outside reviewer retained by an issuer, to the extent that the report assesses a forward-looking statement made by the issuer; or

    F. a statement containing a projection or estimate of such other items as may be specified by rule or regulation of the Commission.

2. Investment company

    The term "investment company" has the same meaning as in section 3(a) of the Investment Company Act of 1940.

3. Going private transaction

    The term "going private transaction" has the meaning given that term under the rules or regulations of the Commission issued pursuant to section 13(e).

4. Person acting on behalf of an issuer

    The term "person acting on behalf of an issuer" means any officer, director, or employee of such issuer.

5. Other terms
The terms "blank check company", "roll-up transaction", "partnership", "limited liability company", "executive officer of an entity" and "direct participation investment program", have the meanings given those terms by rule or regulation of the Commission.

Section 21F – Securities Whistleblower Incentives and Protection

a. **Definitions.** In this section the following definitions shall apply:
1. Covered judicial or administrative action. The term 'covered judicial or administrative action' means any judicial or administrative action brought by the Commission under the securities laws that results in monetary sanctions exceeding $1,000,000.
2. Fund. The term 'Fund' means the Securities and Exchange Commission Investor Protection Fund.
3. Original Information The term 'original information' means information that—
   A. is derived from the independent knowledge or analysis of a whistleblower;
   B. is not known to the Commission from any other source, unless the whistleblower is the original source of the information; and
   C. is not exclusively derived from an allegation made in a judicial or administrative hearing, in a governmental report, hearing, audit, or investigation, or from the news media, unless the whistleblower is a source of the information.
4. Monetary sanctions. The term 'monetary sanctions', when used with respect to any judicial or administrative action, means—
   A. any monies, including penalties, disgorgement, and interest, ordered to be paid; and
   B. any monies deposited into a disgorgement fund or other fund pursuant to section 308(b) of the Sarbanes-Oxley Act of 2002, as a result of such action or any settlement of such action.
5. Related action. The term 'related action', when used with respect to any judicial or administrative action brought by the Commission under the securities laws, means any judicial or administrative action brought by an entity described in subclauses (I) through (IV) of subsection (h)(2)(D)(i) that is based upon the original information provided by a whistleblower pursuant to subsection (a) that led to the successful enforcement of the Commission action.
6. Whistleblower. The term 'whistleblower' means any individual who provides, or 2 or more individuals acting jointly who provide, information relating to a violation of the securities laws to the Commission, in a manner established, by rule or regulation, by the Commission.

b. **Awards**
1. In general. In any covered judicial or administrative action, or related action, the Commission, under regulations prescribed by the Commission and subject to subsection (c), shall pay an award or awards to 1 or more whistleblowers who voluntarily provided original information to the Commission that led to the successful enforcement of the covered judicial or administrative action, or related action, in an aggregate amount equal to—

A. not less than 10 percent, in total, of what has been collected of the monetary sanctions imposed in the action or related actions; and

B. not more than 30 percent, in total, of what has been collected of the monetary sanctions imposed in the action or related actions.

2. Payment of awards. Any amount paid under paragraph (1) shall be paid from the Fund.

c. **Determination of amount of award; denial of award.**

1. Determination of amount of award.

A. Discretion. The determination of the amount of an award made under subsection (b) shall be in the discretion of the Commission.

B. In determining the amount of an award made under subsection (b), the Commission—

i. shall take into consideration—

I. the significance of the information provided by the whistleblower to the success of the covered judicial or administrative action;

II. the degree of assistance provided by the whistleblower and any legal representative of the whistleblower in a covered judicial or administrative action;

III. the programmatic interest of the Commission in deterring violations of the securities laws by making awards to whistleblowers who provide information that lead to the successful enforcement of such laws; and

IV. such additional relevant factors as the Commission may establish by rule or regulation; and

C. shall not take into consideration the balance of the Fund.

2. Denial of award. No award under subsection (b) shall be made—

A. to any whistleblower who is, or was at the time the whistleblower acquired the original information submitted to the Commission, a member, officer, or employee of—

i. an appropriate regulatory agency;

ii. the Department of Justice;

iii. a self-regulatory organization;

iv. the Public Company Accounting Oversight Board; or

v. a law enforcement organization;

B. to any whistleblower who is convicted of a criminal violation related to the judicial or administrative action for which the whistleblower otherwise could receive an award under this section;

C. to any whistleblower who gains the information through the performance of an audit of financial statements required under the securities laws and for whom such submission would be contrary to the requirements of section 10A of the Securities Exchange Act of 1934; or

D. to any whistleblower who fails to submit information to the Commission in such form as the Commission may, by rule, require.

d. **Representation.**

1. Permitted representation. Any whistleblower who makes a claim for an award under subsection (b) may be represented by counsel.

    2.   Required representation.
        A. In general. Any whistleblower who anonymously makes a claim for an award under subsection (b) shall be represented by counsel if the whistleblower anonymously submits the information upon which the claim is based.
        B. Disclosure of identity. Prior to the payment of an award, a whistleblower shall disclose the identity of the whistleblower and provide such other information as the Commission may require, directly or through counsel for the whistleblower.

e. **No contract necessary.** No contract with the Commission is necessary for any whistleblower to receive an award under subsection (b), unless otherwise required by the Commission by rule or regulation.

f. **Appeals.** Any determination made under this section, including whether, to whom, or in what amount to make awards, shall be in the discretion of the Commission. Any such determination, except the determination of the amount of an award if the award was made in accordance with subsection (b), may be appealed to the appropriate court of appeals of the United States not more than 30 days after the determination is issued by the Commission. The court shall review the determination made by the Commission in accordance with section 706 of title 5, United States Code.

g. **Investor protection fund.**
    1.   Fund established. There is established in the Treasury of the United States a fund to be known as the 'Securities and Exchange Commission Investor Protection Fund'.
    2.   Use of fund. The Fund shall be available to the Commission, without further appropriation or fiscal year limitation, for—
        A. paying awards to whistleblowers as provided in subsection (b); and
        B. funding the activities of the Inspector General of the Commission under section 4(i).
    3.   Deposits and credits.
        A. In general. There shall be deposited into or credited to the Fund an amount equal to—
           i. any monetary sanction collected by the Commission in any judicial or administrative action brought by the Commission under the securities laws that is not added to a disgorgement fund or other fund under section 308 of the Sarbanes-Oxley Act of 2002 or otherwise distributed to victims of a violation of the securities laws, or the rules and regulations thereunder, underlying such action, unless the balance of the Fund at the time the monetary sanction is collected exceeds $300,000,000;
          ii. any monetary sanction added to a disgorgement fund or other fund under section 308 of the Sarbanes-Oxley Act of 2002 that is not distributed to the victims for whom the Fund was established, unless the balance of the disgorgement fund at the time the determination is made not to distribute the monetary sanction to such victims exceeds $200,000,000; and

        iii. all income from investments made under paragraph (4).

    B. Additional amounts. If the amounts deposited into or credited to the Fund under subparagraph (A) are not sufficient to satisfy an award made under subsection (b), there shall be deposited into or credited to the Fund an amount equal to the unsatisfied portion of the award from any monetary sanction collected by the Commission in the covered judicial or administrative action on which the award is based.

4. Investments.

    A. Amounts in fund may be invested. The Commission may request the Secretary of the Treasury to invest the portion of the Fund that is not, in the discretion of the Commission, required to meet the current needs of the Fund.

    B. Eligible investments. Investments shall be made by the Secretary of the Treasury in obligations of the United States or obligations that are guaranteed as to principal and interest by the United States, with maturities suitable to the needs of the Fund as determined by the Commission on the record.

    C. Interest and proceeds credited. The interest on, and the proceeds from the sale or redemption of, any obligations held in the Fund shall be credited to the Fund.

5. Reports to Congress. Not later than October 30 of each fiscal year beginning after the date of enactment of this subsection, the Commission shall submit to the Committee on Banking, Housing, and Urban Affairs of the Senate, and the Committee on Financial Services of the House of Representatives a report on—

    A. the whistleblower award program, established under this section, including—

        i. a description of the number of awards granted; and

        ii. the types of cases in which awards were granted during the preceding fiscal year;

    B. the balance of the Fund at the beginning of the preceding fiscal year;

    C. the amounts deposited into or credited to the Fund during the preceding fiscal year;

    D. the amount of earnings on investments made under paragraph (4) during the preceding fiscal year;

    E. the amount paid from the Fund during the preceding fiscal year to whistleblowers pursuant to subsection (b);

    F. the balance of the Fund at the end of the preceding fiscal year; and

    G. a complete set of audited financial statements, including—

        i. a balance sheet;

        ii. income statement; and

        iii. cash flow analysis.

h. **Protection of whistleblowers.**

1. Protection against retaliation.

    A. In general. No employer may discharge, demote, suspend, threaten, harass, directly or indirectly, or in any other manner discriminate against, a whistleblower in the terms and conditions of employment because of any lawful act done by the whistleblower—

      i.   in providing information to the Commission in accordance with this section;

      ii.   in initiating, testifying in, or assisting in any investigation or judicial or administrative action of the Commission based upon or related to such information; or

     iii. in making disclosures that are required or protected under the Sarbanes-Oxley Act of 2002, the Securities Exchange Act of 1934, including section 10A(m) of such Act, section 1513(e) of title 18, United States Code, and any other law, rule, or regulation subject to the jurisdiction of the Commission.

  B. Enforcement.

      i.   Cause of action.   An individual who alleges discharge or other discrimination in violation of subparagraph (A) may bring an action under this subsection in the appropriate district court of the United States for the relief provided in subparagraph (C).

      ii.   Subpoenas. A subpoena requiring the attendance of a witness at a trial or hearing conducted under this section may be served at any place in the United States.

     iii. Statute of limitations.

          I.   In general. An action under this subsection may not be brought—

             aa. more than 6 years after the date on which the violation of subparagraph (A) occurred; or

             bb. more than 3 years after the date when facts material to the right of action are known or reasonably should have been known by the employee alleging a violation of subparagraph (A).

         II.   Required action within 10 years. Notwithstanding subclause (I), an action under this subsection may not in any circumstance be brought more than 10 years after the date on which the violation occurs.

  C. Relief.   Relief for an individual prevailing in an action brought under subparagraph (B) shall include—

      i.   reinstatement with the same seniority status that the individual would have had, but for the discrimination;

      ii.   2 times the amount of back pay otherwise owed to the individual, with interest; and

     iii. compensation for litigation costs, expert witness fees, and reasonable attorneys' fees.

2. Confidentiality.

  A. In general.   Except as provided in subparagraphs (B) and (C), the Commission and any officer or employee of the Commission shall not disclose any information, including information provided by a whistleblower to the Commission, which could reasonably be expected to reveal the identity of a whistleblower, except in accordance with the provisions of section 552a of title 5, United States Code, unless and until required to be disclosed to a defendant or respondent in connection with a public proceeding instituted by the Commission or any entity described in subparagraph (C). For purposes of section 552 of title 5, United States Code, this paragraph shall be considered a statute described in subsection (b)(3)(B) of such section.

B. Exempted statute. For purposes of section 552 of title 5, United States Code, this paragraph shall be considered a statute described in subsection (b)(3)(B) of such section 552.

C. Rule of construction. Nothing in this section is intended to limit, or shall be construed to limit, the ability of the Attorney General to present such evidence to a grand jury or to share such evidence with potential witnesses or defendants in the course of an ongoing criminal investigation.

D. Availability to government agencies.

    i. In general. Without the loss of its status as confidential in the hands of the Commission, all information referred to in subparagraph (A) may, in the discretion of the Commission, when determined by the Commission to be necessary to accomplish the purposes of this Act and to protect investors, be made available to—

       I. the Attorney General of the United States;

       II. an appropriate regulatory authority;

       III. a self-regulatory organization;

       IV. a State attorney general in connection with any criminal investigation;

       V. any appropriate State regulatory authority;

       VI. the Public Company Accounting Oversight Board;

       VII. a foreign securities authority; and

       VIII. a foreign law enforcement authority.

    ii. Confidentiality.

       I. In general. Each of the entities described in subclauses (I) through (VI) of clause (i) shall maintain such information as confidential in accordance with the requirements established under subparagraph (A).

       II. Foreign authorities. Each of the entities described in subclauses (VII) and (VIII) of clause (i) shall maintain such information in accordance with such assurances of confidentiality as the Commission determines appropriate.

3. Rights retained. Nothing in this section shall be deemed to diminish the rights, privileges, or remedies of any whistleblower under any Federal or State law, or under any collective bargaining agreement.

i. **Provision of false information.** A whistleblower shall not be entitled to an award under this section if the whistleblower—

1. knowingly and willfully makes any false, fictitious, or fraudulent statement or representation; or

2. uses any false writing or document knowing the writing or document contains any false, fictitious, or fraudulent statement or entry.

j. **Rulemaking authority.** The Commission shall have the authority to issue such rules and regulations as may be necessary or appropriate to implement the provisions of this section consistent with the purposes of this section.

Section 23 – Rules, Regulations, and Orders; Annual Reports

a. **Power to make rules and regulations; considerations; public disclosure**

1. The Commission, the Board of Governors of the Federal Reserve System, and the other agencies enumerated in section 3(a)(34) shall each have power to make such rules and regulations as may be necessary or appropriate to implement the provisions of this title for which they are responsible or for the execution of the functions vested in them by this title, and may for such purposes classify persons, securities, transactions, statements, applications, reports, and other matters within their respective jurisdictions, and prescribe greater, lesser, or different requirements for different classes thereof. No provision of this title imposing any liability shall apply to any act done or omitted in good faith in conformity with a rule, regulation, or order of the Commission, the Board of Governors of the Federal Reserve System, other agency enumerated in section 3(a)(34), or any self regulatory organization, notwithstanding that such rule, regulation, or order may thereafter be amended or rescinded or determined by judicial or other authority to be invalid for any reason.

2. The Commission and the Secretary of the Treasury, in making rules and regulations pursuant to any provisions of this title, shall consider among other matters the impact any such rule or regulation would have on competition. The Commission and the Secretary of the Treasury shall not adopt any such rule or regulation which would impose a burden on competition not necessary or appropriate in furtherance of the purposes of this title. The Commission and the Secretary of the Treasury shall include in the statement of basis and purpose incorporated in any rule or regulation adopted under this title, the reasons for the Commission's or the Secretary's determination that any burden on competition imposed by such rule or regulation is necessary or appropriate in furtherance of the purposes of this title.

3. The Commission and the Secretary, in making rules and regulations pursuant to any provision of this title, considering any application for registration in accordance with section 19(a), or reviewing any proposed rule change of a self-regulatory organization in accordance with section 19(b), shall keep in a public file and make available for copying all written statements filed with the Commission and the Secretary and all written communications between the Commission or the Secretary and any person relating to the proposed rule, regulation, application, or proposed rule change; *Provided, however,* That the Commission and the Secretary shall not be required to keep in a public file or make available for copying any such statement or communication which it may withhold from the public in accordance with the provisions of section 552 of Title 5.

Section 25 – Court Review of Orders and Rules

a. **Final Commission orders; persons aggrieved; petition; record; findings; affirmance, modification, enforcement, or setting aside of orders; remand to adduce additional evidence**

1. A person aggrieved by a final order of the Commission entered pursuant to this title may obtain review of the order in the United States Court of Appeals for the

circuit in which he resides or has his principal place of business, or for the District of Columbia Circuit, by filing in such court, within sixty days after the entry of the order, a written petition requesting that the order be modified or set aside in whole or in part.

2. A copy of the petition shall be transmitted forthwith by the clerk of the court to a member of the Commission or an officer designated by the Commission for that purpose. Thereupon the Commission shall file in the court the record on which the order complained of is entered, as provided in section 2112 of Title 28 and the Federal Rules of Appellate Procedure.

3. On the filing of the petition, the court has jurisdiction, which becomes exclusive on the filing of the record, to affirm or modify and enforce or to set aside the order in whole or in part.

4. The findings of the Commission as to the facts, if supported by substantial evidence, are conclusive.

5. If either party applies to the court for leave to adduce additional evidence and shows to the satisfaction of the court that the additional evidence is material and that there was reasonable ground for failure to adduce it before the Commission, the court may remand the case to the Commission for further proceedings, in whatever manner and on whatever conditions the court considers appropriate. If the case is remanded to the Commission, it shall file in the court a supplemental record containing any new evidence, any further or modified findings, and any new order.

b. **Commission rules; persons adversely affected; petition; record; affirmance, enforcement, or setting aside of rules; findings; transfer of proceedings**

1. A person adversely affected by a rule of the Commission promulgated pursuant to section 6, 9(h)(2), 11, 11A, 15(c)(5) or (6), 15A, 17, 17A, or 19 may obtain review of this rule in the United States Court of Appeals for the circuit in which he resides or has his principal place of business or for the District of Columbia Circuit, by filing in such court, within sixty days after the promulgation of the rule, a written petition requesting that the rule be set aside.

2. A copy of the petition shall be transmitted forthwith by the clerk of the court to a member of the Commission or an officer designated for that purpose. Thereupon, the Commission shall file in the court the rule under review and any documents referred to therein, the Commission's notice of proposed rulemaking and any documents referred to therein, all written submissions and the transcript of any oral presentations in the rulemaking, factual information not included in the foregoing that was considered by the Commission in the promulgation of the rule or proffered by the Commission as pertinent to the rule, the report of any advisory committee received or considered by the Commission in the rulemaking, and any other materials prescribed by the court.

3. On the filing of the petition, the court has jurisdiction, which becomes exclusive on the filing of the materials set forth in paragraph (2) of this subsection, to affirm and enforce or to set aside the rule.

4. The findings of the Commission as to the facts identified by the Commission as the basis, in whole or in part, of the rule, if supported by substantial evidence, are conclusive. The court shall affirm and enforce the rule unless the Commission's action in promulgating the rule is found to be arbitrary,

capricious, an abuse of discretion, or otherwise not in accordance with law; contrary to constitutional right, power, privilege, or immunity; in excess of statutory jurisdiction, authority, or limitations, or short of statutory right; or without observance of procedure required by law.

5.   If proceedings have been instituted under this subsection in two or more courts of appeals with respect to the same rule, the Commission shall file the materials set forth in paragraph (2) of this subsection in that court in which a proceeding was first instituted. The other courts shall thereupon transfer all such proceedings to the court in which the materials have been filed. For the convenience of the parties in the interest of justice that court may thereafter transfer all the proceedings to any other court of appeals.

c.   **Objections not urged before Commission; stay of orders and rules; transfer of enforcement or review proceedings**

1.   No objection to an order or rule of the Commission, for which review is sought under this section, may be considered by the court unless it was urged before the Commission or there was reasonable ground for failure to do so.

2.   The filing of a petition under this section does not operate as a stay of the Commission's order or rule. Until the court's jurisdiction becomes exclusive, the Commission may stay its order or rule pending judicial review if it finds that justice so requires. After the filing of a petition under this section, the court, on whatever conditions may be required and to the extent necessary to prevent irreparable injury, may issue all necessary and appropriate process to stay the order or rule or to preserve status or rights pending its review; but (notwithstanding section 705 of Title 5) no such process may be issued by the court before the filing of the record or the materials set forth in subsection (b)(2) of this section unless: (A) the Commission has denied a stay or failed to grant requested relief, (B) a reasonable period has expired since the filing of an application for a stay without a decision by the Commission, or (C) there was reasonable ground for failure to apply to the Commission.

3.   When the same order or rule is the subject of one or more petitions for review filed under this section and an action for enforcement filed in a district court of the United States under section 21(d) or (e), that court in which the petition or the action is first filed has jurisdiction with respect to the order or rule to the exclusion of any other court, and thereupon all such proceedings shall be transferred to that court; but, for the convenience of the parties in the interest of justice, that court may thereafter transfer all the proceedings to any other court of appeals or district court of the United States, whether or not a petition for review or an action for enforcement was originally filed in the transferee court. The scope of review by a district court under section 21(d) or (e) is in all cases the same as by a court of appeals under this section.

d.   **Other appropriate regulatory agencies**

1.   For purposes of the preceding subsections of this section, the term "Commission" includes the agencies enumerated in section 3(a)(34) insofar as such agencies are acting pursuant to this title and the Secretary of the Treasury insofar as he is acting pursuant to section 15C.

2. For purposes of subsection (a)(4) of this section and section 706 of Title 5, an order of the Commission pursuant to section 19(a) denying registration to a clearing agency for which the Commission is not the appropriate regulatory agency or pursuant to section 19(b) disapproving a proposed rule change by such a clearing agency shall be deemed to be an order of the appropriate regulatory agency for such clearing agency insofar as such order was entered by reason of a determination by such appropriate regulatory agency pursuant to section 19(a)(2)(C) or 19(b)(4)(C) that such registration or proposed rule change would be inconsistent with the safeguarding of securities or funds.

Section 27 – Jurisdiction of Offenses and Suits

a. **In general.** The district courts of the United States and the United States courts of any Territory or other place subject to the jurisdiction of the United States shall have exclusive jurisdiction of violations of this title or the rules and regulations thereunder, and of all suits in equity and actions at law brought to enforce any liability or duty created by this title or the rules and regulations thereunder. Any criminal proceeding may be brought in the district wherein any act or transaction constituting the violation occurred. Any suit or action to enforce any liability or duty created by this title or rules and regulations thereunder, or to enjoin any violation of such title or rules and regulations, may be brought in any such district or in the district wherein the defendant is found or is an inhabitant or transacts business, and process in such cases may be served in any other district of which the defendant is an inhabitant or wherever the defendant may be found. In any action or proceeding instituted by the Commission under this title in a United States district court for any judicial district, a subpoena issued to compel the attendance of a witness or the production of documents or tangible things (or both) at a hearing or trial may be served at any place within the United States. Rule 45(c)(3)(A)(ii) of the Federal Rules of Civil Procedure shall not apply to a subpoena issued under the preceding sentence. Judgments and decrees so rendered shall be subject to review as provided in sections 1254, 1291, 1292, and 1294 of Title 28. No costs shall be assessed for or against the Commission in any proceeding under this title brought by or against it in the Supreme Court or such other courts.

b. **Extraterritorial jurisdiction.** The district courts of the United States and the United States courts of any Territory shall have jurisdiction of an action or proceeding brought or instituted by the Commission or the United States alleging a violation of the antifraud provisions of this title involving—
1. conduct within the United States that constitutes significant steps in furtherance of the violation, even if the securities transaction occurs outside the United States and involves only foreign investors; or
2. conduct occurring outside the United States that has a foreseeable substantial effect within the United States.

Section 28 – Effect on Existing Law

a. **Limitation on judgments.**
1. **In general.** No person permitted to maintain a suit for damages under the provisions of this title shall recover, through satisfaction of judgment in 1 or

more actions, a total amount in excess of the actual damages to that person on account of the act complained of. Except as otherwise specifically provided in this title, nothing in this title shall affect the jurisdiction of the securities commission (or any agency or officer performing like functions) of any State over any security or any person insofar as it does not conflict with the provisions of this title or the rules and regulations under this title.

2.   **Rule of construction.** Except as provided in subsection (f), the rights and remedies provided by this title shall be in addition to any and all other rights and remedies that may exist at law or in equity.

3.   **State bucket shop laws.** No State law which prohibits or regulates the making or promoting of wagering or gaming contracts, or the operation of 'bucket shops' or other similar or related activities, shall invalidate—

    A.   any put, call, straddle, option, privilege, or other security subject to this title (except any security that has a pari-mutuel payout or otherwise is determined by the Commission, acting by rule, regulation, or order, to be appropriately subject to such laws), or apply to any activity which is incidental or related to the offer, purchase, sale, exercise, settlement, or closeout of any such security;

    B.   any security-based swap between eligible contract participants; or

    C.   any security-based swap effected on a national securities exchange registered pursuant to section 6(b).

Other state provisions. No provision of State law regarding the offer, sale, or distribution of securities shall apply to any transaction in a security-based swap or a security futures product, except that this paragraph may not be construed as limiting any State antifraud law of general applicability. A security-based swap may not be regulated as an insurance contract under any provision of State law.''

b.   **Modification of disciplinary procedures.** Nothing in this title shall be construed to modify existing law with regard to the binding effect (1) on any member of or participant in any self- regulatory organization of any action taken by the authorities of such organization to settle disputes between its members or participants, (2) on any municipal securities dealer or municipal securities broker of any action taken pursuant to a procedure established by the Municipal Securities Rulemaking Board to settle disputes between municipal securities dealers and municipal securities brokers, or (3) of any action described in paragraph (1) or (2) on any person who has agreed to be bound thereby.

c.   **Continuing validity of disciplinary sanctions.** The stay, setting aside, or modification pursuant to section 19(e) of any disciplinary sanction imposed by a self-regulatory organization on a member thereof, person associated with a member, or participant therein, shall not affect the validity or force of any action taken as a result of such sanction by the self-regulatory organization prior to such stay, setting aside, or modification: *Provided,* That such action is not inconsistent with the provisions of this title or the rules or regulations thereunder. The rights of any person acting in good faith which arise out of any such action shall not be affected in any way by such stay, setting aside, or modification.

d. **Physical location of facilities of registered clearing agencies or registered transfer agents not to subject changes in beneficial or record ownership of securities to State or local taxes.** No State or political subdivision thereof shall impose any tax on any change in beneficial or record ownership of securities effected through the facilities of a registered clearing agency or registered transfer agent or any nominee thereof or custodian therefor or upon the delivery or transfer of securities to or through or receipt from such agency or agent or any nominee thereof or custodian therefor, unless such change is in beneficial or record ownership or such transfer or delivery or receipt would otherwise be taxable by such State or political subdivision if the facilities of such registered clearing agency, registered transfer agent, or any nominee thereof or custodian therefor were not physically located in the taxing State or political subdivision. No State or political subdivision thereof shall impose any tax on securities which are deposited in or retained by a registered clearing agency, registered transfer agent, or any nominee thereof or custodian therefor, unless such securities would otherwise be taxable by such State or political subdivision if the facilities of such registered clearing agency, registered transfer agent, or any nominee thereof or custodian therefor were not physically located in the taxing State or political subdivision.

e. **Exchange, broker, and dealer commissions; brokerage and research services**
    1. No person using the mails, or any means or instrumentality of interstate commerce, in the exercise of investment discretion with respect to an account shall be deemed to have acted unlawfully or to have breached a fiduciary duty under State or Federal law unless expressly provided to the contrary by a law enacted by the Congress or any State subsequent to June 4, 1975, solely by reason of his having caused the account to pay a member of an exchange, broker, or dealer an amount of commission for effecting a securities transaction in excess of the amount of commission another member of an exchange, broker, or dealer would have charged for effecting that transaction, if such person determined in good faith that such amount of commission was reasonable in relation to the value of the brokerage and research services provided by such member, broker, or dealer, viewed in terms of either that particular transaction or his overall responsibilities with respect to the accounts as to which he exercises investment discretion. This subsection is exclusive and plenary insofar as conduct is covered by the foregoing, unless otherwise expressly provided by contract: *Provided, however,* That nothing in this subsection shall be construed to impair or limit the power of the Commission under any other provision of this title or otherwise.
    2. A person exercising investment discretion with respect to an account shall make such disclosure of his policies and practices with respect to commissions that will be paid for effecting securities transactions, at such times and in such manner, as the appropriate regulatory agency, by rule, may prescribe as necessary or appropriate in the public interest or for the protection of investors.
    3. For purposes of this subsection a person provides brokerage and research services insofar as he–
        A. furnishes advice, either directly or through publications or writings, as to the value of securities, the advisability of investing in, purchasing, or selling securities, and the availability of securities or purchasers or sellers of securities;

B. furnishes analyses and reports concerning issuers, industries, securities, economic factors and trends, portfolio strategy, and the performance of accounts; or

C. effects securities transactions and performs functions incidental thereto (such as clearance, settlement, and custody) or required in connection therewith by rules of the Commission or a self-regulatory organization of which such person is a member or person associated with a member or in which such person is a participant.

4. The provisions of this subsection shall not apply with regard to securities that are security futures products.

f. **Limitations on remedies**

1. Class action limitations

No covered class action based upon the statutory or common law of any State or subdivision thereof may be maintained in any State or Federal court by any private party alleging–

A. a misrepresentation or omission of a material fact in connection with the purchase or sale of a covered security; or

B. that the defendant used or employed any manipulative or deceptive device or contrivance in connection with the purchase or sale of a covered security.

2. Removal of covered class actions

Any covered class action brought in any State court involving a covered security, as set forth in paragraph (1), shall be removable to the Federal district court for the district in which the action is pending, and shall be subject to paragraph (1).

3. Preservation of certain actions

A. Actions under State law of State of incorporation

i. Actions preserved

Notwithstanding paragraph (1) or (2), a covered class action described in clause (ii) of this subparagraph that is based upon the statutory or common law of the State in which the issuer is incorporated (in the case of a corporation) or organized (in the case of any other entity) may be maintained in a State or Federal court by a private party.

ii. Permissible actions

A covered class action is described in this clause if it involves–

I. the purchase or sale of securities by the issuer or an affiliate of the issuer exclusively from or to holders of equity securities of the issuer; or

II. any recommendation, position, or other communication with respect to the sale of securities of an issuer that–

(aa) is made by or on behalf of the issuer or an affiliate of the issuer to holders of equity securities of the issuer; and
(bb) concerns decisions of such equity holders with respect to voting their securities, acting in response to a tender or exchange offer, or exercising dissenters' or appraisal rights.

B. State actions

i. In general

Notwithstanding any other provision of this subsection, nothing in this subsection may be construed to preclude a State or political subdivision thereof or a State pension plan from bringing an action involving a covered security on its own behalf, or as a member of a class comprised solely of other States, political subdivisions, or State pension plans that are named plaintiffs, and that have authorized participation, in such action.

  ii. State pension plan defined

   For purposes of this subparagraph, the term "State pension plan" means a pension plan established and maintained for its employees by the government of a State or political subdivision thereof, or by any agency or instrumentality thereof.

C. Actions under contractual agreements between issuers and indenture trustees

 Notwithstanding paragraph (1) or (2), a covered class action that seeks to enforce a contractual agreement between an issuer and an indenture trustee may be maintained in a State or Federal court by a party to the agreement or a successor to such party.

D. Remand of removed actions

 In an action that has been removed from a State court pursuant to paragraph (2), if the Federal court determines that the action may be maintained in State court pursuant to this subsection, the Federal court shall remand such action to such State court.

4. Preservation of State jurisdiction

The securities commission (or any agency or office performing like functions) of any State shall retain jurisdiction under the laws of such State to investigate and bring enforcement actions.

5. Definitions

For purposes of this subsection, the following definitions shall apply:

A. Affiliate of the issuer

 The term "affiliate of the issuer" means a person that directly or indirectly, through one or more intermediaries, controls or is controlled by or is under common control with, the issuer.

B. Covered class action

 The term "covered class action" means–

  i. any single lawsuit in which–

   I. damages are sought on behalf of more than 50 persons or prospective class members, and questions of law or fact common to those persons or members of the prospective class, without reference to issues of individualized reliance on an alleged misstatement or omission, predominate over any questions affecting only individual persons or members; or

   II. one or more named parties seek to recover damages on a representative basis on behalf of themselves and other unnamed parties similarly situated, and questions of law or fact common to those persons or members of the prospective class predominate over any questions affecting only individual persons or members; or

            ii. any group of lawsuits filed in or pending in the same court and involving common questions of law or fact, in which–
               I. damages are sought on behalf of more than 50 persons; and
               II. the lawsuits are joined, consolidated, or otherwise proceed as a single action for any purpose.

       C. Exception for derivative actions
Notwithstanding subparagraph (B), the term "covered class action" does not include an exclusively derivative action brought by one or more shareholders on behalf of a corporation.

       D. Counting of certain class members
For purposes of this paragraph, a corporation, investment company, pension plan, partnership, or other entity, shall be treated as one person or prospective class member, but only if the entity is not established for the purpose of participating in the action.

       E. Covered security
The term "covered security" means a security that satisfies the standards for a covered security specified in paragraph (1) or (2) of section 18(b) of the Securities Act of 1933, at the time during which it is alleged that the misrepresentation, omission, or manipulative or deceptive conduct occurred, except that such term shall not include any debt security that is exempt from registration under the Securities Act of 1933 pursuant to rules issued by the Commission under section 4(2) of the Securities Act of 1933.

       F. Rule of construction
Nothing in this paragraph shall be construed to affect the discretion of a State court in determining whether actions filed in such court should be joined, consolidated, or otherwise allowed to proceed as a single action

Section 29 – Validity of Contracts

     a. **Waiver provisions.** Any condition, stipulation, or provision binding any person to waive compliance with any provision of this title or of any rule or regulation thereunder, or of any rule of an exchange required thereby shall be void.

     b. **Contract provisions in violation of title.** Every contract made in violation of any provision of this title or of any rule or regulation thereunder, and every contract (including any contract for listing a security on an exchange) heretofore or hereafter made, the performance of which involves the violation of, or the continuance of any relationship or practice in violation of, any provision of this title or any rule or regulation thereunder, shall be void (1) as regards the rights of any person who, in violation of any such provision, rule, or regulation, shall have made or engaged in the performance of any such contract, and (2) as regards the rights of any person who, not being a party to such contract, shall have acquired any right thereunder with actual knowledge of the facts by reason of which the making or performance of such contract was in violation of any such provision, rule, or regulation: Provided, (A) That no contract shall be void by reason of this subsection because of any violation of any rule or regulation prescribed pursuant to paragraph (3) of subsection (c) of section 15, and (B) that no contract shall be deemed to be void by reason of this subsection in any action maintained in reliance upon this subsection, by any person to or for whom any broker or dealer sells, or from or for whom any broker or dealer purchases, a security in violation of any rule or regulation prescribed pursuant to paragraph (1) or (2) of subsection (c) of section 15, unless such action is brought within one year after the discovery that such sale or purchase involves such violation and within three years after such violation. The Commission may, in a rule or regulation prescribed pursuant to such paragraph (2) of such section 15(c), designate such rule or regulation, or portion thereof, as a rule or regulation, or portion thereof, a contract in violation of which shall not be void by reason of this subsection.

c. **Validity of loans, extensions of credit, and creation of liens; actual knowledge of violation.** Nothing in this title shall be construed (1) to affect the validity of any loan or extension of credit (or any extension or renewal thereof) made or of any lien created prior or subsequent to the enactment of this title, unless at the time of the making of such loan or extension of credit (or extension or renewal thereof) or the creating of such lien, the person making such loan or extension of credit (or extension or renewal thereof) or acquiring such lien shall have actual knowledge of facts by reason of which the making of such loan or extension of credit (or extension or renewal thereof) or the acquisition of such lien is a violation of the provisions of this title or any rule or regulation thereunder, or (2) to afford a defense to the collection of any debt or obligation or the enforcement of any lien by any person who shall have acquired such debt, obligation, or lien in good faith for value and without actual knowledge of the violation of any provision of this title or any rule or regulation thereunder affecting the legality of such debt, obligation, or lien.

Section 32 – Penalties

a. **Willful violations; false and misleading statements.** Any person who willfully violates any provision of this title (other than section 30A), or any rule or regulation thereunder the violation of which is made unlawful or the observance of which is required under the terms of this title, or any person who willfully and knowingly makes, or causes to be made, any statement in any application, report, or document required to be filed under this title or any rule or regulation thereunder or any undertaking contained in a registration statement as provided in subsection (d) of section 15, or by any self-regulatory organization in connection with an application for membership or participation therein or to become associated with a member thereof, which statement was false or misleading with respect to any material fact, shall upon conviction be fined not more than $5,000,000, or imprisoned not more than 20 years, or both, except that when such person is a person other than a natural person, a fine not exceeding $25,000,000 may be imposed; but no person shall be subject to imprisonment under this section for the violation of any rule or regulation if he proves that he had no knowledge of such rule or regulation.

b. **Failure to file information, documents, or reports.** Any issuer which fails to file information, documents, or reports required to be filed under subsection (d) of section 15 or any rule or regulation thereunder shall forfeit to the United States the sum of $100 for each and every day such failure to file shall continue. Such forfeiture, which shall be in lieu of any criminal penalty for such failure to file which might be deemed to arise under subsection (a) of this section, shall be payable into the Treasury of the United States and shall be recoverable in a civil suit in the name of the United States.

c. **Violations by issuers, officers, directors, stockholders, employees, or agents of issuers**

    1.   A.   Any issuer that violates subsection (a) or (g) of section 30A shall be fined not more than $2,000,000.

            B.   Any issuer that violates subsection (a) or (g) of section 30A shall be subject to a civil penalty of not more than $10,000 imposed in an action brought by the Commission.

    2.   A.   Any officer, director, employee, or agent of an issuer, or stockholder acting on behalf of such issuer, who willfully violates subsection (a) or (g) of section 30A shall be fined not more than $100,000, or imprisoned not more than 5 years, or both.

            B.   Any officer, director, employee, or agent of an issuer, or stockholder acting on behalf of such issuer, who violates subsection (a) or (g) of section 30A shall be subject to a civil penalty of not more than $10,000 imposed in an action brought by the Commission.

    3.   Whenever a fine is imposed under paragraph (2) upon any officer, director, employee, agent, or stockholder of an issuer, such fine may not be paid, directly or indirectly, by such issuer.

Section 36 – General Exemptive Authority

a. **Authority**

    1.   In general

        Except as provided in subsection (b) of this section, but notwithstanding any other provision of this title, the Commission, by rule, regulation, or order, may conditionally or unconditionally exempt any person, security, or transaction, or any class or classes of persons, securities, or transactions, from any provision or provisions of this title or of any rule or regulation thereunder, to the extent that such exemption is necessary or appropriate in the public interest, and is consistent with the protection of investors.

    2.   Procedures

        The Commission shall, by rule or regulation, determine the procedures under which an exemptive order under this section shall be granted and may, in its sole discretion, decline to entertain any application for an order of exemption under this section.

b. **Limitation**. The Commission may not, under this section, exempt any person, security, or transaction, or any class or classes of persons, securities, or transactions from section 15C or the rules or regulations issued thereunder or (for purposes of section 15C and the rules and regulations issued thereunder) from any definition in paragraph (42), (43), (44), or (45) of section 3(a).

c. **Derivatives.** Unless the Commission is expressly authorized by any provision described in this subsection to grant exemptions, the Commission shall not grant exemptions, with respect to amendments made by subtitle B of the Wall Street

Transparency and Accountability Act of 2010, with respect to paragraphs (65), (66), (68), (69), (70), (71), (72), (73), (74), (75), (76), and (79) of section 3(a), and sections 10B(a), 10B(b), 10B(c), 13A, 15F, 17A(g), 17A(h), 17A(i), 17A(j), 17A(k), and 17A(l); provided that the Commission shall have exemptive authority under this title with respect to security-based swaps as to the same matters that the Commodity Futures Trading Commission has under the Wall Street Transparency and Accountability Act of 2010 with respect to swaps.

Section 39 – Investor Advisory Committee

a. **Establishment and purpose.**
  1. Establishment. There is established within the Commission the Investor Advisory Committee (referred to in this section as the 'Committee').
  2. Purpose. The Committee shall—
     A. advise and consult with the Commission on—
        i. regulatory priorities of the Commission;
        ii. issues relating to the regulation of securities products, trading strategies, and fee structures, and the effectiveness of disclosure;
        iii. initiatives to protect investor interest; and
        iv. initiatives to promote investor confidence and the integrity of the securities marketplace; and
     B. submit to the Commission such findings and recommendations as the Committee determines are appropriate, including recommendations for proposed legislative changes.

b. **Membership**
  1. In general. The members of the Committee shall be—
     A. the Investor Advocate;
     B. a representative of State securities commissions;
     C. a representative of the interests of senior citizens; and
     D. not fewer than 10, and not more than 20, members appointed by the Commission, from among individuals who—
        i. represent the interests of individual equity and debt investors, including investors in mutual funds;
        ii. represent the interests of institutional investors, including the interests of pension funds and registered investment companies;
        iii. are knowledgeable about investment issues and decisions; and
        iv. have reputations of integrity.
  2. Term. Each member of the Committee appointed under paragraph (1)(B) shall serve for a term of 4 years.
  3. Members not Commission Employees. Members appointed under paragraph (1)(B) shall not be deemed to be employees or agents of the Commission solely because of membership on the Committee.

c. **Chairman; Vice Chairman; Secretary; Assistant Secretary.**
  1. In general. The members of the Committee shall elect, from among the members of the Committee—
     A. a chairman, who may not be employed by an issuer;

          B.   a vice chairman, who may not be employed by an issuer;

          C.   a secretary; and

          D.   an assistant secretary.

     2.   Term. Each member elected under paragraph (1) shall serve for a term of 3 years in the capacity for which the member was elected under paragraph (1).

d.   **Meetings.**

     1.   Frequency of meetings. The Committee shall meet—

          A.   not less frequently than twice annually, at the call of the chairman of the Committee; and

          B.   from time to time, at the call of the Commission.

     2.   Notice. The chairman of the Committee shall give the members of the Committee written notice of each meeting, not later than 2 weeks before the date of the meeting.

e.   **Compensation and travel expenses**. Each member of the Committee who is not a full-time employee of the United States shall—

     1.   be entitled to receive compensation at a rate not to exceed the daily equivalent of the annual rate of basic pay in effect for a position at level V of the Executive Schedule under section 5316 of title 5, United States Code, for each day during which the member is engaged in the actual performance of the duties of the Committee; and

     2.   while away from the home or regular place of business of the member in the performance of services for the Committee, be allowed travel expenses, including per diem in lieu of subsistence, in the same manner as persons employed intermittently in the Government service are allowed expenses under section 5703(b) of title 5, United States Code.

f.   **Staff**. The Commission shall make available to the Committee such staff as the chairman of the Committee determines are necessary to carry out this section.

g.   **Review by Commission**. The Commission shall—

     1.   review the findings and recommendations of the Committee; and

     2.   each time the Committee submits a finding or recommendation to the Commission, promptly issue a public statement—

          A.   assessing the finding or recommendation of the Committee; and

          B.   disclosing the action, if any, the Commission intends to take with respect to the finding or recommendation.

h.   **Committee Findings**. Nothing in this section shall require the Commission to agree to or act upon any finding or recommendation of the Committee.

i.   **Federal Advisory Committee Act**. The Federal Advisory Committee Act (5 U.S.C. App.) shall not apply with respect to the Committee and its activities.

j.   **Authorization of appropriations.** There is authorized to be appropriated to the Commission such sums as are necessary to carry out this section.

Exchange Act – Rules:

Rule 10b-5 – Employment of Manipulative and Deceptive Devices

It shall be unlawful for any person, directly or indirectly, by the use of any means or instrumentality of interstate commerce, or of the mails or of any facility of any national securities exchange,

    a. To employ any device, scheme, or artifice to defraud,

    b.   To make any untrue statement of a material fact or to omit to state a material fact necessary in order to make the statements made, in the light of the circumstances under which they were made, not misleading, or

    c.   To engage in any act, practice, or course of business which operates or would operate as a fraud or deceit upon any person,

in connection with the purchase or sale of any security.

Rule 10b5-1 – Trading "on the Basis of" Material Nonpublic Information in Insider Trading Cases

    a.   **Manipulative or deceptive devices..** The "manipulative and deceptive devices" prohibited by Section 10(b) of the Act and Rule 10b-5 thereunder include, among other things, the purchase or sale of a security of any issuer, on the basis of material nonpublic information about that security or issuer, in breach of a duty of trust or confidence that is owed directly, indirectly, or derivatively, to the issuer of that security or the shareholders of that issuer, or to any other person who is the source of the material nonpublic information.

    b.   **Awareness of material nonpublic information.** Subject to the affirmative defenses in paragraph (c) of this section, a purchase or sale of a security of an issuer is "on the basis of" material nonpublic information about that security or issuer if the person making the purchase or sale was aware of the material nonpublic information when the person made the purchase or sale. The law of insider trading is otherwise defined by judicial opinions construing Rule 10b-5, and Rule 10b5-1 does not modify the scope of insider trading law in any other respect.

    c.   **Affirmative defenses**.
        1.   i.   Subject to paragraph (c)(1)(ii) of this section, a person's purchase or sale is not "on the basis of" material nonpublic information if the person making the purchase or sale demonstrates that:
            A.   Before becoming aware of the information, the person had:
               1.   Entered into a binding contract to purchase or sell the security,
               2.   Instructed another person to purchase or sell the security for the instructing person's account, or
               3.   Adopted a written plan for trading securities;
            B.   The contract, instruction, or plan described in paragraph (c)(1)(i)(A) of this Section:
               1.   Specified the amount of securities to be purchased or sold and the price at which and the date on which the securities were to be purchased or sold;
               2.   Included a written formula or algorithm, or computer program, for determining the amount of securities to be purchased or sold and the price at which and the date on which the securities were to be purchased or sold; or
               3.   Did not permit the person to exercise any subsequent influence over how, when, or whether to effect purchases or sales; provided, in addition, that any other person who, pursuant to the

contract, instruction, or plan, did exercise such influence must not have been aware of the material nonpublic information when doing so; and

C. The purchase or sale that occurred was pursuant to the contract, instruction, or plan. A purchase or sale is not "pursuant to a contract, instruction, or plan" if, among other things, the person who entered into the contract, instruction, or plan altered or deviated from the contract, instruction, or plan to purchase or sell securities (whether by changing the amount, price, or timing of the purchase or sale), or entered into or altered a corresponding or hedging transaction or position with respect to those securities.

ii. Paragraph (c)(1)(i) of this section is applicable only when:

A. The contract, instruction, or plan to purchase or sell securities was given or entered into in good faith and not as part of a plan or scheme to evade the prohibitions of this section, and the person who entered into the contract, instruction, or plan has acted in good faith with resepect to the contract, instruction or plan;

B. If the person who entered into the contract, instruction, or plan is:

1. A director or officer (as defined in Rule16a-1(f) of the issuer, no purchases or sales occur until expiration of a cooling-off period consisting of the later of:

i. Ninety days after the adoption of the contract, instruction, or plan or

ii. Two business days following the disclosure of the issuer's financial results in a Form 10-Q or Form 10-K for the completed fiscal quarter in which the plan was adopted or, for foreign private issuers, in a Form 20-F or Form 6-K that discloses the issuer's financial results (but, in any event, this required cooling-off period is subject to a maximum of 120 days after adoption of the contract, instruction, or plan); or

2. Not the issuer and not a director or officer (as defined in Rule 16a-1(f) of the issuer, no purchases or sales occur until the expiration of a cooling-off period that is 30 days after the adoption of the contract, instruction or plan;.

C. If the person who entered into a plan as described in paragraph (c)(1)(i)(A)(3) of this section is a director or officer (as defined in Rule 16a-1(f) of the issuer of the securities, such director or officer included a representation in the plan certifying that, on the date of adoption of the plan:

1. The individual director or officer is not aware of any material nonpublic information about the security or issuer; and

2. The individual director or officer is adopting the plan in good faith and not as part of a plan or scheme to evade the prohibitions of this section;

D. The person (other than the issuer) who entered into the contract, instruction, or plan has no outstanding (and does not subsequently enter into any additional) contract, instruction, or plan that would qualify for the affirmative defense under paragraph (c)(1) of this section for purchases or sales of the issuer's securities on the open market; except that:

1. For purposes of this paragraph (c)(1)(ii)(D), a series of separate contracts with different broker-dealers or other agents acting on behalf of the person (other than the issuer) to execute trades thereunder may be treated as a single "plan," provided that the individual constituent contracts with each broker-dealer or other agent, when taken together as a whole, meet all of the applicable conditions of and remain collectively subject to the provisions of this rule, including that a modification of any individual contract acts as modification of the whole contract, instruction of plan, as defined in paragraph (c)(1)(iv) of this section. The substitution of a broker-dealer or other agent acting on behalf of the person (other than the issuer) for another broker-dealer that is executing trades pursuant to a contract, instruction or plan shall not be a modification of the contract, instruction, or plan (as defined in paragraph (c)(1)(iv) of this section) as long as the purchase or sales instructions applicable to the substitute and substituted broker are identical with respect to the prices of securities to be purchased or sold, dates of the purchases or sales to be executed, and amount of securities to be purchased or sold; and

2. The person (other than the issuer) may have one later-commencing contract, instruction, or plan for purchases or sales of any securities of the issuer on the open market under which trading is not authorized to begin until after all trades under the earlier-commencing contract, instruction, or plan are completed or expired without execution; provided, however, that if the first trade under the later-commencing contract, instruction, or plan is scheduled during the Effective Cooling-Off Period, the later-commencing contract, instruction, or plan may not rely on this paragraph (c)(1)(ii)(D)(2). For purposes of this paragraph (c)(1)(ii)(D)(2), "Effective Cooling-Off Period" means the cooling-off period that would be applicable under paragraph (c)(1)(ii)(B) of this section with respect to the later-commencing contract, instruction, or plan if the date of adoption of the later-commencing contract, instruction, or plan were deemed to be the date of termination of the earlier-commencing contract, instruction, or plan; and

3. A contract, instruction, or plan providing for an eligible sell-to-cover transaction shall not be considered an outstanding or additional contract, instruction, or plan under paragraph (c)(1)(ii)(D) of this section, and such eligible sell-to-cover transaction shall not be subject to the limitation under paragraph (c)(1)(ii)(D) of this section. A contract, instruction, or plan provides for an eligible sell-to-cover transaction where the contract, instruction, or plan authorizes an agent to sell only such securities as are necessary to satisfy tax withholding obligations

arising exclusively from the vesting of a compensatory award, such as restricted stock or stock appreciation rights, and the insider does not otherwise exercise control over the timing of such sales; and

    E.   With respect to persons (other than the issuer), if the contract, instruction, or plan does not provide for an eligible sell-to-cover transaction as described in paragraph (c)(1)(ii)(D)(3) of this section and is designed to effect the open-market purchase or sale of the total amount of securities as a single transaction, the person who entered into the contract, instruction, or plan has not during the prior 12-month period adopted a contract, instruction, or plan that:

        1.   was designed to effect the open-market purchase or sale of all of the securities covered by such prior contract, instruction or plan, in a single transaction; and

        2.   Would otherwise qualify for the affirmative defense under paragraph (c)(1) of this section.

  iii. This paragraph (c)(1)(iii) defines certain terms as used in paragraph (c) of this Section.

    A.   *Amount.* "Amount" means either a specified number of shares or other securities or a specified dollar value of securities.

    B.   *Price.* "Price" means the market price on a particular date or a limit price, or a particular dollar price.

    C.   *Date.* "Date" means, in the case of a market order, the specific day of the year on which the order is to be executed (or as soon thereafter as is practicable under ordinary principles of best execution). "Date" means, in the case of a limit order, a day of the year on which the limit order is in force.

  iv. Any modification or change to the amount, price, or timing of the purchase or sale of the securities underlying a contract, instruction, or written plan as described in paragraph (c)(1)(i)(A) of this section is a termination of such contract, instruction, or written plan, and the adoption of a new contract, instruction, or written plan. A plan modification, such as the substitution or removal of a broker that is executing trades pursuant to a Rule 10b5-1 arrangement on behalf of the person, that changes the price or date on which purchases or sales are to be executed, is a termination of such plan and the adoption of a new plan.

2.   A person other than a natural person also may demonstrate that a purchase or sale of securities is not "on the basis of" material nonpublic information if the person demonstrates that:

  i. The individual making the investment decision on behalf of the person to purchase or sell the securities was not aware of the information; and

  ii. The person had implemented reasonable policies and procedures, taking into consideration the nature of the person's business, to ensure that individuals making investment decisions would not violate the laws prohibiting trading on the basis of material nonpublic information. These policies and procedures may include those that restrict any purchase, sale, and causing any purchase or sale of any security as to which the person has material nonpublic information, or those that prevent such individuals from becoming aware of such information.

Rule 10b5-2 – Duties of Trust or Confidence in Misappropriation Insider Trading Cases
Preliminary Note:

This section provides a non-exclusive definition of circumstances in which a person has a duty of trust or confidence for purposes of the "misappropriation" theory of insider trading under Section 10(b) of the Act and Rule 10b-5. The law of insider trading is otherwise defined by judicial opinions construing Rule 10b-5, and Rule 10b5-2 does not modify the scope of insider trading law in any other respect.

a.   **Scope of Rule.** This section shall apply to any violation of Section 10(b) of the Act and Rule 10b-5 thereunder that is based on the purchase or sale of securities on the basis of, or the communication of, material nonpublic information misappropriated in breach of a duty of trust or confidence.

b.   **Enumerated "duties of trust or confidence."** For purposes of this section, a *duty of trust or confidence* exists in the following circumstances, among others:
   1.   Whenever a person agrees to maintain information in confidence;
   2.   Whenever the person communicating the material nonpublic information and the person to whom it is communicated have a history, pattern, or practice of sharing confidences, such that the recipient of the information knows or reasonably should know that the person communicating the material nonpublic information expects that the recipient will maintain its confidentiality; or
   3.   Whenever a person receives or obtains material nonpublic information from his or her spouse, parent, child, or sibling; *provided, however*, that the person receiving or obtaining the information may demonstrate that no duty of trust or confidence existed with respect to the information, by establishing that he or she neither knew nor reasonably should have known that the person who was the source of the information expected that the person would keep the information confidential, because of the parties' history, pattern, or practice of sharing and maintaining confidences, and because there was no agreement or understanding to maintain the confidentiality of the information.

Rule 10b-9 – Prohibited Representations in Connection with Certain Offerings

a.   It shall constitute a *manipulative or deception device or contrivance*, as used in section 10(b) of the Act, for any person, directly or indirectly, in connection with the offer or sale of any security, to make any representation:
   1.   To the effect that the security is being offered or sold on an "all-or-none" basis, unless the security is part of an offering or distribution being made on the condition that all or a specified amount of the consideration paid for such security will be promptly refunded to the purchaser unless
      A.   all of the securities being offered are sold at a specified price within a specified time, and
      B.   the total amount due to the seller is received by him by a specified date; or
   2.   To the effect that the security is being offered or sold on any other basis whereby all or part of the consideration paid for any such security will be

refunded to the purchaser if all or some of the securities are not sold, unless the security is part of an offering or distribution being made on the condition that all or a specified part of the consideration paid for such security will be promptly refunded to the purchaser unless

    A.   a specified number of units of the security are sold at a specified price within a specified time, and

    B.   the total amount due to the seller is received by him by a specified date.

    b.   This rule shall not apply to any offer or sale of securities as to which the seller has a firm commitment from underwriters or others (subject only to customary conditions precedent, including "market outs") for the purchase of all the securities being offered.

Rule 10b-18 – Purchases of Certain Equity Securities by the Issuer and Others

Preliminary Notes:

1.   Rule 10b-18 provides an issuer (and its affiliated purchasers) with a "safe harbor" from liability for manipulation under sections 9(a)(2) of the Act and Rule 10b-5 under the Act solely by reason of the manner, timing, price, and volume of their repurchases when they repurchase the issuer's common stock in the market in accordance with the section's manner, timing, price, and volume conditions. As a safe harbor, compliance with Rule 10b-18 is voluntary. To come within the safe harbor, however, an issuer's repurchases must satisfy (on a daily basis) each of the section's four conditions. Failure to meet any one of the four conditions will remove all of the issuer's repurchases from the safe harbor for that day. The safe harbor, moreover, is not available for repurchases that, although made in technical compliance with the section, are part of a plan or scheme to evade the federal securities laws.

2.   Regardless of whether the repurchases are effected in accordance with Rule 10b-18, reporting issuers must report their repurchasing activity as required by Item 703 of Regulation S-K and Item 15(e) of Form 20-F (regarding foreign private issuers), and closed-end management investment companies that are registered under the Investment Company Act of 1940 must report their repurchasing activity as required by Item 8 of Form N-CSR.

    a.   **Definitions.** Unless otherwise provided, all terms used in this section shall have the same meaning as in the Act. In addition, the following definitions shall apply:

        1.   **ADTV** means the average daily trading volume reported for the security during the four calendar weeks preceding the week in which the Rule 10b-18 purchase is to be effected.

        2.   **Affiliate** means any person that directly or indirectly controls, is controlled by, or is under common control with, the issuer.

        3.   **Affiliated purchaser** means:

            i.   A person acting, directly or indirectly, in concert with the issuer for the purpose of acquiring the issuer's securities; or

            ii.   An affiliate who, directly or indirectly, controls the issuer's purchases of such securities, whose purchases are controlled by the issuer, or whose purchases are under common control with those of the issuer; *Provided, however*, that "affiliated purchaser" shall not include a broker, dealer, or other person solely by reason of such broker, dealer, or other person effecting Rule 10b-18 purchases on behalf of the issuer or for its account, and shall not include an officer or director of the issuer solely by reason of that officer or director's participation in the decision to authorize Rule 10b-18 purchases by or on behalf of the issuer.

4. **Agent independent of the issuer** has the meaning contained in Rule 100 of this chapter.

5. **Block** means a quantity of stock that either:
   i. Has a purchase price of $200,000 or more; or
   ii. Is at least 5,000 shares and has a purchase price of at least $50,000; or
   iii. Is at least 20 round lots of the security and totals 150 percent or more of the trading volume for that security or, in the event that trading volume data are unavailable, is at least 20 round lots of the security and totals at least one-tenth of one percent (.001) of the outstanding shares of the security, exclusive of any shares owned by any affiliate;
   Provided, however, That a block under paragraph (a)(5)(i), (ii), and (iii) shall not include any amount a broker or dealer, acting as principal, has accumulated for the purpose of sale or resale to the issuer or to any affiliated purchaser of the issuer if the issuer or such affiliated purchaser knows or has reason to know that such amount was accumulated for such purpose, nor shall it include any amount that a broker or dealer has sold short to the issuer or to any affiliated purchaser of the issuer if the issuer or such affiliated purchaser knows or has reason to know that the sale was a short sale.

6. **Consolidated system** means a consolidated transaction or quotation reporting system that collects and publicly disseminates on a current and continuous basis transaction or quotation information in common equity securities pursuant to an effective transaction reporting plan (Rule 11Aa3-1) or a national market system plan (as defined in Rule 11Aa3-2).

7. **Market-wide trading suspension** means a market-wide trading halt of 30 minutes or more that is:
   i. Imposed pursuant to the rules of a national securities exchange or a national securities association in response to a market-wide decline during a single trading session; or
   ii. Declared by the Commission pursuant to its authority under section 12(k) of the Act.

8. **Plan** has the meaning contained in Rule 100 of this chapter.

9. **Principal market for a security** means the single securities market with the largest reported trading volume for the security during the six full calendar months preceding the week in which the Rule 10b-18 purchase is to be effected.

10. **Public float value** has the meaning contained in Rule 100 of this chapter.

11. **Purchase price** means the price paid per share as reported, exclusive of any commission paid to a broker acting as agent, or commission equivalent, mark-up, or differential paid to a dealer.

12. **Riskless principal transaction** means a transaction in which a broker or dealer after having received an order from an issuer to buy its security, buys the security as principal in the market at the same price to satisfy the issuer's buy order. The issuer's buy order must be effected at the same price per-share at which the

broker or dealer bought the shares to satisfy the issuer's buy order, exclusive of any explicitly disclosed markup or markdown, commission equivalent, or other fee. In addition, only the first leg of the transaction, when the broker or dealer buys the security in the market as principal, is reported under the rules of a self-regulatory organization or under the Act. For purposes of this section, the broker or dealer must have written policies and procedures in place to assure that, at a minimum, the issuer's buy order was received prior to the offsetting transaction; the offsetting transaction is allocated to a riskless principal account or the issuer's account within 60 seconds of the execution; and the broker or dealer has supervisory systems in place to produce records that enable the broker or dealer to accurately and readily reconstruct, in a time-sequenced manner, all orders effected on a riskless principal basis.

13. **Rule 10b-18 purchase** means a purchase (or any bid or limit order that would effect such purchase) of an issuer's common stock (or an equivalent interest, including a unit of beneficial interest in a trust or limited partnership or a depository share) by or for the issuer or any affiliated purchaser (including riskless principal transactions). However, it does not include any purchase of such security:

    i. Effected during the applicable restricted period of a distribution that is subject to Rule 102 of this chapter;

    ii. Effected by or for an issuer plan by an agent independent of the issuer;

    iii. Effected as a fractional share purchase (a fractional interest in a security) evidenced by a script certificate, order form, or similar document;

    iv. Effected during the period from the time of public announcement (as defined in Rule 165(f)) of a merger, acquisition, or similar transaction involving a recapitalization, until the earlier of the completion of such transaction or the completion of the vote by target shareholders. This exclusion does not apply to Rule 10b-18 purchases:

        A. Effected during such transaction in which the consideration is solely cash and there is no valuation period; or

        B. Where:

            1. The total volume of Rule 10b-18 purchases effected on any single day does not exceed the lesser of 25% of the security's four-week ADTV or the issuer's average daily Rule 10b-18 purchases during the three full calendar months preceding the date of the announcement of such transaction;

            2. The issuer's block purchases effected pursuant to paragraph (b)(4) of this section do not exceed the average size and frequency of the issuer's block purchases effected pursuant to paragraph (b)(4) of this section during the three full calendar months preceding the date of the announcement of such transaction; and

            3. Such purchases are not otherwise restricted or prohibited;

    v. Effected pursuant to Rule 13e-1;

    vi. Effected pursuant to a tender offer that is subject to Rule 13e-4 or specifically excepted from Rule 13e-4; or

    vii. Effected pursuant to a tender offer that is subject to section 14(d) of the Act and the rules and regulations thereunder.

b. **Conditions to be met**. Rule 10b-18 purchases shall not be deemed to have violated the anti-manipulation provisions of sections 9(a)(2) or 10(b) of the Act or Rule 10b-5 under the Act, solely by reason of the time, price, or amount of the Rule 10b-18 purchases, or the number of brokers or dealers used in connection with such purchases, if the issuer or affiliated purchaser of the issuer effects the Rule 10b-18 purchases according to each of the following conditions:

1. One broker or dealer. Rule 10b-18 purchases must be effected from or through only one broker or dealer on any single day; *Provided, however*, that:

    i.   The "one broker or dealer" condition shall not apply to Rule 10b-18 purchases that are not solicited by or on behalf of the issuer or its affiliated purchaser(s);

    ii. Where Rule 10b-18 purchases are effected by or on behalf of more than one affiliated purchaser of the issuer (or the issuer and one or more of its affiliated purchasers) on a single day, the issuer and all affiliated purchasers must use the same broker or dealer; and

    iii. Where Rule 10b-18 purchases are effected on behalf of the issuer by a broker-dealer that is not an electronic communication network (ECN) or other alternative trading system (ATS), that broker-dealer can access ECN or other ATS liquidity in order to execute repurchases on behalf of the issuer (or any affiliated purchaser of the issuer) on that day.

2. Time of purchases. Rule 10b-18 purchases must not be:

    i.   The opening (regular way) purchase reported in the consolidated system;

    ii. Effected during the 10 minutes before the scheduled close of the primary trading session in the principal market for the security, and the 10 minutes before the scheduled close of the primary trading session in the market where the purchase is effected, for a security that has an ADTV value of $1 million or more and a public float value of $150 million or more; and

    iii. Effected during the 30 minutes before the scheduled close of the primary trading session in the principal market for the security, and the 30 minutes before the scheduled close of the primary trading session in the market where the purchase is effected, for all other securities;

    iv. However, for purposes of this section, Rule 10b-18 purchases may be effected following the close of the primary trading session until the termination of the period in which last sale prices are reported in the consolidated system so long as such purchases are effected at prices that do not exceed the lower of the closing price of the primary trading session in the principal market for the security and any lower bids or sale prices subsequently reported in the consolidated system, and all of this section's conditions are met. However, for purposes of this section, the issuer may use one broker or dealer to effect Rule 10b-18 purchases during this period that may be different from the broker or dealer that it used during the primary trading session. However, the issuer's Rule 10b-18 purchase may not be the opening transaction of the session following the close of the primary trading session.

516

3. Price of purchases. Rule 10b-18 purchases must be effected at a purchase price that:
   i. Does not exceed the highest independent bid or the last independent transaction price, whichever is higher, quoted or reported in the consolidated system at the time the Rule 10b-18 purchase is effected;
   ii. For securities for which bids and transaction prices are not quoted or reported in the consolidated system, Rule 10b-18 purchases must be effected at a purchase price that does not exceed the highest independent bid or the last independent transaction price, whichever is higher, displayed and disseminated on any national securities exchange or on any inter-dealer quotation system (as defined in Rule 15c2-11) that displays at least two priced quotations for the security, at the time the Rule 10b-18 purchase is effected; and
   iii. For all other securities, Rule 10b-18 purchases must be effected at a price no higher than the highest independent bid obtained from three independent dealers.
4. Volume of purchases. The total volume of Rule 10b-18 purchases effected by or for the issuer and any affiliated purchasers effected on any single day must not exceed 25 percent of the ADTV for that security; However, once each week, in lieu of purchasing under the 25% of ADTV limit for that day, the issuer or an affiliated purchaser of the issuer may effect one block purchase if:
   i. No other Rule 10b-18 purchases are effected that day, and
   ii. The block purchase is not included when calculating a security's four week ADTV under this section.

c. **Alternative conditions.** The conditions of paragraph (b) of this section shall apply in connection with Rule 10b-18 purchases effected during a trading session following the imposition of a market-wide trading suspension, except:
   1. That the time of purchases condition in paragraph (b)(2) of this section shall not apply, either:
      i. From the reopening of trading until the scheduled close of trading on the day that the market-wide trading suspension is imposed; or
      ii. At the opening of trading on the next trading day until the scheduled close of trading that day, if a market-wide trading suspension was in effect at the close of trading on the preceding day; and
   2. The volume of purchases condition in paragraph (b)(4) of this section is modified so that the amount of Rule 10b-18 purchases must not exceed 100 percent of the ADTV for that security.

d. **Other purchases.** No presumption shall arise that an issuer or an affiliated purchaser has violated the anti-manipulation provisions of sections 9(a)(2) or 10(b) of the Act, or Rule 10b-5 under the Act, if the Rule 10b-18 purchases of such issuer or affiliated purchaser do not meet the conditions specified in paragraph (b) or (c) of this section.

Rule 10A-1 – Notice to the Commission Pursuant to Section 10A of the Act

a.

    1.   If any issuer with a reporting obligation under the Act receives a report requiring a notice to the Commission in accordance with section 10A(b)(3) of the Act, the issuer shall submit such notice to the Commission's Office of the Chief Accountant within the time period prescribed in that section. The notice may be provided by facsimile, telegraph, personal delivery, or any other means, provided it is received by the Office of the Chief Accountant within the required time period.

    2.   The notice specified in paragraph (a)(1) of this section shall be in writing and:

        i.   Shall identify the issuer (including the issuer's name, address, phone number, and file number assigned to the issuer's filings by the Commission) and the independent accountant (including the independent accountant's name and phone number, and the address of the independent accountant's principal office);

        ii.   Shall state the date that the issuer received from the independent accountant the report specified in section 10A(b)(2) of the Act;

        iii.   Shall provide, at the election of the issuer, either:

            A.   A summary of the independent accountant's report, including a description of the act that the independent accountant has identified as a likely illegal act and the possible effect of that act on all affected financial statements of the issuer or those related to the most current three-year period, whichever is shorter; or

            B.   A copy of the independent accountant's report; and

        iv.   May provide additional information regarding the issuer's views of and response to the independent accountant's report.

    3.   Reports of the independent accountant submitted by the issuer to the Commission's Office of the Chief Accountant in accordance with paragraph (a)(2)(iii)(B) of this section shall be deemed to have been made pursuant to section 10A(b)(3) or section 10A(b)(4) of the Act, for purposes of the safe harbor provided by section 10A(c) of the Act.

    4.   Submission of the notice in paragraphs (a)(1) and (a)(2) of this section shall not relieve the issuer from its obligations to comply fully with all other reporting requirements, including, without limitation:

        i.   The filing requirements of Form 8-K, and Form N-SAR, regarding a change in the issuer's certifying accountant and

        ii.   The disclosure requirements of Item 304 of Regulation S-K.

b.

    1.   Any independent accountant furnishing to the Commission a copy of a report (or the documentation of any oral report) in accordance with section 10A(b)(3) or section 10A(b)(4) of the Act shall submit that report (or documentation) to the Commission's Office of the Chief Accountant within the time period prescribed by the appropriate section of the Act. The report (or documentation) may be submitted to the Commission's Office of the Chief Accountant by facsimile, telegraph, personal delivery, or any other means, provided it is received by the Office of the Chief Accountant within the time period set forth

in section 10A(b)(3) or 10A(b)(4) of the Act, whichever is applicable in the circumstances.

2.   If the report (or documentation) submitted to the Office of the Chief Accountant in accordance with paragraph (b)(1) of this section does not clearly identify both the issuer (including the issuer's name, address, phone number, and file number assigned to the issuer's filings with the Commission) and the independent accountant (including the independent accountant's name and phone number, and the address of the independent accountant's principal office), then the independent accountant shall place that information in a prominent attachment to the report (or documentation) and shall submit that attachment to the Office of the Chief Accountant at the same time and in the same manner as the report (or documentation) is submitted to that Office.

3.   Submission of the report (or documentation) by the independent accountant as described in paragraphs (b)(1) and (b)(2) of this section shall not replace, or otherwise satisfy the need for, the newly engaged and former accountants' letters under Items 304(a)(2)(D) and 304(a)(3) of Regulation S-K, respectively, and shall not limit, reduce, or affect in any way the independent accountant's obligations to comply fully with all other legal and professional responsibilities, including, without limitation, those under the standards of the Public Company Accounting Oversight Board (United States) ("PCAOB") and the rules or interpretations of the Commission that modify or supplement those auditing standards.

c.   A notice or report submitted to the Office of the Chief Accountant in accordance with paragraphs (a) and (b) of this section shall be deemed to be an investigative record and shall be non-public and exempt from disclosure pursuant to the Freedom of Information Act to the same extent and for the same periods of time that the Commission's investigative records are non-public and exempt from disclosure under, among other applicable provisions, 5 U.S.C. 552(b)(7) and 17 CFR 200.80(b)(7). Nothing in this paragraph, however, shall relieve, limit, delay, or affect in any way, the obligation of any issuer or any independent accountant to make all public disclosures required by law, by any Commission disclosure item, rule, report, or form, or by any applicable accounting, auditing, or professional standard.

     Instruction to Paragraph (c). Issuers and independent accountants may apply for additional bases for confidential treatment for a notice, report, or part thereof, in accordance with 17 CFR 200.83. That section indicates, in part, that any person who, pursuant to any requirement of law, submits any information or causes or permits any information to be submitted to the Commission, may request that the Commission afford it confidential treatment by reason of personal privacy or business confidentiality, or for any other reason permitted by Federal law.

Rule 10A-2 – Auditor Independence

It shall be unlawful for an auditor not to be independent under Rule 2-01(c)(2)(iii)(B), (c)(4), (c)(6), (c)(7), and Rule 2-07 of Regulation S-X.

Rule 10A-3 – Listing Standards Relating to Audit Committees

a.   Pursuant to section 10A(m) of the Act and section 3 of the Sarbanes-Oxley Act:

    1.   National securities exchanges. The rules of each national securities exchange registered pursuant to section 6 of the Act must, in accordance with the provisions of this section, prohibit the initial or continued listing of any security of an issuer that is not in compliance with the requirements of any portion of paragraph (b) or (c) of this section.

***

b.   **Required standards.**

    1.   Independence.

        i.   Each member of the audit committee must be a member of the board of directors of the listed issuer, and must otherwise be independent; provided that, where a listed issuer is one of two dual holding companies, those companies may designate one audit committee for both companies so long as each member of the audit committee is a member of the board of directors of at least one of such dual holding companies.

        ii.   Independence requirements for non-investment company issuers. In order to be considered to be independent for purposes of this paragraph (b)(1), a member of an audit committee of a listed issuer that is not an investment company may not, other than in his or her capacity as a member of the audit committee, the board of directors, or any other board committee:

            A.   Accept directly or indirectly any consulting, advisory, or other compensatory fee from the issuer or any subsidiary thereof, provided that, unless the rules of the national securities exchange or national securities association provide otherwise, compensatory fees do not include the receipt of fixed amounts of compensation under a retirement plan (including deferred compensation) for prior service with the listed issuer (provided that such compensation is not contingent in any way on continued service); or

            B.   Be an affiliated person of the issuer or any subsidiary thereof.

***

        iv.   Exemptions from the independence requirements.

            A.   For an issuer listing securities pursuant to a registration statement under section 12 of the Act, or for an issuer that has a registration statement under the Securities Act of 1933 covering an initial public offering of securities to be listed by the issuer, where in each case the listed issuer was not, immediately prior to the effective date of such registration statement, required to file reports with the Commission pursuant to section 13(a) or 15(d) of the Act:

                1.   All but one of the members of the listed issuer's audit committee may be exempt from the independence requirements of paragraph (b)(1)(ii) of this section for 90 days from the date of effectiveness of such registration statement; and

520

2. A minority of the members of the listed issuer's audit committee may be exempt from the independence requirements of paragraph (b)(1)(ii) of this section for one year from the date of effectiveness of such registration statement.

B. An audit committee member that sits on the board of directors of a listed issuer and an affiliate of the listed issuer is exempt from the requirements of paragraph (b)(1)(ii)(B) of this section if the member, except for being a director on each such board of directors, otherwise meets the independence requirements of paragraph (b)(1)(ii) of this section for each such entity, including the receipt of only ordinary-course compensation for serving as a member of the board of directors, audit committee or any other board committee of each such entity.

C. An employee of a foreign private issuer who is not an executive officer of the foreign private issuer is exempt from the requirements of paragraph (b)(1)(ii) of this section if the employee is elected or named to the board of directors or audit committee of the foreign private issuer pursuant to the issuer's governing law or documents, an employee collective bargaining or similar agreement or other home country legal or listing requirements.

***

2. *Responsibilities relating to registered public accounting firms.* The audit committee of each listed issuer, in its capacity as a committee of the board of directors, must be directly responsible for the appointment, compensation, retention and oversight of the work of any registered public accounting firm engaged (including resolution of disagreements between management and the auditor regarding financial reporting) for the purpose of preparing or issuing an audit report or performing other audit, review or attest services for the listed issuer, and each such registered public accounting firm must report directly to the audit committee.

3. *Complaints.* Each audit committee must establish procedures for:
    i.   The receipt, retention, and treatment of complaints received by the listed issuer regarding accounting, internal accounting controls, or auditing matters; and
    ii. The confidential, anonymous submission by employees of the listed issuer of concerns regarding questionable accounting or auditing matters.

4. *Authority to engage advisers.* Each audit committee must have the authority to engage independent counsel and other advisers, as it determines necessary to carry out its duties.

5. *Funding.* Each listed issuer must provide for appropriate funding, as determined by the audit committee, in its capacity as a committee of the board of directors, for payment of:
    i.   Compensation to any registered public accounting firm engaged for the purpose of preparing or issuing an audit report or performing other audit, review or attest services for the listed issuer;
    ii. Compensation to any advisers employed by the audit committee under paragraph (b)(4) of this section; and

    iii.   Ordinary administrative expenses of the audit committee that are necessary or appropriate in carrying out its duties.

c. **General exemptions**.

    1.   At any time when an issuer has a class of securities that is listed on a national securities exchange or national securities association subject to the requirements of this section, the listing of other classes of securities of the listed issuer on a national securities exchange or national securities association is not subject to the requirements of this section.

    2.   At any time when an issuer has a class of common equity securities (or similar securities) that is listed on a national securities exchange or national securities association subject to the requirements of this section, the listing of classes of securities of a direct or indirect consolidated subsidiary or an at least 50% beneficially owned subsidiary of the issuer (except classes of equity securities, other than non-convertible, non-participating preferred securities, of such subsidiary) is not subject to the requirements of this section.

    3.   The listing of securities of a foreign private issuer is not subject to the requirements of paragraphs (b)(1) through (b)(5) of this section if the foreign private issuer meets the following requirements:

        i.   The foreign private issuer has a board of auditors (or similar body), or has statutory auditors, established and selected pursuant to home country legal or listing provisions expressly requiring or permitting such a board or similar body;

        ii.   The board or body, or statutory auditors is required under home country legal or listing requirements to be either:

            A. Separate from the board of directors; or

            B. Composed of one or more members of the board of directors and one or more members that are not also members of the board of directors;

        iii.   The board or body, or statutory auditors, are not elected by management of such issuer and no executive officer of the foreign private issuer is a member of such board or body, or statutory auditors;

        iv.   Home country legal or listing provisions set forth or provide for standards for the independence of such board or body, or statutory auditors, from the foreign private issuer or the management of such issuer;

        v.   Such board or body, or statutory auditors, in accordance with any applicable home country legal or listing requirements or the issuer's governing documents, are responsible, to the extent permitted by law, for the appointment, retention and oversight of the work of any registered public accounting firm engaged (including, to the extent permitted by law, the resolution of disagreements between management and the auditor regarding financial reporting) for the purpose of preparing or issuing an audit report or performing other audit, review or attest services for the issuer; and

        vi.   The audit committee requirements of paragraphs (b)(3), (b)(4) and (b)(5) of this section apply to such board or body, or statutory auditors, to the extent permitted by law.

***

e.   **Definitions**. Unless the context otherwise requires, all terms used in this section have the same meaning as in the Act. In addition, unless the context otherwise requires, the following definitions apply for purposes of this section:

1.

   i.   The term **affiliate** of, or a person **affiliated** with, a specified person, means a person that directly, or indirectly through one or more intermediaries, controls, or is controlled by, or is under common control with, the person specified.

   ii.

   A. A person will be deemed not to be in control of a specified person for purposes of this section if the person:
   1.   Is not the beneficial owner, directly or indirectly, of more than 10% of any class of voting equity securities of the specified person; and
   2.   Is not an executive officer of the specified person.

   B. Paragraph (e)(1)(ii)(A) of this section only creates a safe harbor position that a person does not control a specified person. The existence of the safe harbor does not create a presumption in any way that a person exceeding the ownership requirement in paragraph (e)(1)(ii)(A)(1) of this section controls or is otherwise an affiliate of a specified person.

   iii. The following will be deemed to be affiliates:
   A. An executive officer of an affiliate;
   B. A director who also is an employee of an affiliate;
   C. A general partner of an affiliate; and
   D. A managing member of an affiliate.

   iv. For purposes of paragraph (e)(1)(i) of this section, dual holding companies will not be deemed to be affiliates of or persons affiliated with each other by virtue of their dual holding company arrangements with each other, including where directors of one dual holding company are also directors of the other dual holding company, or where directors of one or both dual holding companies are also directors of the businesses jointly controlled, directly or indirectly, by the dual holding companies (and, in each case, receive only ordinary-course compensation for serving as a member of the board of directors, audit committee or any other board committee of the dual holding companies or any entity that is jointly controlled, directly or indirectly, by the dual holding companies).

***

4.   The term **control** (including the terms **controlling, controlled by** and under **common control with**) means the possession, direct or indirect, of the power to direct or cause the direction of the management and policies of a person, whether through the ownership of voting securities, by contract, or otherwise.

***

6.   The term **executive officer** has the meaning set forth in Rule 3b-7.

***

8.   The term **indirect** acceptance by a member of an audit committee of any consulting, advisory or other compensatory fee includes acceptance of such a fee by a spouse, a minor child or stepchild or a child or stepchild sharing a home with the member or by an entity in which such member is a partner, member, an officer such as a managing director occupying a comparable position or executive officer, or occupies a similar position (except limited partners, non-managing members and those occupying similar positions who, in each case, have no active role in providing services to the entity) and which provides accounting, consulting, legal, investment banking or financial advisory services to the issuer or any subsidiary of the issuer.

9.   The terms **listed** and **listing** refer to securities listed on a national securities exchange or listed in an automated inter-dealer quotation system of a national securities association or to issuers of such securities.

Instructions to Rule 10A-3:

1.   The requirements in paragraphs (b)(2) through (b)(5), (c)(3)(v) and (c)(3)(vi) of this section do not conflict with, and do not affect the application of, any requirement or ability under a listed issuer's governing law or documents or other home country legal or listing provisions that requires or permits shareholders to ultimately vote on, approve or ratify such requirements. The requirements instead relate to the assignment of responsibility as between the audit committee and management. In such an instance, however, if the listed issuer provides a recommendation or nomination regarding such responsibilities to shareholders, the audit committee of the listed issuer, or body performing similar functions, must be responsible for making the recommendation or nomination.

2.   The requirements in paragraphs (b)(2) through (b)(5), (c)(3)(v), (c)(3)(vi) and Instruction 1 of this section do not conflict with any legal or listing requirement in a listed issuer's home jurisdiction that prohibits the full board of directors from delegating such responsibilities to the listed issuer's audit committee or limits the degree of such delegation. In that case, the audit committee, or body performing similar functions, must be granted such responsibilities, which can include advisory powers, with respect to such matters to the extent permitted by law, including submitting nominations or recommendations to the full board.

3.   The requirements in paragraphs (b)(2) through (b)(5), (c)(3)(v) and (c)(3)(vi) of this section do not conflict with any legal or listing requirement in a listed issuer's home jurisdiction that vests such responsibilities with a government entity or tribunal. In that case, the audit committee, or body performing similar functions, must be granted such responsibilities, which can include advisory powers, with respect to such matters to the extent permitted by law.

For purposes of this section, the determination of a person's beneficial ownership must be made in accordance with Rule 13d-3.

Rule 10C-1 – Listing Standards Relating to Compensation Committees

a.   Pursuant to section 10C(a) of the Act and section 952 of the Dodd-Frank Wall Street Reform and Consumer Protection Act of 2010:

1.   National securities exchanges. The rules of each national securities exchange registered pursuant to section 6 of the Act, to the extent such national securities exchange lists equity securities, must, in accordance with the provisions of this

section, prohibit the initial or continued listing of any equity security of an issuer that is not in compliance with the requirements of any portion of paragraph (b) or (c) of this section.

***

b. **Required standards.** The requirements of this section apply to the compensation committees of listed issuers.

1. Independence.
    i.   Each member of the compensation committee must be a member of the board of directors of the listed issuer, and must otherwise be independent.
    ii. Independence requirements. In determining independence requirements for members of compensation committees, the national securities exchanges and national securities associations shall consider relevant factors, including, but not limited to:
        A. The source of compensation of a member of the board of directors of an issuer, including any consulting, advisory or other compensatory fee paid by the issuer to such member of the board of directors; and
        B. Whether a member of the board of directors of an issuer is affiliated with the issuer, a subsidiary of the issuer or an affiliate of a subsidiary of the issuer.

***

2. Authority to retain compensation consultants, independent legal counsel and other compensation advisers.
    i.   The compensation committee of a listed issuer, in its capacity as a committee of the board of directors, may, in its sole discretion, retain or obtain the advice of a compensation consultant, independent legal counsel or other adviser.
    ii. The compensation committee shall be directly responsible for the appointment, compensation and oversight of the work of any compensation consultant, independent legal counsel and other adviser retained by the compensation committee.
    iii. Nothing in this paragraph (b)(2) shall be construed:
        A. To require the compensation committee to implement or act consistently with the advice or recommendations of the compensation consultant, independent legal counsel or other adviser to the compensation committee; or
        B. To affect the ability or obligation of a compensation committee to exercise its own judgment in fulfillment of the duties of the compensation committee.

3. Funding. Each listed issuer must provide for appropriate funding, as determined by the compensation committee, in its capacity as a committee of the board of directors, for payment of reasonable compensation to a compensation consultant, independent legal counsel or any other adviser retained by the compensation committee.

4. Independence of compensation consultants and other advisers. The compensation committee of a listed issuer may select a compensation consultant, legal counsel or other adviser to the compensation committee only after taking

into consideration the following factors, as well as any other factors identified by the relevant national securities exchange or national securities association in its listing standards:

i.   The provision of other services to the issuer by the person that employs the compensation consultant, legal counsel or other adviser;

ii.   The amount of fees received from the issuer by the person that employs the compensation consultant, legal counsel or other adviser, as a percentage of the total revenue of the person that employs the compensation consultant, legal counsel or other adviser;

iii. The policies and procedures of the person that employs the compensation consultant, legal counsel or other adviser that are designed to prevent conflicts of interest;

iv.   Any business or personal relationship of the compensation consultant, legal counsel or other adviser with a member of the compensation committee;

v.   Any stock of the issuer owned by the compensation consultant, legal counsel or other adviser; and

vi.   Any business or personal relationship of the compensation consultant, legal counsel, other adviser or the person employing the adviser with an executive officer of the issuer.

Instruction to paragraph (b)(4) of this section: A listed issuer's compensation committee is required to conduct the independence assessment outlined in paragraph (b)(4) of this section with respect to any compensation consultant, legal counsel or other adviser that provides advice to the compensation committee, other than in-house legal counsel.

***

Rule 10D-1 – Listing standards relating to recovery of erroneously awarded compensation

a.   Each national securities exchange registered pursuant to section 6 of the Act and each national securities association registered pursuant to section 15A of the Act to the extent such national securities exchange or association lists securities, must:

1.   In accordance with the provisions of this section, prohibit the initial or continued listing of any security of an issuer that is not in compliance with the requirements of any portion of this section;

2.   No later than February 27, 2023, propose rules or rule amendments that comply with this section. Such rules or rule amendments that comply with this section must be effective no later than one year after November 28, 2022;

3.   Require that each listed issuer:

i.   Adopt the recovery policy required by this section no later than 60 days following the effective date of the listing standard referenced in paragraph (a)(2) of this section to which the issuer is subject;

ii.   Comply with that recovery policy for all incentive-based compensation received (as defined in paragraph (d) of this section) by executive officers on or after the effective date of the applicable listing standard;

iii. Provide the disclosures required by this section and in the applicable Commission filings required on or after the effective date of the listing standard referenced in paragraph (a)(2) of this section to which the issuer is subject.

b. **Recovery of Erroneously Awarded Compensation**. The issuer must:

    1.   Adopt and comply with a written policy providing that the issuer will recover reasonably promptly the amount of erroneously awarded incentive-based compensation in the event that the issuer is required to prepare an accounting restatement due to the material noncompliance of the issuer with any financial reporting requirement under the securities laws, including any required accounting restatement to correct an error in previously issued financial statements that is material to the previously issued financial statements, or that would result in a material misstatement if the error were corrected in the current period or left uncorrected in the current period.

        i.   The issuer's recovery policy must apply to all incentive-based compensation received by a person:

            A.   After beginning service as an executive officer;

            B.   Who served as an executive officer at any time during the performance period for that incentive-based compensation;

            C.   While the issuer has a class of securities listed on a national securities exchange or a national securities association; and

            D.   During the three completed fiscal years immediately preceding the date that the issuer is required to prepare an accounting restatement as described in paragraph (b)(1) of this section. In addition to these last three completed fiscal years, the recovery policy must apply to any transition period (that results from a change in the issuer's fiscal year) within or immediately following those three completed fiscal years. However, a transition period between the last day of the issuer's previous fiscal year end and the first day of its new fiscal year that comprises a period of nine to 12 months would be deemed a completed fiscal year. An issuer's obligation to recover erroneously awarded compensation is not dependent on if or when the restated financial statements are filed.

        ii.   For purposes of determining the relevant recovery period, the date that an issuer is required to prepare an accounting restatement as described in paragraph (b)(1) of this section is the earlier to occur of:

            A.   The date the issuer's board of directors, a committee of the board of directors, or the officer or officers of the issuer authorized to take such action if board action is not required, concludes, or reasonably should have concluded, that the issuer is required to prepare an accounting restatement as described in paragraph (b)(1) of this section; or

            B.   The date a court, regulator, or other legally authorized body directs the issuer to prepare an accounting restatement as described in paragraph (b)(1) of this section.

        iii.   The amount of incentive-based compensation that must be subject to the issuer's recovery policy ("erroneously awarded compensation") is the amount of incentive-based compensation received that exceeds the amount of incentive-based compensation that otherwise would have been received had it been determined based on the restated amounts, and must be computed without regard to any taxes paid. For incentive-based compensation based on stock price or total shareholder return, where the amount of erroneously awarded compensation is not subject to mathematical recalculation directly from the information in an accounting restatement:

 A. The amount must be based on a reasonable estimate of the effect of the accounting restatement on the stock price or total shareholder return upon which the incentive-based compensation was received; and

 B. The issuer must maintain documentation of the determination of that reasonable estimate and provide such documentation to the exchange or association.

iv. The issuer must recover erroneously awarded compensation in compliance with its recovery policy except to the extent that the conditions of paragraphs (b)(1)(iv)(A), (B), or (C) of this section are met, and the issuer's committee of independent directors responsible for executive compensation decisions, or in the absence of such a committee, a majority of the independent directors serving on the board, has made a determination that recovery would be impracticable.

 A. The direct expense paid to a third party to assist in enforcing the policy would exceed the amount to be recovered. Before concluding that it would be impracticable to recover any amount of erroneously awarded compensation based on expense of enforcement, the issuer must make a reasonable attempt to recover such erroneously awarded compensation, document such reasonable attempt(s) to recover, and provide that documentation to the exchange or association.

 B. Recovery would violate home country law where that law was adopted prior to November 28, 2022. Before concluding that it would be impracticable to recover any amount of erroneously awarded compensation based on violation of home country law, the issuer must obtain an opinion of home country counsel, acceptable to the applicable national securities exchange or association, that recovery would result in such a violation, and must provide such opinion to the exchange or association.

 C. Recovery would likely cause an otherwise tax-qualified retirement plan, under which benefits are broadly available to employees of the registrant, to fail to meet the requirements of 26 U.S.C. 401(a)(13) or 26 U.S.C. 411(a) and regulations thereunder.

v. The issuer is prohibited from indemnifying any executive officer or former executive officer against the loss of erroneously awarded compensation.

2. File all disclosures with respect to such recovery policy in accordance with the requirements of the Federal securities laws, including the disclosure required by the applicable Commission filings.

c. **General Exemptions**. The requirements of this section do not apply to the listing of:

1. A security futures product cleared by a clearing agency that is registered pursuant to section 17A of the Act or that is exempt from the registration requirements of section 17A(b)(7)(A);

2.   A standardized option, as defined in Rule 9b-1(a)(4), issued by a clearing agency that is registered pursuant to section 17A of the Act;

3.   Any security issued by a unit investment trust, as defined in 15 U.S.C. 80a-4(2);

4.   Any security issued by a management company, as defined in 15 U.S.C. 80a-4(3), that is registered under section 8 of the Investment Company Act of 1940, if such management company has not awarded incentive-based compensation to any executive officer of the company in any of the last three fiscal years, or in the case of a company that has been listed for less than three fiscal years, since the listing of the company.

d.   **Definitions**. Unless the context otherwise requires, the following definitions apply for purposes of this section:

Executive Officer. An executive officer is the issuer's president, principal financial officer, principal accounting officer (or if there is no such accounting officer, the controller), any vice-president of the issuer in charge of a principal business unit, division, or function (such as sales, administration, or finance), any other officer who performs a policy-making function, or any other person who performs similar policy-making functions for the issuer. Executive officers of the issuer's parent(s) or subsidiaries are deemed executive officers of the issuer if they perform such policy making functions for the issuer. In addition, when the issuer is a limited partnership, officers or employees of the general partner(s) who perform policy-making functions for the limited partnership are deemed officers of the limited partnership. When the issuer is a trust, officers, or employees of the trustee(s) who perform policy-making functions for the trust are deemed officers of the trust. Policy-making function is not intended to include policy-making functions that are not significant. Identification of an executive officer for purposes of this section would include at a minimum executive officers identified pursuant to Rule 401(b).

Financial reporting measures. Financial reporting measures are measures that are determined and presented in accordance with the accounting principles used in preparing the issuer's financial statements, and any measures that are derived wholly or in part from such measures. Stock price and total shareholder return are also financial reporting measures. A financial reporting measure need not be presented within the financial statements or included in a filing with the Commission.

Incentive-based compensation. Incentive-based compensation is any compensation that is granted, earned, or vested based wholly or in part upon the attainment of a financial reporting measure.

Received. Incentive-based compensation is deemed received in the issuer's fiscal period during which the financial reporting measure specified in the incentive-based compensation award is attained, even if the payment or grant of the incentive-based compensation occurs after the end of that period.

Rule 12b-2 – Definitions

Unless the context otherwise requires, the following terms, when used in the rules contained in this regulation or in Regulation 13A or 15D or in the forms for statements and reports filed pursuant to Sections 12, 13 or 15(d) of the act, shall have the respective meanings indicated in this rule:

Accelerated filer and large accelerated filer.

1. The term "accelerated filer" means an issuer after it first meets the following conditions as of the end of its fiscal year:

    i.   The issuer had an aggregate worldwide market value of the voting and non-voting common equity held by its non-affiliates of $75 million or more, but less than $700 million, as of the last business day of the issuer's most recently completed second fiscal quarter;

    ii. The issuer has been subject to the requirements of section 13(a) or 15(d) of the Act for a period of at least twelve calendar months;

    iii. The issuer has filed at least one annual report pursuant to section 13(a) or 15(d) of the Act; and

    iv. The issuer is not eligible to use the requirements for smaller reporting companies under the revenue test in paragraph (2) or (3)(iii)(B) of the "smaller reporting company" definition in this section, as applicable..

2. *Large accelerated filer.* The term large accelerated filer means an issuer after it first meets the following conditions as of the end of its fiscal year:

    i.   The issuer had an aggregate worldwide market value of the voting and non-voting common equity held by its non-affiliates of $700 million or more, as of the last business day of the issuer's most recently completed second fiscal quarter;

    ii. The issuer has been subject to the requirements of section 13(a) or 15(d) of the Act for a period of at least twelve calendar months;

    iii. The issuer has filed at least one annual report pursuant to section 13(a) or 15(d) of the Act; and

    iv. The issuer is not eligible to use the requirements for smaller reporting companies under the revenue test in paragraph (2) or (3)(iii)(B) of the "smaller reporting company" definition in this section, as applicable.

3. *Entering and Exiting Accelerated Filer Status.*

    i.   The determination at the end of the issuer's fiscal year for whether a nonaccelerated filer becomes an accelerated filer, or whether a non-accelerated filer or accelerated filer becomes a large accelerated filer, governs the deadlines for the annual report to be filed for that fiscal year, the quarterly and annual reports to be filed for the subsequent fiscal year and all annual and quarterly reports to be filed thereafter while the issuer remains an accelerated filer or large accelerated filer.

    ii. Once an issuer becomes an accelerated filer, it will remain an accelerated filer unless: the issuer determines, at the end of a fiscal year, that the aggregate worldwide market value of the voting and non-voting common equity held by its non-affiliates was less than $60 million, as of the last business day of the issuer's most recently completed second fiscal quarter; or it determines that it is eligible to use the requirements for smaller reporting companies under the revenue test in paragraph (2) or (3)(iii)(B) of the "smaller reporting company" definition in this section, as applicable. An issuer that makes either of these determinations becomes a non-accelerated filer. The issuer will not become an accelerated filer again unless it subsequently meets the conditions in paragraph (1) of this definition.

iii.   Once an issuer becomes a large accelerated filer, it will remain a large accelerated filer unless: it determines, at the end of a fiscal year, that the aggregate worldwide market value of the voting and non-voting common equity held by its non-affiliates ("aggregate worldwide market value") was less than $560 million, as of the last business day of the issuer's most recently completed second fiscal quarter or it determines that it is eligible to use the requirements for smaller reporting companies under the revenue test in paragraph (2) or (3)(iii)(B) of the "smaller reporting company" definition in this section, as applicable. If the issuer's aggregate worldwide market value was $60 million or more, but less than $560 million, as of the last business day of the issuer's most recently completed second fiscal quarter, and it is not eligible to use the requirements for smaller reporting companies under the revenue test in paragraph (2) or (3)(iii)(B) of the "smaller reporting company" definition in this section, as applicable, it becomes an accelerated filer. If the issuer's aggregate worldwide market value was less than $60 million, as of the last business day of the issuer's most recently completed second fiscal quarter, or it is eligible to use the requirements for smaller reporting companies under the revenue test in paragraph (2) or (3)(iii)(B) of the "smaller reporting company" definition in this section, it becomes a non-accelerated filer. An issuer will not become a large accelerated filer again unless it subsequently meets the conditions in paragraph (2) of this definition..

iv.   The determination at the end of the issuer's fiscal year for whether an accelerated filer becomes a nonaccelerated filer, or a large accelerated filer becomes an accelerated filer or a non-accelerated filer, governs the deadlines for the annual report to be filed for that fiscal year, the quarterly and annual reports to be filed for the subsequent fiscal year and all annual and quarterly reports to be filed thereafter while the issuer remains an accelerated filer or non-accelerated filer.

Note to paragraphs (1), (2) and (3): The aggregate worldwide market value of the issuer's outstanding voting and non-voting common equity shall be computed by use of the price at which the common equity was last sold, or the average of the bid and asked prices of such common equity, in the principal market for such common equity.

4.   For purposes of paragraphs (1), (2), and (3) of this definition only, a business development company is considered to be eligible to use the requirements for smaller reporting companies under the revenue test in paragraph (2) or (3)(iii)(B) of the "smaller reporting company" definition in this section, provided that the business development company meets the requirements of the test using annual investment income under Rule 6-07.1 of Regulation S-X as the measure of its "annual revenues" for purposes of the test.

Affiliate. An "affiliate" of, or a person "affiliated" with, a specified person, is a person that directly, or indirectly through one or more intermediaries, controls, or is controlled by, or is under common control with, the person specified.

Amount. The term "amount," when used in regard to securities, means the principal amount if relating to evidences of indebtedness, the number of shares if relating to shares, and the number of units if relating to any other kind of security.

Associate. The term "associate" used to indicate a relationship with any person, means

1. any corporation or organization (other than the registrant or a majority-owned subsidiary of the registrant) of which such person is an officer or partner or is, directly or indirectly, the beneficial owner of 10 percent or more of any class of equity securities,
2. any trust or other estate in which such person has a substantial beneficial interest or as to which such person serves as trustee or in a similar fiduciary capacity, and
3. any relative or spouse of such person, or any relative of such spouse, who has the same home as such person or who is a director or officer of the registrant or any of its parents or subsidiaries.

Business combination related shell company: The term business combination related shell company means a shell company (as defined in Rule 12b-2) that is:

1. Formed by an entity that is not a shell company solely for the purpose of changing the corporate domicile of that entity solely within the United States; or
2. Formed by an entity that is not a shell company solely for the purpose of completing a business combination transaction (as defined in Rule 165(f) of this chapter) among one or more entities other than the shell company, none of which is a shell company.

Certified. The term "certified," when used in regard to financial statements, means examined and reported upon with an opinion expressed by an independent public or certified public accountant.

Charter. The term "charter" includes articles of incorporation, declarations of trust, articles of association or partnership, or any similar instrument, as amended, effecting (either with or without filing with any governmental agency) the organization or creation of an incorporated or unincorporated person.

Common equity. The term "common equity" means any class of common stock or an equivalent interest, including but not limited to a unit of beneficial interest in a trust or a limited partnership interest.

Control. The term "control" (including the terms "controlling," "controlled by" and "under common control with") means the possession, direct or indirect, of the power to direct or cause the direction of the management and policies of a person, whether through the ownership of voting securities, by contract, or otherwise.

Depositary share. The term "depositary share" means a security, evidenced by an American Depositary Receipt, that represents a foreign security or a multiple of or fraction thereof deposited with a depositary.

Emerging growth company.

1   The term *emerging growth company* means an issuer that had total annual gross revenues of less than $1,235,000,000 during its most recently completed fiscal year.

2   An issuer that is an emerging growth company as of the first day of that fiscal year shall continue to be deemed an emerging growth company until the earliest of:

      i.   the last day of the fiscal year of the issuer during which it had total annual gross revenues of $1,235,000,000 or more;

      ii   the last day of the fiscal year of the issuer following the fifth anniversary of the date of the first sale of common equity securities of the issuer pursuant to an effective registration statement under the Securities Act of 1933;

      iii   the date on which such issuer has, during the previous three year period, issued more than $1,000,000,000 in non-convertible debt; or

      iv   the date on which such issuer is deemed to be a large accelerated filer, as defined in Rule 12b-2, or any successor thereto

Employee. The term "employee" does not include a director, trustee, or officer.

Fiscal year. The term "fiscal year" means the annual accounting period or, if no closing date has been adopted, the calendar year ending on December 31.

Majority-owned subsidiary. The term "majority-owned subsidiary" means a subsidiary more than 50 percent of whose outstanding securities representing the right, other than as affected by events of default, to vote for the election of directors, is owned by the subsidiary's parent and/or one or more of the parent's other majority-owned subsidiaries.

Managing underwriter. The term "managing underwriter" includes an underwriter (or underwriters) who, by contract or otherwise, deals with the registrant; organizes the selling effort; receives some benefit directly or indirectly in which all other underwriters similarly situated do not share in proportion to their respective interests in the underwriting; or represents any other underwriters in such matters as maintaining the records of the distribution, arranging the allotments of securities offered or arranging for appropriate stabilization activities, if any.

Material. The term "material," when used to qualify a requirement for the furnishing of information as to any subject, limits the information required to those matters to which there is a substantial likelihood that a reasonable investor would attach importance in determining whether to buy or sell the securities registered.

Material weakness. The term material weakness is a deficiency, or a combination of deficiencies, in internal control over financial reporting such that there is a reasonable possibility that a material misstatement of the registrant's annual or interim financial statements will not be prevented or detected on a timely basis.

Parent. A "parent" of a specified person is an affiliate controlling such person directly, or indirectly through one or more intermediaries.

Predecessor. The term "predecessor" means a person the major portion of the business and assets of which another person acquired in a single succession or in a series of related successions in each of which the acquiring person acquired the major portion of the business and assets of the acquired person.

Previously filed or reported. The terms "previously filed" and "previously reported" mean previously filed with, or reported in, a statement under Section 12, a report under Section 13 or 15(d), a definitive proxy statement or information statement under Section 14 of the act, or a registration statement under the Securities Act of 1933: *Provided,* That information contained in any such document shall be deemed to have been previously filed with, or reported to, an exchange only if such document is filed with such exchange.

Principal underwriter. The term "principal underwriter" means an underwriter in privity of contract with the issuer of the securities as to which he is underwriter.

Promoter.
1. The term "promoter" includes:
   i. Any person who, acting alone or in conjunction with one or more other persons, directly or indirectly takes initiative in founding and organizing the business or enterprise of an issuer; or
   ii. Any person who, in connection with the founding and organizing of the business or enterprise of an issuer, directly or indirectly receives in consideration of services or property, or both services and property, 10 percent or more of any class of securities of the issuer or 10 percent or more of the proceeds from the sale of any class of such securities. However, a person who receives such securities or proceeds either solely as underwriting commissions or solely in consideration of property shall not be deemed a promoter within the meaning of this paragraph if such person does not otherwise take part in founding and organizing the enterprise.
2. All persons coming within the definition of "promoter" in paragraph 1 of this definition may be referred to as "founders" or "organizers" or by another term provided that such term is reasonably descriptive of those persons' activities with respect to the issuer.

Prospectus. Unless otherwise specified or the context otherwise requires, the term "prospectus" means a prospectus meeting the requirements of Section 10(a) of the Securities Act of 1933 as amended.

Registrant. The term "registrant" means an issuer of securities with respect to which a registration statement or report is to be filed.

Registration statement. The term "registration statement" or "statement", when used with reference to registration pursuant to Section 12 of the act, includes both an application for registration of securities on a national securities exchange pursuant to Section 12(b) of the act and a registration statement filed pursuant to Section 12(g) of the act.

Share. The term "share" means a share of stock in a corporation or unit of interest in an unincorporated person.

Shell Company: The term shell company means a registrant, other than an asset-backed issuer as defined in Item 1101(b) of Regulation AB, that has:
  1.   No or nominal operations; and
  2.   Either:
        i.   No or nominal assets;
        ii.   Assets consisting solely of cash and cash equivalents; or
        iii. Assets consisting of any amount of cash and cash equivalents and nominal other assets.
Note: For purposes of this definition, the determination of a registrant's assets (including cash and cash equivalents) is based solely on the amount of assets that would be reflected on the registrant's balance sheet prepared in accordance with generally accepted accounting principles on the date of that determination.

Significant deficiency. The term significant deficiency is a deficiency, or a combination of deficiencies, in internal control over financial reporting that is less severe than a material weakness, yet important enough to merit attention by those responsible for oversight of the registrant's financial reporting.

Significant subsidiary. The term "significant subsidiary" means a subsidiary, including its subsidiaries, which meets any of the following conditions:
  1.   The registrant's and its other subsidiaries' investments in and advances to the subsidiary exceed 10 percent of the total assets of the registrant and its subsidiaries consolidated as of the end of the most recently completed fiscal year (for a proposed combination between entities under common control, this condition is also met when the number of common shares exchanged or to be exchanged by the registrant exceeds 10 percent of its total common shares outstanding at the date the combination is initiated); or
  2.   The registrant's and its other subsidiaries' proportionate share of the total assets (after intercompany eliminations) of the subsidiary exceeds 10 percent of the total assets of the registrant and its subsidiaries consolidated as of the end of the most recently completed fiscal year; or
  3.   The registrant's and its other subsidiaries' equity in the income from continuing operations before income taxes of the subsidiary exclusive of amounts attributable to any noncontrolling interests exceeds 10 percent of such income of the registrant and its subsidiaries consolidated for the most recently completed fiscal year.
Note 1: A registrant that files its financial statements in accordance with or provides a reconciliation to U.S. Generally Accepted Accounting Principles shall make the prescribed tests using amounts determined under U.S. Generally Accepted Accounting Principles. A foreign private issuer that files its financial statements in accordance with IFRS as issued by the IASB shall make the prescribed tests using amounts determined under IFRS as issued by the IASB.
Computational note 1 to paragraph (3): For purposes of making the prescribed income test the following guidance should be applied:

1.   When a loss exclusive of amounts attributable to any noncontrolling interests has been incurred by either the parent and its subsidiaries consolidated or the tested subsidiary, but not both, the equity in the income or loss of the tested subsidiary exclusive of amounts attributable to any noncontrolling interests should be excluded from such income of the registrant and its subsidiaries consolidated for purposes of the computation.

2.   If income of the registrant and its subsidiaries consolidated exclusive of amounts attributable to any noncontrolling interests for the most recent fiscal year is at least 10 percent lower than the average of the income for the last five fiscal years, such average income should be substituted for purposes of the computation. Any loss years should be omitted for purposes of computing average income.

Smaller reporting company. As used in this part, the term smaller reporting company means an issuer that is not an investment company, an asset-backed issuer (as defined in Item 1101 of this chapter), or a majority-owned subsidiary of a parent that is not a smaller reporting company and that:

1.   Had a public float of less than $ 250 million; or

2.   Had annual revenues of less than $100 million and either:

     i.   no public float; or

     ii.   A public float of less than $700 million.

3.   Whether an issuer is a smaller reporting company is determined on an annual basis.

     i.   For issuers that are required to file reports under section 13(a) or 15(d) of the Exchange Act:

          A.   Public float is measured as of the last business day of the issuer's most recently completed second fiscal quarter and computed by multiplying the aggregate worldwide number of shares of its voting and non-voting common equity held by non-affiliates by the price at which the common equity was last sold, or the average of the bid and asked prices of common equity, in the principal market for the common equity;

          B.   Annual revenues are as of the most recently completed fiscal year for which audited financial statements are available; and

          C.   An issuer must reflect the determination of whether it came within the definition of smaller reporting company in its quarterly report on Form 10-Q for the first fiscal quarter of the next year, indicating on the cover page of that filing, and in subsequent filings for that fiscal year, whether it is a smaller reporting company, except that, if a determination based on public float indicates that the issuer is newly eligible to be a smaller reporting company, the issuer may choose to reflect this determination beginning with its first quarterly report on Form 10-Q following the determination, rather than waiting until the first fiscal quarter of the next year.

     ii.   For determinations based on an initial registration statement under the Securities Act or Exchange Act for shares of its common equity:

          A.   Public float is measured as of a date within 30 days of the date of the filing of the registration statement and computed by multiplying the aggregate worldwide number of shares of its voting and non-voting common equity held by non-affiliates before the registration plus, in the case of a Securities Act registration statement, the number of shares of its voting and non-voting common equity included in the registration statement by the estimated public offering price of the shares;

B. Annual revenues are as of the most recently completed fiscal year for which audited financial statements are available; and

C. The issuer must reflect the determination of whether it came within the definition of smaller reporting company in the registration statement and must appropriately indicate on the cover page of the filing, and subsequent filings for the fiscal year in which the filing is made, whether it is a smaller reporting company. The issuer must re-determine its status at the end of its second fiscal quarter and then reflect any change in status as provided in paragraph (3)(i)(C) of this definition. In the case of a determination based on an initial Securities Act registration statement, an issuer that was not determined to be a smaller reporting company has the option to re-determine its status at the conclusion of the offering covered by the registration statement based on the actual offering price and number of shares sold.

iii. Once an issuer determines that it does not qualify for smaller reporting company status because it exceeded one or more of the current thresholds, it will remain unqualified unless when making its annual determination either:

A. It determines that its public float was less than $200 million; or

B. It determines that its public float and its annual revenues meet the requirements for subsequent qualification included in the following chart:

Prior Annual Revenues	Prior Public Float			
	None or less than $700 million		$700 million or more	
Less than $100 million	Neither threshold exceeded		Public float	Less than $560 million; and
			Revenues	Less than $100 million
$100 million or more	Public Float	None or less than $700 million; and	Public Float	Less than $560 million; and
	Revenues	Less than $80 million	Revenues	Less than $80 million

Instruction 1 to definition of "smaller reporting company": A registrant that qualifies as a smaller reporting company under the public float thresholds identified in paragraphs (1) and (3)(iii)(A) of this definition will qualify as a smaller reporting company regardless of its revenues.

Instruction 2 to definition of "smaller reporting company": A foreign private issuer is not eligible to use the requirements for smaller reporting companies unless it uses the forms and rules designated for domestic issuers and provides financial statements prepared in accordance with U.S. Generally Accepted Accounting Principles.

Subsidiary. A "subsidiary" of a specified person is an affiliate controlled by such person directly, or indirectly through one or more intermediaries. (See also "majority-owned subsidiary," "significant subsidiary," and "totally-held subsidiary.")

Succession. The term "succession" means the direct acquisition of the assets comprising a going business, whether by merger, consolidation, purchase, or other direct transfer. The term does not include the acquisition of control of a business unless followed by the direct acquisition of its assets. The terms "succeed" and "successor" have meanings correlative to the foregoing.

Totally held subsidiary. The term "totally held subsidiary" means a subsidiary (1) substantially all of whose outstanding securities are owned by its parent and/or the parent's other totally held subsidiaries, and (2) which is not indebted to any person other than its parent and/or the parent's other totally held subsidiaries in an amount which is material in relation to the particular subsidiary, excepting indebtedness incurred in the ordinary course of business which is not overdue and which matures within one year from the date of its creation, whether evidenced by securities or not.

Voting securities. The term "voting securities" means securities the holders of which are presently entitled to vote for the election of directors.

Wholly-owned subsidiary. The term "wholly-owned subsidiary" means a subsidiary substantially all of whose outstanding voting securities are owned by its parent and/or the parent's other wholly-owned subsidiaries.

Rule 12b-20 – Additional Information

In addition to the information expressly required to be included in a statement or report, there shall be added such further material information, if any, as may be necessary to make the required statements, in the light of the circumstances under which they are made not misleading.

Rule 12g-1 – Registration of Securities; Exemption from Section 12(g)

An issuer is not required to register a class of equity securities pursuant to section 12(g)(1) of the Act if on the last day of its most recent fiscal year:

a.   The issuer had total assets not exceeding $10 million; or

b.
1.   The class of equity securities was held of record by fewer than 2,000 persons and fewer than 500 of those persons were not accredited investors (as such term is defined in § 501(a) of this chapter, determined as of such day rather than at the time of the sale of the securities); or
2.   The class of equity securities was held of record by fewer than 2,000 persons in the case of a bank; a savings and loan holding company, as such term is defined in section 10 of the Home Owners' Loan Act; or a bank holding company, as such term is defined in section 2 of the Bank Holding Company Act of 1956.

Rule 12g-2 – Securities Deemed to be Registered Pursuant to Section 12(g)(1) upon Termination of Exemption Pursuant to Section 12(g)(2)(A) or (B)

Any class of securities that would have been required to be registered pursuant to section 12(g)(1) of the Act except for the fact that it was exempt from such registration by section 12(g)(2)(A) of the Act because it was listed and registered on a national securities exchange, or by section 12(g)(2)(B) of the Act because it was issued by an investment company registered pursuant to section 8 of the Investment Company Act of 1940, shall upon the termination of the listing and registration of such class or the termination of the registration of such company and without the filing of an additional registration statement be deemed to be registered pursuant to section 12(g)(1) of the Act if at the time of such termination:

a.   The issuer of such class of securities has elected to be regulated as a business development company pursuant to sections 55 through 65 of the Investment Company Act of 1940 and such election has not been withdrawn; or

b.   Securities of the class are not exempt from such registration pursuant to section 12 of the Act or rules thereunder and all securities of such class are held of record by 300 or more persons, or 1,200 or more persons in the case of a bank; a savings and loan holding company, as such term is defined in section 10 of the Home Owners' Loan Act; or a bank holding company, as such term is defined in section 2 of the Bank Holding Company Act of 1956.

Rule 12g3-2 – Exemptions for American Depositary Receipts and Certain Foreign Securities

a.   Securities of any class issued by any foreign private issuer shall be exempt from section 12(g) of the Act if the class has fewer than 300 holders resident in the United States. This exemption shall continue until the next fiscal year end at which the issuer has a class of equity securities held by 300 or more persons resident in the United States. For the purpose of determining whether a security is exempt pursuant to this paragraph:
1.   Securities held of record by persons resident in the United States shall be determined as provided in Rule 12g5-1 except that securities held of record by a broker, dealer, bank or nominee for any of them for the accounts of customers resident in the United States shall be counted as held in the United States by the number of separate accounts for which the securities are held. The issuer may rely in good faith on information as to the number of such separate accounts supplied by all owners of the class of its securities which are brokers, dealers, or banks or a nominee for any of them.
2.   Persons in the United States who hold the security only through a Canadian Retirement Account (as that term is defined in Rule 237(a)(2) under the Securities Act of 1933, shall not be counted as holders resident in the United States.

b.   1.   A foreign private issuer shall be exempt from the requirement to register a class of equity securities under section 12(g) of the Act if:
i.   The issuer is not required to file or furnish reports under section 13(a) of the Act or section 15(d) of the Act;

ii.   The issuer currently maintains a listing of the subject class of securities on one or more exchanges in a foreign jurisdiction that, either singly or together with the trading of the same class of the issuer's securities in another foreign jurisdiction, constitutes the primary trading market for those securities; and

iii. The issuer has published in English, on its Internet Web site or through an electronic information delivery system generally available to the public in its primary trading market, information that, since the first day of its most recently completed fiscal year, it:

   A. Has made public or been required to make public pursuant to the laws of the country of its incorporation, organization or domicile

   B. Has filed or been required to file with the principal stock exchange in its primary trading market on which its securities are traded and which has been made public by that exchange; and

   C. Has distributed or been required to distribute to its security holders.

Note 1 to Paragraph (b)(1):

For the purpose of paragraph (b) of this section, primary trading market means that at least 55 percent of the trading in the subject class of securities on a worldwide basis took place in, on or through the facilities of a securities market or markets in a single foreign jurisdiction or in no more than two foreign jurisdictions during the issuer's most recently completed fiscal year. If a foreign private issuer aggregates the trading of its subject class of securities in two foreign jurisdictions for the purpose of this paragraph, the trading for the issuer's securities in at least one of the two foreign jurisdictions must be larger than the trading in the United States for the same class of the issuer's securities. When determining an issuer's primary trading market under this paragraph, calculate average daily trading volume in the United States and on a worldwide basis as under Rule 12h-6 under the Act.

Note 2 to Paragraph (b)(1):

Paragraph (b)(1)(iii) of this section does not apply to an issuer when claiming the exemption under paragraph (b) of this section upon the effectiveness of the termination of its registration of a class of securities under section 12(g) of the Act, or the termination of its obligation to file or furnish reports under section 15(d) of the Act.

Note 3 to Paragraph (b)(1):

Compensatory stock options for which the underlying securities are in a class exempt under paragraph (b) of this section are also exempt under that paragraph.

2.

i.   In order to maintain the exemption under paragraph (b) of this section, a foreign private issuer shall publish, on an ongoing basis and for each subsequent fiscal year, in English, on its Internet Web site or through an electronic information delivery system generally available to the public in its primary trading market, the information specified in paragraph (b)(1)(iii) of this section.

ii. An issuer must electronically publish the information required by paragraph (b)(2) of this secti on promptly after the information has been made public.

3.
    i.   The information required to be published electronically under paragraph (b) of this section is information that is material to an investment decision regarding the subject securities, such as information concerning:
        A. Results of operations or financial condition;
        B. Changes in business;
        C. Acquisitions or dispositions of assets;
        D. The issuance, redemption or acquisition of securities;
        E. Changes in management or control;
        F. The granting of options or the payment of other remuneration to directors or officers; and
        G. Transactions with directors, officers or principal security holders
    ii. At a minimum, a foreign private issuer shall electronically publish English translations of the following documents required to be published under paragraph (b) of this section if in a foreign language:
        A. Its annual report, including or accompanied by annual financial statements;
        B. Interim reports that include financial statements;
        C. Press releases; and
        D. All other communications and documents distributed directly to security holders of each class of securities to which the exemption relates.

c.   The exemption under paragraph (b) of this section shall remain in effect until:
    1.   The issuer no longer satisfies the electronic publication condition of paragraph (b)(2) of this section;
    2.   The issuer no longer maintains a listing of the subject class of securities on one or more exchanges in a primary trading market, as defined under paragraph (b)(1) of this section; or
    3.   The issuer registers a class of securities under section 12 of the Act or incurs reporting obligations under section 15(d) of the Act.

d.   Depositary shares registered on Form F-6, but not the underlying deposited securities, are exempt from section 12(g) of the Act under this paragraph.

Rule 12g-4 – Certifications of Termination of Registration Under Section 12(g)

a.   Termination of registration of a class of securities under section 12(g) of the Act shall take effect 90 days, or such shorter period as the Commission may determine, after the issuer certifies to the Commission on Form 15 that the class of securities is held of record by:
    1.   Fewer than 300 persons, or in the case of a bank; a savings and loan holding company, as such term is defined in section 10 of the Home Owners' Loan Act; or a bank holding company, as such term is defined in section 2 of the Bank Holding Company Act of 1956, 1,200 persons; or
    2.   Fewer than 500 persons, where the total assets of the issuer have not exceeded $10 million on the last day of each of the issuer's most recent three fiscal years.

b. The issuer's duty to file any reports required under section 13(a) shall be suspended immediately upon filing a certification on Form 15; *Provided, however,* That if the certification on Form 15 is subsequently withdrawn or denied, the issuer shall, within 60 days after the date of such withdrawal or denial, file with the Commission all reports which would have been required had the certification on Form 15 not been filed. If the suspension resulted from the issuer's merger into, or consolidation with, another issuer or issuers, the certification shall be filed by the successor issuer.

Rule 12g5-1 – Definition of Securities "Held of Record"

a. For the purpose of determining whether an issuer is subject to the provisions of Sections 12(g) and 15(d) of the Act, securities shall be deemed to be "held of record" by each person who is identified as the owner of such securities on records of security holders maintained by or on behalf of the issuer, subject to the following:

   1. In any case where the records of security holders have not been maintained in accordance with accepted practice, any additional person who would be identified as such an owner on such records if they had been maintained in accordance with accepted practice shall be included as a holder of record.

   2. Except as specified in paragraph (a)(9) of this section, securities identified as held of record by a corporation, a partnership, a trust whether or not the trustees are named, or other organization shall be included as so held by one person.

   3. Securities identified as held of record by one or more persons as trustees, executors, guardians, custodians or in other fiduciary capacities with respect to a single trust, estate or account shall be included as held of record by one person.

   4. Securities held by two or more persons as co-owners shall be included as held by one person.

   5. Each outstanding unregistered or bearer certificate shall be included as held of record by a separate person, except to the extent that the issuer can establish that, if such securities were registered, they would be held of record, under the provisions of this rule, by a lesser number of persons.

   6. Securities registered in substantially similar names where the issuer has reason to believe because of the address or other indications that such names represent the same person, may be included as held of record by one person.

   7. Other than when determining compliance with Rule 257(d)(2) of Regulation A, the definition of "held of record" shall not include securities issued in a Tier 2 offering pursuant to Regulation A by an issuer that:

      i.   Is required to file reports pursuant to Rule 257(b) of Regulation A of the Securities Act;

      ii. Is current in filing annual, semiannual and special financial reports pursuant to such rule as of its most recently completed fiscal year end;

      iii. Has engaged a transfer agent registered pursuant to Section 17A(c) of the Act to perform the function of a transfer agent with respect to such securities; and

      iv. Had a public float of less than $75 million as of the last business day of its most recently completed semiannual period, computed by multiplying the aggregate worldwide number of shares of its common equity securities held by non-affiliates by the price at which such securities were last sold (or the average bid and asked prices of such securities) in the principal market for such securities or, in the event the result of such public float calculation was zero, had annual revenues of less than $50 million as of its most recently completed fiscal year. An issuer that would be required to register a class of securities under Section 12(g) of the Act as a result of exceeding the applicable threshold in this paragraph (a)(7)(iv), may continue to exclude the relevant securities from the definition of "held of record" for a transition period ending on the penultimate day of the fiscal year two years after the date it became ineligible. The transition period terminates immediately upon the failure of an issuer to timely file any periodic report due pursuant to Rule 257 at which time the issuer must file a registration statement that registers that class of securities under the Act within 120 days.

8.
    i.   For purposes of determining whether an issuer is required to register a class of equity securities with the Commission pursuant to section 12(g)(1) of the Act, an issuer may exclude securities:

        A. Held by persons who received the securities pursuant to an employee compensation plan in transactions exempt from, or not subject to, the registration requirements of section 5 of the Securities Act of 1933; and

        B. Held by persons who received the securities in a transaction exempt from, or not subject to, the registration requirements of section 5 of the Securities Act from the issuer, a predecessor of the issuer or an acquired company in substitution or exchange for excludable securities under paragraph (a)(8)(i)(A) of this section, as long as the persons were eligible to receive securities pursuant to Rule 701(c) of this chapter at the time the excludable securities were originally issued to them.

    ii. As a non-exclusive safe harbor under this paragraph (a)(8):

        A. An issuer may deem a person to have received the securities pursuant to an employee compensation plan if such plan and the person who received the securities pursuant to the plan met the plan and participant conditions of § 230.701(c) of this chapter; and

        B. An issuer may, solely for the purposes of Section 12(g) of the Act, deem the securities to have been issued in a transaction exempt from, or not subject to, the registration requirements of Section 5 of the Securities Act if the issuer had a reasonable belief at the time of the issuance that the securities were issued in such a transaction.

9.   For purposes of determining whether a crowdfunding issuer, as defined in Rule 3a-9(b)(1) of this chapter, or a crowdfunding vehicle, as defined in Rule 3a-9(b)(2) of this chapter, is required to register a class of equity securities with the Commission pursuant to section 12(g)(1) of the Act, both the crowdfunding issuer and the crowdfunding vehicle:

    i.   May exclude securities issued by a crowdfunding vehicle, as defined in Rule 3a-9(b)(2) of this chapter, in an offering under Regulation Crowdfunding in which the crowdfunding vehicle and the crowdfunding issuer are deemed to be co-issuers under the Securities Act and that are held by natural persons; and

    ii. Shall include securities issued by a crowdfunding vehicle, as defined in Rule 3a-9(b)(2) of this chapter, in an offering under Regulation Crowdfunding in which the crowdfunding vehicle and the crowdfunding issuer are deemed to be co-issuers under the Securities Act and that are held by investors that are not natural persons.

b. Notwithstanding paragraph (a) of this section:

    1. Securities held, to the knowledge of the issuer, subject to a voting trust, deposit agreement or similar arrangement shall be included as held of record by the record holders of the voting trust certificates, certificates of deposit, receipts or similar evidences of interest in such securities: *Provided, however,* That the issuer may rely in good faith on such information as is received in response to its request from a non-affiliated issuer of the certificates or evidences of interest.

    2. Whole or fractional securities issued by a savings and loan association, building and loan association, cooperative bank, homestead association, or similar institution for the sole purpose of qualifying a borrower for membership in the issuer, and which are to be redeemed or repurchased by the issuer when the borrower's loan is terminated, shall not be included as held of record by any person.

    3. If the issuer knows or has reason to know that the form of holding securities of record is used primarily to circumvent the provisions of Section 12(g) or 15(d) of the Act, the beneficial owners of such securities shall be deemed to be the record owners thereof.

Rule 12g-6 – Exemption for Securities Issued Pursuant to Section 4(a)(6) of the Securities Act of 1933 or Regulation Crowdfunding

a. For purposes of determining whether an issuer is required to register a security with the Commission pursuant to Section 12(g)(1) of the Act, the definition of held of record shall not include securities issued pursuant to the offering exemption under section 4(a)(6) of the Securities Act or Regulation Crowdfunding by an issuer that:

    1. Is current in filing its ongoing annual reports required pursuant to Rule 202 of this chapter;

    2. Has total assets not in excess of $25 million as of the end of its most recently completed fiscal year; and

    3. Has engaged a transfer agent registered pursuant to Section 17A(c) of the Act to perform the function of a transfer agent with respect to such securities.

b. An issuer that would be required to register a class of securities under Section 12(g) of the Act as a result of exceeding the asset threshold in paragraph (2) may continue to exclude the relevant securities from the definition of "held of record" for a transition period ending on the penultimate day of the fiscal year two years after the date it became ineligible. The transition period terminates immediately upon the failure of an issuer to timely file any periodic report due pursuant to [Regulation Crowdfunding] Rule 202 at which time the issuer must file a registration statement that registers that class of securities under the Act within 120 days.

Rule 12h-3 – Suspension of Duty to File Reports under Section 15(d)

a. Subject to paragraphs (c) and (d) of this section, the duty under Section 15(d) to file reports required by Section 13(a) of the Act with respect to a class of securities specified in paragraph (b) of this section shall be suspended for such class of securities immediately upon filing with the Commission a certification on Form 15 if the issuer of such class has filed all reports required by Section 13(a), without regard to Rule 12b-25, for the shorter of its most recent three fiscal years and the portion of the current year preceding the date of filing Form 15, or the period since the issuer became subject to such reporting obligation. If the certification on Form 15 is subsequently withdrawn or denied, the issuer shall, within 60 days, file with the Commission all reports which would have been required if such certification had not been filed.

b. The classes of securities eligible for the suspension provided in paragraph (a) of this section are:
    1. Any class of securities, other than any class of asset-backed securities, held of record by:
        i.   Fewer than 300 persons; or in the case of a bank; a savings and loan holding company, as such term is defined in section 10 of the Home Owners' Loan Act; or a bank holding company, as such term is defined in section 2 of the Bank Holding Company Act of 1956 1,200 persons; or
        ii. Fewer than 500 persons, where the total assets of the issuer have not exceeded $10 million on the last day of each of the issuer's three most recent fiscal years; and
    2. Any class or securities deregistered pursuant to Section 12(d) of the Act if such class would not thereupon be deemed registered under Section 12(g) of the Act or the rules thereunder.

c. This section shall not be available for any class of securities for a fiscal year in which a registration statement relating to that class becomes effective under the Securities Act of 1933, or is required to be updated pursuant to Section 10(a)(3) of the Act, and, in the case of paragraph (b)(1)(ii), the two succeeding fiscal years; *Provided, however,* That this paragraph shall not apply to the duty to file reports which arises solely from a registration statement filed by an issuer with no significant assets, for the reorganization of a non-reporting issuer into a one subsidiary holding company in which equity security holders receive the same proportional interest in the holding company as they held in the non-reporting issuer, except for changes resulting from the exercise of dissenting shareholder rights under state law.

d. The suspension provided by this rule relates only to the reporting obligation under section 15(d) with respect to a class of securities, does not affect any other duties imposed on that class of securities, and shall continue as long as either criteria (i) or (ii) in paragraph (b)(1) is met on the first day of any subsequent fiscal year; *Provided, however,* That such criteria need not be met if the duty to file reports arises solely from a registration statement filed by an issuer with no significant assets in a reorganization of a non-reporting company into a one subsidiary holding company in which equity security holders receive the same proportional interest in the holding company as they held in the non-reporting issuer except for changes resulting from the exercise of dissenting shareholder rights under state law.

e. If the suspension provided by this rule is discontinued because a class of securities does not meet the eligibility criteria of paragraph (b) on the first day of an issuer's fiscal year, then the issuer shall resume periodic reporting pursuant to Section 15(d) by filing an annual report on Form 10-K for its preceding fiscal year, not later than 120 days after the end of such fiscal year.

Rule 13a-1 – Requirements of Annual Reports

Every issuer having securities registered pursuant to section 12 of the Act shall file an annual report on the appropriate form authorized or prescribed therefor for each fiscal year after the last full fiscal year for which financial statements were filed in its registration statement. Annual reports shall be filed within the period specified in the appropriate form.

Rule 13a-11 – Current Reports on Form 8-K

a. Except as provided in paragraph (b) of this section, every registrant subject to Rule 13a-1 shall file a current report on Form 8-K within the period specified in that form unless substantially the same information as that required by Form 8-K has been previously reported by the registrant.

b. This section shall not apply to foreign governments, foreign private issuers required to make reports on Form 6-K pursuant to Rule 13a-16, issuers of American Depositary Receipts for securities of any foreign issuer, or investment companies required to file reports pursuant to Rule 30b1-1 under the Investment Company Act of 1940, except where such investment companies are required to file:.
1. Notice of a blackout period pursuant to Rule 104 of this chapter;
2. Disclosure pursuant to Instruction 2 to Rule 14a-11(b)(1) of information concerning outstanding shares and voting; or
3. Disclosure pursuant to Instruction 2 to Rul1 14a-11(b)(10) of the date by which a nominating shareholder or nominating shareholder group must submit the notice required pursuant to Rule 14a-11(b)(10).

c. No failure to file a report on Form 8-K that is required solely pursuant to Item 1.01, 1.02, 2.03, 2.04, 2.05, 2.06, 4.02(a), 5.02(e) or 6.03 of Form 8-K shall be deemed to be a violation of Section 10(b) and Rule 10b-5.

Rule 13a-13 – Quarterly Reports on Form 10-Q

a. Except as provided in paragraphs (b) and (c) of this section, every issuer that has securities registered pursuant to section 12 of the Act and is required to file annual reports pursuant to section 13 of the Act, and has filed or intends to file such reports on Form 10-K shall file a quarterly report on Form 10-Q within the period specified in General Instruction A.1. to that form for each of the first three quarters of each fiscal year of the issuer, commencing with the first fiscal quarter following the most recent fiscal year for which full financial statements were included in the registration statement, or, if the registration statement included financial statements for an interim period subsequent to the most recent fiscal year end meeting the requirements of Article 10 of Regulation S-X, for the first fiscal quarter subsequent to the quarter reported upon in the registration statement. The first quarterly report of the issuer shall be filed either within 45 days after the effective date of the registration statement or on or before the date on which such report would have been required to be filed if the issuer has been required to file reports on Form 10-Q as of its last fiscal quarter, whichever is later.

b. The provisions of this rule shall not apply to the following issuers:
1. Investment companies required to file reports pursuant to Rule 30b1-1; or
2. Foreign private issuers required to file reports pursuant to Rule 13a-16; and
3. Asset-backed issuers required to file reports pursuant to Rule 13a-17.

c. Part I of the quarterly reports on Form 10-Q need not be filed by:
1. Mutual life insurance companies; or
2. Mining companies not in the production stage but engaged primarily in the exploration for the development of mineral deposits other than oil, gas or coal, if all the following conditions are met:
    i.   The registrant has not been in production during the current fiscal year or the two years immediately prior thereto; except that being in production for an aggregate period of not more than eight months over the three-year period shall not be a violation of this condition.
    ii. Receipts from the sale of mineral products or from the operations of mineral producing properties by the registrant and its subsidiaries combined have not exceeded $500,000 in any of the most recent six years and have not aggregated more than $1,500,000 in the most recent six fiscal years.

d. Notwithstanding the foregoing provisions of this section, the financial information required by Part I of Form 10-Q shall not be deemed to be "filed" for the purpose of section 18 of the Act or otherwise subject to the liabilities of that section of the Act but shall be subject to all other provisions of the Act.

Rule 13a-14 – Certification of Disclosure in Annual and Quarterly Reports

a. Each report, including transition reports, filed on Form 10-Q, Form 10-K, Form 20-F or Form 40-F under section 13(a) of the Act, other than a report filed by an Asset-Backed Issuer (as defined in 1101 of this chapter), must include certifications in the form specified in the applicable exhibit filing requirements of such report and such certifications must be filed as an exhibit to such report. Each principal executive and principal financial officer of the issuer, or persons performing similar functions, at the time of filing of the report must sign a certification.

b. Each periodic report containing financial statements filed by an issuer pursuant to section 13(a) of the Act must be accompanied by the certifications required by Section 1350 of Chapter 63 of Title 18 of the United States Code and such certifications must be furnished as an exhibit to such report as specified in the applicable exhibit requirements for such report. Each principal executive and principal financial officer of the issuer (or equivalent thereof) must sign a certification. This requirement may be satisfied by a single certification signed by an issuer's principal executive and principal financial officers.

c.   A person required to provide a certification specified in paragraph (a) or (b) of this section may not have the certification signed on his or her behalf pursuant to a power of attorney or other form of confirming authority.

Rule 13a-15 – Issuer's Disclosure Controls and Procedures Related to Preparation of Required Reports

a.   Every issuer that has a class of securities registered pursuant to section 12 of the Act, other than an Asset-Backed Issuer (as defined in Rule 13a-14(g)), a small business investment company registered on Form N-5, or a unit investment trust as defined by section 4(2) of the Investment Company Act of 1940, must maintain disclosure controls and procedures (as defined in paragraph (e) of this section) and internal control over financial reporting (as defined in paragraph (f) of this section).

b.   Each such issuer's management must evaluate, with the participation of the issuer's principal executive and principal financial officers, or persons performing similar functions, the effectiveness of the issuer's disclosure controls and procedures, as of the end of each fiscal quarter, except that management must perform this evaluation:
   1.   In the case of a foreign private issuer (as defined in Rule 3b-4) as of the end of each fiscal year; and
   2.   In the case of an investment company registered under section 8 of the Investment Company Act of 1940, within the 90-day period prior to the filing date of each report requiring certification under Investment Company Act Rule 30a-2.

c.   The management of each such issuer, that either had been required to file an annual report pursuant to section 13(a) or 15(d) of the Act for the prior fiscal year or previously had filed an annual report with the Commission for the prior fiscal year, other than an investment company registered under section 8 of the Investment Company Act of 1940, must evaluate, with the participation of the issuer's principal executive and principal financial officers, or persons performing similar functions, the effectiveness, as of the end of each fiscal year, of the issuer's internal control over financial reporting. The framework on which management's evaluation of the issuer's internal control over financial reporting is based must be a suitable, recognized control framework that is established by a body or group that has followed due-process procedures, including the broad distribution of the framework for public comment. Although there are many different ways to conduct an evaluation of the effectiveness of internal control over financial reporting to meet the requirements of this paragraph, an evaluation that is conducted in accordance with the interpretive guidance issued by the Commission in Release No. 34-55929 will satisfy the evaluation required by this paragraph.

d.   The management of each such issuer, other than an investment company registered under section 8 of the Investment Company Act of 1940, must evaluate, with the participation of the issuer's principal executive and principal financial officers, or persons performing similar functions, any change in the issuer's internal control over financial reporting, that occurred during each of the issuer's fiscal quarters, or fiscal year in the case of a foreign private issuer, that has materially affected, or is reasonably likely to materially affect, the issuer's internal control over financial reporting.

e. For purposes of this section, the term *disclosure controls and procedures* means controls and other procedures of an issuer that are designed to ensure that information required to be disclosed by the issuer in the reports that it files or submits under the Act is recorded, processed, summarized and reported, within the time periods specified in the Commission's rules and forms. Disclosure controls and procedures include, without limitation, controls and procedures designed to ensure that information required to be disclosed by an issuer in the reports that it files or submits under the Act is accumulated and communicated to the issuer's management, including its principal executive and principal financial officers, or persons performing similar functions, as appropriate to allow timely decisions regarding required disclosure.

f. The term *internal control over financial reporting* is defined as a process designed by, or under the supervision of, the issuer's principal executive and principal financial officers, or persons performing similar functions, and effected by the issuer's board of directors, management and other personnel, to provide reasonable assurance regarding the reliability of financial reporting and the preparation of financial statements for external purposes in accordance with generally accepted accounting principles and includes those policies and procedures that:
   1. Pertain to the maintenance of records that in reasonable detail accurately and fairly reflect the transactions and dispositions of the assets of the issuer;
   2. Provide reasonable assurance that transactions are recorded as necessary to permit preparation of financial statements in accordance with generally accepted accounting principles, and that receipts and expenditures of the issuer are being made only in accordance with authorizations of management and directors of the issuer; and
   3. Provide reasonable assurance regarding prevention or timely detection of unauthorized acquisition, use or disposition of the issuer's assets that could have a material effect on the financial statements.

Rule 13a-20 – Plain English Presentation of Specified Information

a. Any information included or incorporated by reference in a report filed under section 13(a) of the Act that is required to be disclosed pursuant to Item 402, 403, 404 or 407 of Regulation S-K must be presented in a clear, concise and understandable manner. You must prepare the disclosure using the following standards:
   1. Present information in clear, concise sections, paragraphs and sentences;
   2. Use short sentences;
   3. Use definite, concrete, everyday words;
   4. Use the active voice;
   5. Avoid multiple negatives;
   6. Use descriptive headings and subheadings;
   7. Use a tabular presentation or bullet lists for complex material, wherever possible;
   8. Avoid legal jargon and highly technical business and other terminology;

9. Avoid frequent reliance on glossaries or defined terms as the primary means of explaining information. Define terms in a glossary or other section of the document only if the meaning is unclear from the context. Use a glossary only if it facilitates understanding of the disclosure; and

10. In designing the presentation of the information you may include pictures, logos, charts, graphs and other design elements so long as the design is not misleading and the required information is clear. You are encouraged to use tables, schedules, charts and graphic illustrations that present relevant data in an understandable manner, so long as such presentations are consistent with applicable disclosure requirements and consistent with other information in the document. You must draw graphs and charts to scale. Any information you provide must not be misleading.

b. Reserved.

Note to Rule 13a-20. In drafting the disclosure to comply with this section, you should avoid the following:

1. Legalistic or overly complex presentations that make the substance of the disclosure difficult to understand;

2. Vague "boilerplate" explanations that are imprecise and readily subject to different interpretations;

3. Complex information copied directly from legal documents without any clear and concise explanation of the provision(s); and

4. Disclosure repeated in different sections of the document that increases the size of the document but does not enhance the quality of the information.

Rule 13b2-1 – Falsification of Accounting Records

No person shall directly or indirectly, falsify or cause to by falsified, any book, record or account subject to section 13(b)(2)(A) of the Securities Exchange Act.

Rule 13b2-2 – Representations and Conduct in Connection with the Preparation of Required Reports and Documents

a. No director or officer of an issuer shall, directly or indirectly:

1. Make or cause to be made a materially false or misleading statement to an accountant in connection with; or

2. Omit to state, or cause another person to omit to state, any material fact necessary in order to make statements made, in light of the circumstances under which such statements were made, not misleading, to an accountant in connection with:

    i. Any audit, review or examination of the financial statements of the issuer required to be made pursuant to this subpart; or

    ii. The preparation or filing of any document or report required to be filed with the Commission pursuant to this subpart or otherwise.

b.

1. No officer or director of an issuer, or any other person acting under the direction thereof, shall directly or indirectly take any action to coerce, manipulate, mislead, or fraudulently influence any independent public or certified public

accountant engaged in the performance of an audit or review of the financial statements of that issuer that are required to be filed with the Commission pursuant to this subpart or otherwise if that person knew or should have known that such action, if successful, could result in rendering the issuer's financial statements materially misleading.

2.   For purposes of paragraphs (b)(1) and (c)(2) of this section, actions that, "if successful, could result in rendering the issuer's financial statements materially misleading" include, but are not limited to, actions taken at any time with respect to the professional engagement period to coerce, manipulate, mislead, or fraudulently influence an auditor:

    i.   To issue or reissue a report on an issuer's financial statements that is not warranted in the circumstances (due to material violations of generally accepted accounting principles, the standards of the PCAOB, or other professional or regulatory standards);

    ii.   Not to perform audit, review or other procedures required by standards of the PCAOB or other professional standards;

    iii.   Not to withdraw an issued report; or

    iv.   Not to communicate matters to an issuer's audit committee.

c.   In addition, in the case of an investment company registered under section 8 of the Investment Company Act of 1940, or a business development company as defined in section 2(a)(48) of the Investment Company Act of 1940, no officer or director of the company's investment adviser, sponsor, depositor, trustee, or administrator (or, in the case of paragraph (c)(2) of this section, any other person acting under the direction thereof) shall, directly or indirectly:

1.

    i.   Make or cause to be made a materially false or misleading statement to an accountant in connection with; or

    ii.   Omit to state, or cause another person to omit to state, any material fact necessary in order to make statements made, in light of the circumstances under which such statements were made, not misleading to an accountant in connection with:

    A.   Any audit, review, or examination of the financial statements of the investment company required to be made pursuant to this subpart; or

    B.   The preparation or filing of any document or report required to be filed with the Commission pursuant to this subpart or otherwise; or

Take any action to coerce, manipulate, mislead, or fraudulently influence any independent public or certified public accountant engaged in the performance of an audit or review of the financial statements of that investment company that are required to be filed with the Commission pursuant to this subpart or otherwise if that person knew or should have known that such action, if successful, could result in rendering the investment company's financial statements materially misleading.

Rule 13q-1 – Disclosure of Payments Made by Resource Extraction Issuers

a.   *Resource extraction issuers.* Every issuer that is required to file an annual report with the Commission pursuant to Section 13 or 15(d) of the Exchange Act and engages in the commercial development of oil, natural gas, or minerals must file a report on within the period specified in that Form disclosing the information required by the applicable items of Form SD as specified in that Form.

b.   *Anti-evasion.* Disclosure is required under this section in circumstances in which an activity related to the commercial development of oil, natural gas, or minerals, or a payment or series of payments made by a resource extraction issuer to a foreign government or the Federal Government for the purpose of commercial development of oil, natural gas, or minerals is not, in form or characterization, within one of the categories of activities or payments specified in Form SD, but is part of a plan or scheme to evade the disclosure required under this section.

c.   *Alternative reporting.* An application for recognition of a regime as substantially similar for purposes of alternative reporting must be filed in accordance with the procedures set forth in Rule 0-13, except that, for purposes of this paragraph (c), applications may be submitted by resource extraction issuers, governments, industry groups, or trade associations.

d.   *Exemptive relief.* An application for exemptive relief under this section may be filed in accordance with the procedures set forth in Rule 0-12.

e.   *Public compilation.* To the extent practicable, the staff will periodically make a compilation of the information required to be filed under this section publicly available online. The staff may determine the form, manner and timing of the compilation, except that no information included therein may be anonymized (whether by redacting the names of the resource extraction issuer or otherwise).

Rule 14a-1 – Definitions

Unless the context otherwise requires, all terms used in this regulation have the same meanings as in the Act or elsewhere in the general rules and regulations thereunder. In addition, the following definitions apply unless the context otherwise requires:

a.   **Associate**. The term *associate*, used to indicate a relationship with any person, means:
    1.   Any corporation or organization (other than the registrant or a majority owned subsidiary of the registrant) of which such person is an officer or partner or is, directly or indirectly, the beneficial owner of 10 percent or more of any class of equity securities;
    2.   Any trust or other estate in which such person has a substantial beneficial interest or as to which such person serves as trustee or in a similar fiduciary capacity; and
    3.   Any relative or spouse of such person, or any relative of such spouse, who has the same home as such person or who is a director or officer of the registrant or any of its parents or subsidiaries.

b.   **Employee benefit plan**. For purposes of Rules 14a-13, 14b-1 and 14b-2, the term *employee benefit plan* means any purchase, savings, option, bonus, appreciation, profit sharing, thrift, incentive, pension or similar plan primarily for employees, directors, trustees or officers.

c.   **Entity that exercises fiduciary powers.** The term *entity that exercises fiduciary powers* means any entity that holds securities in nominee name or otherwise on behalf of a beneficial owner but does not include a clearing agency registered pursuant to section 17A of the Act or a broker or a dealer.

d.   **Exempt employee benefit plan securities.** For purposes of Rules 14a-13, 14b-1 and 14b-2, the term *exempt employee benefit plan securities* means:
1.   Securities of the registrant held by an employee benefit plan, as defined in paragraph (b) of this section, where such plan is established by the registrant; or
2.   If notice regarding the current solicitation has been given pursuant to Rule 14a-13(a)(1)(ii)(C) or if notice regarding the current request for a list of names, addresses and securities positions of beneficial owners has been given pursuant to Rule 14a-13(b)(3), securities of the registrant held by an employee benefit plan, as defined in paragraph (b) of this section, where such plan is established by an affiliate of the registrant.

e.   **Last fiscal year.** The term *last fiscal year* of the registrant means the last fiscal year of the registrant ending prior to the date of the meeting for which proxies are to be solicited or if the solicitation involves written authorizations or consents in lieu of a meeting, the earliest date they may be used to effect corporate action.

f.   **Proxy.** The term *proxy* includes every proxy, consent or authorization within the meaning of section 14(a) of the Act. The consent or authorization may take the form of failure to object or to dissent.

g.   **Proxy statement.** The term *proxy statement* means the statement required by Rule 14a-3(a) whether or not contained in a single document.

h.   **Record date.** The term *record date* means the date as of which the record holders of securities entitled to vote at a meeting or by written consent or authorization shall be determined.

i.   **Record holder.** For purposes of Rules 14a-13, 14b-1 and 14b-2, the term *record holder* means any broker, dealer, voting trustee, bank, association or other entity that exercises fiduciary powers which holds securities of record in nominee name or otherwise or as a participant in a clearing agency registered pursuant to section 17A of the Act.

j.   **Registrant.** The term *registrant* means the issuer of the securities in respect of which proxies are to be solicited.

k.   **Respondent bank.** For purposes of Rules 14a-13, 14b-1 and 14b-2, the term *respondent bank* means any bank, association or other entity that exercises fiduciary powers which holds securities on behalf of beneficial owners and deposits such securities for safekeeping with another bank, association or other entity that exercises fiduciary powers.

l. **Solicitation.**
1. The terms *solicit* and *solicitation* include:
    i. Any request for a proxy whether or not accompanied by or included in a form of proxy:
    ii. Any request to execute or not to execute, or to revoke, a proxy; or
    iii. The furnishing of a form of proxy or other communication to security holders under circumstances reasonably calculated to result in the procurement, withholding or revocation of a proxy, including:
        A. Any proxy voting advice that makes a recommendation to a security holder as to its vote, consent, or authorization on a specific matter for which security holder approval is solicited, and that is furnished by a person that markets its expertise as a provider of such proxy voting advice, separately from other forms of investment advice, and sells such proxy voting advice for a fee.
        B. [Reserved].
2. The terms do not apply, however, to:
    i. The furnishing of a form of proxy to a security holder upon the unsolicited request of such security holder;
    ii. The performance by the registrant of acts required by Rule 14a-7;
    iii. The performance by any person of ministerial acts on behalf of a person soliciting a proxy; or
    iv. A communication by a security holder who does not otherwise engage in a proxy solicitation (other than a solicitation exempt under Rule 14a-2) stating how the security holder intends to vote and the reasons therefor, provided that the communication:
        A. Is made by means of speeches in public forums, press releases, published or broadcast opinions, statements, or advertisements appearing in a broadcast media, or newspaper, magazine or other bona fide publication disseminated on a regular basis,
        B. Is directed to persons to whom the security holder owes a fiduciary duty in connection with the voting of securities of a registrant held by the security holder, or
        C. Is made in response to unsolicited requests for additional information with respect to a prior communication by the security holder made pursuant to this paragraph (l)(2)(iv).
    v. The furnishing of any proxy voting advice by a person who furnishes such advice only in response to an unprompted request.

Rule 14a-2 – Solicitations to Which Rule 14a-3 to Rule 14a-15 Apply

Rules 14a-3 to 14a-15, except as specified, apply to every solicitation of a proxy with respect to securities registered pursuant to section 12 of the Act, whether or not trading in such securities has been suspended. To the extent specified below, certain of these sections also apply to roll-up transactions that do not involve an entity with securities registered pursuant to section 12 of the Act.

a.   Rules 14a-3 to 14a-15 do not apply to the following:
1.   Any solicitation by a person in respect to securities carried in his name or in the name of his nominee (otherwise than as voting trustee) or held in his custody, if such person-
     i.   Receives no commission or remuneration for such solicitation, directly or indirectly, other than reimbursement of reasonable expenses,
     ii.   Furnishes promptly to the person solicited (or such person's household in accordance with Rule 14a-3(e)(1)) a copy of all soliciting material with respect to the same subject matter or meeting received from all persons who shall furnish copies thereof for such purpose and who shall, if requested, defray the reasonable expenses to be incurred in forwarding such material, and
     iii. In addition, does no more than impartially instruct the person solicited to forward a proxy to the person, if any, to whom the person solicited desires to give a proxy, or impartially request from the person solicited instructions as to the authority to be conferred by the proxy and state that a proxy will be given if no instructions are received by a certain date.
2.   Any solicitation by a person in respect of securities of which he is the beneficial owner;
3.   Any solicitation involved in the offer and sale of securities registered under the Securities Act of 1933: *Provided,* That this paragraph shall not apply to securities to be issued in any transaction of the character specified in paragraph (a) of Rule 145 under that Act;
4.   Any solicitation with respect to a plan of reorganization under Chapter 11 of the Bankruptcy Reform Act of 1978, as amended, if made after the entry of an order approving the written disclosure statement concerning a plan of reorganization pursuant to section 1125 of said Act and after, or concurrently with, the transmittal of such disclosure statement as required by section 1125 of said Act;
5.   [Reserved]
6.   Any solicitation through the medium of a newspaper advertisement which informs security holders of a source from which they may obtain copies of a proxy statement, form of proxy and any other soliciting material and does no more than:
     i.   Name the registrant,
     ii.   State the reason for the advertisement, and
     iii. Identify the proposal or proposals to be acted upon by security holders.

b.   Rules 14a-3 to 14a-6 (other than Rule 14a-6(g) and 14a-6(p)), Rule 14a-8, Rule 14a-10, and Rule 14a-12 through Rule 14a-15, and Rule 14a-19 do not apply to the following:
1.   Any solicitation by or on behalf of any person who does not, at any time during such solicitation, seek directly or indirectly, either on its own or another's behalf, the power to act as proxy for a security holder and does not furnish or otherwise request, or act on behalf of a person who furnishes or requests, a form of revocation, abstention, consent or authorization. *Provided, however,* That the exemption set forth in this paragraph shall not apply to:
     i.   The registrant or an affiliate or associate of the registrant (other than an officer or director or any person serving in a similar capacity);

555

    ii.   An officer or director of the registrant or any person serving in a similar capacity engaging in a solicitation financed directly or indirectly by the registrant;

    iii.   An officer, director, affiliate or associate of a person that is ineligible to rely on the exemption set forth in this paragraph (other than persons specified in paragraph (b)(1)(i) of this section), or any person serving in a similar capacity;

    iv.   Any nominee for whose election as a director proxies are solicited;

    v.   Any person soliciting in opposition to a merger, recapitalization, reorganization, sale of assets or other extraordinary transaction recommended or approved by the board of directors of the registrant who is proposing or intends to propose an alternative transaction to which such person or one of its affiliates is a party;

    vi.   Any person who is required to report beneficial ownership of the registrant's equity securities on a Schedule 13D, unless such person has filed a Schedule 13D and has not disclosed pursuant to Item 4 thereto an intent, or reserved the right, to engage in a control transaction, or any contested solicitation for the election of directors;

    vii.   Any person who receives compensation from an ineligible person directly related to the solicitation of proxies, other than pursuant to Rule 14a-13;

    viii.   Where the registrant is an investment company registered under the Investment Company Act of 1940, an "interested person" of that investment company, as that term is defined in section 2(a)(19) of the Investment Company Act;

    ix.   Any person who, because of a substantial interest in the subject matter of the solicitation, is likely to receive a benefit from a successful solicitation that would not be shared pro rata by all other holders of the same class of securities, other than a benefit arising from the person's employment with the registrant; and

    x.   Any person acting on behalf of any of the foregoing.

2.   Any solicitation made otherwise than on behalf of the registrant where the total number of persons solicited is not more than ten; and

3.   The furnishing of proxy voting advice by any person (the "advisor") to any other person with whom the advisor has a business relationship, if:

    i.   The advisor renders financial advice in the ordinary course of his business;

    ii.   The advisor discloses to the recipient of the advice any significant relationship with the registrant or any of its affiliates, or a security holder proponent of the matter on which advice is given, as well as any material interests of the advisor in such matter;

    iii.   The advisor receives no special commission or remuneration for furnishing the proxy voting advice from any person other than a recipient of the advice and other persons who receive similar advice under this subsection; and

    iv.   The proxy voting advice is not furnished on behalf of any person soliciting proxies or on behalf of a participant in an election subject to the provisions of Rule 14a-12(c).

4. Any solicitation in connection with a roll-up transaction as defined in Item 901(c) of Regulation S-K in which the holder of a security that is the subject of a proposed roll-up transaction engages in preliminary communications with other holders of securities that are the subject of the same limited partnership roll-up transaction for the purpose of determining whether to solicit proxies, consents, or authorizations in opposition to the proposed limited partnership roll-up transaction; *Provided, however,* that:

    i. This exemption shall not apply to a security holder who is an affiliate of the registrant or general partner or sponsor; and

    ii. This exemption shall not apply to a holder of five percent 5% or more of the outstanding securities of a class that is the subject of the proposed roll-up transaction who engages in the business of buying and selling limited partnership interests in the secondary market unless that holder discloses to the persons to whom the communications are made such ownership interest and any relations of the holder to the parties of the transaction or to the transaction itself, as required by Rule 14a-6(n)(1) and specified in the Notice of Exempt Preliminary Roll-up Communication. If the communication is oral, this disclosure may be provided to the security holder orally. Whether the communication is written or oral, the notice required by Rule 14a-6(n) and Rule 14a-104 shall be furnished to the Commission.

5. Publication or distribution by a broker or a dealer of a research report in accordance with Rule 138 or Rule 139 during a transaction in which the broker or dealer or its affiliate participates or acts in an advisory role.

6. Any solicitation by or on behalf of any person who does not seek directly or indirectly, either on its own or another's behalf, the power to act as proxy for a shareholder and does not furnish or otherwise request, or act on behalf of a person who furnishes or requests, a form of revocation, abstention, consent, or authorization in an electronic shareholder forum that is established, maintained or operated pursuant to the provisions of Rule 14a-17, provided that the solicitation is made more than 60 days prior to the date announced by a registrant for its next annual or special meeting of shareholders. If the registrant announces the date of its next annual or special meeting of shareholders less than 60 days before the meeting date, then the solicitation may not be made more than two days following the date of the registrant's announcement of the meeting date. Participation in an electronic shareholder forum does not eliminate a person's eligibility to solicit proxies after the date that this exemption is no longer available, or is no longer being relied upon, provided that any such solicitation is conducted in accordance with this regulation.

7. Any solicitation by or on behalf of any shareholder in connection with the formation of a nominating shareholder group pursuant to Rule 14a-11, provided that:

    i. The soliciting shareholder is not holding the registrant's securities with the purpose, or with the effect, of changing control of the registrant or to gain a number of seats on the board of directors that exceeds the maximum number of nominees that the registrant could be required to include under Rule 14a-11(d);

    ii.   Each written communication includes no more than:

        A. A statement of each soliciting shareholder's intent to form a nominating shareholder group in order to nominate one or more directors under Rule 14a-11;

        B. Identification of, and a brief statement regarding, the potential nominee or nominees or, where no nominee or nominees have been identified, the characteristics of the nominee or nominees that the shareholder intends to nominate, if any;

        C. The percentage of voting power of the registrant's securities that are entitled to be voted on the election of directors that each soliciting shareholder holds or the aggregate percentage held by any group to which the shareholder belongs; and

        D. The means by which shareholders may contact the soliciting party.

    iii. Any written soliciting material published, sent or given to shareholders in accordance with this paragraph must be filed by the shareholder with the Commission, under the registrant's Exchange Act file number, or, in the case of a registrant that is an investment company registered under the Investment Company Act of 1940, under the registrant's Investment Company Act file number, no later than the date the material is first published, sent or given to shareholders. Three copies of the material must at the same time be filed with, or mailed for filing to, each national securities exchange upon which any class of securities of the registrant is listed and registered. The soliciting material must include a cover page in the form set forth in Schedule 14N and the appropriate box on the cover page must be marked.

    iv. In the case of an oral solicitation made in accordance with the terms of this section, the nominating shareholder must file a cover page in the form set forth in Schedule 14N, with the appropriate box on the cover page marked, under the registrant's Exchange Act file number (or in the case of an investment company registered under the Investment Company Act of 1940, under the registrant's Investment Company Act file number), no later than the date of the first such communication.

Instruction to paragraph (b)(7): The exemption provided in paragraph (b)(7) of this section shall not apply to a shareholder that subsequently engages in soliciting or other nominating activities outside the scope of Rule 14a-2(b)(8) and Rule 14a-11 in connection with the subject election of directors or is or becomes a member of any other group, as determined under section 13(d)(3) of the Act and Rule 13d-5(b)), or otherwise, with persons engaged in soliciting or other nominating activities in connection with the subject election of directors.

8.   Any solicitation by or on behalf of a nominating shareholder or nominating shareholder group in support of its nominee that is included or that will be included on the registrant's form of proxy in accordance with § 240.14a-11 or for or against the registrant's nominee or nominees, provided that:

    i.   The soliciting party does not, at any time during such solicitation, seek directly or indirectly, either on its own or another's behalf, the power to act as proxy for a shareholder and does not furnish or otherwise request, or act on behalf of a person who furnishes or requests, a form of revocation, abstention, consent or authorization;

     ii. Any written communication includes:

        A. The identity of each nominating shareholder and a description of his or her direct or indirect interests, by security holdings or otherwise;

        B. A prominent legend in clear, plain language advising shareholders that a shareholder nominee is or will be included in the registrant's proxy statement and that they should read the registrant's proxy statement when available because it includes important information (or, if the registrant's proxy statement is publicly available, advising shareholders of that fact and encouraging shareholders to read the registrant's proxy statement because it includes important information). The legend also must explain to shareholders that they can find the registrant's proxy statement, other soliciting material, and any other relevant documents at no charge on the Commission's Web site; and

     iii. Any written soliciting material published, sent or given to shareholders in accordance with this paragraph must be filed by the nominating shareholder or nominating shareholder group with the Commission, under the registrant's Exchange Act file number, or, in the case of a registrant that is an investment company registered under the Investment Company Act of 1940, under the registrant's Investment Company Act file number, no later than the date the material is first published, sent or given to shareholders. Three copies of the material must at the same time be filed with, or mailed for filing to, each national securities exchange upon which any class of securities of the registrant is listed and registered. The soliciting material must include a cover page in the form set forth in Schedule 14N and the appropriate box on the cover page must be marked.

Instruction 1 to paragraph (b)(8): A nominating shareholder or nominating shareholder group may rely on the exemption provided in paragraph (b)(8) of this section only after receiving notice from the registrant in accordance with Rule14a-11(g)(1) or Rule 14a-11(g)(3)(iv) that the registrant will include the nominating shareholder's or nominating shareholder group's nominee or nominees in its form of proxy.

Instruction 2 to paragraph (b)(8): Any solicitation by or on behalf of a nominating shareholder or nominating shareholder group in support of its nominee included or to be included on the registrant's form of proxy in accordance with Rule 14a-11 or for or against the registrant's nominee or nominees must be made in reliance on the exemption provided in paragraph (b)(8) of this section and not on any other exemption.

Instruction 3 to paragraph (b)(8): The exemption provided in paragraph (b)(8) of this section shall not apply to a person that subsequently engages in soliciting or other nominating activities outside the scope of Rule 14a-11 in connection with the subject election of directors or is or becomes a member of any other group, as determined under section 13(d)(3) of the Act and Rule 13d-5(b)), or otherwise, with persons engaged in soliciting or other nominating activities in connection with the subject election of directors.

9. Paragraphs (b)(1) and (b)(3) of this section shall not be available to a person furnishing proxy voting advice covered by Rule 14a-1(l)(1)(iii)(A) ("proxy voting advice business") unless the proxy voting advice business includes in its

proxy voting advice or in an electronic medium used to deliver the proxy voting advice prominent disclosure of:

    i.   Any information regarding an interest, transaction, or relationship of the proxy voting advice business (or its affiliates) that is material to assessing the objectivity of the proxy voting advice in light of the circumstances of the particular interest, transaction, or relationship; and

    ii.   Any policies and procedures used to identify, as well as the steps taken to address, any such material conflicts of interest arising from such interest, transaction, or relationship.; and

Rule 14a-3 – Information to be Furnished to Security Holders

a.   No solicitation subject to this regulation shall be made unless each person solicited is concurrently furnished or has previously been furnished with:

    1.   A publicly-filed preliminary or definitive written proxy statement containing the information specified in Schedule 14A;

    2.   A preliminary or definitive written proxy statement included in a registration statement filed under the Securities Act of 1933 on Form S-4 or F-4 or Form N–14 and containing the information specified in such Form; or

    3.   A publicly-filed preliminary or definitive proxy statement, not in the form and manner described in Rule 14a-16, containing the information specified in Schedule 14A, if:

        i.   The solicitation relates to a business combination transaction as that term is defined in Rule 165 of this chapter, as well as transactions for cash consideration requiring disclosure under Item 14 of Rule 14a-101; or

        ii.   The solicitation may not follow the form and manner described in Rule 14a-16 pursuant to the laws of the state of incorporation of the registrant.

b.   If the solicitation is made on behalf of the registrant, other than an investment company registered under the Investment Company Act of 1940, and relates to an annual (or special meeting in lieu of the annual) meeting of security holders, or written consent in lieu of such meeting, at which directors are to be elected, each proxy statement furnished pursuant to paragraph (a) of this section shall be accompanied or preceded by an annual report to security holders as follows:

    1.   The report shall include, for the registrant and its subsidiaries consolidated, audited balance sheets as of the end of each of the two most recent fiscal years and audited statements of income and cash flows for each of the three most recent fiscal years prepared in accordance with Regulation S-X, except that the provisions of Article 3 (other than Rules 3-03(e), 3-04 and 3-20) and Article 11 shall not apply. Any financial statement schedules or exhibits or separate financial statements which may otherwise be required in filings with the Commission may be omitted. If the financial statements of the registrant and its subsidiaries consolidated in the annual report filed or to be filed with the Commission are not required to be audited, the financial statements required by this paragraph may be unaudited.

    Note 1: If the financial statements for a period prior to the most recently completed fiscal year have been examined by a predecessor accountant, the separate report of the predecessor accountant may be omitted in the report to security holders provided the registrant has obtained from the predecessor accountant a reissued report covering the prior period presented and the successor accountant clearly indicates in the scope paragraph of his report

a.   that the financial statements of the prior period were examined by other accountants,
b.   the date of their report,
c.   the type of opinion expressed by the predecessor accountant and
d.   the substantive reasons therefor, if it was other than unqualified.

It should be noted, however, that the separate report of any predecessor accountant is required in filings with the Commission. If, for instance, the financial statements in the annual report to security holders are incorporated by reference in a Form 10-K the separate report of a predecessor accountant shall be filed in Part II or in Part IV as a financial statement schedule.

Note 2: For purposes of complying with Rule 14a-3, if the registrant has changed its fiscal closing date, financial statements covering two years and one period of 9 to 12 months shall be deemed to satisfy the requirements for statements of income and cash flows for the three most recent fiscal years.

2.   Financial statements and notes thereto shall be presented in roman type at least as large and as legible as 10-point modern type. If necessary for convenient presentation, the financial statements may be in roman type as large and as legible as 8-point modern type. All type shall be leaded at least 2 points.

3.   The report shall contain the supplementary financial information required by Item 302 of Regulation S-K.

4.   The report shall contain information concerning changes in and disagreements with accountants on accounting and financial disclosure required by Item 304 of Regulation S-K.

5.
    a.   [Reserved].
    b.   The report shall contain management's discussion and analysis of financial condition and results of operations required by Item 303 of Regulation S-K.
    c.   The report shall contain the quantitative and qualitative disclosures about market risk required by Item 305 of Regulation S-K.

6.   The report shall contain a brief description of the business done by the registrant and its subsidiaries during the most recent fiscal year which will, in the opinion of management, indicate the general nature and scope of the business of the registrant and its subsidiaries.

7.   The report shall contain information relating to the registrant's industry segments, classes of similar products or services, foreign and domestic operations and exports sales required by paragraphs (b), (c)(1)(i) and (d) of Item 101 of Regulation S-K.

8.   The report shall identify each of the registrant's directors and executive officers, and shall indicate the principal occupation or employment of each such person and the name and principal business of any organization by which such person is employed.

9.   The report shall contain the market price of and dividends on the registrant's common equity and related security holder matters required by Items 201(a), (b) and (c) of Regulation S-K. If the report precedes or accompanies a proxy statement or information statement relating to an annual meeting of security holders at which directors are to be elected (or special meeting or written consents in lieu of such meeting), furnish the performance graph required by Item 201(e).

10.   The registrant's proxy statement, or the report, shall contain an undertaking in bold face or otherwise reasonably prominent type to provide without charge to each person solicited upon the written request of any such person, a copy of the registrant's annual report on Form 10-K including the financial statements and the financial statement schedules, required to be filed with the Commission pursuant to Rule 13a-1 under the Act for the registrant's most recent fiscal year, and shall indicate the name and address of the person to whom such a written request is to be directed. In the discretion of management, a registrant need not undertake to furnish without charge copies of all exhibits to its Form 10-K provided the that copy of the annual report on Form 10-K furnished without charge to requesting security holders is accompanied by a list briefly describing all the exhibits not contained therein and indicating that the registrant will furnish any exhibit upon the payment of a specified reasonable fee which fee shall be limited to the registrant's reasonable expenses in furnishing such exhibit. If the registrant's annual report to security holders complies with all of the disclosure requirements of Form 10-K and is filed with the Commission in satisfaction of its Form 10-K filing requirements, such registrant need not furnish a separate Form 10-K to security holders who receive a copy of such annual report.

Note: Pursuant to the undertaking required by paragraph (b)(10) of this section, a registrant shall furnish a copy of its annual report on Form 10-K to a beneficial owner of its securities upon receipt of a written request from such person. Each request must set forth a good faith representation that, as of the record date for the solicitation requiring the furnishing of the annual report to security holders pursuant to paragraph (b) of this section, the person making the request was a beneficial owner of securities entitled to vote. Subject to the foregoing requirements, the report may be in any form deemed suitable by management and the information required by paragraphs (b)(5) to (10) of this section may be presented in an appendix or other separate section of the report, provided that the attention of security holders is called to such presentation.

Note: Registrants are encouraged to utilize tables, schedules, charts and graphic illustrations of present financial information in an understandable manner. Any presentation of financial information must be consistent with the data in the financial statements contained in the report and, if appropriate, should refer to relevant portions of the financial statements and notes thereto.

11.   [Reserved]

12.   Paragraph (b) of this section shall not apply, however, to solicitations made on behalf of the registrant before the financial statements are available if a solicitation is being made at the same time in opposition to the registrant and if the registrant's proxy statement includes an undertaking in bold face type to furnish such annual report to security holders to all persons being solicited at

least 20 calendar days before the date of the meeting or, if the solicitation refers to a written consent or authorization in lieu of a meeting, at least 20 calendar days prior to the earliest date on which it may be used to effect corporate action.

c.   The report sent to security holders pursuant to this rule shall be submitted in electronic format, in accordance with the EDGAR Filer Manual, to the Commission, solely for its information, not later than the date on which such report is first sent or given to security holders or the date on which preliminary copies, or definitive copies, if preliminary filing was not required, of solicitation material are filed with the Commission pursuant to Rule 14a-6, whichever date is later. The report is not deemed to be "soliciting material" or to be "filed" with the Commission or subject to this regulation otherwise than as provided in this Rule, or to the liabilities of section 18 of the Act, except to the extent that the registrant specifically requests that it be treated as a part of the proxy soliciting material or incorporates it in the proxy statement or other filed report by reference.

d.   An annual report to security holders prepared on an integrated basis pursuant to General Instruction H to Form 10-K may also be submitted in satisfaction of this rule. When filed as the annual report on Form 10-K responses to the Items of that form are subject to section 18 of the Act notwithstanding paragraph (c) of this section.

e.

   1.   i.   A registrant will be considered to have delivered an annual report to security holders, proxy statement or Notice of Internet Availability of Proxy Materials, as described in Rule 14a-16, to all security holders of record who share an address if:

      A. The registrant delivers one annual report to security holders, proxy statement or Notice of Internet Availability of Proxy Materials, as applicable, to the shared address;

      B. The registrant addresses the annual report to security holders, proxy statement or Notice of Internet Availability of Proxy Materials, as applicable, to the security holders as a group (for example, "ABC Fund [or Corporation] Security Holders," "Jane Doe and Household," "The Smith Family"), to each of the security holders individually (for example, "John Doe and Richard Jones") or to the security holders in a form to which each of the security holders has consented in writing;

      Note to paragraph (e)(1)(i)(B): Unless the registrant addresses the annual report to security holders, proxy statement or Notice of Internet Availability of Proxy Materials to the security holders as a group or to each of the security holders individually, it must obtain, from each security holder to be included in the householded group, a separate affirmative written consent to the specific form of address the registrant will use.

      C. The security holders consent, in accordance with paragraph (e)(1)(ii) of this section, to delivery of one annual report to security holders or proxy statement, as applicable;

      D. With respect to delivery of the proxy statement or Notice of Internet Availability of Proxy Materials, the registrant delivers, together with or subsequent to delivery of the proxy statement, a separate proxy card for each security holder at the shared address; and

E. The registrant includes an undertaking in the proxy statement to deliver promptly upon written or oral request a separate copy of the annual report to security holders, proxy statement or Notice of Internet Availability of Proxy Materials, as applicable, to a security holder at a shared address to which a single copy of the document was delivered.

ii. Consent.

A. Affirmative written consent. Each security holder must affirmatively consent, in writing, to delivery of one annual report to security holders or proxy statement, as applicable. A security holder's affirmative written consent will be considered valid only if the security holder has been informed of:

1. The duration of the consent;
2. The specific types of documents to which the consent will apply;
3. The procedures the security holder must follow to revoke consent; and
4. The registrant's obligation to begin sending individual copies to a security holder within thirty days after the security holder revokes consent.

B. Implied consent. The registrant need not obtain affirmative written consent from a security holder for purposes of paragraph (e)(1)(ii)(A) of this section if all of the following conditions are met:

1. The security holder has the same last name as the other security holders at the shared address or the registrant reasonably believes that the security holders are members of the same family;
2. The registrant has sent the security holder a notice at least 60 days before the registrant begins to rely on this section concerning delivery of annual reports and proxy statements or Notice of Internet Availability of Proxy Materials to that security holder. The notice must:

    i.   Be a separate written document;
    ii. State that only one annual report or proxy statement or Notice of Internet Availability of Proxy Materials, as applicable, will be delivered to the shared address unless the registrant receives contrary instructions;
    iii. Include a toll-free telephone number, or be accompanied by a reply form that is pre-addressed with postage provided, that the security holder can use to notify the registrant that the security holder wishes to receive a separate annual report or proxy statement or Notice of Internet Availability of Proxy Materials,;
    iv. State the duration of the consent;
    v.   Explain how a security holder can revoke consent;
    vi. State that the registrant will begin sending individual copies to a security holder within thirty days after the security holder revokes consent; and

        vii.   Contain the following prominent statement, or similar clear and understandable statement, in bold-face type: "Important Notice Regarding Delivery of Security Holder Documents." This statement also must appear on the envelope in which the notice is delivered. Alternatively, if the notice is delivered separately from other communications to security holders, this statement may appear either on the notice or on the envelope in which the notice is delivered.

Note to paragraph (e)(1)(ii)(B)(2): The notice should be written in plain English. See Rule 421(d)(2) for a discussion of plain English principles.

      3.   The registrant has not received the reply form or other notification indicating that the security holder wishes to continue to receive an individual copy of the annual report or proxy statement or Notice of Internet Availability of Proxy Materials,, as applicable, within 60 days after the registrant sent the notice required by paragraph (e)(1)(ii)(B)(2) of this section; and

      4.   The registrant delivers the document to a post office box or residential street address.

Note to paragraph (e)(1)(ii)(B)(4): The registrant can assume that a street address is residential unless the registrant has information that indicates the street address is a business.

    iii. Revocation of consent. If a security holder, orally or in writing, revokes consent to delivery of one annual report to security holder, proxy statement or Notice of Internet Availability of Proxy Materials to a shared address, the registrant must begin sending individual copies to that security holder within 30 days after the registrant receives revocation of the security holder's consent.

    iv. Definition of address. Unless otherwise indicated, for purposes of this section, address means a street *address,* a post office box number, an electronic mail address, a facsimile telephone number or other similar destination to which paper or electronic documents are delivered, unless otherwise provided in this section. If the registrant has reason to believe that the address is a street address of a multi-unit building, the address must include the unit number.

Note to paragraph (e)(1): A person other than the registrant making a proxy solicitation may deliver a single proxy statement to security holders of record or beneficial owners who have separate accounts and share an address if: (a) the registrant or intermediary has followed the procedures in this section; and (b) the registrant or intermediary makes available the shared address information to the person in accordance with Rule 14a-7(a)(2)(i) and (ii).

2.   Notwithstanding paragraphs (a) and (b) of this section, unless state law requires otherwise, a registrant is not required to send an annual report to security holders or proxy statement or Notice of Internet Availability of Proxy Materials to a security holder if:

    i.   An annual report and a proxy statement, or Notice of Internet Availability of Proxy Materials, for two consecutive annual meetings; or

ii.   All, and at least two, payments (if sent by first class mail) of dividends or interest on securities, or dividend reinvestment confirmations, during a twelve month period, have been mailed to such security holder's address and have been returned as undeliverable. If any such security holder delivers or causes to be delivered to the registrant written notice setting forth his then current address for security holder communications purposes, the registrant's obligation to deliver an annual report to security holders or a proxy statement or Notice of Internet Availability of Proxy Materials under this section is reinstated.

f.   The provisions of paragraph (a) of this section shall not apply to a communication made by means of speeches in public forums, press releases, published or broadcast opinions, statements, or advertisements appearing in a broadcast media, newspaper, magazine or other bona fide publication disseminated on a regular basis, provided that:

1.   No form of proxy, consent or authorization or means to execute the same is provided to a security holder in connection with the communication; and

2.   At the time the communication is made, a definitive proxy statement is on file with the Commission pursuant to Rule 14a-6(b).

Rule 14a-4 – Requirements as to a Proxy

a.   The form of proxy

1.   Shall indicate in bold-face type whether or not the proxy is solicited on behalf of the registrant's board of directors or, if provided other than by a majority of the board of directors, shall indicate in bold-face type on whose behalf the solicitation is made;

2.   Shall provide a specifically designated blank space for dating the proxy card; and

3.   Shall identify clearly and impartially each separate matter intended to be acted upon, whether or not related to or conditioned on the approval of other matters, and whether proposed by the registrant or by security holders. No reference need be made, however, to proposals as to which discretionary authority is conferred pursuant to paragraph (c) of this section.

Note to paragraph (a)(3) (Electronic filers):
Electronic filers shall satisfy the filing requirements of Rule 14a-6(a) or (b) with respect to the form of proxy by filing the form of proxy as an appendix at the end of the proxy statement. Forms of proxy shall not be filed as exhibits or separate documents within an electronic submission.

b.   1.   Means shall be provided in the form of proxy whereby the person solicited is afforded an opportunity to specify by boxes a choice between approval or disapproval of, or abstention with respect to each separate matter referred to therein as intended to be acted upon, other than elections to office. A proxy may confer discretionary authority with respect to matters as to which a choice is not specified by the security holder provided that the form of proxy states in bold-face type how it is intended to vote the shares represented by the proxy in each such case.

2.   A form of proxy that provides for the election of directors shall set forth the names of persons nominated for election as directors, including any person whose nomination by a shareholder or shareholder group satisfies the requirements of an applicable state or foreign law provision, or a registrant's governing documents as they relate to the inclusion of shareholder director nominees in the registrant's proxy materials.

3.   Except as otherwise provided in Rule 14a-19, a form of proxy that provides for the election of directors may provide a means for the security holder to grant authority to vote for the nominees set forth, as a group, provided that there is a similar means for the security holder to withhold authority to vote for such group of nominees (or, when applicable state law gives legal effect to votes cast against a nominee, a similar means for the security holder to vote against such group of nominees and a means for security holders to abstain from voting for such group of nominees). Any such form of proxy which is executed by the security holder in such manner as not to withhold authority to vote for the election of any nominee, or not to grant authority to vote against the election of any nominee, shall be deemed to grant authority to vote for the election of any nominee, provided that the form of proxy so states in bold-face type. Means to grant authority to vote for any nominees as a group or to withhold authority for any nominees as a group or to vote against any nominees as a group may not be provided if the form of proxy includes one or more shareholder nominees in accordance with an applicable state or foreign law provision, or a registrant's governing documents as they relate to the inclusion of shareholder director nominees in the registrant's proxy materials.

4.   When applicable state law gives legal effect to votes cast against a nominee, then in lieu of providing a means for security holders to withhold authority to vote, the form of proxy shall provide a means for security holders to vote against each nominee and a means for security holders to abstain from voting. When applicable state law does not give legal effect to votes cast against a nominee, such form of proxy shall not provide a means for security holders to vote against any nominee and such form of proxy shall clearly provide any of the following means for security holders to withhold authority to vote for each nominee:

    i.   A box opposite the name of each nominee which may be marked to indicate that authority to vote for such nominee is withheld; or

    ii.   An instruction in bold-face type which indicates that the security holder may withhold authority to vote for any nominee by lining through or otherwise striking out the name of any nominee; or

    iii.   Designated blank spaces in which the security holder may enter the names of nominees with respect to whom the security holder chooses to withhold authority to vote; or

    iv.   Any other similar means, provided that clear instructions are furnished indicating how the security holder may withhold authority to vote for any nominee.

Instruction 1 to paragraphs (b)(2), (3), and (4). Paragraphs (b)(2), (3), and (4) do not apply in the case of a merger, consolidation or other plan if the election of directors is an integral part of the plan.

5.   A form of proxy which provides for a shareholder vote on the frequency of shareholder votes to approve the compensation of executives required by section

14A(a)(2) of the Securities Exchange Act of 1934 shall provide means whereby the person solicited is afforded an opportunity to specify by boxes a choice among 1, 2 or 3 years, or abstain.

c. A proxy may confer discretionary authority to vote on any of the following matters:

1. For an annual meeting of shareholders, if the registrant did not have notice of the matter at least 45 days before the date on which the registrant first sent its proxy materials for the prior year's annual meeting of shareholders (or date specified by an advance notice provision), and a specific statement to that effect is made in the proxy statement or form of proxy. If during the prior year the registrant did not hold an annual meeting, or if the date of the meeting has changed more than 30 days from the prior year, then notice must not have been received a reasonable time before the registrant sends its proxy materials for the current year.

2. In the case in which the registrant has received timely notice in connection with an annual meeting of shareholders (as determined under paragraph (c)(1) of this section), if the registrant includes, in the proxy statement, advice on the nature of the matter and how the registrant intends to exercise its discretion to vote on each matter. However, even if the registrant includes this information in its proxy statement, it may not exercise discretionary voting authority on a particular proposal if the proponent:

   i. Provides the registrant with a written statement, within the time-frame determined under paragraph (c)(1) of this section, that the proponent intends to deliver a proxy statement and form of proxy to holders of at least the percentage of the company's voting shares required under applicable law to carry the proposal;

   ii. Includes the same statement in its proxy materials filed under Rule 14a-6; and

   iii. Immediately after soliciting the percentage of shareholders required to carry the proposal, provides the registrant with a statement from any solicitor or other person with knowledge that the necessary steps have been taken to deliver a proxy statement and form of proxy to holders of at least the percentage of the company's voting shares required under applicable law to carry out the proposal.

3. For solicitations other than for annual meetings or for solicitations by persons other than the registrant, matters which the persons making the solicitation do not know, a reasonable time before the solicitation, are to be presented at the meeting, if a specific statement to that effect is made in the proxy statement or form of proxy.

4. Approval of the minutes of the prior meeting if such approval does not amount to ratification of the action taken at that meeting;

5. The election of any person to any office for which a bona fide nominee is named in the proxy statement and such nominee is unable to serve or for good cause will not serve.

6. Any proposal omitted from the proxy statement and form of proxy pursuant to Rule 14a-8 or 14a-9 of this chapter.

7. Matters incident to the conduct of the meeting.

d.   No proxy shall confer authority:
    1.   To vote for the election of any person to any office for which a bona fide nominee is not named in the proxy statement,
        i.   A person shall not be deemed to be a bona fide nominee and shall not be named as such unless the person has consented to being named in a proxy statement relating to the registrant's next annual meeting of shareholders at which directors are to be elected (or a special meeting in lieu of such meeting) and to serve if elected.
        ii. Notwithstanding paragraph (d)(1)(i) of this section, if the registrant is an investment company registered under the Investment Company Act of 1940 or a business development company as defined by section 2(a)(48) of the Investment Company Act of 1940, a person shall not be deemed to be a bona fide nominee and shall not be named as such unless the person has consented to being named in the proxy statement and to serve if elected. Provided, however, that nothing in this section shall prevent any person soliciting in support of nominees who, if elected, would constitute a minority of the board of directors of an investment company registered under the Investment Company Act of 1940 or a business development company as defined by section 2(a)(48) of the Investment Company Act of 1940, from seeking authority to vote for nominees named in the registrant's proxy statement, so long as the soliciting party:
           A.   Seeks authority to vote in the aggregate for the number of director positions then subject to election;
           B.   Represents that it will vote for all the registrant nominees, other than those registrant nominees specified by the soliciting party;
           C.   Provides the security holder an opportunity to withhold authority with respect to any other registrant nominee by writing the name of that nominee on the form of proxy; and
           D.   States on the form of proxy and in the proxy statement that there is no assurance that the registrant's nominees will serve if elected with any of the soliciting party's nominees;
    2.   To vote at any annual meeting other than the next annual meeting (or any adjournment thereof) to be held after the date on which the proxy statement and form of proxy are first sent or given to security holders,
    3.   To vote with respect to more than one meeting (and any adjournment thereof) or more than one consent solicitation or
    4.   To consent to or authorize any action other than the action proposed to be taken in the proxy statement, or matters referred to in paragraph (c) of this rule.

e.   The proxy statement or form of proxy shall provide, subject to reasonable specified conditions, that the shares represented by the proxy will be voted and that where the person solicited specifies by means of a ballot provided pursuant to paragraph (b) of this section a choice with respect to any matter to be acted upon, the shares will be voted in accordance with the specifications so made.

f.   No person conducting a solicitation subject to this regulation shall deliver a form of proxy, consent or authorization to any security holder unless the security holder concurrently receives, or has previously received, a definitive proxy statement that has been filed with the Commission pursuant to Rule 14a-6(b).

Rule 14a-5 – Presentation of Information in Proxy Statement

a. The information included in the proxy statement shall be clearly presented and the statements made shall be divided into groups according to subject matter and the various groups of statements shall be preceded by appropriate headings. The order of items and sub-items in the schedule need not be followed. Where practicable and appropriate, the information shall be presented in tabular form. All amounts shall be stated in figures. Information required by more than one applicable item need not be repeated. No statement need be made in response to any item or sub-item which is inapplicable.

b. Any information required to be included in the proxy statement as to terms of securities or other subject matter which from a standpoint of practical necessity must be determined in the future may be stated in terms of present knowledge and intention. To the extent practicable, the authority to be conferred concerning each such matter shall be confined within limits reasonably related to the need for discretionary authority. Subject to the foregoing, information which is not known to the persons on whose behalf the solicitation is to be made and which it is not reasonably within the power of such persons to ascertain or procure may be omitted, if a brief statement of the circumstances rendering such information unavailable is made.

c. Any information contained in any other proxy soliciting material which has been furnished to each person solicited in connection with the same meeting or subject matter may be omitted from the proxy statement, if a clear reference is made to the particular document containing such information.

d.
  1. All printed proxy statements shall be in roman type at least as large and as legible as 10-point modern type, except that to the extent necessary for convenient presentation financial statements and other tabular data, but not the notes thereto, may be in roman type at least as large and as legible as 8-point modern type. All such type shall be leaded at least 2 points.
  2. Where a proxy statement is delivered through an electronic medium, issuers may satisfy legibility requirements applicable to printed documents, such as type size and font, by presenting all required information in a format readily communicated to investors.

e. All proxy statements shall disclose, under an appropriate caption, the following dates:
  1. The deadline for submitting shareholder proposals for inclusion in the registrant's proxy statement and form of proxy for the registrant's next annual meeting, calculated in the manner provided in Rule 14a- 8(d)(Question 5);
  2. The date after which notice of a shareholder proposal submitted outside the processes of Rule 14a-8 is considered untimely, either calculated in the manner provided by Rule 14a-4(c)(1) or as established by the registrant's advance notice provision, if any, authorized by applicable state law;

3.   The deadline for submitting nominees for inclusion in the registrant's proxy statement and form of proxy pursuant to Rule 14a-11, an applicable state or foreign law provision, or a registrant's governing documents as they relate to the inclusion of shareholder director nominees in the registrant's proxy materials for the registrant's next annual meeting of shareholders; and

4.   The deadline for providing notice of a solicitation of proxies in support of director nominees other than the registrant's nominees pursuant to Rule14a-19 for the registrant's next annual meeting unless the registrant is an investment company registered under the Investment Company Act of 1940 or a business development company as defined by section 2(a)(48) of the Investment Company Act of 1940.

f.   If the date of the next annual meeting is subsequently advanced or delayed by more than 30 calendar days from the date of the annual meeting to which the proxy statement relates, the registrant shall, in a timely manner, inform shareholders of such change, and the new dates referred to in paragraphs (e)(1) and (e)(2) of this section, by including a notice, under Item 5, in its earliest possible quarterly report on Form 10-Q or, in the case of investment companies, in a shareholder report under Rule 30e-1 under the Investment Company Act of 1940, or, if impracticable, any means reasonably calculated to inform shareholders.

Rule 14a-6 – Filing Requirements

a.   **Preliminary proxy statement.** Five preliminary copies of the proxy statement and form of proxy shall be filed with the Commission at least 10 calendar days prior to the date definitive copies of such material are first sent or given to security holders, or such shorter period prior to that date as the Commission may authorize upon a showing of good cause thereunder. A registrant, however, shall not file with the Commission a preliminary proxy statement, form of proxy or other soliciting material to be furnished to security holders concurrently therewith if the solicitation relates to an annual (or special meeting in lieu of the annual) meeting, or for an investment company registered under the Investment Company Act of 1940 or a business development company, if the solicitation relates to any meeting of security holders at which the only matters to be acted upon are:

1.   The election of directors;
2.   The election, approval or ratification of accountant(s);
3.   A security holder proposal included pursuant to Rule 14a-8;
4.   A shareholder nominee for director included pursuant to Rule 14a-11, an applicable state or foreign law provision, or a registrant's governing documents as they relate to the inclusion of shareholder director nominees in the registrant's proxy materials.
5.   The approval or ratification of a plan as defined in paragraph (a)(6)(ii) of Item 402 of Regulation S-K or amendments to such a plan;
6.   With respect to an investment company registered under the Investment Company Act of 1940 or a business development company, a proposal to continue, without change, any advisory or other contract or agreement that previously has been the subject of a proxy solicitation for which proxy material was filed with the Commission pursuant to this section; and/or

7.   A vote to approve the compensation of executives as required pursuant to section 14A(a)(1) of the Securities Exchange Act of 1934 and Rule 14a-21(a) of this chapter, or pursuant to section 111(e)(1) of the Emergency Economic Stabilization Act of 2008 and Rule 14a-20 of this chapter, a vote to determine the frequency of shareholder votes to approve the compensation of executives as required pursuant to Section 14A(a)(2) of the Securities Exchange Act of 1934 and Rule 14a-21(b) of this chapter, or any other shareholder advisory vote on executive compensation.

This exclusion from filing preliminary proxy material does not apply if the registrant comments upon or refers to a solicitation in opposition in connection with the meeting in its proxy material.

Note 1 to paragraph (a): The filing of revised material does not recommence the ten day time period unless the revised material contains material revisions or material new proposal(s) that constitute a fundamental change in the proxy material.

Note 2 to paragraph (a): The official responsible for the preparation of the proxy material should make every effort to verify the accuracy and completeness of the information required by the applicable rules. The preliminary material should be filed with the Commission at the earliest practicable date.

Note 3 to paragraph (a)*: Solicitation in Opposition.*

For purposes of the exclusion from filing preliminary proxy material, a "solicitation in opposition" includes:

a.   Any solicitation opposing a proposal supported by the registrant; and

b.   any solicitation supporting a proposal that the registrant does not expressly support, other than a security holder proposal included in the registrant's proxy material pursuant to Rule14a-8. The inclusion of a security holder proposal in the registrant's proxy material pursuant to Rule 14a-8 does not constitute a "solicitation in opposition," even if the registrant opposes the proposal and/or includes a statement in opposition to the proposal. The inclusion of a shareholder nominee in the registrant's proxy materials pursuant to an applicable state or foreign law provision, or a registrant's governing documents as they relate to the inclusion of shareholder director nominees in the registrant's proxy materials does not constitute a "solicitation in opposition" for purposes of paragraph (a) of this section, even if the registrant opposes the shareholder nominee and solicits against the shareholder nominee and in favor of a registrant nominee.

Note 4 to paragraph (a): A registrant that is filing proxy material in preliminary form only because the registrant has commented on or referred to a solicitation in opposition should indicate that fact in a transmittal letter when filing the preliminary material with the Commission.

b.   **Definitive proxy statement and other soliciting material.** Eight definitive copies of the proxy statement, form of proxy and all other soliciting materials, in the same form as the materials sent to security holders, must be filed with the Commission no later than the date they are first sent or given to security holders. Three copies of these materials also must be filed with, or mailed for filing to, each national securities exchange on which the registrant has a class of securities listed and registered.

c.   **Personal solicitation materials.** If part or all of the solicitation involves personal solicitation, then eight copies of all written instructions or other materials that discuss, review or comment on the merits of any matter to be acted on, that are furnished to persons making the actual solicitation for their use directly or indirectly in connection with the solicitation, must be filed with the Commission no later than the date the materials are first sent or given to these persons.

d. **Release dates.** All preliminary proxy statements and forms of proxy filed pursuant to paragraph (a) of this section shall be accompanied by a statement of the date on which definitive copies thereof filed pursuant to paragraph (b) of this section are intended to be released to security holders. All definitive material filed pursuant to paragraph (b) of this section shall be accompanied by a statement of the date on which copies of such material were released to security holders, or, if not released, the date on which copies thereof are intended to be released. All material filed pursuant to paragraph (c) of this section shall be accompanied by a statement of the date on which copies thereof were released to the individual who will make the actual solicitation or if not released, the date on which copies thereof are intended to be released.

e.

1. **Public availability of information.** All copies of preliminary proxy statements and forms of proxy filed pursuant to paragraph (a) of this section shall be clearly marked "Preliminary Copies," and shall be deemed immediately available for public inspection unless confidential treatment is obtained pursuant to paragraph (e)(2) of this section.

2. **Confidential treatment.** If action will be taken on any matter specified in Item 14 of Schedule 14A, all copies of the preliminary proxy statement and form of proxy filed under paragraph (a) of this section will be for the information of the Commission only and will not be deemed available for public inspection until filed with the Commission in definitive form so long as:

   i. The proxy statement does not relate to a matter or proposal subject to Rule 13e-3 or a roll-up transaction as defined in Item 901(c) of Reg. S-K;

   ii. Neither the parties to the transaction nor any persons authorized to act on their behalf have made any public communications relating to the transaction except for statements where the content is limited to the information specified in Rule 135; and

   iii. The materials are filed in paper and marked "Confidential, For Use of the Commission Only." In all cases, the materials may be disclosed to any department or agency of the United States Government and to the Congress, and the Commission may make any inquiries or investigation into the materials as may be necessary to conduct an adequate review by the Commission.

   Instruction to paragraph (e)(2): If communications are made publicly that go beyond the information specified in Rule 135, the preliminary proxy materials must be re-filed promptly with the Commission as public materials.

f. **Communications not required to be filed.** Copies of replies to inquiries from security holders requesting further information and copies of communications which do no more than request that forms of proxy theretofore solicited be signed and returned need not be filed pursuant to this section.

g. **Solicitations subject to Rule 14a-2(b)(1)**

    1.   Any person who:

        i.   Engages in a solicitation pursuant to Rule 14a-2(b)(1), and

        ii.   At the commencement of that solicitation owns beneficially securities of the class which is the subject of the solicitation with a market value of over $5 million,

shall furnish or mail to the Commission, not later than three days after the date the written solicitation is first sent or given to any security holder, five copies of a statement containing the information specified in the Notice of Exempt Solicitation (Rule 14a-103) which statement shall attach as an exhibit all written soliciting materials. Five copies of an amendment to such statement shall be furnished or mailed to the Commission, in connection with dissemination of any additional communications, not later than three days after the date the additional material is first sent or given to any security holder. Three copies of the Notice of Exempt Solicitation and amendments thereto shall, at the same time the materials are furnished or mailed to the Commission, be furnished or mailed to each national securities exchange upon which any class of securities of the registrant is listed and registered.

    2.   Notwithstanding paragraph (g)(1) of this section, no such submission need be made with respect to oral solicitations (other than with respect to scripts used in connection with such oral solicitations), speeches delivered in a public forum, press releases, published or broadcast opinions, statements, and advertisements appearing in a broadcast media, or a newspaper, magazine or other bona fide publication disseminated on a regular basis.

h. **Revised material.** Where any proxy statement, form of proxy or other material filed pursuant to this section is amended or revised, two of the copies of such amended or revised material filed pursuant to this section (or in the case of investment companies registered under the Investment Company Act of 1940, three of such copies) shall be marked to indicate clearly and precisely the changes effected therein. If the amendment or revision alters the text of the material the changes in such text shall be indicated by means of underscoring or in some other appropriate manner.

i. **Fees.** At the time of filing the proxy solicitation material, the persons upon whose behalf the solicitation is made, other than investment companies registered under the Investment Company Act of 1940, shall pay to the Commission the following applicable fee:

    1.   For preliminary proxy material involving acquisitions, mergers, spinoffs, consolidations or proposed sales or other dispositions of substantially all the assets of the company, a fee established in accordance with Rule 0-11 shall be paid. No refund shall be given.

    2.   For all other proxy submissions and submissions made pursuant to Rule 14a-6(g), no fee shall be required.

j. **Merger proxy materials.**

    1.   Any proxy statement, form of proxy or other soliciting material required to be filed by this section that also is either

i.   Included in a registration statement filed under the Securities Act of 1933 on Forms S-4, F-4 or N-14; or

ii.   Filed under Rule 424, Rule 425 or Rule 497 is required to be filed only under the Securities Act, and is deemed filed under this section.

2.   Under paragraph (j)(1) of this section, the fee required by paragraph (i) of this section need not be paid.

k.   **Computing time periods.** In computing time periods beginning with the filing date specified in Regulation 14A , the filing date shall be counted as the first day of the time period and midnight of the last day shall constitute the end of the specified time period.

l.   **Roll-up transactions.** If a transaction is a roll-up transaction as defined in Item 901(c) of Regulation S-K and is registered (or authorized to be registered) on Form S-4 or Form F-4, the proxy statement of the sponsor or the general partner as defined in Item 901(d) and Item 901(a), respectively, of Regulation S-K must be distributed to security holders no later than the lesser of 60 calendar days prior to the date on which the meeting of security holders is held or action is taken, or the maximum number of days permitted for giving notice under applicable state law.

m.   **Cover page.** Proxy materials filed with the Commission shall include a cover page in the form set forth in Schedule 14A. The cover page required by this paragraph need not be distributed to security holders.

n.   **Solicitations subject to Rule 14a-2(b)(4).** Any person who:

1.   Engages in a solicitation pursuant to Rule 14a-2(b)(4); and

2.   At the commencement of that solicitation both owns five percent 5% or more of the outstanding securities of a class that is the subject of the proposed roll-up transaction, and engages in the business of buying and selling limited partnership interests in the secondary market, shall furnish or mail to the Commission, not later than three days after the date an oral or written solicitation by that person is first made, sent or provided to any security holder, five copies of a statement containing the information specified in the Notice of Exempt Preliminary Roll-up Communication (Rule 14a-104). Five copies of any amendment to such statement shall be furnished or mailed to the Commission not later than three days after a communication containing revised material is first made, sent or provided to any security holder.

o.   **Solicitations before furnishing a definitive proxy statement.** Solicitations that are published, sent or given to security holders before they have been furnished a definitive proxy statement must be made in accordance with Rule 14a-12 unless there is an exemption available under Rule 14a-2.

p.   **Solicitations subject to Rule 14a-11.** Any soliciting material that is published, sent or given to shareholders in connection with Rule 14a-2(b)(7) or (b)(8) must be filed with the Commission as specified in that section.

Rule 14a-7 – Obligations of Registrants to Provide a List of, or Mail Soliciting Material to, Security Holders

a. If the registrant has made or intends to make a proxy solicitation in connection with a security holder meeting or action by consent or authorization, upon the written request by any record or beneficial holder of securities of the class entitled to vote at the meeting or to execute a consent or authorization to provide a list of security holders or to mail the requesting security holder's materials, regardless of whether the request references this section, the registrant shall:

1. Deliver to the requesting security holder within five business days after receipt of the request:

    i. Notification as to whether the registrant has elected to mail the security holder's soliciting materials or provide a security holder list if the election under paragraph (b) of this section is to be made by the registrant;

    ii. A statement of the approximate number of record holders and beneficial holders, separated by type of holder and class, owning securities in the same class or classes as holders which have been or are to be solicited on management's behalf, or any more limited group of such holders designated by the security holder if available or retrievable under the registrant's or its transfer agent's security holder data systems; and

    iii. The estimated cost of mailing a proxy statement, form of proxy or other communication to such holders, including to the extent known or reasonably available, the estimated costs of any bank, broker, and similar person through whom the registrant has solicited or intends to solicit beneficial owners in connection with the security holder meeting or action;

2. Perform the acts set forth in either paragraphs (a)(2)(i) or (a)2(ii) of this section, at the registrant's or requesting security holder's option, as specified in paragraph (b) of this section:

    i. Send copies of any proxy statement, form of proxy, or other soliciting material, including a Notice of Internet Availability of Proxy Materials (as described in Rule 14a-16), furnished by the security holder to the record holders, including banks, brokers, and similar entities, designated by the security holder. A sufficient number of copies must be sent to the banks, brokers, and similar entities for distribution to all beneficial owners designated by the security holder. The security holder may designate only record holders and/or beneficial owners who have not requested paper and/or e-mail copies of the proxy statement. If the registrant has received affirmative written or implied consent to deliver a single proxy statement to security holders at a shared address in accordance with the procedures in Rule 14a-3(e)(1), a single copy of the proxy statement or Notice of Internet Availability of Proxy Materials furnished by the security holder shall be sent to that address, provided that if multiple copies of the Notice of Internet Availability of Proxy Materials are furnished by the security holder for that address, the registrant shall deliver those copies in a single envelope to that address. The registrant shall send the security holder material with reasonable promptness after tender of the material to be sent, envelopes or other containers therefore, postage or payment for postage and other reasonable expenses of effecting such distribution. The registrant shall not be responsible for the content of the material; or

ii. Deliver the following information to the requesting security holder within five business days of receipt of the request:

    A. A reasonably current list of the names, addresses and security positions of the record holders, including banks, brokers and similar entities holding securities in the same class or classes as holders which have been or are to be solicited on management's behalf, or any more limited group of such holders designated by the security holder if available or retrievable under the registrant's or its transfer agent's security holder data systems;

    B. The most recent list of names, addresses and security positions of beneficial owners as specified in Rule 14a-13(b), in the possession, or which subsequently comes into the possession, of the registrant;

    C. The names of security holders at a shared address that have consented to delivery of a single copy of proxy materials to a shared address, if the registrant has received written or implied consent in accordance with Rule 14a-3(e)(1); and

    D. If the registrant has relied on Rule 14a-16, the names of security holders who have requested paper copies of the proxy materials for all meetings and the names of security holders who, as of the date that the registrant receives the request, have requested paper copies of the proxy materials only for the meeting to which the solicitation relates.

iii. All security holder list information shall be in the form requested by the security holder to the extent that such form is available to the registrant without undue burden or expense. The registrant shall furnish the security holder with updated record holder information on a daily basis or, if not available on a daily basis, at the shortest reasonable intervals; provided, however, the registrant need not provide beneficial or record holder information more current than the record date for the meeting or action.

b. 1. The requesting security holder shall have the options set forth in paragraph (a)(2) of this section, and the registrant shall have corresponding obligations, if the registrant or general partner or sponsor is soliciting or intends to solicit with respect to:

i. A proposal that is subject to Rule 13e-3;

ii. A roll-up transaction as defined in Item 901(c) of Regulation S-K that involves an entity with securities registered pursuant to Section 12 of the Act; or

iii. A roll-up transaction as defined in Item 901(c) of Regulation S-K that involves a limited partnership, unless the transaction involves only:

    A. Partnerships whose investors will receive new securities or securities in another entity that are not reported under a transaction reporting plan declared effective before December 17, 1993 by the Commission under Section 11A of the Act; or

        B. Partnerships whose investors' securities are reported under a transaction reporting plan declared effective before December 17, 1993 by the Commission under Section 11A of the Act.

    2. With respect to all other requests pursuant to this section, the registrant shall have the option to either mail the security holder's material or furnish the security holder list as set forth in this section.

c. At the time of a list request, the security holder making the request shall:

    1. If holding the registrant's securities through a nominee, provide the registrant with a statement by the nominee or other independent third party, or a copy of a current filing made with the Commission and furnished to the registrant, confirming such holder's beneficial ownership; and

    2. Provide the registrant with an affidavit, declaration, affirmation or other similar document provided for under applicable state law identifying the proposal or other corporate action that will be the subject of the security holder's solicitation or communication and attesting that:

        i. The security holder will not use the list information for any purpose other than to solicit security holders with respect to the same meeting or action by consent or authorization for which the registrant is soliciting or intends to solicit or to communicate with security holders with respect to a solicitation commenced by the registrant; and

        ii. The security holder will not disclose such information to any person other than a beneficial owner for whom the request was made and an employee or agent to the extent necessary to effectuate the communication or solicitation.

d. The security holder shall not use the information furnished by the registrant pursuant to paragraph (a)(2)(ii) of this section for any purpose other than to solicit security holders with respect to the same meeting or action by consent or authorization for which the registrant is soliciting or intends to solicit or to communicate with security holders with respect to a solicitation commenced by the registrant; or disclose such information to any person other than an employee, agent, or beneficial owner for whom a request was made to the extent necessary to effectuate the communication or solicitation. The security holder shall return the information provided pursuant to paragraph (a)(2)(ii) of this section and shall not retain any copies thereof or of any information derived from such information after the termination of the solicitation.

e. The security holder shall reimburse the reasonable expenses incurred by the registrant in performing the acts requested pursuant to paragraph (a) of this section.

Notes to Rule 14a-7:

1. Reasonably prompt methods of distribution to security holders may be used instead of mailing. If an alternative distribution method is chosen, the costs of that method should be considered where necessary rather than the costs of mailing.

2. When providing the information required by Rule 14a-7(a)(1)(ii), if the registrant has received affirmative written or implied consent to delivery of a single copy of proxy materials to a shared address in accordance with Rule 14a-3(e)(1), it shall exclude from the number of record holders those to whom it does not have to deliver a separate proxy statement.

Rule 14a-8 – Proposals of Security Holders

This section addresses when a company must include a shareholder's proposal in its proxy statement and identify the proposal in its form of proxy when the company holds an annual or special meeting of shareholders. In summary, in order to have your shareholder proposal included on a company's proxy card, and included along with any supporting statement in its proxy statement, you must be eligible and follow certain procedures. Under a few specific circumstances, the company is permitted to exclude your proposal, but only after submitting its reasons to the Commission. We structured this section in a question-and- answer format so that it is easier to understand. The references to "you" are to a shareholder seeking to submit the proposal.

a.   **Question 1:** What is a proposal? A shareholder proposal is your recommendation or requirement that the company and/or its board of directors take action, which you intend to present at a meeting of the company's shareholders. Your proposal should state as clearly as possible the course of action that you believe the company should follow. If your proposal is placed on the company's proxy card, the company must also provide in the form of proxy means for shareholders to specify by boxes a choice between approval or disapproval, or abstention. Unless otherwise indicated, the word "proposal" as used in this section refers both to your proposal, and to your corresponding statement in support of your proposal (if any).

b.   **Question 2**: Who is eligible to submit a proposal, and how do I demonstrate to the company that I am eligible?
   1.   To be eligible to submit a proposal, you must satisfy the following requirements:
       i.   You must have continuously held:
           A.   At least $2,000 in market value of the company's securities entitled to vote on the proposal for at least three years; or
           B.   At least $15,000 in market value of the company's securities entitled to vote on the proposal for at least two years; or
           C.   At least $25,000 in market value of the company's securities entitled to vote on the proposal for at least one year; or
           D.   The amounts specified in paragraph (b)(3) of this section. This paragraph (b)(1)(i)(D) will expire on the same date that § 240.14a-8(b)(3) expires; and
       ii.   You must provide the company with a written statement that you intend to continue to hold the requisite amount of securities, determined in accordance with paragraph (b)(1)(i)(A) through (C) of this section, through the date of the shareholders' meeting for which the proposal is submitted; and
       iii.   You must provide the company with a written statement that you are able to meet with the company in person or via teleconference no less than 10 calendar days, nor more than 30 calendar days, after submission of the shareholder proposal. You must include your contact information as well as business days and specific times that you are available to discuss the proposal with the company. You must identify times that are within the regular business hours of the company's principal executive offices. If these hours are not disclosed in the company's proxy statement for the prior year's

annual meeting, you must identify times that are between 9 a.m. and 5:30 p.m. in the time zone of the company's principal executive offices. If you elect to co-file a proposal, all co-filers must either:

    A. Agree to the same dates and times of availability, or

    B. Identify a single lead filer who will provide dates and times of the lead filer's availability to engage on behalf of all co-filers; and

iv. If you use a representative to submit a shareholder proposal on your behalf, you must provide the company with written documentation that:

    A. Identifies the company to which the proposal is directed;

    B. Identifies the annual or special meeting for which the proposal is submitted;

    C. Identifies you as the proponent and identifies the person acting on your behalf as your representative;

    D. Includes your statement authorizing the designated representative to submit the proposal and otherwise act on your behalf;

    E. Identifies the specific topic of the proposal to be submitted;

    F. Includes your statement supporting the proposal; and

    G. Is signed and dated by you.

v. The requirements of paragraph (b)(1)(iv) of this section shall not apply to shareholders that are entities so long as the representative's authority to act on the shareholder's behalf is apparent and self-evident such that a reasonable person would understand that the agent has authority to submit the proposal and otherwise act on the shareholder's behalf.

vi. For purposes of paragraph (b)(1)(i) of this section, you may not aggregate your holdings with those of another shareholder or group of shareholders to meet the requisite amount of securities necessary to be eligible to submit a proposal.

2. One of the following methods must be used to demonstrate your eligibility to submit a proposal:

i. If you are the registered holder of your securities, which means that your name appears in the company's records as a shareholder, the company can verify your eligibility on its own, although you will still have to provide the company with a written statement that you intend to continue to hold the requisite amount of securities, determined in accordance with paragraph (b)(1)(i)(A) through (C) of this section, through the date of the meeting of shareholders. .

ii. If, like many shareholders, you are not a registered holder, the company likely does not know that you are a shareholder, or how many shares you own. In this case, at the time you submit your proposal, you must prove your eligibility to the company in one of two ways:

    A. The first way is to submit to the company a written statement from the "record" holder of your securities (usually a broker or bank) verifying that, at the time you submitted your proposal, you continuously held at least $2,000, $15,000, or $25,000 in market value of the company's securities entitled to vote on the proposal for at least three years, two years, or one year, respectively. You must also include your own written statement that you intend to continue to hold the requisite amount of securities, determined in accordance with paragraph (b)(1)(i)(A) through (C) of this section, through the date of the shareholders' meeting for which the proposal is submitted; or

B. The second way to prove ownership applies only if you have filed a Schedule 13D, Schedule 13G, Form 3, Form 4 and/or Form 5, or amendments to those documents or updated forms, demonstrating that you meet at least one of the share ownership requirements under paragraph (b)(1)(i)(A) through (C) of this section . If you have filed one of these documents with the SEC, you may demonstrate your eligibility by submitting to the company:

1. A copy of the schedule and/or form, and any subsequent amendments reporting a change in your ownership level;

2. Your written statement that you continuously held at least $2,000, $15,000, or $25,000 in market value of the company's securities entitled to vote on the proposal for at least three years, two years, or one year, respectively; and

3. Your written statement that you intend to continue to hold the requisite amount of securities, determined in accordance with paragraph (b)(1)(i)(A) through (C) of this section, through the date of the company's annual or special meeting.

***

c. **Question 3:** How many proposals may I submit? Each person may submit no more than one proposal, directly or indirectly, to a company for a particular shareholders' meeting. A person may not rely on the securities holdings of another person for the purpose of meeting the eligibility requirements and submitting multiple proposals for a particular shareholders' meeting.

d. **Question 4:** How long can my proposal be? The proposal, including any accompanying supporting statement, may not exceed 500 words.

e. **Question 5:** What is the deadline for submitting a proposal?

1. If you are submitting your proposal for the company's annual meeting, you can in most cases find the deadline in last year's proxy statement. However, if the company did not hold an annual meeting last year, or has changed the date of its meeting for this year more than 30 days from last year's meeting, you can usually find the deadline in one of the company's quarterly reports on Form 10-Q or in shareholder reports of investment companies under Rule 30e-1 of the Investment Company Act of 1940. In order to avoid controversy, shareholders should submit their proposals by means, including electronic means, that permit them to prove the date of delivery.

2. The deadline is calculated in the following manner if the proposal is submitted for a regularly scheduled annual meeting. The proposal must be received at the company's principal executive offices not less than 120 calendar days before the date of the company's proxy statement released to shareholders in connection with the previous year's annual meeting. However, if the company did not hold an annual meeting the previous year, or if the date of this year's annual meeting has been changed by more than 30 days from the date of the previous year's

meeting, then the deadline is a reasonable time before the company begins to print and send its proxy materials.

3. If you are submitting your proposal for a meeting of shareholders other than a regularly scheduled annual meeting, the deadline is a reasonable time before the company begins to print and mail its proxy materials.

f. **Question 6:** What if I fail to follow one of the eligibility or procedural requirements explained in answers to Questions 1 through 4 of this section?

1. The company may exclude your proposal, but only after it has notified you of the problem, and you have failed adequately to correct it. Within 14 calendar days of receiving your proposal, the company must notify you in writing of any procedural or eligibility deficiencies, as well as of the time frame for your response. Your response must be postmarked, or transmitted electronically, no later than 14 days from the date you received the company's notification. A company need not provide you such notice of a deficiency if the deficiency cannot be remedied, such as if you fail to submit a proposal by the company's properly determined deadline. If the company intends to exclude the proposal, it will later have to make a submission under Rule 14a-8 and provide you with a copy under Question 10 below, Rule 14a-8(j).

2. If you fail in your promise to hold the required number of securities through the date of the meeting of shareholders, then the company will be permitted to exclude all of your proposals from its proxy materials for any meeting held in the following two calendar years.

g. **Question 7:** Who has the burden of persuading the Commission or its staff that my proposal can be excluded? Except as otherwise noted, the burden is on the company to demonstrate that it is entitled to exclude a proposal.

h. **Question 8:** Must I appear personally at the shareholders' meeting to present the proposal?

1. Either you, or your representative who is qualified under state law to present the proposal on your behalf, must attend the meeting to present the proposal. Whether you attend the meeting yourself or send a qualified representative to the meeting in your place, you should make sure that you, or your representative, follow the proper state law procedures for attending the meeting and/or presenting your proposal.

2. If the company holds it shareholder meeting in whole or in part via electronic media, and the company permits you or your representative to present your proposal via such media, then you may appear through electronic media rather than traveling to the meeting to appear in person.

3. If you or your qualified representative fail to appear and present the proposal, without good cause, the company will be permitted to exclude all of your proposals from its proxy materials for any meetings held in the following two calendar years.

i. **Question 9:** If I have complied with the procedural requirements, on what other bases may a company rely to exclude my proposal?

1. **Improper under state law**: If the proposal is not a proper subject for action by shareholders under the laws of the jurisdiction of the company's organization;
    Note to paragraph (i)(1): Depending on the subject matter, some proposals are not considered proper under state law if they would be binding on the company if approved by shareholders. In our experience, most proposals that are cast as recommendations or requests that the board of directors take specified action are proper under state law. Accordingly, we will assume that a proposal drafted as a recommendation or suggestion is proper unless the company demonstrates otherwise.

2. **Violation of law**: If the proposal would, if implemented, cause the company to violate any state, federal, or foreign law to which it is subject;
    Note to paragraph (i)(2): We will not apply this basis for exclusion to permit exclusion of a proposal on grounds that it would violate foreign law if compliance with the foreign law could result in a violation of any state or federal law.

3. **Violation of proxy rules**: If the proposal or supporting statement is contrary to any of the Commission's proxy rules, including Rule 14a-9, which prohibits materially false or misleading statements in proxy soliciting materials;

4. **Personal grievance; special interest**: If the proposal relates to the redress of a personal claim or grievance against the company or any other person, or if it is designed to result in a benefit to you, or to further a personal interest, which is not shared by the other shareholders at large;

5. **Relevance**: If the proposal relates to operations which account for less than 5 percent of the company's total assets at the end of its most recent fiscal year, and for less than 5 percent of its net earnings and gross sales for its most recent fiscal year, and is not otherwise significantly related to the company's business;

6. **Absence of power/authority**: If the company would lack the power or authority to implement the proposal;

7. **Management functions**: If the proposal deals with a matter relating to the company's ordinary business operations;

8. **Director elections**: If the proposal:
    i.   Would disqualify a nominee who is standing for election;
    ii. Would remove a director from office before his or her term expired;
    iii. Questions the competence, business judgment, or character of one or more nominees or directors;
    iv. Seeks to include a specific individual in the company's proxy materials for election to the board of directors; or
    v.   Otherwise could affect the outcome of the upcoming election of directors.;

9. **Conflicts with company's proposal**: If the proposal directly conflicts with one of the company's own proposals to be submitted to shareholders at the same meeting.
    Note to paragraph (i)(9): Note to paragraph (i)(9): A company's submission to the Commission under this section should specify the points of conflict with the company's proposal.

10. **Substantially implemented**: If the company has already substantially implemented the proposal;

Note to paragraph (i)(10): A company may exclude a shareholder proposal that would provide an advisory vote or seek future advisory votes to approve the compensation of executives as disclosed pursuant to Item 402 of Regulation S-K or any successor to Item 402 (a "say-on-pay vote") or that relates to the frequency of say-on-pay votes, provided that in the most recent shareholder vote required by Rule 14a-21(b) of this chapter a single year (i.e., one, two, or three years) received approval of a majority of votes cast on the matter and the company has adopted a policy on the frequency of say-on-pay votes that is consistent with the choice of the majority of votes cast in the most recent shareholder vote required by Rule 14a-21(b) of this chapter.

11. **Duplication**: If the proposal substantially duplicates another proposal previously submitted to the company by another proponent that will be included in the company's proxy materials for the same meeting;

12. **Resubmissions**: If the proposal addresses substantially the same subject matter as a proposal, or proposals, previously included in the company's proxy materials within the preceding five calendar years if the most recent vote occurred within the preceding three calendar years and the most recent vote was:
    i. Less than 5 percent of the votes cast if previously voted on once;
    ii. Less than 15 percent of the votes cast if previously voted on twice; or
    iii. Less than 25 percent of the votes cast if previously voted on three or more times.

13. **Specific amount of dividends**: If the proposal relates to specific amounts of cash or stock dividends.

j. **Question 10:** What procedures must the company follow if it intends to exclude my proposal?

1. If the company intends to exclude a proposal from its proxy materials, it must file its reasons with the Commission no later than 80 calendar days before it files its definitive proxy statement and form of proxy with the Commission. The company must simultaneously provide you with a copy of its submission. The Commission staff may permit the company to make its submission later than 80 days before the company files its definitive proxy statement and form of proxy, if the company demonstrates good cause for missing the deadline.

2. The company must file six paper copies of the following:
    i. The proposal;
    ii. An explanation of why the company believes that it may exclude the proposal, which should, if possible, refer to the most recent applicable authority, such as prior Division letters issued under the rule; and
    iii. A supporting opinion of counsel when such reasons are based on matters of state or foreign law.

k. **Question 11:** May I submit my own statement to the Commission responding to the company's arguments?

Yes, you may submit a response, but it is not required. You should try to submit any response to us, with a copy to the company, as soon as possible after the company makes its submission. This way, the Commission staff will have time to consider fully your submission before it issues its response. You should submit six paper copies of your response.

l. **Question 12:** If the company includes my shareholder proposal in its proxy materials, what information about me must it include along with the proposal itself?

    1. The company's proxy statement must include your name and address, as well as the number of the company's voting securities that you hold. However, instead of providing that information, the company may instead include a statement that it will provide the information to shareholders promptly upon receiving an oral or written request.

    2. The company is not responsible for the contents of your proposal or supporting statement.

m. **Question 13:** What can I do if the company includes in its proxy statement reasons why it believes shareholders should not vote in favor of my proposal, and I disagree with some of its statements?

    1. The company may elect to include in its proxy statement reasons why it believes shareholders should vote against your proposal. The company is allowed to make arguments reflecting its own point of view, just as you may express your own point of view in your proposal's supporting statement.

    2. However, if you believe that the company's opposition to your proposal contains materially false or misleading statements that may violate our anti- fraud rule, Rule 14a-9, you should promptly send to the Commission staff and the company a letter explaining the reasons for your view, along with a copy of the company's statements opposing your proposal. To the extent possible, your letter should include specific factual information demonstrating the inaccuracy of the company's claims. Time permitting, you may wish to try to work out your differences with the company by yourself before contacting the Commission staff.

    3. We require the company to send you a copy of its statements opposing your proposal before it sends its proxy materials, so that you may bring to our attention any materially false or misleading statements, under the following timeframes:

        i.   If our no-action response requires that you make revisions to your proposal or supporting statement as a condition to requiring the company to include it in its proxy materials, then the company must provide you with a copy of its opposition statements no later than 5 calendar days after the company receives a copy of your revised proposal; or

        ii. In all other cases, the company must provide you a copy of its opposition statements no later than 30 calendar days before it files definitive copies of its proxy statement and form of proxy under Rule 14a-6.

Rule 14a-9 – False or Misleading Statements

a. No solicitation subject to this regulation shall be made by means of any proxy statement, form of proxy, notice of meeting or other communication, written or oral, containing any statement which, at the time and in the light of the circumstances under which it is made, is false or misleading with respect to any material fact, or which omits to state any material fact necessary in order to make the statements therein not false or misleading or necessary to correct any statement in any earlier communication with respect to the solicitation of a proxy for the same meeting or subject matter which has become false or misleading.

b. The fact that a proxy statement, form of proxy or other soliciting material has been filed with or examined by the Commission shall not be deemed a finding by the Commission that such material is accurate or complete or not false or misleading, or that the Commission has passed upon the merits of or approved any statement contained therein or any matter to be acted upon by security holders. No representation contrary to the foregoing shall be made.

c. No nominee, nominating shareholder or nominating shareholder group, or any member thereof, shall cause to be included in a registrant's proxy materials, either pursuant to the federal proxy rules, an applicable state or foreign law provision, or a registrant's governing documents as they relate to including shareholder nominees for director in a registrant's proxy materials, include in a notice on Schedule 14N, or include in any other related communication, any statement which, at the time and in the light of the circumstances under which it is made, is false or misleading with respect to any material fact, or which omits to state any material fact necessary in order to make the statements therein not false or misleading or necessary to correct any statement in any earlier communication with respect to a solicitation for the same meeting or subject matter which has become false or misleading.

Note: The following are some examples of what, depending upon particular facts and circumstances, may be misleading within the meaning of this section.

1. Predictions as to specific future market values.
2. Material which directly or indirectly impugns character, integrity or personal reputation, or directly or indirectly makes charges concerning improper, illegal or immoral conduct or associations, without factual foundation.
3. Failure to so identify a proxy statement, form of proxy and other soliciting material as to clearly distinguish it from the soliciting material of any other person or persons soliciting for the same meeting or subject matter.
4. Claims made prior to a meeting regarding the results of a solicitation.

Rule 14a-10 – Prohibition of Certain Solicitations

No person making a solicitation which is subject to Rule 14a-1 to Rule 14a-10 shall solicit:

a. Any undated or postdated proxy; or

b. Any proxy which provides that it shall be deemed to be dated as of any date subsequent to the date on which it is signed by the security holder.

Rule 14a-11 – Shareholder Nominations (Vacated)

a. **Applicability**. In connection with an annual (or a special meeting in lieu of an annual) meeting of shareholders, or a written consent in lieu of such meeting, at which directors are elected, a registrant will be required to include in its proxy statement and form of proxy the name of a person or persons nominated by a shareholder or group of shareholders for election to the board of directors and include in its proxy statement the disclosure about such nominee or nominees and the nominating shareholder or members of the nominating shareholder group as specified in Item 5 of Schedule 14N, provided that the conditions set forth in paragraph (b) of this section are satisfied. This rule will not apply to a registrant if:

1.   The registrant is subject to the proxy rules solely because it has a class of debt securities registered under section 12 of the Exchange Act; or

2.   Applicable state or foreign law or a registrant's governing documents prohibit the registrant's shareholders from nominating a candidate or candidates for election as director.

b.   **Eligibility**. A shareholder nominee or nominees shall be included in a registrant's proxy statement and form of proxy if the following requirements are satisfied:

1.   The nominating shareholder individually, or the nominating shareholder group in the aggregate, holds at least 3% of the total voting power of the registrant's securities that are entitled to be voted on the election of directors at the annual (or a special meeting in lieu of the annual) meeting of shareholders or on a written consent in lieu of such meeting, on the date the nominatingshareholder or nominating shareholder group files the notice on Schedule 14N with the Commission and transmits the notice to the registrant;

Instruction 1 to paragraph (b)(1). In the case of a registrant other than an investment company registered under the Investment Company Act of 1940, for purposes of (b)(1) of this section, in determining the total voting power of the registrant's securities that are entitled to be voted on the election of directors, the nominating shareholder or nominating shareholder group may rely on information set forth in the registrant's most recent quarterly or annual report, and any current report subsequent thereto, filed with the Commission pursuant to this Act, unless the nominating shareholder or nominating shareholder group knows or has reason to know that the information contained therein is inaccurate. In the case of a registrant that is an investment company registered under the Investment Company Act of 1940, for purposes of (b)(1) of this section, in determining the total voting power of the registrant's securities that are entitled to be voted on the election of directors, the nominating shareholder or nominating shareholder group may rely on information set forth in the following documents, unless the nominating shareholder or nominating shareholder group knows or has reason to know that the information contained therein is inaccurate:

a.   In the case of a registrant that is a series company as defined in Rule 18f-2(a) under the Investment Company Act of 1940, the Form 8-K described in Instruction 2 to paragraph (b)(1) of this section; or

b.   In the case of other investment companies, the registrant's most recent annual or semiannual report filed with the Commission on Form N-CSR.

Instruction 2 to paragraph (b)(1). If the registrant is an investment company that is a series company (as defined in Rule 18f-2(a) of this chapter), the registrant must disclose pursuant to Item 5.08 of Form 8-K the total number of shares of the registrant outstanding and entitled to be voted (or if the votes are to be cast on a basis other than one vote per share, then the total number of votes entitled to be voted and the basis for allocating such votes) on the election of directors as of the end of the most recent calendar quarter.

Instruction 3 to paragraph (b)(1).

a. When determining the total voting power of the registrant's securities, which is the denominator in the calculation of the percentage of voting power held by the nominating shareholder individually or the nominating shareholder group in the aggregate, calculate the aggregate number of votes derived from all classes of securities of the registrant that are entitled to vote on the election of directors regardless of whether solicitation of a proxy with respect to those securities would require compliance with Exchange Act Regulation 14A.

b. When determining the total voting power of the registrant's securities held by the nominating shareholder or any member of the nominating shareholder group, which is the numerator in the calculation of the percentage:

   1. Calculate the number of votes derived only from securities with respect to which solicitation of a proxy would require compliance with Exchange Act Regulation 14A and over which the nominating shareholder or any the member of the nominating shareholder group, as the case may be, has voting power and investment power, either directly or through any person acting on their behalf;

   2. Notwithstanding the voting power calculation specified in paragraph b.1. of this instruction, add to the result of the calculation specified in paragraph b.1. of this instruction any votes attributable to securities with respect to which solicitation of a proxy would require compliance with Exchange Act Regulation 14A that have been loaned by or on behalf of the nominating shareholder or any member of the nominating shareholder group to another person, if the nominating shareholder or member of the nominating shareholder group, as the case may be, or any person acting on their behalf, has the right to recall the loaned securities, and will recall the loaned securities upon being notified that any of the nominating shareholder's or group's nominees will be included in the registrant's proxy statement and proxy card; and

   3. Subtract from the result of the calculation specified in paragraphs b.1. and b.2. of this instruction the number of votes attributable to securities of the registrant entitled to vote on the election of directors, regardless of whether solicitation of a proxy with respect to those securities would require compliance Exchange Act Regulation 14A, that the nominating shareholder or any member of the nominating shareholder group, as the case may be, or any person acting on their behalf, has sold in a short sale, as defined in Regulation SHO 200(a), that is not closed out, or has borrowed for purposes other than a short sale.

c. For purposes of the voting power calculation in paragraph b.1. of this instruction:

   1. A shareholder has voting power directly only when the shareholder has the power to vote or direct the voting, and investment power directly only when the shareholder has the power to dispose or direct the disposition, of the securities; and

   2. A securities intermediary (as defined in Rule 17Ad-20(b)) shall not have voting power or investment power over securities for purposes of

paragraph b.1. of this instruction solely because such intermediary holds such securities by or on behalf of another person, notwithstanding that pursuant to the rules of a national securities exchange such intermediary may vote or direct the voting of such securities without instruction.

Instruction 4 to paragraph (b)(1). If a registrant has more than one class of outstanding securities entitled to vote on the election of directors and those classes do not vote together in the election of all directors, then the voting power of the registrant's securities for purposes of the calculation of both the numerator and denominator specified in Instruction 3 to paragraph (b)(1) should be determined only on the basis of the voting power of the class or classes of securities that would be voting together on the election of the person or persons sought to be nominated by the nominating shareholder or the nominating shareholder group.

2.   The nominating shareholder or each member of the nominating shareholder group has held the amount of securities that are used for purposes of satisfying the minimum ownership requirement of paragraph (b)(1) of this section continuously for at least three years as of the date the notice on Schedule 14N is filed with the Commission and transmitted to the registrant and must continue to hold that amount of securities through the date of the subject election of directors;

Instruction to paragraph (b)(2). To determine whether the amount of securities that are used for purposes of satisfying the minimum ownership requirement of paragraph (b)(1) has been held continuously during the three year period prior to the date the Schedule 14N is filed and during the period after the Schedule 14N is filed through the date of the subject election of directors, and with respect to all points in time during those periods:

a.   Include only the amount of securities with respect to which a solicitation of a proxy would require compliance with Exchange Act Regulation 14A and over which the nominating shareholder or the member of the nominating shareholder group, as the case may be, has voting power and investment power, either directly or through any person acting on their behalf;

b.   Notwithstanding the voting power determination specified in paragraph a. of this instruction, include the amount of securities that have been loaned by or on behalf of the nominating shareholder or any member of the nominating shareholder group to another person, if the nominating shareholder or member of the nominating shareholder group, as the case may be, or any person acting on their behalf:

1.   Has the right to recall the loaned securities; and

2.   With respect to the period from the date the Schedule 14Nis filed through the date of the subject election of directors, will recall the loaned securities upon being notified that any of the person's nominees will be included in the registrant's proxy statement and proxy card;

c.   Reduce the amount of securities held by the amount of securities, on a class basis, that the nominating shareholder or any member of the nominating shareholder group, as the case may be, or any person acting on their behalf, sold in a short sale, as defined in Reg SHO 200(a), during the periods, or borrowed for purposes other than a short sale; and

    d.   Adjust the amount of securities held to give effect to any changes in the amount of securities during the periods resulting from stock splits, reclassifications or other similar adjustments by the registrant.

3.   The nominating shareholder or each member of the nominating shareholder group provides proof of ownership of the amount of securities that are used for purposes of satisfying the ownership and holding period requirements of paragraphs (b)(1) and (b)(2) of this section. If the nominating shareholder or each member of the nominating shareholder group is not the registered holder of the securities, the nominating shareholder or each member of the nominating shareholder group must provide proof of ownership in the form of one or more written statements from the registered holder of the nominating shareholder's securities (or the brokers or banks through which those securities are held) verifying that, as of a date within seven calendar days prior to filing the notice on Schedule 14N with the Commissionand transmitting the notice to the registrant, the nominating shareholder or each member of the nominating shareholder group, continuously held the amount of securities being used to satisfy the ownership threshold for a period of at least three years. The written statement or statements proving ownership must be attached as an appendix to Schedule 14N on the date the notice is filed with the Commission and transmitted to the registrant, and provide the information specified in Item 4 of Schedule 14N. In the alternative, if the nominating shareholder or member of the nominating shareholder group has filed a Schedule 13D, Schedule 13G, Form 3, Form 4, and/or Form 5, or amendments to those documents, reflecting ownership of the securities as of or before the date on which the three-year eligibility period begins, the nominating shareholder or member of the nominating shareholder group may attach the filing as an appendix to the Schedule 14N or incorporate the filing by reference into the Schedule 14N;

Instruction to paragraph (b)(3). If the nominating shareholder or member of the nominating shareholder group must provide proof of ownership in the form of a written statement with respect to securities held through a broker or bank that is a participant in the Depository Trust Company or other clearing agency acting as a securities depository, then a statement from such broker or bank will satisfy the requirements of paragraph (b)(3) of this section. If the securities are held through a broker or bank (e.g., in an omnibus account) that is not a participant in a clearing agency acting as a securities depository, the nominating shareholder or member of the nominating shareholder group must also obtain and submit a separate written statement specified in the Instruction to Item 4 of Schedule 14N.

4.   The nominating shareholder or each member of the nominating shareholder group provides a statement, as specified in Item 4(b) of Schedule 14N, on the date the notice on Schedule 14N is filed with the Commission and transmitted to the registrant, that the nominating shareholder or each member of the nominating shareholder group intends to continue to hold the amount of securities that are used for purposes of satisfying the minimum ownership requirement of paragraph (b)(1) of this section through the date of the meeting;

5.   The nominating shareholder or each member of the nominating shareholder group provides a statement, as specified in Item 4(b) of Schedule 14N, on the date the notice on Schedule 14N is filed with the Commission and transmitted

to the registrant, regarding the nominating shareholder's or group's intent with respect to continued ownership of the registrant's securities after the election;

6.   The nominating shareholder (or where there is a nominating shareholder group, each member of the nominating shareholder group) is not holding any of the registrant's securities with the purpose, or with the effect, of changing control of the registrant or to gain a number of seats on the board of directors that exceeds the maximum number of nominees that the registrant could be required to include under paragraph (d) of this section;

7.   Neither the nominee nor the nominating shareholder (or where there is a nominating shareholder group, any member of the nominating shareholder group) has an agreement with the registrant regarding the nomination of the nominee;

Instruction to paragraph (b)(7). Negotiations between the nominee, the nominating shareholder or nominating shareholder group and the nominating committee or board of the registrant to have the nominee included in the registrant's proxy statement and form of proxy as a registrant nominee, where those negotiations are unsuccessful, or negotiations that are limited to whether the registrant is required to include the shareholder nominee in the registrant's proxy statement and form of proxy in accordance with this section, will not represent a direct or indirect agreement with the registrant.

8.   The nominee's candidacy or, if elected, board membership would not violate controlling federal law, state law, foreign law, or rules of a national securities exchange or national securities association (other than rules regarding director independence) or, in the case that the nominee's candidacy or, if elected, board membership would violate such laws or rules, such violation could not be cured by the time provided in paragraph (g)(2) of this section;

9.   In the case of a registrant other than an investment company, the nominee meets the objective criteria for "independence" of the national securities exchange or national securities association rules applicable to the registrant, if any, or, in the case of a registrant that is an investment company, the nominee is not an "interested person" of the registrant as defined in section 2(a)(19) of the Investment Company Act of 1940;

Instruction to paragraph (b)(9). For purposes of this provision, the nominee would be required to meet the definition of "independence" that is generally applicable to directors of the registrant and not any particular definition of independence applicable to members of the audit committee of the registrant's board of directors. To the extent a national securities exchange or national securities association rule imposes a standard regarding independence that requires a subjective determination by the board or a group or committee of the board (for example, requiring that the board of directors or any group or committee of the board of directors make a determination regarding the existence of factors material to a determination of a nominee's independence), the nominee would not be required to meet the subjective determination of independence as part of the shareholder nomination process.

10.   The nominating shareholder or nominating shareholder group provides notice to the registrant on Schedule 14N, as specified by Rule 14n-1, of its intent to require that the registrant include that shareholder's or group's nominee in the registrant's proxy statement and form of proxy. This notice must be transmitted

to the registrant on the date it is filed with the Commission. The notice must be filed with the Commission and transmitted to the registrant no earlier than 150 calendar days, and no later than 120 calendar days, before the anniversary of the date that the registrant mailed its proxy materials for the prior year's annual meeting, except that, if the registrant did not hold an annual meeting during the prior year, or if the date of the meeting has changed by more than 30 calendar days from the prior year, or if the registrant is holding a special meeting or conducting an election of directors by written consent, then the nominating shareholder or nominating shareholder group must transmit the notice to the registrant and file its notice with the Commission a reasonable time before the registrant mails its proxy materials, as specified by the registrant in a Form 8-K filed pursuant to Item 5.08 of Form 8-K; and

Instruction 1 to paragraph (b)(10). If the registrant held a meeting the previous year and the date of the current year's annual meeting has not changed by more than 30 calendar days from the date of the previous year's annual meeting, the window period for filing a notice on Schedule 14N with the Commission and transmitting that notice to the registrant should be calculated by determining the release date disclosed in the registrant's previous year's proxy statement, increasing the year by one, and counting back 150 calendar days and 120 calendar days for the beginning and end of the window period, respectively. Where the 120 calendar day deadline falls on a Saturday, Sunday or holiday, the deadline will be treated as the first business day following the Saturday, Sunday or holiday.

Instruction 2 to paragraph (b)(10). If the registrant did not hold an annual meeting the previous year, or if the date of the current year's annual meeting has been changed by more than 30 calendar days from the date of the previous year's annual meeting, or if the registrant is holding a special meeting or conducting the election of directors by written consent, the registrant must disclose pursuant to Item 5.08 of Form 8-K the date by which a shareholder or group must submit the notice required pursuant to paragraph (b)(10) of this section, which date shall be a reasonable time prior to the date the registrant mails its proxy materials for the meeting.

11.   The nominating shareholder or nominating shareholder group provides the certifications required by Schedule 14N on the date the notice on Schedule 14N is filed with the Commission and transmitted to the registrant.

Instruction to paragraph (b). A registrant will not be required to include a nominee or nominees submitted by a nominating shareholder or nominating shareholder group pursuant to this section if the nominating shareholder or any member of the nominating shareholder group also submits any other nomination to that registrant and/or is participating in more than one nominating shareholder group for that registrant. In addition, a registrant will not be required to include a nominee or nominees if a nominating shareholder or member of a nominating shareholder group:

a.   Is or becomes a member of any other group, as determined under section 13(d)(3) of the Act Rule 13d-5(b)), or otherwise, with persons engaged in soliciting or other nominating activities in connection with the subject election of directors;

b.   Is separately conducting a solicitation in connection with the subject election of directors other than a solicitation subject to Rule 14a-2(b)(8) in relation to those nominees it has nominated pursuant to this section or for or against the registrant's nominees; or

c.   Is acting as a participant in another person's solicitation in connection with the subject election of directors.

c.   **Statement of support.** A registrant will be required to include a statement of support submitted by a nominating shareholder or nominating shareholder group in Item 5(i) of the notice on Schedule 14N, provided that the statement of support does not exceed 500 words per nominee. If a statement of support submitted by a nominating shareholder or nominating shareholder group exceeds 500 words per nominee, the registrant will be required to include the nominee or nominees, provided that the eligibility requirements and other conditions of the rule are satisfied, but the registrant may exclude the supporting statement(s).

d.   **Maximum number of shareholder nominees.**

1.   A registrant will be required to include in its proxy statement and form of proxy one shareholder nominee or the number of nominees that represents 25% of the total number of the registrant's board of directors, whichever is greater, submitted by a nominating shareholder or nominating shareholder group pursuant to this section, subject to the limitations in paragraphs (d)(2), (d)(3), (d)(4), and (d)(5) of this section. A registrant may exclude a nominee or nominees if including the nominee or nominees would result in the registrant exceeding the maximum number of nominees it is required to include in its proxy statement and form of proxy pursuant to this provision.

Instruction to paragraph (d)(1). Depending on board size, 25% of the board may not result in a whole number. In those instances, the registrant will round down to the closest whole number below 25% to determine the maximum number of shareholder nominees for director that the registrant is required to include in its proxy statement and form of proxy.

2.   Where the registrant has one or more directors currently serving on its board of directors who were elected as a shareholder nominee pursuant to this section, and the term of that director or directors extends past the election of directors for which it is soliciting proxies, the registrant will not be required to include in the proxy statement and form of proxy more shareholder nominees than could result in the total number of directors who were elected as shareholder nominees pursuant to this section and serving on the board being more than one shareholder nominee or 25% of the total number of the registrant's board of directors, whichever is greater.

3.   Where the registrant has multiple classes of securities and each class is entitled to elect a specified number of directors, the registrant will be required to include the lesser of the number of nominees that the nominating shareholder's or group's class is entitled to elect or 25% of the registrant's board of directors, but in no case less than one nominee.

4.   Where the registrant agrees to include in its proxy statement and form of proxy, as an unopposed registrant nominee, the nominee or nominees of the nominating shareholder or nominating shareholder group that otherwise would be eligible under this section to have its nominees included in the registrant's proxy materials, the nominee will be considered a shareholder nominee for purposes

of calculating the maximum number of shareholder nominees that must be included in the registrant's proxy statement and form of proxy, provided that the nominating shareholder or nominating shareholder group filed its notice on Schedule 14N before beginning communications with the registrant about the nomination.

5.   A nominee included in a registrant's proxy statement and form of proxy as a result of an agreement between the nominee or nominating shareholder (or where there is a nominating shareholder group, any member of the nominating shareholder group) and the registrant, other than as specified in paragraph (d)(4) of this section, will not be counted as a shareholder nominee for purposes of calculating the maximum number of shareholder nominees that the registrant is required to include in its proxy statement and form of proxy.

Instruction to paragraph (d)(5). Negotiations between the nominee, the nominating shareholder or nominating shareholder group and the nominating committee or board of the registrant to have the nominee included in the registrant's proxy statement and form of proxy as a registrant nominee, where those negotiations are unsuccessful, or negotiations that are limited to whether the registrant is required to include the shareholder nominee in the registrant's proxy statement and form of proxy in accordance with this section, will not represent a direct or indirect agreement with the registrant.

e.   **Order of priority for shareholder nominees**.

1.   In the event that more than one eligible shareholder or group of shareholders submits a nominee or nominees for inclusion in the registrant's proxy materials pursuant to this section, the registrant shall include in the proxy statement and form of proxy the nominee or nominees of the nominating shareholder or nominating shareholder group with the highest qualifying voting power percentage disclosed as of the date of filing the Schedule 14N (as determined in calculating ownership to satisfy the requirement as specified in paragraph (b)(1) of this section) from which the registrant received a notice filed and transmitted as specified in paragraph (b)(10) of this section, up to and including the total number of nominees required to be included by the registrant pursuant to this section. Where the nominating shareholder or nominating shareholder group with the highest qualifying voting power percentage that is otherwise eligible to rely on this section and that filed and transmitted the notice as specified in paragraph (b)(10) of this section does not nominate the maximum number of individuals required to be included by the registrant, the nominee or nominees of the nominating shareholder or nominating shareholder group with the next highest qualifying voting power percentage from which the registrant received the notice filed and transmitted as specified in paragraph (b)(10) of this section would be included in the registrant's proxy statement and form of proxy, if any, up to and including the total number required to be included by the registrant. This process would continue until the registrant has included the maximum number of nominees it is required to include in its proxy statement and form of proxy pursuant to paragraph (d) of this section or the registrant exhausts the list of eligible nominees.

2.   Prior to the time a registrant has commenced printing its proxy statement and form of proxy, if a nominating shareholder or nominating shareholder group

withdraws or is disqualified, a registrant will be required to include in its proxy statement and form of proxy the nominee or nominees of the nominating shareholder or nominating shareholder group with the next highest qualifying voting power percentage, disclosed as of the date of filing the Schedule 14N (as determined in calculating ownership to satisfy the requirement as specified in paragraph (b)(1) of this section), from which the registrant received a notice filed and transmitted as specified in paragraph (b)(10) of this section, if any, up to and including the total number required to be included by the registrant. This process would continue until the registrant included the maximum number of nominees it is required to include in its proxy statement and form of proxy pursuant to paragraph (d) of this section or the registrant exhausts the list of eligible nominees. If the registrant has commenced printing its proxy statement and form of proxy, the registrant will not be required to include a nominee or nominees in its proxy statement and form of proxy in place of a nominee or nominees that has withdrawn or has been disqualified.

3.   If a nominee or nominees withdraws or is disqualified after the registrant provides notice to the nominating shareholder or nominating shareholder group of the registrant's intent to include the nominee or nominees in its proxy statement and form of proxy, the registrant will be required to include in its proxy statement and form of proxy any other eligible nominee submitted by that nominating shareholder or nominating shareholder group. If that nominating shareholder or nominating shareholder group did not include any other eligible nominees in its notice filed on Schedule 14N, then the registrant will be required to include the nominee or nominees of the nominating shareholder or nominating shareholder group with the next highest voting power percentage, disclosed as of the date of filing the Schedule 14N (as determined in calculating ownership to satisfy the requirement as specified in paragraph (b)(1) of this section), from which the registrant received a notice filed and transmitted as specified in paragraph (b)(10) of this section, if any, up to and including the total number required to be included by the registrant. This process would continue until the registrant included the maximum number of nominees it is required to include in its proxy statement and form of proxy pursuant to paragraph (d) of this section or the registrant exhausts the list of eligible nominees. If the registrant has commenced printing its proxy statement and form of proxy, the registrant will not be required to include a nominee or nominees in its proxy statement and form of proxy in place of a nominee or nominees that has withdrawn or has been disqualified.

4.   Notwithstanding the other provisions of this paragraph, if a registrant has multiple classes of securities and each class is entitled to elect a specified number of directors, and nominating shareholders or groups of nominating shareholders of more than one of those classes submit a number of eligible nominees for inclusion in the registrant's proxy materials pursuant to this section that is greater than 25% of the total number of the registrant's board of directors, the registrant shall include in the proxy statement and form of proxy the nominee or nominees of the nominating shareholders or groups on the basis of the proportion of total voting power in the election of directors attributable to each class, rounding to the closest whole number, if necessary, and otherwise in accordance with paragraph (e) of this section.

Instruction 1 to paragraph (e). In determining the priority of the nominee or nominees to be included in the registrant's proxy materials, the registrant will be required to consider only the nominee or nominees that would otherwise be required to be included under the provisions of this section.

Instruction 2 to paragraph (e). If the registrant is including shareholder director nominees from more than one nominating shareholder or nominating shareholder group, as described in this paragraph, and including all of the shareholder director nominees of the nominating shareholder or nominating shareholder group that is last in priority would result in exceeding the maximum number required under paragraph (d) of this section, the nominating shareholder or nominating shareholder group that is last in priority may specify which of its nominees are to be included in the registrant's proxy materials.

f.   **False or misleading statements.** The registrant is not responsible for any information in the notice from the nominating shareholder or nominating shareholder group submitted as required by paragraph (b)(10) of this section or otherwise provided by the nominating shareholder or nominating shareholder group that is included in the registrant's proxy materials.

g.   **Determinations regarding eligibility.**

1.   If the registrant determines that it will include a shareholder nominee, it must notify the nominating shareholder or nominating shareholder group (or their authorized representative) upon making this determination. In no event should the notification be postmarked or transmitted electronically later than 30 calendar days before it files its definitive proxy statement and form of proxy with the Commission.

2.   If the registrant determines that it may exclude a shareholder nominee pursuant to a provision in paragraph (a), (b), (d), or (e) of this section, or exclude a statement of support pursuant to paragraph (c) of this section, the registrant must notify in writing the nominating shareholder or nominating shareholder group (or their authorized representative) of this determination. This notice must be postmarked or transmitted electronically to the nominating shareholder or nominating shareholder group (or their authorized representative) no later than 14 calendar days after the close of the period for submission specified in paragraph (b)(10) of this section.

   i.   The registrant's notice to the nominating shareholder or nominating shareholder group (or their authorized representative) that it has determined that it may exclude a shareholder nominee or statement of support must include an explanation of the registrant's basis for determining that it may exclude the nominee or statement of support.

   ii.   The nominating shareholder or nominating shareholder group shall have 14 calendar days after receipt of the registrant's notice pursuant to paragraph (g)(2)(i) of this section to respond to the registrant's notice and correct any eligibility or procedural deficiencies identified in that notice. The nominating shareholder's or nominating shareholder group's response must be postmarked or transmitted electronically to the registrant no later than 14 calendar days after receipt of the registrant's notice.

3. If the registrant intends to exclude a shareholder nominee or statement of support, after providing the requisite notice of and time for the nominating shareholder or nominating shareholder group to remedy any eligibility or procedural deficiencies in the nomination or statement, the registrant must provide notice of the basis for its determination to the Commission no later than 80 calendar days before it files its definitive proxy statement and form of proxy with the Commission. The Commission staff may permit the registrant to make its submission later than 80 calendar days before the registrant files its definitive proxy statement and form of proxy if the registrant demonstrates good cause for missing the deadline.

    i.   The registrant's notice to the Commission shall include:

         A. Identification of the nominating shareholder or each member of the nominating shareholder group, as applicable;

         B. The name of the nominee or nominees;

         C. An explanation of the registrant's basis for determining that the registrant may exclude the nominee or nominees or a statement of support; and

         D. A supporting opinion of counsel when the registrant's basis for excluding a nominee or nominees relies on a matter of state or foreign law.

    ii. The registrant must file its notice to the Commission and simultaneously provide a copy to the nominating shareholder or each member of the nominating shareholder group (or their authorized representative). At the time the registrant files its notice, the registrant also may seek an informal statement of the Commission staff's views with regard to its determination to exclude from its proxy materials a nominee or nominees or a statement of support. The Commission staff may provide an informal statement of its views to the registrant along with a copy to the nominating shareholder or nominating shareholder group (or their authorized representative);

    iii. The nominating shareholder or nominating shareholder group may submit a response to the registrant's notice to the Commission. This response must be postmarked or transmitted electronically to the Commission no later than 14 calendar days after the nominating shareholder's or nominating shareholder group's receipt of the registrant's notice to the Commission. The nominating shareholder or nominating shareholder group must simultaneously provide to the registrant a copy of its response to the Commission.

    iv. If the registrant seeks an informal statement of the Commission staff's views with regard to its determination to exclude a shareholder nominee or nominees, the registrant shall provide the nominating shareholder or nominating shareholder group (or their authorized representative) with notice, either postmarked or transmitted electronically, promptly following receipt of the staff's response, of whether it will include or exclude the shareholder nominee; and

    v.   The exclusion of a shareholder nominee or a statement of support by a registrant where that exclusion is not permissible under paragraph (a), (b), (c), (d), or (e) of this section shall be a violation of this section.

Instruction 1 to paragraph (g). When a registrant must provide a notice to a nominating shareholder, member of a nominating shareholder group, or authorized representative of a nominating shareholder group, the registrant is responsible for providing the notice in a manner that evidences timely transmission. Where a nominating shareholder, member of a nominating shareholder group, or authorized representative of a nominating shareholder group responds to a notice, the nominating shareholder, member of a nominating shareholder group, or authorized representative of a nominating shareholder group is responsible for providing the response in a manner that evidences timely transmission.

Instruction 2 to paragraph (g). Neither the composition of the nominating shareholder group nor the shareholder nominee may be changed as a means to correct a deficiency identified in the registrant's notice to the nominating shareholder or nominating shareholder group under paragraph (g)(2) of this section; however, where a nominating shareholder or nominating shareholder group submits a number of nominees that exceeds the maximum number required to be included by the registrant under the circumstances set forth in paragraph (d) of this section, the nominating shareholder or nominating shareholder group may specify which nominee or nominees are not to be included in the registrant's proxy materials.

Instruction 3 to paragraph (g). Unless otherwise indicated in this section, the burden is on the registrant to demonstrate that it may exclude a nominee or statement of support.

Rule 14a-12 – Solicitation Before Furnishing a Proxy Statement

a. Notwithstanding the provisions of Rule 14a-3(a), a solicitation may be made before furnishing security holders with a proxy statement meeting the requirements of Rule 14a-3(a) if:
   1. Each written communication includes:
      i.   The identity of the participants in the solicitation (as defined in Instruction 3 to Item 4 of Schedule 14A (Rule 14a-101)) and a description of their direct or indirect interests, by security holdings or otherwise, or a prominent legend in clear, plain language advising security holders where they can obtain that information; and
      ii. A prominent legend in clear, plain language advising security holders to read the proxy statement when it is available because it contains important information. The legend also must explain to investors that they can get the proxy statement, and any other relevant documents, for free at the Commission's web site and describe which documents are available free from the participants; and
   2. A definitive proxy statement meeting the requirements of Rule 14a-3(a) is sent or given to security holders solicited in reliance on this section before or at the same time as the forms of proxy, consent or authorization are furnished to or requested from security holders.

b. Any soliciting material published, sent or given to security holders in accordance with paragraph (a) of this section must be filed with the Commission no later than the date the material is first published, sent or given to security holders. Three copies of the material must at the same time be filed with, or mailed for filing to, each national securities exchange upon which any class of securities of the registrant is listed and registered. The soliciting material must include a cover page in the form set forth in Schedule 14A (Rule 14a-101) and the appropriate box on the cover page must be marked. Soliciting material in connection with a registered offering is required to be filed only under Rule 424 or Rule 425, and will be deemed filed under this section.

c. Solicitations by any person or group of persons for the purpose of opposing a solicitation subject to this regulation by any other person or group of persons with respect to the election or removal of directors at any annual or special meeting of security holders also are subject to the following provisions:

  1. Application of this rule to annual report to security holders. Notwithstanding the provisions of Rule 14a-3(b) and (c), any portion of the annual report to security holders referred to in Rule 14a-3(b) that comments upon or refers to any solicitation subject to this rule, or to any participant in the solicitation, other than the solicitation by the management, must be filed with the Commission as proxy material subject to this regulation. This must be filed in electronic format unless an exemption is available under Rules 201 or 202 of Regulation S-T.

  2. Use of reprints or reproductions. In any solicitation subject to this Rule 14a-12(c), soliciting material that includes, in whole or part, any reprints or reproductions of any previously published material must:

      i.   State the name of the author and publication, the date of prior publication, and identify any person who is quoted without being named in the previously published material.

      ii. Except in the case of a public or official document or statement, state whether or not the consent of the author and publication has been obtained to the use of the previously published material as proxy soliciting material.

      iii. If any participant using the previously published material, or anyone on his or her behalf, paid, directly or indirectly, for the preparation or prior publication of the previously published material, or has made or proposes to make any payments or give any other consideration in connection with the publication or republication of the material, state the circumstances.

Instructions to Rule 14a-12

1. If paper filing is permitted, file eight copies of the soliciting material with the Commission, except that only three copies of the material specified by Rule 14a-12(c)(1) need be filed.

2. Any communications made under this section after the definitive proxy statement is on file but before it is disseminated also must specify that the proxy statement is publicly available and the anticipated date of dissemination.

3. Inclusion of a nominee pursuant to Rule 14a-11, an applicable state or foreign law provision, or a registrant's governing documents as they relate to the inclusion of shareholder director nominees in the registrant's proxy materials, or solicitations by a nominating shareholder or nominating shareholder group that are made in connection with that nomination constitute solicitations in opposition subject to Rule 14a-12(c), except for purposes of Rule 14a-6(a).

Rule 14a-13 – Obligation of Registrants in Communicating with Beneficial Owners

a. If the registrant knows that securities of any class entitled to vote at a meeting (or by written consents or authorizations if no meeting is held) with respect to which the registrant intends to solicit proxies, consents or authorizations are held of record by a broker, dealer, voting trustee, bank, association, or other entity that exercises fiduciary powers in nominee name or otherwise, the registrant shall:

1. By first class mail or other equally prompt means:

   i.   Inquire of each such record holder:

   A. Whether other persons are the beneficial owners of such securities and if so, the number of copies of the proxy and other soliciting material necessary to supply such material to such beneficial owners;

   B. In the case of an annual (or special meeting in lieu of the annual) meeting, or written consents in lieu of such meeting, at which directors are to be elected, the number of copies of the annual report to security holders necessary to supply such report to beneficial owners to whom such reports are to be distributed by such record holder or its nominee and not by the registrant;

   C. If the record holder has an obligation under Rule 14b-1(b)(3) or Rule 14b-2(b)(4)(ii) and (iii), whether an agent has been designated to act on its behalf in fulfilling such obligation and, if so, the name and address of such agent; and

   D. Whether it holds the registrant's securities on behalf of any respondent bank and, if so, the name and address of each such respondent bank; and

   ii. Indicate to each such record holder:

   A. Whether the registrant, pursuant to paragraph (c) of this section, intends to distribute the annual report to security holders to beneficial owners of its securities whose names, addresses and securities positions are disclosed pursuant to Rule 14b-1(b)(3) or Rule 14b-2(b)(4)(ii) and (iii);

   B. The record date; and

   C. At the option of the registrant, any employee benefit plan established by an affiliate of the registrant that holds securities of the registrant that the registrant elects to treat as exempt employee benefit plan securities;

2. Upon receipt of a record holder's or respondent bank's response indicating, pursuant to Rule 14b-2(b)(1)(i), the names and addresses of its respondent banks, within one business day after the date such response is received, make an inquiry of and give notification to each such respondent bank in the same manner required by paragraph (a)(1) of this section; *Provided, however,* the inquiry required by paragraphs(a)(1) and (a)(2) of this section shall not cover beneficial owners of exempt employee benefit plan securities;

3. Make the inquiry required by paragraph (a)(1) of this section at least 20 business days prior to the record date of the meeting of security holders, or

   i.   If such inquiry is impracticable 20 business days prior to the record date of a special meeting, as many days before the record date of such meeting as is practicable or,

ii. If consents or authorizations are solicited, and such inquiry is impracticable 20 business days before the earliest date on which they may be used to effect corporate action, as many days before that date as is practicable, or

iii. At such later time as the rules of a national securities exchange on which the class of securities in question is listed may permit for good cause shown;

Provided, however, That if a record holder or respondent bank has informed the registrant that a designated office(s) or department(s) is to receive such inquiries, the inquiry shall be made to such designated office(s) or department(s); and

4. Supply, in a timely manner, each record holder and respondent bank of whom the inquiries required by paragraphs(a)(1) and (a)(2) of this section are made with copies of the proxy, other proxy soliciting material, and/or the annual report to security holders, in such quantities, assembled in such form and at such place(s), as the record holder or respondent bank may reasonably request in order to send such material to each beneficial owner of securities who is to be furnished with such material by the record holder or respondent bank; and

5. Upon the request of any record holder or respondent bank that is supplied with proxy soliciting material and/or annual reports to security holders pursuant to paragraph (a)(4) of this section, pay its reasonable expenses for completing the sending of such material to beneficial owners.

Note 1: If the registrant's list of security holders indicates that some of its securities are registered in the name of a clearing agency registered pursuant to Section 17A of the Act (e.g., "Cede & Co.", nominee for the Depository Trust Company), the registrant shall make appropriate inquiry of the clearing agency and thereafter of the participants in such clearing agency who may hold on behalf of a beneficial owner or respondent bank, and shall comply with the above paragraph with respect to any such participant (*see* Rule 14a-1(i)).

Note 2: The attention of registrants is called to the fact that each broker, dealer, bank, association, and other entity that exercises fiduciary powers has an obligation pursuant to Rule 14b-1 and Rule 14b-2 (except as provided therein with respect to exempt employee benefit plan securities held in nominee name) and, with respect to brokers and dealers, applicable self-regulatory organization requirements to obtain and forward, within the time periods prescribed therein,

i. proxies (or in lieu thereof requests for voting instructions) and proxy soliciting materials to beneficial owners on whose behalf it holds securities, and

ii. annual reports to security holders to beneficial owners on whose behalf it holds securities,

unless the registrant has notified the record holder or respondent bank that it has assumed responsibility to send such material to beneficial owners whose names, addresses, and securities positions are disclosed pursuant to Rule 14b-1(b)(3) and Rule 14b-2(b)(4)(ii) and (iii).

Note 3: The attention of registrants is called to the fact that registrants have an obligation, pursuant to paragraph (d) of this section, to cause proxies (or in lieu thereof requests for voting instructions), proxy soliciting material and annual reports to security holders to be furnished, in a timely manner, to beneficial owners of exempt employee benefit plan securities.

b. Any registrant requesting pursuant to Rule 14b-1(b)(3) or Rule 14b-2(b)(4)(ii) and (iii) a list of names, addresses and securities positions of beneficial owners of its securities who either have consented or have not objected to disclosure of such information shall:

   1. By first class mail or other equally prompt means, inquire of each record holder and each respondent bank identified to the registrant pursuant to Rule 14b-2(b)(4)(i) whether such record holder or respondent bank holds the registrant's securities on behalf of any respondent banks and, if so, the name and address of each such respondent bank;

   2. Request such list to be compiled as of a date no earlier than five business days after the date the registrant's request is received by the record holder or respondent bank; *Provided, however,* That if the record holder or respondent bank has informed the registrant that a designated office(s) or department(s) is to receive such requests, the request shall be made to such designated office(s) or department(s);

   3. Make such request to the following persons that hold the registrant's securities on behalf of beneficial owners: all brokers, dealers, banks, associations and other entities that exercises fiduciary powers; *Provided however,* such request shall not cover beneficial owners of exempt employee benefit plan securities as defined in Rule 14a-1(d)(1); and, at the option of the registrant, such request may give notice of any employee benefit plan established by an affiliate of the registrant that holds securities of the registrant that the registrant elects to treat as exempt employee benefit plan securities;

   4. Use the information furnished in response to such request exclusively for purposes of corporate communications; and

   5. Upon the request of any record holder or respondent bank to whom such request is made, pay the reasonable expenses, both direct and indirect, of providing beneficial owner information.

       Note: A registrant will be deemed to have satisfied its obligations under paragraph (b) of this section by requesting consenting and non-objecting beneficial owner lists from a designated agent acting on behalf of the record holder or respondent bank and paying to that designated agent the reasonable expenses of providing the beneficial owner information.

c. A registrant, at its option, may send its annual report to security holders to the beneficial owners whose identifying information is provided by record holders and respondent banks, pursuant to Rule 14b-1(b)(3) or Rule 14b-2(b)(4)(ii) and (iii), provided that such registrant notifies the record holders and respondent banks, at the time it makes the inquiry required by paragraph (a) of this section, that the registrant will send the annual report to security holders to the beneficial owners so identified.

d. If a registrant solicits proxies, consents or authorizations from record holders and respondent banks who hold securities on behalf of beneficial owners, the registrant shall cause proxies (or in lieu thereof requests or voting instructions), proxy soliciting material and annual reports to security holders to be furnished, in a timely manner, to beneficial owners of exempt employee benefit plan securities.

Rule 14a-14 – Modified or Superseded Documents

a. Any statement contained in a document incorporated or deemed to be incorporated by reference shall be deemed to be modified or superseded, for purposes of the proxy statement, to the extent that a statement contained in the proxy statement or in any other subsequently filed document that also is or is deemed to be incorporated by reference modifies or replaces such statement.

b. The modifying or superseding statement may, but need not, state it has modified or superseded a prior statement or include any other information set forth in the document that is not so modified or superseded. The making of a modifying or superseding statement shall not be deemed an admission that the modified or superseded statement, when made, constituted an untrue statement of a material fact, an omission to state a material fact necessary to make a statement not misleading, or the employment of a manipulative, deceptive, or fraudulent device, contrivance, scheme, transaction, act, practice, course of business or artifice to defraud, as those terms are used in the Securities Act of 1933, the Securities Exchange Act of 1934 ("the Act"), the Investment Company Act of 1940, or the rules and regulations thereunder.

c. Any statement so modified shall not be deemed in its unmodified form to constitute part of the proxy statement for purposes of the Act. Any statement so superseded shall not be deemed to constitute a part of the proxy statement for purposes of the Act.

Rule 14a-15 – Differential and Contingent Compensation in Connection with Roll-Up Transactions

a. It shall be unlawful for any person to receive compensation for soliciting proxies, consents, or authorizations directly from security holders in connection with a roll-up transaction as provided in paragraph (b) of this section, if the compensation is:
    1. Based on whether the solicited proxy, consent, or authorization either approves or disapproves the proposed roll-up transaction; or
    2. Contingent on the approval, disapproval, or completion of the roll-up transaction.

b. This section is applicable to a roll-up transaction as defined in Item 901(c) of Regulation S-K, except for a transaction involving only:
    1. Finite-life entities that are not limited partnerships;
    2. Partnerships whose investors will receive new securities or securities in another entity that are not reported under a transaction reporting plan declared effective before December 17, 1993 by the Commission under section 11A of the Act; or
    3. Partnerships whose investors' securities are reported under a transaction reporting plan declared effective before December 17, 1993 by the Commission under section 11A of the Act.

Rule 14a-16 – Internet availability of proxy materials.

a. 1. A registrant shall furnish a proxy statement pursuant to Rule14a–3(a), or an annual report to security holders pursuant to Rule 14a–3(b), to a security holder by sending the security holder a Notice of Internet Availability of Proxy Materials, as described in this section, 40 calendar days or more prior to the security holder meeting date, or if no meeting is to be held, 40 calendar days or more prior to the date the votes, consents or authorizations may be used to effect the corporate action, and complying with all other requirements of this section.

2. Unless the registrant chooses to follow the full set delivery option set forth in paragraph (n) of this section, it must provide the record holder or respondent bank with all information listed in paragraph (d) of this section in sufficient time for the record holder or respondent bank to prepare, print and send a Notice of Internet Availability of Proxy Materials to beneficial owners at least 40 calendar days before the meeting date.

b. 1. All materials identified in the Notice of Internet Availability of Proxy Materials must be publicly accessible, free of charge, at the Web site address specified in the notice on or before the time that the notice is sent to the security holder and such materials must remain available on that Web site through the conclusion of the meeting of security holders.

2. All additional soliciting materials sent to security holders or made public after the Notice of Internet Availability of Proxy Materials has been sent must be made publicly accessible at the specified Web site address no later than the day on which such materials are first sent to security holders or made public.

3. The Web site address relied upon for compliance under this section may not be the address of the Commission's electronic filing system.

4. The registrant must provide security holders with a means to execute a proxy as of the time the Notice of Internet Availability of Proxy Materials is first sent to security holders.

c. The materials must be presented on the Web site in a format, or formats, convenient for both reading online and printing on paper.

d. The Notice of Internet Availability of Proxy Materials must contain the following:
1. A prominent legend in bold-face type that states: **"Important Notice Regarding the Availability of Proxy Materials for the Shareholder Meeting to Be Held on [insert meeting date]."**

2. An indication that the communication is not a form for voting and presents only an overview of the more complete proxy materials, which contain important information and are available on the Internet or by mail, and encouraging a security holder to access and review the proxy materials before voting;

3. The Internet Web site address where the proxy materials are available;

4. Instructions regarding how a security holder may request a paper or email copy of the proxy materials at no charge, including the date by which they should make the request to facilitate timely delivery, and an indication that they will not otherwise receive a paper or email copy;

5. The date, time, and location of the meeting, or if corporate action is to be taken by written consent, the earliest date on which the corporate action may be effected;

6. A clear and impartial identification of each separate matter intended to be acted on and the soliciting person's recommendations, if any, regarding those matters, but no supporting statements;

7. A list of the materials being made available at the specified Web site;

8. A toll-free telephone number, an e-mail address, and an Internet Web site where the security holder can request a copy of the proxy statement, annual report to security holders, and form of proxy, relating to all of the registrant's future security holder meetings and for the particular meeting to which the proxy materials being furnished relate;

9. Any control/identification numbers that the security holder needs to access his or her form of proxy;

10. Instructions on how to access the form of proxy, provided that such instructions do not enable a security holder to execute a proxy without having access to the proxy statement and, if required by Rule 14a-3(b), the annual report to security holders; and

11. Information on how to obtain directions to be able to attend the meeting and vote in person.

e. 1. The Notice of Internet Availability of Proxy Materials may not be incorporated into, or combined with, another document, except that it may be incorporated into, or combined with, a notice of security holder meeting required under state law, unless state law prohibits such incorporation or combination.

2. The Notice of Internet Availability of Proxy Materials may contain only the information required by paragraph (d) of this section and any additional information required to be included in a notice of security holders meeting under state law; provided that:

 i. The registrant must revise the information on the Notice of Internet Availability of Proxy Materials, including any title to the document, to reflect the fact that:

  A. The registrant is conducting a consent solicitation rather than a proxy solicitation; or

  B. The registrant is not soliciting proxy or consent authority, but is furnishing an information statement pursuant to Rule 14c-2; and

 ii. The registrant may include a statement on the Notice to educate security holders that no personal information other than the identification or control number is necessary to execute a proxy.

f. 1. Except as provided in paragraph (h) of this section, the Notice of Internet Availability of Proxy Materials must be sent separately from other types of security holder communications and may not accompany any other document or materials, including the form of proxy.

2. Notwithstanding paragraph (f)(1) of this section, the registrant may accompany the Notice of Internet Availability of Proxy Materials with:

        i.   A pre-addressed, postage-paid reply card for requesting a copy of the proxy materials;

        ii.   A copy of any notice of security holder meeting required under state law if that notice is not combined with the Notice of Internet Availability of Proxy Materials; and

        iii.   In the case of an investment company registered under the Investment Company Act of 1940, the company's prospectus or a report that is required to be transmitted to stockholders by section 30(e) of the Investment Company Act and the rules thereunder; and

        iv.   An explanation of the reasons for a registrant's use of the rules detailed in this section and the process of receiving and reviewing the proxy materials and voting as detailed in this section.

g.   **Plain English**

     1.   To enhance the readability of the Notice of Internet Availability of Proxy Materials, the registrant must use plain English principles in the organization, language, and design of the notice.

     2.   The registrant must draft the language in the Notice of Internet Availability of Proxy Materials so that, at a minimum, it substantially complies with each of the following plain English writing principles:

        i.   Short sentences;

        ii.   Definite, concrete, everyday words;

        iii.   Active voice;

        iv.   Tabular presentation or bullet lists for complex material, whenever possible;

        v.   No legal jargon or highly technical business terms; and

        vi.   No multiple negatives.

     3.   In designing the Notice of Internet Availability of Proxy Materials, the registrant may include pictures, logos, or similar design elements so long as the design is not misleading and the required information is clear.

h.   The registrant may send a form of proxy to security holders if:

     1.   At least 10 calendar days or more have passed since the date it first sent the Notice of Internet Availability of Proxy Materials to security holders and the form of proxy is accompanied by a copy of the Notice of Internet Availability of Proxy Materials; or

     2.   The form of proxy is accompanied or preceded by a copy, via the same medium, of the proxy statement and any annual report to security holders that is required by Rule 14a-3(b).

i.   The registrant must file a form of the Notice of Internet Availability of Proxy Materials with the Commission pursuant to Rule 14a-6(b) no later than the date that the registrant first sends the notice to security holders.

j.   **Obligation to provide copies**

     1.   The registrant must send, at no cost to the record holder or respondent bank and by U.S. first class mail or other reasonably prompt means, a paper copy of the proxy statement, information statement, annual report to security

holders, and form of proxy (to the extent each of those documents is applicable) to any record holder or respondent bank requesting such a copy within three business days after receiving a request for a paper copy.

2. The registrant must send, at no cost to the record holder or respondent bank and via e-mail, an electronic copy of the proxy statement, information statement, annual report to security holders, and form of proxy (to the extent each of those documents is applicable) to any record holder or respondent bank requesting such a copy within three business days after receiving a request for an electronic copy via e-mail.

3. The registrant must provide copies of the proxy materials for one year after the conclusion of the meeting or corporate action to which the proxy materials relate, provided that, if the registrant receives the request after the conclusion of the meeting or corporate action to which the proxy materials relate, the registrant need not send copies via First Class mail and need not respond to such request within three business days.

4. The registrant must maintain records of security holder requests to receive materials in paper or via e-mail for future solicitations and must continue to provide copies of the materials to a security holder who has made such a request until the security holder revokes such request.

k. **Security holder information**

1. A registrant or its agent shall maintain the Internet Web site on which it posts its proxy materials in a manner that does not infringe on the anonymity of a person accessing such Web site.

2. The registrant and its agents shall not use any e-mail address obtained from a security holder solely for the purpose of requesting a copy of proxy materials pursuant to paragraph (j) for any purpose other than to send a copy of those materials to that security holder. The registrant shall not disclose such information to any person other than an employee or agent to the extent necessary to send a copy of the proxy materials pursuant to para. (j).

l. A person other than the registrant may solicit proxies pursuant to the conditions imposed on registrants by this section, provided that:

1. A soliciting person other than the registrant is required to provide copies of its proxy materials only to security holders to whom it has sent a Notice of Internet Availability of Proxy Materials; and

2. A soliciting person other than the registrant must send its Notice of Internet Availability of Proxy Materials by the later of:

    i.   40 calendar days prior to the security holder meeting date or, if no meeting is to be held, 40 calendar days prior to the date the votes, consents, or authorizations may be used to effect the corporate action; or

    ii. The date on which it files its definitive proxy statement with the Commission, provided its preliminary proxy statement is filed no later than 10 calendar days after the date that the registrant files its definitive proxy statement.

3. Content of the soliciting person's Notice of Internet Availability of Proxy Materials.

      i.   If, at the time a soliciting person other than the registrant sends its Notice of Internet Availability of Proxy Materials, the soliciting person is not aware of all matters on the registrant's agenda for the meeting of security holders, the soliciting person's Notice on Internet Availability of Proxy Materials must provide a clear and impartial identification of each separate matter on the agenda to the extent known by the soliciting person at that time. The soliciting person's notice also must include a clear statement indicating that there may be additional agenda items of which the soliciting person is not aware and that the security holder cannot direct a vote for those items on the soliciting person's proxy card provided at that time.

     ii.   If a soliciting person other than the registrant sends a form of proxy not containing all matters intended to be acted upon, the Notice of Internet Availability of Proxy Materials must clearly state whether execution of the form of proxy will invalidate a security holder's prior vote on matters not presented on the form of proxy.

m.   This section shall not apply to a proxy solicitation in connection with a business combination transaction, as defined in Rule 165 of this chapter, as well as transactions for cash consideration requiring disclosure under Item 14 of Rule 14a-101.

n.   **Full Set Delivery Option**
1.   For purposes of this paragraph (n), the term full set of proxy materials shall include all of the following documents:
    i.   A copy of the proxy statement;
    ii. A copy of the annual report to security holders if required by 14a-3(b); and
    iii. A form of proxy.
2.   Notwithstanding paragraphs (e) and (f)(2) of this section, a registrant or other soliciting person may:
    i.   Accompany the Notice of Internet Availability of Proxy Materials with a full set of proxy materials; or
    ii. Send a full set of proxy materials without a Notice of Internet Availability of Proxy Materials if all of the information required in a Notice of Internet Availability of Proxy Materials pursuant to paragraphs (d) and (n)(4) is incorporated in the proxy statement and the form of proxy.
3.   A registrant or other soliciting person that sends a full set of proxy materials to a security holder pursuant to this paragraph (n) need not comply with
    i.   The timing provisions of paragraphs (a) and (l)(2); and
    ii. The obligation to provide copies pursuant to paragraph (j).
4.   A registrant or other soliciting person that sends a full set of proxy materials to a security holder pursuant to this paragraph (n) need not include in its Notice of Internet Availability of Proxy Materials, proxy statement, or form of proxy the following disclosures:
    i.   Instructions regarding the nature of the communication pursuant to paragraph (d)(2) of this section;

ii.   Instructions on how to request a copy of the proxy materials; and

iii.   Instructions on how to access the form of proxy pursuant to paragraph (d)(7).

Rule 14a-17 – Electronic Shareholder Forums

a.   A shareholder, registrant, or third party acting on behalf of a shareholder or registrant may establish, maintain, or operate an electronic shareholder forum to facilitate interaction among the registrant's shareholders and between the registrant and its shareholders as the shareholder or registrant deems appropriate. Subject to paragraphs (b) and (c) of this section, the forum must comply with the federal securities laws, including Section 14(a) of the Act and its associated regulations, other applicable federal laws, applicable state laws, and the registrant's governing documents.

b.   No shareholder, registrant, or third party acting on behalf of a shareholder or registrant, by reason of establishing, maintaining, or operating an electronic shareholder forum, will be liable under the federal securities laws for any statement or information provided by another person to the electronic shareholder forum. Nothing in this section prevents or alters the application of the federal securities laws, including the provisions for liability for fraud, deception, or manipulation, or other applicable federal and state laws to the person or persons that provide a statement or information to an electronic shareholder forum.

c.   Reliance on the exemption in Rule 14a-2(b)(6) to participate in an electronic shareholder forum does not eliminate a person's eligibility to solicit proxies after the date that the exemption in Rule 14a-2(b)(6) is no longer available, or is no longer being relied upon, provided that any such solicitation is conducted in accordance with this regulation.

Rule 14a-18 – Disclosure regarding nominating shareholders and nominees submitted for inclusion in a registrant's proxy materials pursuant to applicable state or foreign law, or a registrant's governing documents

To have a nominee included in a registrant's proxy materials pursuant to a procedure set forth under applicable state or foreign law, or the registrant's governing documents addressing the inclusion of shareholder director nominees in the registrant's proxy materials, the nominating shareholder or nominating shareholder group must provide notice to the registrant of its intent to do so on a Schedule 14N and file that notice, including the required disclosure, with the Commission on the date first transmitted to the registrant. This notice shall be postmarked or transmitted electronically to the registrant by the date specified by the registrant's advance notice provision or, where no such provision is in place, no later than 120 calendar days before the anniversary of the date that the registrant mailed its proxy materials for the prior year's annual meeting, except that, if the registrant did not hold an annual meeting during the prior year, or if the date of the meeting has changed by more than 30 calendar days from the prior year, then the nominating shareholder or nominating shareholder group must provide notice a reasonable time before the registrant mails its proxy materials, as specified by the registrant in a Form 8-K filed pursuant to Item 5.08 of Form 8-K.

Instruction to Rule 14a-18. The registrant is not responsible for any information provided in the Schedule 14N by the nominating shareholder or nominating shareholder group, which is submitted as required by this section or otherwise provided by the nominating shareholder or nominating shareholder group that is included in the registrant's proxy materials.

Rule 14a-19 Solicitation of proxies in support of director nominees other than the registrant's nominees

    a.   No person may solicit proxies in support of director nominees other than the registrant's nominees unless such person:

        1.   Provides notice to the registrant in accordance with paragraph (b) of this section unless the information required by paragraph (b) of this section has been provided in a preliminary or definitive proxy statement previously filed by such person;

        2.   Files a definitive proxy statement with the Commission in accordance with Rule 14a-6(b) by the later of:

            i.   25 calendar days prior to the security holder meeting date; or

            ii.   Five (5) calendar days after the date that the registrant files its definitive proxy statement; and

        3.   Solicits the holders of shares representing at least 67% of the voting power of shares entitled to vote on the election of directors and includes a statement to that effect in the proxy statement or form of proxy.

    b.   The notice shall:

        1.   Be postmarked or transmitted electronically to the registrant at its principal executive office no later than 60 calendar days prior to the anniversary of the previous year's annual meeting date, except that, if the registrant did not hold an annual meeting during the previous year, or if the date of the meeting has changed by more than 30 calendar days from the previous year, then notice must be provided by the later of 60 calendar days prior to the date of the annual meeting or the 10th calendar day following the day on which public announcement of the date of the annual meeting is first made by the registrant;

        2.   Include the names of all nominees for whom such person intends to solicit proxies; and

        3.   Include a statement that such person intends to solicit the holders of shares representing at least 67% of the voting power of shares entitled to vote on the election of directors in support of director nominees other than the registrant's nominees.

    c.   If any change occurs with respect to such person's intent to solicit the holders of shares representing at least 67% of the voting power of shares entitled to vote on the election of directors in support of director nominees other than the registrant's nominees or with respect to the names of such person's nominees, such person shall notify the registrant promptly.

d.   A registrant shall notify the person conducting a proxy solicitation subject to this section of the names of all nominees for whom the registrant intends to solicit proxies unless the names have been provided in a preliminary or definitive proxy statement previously filed by the registrant. The notice shall be postmarked or transmitted electronically no later than 50 calendar days prior to the anniversary of the previous year's annual meeting date, except that, if the registrant did not hold an annual meeting during the previous year, or if the date of the meeting has changed by more than 30 calendar days from the previous year, then notice must be provided no later than 50 calendar days prior to the date of the annual meeting. If any change occurs with respect to the names of the registrant's nominees, the registrant shall notify the person conducting a proxy solicitation subject to this section promptly.

e.   Notwithstanding the provisions of Rule 14a-4(b)(2), if any person is conducting a proxy solicitation subject to this section, the form of proxy of the registrant and the form of proxy of any person soliciting proxies pursuant to this section shall:

    1.   Set forth the names of all persons nominated for election by the registrant and by any person or group of persons that has complied with this section and the name of any person whose nomination by a shareholder or shareholder group satisfies the requirements of an applicable state or foreign law provision or a registrant's governing documents as they relate to the inclusion of shareholder director nominees in the registrant's proxy materials;

    2.   Provide a means for the security holder to grant authority to vote for the nominees set forth;

    3.   Clearly distinguish between the nominees of the registrant, the nominees of the person or group of persons that has complied with this section and the nominees of any shareholder or shareholder group whose nominees are included in a registrant's proxy materials pursuant to the requirements of an applicable state or foreign law provision or a registrant's governing documents;

    4.   Within each group of nominees referred to in paragraph (e)(3) of this section, list nominees in alphabetical order by last name;

    5.   Use the same font type, style and size for all nominees;

    6.   Prominently disclose the maximum number of nominees for which authority to vote can be granted; and

    7.   Prominently disclose the treatment and effect of a proxy executed in a manner that grants authority to vote for the election of fewer or more nominees than the number of directors being elected and the treatment and effect of a proxy executed in a manner that does not grant authority to vote with respect to any nominees.

f.   If any person is conducting a proxy solicitation subject to this section, the form of proxy of the registrant and the form of proxy of any person soliciting proxies pursuant to this section may provide a means for the security holder to grant authority to vote for the nominees of the registrant set forth, as a group, and a means for the security holder to grant authority to vote for the nominees of any other soliciting person set forth, as a group, provided that there is a similar means for the security holder to withhold authority to vote for such groups of nominees unless the number of nominees of the registrant or of any other soliciting person is less than the number of directors being elected. Means to grant authority to vote for any nominees as a group or to withhold authority for any nominees as a group may not be provided if the form of proxy includes one or more shareholder nominees in accordance with an applicable state or foreign law provision or a registrant's governing documents as they relate to the inclusion of shareholder director nominees in the registrant's proxy materials.

g.   This section shall not apply to:
   1.   A consent solicitation; or
   2.   A solicitation in connection with an election of directors at an investment company registered under the Investment Company Act of 1940 or a business development company as defined by section 2(a)(48) of the Investment Company Act of 1940.

Instruction 1 to paragraphs (b)(1) and (d). Where the deadline falls on a Saturday, Sunday, or holiday, the deadline will be treated as the first business day following the Saturday, Sunday, or holiday.

Instruction 2 to paragraph (f). Where applicable state law gives legal effect to votes cast against a nominee, the form of proxy may provide a means for the security holder to grant authority to vote for the nominees of the registrant set forth, as a group, and a means for the security holder to grant authority to vote for the nominees of any other soliciting person set forth, as a group, provided that, in lieu of the ability to withhold authority to vote as a group, there is a similar means for the security holder to vote against such group of nominees (as well as a means for security holders to abstain from voting for such group of nominees).

Rule 14a-21 – Shareholder approval of executive compensation, frequency of votes for approval of executive compensation and shareholder approval of golden parachute compensation

a.   If a solicitation is made by a registrant, other than an emerging growth company as defined in Rule 12b-2, and the solicitation relates to an annual or other meeting of shareholders at which directors will be elected and for which the rules of the Commission require executive compensation disclosure pursuant to Item 402 of Regulation S-K, the registrant shall, for the first annual or other meeting of shareholders on or after January 21, 2011, or for the first annual or other meeting of shareholders on or after January 21, 2013 if the registrant is a smaller reporting company, and thereafter no later than the annual or other meeting of shareholders held in the third calendar year after the immediately preceding vote under this subsection, include a separate resolution subject to shareholder advisory vote to approve the compensation of its named executive officers, as disclosed pursuant to Item 402 of Regulation S-K.

Instruction to Rule 14a-21(a):
The registrant's resolution shall indicate that the shareholder advisory vote under this subsection is to approve the compensation of the registrant's named executive officers as disclosed pursuant to Item 402 of Regulation S-K. The following is a

non-exclusive example of a resolution that would satisfy the requirements of this subsection: "RESOLVED, that the compensation paid to the company's named executive officers, as disclosed pursuant to Item 402 of Regulation S-K, includingthe Compensation Discussion and Analysis, compensation tables and narrative discussion is hereby APPROVED."

b. If a solicitation is made by a registrant, other than an emerging growth company as defined in Rule 12b-2, and the solicitation relates to an annual or other meeting of shareholders at which directors will be elected and for which the rules of the Commission require executive compensation disclosure pursuant to Item 402 of Regulation S-K of this chapter), the registrant shall, for the first annual or other meeting of shareholders on or after January 21, 2011, or for the first annual or other meeting of shareholders on or after January 21, 2013 if the registrant is a smaller reporting company, and thereafter no later than the annual or other meeting of shareholders held in the sixth calendar year after the immediately preceding vote under this subsection, include a separate resolution subject to shareholder advisory vote as to whether the shareholder vote required by paragraph (a) of this section should occur every 1, 2 or 3 years. Registrants required to provide a separate shareholder vote pursuant to Rule 14a-20 of this chapter shall include the separate resolution required by this section for the first annual or other meeting of shareholders after the registrant has repaid all obligations arising from financial assistance provided under the TARP, as defined in section 3(8) of the Emergency Economic Stabilization Act of 2008, and thereafter no later than the annual or other meeting of shareholders held in the sixth calendar year after the immediately preceding vote under this subsection.

c. If a solicitation is made by a registrant, other than an emerging growth company as defined in Rule 12b-2, for a meeting of shareholders at which shareholders are asked to approve an acquisition, merger, consolidation or proposed sale or other disposition of all or substantially all the assets of the registrant, the registrant shall include a separate resolution subject to shareholder advisory vote to approve any agreements or understandings and compensation disclosed pursuant to Item 402(t) of Regulation S-K, unless such agreements or understandings have been subject to a shareholder advisory vote under paragraph (a) of this section. Consistent with section 14A(b) of the Exchange Act, any agreements or understandings between an acquiring company and the named executive officers of the registrant, where the registrant is not the acquiring company, are not required to be subject to the separate shareholder advisory vote under this paragraph.

Instructions to Rule 14a-21:

1. Disclosure relating to the compensation of directors required by Item 402(k) and Item 402(r) of Regulation S-K is not subject to the shareholder vote required by paragraph (a) of this section. If a registrant includes disclosure pursuant to Item 402(s) of Regulation S-K about the registrant's compensation policies and practices as they relate to risk management and risk-taking incentives, these policies and practices would not be subject to the shareholder vote required by paragraph (a) of this section. To the extent that risk considerations are a material aspect of the registrant's compensation policies or decisions for named executive officers, the registrant is required to discuss them as part of its Compensation Discussion and Analysis under

402(b), and therefore such disclosure would be considered by shareholders when voting on executive compensation.

2. If a registrant includes disclosure of golden parachute compensation arrangements pursuant to Item 402(t) in an annual meeting proxy statement, such disclosure would be subject to the shareholder advisory vote required by paragraph (a) of this section.

3. Registrants that are smaller reporting companies entitled to provide scaled disclosure in accordance with Item 402(l) of Regulation S-K are not required to include a Compensation Discussion and Analysis in their proxy statements in order to comply with this section. For smaller reporting companies, the vote required by paragraph (a) of this section must be to approve the compensation of the named executive officers as disclosed pursuant to Item 402(m) through (q) of Regulation S-K.

4. A registrant that has ceased being an emerging growth company shall include the first separate resolution described under Rule 14a-21(a) not later than the end of (i) in the case of a registrant that was an emerging growth company for less than two years after the date of first sale of common equity securities of the registrant pursuant to an effective registration statement under the Securities Act of 1933, the three-year period beginning on such date; and (ii) in the case of any other registrant, the one-year period beginning on the date the registrant is no longer an emerging growth company.

Rule 14e-3 – Transactions in Securities on the Basis of Material, Nonpublic Information in the Context of Tender Offers

a. If any person has taken a substantial step or steps to commence, or has commenced, a tender offer (the "offering person"), it shall constitute a fraudulent, deceptive or manipulative act or practice within the meaning of section 14(e) of the Act for any other person who is in possession of material information relating to such tender offer which information he knows or has reason to know is nonpublic and which he knows or has reason to know has been acquired directly or indirectly from:

1. The offering person,
2. The issuer of the securities sought or to be sought by such tender offer, or
3. Any officer, director, partner or employee or any other person acting on behalf of the offering person or such issuer, to purchase or sell or cause to be purchased or sold any of such securities or any securities convertible into or exchangeable for any such securities or any option or right to obtain or to dispose of any of the foregoing securities, unless within a reasonable time prior to any purchase or sale such information and its source are publicly disclosed by press release or otherwise.

b. A person other than a natural person shall not violate paragraph (a) of this section if such person shows that:

1. The individual(s) making the investment decision on behalf of such person to purchase or sell any security described in paragraph (a) of this section or to cause any such security to be purchased or sold by or on behalf of others did not know the material, nonpublic information; and
2. Such person had implemented one or a combination of policies and procedures, reasonable under the circumstances, taking into consideration the nature of the person's business, to ensure that individual(s) making

investment decision(s) would not violate paragraph (a) of this section, which policies and procedures may include, but are not limited to,

    i.   those which restrict any purchase, sale and causing any purchase and sale of any such security or

    ii.   those which prevent such individual(s) from knowing such information.

c. Notwithstanding anything in paragraph (a) of this section to contrary, the following transactions shall not be violations of paragraph (a) of this section:

    1.   Purchase(s) of any security described in paragraph (a) of this section by a broker or by another agent on behalf of an offering person; or

    2.   Sale(s) by any person of any security described in paragraph (a) of this section to the offering person.

d.

    1.   As a means reasonably designed to prevent fraudulent, deceptive or manipulative acts or practices within the meaning of section 14(e) of the Act, it shall be unlawful for any person described in paragraph (d)(2) of this section to communicate material, nonpublic information relating to a tender offer to any other person under circumstances in which it is reasonably foreseeable that such communication is likely to result in a violation of this section *except* that this paragraph shall not apply to a communication made in good faith,

        i.   To the officers, directors, partners or employees of the offering person, to its advisors or to other persons, involved in the planning, financing, preparation or execution of such tender offer;

        ii.   To the issuer whose securities are sought or to be sought by such tender offer, to its officers, directors, partners, employees or advisors or to other persons, involved in the planning, financing, preparation or execution of the activities of the issuer with respect to such tender offer; or

        iii.   To any person pursuant to a requirement of any statute or rule or regulation promulgated thereunder.

    2.   The persons referred to in paragraph (d)(1) of this section are:

        i.   The offering person or its officers, directors, partners, employees or advisors;

        ii.   The issuer of the securities sought or to be sought by such tender offer or its officers, directors, partners, employees or advisors;

        iii.   Anyone acting on behalf of the persons in paragraph (d)(2)(i) of this section or the issuer or persons in paragraph (d)(2)(ii) of this section; and

        iv.   Any person in possession of material information relating to a tender offer which information he knows or has reason to know is nonpublic and which he knows or has reason to know has been acquired directly or indirectly from any of the above.

Rule 15c2-8 – Delivery of Prospectus

a.   It shall constitute a deceptive act or practice, as those terms are used in Section 15(c)(2) of the Act, for a broker or dealer to participate in a distribution of securities with respect to which a registration statement has been filed under the Securities Act of 1933 unless he complies with the requirements set forth in paragraphs (b) through (g) of this section. For the purposes of this section, a broker or dealer participating in the distribution shall mean any underwriter and any member or proposed member of the selling group.

b.   In connection with an issue of securities, the issuer of which has not previously been required to file reports pursuant to Sections 13(a) or 15(d) of the Securities Exchange Act of 1934, unless such issuer has been exempted from the requirement to file reports thereunder pursuant to Section 12(h) of the Act, such broker or dealer shall deliver a copy of the preliminary prospectus to any person who is expected to receive a confirmation of sale at least 48 hours prior to the sending of such confirmation. Provided, however, this paragraph (b) shall apply to all issuances of asset-backed securities (as defined in Rule 1101(c) of the Securities Act) regardless of whether the issuer has previously been required to file reports pursuant to sections 13(a) or 15(d) of the Securities Exchange Act of 1934, or exempted from the requirement to file reports thereunder pursuant to section 12(h) of the Act.

c.   Such broker or dealer shall take reasonable steps to furnish to any person who makes written request for a preliminary prospectus between the filing date and a reasonable time prior to the effective date of the registration statement to which such prospectus relates, a copy of the latest preliminary prospectus on file with the Commission. Reasonable steps shall include receiving an undertaking by the managing underwriter or underwriters to send such copy to the address given in the requests.

d.   Such broker or dealer shall take reasonable steps to comply promptly with the written request of any person for a copy of the final prospectus relating to such securities during the period between the effective date of the registration statement and the later of either the termination of such distribution, or the expiration of the applicable 40- or 90-day period under Section 4(a)(3) of the Securities Act of 1933. Reasonable steps shall include receiving an undertaking by the managing underwriter or underwriters to send such copy to the address given in the requests. (The 40-day and 90-day periods referred to above shall be deemed to apply for purposes of this rule irrespective of the provisions of paragraphs (b) and (d) of Rule 174 under the Securities Act of 1933).

e.   Such broker or dealer shall take reasonable steps
      i.   to make available a copy of the preliminary prospectus relating to such securities to each of his associated persons who is expected, prior to the effective date, to solicit customers' order for such securities before the making of any such solicitation by such associated persons and 2 to make

616

available to each such associated person a copy of any amended preliminary prospectus promptly after the filing thereof.

f.   Such broker or dealer shall take reasonable steps to make available a copy of the final prospectus relating to such securities to each of his associated persons who is expected, after the effective date, to solicit customers' orders for such securities prior to the making of any such solicitation by such associated persons, unless a preliminary prospectus which is substantially the same as the final prospectus except for matters relating to the price of the stocks, has been so made available.

g.   If the broker or dealer is a managing underwriter of such distribution, he shall take reasonable steps to see to it that all other brokers or dealers participating in such distribution are promptly furnished with sufficient copies, as requested by them, of each preliminary prospectus, each amended preliminary prospectus and the final prospectus to enable them to comply with paragraphs (b), (c), (d), and (e) of this section.

h.   If the broker or dealer is a managing underwriter of such distribution, he shall take reasonable steps to see that any broker or dealer participating in the distribution or trading in the registered security is furnished reasonable quantities of the final prospectus relating to such securities, as requested by him, in order to enable him to comply with the prospectus delivery requirements of Section 5(b)(1) and (2) of the Securities Act of 1933.

i.   This rule shall not require the furnishing of prospectuses in any state where such furnishing would be unlawful under the laws of such state: *Provided, however,* That this provision is not to be construed to relieve a broker or dealer from complying with the requirements of Section 5(b)(1) and (2) of the Securities Act of 1933. Prospectuses shall not be furnished pursuant to this rule while the registration statement is subject to an examination, proceeding, or stop order pursuant to Section 8 of the securities act of 1933.

j.   For purposes of this section, the term **preliminary prospectus** shall include the term *prospectus subject to completion* as used in Rule 434(a), and the term *final prospectus* shall include the term *Section 10(a) prospectus* as used in Rule 434(a).

Rule 15c2-11 – Initiation or Resumption of Quotations without Specific Information

a.   **Unlawful activity.** As a means reasonably designed to prevent fraudulent, deceptive, or manipulative acts or practices, it shall be unlawful:

1.   **Brokers or dealers.** For a broker or dealer to publish any quotation for a security or, directly or indirectly, to submit any such quotation for publication, in any quotation medium unless:

i.

A.   Such broker or dealer has in its records the documents and information specified by paragraph (b) of this section;

B.   Such documents and information specified by paragraph (b) of this section (excluding paragraphs (b)(5)(i)(N) through (P) of this section) are current and publicly available; and;

C.   Based upon a review of the documents and information specified in paragraph (b) of this section, together with any other documents and information required by paragraph (c) of this section, such broker or dealer has a reasonable basis under the circumstances for believing that:

(1) The documents and information specified in paragraph (b) of this section are accurate in all material respects; and

(2) The sources of the documents and information specified in paragraph (b) of this section are reliable; or

ii.

A.   The quotation medium is a qualified interdealer quotation system that made a publicly available determination that it has performed the activities described in paragraph (a)(2)(i) through (iii) of this section; and

B.   Such quotation is published or submitted for publication within three business days after such qualified interdealer quotation system makes such publicly available determination.

2.   **Qualified interdealer quotation systems.** A qualified interdealer quotation system to make known to others the quotation of a broker or dealer that is published or submitted for publication pursuant to paragraph (a)(1)(ii) of this section, unless:

i.   Such qualified interdealer quotation system has in its records the documents and information specified in paragraph (b) of this section (excluding paragraphs (b)(5)(i)(N) through (P) of this section except where the qualified interdealer quotation system has knowledge or possession of this information);

ii. Such documents and information specified in paragraph (b) of this section (excluding paragraphs (b)(5)(i)(N) through (P) of this section) are current and publicly available;

iii. Based upon a review of the documents and information specified in paragraph (b) of this section (excluding paragraphs (b)(5)(i)(N) through (P) of this section, except where the qualified interdealer quotation system has knowledge or possession of this information), together with any other documents and information required by paragraph (c) of this section, such qualified interdealer quotation system has a reasonable basis under the circumstances for believing that:

A.   The documents and information specified in paragraph (b) of this section are accurate in all material respects; and

B.   The sources of the documents and information specified in paragraph (b) of this section are reliable; and

iv. The qualified interdealer quotation system makes a publicly available determination that it has performed the activities described in paragraphs (i) through (iii) of this paragraph (a)(2); or

3. **Qualified interdealer quotation systems or registered national securities Associations.** A qualified interdealer quotation system or registered national securities association to make a publicly available determination described in paragraph (f)(2)(iii)(B), (f)(3)(ii)(A), or (f)(7) of this section, unless such qualified interdealer quotation system or registered national securities association establishes, maintains, and enforces reasonably designed written policies and procedures to determine whether:
    i.   The documents and information specified in paragraph (b) of this section are current and publicly available; and
    ii. The requirements of an exception under paragraph (f) of this section are met, if it makes a publicly available determination described in paragraph (f)(7) of this section.

b. **Specified information.**
    1. A copy of the prospectus specified by Section 10(a) of the Securities Act of 1933 for an issuer that has filed a registration statement under the Securities Act of 1933, other than a registration statement on Form F-6, that became effective less than 90 calendar days prior to the day on which such broker or dealer publishes or submits the quotation to the quotation medium, *Provided* That such registration statement has not thereafter been the subject of a stop order which is still in effect when the quotation is published or submitted; or
    2. A copy of the offering circular provided for under Regulation A under the Securities Act of 1933 for an issuer that has filed a notification under Regulation A and was authorized to commence the offering less than 40 calendar days prior to the day on which such broker or dealer publishes or submits the quotation to the quotation medium, *Provided,* That the Regulation A exemption, with respect to such issuer, has not thereafter become subject to a suspension order that is still in effect when the quotation is published or submitted;; or
    3. A current copy of:
        i.   An annual report filed pursuant to section 13 or 15(d) of the Act, together with any periodic and current reports that have been filed thereafter under the Act by the issuer, except for current reports filed during the three business days prior to the publication or submission of the quotation; *Provided, however,* That, until such issuer has filed its first such annual report, the broker, dealer, or qualified interdealer quotation system has in its records a copy of the registration statement filed by the issuer under the Securities Act of 1933, other than a registration statement on Form F-6, that became effective within the prior 16 months, or a copy of any registration statement filed by the issuer under section 12 of the Act that became effective within the prior 16 months, together with any periodic and current reports filed thereafter under section 13 or 15(d) of the Act;
        ii. An annual report filed pursuant to Regulation A, together with any periodic and current reports filed thereafter under Regulation A by the issuer, except for current reports filed during the three business days prior to the publication or submission of the quotation; *Provided,*

however, That, until such issuer has filed its first such annual report, the broker, dealer, or qualified interdealer quotation system has in its records a copy of the offering statement filed by the issuer under Regulation A, that was qualified within the prior 16 months, together with any periodic and current reports filed thereafter under Reg. A;

iii. An annual report filed pursuant to Regulation Crowdfunding; *Provided, however,* That, until such issuer has filed its first such annual report, the broker, dealer, or qualified interdealer quotation system has in its records a copy of the Form C filed by the issuer under Regulation Crowdfunding within the prior 16 months, together with any Form C/A and Form C/U filed thereafter under Regulation Crowdfunding;

iv. An annual statement referred to in section 12(g)(2)(G)(i) of the Act (in the case of an issuer required to file reports pursuant to section 13 or 15(d) of the Act), together with any periodic and current reports filed thereafter under the Act by the issuer, except for current reports filed during the three business days prior to the publication or submission of the quotation; *Provided, however,* That, until such issuer has filed its first such annual statement, the broker, dealer, or qualified interdealer quotation system has in its records a copy of the registration statement filed by the issuer under the Securities Act of 1933, other than a registration statement on Form F-6, that became effective within the prior 16 months, or a copy of any registration statement filed by the issuer under section 12 of the Act, that became effective within the prior 16 months, together with any periodic and current reports filed thereafter under section 13 or 15(d) of the Act; or

v. An annual statement referred to in section 12(g)(2)(G)(i) of the Act (in the case of an issuer of a security that falls within the provisions of section 12(g)(2)(G) of the Act); or

4. A copy of the information that, since the first day of its most recently completed fiscal year, the issuer has published as required to establish the exemption from registration under section 12(g) of the Act pursuant to Rule 12g3-2(b) of this chapter, which the broker or dealer must make available upon the request of a person expressing an interest in a proposed transaction in the issuer's security with the broker or dealer, such as by providing the requesting person with appropriate instructions regarding how to obtain the information electronically; or

5.

i. The following information, which must be (excluding paragraphs (b)(5)(i)(N) through (P) of this section) as of a date within 12 months prior to the publication or submission of the quotation, unless otherwise specified:

    A. The name of the issuer and any predecessors during the past five years;

    B. The address(es) of the issuer's principal executive office and of its principal place of business;

    C. The state of incorporation or registration of the issuer and of each of its predecessors (if any) during the past five years;

    D. The title, class, and ticker symbol (if assigned) of the security;

E.   The par or stated value of the security;

F.   The number of shares or total amount of the securities outstanding as of the end of the issuer's most recent fiscal year;

G.   The name and address of the transfer agent;

H.   A description of the issuer's business;

I.   A description of products or services offered by the issuer;

J.   A description and extent of the issuer's facilities;

K.   The name and title of all company insiders;

L.   The issuer's most recent balance sheet (as of a date less than 16 months before the publication or submission of the quotation) and profit and loss and retained earnings statements (for the 12 months preceding the date of the most recent balance sheet);

M.   Similar financial information for such part of the two preceding fiscal years as the issuer or its predecessors has been in existence;

N.   Whether the broker or dealer or any associated person of the broker or dealer is affiliated, directly or indirectly, with the issuer;

O.   Whether the quotation is being published or submitted on behalf of any other broker or dealer and, if so, the name of such broker or dealer; and

P.   Whether the quotation is being submitted or published, directly or indirectly, by or on behalf of the issuer or a company insider and, if so, the name of such person and the basis for any exemption under the federal securities laws for any sales of such securities on behalf of such person.

ii.   The broker or dealer must make the documents and information specified in paragraph (b)(5)(i) of this section available upon the request of a person expressing an interest in a proposed transaction in the issuer's security with the broker or dealer, such as by providing the requesting person with appropriate instructions regarding how to obtain such publicly available documents and information electronically. If such information is made available to others upon request pursuant to this paragraph, such delivery, unless otherwise represented, shall not constitute a representation by such broker or dealer that such information is accurate but shall constitute a representation by such broker or dealer that the information is current in relation to the day the quotation is submitted, the broker or dealer has a reasonable basis under the circumstances for believing the information is accurate in all material respects, and the information was obtained from sources that the broker or dealer has a reasonable basis under the circumstances for believing are reliable. The documents and information specified in paragraph (b)(5) of this section must be reviewed where paragraphs (b)(1) through (b)(4) of this section do not apply to such issuer. For purposes of compliance with paragraph (a)(1)(i)(B) or (a)(2)(ii) of this section, the documents and information specified in paragraph (b)(5) of this section must be reviewed for an issuer for which the documents and information specified in paragraph (b)(1), (b)(2), (b)(3), or (b)(4) of this section regarding such issuer are not current.

c. **Supplemental information.** With respect to any security the quotation of which is within the provisions of this section, the broker or dealer submitting or publishing such quotation, or any qualified interdealer quotation system that makes known to others the quotation of a broker or dealer pursuant to paragraph (a)(2) of this section, shall have in its records the following documents and information:

    1. Records related to the submission or publication of such quotation, including the identity of the person or persons for whom the quotation is being published or submitted, whether such person or persons is the issuer or a company insider, and any information regarding the transactions provided to the broker, dealer, or qualified interdealer quotation system by such person or persons;

    2. A copy of any trading suspension order issued by the Commission pursuant to section 12(k) of the Act regarding any securities of the issuer or its predecessor (if any) during the 12 months preceding the date of the publication or submission of the quotation or a copy of the public release issued by the Commission announcing such trading suspension order; and

    3. A copy or a written record of any other material information (including adverse information) regarding the issuer that comes to the knowledge or possession of the broker, dealer, or qualified interdealer quotation system before the publication or submission of the quotation.

d. **Recordkeeping.**

    1.

        i. The following persons shall preserve for a period of not less than three years, the first two years in an easily accessible place, the documents and information required under paragraphs (a), (b), and (c) of this section, except for the documents and information that are available on the Commission's *Electronic Data Gathering, Analysis and Retrieval System* (EDGAR):

            A. Any broker or dealer that publishes or submits a quotation pursuant to paragraph (a)(1) of this section for a security; or

            B. Any qualified interdealer quotation system that makes known to others the quotation of a broker or dealer pursuant to paragraph (a)(2) of this section for a security;

        ii. Any broker or dealer that publishes or submits a quotation pursuant to paragraph (a)(1)(ii) of this section shall preserve for a period of not less than three years, the first two years in an easily accessible place, the name of the qualified interdealer quotation system that made a publicly available determination that it has performed the activities described in paragraph (a)(2)(i) through (iii) of this section.

    2. The following persons shall preserve for a period of not less than three years, the first two years in an easily accessible place, the documents and information that demonstrate that the requirements for an exception under

paragraph (f)(2), (f)(3), (f)(5), (f)(6), or (f)(7) of this section are met, except for the documents and information that are available on EDGAR:

i. Any qualified interdealer quotation system or registered national securities association that makes a publicly available determination described in paragraph (f)(2)(iii)(B), (f)(3)(ii)(A), or (f)(7) of this section; and

ii. Any broker or dealer that publishes or submits a quotation pursuant to paragraph (f) of this section; *Provided, however,* That any broker or dealer that relies on a publicly available determination described in paragraph (f)(2)(iii)(B) or (f)(3)(ii)(A) of this section shall preserve only a record of the name of the qualified interdealer quotation system or registered national securities association that determined whether the documents and information specified in paragraph (b) of this section are current and publicly available in addition to the documents and information that demonstrate that the other requirements of the exception provided in paragraph (f)(2) or (f)(3), respectively, are met; and that any broker or dealer that relies on a publicly available determination described in paragraph (f)(7) of this section shall preserve only a record of the exception provided in paragraph (f)(1), (f)(3)(i), (f)(4), or (f)(5) for which the publicly available determination is made and the name of the qualified interdealer quotation system or registered national securities association that determined that the requirements of that exception are met.

e. **Definitions**. For purposes of this section:

1. *Company insider* shall mean any officer or director of the issuer, or person that performs a similar function, or any person who is, directly or indirectly, the beneficial owner of more than 10 percent of the outstanding units or shares of any class of any equity security of the issuer.

2. *Current* shall mean, for the documents and information specified in:

   i. Paragraph (b)(1), (b)(2), (b)(4), or (b)(5) of this section, filed, published, or are as of a date in accordance with the time frames specified in the applicable paragraph for such documents and information; or

   ii. Paragraph (b)(3) of this section, the most recently required annual report or statement filed pursuant to section 13 or 15(d) of the Act and any rule(s) thereunder, Regulation A, Regulation Crowdfunding, or section 12(G)(2)(g) of the Act, together with any subsequently required periodic reports or statements, filed pursuant to section 13 or 15(d) of the Act and any rule(s) thereunder, Regulation A, Regulation Crowdfunding, or section 12(G)(2)(g) of the Act.

3. *Interdealer quotation system* shall mean any system of general circulation to brokers or dealers that regularly disseminates quotations of identified brokers or dealers.

4. *Issuer*, in the case of quotations for American Depositary Receipts, shall mean the issuer of the deposited shares represented by such American Depositary Receipts.

5.   *Publicly available* shall mean available on EDGAR; on the website of a state or federal agency, a qualified interdealer quotation system, a registered national securities association, an issuer, or a registered broker or dealer; or through an electronic information delivery system that is generally available to the public in the primary trading market of a foreign private issuer as defined in § 240.3b-4 of this chapter; *Provided, however*, That *publicly available* shall mean where access is not restricted by user name, password, fees, or other restraints.

6.   *Qualified interdealer quotation system* shall mean any interdealer quotation system that meets the definition of an "alternative trading system" under Rule 300(a) of this chapter and operates pursuant to the exemption from the definition of an "exchange" under Rule 3a1-1(a)(2) of this chapter.

7.   Except as otherwise specified in this rule, *quotation* shall mean any bid or offer at a specified price with respect to a security, or any indication of interest by a broker or dealer in receiving bids or offers from others for a security, or any indication by a broker or dealer that wishes to advertise its general interest in buying or selling a particular security.

8.   *Quotation medium* shall mean any "interdealer quotation system" or any publication or electronic communications network or other device that is used by brokers or dealers to make known to others their interest in transactions in any security, including offers to buy or sell at a stated price or otherwise, or invitations of offers to buy or sell.

9.   *Shell company* shall mean any issuer, other than a business combination related shell company, as defined in Rule 405 of this chapter, or an asset-backed issuer as defined in Item 1101(b) of Regulation AB of this chapter, that has:

   i.   No or nominal operations; and
   ii. Either:
      A.   No or nominal assets;
      B.   Assets consisting solely of cash and cash equivalents; or
      C.   Assets consisting of any amount of cash and cash equivalents and nominal other assets. .

f.   **Exceptions.** Except as provided in paragraph (d)(2) of this section, the provisions of this section shall not apply to:

1.   The publication or submission of a quotation for a security that is admitted to trading on a national securities exchange and that is traded on such an exchange on the same day as, or on the business day next preceding, the day the quotation is published or submitted.

2.

   i.   The publication or submission by a broker or dealer, solely on behalf of a customer (other than a person acting as or for a dealer), of a quotation that represents the customer's unsolicited indication of interest;

   ii. *Provided, however*, That this paragraph (f)(2) shall not apply to a quotation:
      A.   Consisting of both a bid and an offer, each of which is at a specified price, unless the quotation medium specifically

identifies the quotation as representing such an unsolicited customer interest; or

B. Published or submitted, directly or indirectly on behalf of a company insider or affiliate as defined in Rule 144(a)(1) of this chapter, unless the documents and information specified in paragraph (b) of this section are current and publicly available.

iii. For purposes of this paragraph (f)(2)(ii)(B), a broker or dealer that publishes or submits quotations may rely on either a:

A. Written representation from the customer's broker that such customer is not a company insider or an affiliate if:

1. Such representation is received prior to, and on the same day that, the quotation representing the customer's unsolicited indication of interest is published or submitted; and

2. The broker or dealer has a reasonable basis under the circumstances for believing that the customer's broker is a reliable source; or

B. Publicly available determination by a qualified interdealer quotation system or registered national securities association that the documents and information specified in paragraph (b) of this section are current and publicly available.

3.

    i.

A. The publication or submission, in an interdealer quotation system that specifically identifies as such unsolicited customer indications of interest of the kind described in paragraph (f)(2) of this section, of a quotation for a security that has been the subject of a bid or offer quotation (exclusive of any identified customer interests) in such a system at a specified price, with no more than four business days in succession without such a quotation;

B. *Provided, however,* That this paragraph (f)(3) shall not apply to a quotation that is published or submitted by a broker or dealer for the security of an issuer that:

1. Was the subject of a trading suspension order issued by the Commission pursuant to section 12(k) of the Act until 60 calendar days after the expiration of such order;

2. Such broker or dealer, or any qualified interdealer quotation system or registered national securities association, has a reasonable basis under the circumstances for believing is a shell company, unless such quotation is published or submitted within the 18 months following the initial quotation for such issuer's security that is the subject of a bid or offer quotation in an interdealer quotation system at a specified price;

C. *Provided further,* That this paragraph (f)(3) shall apply to the publication or submission of a quotation for a security of an issuer only if the documents and information regarding such issuer that are specified in:

1. Paragraph (b)(3)(i), (b)(3)(iv), or (b)(3)(v) of this section are filed within 180 calendar days from the end of the issuer's most recent fiscal year or any quarterly reporting period that is covered by a report required by section 13 or 15(d) of the Act, as applicable;

2. Paragraph (b)(3)(ii) or (b)(3)(iii) of this section are timely filed;

3. Paragraph (b)(4) or (b)(5)(i) (excluding paragraphs (b)(5)(i)(N) through (P)) are current and publicly available; or

4. Paragraph (b)(3)(i), (b)(3)(ii), (b)(3)(iii), (b)(3)(iv), or (b)(3)(v) are filed within 15 calendar days starting on the date on which a publicly available determination is made pursuant to paragraph (f)(3)(ii)(A) of this section; or

ii. If the documents and information specified in paragraph (b) of this section (excluding paragraphs (b)(5)(i)(N) through (P)) regarding an issuer are no longer current and publicly available, timely filed, or filed within 180 calendar days, as specified in paragraph (f)(3)(i)(C) of this section, a broker or dealer may continue to publish or submit a quotation for such issuer's security in an interdealer quotation system during the time frame specified in in paragraph (f)(3)(ii)(C) if:

A. Within the first four business days that such documents and information are no longer current and publicly available, timely filed, or filed within 180 calendar days, as applicable, a qualified interdealer quotation system or registered national securities association makes a publicly available determination that:

1. Such documents and information are no longer current and publicly available, timely filed, or filed within 180 calendar days, as specified in paragraph (f)(3)(i)(C) of this section; and

2. The exception provided in paragraph (f)(3)(ii) of this section is available only during the 15 calendar days starting on the date on which the publicly available determination described in paragraph (f)(3)(ii)(A)(*1*) of this section is made; and

B. The broker or dealer complies with the requirements of paragraphs (d)(2) and (f)(3)(i) of this section, except for the requirement that the documents and information specified in paragraph (b) (excluding paragraphs (b)(5)(i)(N) through (P)) regarding such issuer be current and publicly available, timely filed, or filed within 180 calendar days, as applicable;

C. *Provided, however*, That the provisions of this paragraph (f)(3)(ii) shall apply only during the shorter of the period beginning with the date on which a qualified interdealer quotation system or registered national securities association

626

makes a publicly available determination identified in paragraph (f)(3)(ii)(A) and ending on:

1. The date on which the documents and information specified in paragraph (b) (excluding paragraphs (b)(5)(i)(N) through (P)) regarding such issuer become current and publicly available or filed; or

2. The fourteenth calendar day following the date on which such publicly available determination was made.

4. The publication or submission of a quotation for a municipal security.

5. The publication or submission of a quotation for:

   i. A security with a worldwide average daily trading volume value of at least $100,000 reported during the 60 calendar days immediately before the publication of the quotation of such security; and

   ii. The issuer of such security has at least $50 million in total assets and $10 million in shareholders' equity as reflected in the issuer's publicly available audited balance sheet issued within six months after the end of its most recent fiscal year.

6. The publication or submission of a quotation for a security by a broker or dealer that is named as an underwriter in a registration statement for an offering of that class of security referenced in paragraph (b)(1) of this section or in an offering statement for an offering of that class of security referenced in paragraph (b)(2) of this section; *Provided, however*, That this paragraph (f)(6) shall apply only to the publication or submission of a quotation for such security within the time frames specified in paragraph (b)(1) or (b)(2) of this section.

7. The publication or submission of a quotation by a broker or dealer that relies on a publicly available determination by a qualified interdealer quotation system or registered national securities association that the requirements of an exception provided in paragraph (f)(1), (f)(3)(i), (f)(4), or (f)(5) of this section are met; *Provided, however*, That any qualified interdealer quotation system or registered national securities association that makes a publicly available determination that the requirements of the exception provided in paragraph (f)(3)(i) of this section are met must subsequently make a publicly available determination under paragraph (f)(3)(ii)(A) of this section, as applicable.

g. **Exemptive authority**. Upon written application or upon its own motion, the Commission may, conditionally or unconditionally, exempt by order any person, security, or transaction, or any class or classes of persons, securities, or transactions, from any provision or provisions of this section, to the extent that such exemption is necessary or appropriate in the public interest, and is consistent with the protection of investors.

Rule 15d-3 – Reports for Depositary Shares Registered on Form F-6

Annual and other reports are not required with respect to Depositary Shares registered on Form F-6. The exemption in this section does not apply to any deposited securities registered on any other form under the Securities Act of 1933.

Rule 15d-14 – Certification of Disclosure in Annual and Quarterly Reports

a. Each report, including transition reports, filed on Form 10-Q, Form 10-K, Form 20-F or Form 40-F under section 15(d) of the Act, other than a report filed by an Asset-Backed Issuer (as defined in paragraph (g) of this section), must include certifications in the form specified in the applicable exhibit filing requirements of such report and such certifications must be filed as an exhibit to such report. Each principal executive and principal financial officer of the issuer, or persons performing similar functions, at the time of filing of the report must sign a certification.

b. Each periodic report containing financial statements filed by an issuer pursuant to section 15(d) of the Act must be accompanied by the certifications required by Section 1350 of Chapter 63 of Title 18 of the United States Code and such certifications must be furnished as an exhibit to such report as specified in the applicable exhibit requirements for such report. Each principal executive and principal financial officer of the issuer (or equivalent thereof) must sign a certification. This requirement may be satisfied by a single certification signed by an issuer's principal executive and principal financial officers.

c. A person required to provide a certification specified in paragraph (a) or (b) of this section may not have the certification signed on his or her behalf pursuant to a power of attorney or other form of confirming authority.

* * *

Rule 15d-15 – Controls and Procedures

a. Every issuer that files reports under section 15(d) of the Act, other than an Asset-Backed Issuer (as defined in Rule 15d-14(g)), a small business investment company registered on Form N-5, or a unit investment trust as defined in section 4(2) of the Investment Company Act of 1940, must maintain disclosure controls and procedures (as defined in paragraph (e) of this section) and internal control over financial reporting (as defined in paragraph (f) of this section).

b. Each such issuer's management must evaluate, with the participation of the issuer's principal executive and principal financial officers, or persons performing similar functions, the effectiveness of the issuer's disclosure controls and procedures, as of the end of each fiscal quarter, except that management must perform this evaluation:
    1. In the case of a foreign private issuer (as defined in Rule 3b-4) as of the end of each fiscal year; and

2.   In the case of an investment company registered under section 8 of the Investment Company Act of 1940, within the 90-day period prior to the filing date of each report requiring certification under Investment Company Act Rule 30a-2.

c.   The management of each such issuer, that either had been required to file an annual report pursuant to section 13(a) or 15(d) of the Act for the prior fiscal year or previously had filed an annual report with the Commission for the prior fiscal year, other than an investment company registered under section 8 of the Investment Company Act of 1940, must evaluate, with the participation of the issuer's principal executive and principal financial officers, or persons performing similar functions, the effectiveness, as of the end of each fiscal year, of the issuer's internal control over financial reporting. The framework on which management's evaluation of the issuer's internal control over financial reporting is based must be a suitable, recognized control framework that is established by a body or group that has followed due-process procedures, including the broad distribution of the framework for public comment. Although there are many different ways to conduct an evaluation of the effectiveness of internal control over financial reporting to meet the requirements of this paragraph, an evaluation that is conducted in accordance with the interpretive guidance issued by the Commission in Release No. 34-55929 will satisfy the evaluation required by this paragraph.

d.   The management of each such issuer, other than an investment company registered under section 8 of the Investment Company Act of 1940, must evaluate, with the participation of the issuer's principal executive and principal financial officers, or persons performing similar functions, any change in the issuer's internal control over financial reporting, that occurred during each of the issuer's fiscal quarters, or fiscal year in the case of a foreign private issuer, that has materially affected, or is reasonably likely to materially affect, the issuer's internal control over financial reporting.

e.   For purposes of this section, the term *disclosure controls and procedures* means controls and other procedures of an issuer that are designed to ensure that information required to be disclosed by the issuer in the reports that it files or submits under the Act is recorded, processed, summarized and reported, within the time periods specified in the Commission's rules and forms. Disclosure controls and procedures include, without limitation, controls and procedures designed to ensure that information required to be disclosed by an issuer in the reports that it files or submits under the Act is accumulated and communicated to the issuer's management, including its principal executive and principal financial officers, or persons performing similar functions, as appropriate to allow timely decisions regarding required disclosure.

f.   The term *internal control over financial reporting* is defined as a process designed by, or under the supervision of, the issuer's principal executive and principal financial officers, or persons performing similar functions, and effected by the issuer's board of directors, management and other personnel, to provide reasonable assurance regarding the reliability of financial reporting and the preparation of financial statements for external purposes in accordance with generally accepted accounting principles and includes those policies and procedures that:

1.   Pertain to the maintenance of records that in reasonable detail accurately and fairly reflect the transactions and dispositions of the assets of the issuer;

2.   Provide reasonable assurance that transactions are recorded as necessary to permit preparation of financial statements in accordance with generally accepted accounting principles, and that receipts and expenditures of the issuer are being made only in accordance with authorizations of management and directors of the issuer; and

3.   Provide reasonable assurance regarding prevention or timely detection of unauthorized acquisition, use or disposition of the issuer's assets that could have a material effect on the financial statements.

Rule 16a-1 – Definitions of Terms

Terms defined in this rule shall apply solely to section 16 of the Act and the rules thereunder. These terms shall not be limited to section 16(a) of the Act but also shall apply to all other subsections under section 16 of the Act.

    a.   The term **beneficial owner** shall have the following applications:

        1.   Solely for purposes of determining whether a person is a beneficial owner of more than ten percent of any class of equity securities registered pursuant to section 12 of the Act, the term "beneficial owner" shall mean any person who is deemed a beneficial owner pursuant to section 13(d) of the Act and the rules thereunder; *provided, however,* that the following institutions or persons shall not be deemed the beneficial owner of securities of such class held for the benefit of third parties or in customer or fiduciary accounts in the ordinary course of business (or in the case of an employee benefit plan specified in paragraph (a)(1)(vi) of this section, of securities of such class allocated to plan participants where participants have voting power) as long as such shares are acquired by such institutions or persons without the purpose or effect of changing or influencing control of the issuer or engaging in any arrangement subject to Rule 13d-3(b):

          i.   A broker or dealer registered under section 15 of the Act;

          ii.   A bank as defined in section 3(a)(6) of the Act;

          iii.   An insurance company as defined in section 3(a)(19) of the Act;

          iv.   An investment company registered under section 8 of the Investment Company Act of 1940;

          v.   Any person registered as an investment adviser under Section 203 of the Investment Advisers Act of 1940 or under the laws of any state;

          vi.   An employee benefit plan as defined in Section 3(3) of the Employee Retirement Income Security Act of 1974 ("ERISA") that is subject to the provisions of ERISA, or any such plan that is not subject to ERISA that is maintained primarily for the benefit of the employees of a state or local government or instrumentality, or an endowment fund;

vii.   A parent holding company or control person, provided the aggregate amount held directly by the parent or control person, and directly and indirectly by their subsidiaries or affiliates that are not persons specified in paragraphs (a)(1)(i) through (ix), does not exceed one percent of the securities of the subject class;

viii.   A savings association as defined in Section 3(b) of the Federal Deposit Insurance Act;

ix.   A church plan that is excluded from the definition of an investment company under section 3(c)(14) of the Investment Company Act of 1940; and

x.   A group, provided that all the members are persons specified in Rule 16a-1(a)(1)(i) through (ix).

xi.   A group, provided that all the members are persons specified in Rule 16a-1(a)(1) (i) through (vii).

Note to paragraph (a). Pursuant to this section, a person deemed a beneficial owner of more than ten percent of any class of equity securities registered under section 12 of the Act would file a Form 3, but the securities holdings disclosed on Form 3, and changes in beneficial ownership reported on subsequent Forms 4 or 5, would be determined by the definition of "beneficial owner" in paragraph (a)(2) of this section.

2.   Other than for purposes of determining whether a person is a beneficial owner of more than ten percent of any class of equity securities registered under Section 12 of the Act, the term *beneficial owner* shall mean any person who, directly or indirectly, through any contract, arrangement, understanding, relationship or otherwise, has or shares a direct or indirect pecuniary interest in the equity securities, subject to the following:

i.   The term *pecuniary interest* in any class of equity securities shall mean the opportunity, directly or indirectly, to profit or share in any profit derived from a transaction in the subject securities.

ii.   The term *indirect pecuniary interest* in any class of equity securities shall include, but not be limited to:

A.   Securities held by members of a person's immediate family sharing the same household; *provided, however*, that the presumption of such beneficial ownership may be rebutted; *see also* Rule 16a-1(a)(4);

B.   A general partner's proportionate interest in the portfolio securities held by a general or limited partnership. The general partner's proportionate interest, as evidenced by the partnership agreement in effect at the time of the transaction and the partnership's most recent financial statements, shall be the greater of:

1.   The general partner's share of the partnership's profits, including profits attributed to any limited partnership interests held by the general partner and any other interests in profits that arise from the purchase and sale of the partnership's portfolio securities; or

      2.   The general partner's share of the partnership capital account, including the share attributable to any limited partnership interest held by the general partner.

   C.   A performance-related fee, other than an asset-based fee, received by any broker, dealer, bank, insurance company, investment company, investment adviser, investment manager, trustee or person or entity performing a similar function; *provided, however,* that no pecuniary interest shall be present where:

      1.   The performance-related fee, regardless of when payable, is calculated based upon net capital gains and/or net capital appreciation generated from the portfolio or from the fiduciary's overall performance over a period of one year or more; and

      2.   Equity securities of the issuer do not account for more than ten percent of the market value of the portfolio. A right to a nonperformance-related fee alone shall not represent a pecuniary interest in the securities;

   D.   A person's right to dividends that is separated or separable from the underlying securities. Otherwise, a right to dividends alone shall not represent a pecuniary interest in the securities;

   E.   A person's interest in securities held by a trust, as specified in Rule 16a-8(b); and

   F.   A person's right to acquire equity securities through the exercise or conversion of any derivative security, whether or not presently exercisable.

   iii.   A shareholder shall not be deemed to have a pecuniary interest in the portfolio securities held by a corporation or similar entity in which the person owns securities if the shareholder is not a controlling shareholder of the entity and does not have or share investment control over the entity's portfolio.

3.   Where more than one person subject to section 16 of the Act is deemed to be a beneficial owner of the same equity securities, all such persons must report as beneficial owners of the securities, either separately or jointly, as provided in Rule 16a-3(j). In such cases, the amount of short-swing profit recoverable shall not be increased above the amount recoverable if there were only one beneficial owner.

4.   Any person filing a statement pursuant to section 16(a) of the Act may state that the filing shall not be deemed an admission that such person is, for purposes of section 16 of the Act or otherwise, the beneficial owner of any equity securities covered by the statement.

5.   The following interests are deemed not to confer beneficial ownership for purposes of section 16 of the Act:

   i.   Interests in portfolio securities held by any investment company registered under the Investment Company Act of 1940; and

   ii.   Interests in securities comprising part of a broad-based, publicly traded market basket or index of stocks, approved for trading by the appropriate federal governmental authority.

b. The term **call equivalent position** shall mean a derivative security position that increases in value as the value of the underlying equity increases, including, but not limited to, a long convertible security, a long call option, and a short put option position.

c. The term **derivative securities** shall mean any option, warrant, convertible security, stock appreciation right, or similar right with an exercise or conversion privilege at a price related to an equity security, or similar securities with a value derived from the value of an equity security, but shall not include:
    1. Rights of a pledgee of securities to sell the pledged securities;
    2. Rights of all holders of a class of securities of an issuer to receive securities pro rata, or obligations to dispose of securities, as a result of a merger, exchange offer, or consolidation involving the issuer of the securities;
    3. Rights or obligations to surrender a security, or have a security withheld, upon the receipt or exercise of a derivative security or the receipt or vesting of equity securities, in order to satisfy the exercise price or the tax withholding consequences of receipt, exercise or vesting;
    4. Interests in broad-based index options, broad-based index futures, and broad-based publicly traded market baskets of stocks approved for trading by the appropriate federal governmental authority;
    5. Interests or rights to participate in employee benefit plans of the issuer;
    6. Rights with an exercise or conversion privilege at a price that is not fixed; or
    7. Options granted to an underwriter in a registered public offering for the purpose of satisfying over-allotments in such offering.

d. The term **equity security of such issuer** shall mean any equity security or derivative security relating to an issuer, whether or not issued by that issuer.

e. The term **immediate family** shall mean any child, stepchild, grandchild, parent, stepparent, grandparent, spouse, sibling, mother-in-law, father-in-law, son-in-law, daughter-in-law, brother-in-law, or sister-in-law, and shall include adoptive relationships.

f. The term **officer** shall mean an issuer's president, principal financial officer, principal accounting officer (or, if there is no such accounting officer, the controller), any vice-president of the issuer in charge of a principal business unit, division or function (such as sales, administration or finance), any other officer who performs a policy-making function, or any other person who performs similar policy-making functions for the issuer. Officers of the issuer's parent(s) or subsidiaries shall be deemed officers of the issuer if they perform such policy-making functions for the issuer. In addition, when the issuer is a limited partnership, officers or employees of the general partner(s) who perform policy-making functions for the limited partnership are deemed officers of the limited partnership. When the issuer is a trust, officers or employees of the trustee(s) who perform policy-making functions for the trust are deemed officers of the trust.

Note: "Policy-making function" is not intended to include policy-making functions that are not significant. If pursuant to Item 401(b) of Regulation S-K the issuer identifies a person as an "executive officer," it is presumed that the Board of Directors has made that judgment and that the persons so identified are the officers for purposes of Section 16 of the Act, as are such other persons enumerated in this paragraph (f) but not in Item 401(b).

g. The term **portfolio securities** shall mean all securities owned by an entity, other than securities issued by the entity.

h. The term **put equivalent position** shall mean a derivative security position that increases in value as the value of the underlying equity decreases, including, but not limited to, a long put option and a short call option position.

Rule 16a-2 – Persons and Transactions Subject to Section 16

Any person who is the beneficial owner, directly or indirectly, of more than ten percent of any class of equity securities ("ten percent beneficial owner") registered pursuant to section 12 of the Act, any director or officer of the issuer of such securities, and any person specified in section 30(h) of the Investment Company Act of 1940, including any person specified in Rule 16a-8, shall be subject to the provisions of section 16 of the Act. The rules under section 16 apply to any class of equity securities of an issuer whether or not registered under section 12 of the Act. The rules under section 16 of the Act also apply to non-equity securities as provided by the Investment Company Act of 1940. With respect to transactions by persons subject to section 16 of the Act:

a. A transaction(s) carried out by a director or officer in the six months prior to the director or officer becoming subject to section 16 of the Act shall be subject to section 16 of the Act and reported on the first required Form 4 only if the transaction(s) occurred within six months of the transaction giving rise to the Form 4 filing obligation and the director or officer became subject to section 16 of the Act solely as a result of the issuer registering a class of equity securities pursuant to section 12 of the Act.

b. A transaction(s) following the cessation of director or officer status shall be subject to section 16 of the Act only if :
    1. Executed within a period of less than six months of an opposite transaction subject to section 16(b) of the Act that occurred while that person was a director or officer.
    2. Not otherwise exempted form section 16(b) of the Act pursuant to the provisions of this chapter.
    Note to Paragraph (b): For the purposes of this paragraph, an acquisition and a disposition each shall be an opposite transaction with respect to the other.

c. The transaction that results in a person becoming a ten percent beneficial owner is not subject to section 16 of the Act unless the person otherwise is subject to section 16 of the Act. A ten percent beneficial owner not otherwise subject to section 16 of the Act must report only those transactions conducted while the beneficial owner of more than ten percent of a class of equity securities of the issuer registered pursuant to section 12 of the Act.

d.

    1.   Transactions by a person or entity shall be exempt from the provisions of section 16 of the Act for the 12 months following appointment and qualification, to the extent such person or entity is acting as:

        i.   Executor or administrator of the estate of a decedent;

        ii.   Guardian or member of a committee for an incompetent;

        iii.   Receiver, trustee in bankruptcy, assignee for the benefit of creditors, conservator, liquidating agent, or other similar person duly authorized by law to administer the estate or assets of another person; or

        iv.   Fiduciary in a similar capacity.

    2.   Transactions by such person or entity acting in a capacity specified in paragraph (d)(1) of this section after the period specified in that paragraph shall be subject to section 16 of the Act only where the estate, trust or other entity is a beneficial owner of more than ten percent of any class of equity security registered pursuant to section 12 of the Act.

Rule 16a-3 – Reporting Transactions and Holdings

a.   Initial statements of beneficial ownership of equity securities required by section 16(a) of the Act shall be filed on Form 3. Statements of changes in beneficial ownership required by that section shall be filed on Form 4. Annual statements shall be filed on Form 5. At the election of the reporting person, any transaction required to be reported on Form 5 may be reported on an earlier filed Form 4. All such statements shall be prepared and filed in accordance with the requirements of the applicable form.

b.   A person filing statements pursuant to section 16(a) of the Act with respect to any class of equity securities registered pursuant to section 12 of the Act need not file an additional statement on Form 3:

    1.   When an additional class of equity securities of the same issuer becomes registered pursuant to section 12 of the Act; or

    2.   When such person assumes a different or an additional relationship to the same issuer (for example, when an officer becomes a director).

c.   Any issuer that has equity securities listed on more than one national securities exchange may designate one exchange as the only exchange with which reports pursuant to section 16(a) of the Act need be filed. Such designation shall be made in writing and shall be filed with the Commission and with each national securities exchange on which any equity security of the issuer is listed at the time of such election. The reporting person's obligation to file reports with each national securities exchange on which any equity security of the issuer is listed shall be satisfied by filing with the exchange so designated.

d. Any person required to file a statement with respect to securities of a single issuer under both section 16(a) of the Act and section 30(h) of the Investment Company Act of 1940 may file a single statement containing the required information, which will be deemed to be filed under both Acts.

e. Any person required to file a statement under section 16(a) of the Act shall, not later than the time the statement is transmitted for filing with the Commission, send or deliver a duplicate to the person designated by the issuer to receive such statements, or, in the absence of such a designation, to the issuer's corporate secretary or person performing equivalent functions.

f.

 1. A Form 5 shall be filed by every person who at any time during the issuer's fiscal year was subject to section 16 of the Act with respect to such issuer, except as provided in paragraph (f)(2) of this section. The Form shall be filed within 45 days after the issuer's fiscal year end, and shall disclose the following holdings and transactions not reported previously on Forms 3, 4 or 5:

  i. All transactions during the most recent fiscal year that were exempt from Section 16(b) of the Act, except:

   A. Exercises and conversions of derivative securities exempt under either Rule 16b-3 or Rule 16b-6(b), and any transaction exempt under Rule 16b-3(d), Rule 16b-3(e), or Rule 16b-3(f) (these are required to be reported on Form 4);

   B. Transactions exempt from Section 16(b) of the Act pursuant to Rule 16b-3(c) which shall be exempt from Section 16(a) of the Act; and

   C. Transactions exempt from Section 16(a) of the Act pursuant to another rule;

  ii. Transactions that constituted small acquisitions pursuant to Rule 16a-6(a);

  iii. All holdings and transactions that should have been reported during the most recent fiscal year, but were not; and

  iv. With respect to the first Form 5 requirement for a reporting person, all holdings and transactions that should have been reported in each of the issuer's last two fiscal years but were not, based on the reporting person's reasonable belief in good faith in the completeness and accuracy of the information.

 2. Notwithstanding the above, no Form 5 shall be required where all transactions otherwise required to be reported on the Form 5 have been reported before the due date of the Form 5.

Note: Persons no longer subject to section 16 of the Act, but who were subject to the Section at any time during the issuer's fiscal year, must file a Form 5 unless paragraph (f)(2) is satisfied. *See also* Rule 16a-2(b) regarding the reporting obligations of persons ceasing to be officers or directors.

g.

    1.   A Form 4 must be filed to report: All transactions not exempt from section 16(b) of the Act; All transactions exempt from section 16(b) of the Act pursuant to Rule 16b-3(d), Rule 16b-3(e), or Rule 16b-3(f); and all exercises and conversions of derivative securities, regardless of whether exempt from section 16(b) of the Act. Form 4 must be filed before the end of the second business day following the day on which the subject transaction has been executed.

    2.   Solely for purposes of section 16(a)(2)(C) of the Act and paragraph (g)(1) of this section, the date on which the executing broker, dealer or plan administrator notifies the reporting person of the execution of the transaction is deemed the date of execution for a transaction where the following conditions are satisfied:

        i.   the transaction is pursuant to a contract, instruction or written plan for the purchase or sale of equity securities of the issuer (as defined in Rule 16a-1(d)) that satisfies the affirmative defense conditions of Rule 10b5-1(c); and

        ii. the reporting person does not select the date of execution.

    3.   Solely for purposes of section 16(a)(2)(C) of the Act and paragraph (g)(1) of this section, the date on which the plan administrator notifies the reporting person that the transaction has been executed is deemed the date of execution for a discretionary transaction (as defined in Rule 16b-3(b)(1)) for which the reporting person does not select the date of execution.

    4.   In the case of the transactions described in paragraphs (g)(2) and (g)(3) of this section, if the notification date is later than the third business day following the trade date of the transaction, the date of execution is deemed to be the third business day following the trade date of the transaction.

    5.   At the option of the reporting person, transactions that are reportable on Form 5 may be reported on Form 4, so long as the Form 4 is filed no later than the due date of the Form 5 on which the transaction is otherwise required to be reported.

h.   The date of filing with the Commission shall be the date of receipt by the Commission.

i.   Duplicated or facsimile versions of manual signatures of persons required to sign any document pursuant to Section 16 of the Act that is filed or submitted to the Commission under the Act shall be considered manual signatures for purposes of the Act and rules and regulations thereunder; provided that, the original signed document is retained by the filer for a period of five years and, upon request, the filer furnishes to the Commission or the staff the original manually signed document.

j.   Where more than one person subject to section 16 of the Act is deemed to be a beneficial owner of the same equity securities, all such persons must report as beneficial owners of the securities, either separately or jointly. Where persons in a group are deemed to be beneficial owners of equity securities pursuant to Rule 16a-1(a)(1) due to the aggregation of holdings, a single Form 3, 4 or 5 may be filed on behalf of all persons in the group. Joint and group filings must include all required information for each beneficial owner, and such filings must be signed by each beneficial owner, or on behalf of such owner by an authorized person.

k. Any issuer that maintains a corporate Web site shall post on that Web site by the end of the business day after filing any Form 3, 4, or 5 filed under section 16(a) of the Act as to the equity securities of that issuer. Each such form shall remain accessible on such issuer's Web site for at least a 12-month period. In the case of an issuer that is an investment company and that does not maintain its own Web site, if any of the issuer's investment adviser, sponsor, depositor, trustee, administrator, principal underwriter, or any affiliated person of the investment company maintains a Web site that includes the name of the issuer, the issuer shall comply with the posting requirements by posting the forms on one such Web site.

Rule 16a-4 – Derivative Securities

a. For purposes of section 16 of the Act, both derivative securities and the underlying securities to which they relate shall be deemed to be the same class of equity securities, except that the acquisition or disposition of any derivative security shall be separately reported.

b. The exercise or conversion of a call equivalent position shall be reported on Form 4 and be treated for reporting purposes as:
    1. A purchase of the underlying security; and
    2. A closing of the derivative security position.

c. The exercise or conversion of a put equivalent position shall be reported on Form 4 and shall be treated for reporting purposes as:
    1. A sale of the underlying security; and
    2. A closing of the derivative security position.

d. The disposition or closing of a long derivative security position, as a result of cancellation or expiration, shall be exempt from section 16(a) of the Act if exempt from section 16(b) of the Act pursuant to Rule .

Note: Under Rule 16b-6(b), a purchase or sale resulting from an exercise or conversion of a derivative security generally is exempt from section 16(b) of the Act.

Rule 16b-3 – Transactions Between an Issuer and its Officers or Directors

Transactions between an issuer and its officers or directors.

a. **General**. A transaction between the issuer (including an employee benefit plan sponsored by the issuer) and an officer or director of the issuer that involves issuer equity securities shall be exempt from Section 16(b) of the Act if the transaction satisfies the applicable conditions set forth in this section.

b. **Definitions**.
1. A **Discretionary Transaction** shall mean a transaction pursuant to an employee benefit plan that:
    i.   Is at the volition of a plan participant;
    ii. Is not made in connection with the participant's death, disability, retirement or termination of employment;
    iii. Is not required to be made available to a plan participant pursuant to a provision of the Internal Revenue Code; and
    iv. Results in either an intra-plan transfer involving an issuer equity securities fund, or a cash distribution funded by a volitional disposition of an issuer equity security.
2. An **Excess Benefit Plan** shall mean an employee benefit plan that is operated in conjunction with a Qualified Plan, and provides only the benefits or contributions that would be provided under a Qualified Plan but for any benefit or contribution limitations set forth in the Internal Revenue Code of 1986, or any successor provisions thereof.
    i.   A **Non-Employee Director** shall mean a director who:
        A. Is not currently an officer (as defined in Rule 16a-1(f)) of the issuer or a parent or subsidiary of the issuer, or otherwise currently employed by the issuer or a parent or subsidiary of the issuer;
        B. Does not receive compensation, either directly or indirectly, from the issuer or a parent or subsidiary of the issuer, for services rendered as a consultant or in any capacity other than as a director, except for an amount that does not exceed the dollar amount for which disclosure would be required pursuant to Item 404(a) of Regulation S-K.
        C. Does not possess an interest in any other transaction for which disclosure would be required pursuant to Item 404(a) of Regulation S-K; and
        D. Is not engaged in a business relationship for which disclosure would be required pursuant to Item 404(b) of Regulation S-K.
    ii. Notwithstanding paragraph (b)(3)(i) of this section, a Non-Employee Director of a closed-end investment company shall mean a director who is not an interested person of the issuer, as that term is defined in Section 2(a)(19) of the Investment Company Act of 1940.
3. A **Qualified Plan** shall mean an employee benefit plan that satisfies the coverage and participation requirements of Sections 410 and 401(a)(26) of the Internal Revenue Code of 1986, or any successor provisions thereof.
4. A **Stock Purchase Plan** shall mean an employee benefit plan that satisfies the coverage and participation requirements of Sections 423(b)(3) and 423(b)(5), or Section 410, of the Internal Revenue Code of 1986, or any successor provisions thereof.

c.   **Tax-conditioned plans**. Any transaction (other than a Discretionary Transaction) pursuant to a Qualified Plan, an Excess Benefit Plan, or a Stock Purchase Plan shall be exempt without condition.

d.   **Acquisitions from the issuer**. Any transaction, other than a Discretionary Transaction, involving an acquisition from the issuer (including without limitation a grant or award), whether or not intended for a compensatory or other particular purpose, shall be exempt if:
1.   The transaction is approved by the board of directors of the issuer, or a committee of the board of directors that is composed solely of two or more Non-Employee Directors;
2.   The transaction is approved or ratified, in compliance with Section 14 of the Act, by either: the affirmative votes of the holders of a majority of the securities of the issuer present, or represented, and entitled to vote at a meeting duly held in accordance with the applicable laws of the state or other jurisdiction in which the issuer is incorporated; or the written consent of the holders of a majority of the securities of the issuer entitled to vote; provided that such ratification occurs no later than the date of the next annual meeting of shareholders; or
3.   The issuer equity securities so acquired are held by the officer or director for a period of six months following the date of such acquisition, provided that this condition shall be satisfied with respect to a derivative security if at least six months elapse from the date of acquisition of the derivative security to the date of disposition of the derivative security (other than upon exercises or conversion) or its underlying equity security.

e.   **Dispositions to the issuer**. Any transaction, other than a Discretionary Transaction, involving the disposition to the issuer of issuer equity securities, whether or not intended for a compensatory or other particular purpose, shall be exempt, provided that the terms of such disposition are approved in advance in the manner prescribed by either paragraph (d)(1) or (d)(2) of this section.

f.   **Discretionary Transactions**. A Discretionary Transaction shall be exempt only if effected pursuant to an election made at least six months following the date of the most recent election, with respect to any plan of the issuer, that effected a Discretionary Transaction that was:
1.   An acquisition, if the transaction to be exempted would be a disposition; or
2.   A disposition, if the transaction to be exempted would be an acquisition.

Notes to Rule 16b-3:
1.   The exercise or conversion of a derivative security that does not satisfy the conditions of this section is eligible for exemption from Section 16(b) of the Act to the extent that the conditions of Rule 16b-6(b) are satisfied.
2.   Section 16(a) reporting requirements applicable to transactions exempt pursuant to this section are set forth in Rule 16a-3(f) and (g) and Rule 16a-4.
3.   The approval conditions of paragraphs (d)(1), (d)(2) and (e) of this section require the approval of each specific transaction, and are not satisfied by approval of a plan in its entirety except for the approval of a plan pursuant to which the terms and conditions of each transaction are fixed in advance, such as a formula plan.

Where the terms of a subsequent transaction (such as the exercise price of an option, or the provision of an exercise or tax with-holding right) are provided for in a transaction as initially approved pursuant to paragraphs (d)(1), (d)(2) or (e), such subsequent transaction shall not require further specific approval.

4. For purposes of determining a director's status under those portions of paragraph (b)(3)(i) that reference Item 404(a) of this chapter, an issuer may rely on the disclosure provided under Item 404(a) of this chapter for the issuer's most recent fiscal year contained in the most recent filing in which disclosure required under Item 404(a) is presented. Where a transaction disclosed in that filing was terminated before the director's proposed service as a Non-Employee Director, that transaction will not bar such service. The issuer must believe in good faith that any current or contemplated transaction in which the director participates will not be required to be disclosed under Item 404(a) of this chapter, based on information readily available to the issuer and the director at the time such director proposes to act as a Non-Employee Director. At such time as the issuer believes in good faith, based on readily available information, that a current or contemplated transaction with a director will be required to be disclosed under Item 404(a) in a future filing, the director no longer is eligible to serve as a Non-Employee Director; provided, however, that this determination does not result in retroactive loss of a Rule 16b-3 exemption for a transaction previously approved by the director while serving as a Non-Employee Director consistent with this note. In making the determinations specified in this Note, the issuer may rely on information it obtains from the director, for example, pursuant to a response to an inquiry.

Rule 16b-6 – Derivative Securities

a. The establishment of or increase in a call equivalent position or liquidation of or decrease in a put equivalent position shall be deemed a purchase of the underlying security for purposes of Section 16(b) of the Act, and the establishment of or increase in a put equivalent position or liquidation of or decrease in a call equivalent position shall be deemed a sale of the underlying securities for purposes of Section 16(b) of the Act; *Provided, however,* That if the increase or decrease occurs as a result of the fixing of the exercise price of a right initially issued without a fixed price, where the date the price is fixed is not known in advance and is outside the control of the recipient, the increase or decrease shall be exempt from Section 16(b) of the Act with respect to any offsetting transaction within the six months prior to the date the price is fixed.

b. The closing of a derivative security position as a result of its exercise or conversion shall be exempt from the operation of Section 16(b) of the Act, and the acquisition of underlying securities at a fixed exercise price due to the exercise or conversion of a call equivalent position or the disposition of underlying securities at a fixed exercise price due to the exercise of a put equivalent position shall be exempt from the operation of Section 16(b) of the Act: *Provided, however,* That the acquisition of underlying securities from the exercise of an out-of-the-money option, warrant, or right shall not be exempt unless the exercise is necessary to comport with the sequential exercise provisions of the Internal Revenue Code.

    c. In determining the short-swing profit recoverable pursuant to Section 16(b) of the Act from transactions involving the purchase and sale or sale and purchase of derivative and other securities, the following rules apply:

        1. Short-swing profits in transactions involving the purchase and sale or sale and purchase of derivative securities that have identical characteristics (*e.g.*, purchases and sales of call options of the same strike price and expiration date, or purchases and sales of the same series of convertible debentures) shall be measured by the actual prices paid or received in the short-swing transactions.

        2. Short-swing profits in transactions involving the purchase and sale or sale and purchase of derivative securities having different characteristics but related to the same underlying security (*e.g.,* the purchase of a call option and the sale of a convertible debenture) or derivative securities and underlying securities shall not exceed the difference in price of the underlying security on the date of purchase or sale and the date of sale or purchase. Such profits may be measured by calculating the short-swing profits that would have been realized had the subject transactions involved purchases and sales solely of the derivative security that was purchased or solely of the derivative security that was sold, valued as of the time of the matching purchase or sale, and calculated for the lesser of the number of underlying securities actually purchased or sold.

    d. Upon cancellation or expiration of an option within six months of the writing of the option, any profit derived from writing the option shall be recoverable under Section 16(b) of the Act. The profit shall not exceed the premium received for writing the option. The disposition or closing of a long derivative security position, as a result of cancellation or expiration, shall be exempt from Section 16(b) of the Act where no value is received from the cancellation or expiration.

Rule 21F-1 – General

Section 21F of the Securities Exchange Act of 1934, entitled "Securities Whistleblower Incentives and Protection," requires the Securities and Exchange Commission to pay awards, subject to certain limitations and conditions, to whistleblowers who provide the Commission with original information about violations of the federal securities laws. These rules describe the whistleblower program that the Commission has established to implement the provisions of Section 21F, and explain the procedures you will need to follow in order to be eligible for an award. You should read these procedures carefully because the failure to take certain required steps within the time frames described in these rules may disqualify you from receiving an award for which you otherwise may be eligible. Unless expressly provided for in these rules, no person is authorized to make any offer or promise, or otherwise to bind the Commission with respect to the payment of any award or the amount thereof. The Securities and Exchange Commission's Office of the Whistleblower administers our whistleblower program. Questions about the program or these rules should be directed to the SEC Office of the Whistleblower, 100 F Street, N.E., Washington, DC 20549-5631.

Rule 21F-2 – Whistleblower Status and Retaliation Protection

a. **Whistleblower status.**

    1.   You are a whistleblower for purposes of Section 21F of the Exchange Act as of the time that, alone or jointly with others, you provide the Commission with information in writing that relates to a possible violation of the federal securities laws (including any law, rule, or regulation subject to the jurisdiction of the Commission) that has occurred, is ongoing, or is about to occur.

    2.   A whistleblower must be an individual. A company or other entity is not eligible to be a whistleblower.

b. **Award eligibility.** To be eligible for an award under Section 21F(b) of the Exchange Act based on any information you provide that relates to a possible violation of the federal securities laws, you must comply with the procedures and the conditions described in Rules 21F-4, 21F-8, and 21F-9. You should carefully review those rules before you submit any information that you may later wish to rely upon to claim an award.

c. **Confidentiality protections.** To qualify for the confidentiality protections afforded by Section 21F(h)(2) of the Exchange Act based on any information you provide that relates to a possible violation of the federal securities laws, you must comply with the procedures and the conditions described in Rule 21F-9(a).

d. **Retaliation protections.**

    1.   To qualify for the retaliation protections afforded by Section 21F(h)(1) of the Exchange Act, you must satisfy all of the following criteria:

        i.   You must qualify as a whistleblower under paragraph (a) of this section before experiencing the retaliation for which you seek redress;

        ii.   You must reasonably believe that the information you provide to the Commission under paragraph (a) of this section relates to a possible violation of the federal securities laws; and

        iii.   You must perform a lawful act that meets the following two criteria:

            A.   First, the lawful act must be performed in connection with any of the activities described in Section 21F(h)(1)(A)(i) through (iii) of the Exchange Act; and

            B.   Second, the lawful act must relate to the subject matter of your submission to the Commission under paragraph (a) of this section.

    2.   To receive retaliation protection for a lawful act described in paragraph (d)(1)(iii) of this section, you do not need to qualify as a whistleblower under paragraph (a) of this section before performing the lawful act, but you must qualify as a whistleblower under paragraph (a) of this section before experiencing retaliation for the lawful act.

    3.   To qualify for retaliation protection, you do not need to satisfy the procedures and conditions for award eligibility in Rules 21F-4, 21F-8, and 21F-9.

4.   Section 21F(h)(1) of the Exchange Act. including any rules promulgated thereunder, shall be enforceable in an action or proceeding brought by the Commission.

Rule 21F-3 – Payment of Awards

a.   **Commission actions**: Subject to the eligibility requirements described in Rules 21F-2, 21F-8, and F-16 of this chapter, the Commission will pay an award or awards to one or more whistleblowers who:
1.   Voluntarily provide the Commission
2.   With original information
3.   That leads to the successful enforcement by the Commission of a federal court or administrative action
4.   In which the Commission obtains monetary sanctions totaling more than $1,000,000.
Note to paragraph (a): The terms voluntarily, original information, leads to successful enforcement, action, and monetary sanctions are defined in Rule 21F-4 of this chapter.

b.   **Related actions**: The Commission will also pay an award based on amounts collected in certain related actions.
1.   A related action is a judicial or administrative action that is brought by one of the governmental entities listed in paragraphs (b)(1)(i) through (iii) of this section or a self-regulatory organization as specified in paragraph (b)(1)(iv) of this section (collectively "governmental/SRO authority"), that yields monetary sanctions, and that is based upon information that either the whistleblower provided directly to a governmental/SRO entity or the Commission itself passed along to the governmental/SRO entity pursuant to the Commission's procedures for sharing information, and which is the same original information that the whistleblower voluntarily provided to the Commission and that led the Commission to obtain monetary sanctions totaling more than $1,000,000.
      i.   The Attorney General of the United States;
      ii.   An appropriate regulatory authority (as defined in Rule 21F-4);
      iii. A state attorney general in a criminal case; or
      iv.   A self-regulatory organization (as defined in Rule 21F-4).
2.   In order for the Commission to make an award in connection with a related action, the Commission must determine that the same original information that the whistleblower gave to the Commission also led to the successful enforcement of the related action under the same criteria described in these rules for awards made in connection with Commission actions. The Commission may seek assistance and confirmation from the authority bringing the related action in making this determination. The Commission will deny an award in connection with the related action if:
      i.   The Commission determines that the criteria for an award are not satisfied; or
      ii.   The Commission is unable to make a determination because the Office of the Whistleblower could not obtain sufficient and reliable

information that could be used as the basis for an award determination pursuant to Rule 21F-12(a) of this chapter. Additional procedures apply to the payment of awards in related actions. These procedures are described in Rules 21F-11 and 21F-14 of this chapter.

3. The following provision shall apply where a claimant's application for a potential related action may also involve a potential recovery from another whistleblower award program for that same action.

    i.   Notwithstanding paragraph (b)(1) of this section, if a judicial or administrative action is subject to a separate monetary award program established by the Federal Government, a state government, or a self-regulatory organization, the Commission will deem the action a related action only if the Commission finds (based on the facts and circumstances of the action) that its whistleblower program has the more direct or relevant connection to the action.

    ii. In determining whether a potential related action has a more direct or relevant connection to the Commission's whistleblower program than another award program, the Commission will consider the nature, scope, and impact of the misconduct charged in the potential related action, and its relationship to the Federal securities laws. This inquiry may include consideration of, among other things:

        A. The relative extent to which the misconduct charged in the potential related action implicates the public policy interests underlying the Federal securities laws (such as investor protection) rather than other law-enforcement or regulatory interests (such as tax collection or fraud against the Federal Government);

        B. The degree to which the monetary sanctions imposed in the potential related action are attributable to conduct that also underlies the Federal securities law violations that were the subject of the Commission's enforcement action; and

        C. Whether the potential related action involves state-law claims and the extent to which the state may have a whistleblower award program that potentially applies to that type of law-enforcement action.

    iii. If the Commission determines to deem the action a related action, the Commission will not make an award to you for the related action if you have already been granted an award by the governmental/SRO entity responsible for administering the other whistleblower award program. Further, if you were denied an award by the other award program, you will not be permitted to readjudicate any issues before the Commission that the governmental/SRO entity responsible for administering the other whistleblower award program resolved against you as part of the award denial. Additionally, if the Commission makes an award before an award determination is finalized by the governmental/SRO entity responsible for administering the other award program, the Commission shall condition its award on the meritorious whistleblower making a prompt, irrevocable waiver of any claim to an award from the other award program.

Rule 21F-4 – Other Definitions

a. **Voluntary submission of information.**
1. Your submission of information is made voluntarily within the meaning of Rules 21F-1 through 21F-17 of this chapter if you provide your submission before a request, inquiry, or demand that relates to the subject matter of your submission is directed to you or anyone representing you (such as an attorney):
   i. By the Commission;
   ii. In connection with an investigation, inspection, or examination by the Public Company Accounting Oversight Board, or any self-regulatory organization; or
   iii. In connection with an investigation by Congress, any other authority of the federal government, or a state Attorney General or securities regulatory authority.
2. If the Commission or any of these other authorities direct a request, inquiry, or demand as described in paragraph (1) of this section to you or your representative first, your submission will not be considered voluntary, and you will not be eligible for an award, even if your response is not compelled by subpoena or other applicable law. However, your submission of information to the Commission will be considered voluntary if you voluntarily provided the same information to one of the other authorities identified above prior to receiving a request, inquiry, or demand from the Commission.
3. In addition, your submission will not be considered voluntary if you are required to report your original information to the Commission as a result of a pre-existing legal duty, a contractual duty that is owed to the Commission or to one of the other authorities set forth in paragraph (1) of this section, or a duty that arises out of a judicial or administrative order.

b. **Original information.**
1. In order for your whistleblower submission to be considered original information, it must be:
   i. Derived from your independent knowledge or independent analysis;
   ii. Not already known to the Commission from any other source, unless you are the original source of the information;
   iii. Not exclusively derived from an allegation made in a judicial or administrative hearing, in a governmental report, hearing, audit, or investigation, or from the news media, unless you are a source of the information; and
   iv. Provided to the Commission for the first time after July 21, 2010 (the date of enactment of the *Dodd-Frank Wall Street Reform and Consumer Protection Act*).
2. Independent knowledge means factual information in your possession that is not derived from publicly available sources. You may gain independent knowledge from your experiences, communications and observations in your business or social interactions.

3. Independent analysis means your own analysis, whether done alone or in combination with others. Analysis means your examination and evaluation of information that may be publicly available, but which reveals information that is not generally known or available to the public.

4. The Commission will not consider information to be derived from your independent knowledge or independent analysis in any of the following circumstances:

    i.   If you obtained the information through a communication that was subject to the attorney-client privilege, unless disclosure of that information would otherwise be permitted by an attorney pursuant to Rule 205.3(d)(2) of this chapter, the applicable state attorney conduct rules, or otherwise;

    ii. If you obtained the information in connection with the legal representation of a client on whose behalf you or your employer or firm are providing services, and you seek to use the information to make a whistleblower submission for your own benefit, unless disclosure would otherwise be permitted by an attorney pursuant to Rule 205.3(d)(2) of this chapter, the applicable state attorney conduct rules, or otherwise; or

    iii. In circumstances not covered by paragraphs (b)(4)(i) or (b)(4)(ii) of this section, if you obtained the information because you were:

         A. An officer, director, trustee, or partner of an entity and another person informed you of allegations of misconduct, or you learned the information in connection with the entity's processes for identifying, reporting, and addressing possible violations of law;

         B. An employee whose principal duties involve compliance or internal audit responsibilities, or you were employed by or otherwise associated with a firm retained to perform compliance or internal audit functions for an entity;

         C. Employed by or otherwise associated with a firm retained to conduct an inquiry or investigation into possible violations of law; or

         D. An employee of, or other person associated with, a public accounting firm, if you obtained the information through the performance of an engagement required of an independent public accountant under the federal securities laws (other than an audit subject to Rule 21F-8(c)(4) of this chapter), and that information related to a violation by the engagement client or the client's directors, officers or other employees.

    iv. If you obtained the information by a means or in a manner that is determined by a United States court to violate applicable federal or state criminal law; or

    v.   **Exceptions.** Paragraph (b)(4)(iii) of this section shall not apply if:

         A. You have a reasonable basis to believe that disclosure of the information to the Commission is necessary to prevent the relevant entity from engaging in conduct that is likely to cause substantial injury to the financial interest or property of the entity or investors;

        B. You have a reasonable basis to believe that the relevant entity is engaging in conduct that will impede an investigation of the misconduct; or

        C. At least 120 days have elapsed since you provided the information to the relevant entity's audit committee, chief legal officer, chief compliance officer (or their equivalents), or your supervisor, or since you received the information, if you received it under circumstances indicating that the entity's audit committee, chief legal officer, chief compliance officer (or their equivalents), or your supervisor was already aware of the information.

    vi. If you obtained the information from a person who is subject to this section, unless the information is not excluded from that person's use pursuant to this section, or you are providing the Commission with information about possible violations involving that person.

5.   The Commission will consider you to be an original source of the same information that we obtain from another source if the information satisfies the definition of original information and the other source obtained the information from you or your representative. In order to be considered an original source of information that the Commission receives from Congress, any other authority of the federal government, a state Attorney General or securities regulatory authority, any self-regulatory organization, or the Public Company Accounting Oversight Board, you must have voluntarily given such authorities the information within the meaning of these rules. You must establish your status as the original source of information to the Commission's satisfaction. In determining whether you are the original source of information, the Commission may seek assistance and confirmation from one of the other authorities described above, or from another entity (including your employer), in the event that you claim to be the original source of information that an authority or another entity provided to the Commission.

6.   If the Commission already knows some information about a matter from other sources at the time you make your submission, and you are not an original source of that information under paragraph (b)(5) of this section, the Commission will consider you an original source of any information you provide that is derived from your independent knowledge or analysis and that materially adds to the information that the Commission already possesses.

7.   If you provide information to the Congress, any other authority of the federal government, a state Attorney General or securities regulatory authority, any self-regulatory organization, or the Public Company Accounting Oversight Board, or to an entity's internal whistleblower, legal, or compliance procedures for reporting allegations of possible violations of law, and you, within 120 days, submit the same information to the Commission pursuant to Rul 21F-9 of this chapter, as you must do in order for you to be eligible to be considered for an award, then, for purposes of evaluating your claim to an award under Rules 21F-10 and 21F-11 of this chapter, the Commission will consider that you provided information as of the date of your original disclosure, report or submission to one of these

other authorities or persons. You must establish the effective date of any prior disclosure, report, or submission, to the Commission's satisfaction. The Commission may seek assistance and confirmation from the other authority or person in making this determination.

c.   **Information that leads to successful enforcement.** The Commission will consider that you provided original information that led to the successful enforcement of a judicial or administrative action in any of the following circumstances:

1.   You gave the Commission original information that was sufficiently specific, credible, and timely to cause the staff to commence an examination, open an investigation, reopen an investigation that the Commission had closed, or to inquire concerning different conduct as part of a current examination or investigation, and the Commission brought a successful judicial or administrative action based in whole or in part on conduct that was the subject of your original information; or

2.   You gave the Commission original information about conduct that was already under examination or investigation by the Commission, the Congress, any other authority of the federal government, a state Attorney General or securities regulatory authority, any self-regulatory organization, or the PCAOB (except in cases where you were an original source of this information as defined in paragraph (b)(5) of this section), and your submission significantly contributed to the success of the action..

3.   You reported original information through an entity's internal whistleblower, legal, or compliance procedures for reporting allegations of possible violations of law before or at the same time you reported them to the Commission; the entity later provided your information to the Commission, or provided results of an audit or investigation initiated in whole or in part in response to information you reported to the entity; and the information the entity provided to the Commission satisfies either paragraph (c)(1) or (c)(2) of this section. Under this paragraph (c)(3), you must also submit the same information to the Commission in accordance with the procedures set forth in Rule 21F-9 within 120 days of providing it to the entity.

d.   An **action** generally means a single captioned judicial or administrative proceeding brought by the Commission. Notwithstanding the foregoing:

1.   For purposes of making an award under Rule 21F-10 of this chapter, the Commission will treat as a Commission action two or more administrative or judicial proceedings brought by the Commission if these proceedings arise out of the same nucleus of operative facts; or

2.   For purposes of determining the payment on an award under Rule 21F-14 of this chapter, the Commission will deem as part of the Commission action upon which the award was based any subsequent Commission proceeding that, individually, results in a monetary sanction of $1,000,000 or less, and that arises out of the same nucleus of operative facts.

3.   For purposes of making an award under Rules 21F-10 and 21F-11, the following will be deemed to be an administrative action and any money

required to be paid thereunder will be deemed a monetary sanction under §
Rule 21F-4(e):

i.   A non-prosecution agreement or deferred prosecution agreement
     entered into by the U.S. Department of Justice; or

ii. A similar settlement agreement entered into by the Commission
     outside of the context of a judicial or administrative proceeding to
     address violations of the securities laws.

e.   **Monetary sanctions** means:

1.   An order to pay money that results from a Commission action or related
     action and which is either:

     i.   Expressly designated as a penalty, disgorgement, or interest; or

     ii. Otherwise ordered as relief for the violations that are the subject of the
          covered action or related action; or

2.   Any money deposited into a disgorgement fund or other fund pursuant to
     section 308(b) of the Sarbanes-Oxley Act of 2002, as a result of such action
     or any settlement of such action.

f.   **Appropriate regulatory agency** means the Commission, the Comptroller of the
     Currency, the Board of Governors of the Federal Reserve System, the Federal
     Deposit Insurance Corporation, the Office of Thrift Supervision, and any other
     agencies that may be defined as appropriate regulatory agencies under Section
     3(a)(34) of the Exchange Act.

g.   **Appropriate regulatory authority** means an appropriate regulatory agency other
     than the Commission.

h.   **Self-regulatory organization** means any national securities exchange, registered
     securities association, registered clearing agency, the Municipal Securities
     Rulemaking Board, and any other organizations that may be defined as self-
     regulatory organizations under Section 3(a)(26) of the Exchange Act.

Rule 21F-5 – Amount of Award

a.   The determination of the amount of an award is in the discretion of the
     Commission.

b.   If all of the conditions are met for a whistleblower award in connection with a
     Commission action or a related action, the Commission will then decide the
     percentage amount of the award applying the criteria set forth in Rule 21F-6 of
     this chapter and pursuant to the procedures set forth in Rules 21F-10 and 21F-11
     of this chapter. The amount will be at least 10 percent and no more than 30 percent
     of the monetary sanctions that the Commission and the other authorities are able
     to collect. The percentage awarded in connection with a Commission action may
     differ from the percentage awarded in connection with a related action.

c.   If the Commission makes awards to more than one whistleblower in connection
     with the same action or related action, the Commission will determine an

individual percentage award for each whistleblower, but in no event will the total amount awarded to all whistleblowers in the aggregate be less than 10 percent or greater than 30 percent of the amount the Commission or the other authorities collect.

Rule 21F-15 – No Amnesty

The Securities Whistleblower Incentives and Protection provisions do not provide amnesty to individuals who provide information to the Commission. The fact that you may become a whistleblower and assist in Commission investigations and enforcement actions does not preclude the Commission from bringing an action against you based upon your own conduct in connection with violations of the federal securities laws. If such an action is determined to be appropriate, however, the Commission will take your cooperation into consideration in accordance with its Policy Statement Concerning Cooperation by Individuals in Investigations and Related Enforcement Actions (17 CFR § 202.12).

Rule 21F-17 – Staff Communications with Individuals Reporting Possible Securities Law Violations

a. No person may take any action to impede an individual from communicating directly with the Commission staff about a possible securities law violation, including enforcing, or threatening to enforce, a confidentiality agreement (other than agreements dealing with information covered by Rule 21F-4(b)(4)(i) and Rule 21F-4(b)(4)(ii) of this chapter related to the legal representation of a client) with respect to such communications.

b. If you are a director, officer, member, agent, or employee of an entity that has counsel, and you have initiated communication with the Commission relating to a possible securities law violation, the staff is authorized to communicate directly with you regarding the possible securities law violation without seeking the consent of the entity's counsel.

Regulation FD

Rule 100 – General Rule Regarding Selective Disclosure

a. Whenever an issuer, or any person acting on its behalf, discloses any material nonpublic information regarding that issuer or its securities to any person described in paragraph (b)(1) of this section, the issuer shall make public disclosure of that information as provided in Rule 101(e):

1. Simultaneously, in the case of an intentional disclosure; and

2. Promptly, in the case of a non-intentional disclosure.

b.

1. Except as provided in paragraph (b)(2) of this section, paragraph (a) of this section shall apply to a disclosure made to any person outside the issuer:

    i.   Who is a broker or dealer, or a person associated with a broker or dealer, as those terms are defined in Section 3(a) of the Securities Exchange Act of 1934;

    ii. Who is an investment adviser, as that term is defined in Section 202(a)(11) of the Investment Advisers Act of 1940; an institutional investment manager, as that term is defined in Section 13(f)(6) of the Securities Exchange Act of 1934, that filed a report on Form 13F with the Commission for the most recent quarter ended prior to the date of the disclosure; or a person associated with either of the foregoing. For purposes of this paragraph, a "person associated with an investment adviser or institutional investment manager" has the meaning set forth in Section 202(a)(17) of the Investment Advisers Act of 1940, assuming for these purposes that an institutional investment manager is an investment adviser;

    iii. Who is an investment company, as defined in Section 3 of the Investment Company Act of 1940, or who would be an investment company but for Section 3(c)(1) or Section 3(c)(7) thereof, or an affiliated person of either of the foregoing. For purposes of this paragraph, "affiliated person" means only those persons described in Section 2(a)(3)(C), (D), (E), and (F) of the Investment Company Act of 1940, assuming for these purposes that a person who would be an investment company but for Section 3(c)(1) or Section 3(c)(7) of the Investment Company Act of 1940 is an investment company; or

    iv. Who is a holder of the issuer's securities, under circumstances in which it is reasonably foreseeable that the person will purchase or sell the issuer's securities on the basis of the information.

2. Paragraph (a) of this section shall not apply to a disclosure made:

    i.   To a person who owes a duty of trust or confidence to the issuer (such as an attorney, investment banker, or accountant);

    ii. To a person who expressly agrees to maintain the disclosed information in confidence;

    iii. In connection with a securities offering registered under the Securities Act, other than an offering of the type described in any of Rule 415(a)(1)(i) through (vi) under the Securities Act (except an offering of the type described in Rule 415(a)(1)(i) under the Securities Act also involving a registered offering, whether or not underwritten, for capital formation purposes for the account of the issuer (unless the issuer's offering is being registered for the purpose of evading the requirements of this section)), if the disclosure is by any of the following means:

(A)   A registration statement filed under the Securities Act, including a prospectus contained therein;

(B)   A free writing prospectus used after filing of the registration statement for the offering or a communication falling within the exception to the definition of prospectus contained in clause (a) of section 2(a)(10) of the Securities Act;

(C)   Any other Section 10(b) prospectus;

(D)   A notice permitted by Rule 135 under the Securities Act;

(E)   A communication permitted by Rule 134 under the Securities Act; or

(F)   An oral communication made in connection with the registered securities offering after filing of the registration statement for the offering under the Securities Act.

Rule 101 – Definitions

This section defines certain terms as used in Regulation FD (Rule 100 through Rule 103).

a.   **Intentional.** A selective disclosure of material nonpublic information is *intentional* when the person making the disclosure either knows, or is reckless in not knowing, that the information he or she is communicating is both material and nonpublic.

b.   **Issuer.** An *issuer* subject to this regulation is one that has a class of securities registered under Section 12 of the Securities Exchange Act of 1934, or is required to file reports under Section 15(d) of the Securities Exchange Act of 1934, including any closed-end investment company (as defined in Section 5(a)(2) of the Investment Company Act of 1940), but not including any other investment company or any foreign government or foreign private issuer, as those terms are defined in Rule 405 under the Securities Act.

c.   **Person acting on behalf of an issuer.** *Person acting on behalf of an issuer* means any senior official of the issuer (or, in the case of a closed-end investment company, a senior official of the issuer's investment adviser), or any other officer, employee, or agent of an issuer who regularly communicates with any person described in Rule 100(b)(1)(i), (ii), or (iii), or with holders of the issuer's securities. An officer, director, employee, or agent of an issuer who discloses material nonpublic information in breach of a duty of trust or confidence to the issuer shall not be considered to be acting on behalf of the issuer.

d.   **Promptly.** *Promptly* means as soon as reasonably practicable (but in no event after the later of 24 hours or the commencement of the next day's trading on the New York Stock Exchange) after a senior official of the issuer (or, in the case of a closed-end investment company, a senior official of the issuer's investment adviser) learns that there has been a non-intentional disclosure by the issuer or person acting on behalf of the issuer of information that the senior official knows, or is reckless in not knowing, is both material and nonpublic.

e. **Public disclosure.**
   1. Except as provided in paragraph (e)(2) of this section, an issuer shall make the *public disclosure* of information required by Rule 100(a) by furnishing to or filing with the Commission a Form 8-K disclosing that information.
   2. An issuer shall be exempt from the requirement to furnish or file a Form 8-K if it instead disseminates the information through another method (or combination of methods) of disclosure that is reasonably designed to provide broad, non-exclusionary distribution of the information to the public.

f. **Senior official.** *Senior official* means any director, executive officer (as defined in Rule 3b-7 under the Securities Exchange Act of 1934), investor relations or public relations officer, or other person with similar functions.

g. **Securities offering.** For purposes of Rule 100(b)(2)(iv):
   1. Underwritten offerings. A *securities offering* that is underwritten commences when the issuer reaches an understanding with the broker-dealer that is to act as managing underwriter and continues until the later of the end of the period during which a dealer must deliver a prospectus or the sale of the securities (unless the offering is sooner terminated);
   2. Non-underwritten offerings. A securities offering that is not underwritten:
      i. If covered by Rule 415(a)(1)(x), commences when the issuer makes its first bona fide offer in a takedown of securities and continues until the later of the end of the period during which each dealer must deliver a prospectus or the sale of the securities in that takedown (unless the takedown is sooner terminated);
      ii. If a business combination as defined in Rule 165(f)(1), commences when the first public announcement of the transaction is made and continues until the completion of the vote or the expiration of the tender offer, as applicable (unless the transaction is sooner terminated);
      iii. If an offering other than those specified in paragraphs (a) and (b) of this section, commences when the issuer files a registration statement and continues until the later of the end of the period during which each dealer must deliver a prospectus or the sale of the securities (unless the offering is sooner terminated).

Rule 102 – No Effect on Antifraud Liability

No failure to make a public disclosure required solely by Rule 100 shall be deemed to be a violation of Rule 10b-5 under the Securities Exchange Act.

Rule 103 – No Effect on Exchange Act Reporting Status

A failure to make a public disclosure required solely by Rule 100 shall not affect whether:

a. For purposes of Forms S-3, S-8 and SF-3 under the Securities Act, an issuer is deemed to have filed all the material required to be filed pursuant to Section 13 or 15(d) of the Securities Exchange Act of 1934 or, where applicable, has made those filings in a timely manner; or

b. There is adequate current public information about the issuer for purposes of Rule 144(c).

Regulation G

Rule 100 – General Rules Regarding Disclosure of Non-GAAP Financial Measures

a. Whenever a registrant, or person acting on its behalf, publicly discloses material information that includes a non-GAAP financial measure, the registrant must accompany that non-GAAP financial measure with:

    1. A presentation of the most directly comparable financial measure calculated and presented in accordance with Generally Accepted Accounting Principles (GAAP); and

    2. A reconciliation (by schedule or other clearly understandable method), which shall be quantitative for historical non-GAAP measures presented, and quantitative, to the extent available without unreasonable efforts, for forward-looking information, of the differences between the non-GAAP financial measure disclosed or released with the most comparable financial measure or measures calculated and presented in accordance with GAAP identified in paragraph (a)(1) of this section.

b. A registrant, or a person acting on its behalf, shall not make public a non-GAAP financial measure that, taken together with the information accompanying that measure and any other accompanying discussion of that measure, contains an untrue statement of a material fact or omits to state a material fact necessary in order to make the presentation of the non-GAAP financial measure, in light of the circumstances under which it is presented, not misleading.

c. This section shall not apply to a disclosure of a non-GAAP financial measure that is made by or on behalf of a registrant that is a foreign private issuer if the following conditions are satisfied:

    1. The securities of the registrant are listed or quoted on a securities exchange or inter-dealer quotation system outside the United States;

    2. The non-GAAP financial measure is not derived from or based on a measure calculated and presented in accordance with generally accepted accounting principles in the United States; and

    3. The disclosure is made by or on behalf of the registrant outside the United States, or is included in a written communication that is released by or on behalf of the registrant outside the United States.

d. This section shall not apply to a non-GAAP financial measure included in disclosure relating to a proposed business combination, the entity resulting therefrom or an entity that is a party thereto, if the disclosure is contained in a communication that is subject to Rule 425 under the Securities Act, Rules 14a-12 or 14d-2(b)(2) under the Exchange Act or Item 1015 of Regulation M-A.

Notes to Rule 100:

    1. If a non-GAAP financial measure is made public orally, telephonically, by Web cast, by broadcast, or by similar means, the requirements of paragraphs (a)(1)(i) and (a)(1)(ii) of this section will be satisfied if:

       i. The required information in those paragraphs is provided on the registrant's Web site at the time the non-GAAP financial measure is made public; and

       ii. The location of the web site is made public in the same presentation in which the non-GAAP financial measure is made public.

2. The provisions of paragraph (c) of this section shall apply notwithstanding the existence of one or more of the following circumstances:

       i. A written communication is released in the United States as well as outside the United States, so long as the communication is released in the United States contemporaneously with or after the release outside the United States and is not otherwise targeted at persons located in the United States;

       ii. Foreign journalists, U.S. journalists or other third parties have access to the information;

       iii. The information appears on one or more web sites maintained by the registrant, so long as the web sites, taken together, are not available exclusively to, or targeted at, persons located in the United States; or

       iv. Following the disclosure or release of the information outside the United States, the information is included in a submission by the registrant to the Commission made under cover of a Form 6-K.

Rule 101 – Definitions

This section defines certain terms as used in Regulation G (Rule 100 through Rule 102).

a.

1. **Non-GAAP financial measure**. A *non-GAAP financial measure* is a numerical measure of a registrant's historical or future financial performance, financial position or cash flows that:

       i. Excludes amounts, or is subject to adjustments that have the effect of excluding amounts, that are included in the most directly comparable measure calculated and presented in accordance with GAAP in the statement of income, balance sheet or statement of cash flows (or equivalent statements) of the issuer; or

       ii. Includes amounts, or is subject to adjustments that have the effect of including amounts, that are excluded from the most directly comparable measure so calculated and presented.

2. A non-GAAP financial measure does not include operating and other financial measures and ratios or statistical measures calculated using exclusively one or both of:

       i. Financial measures calculated in accordance with GAAP; and

       ii. Operating measures or other measures that are not non-GAAP financial measures.

3. A non-GAAP financial measure does not include financial measures required to be disclosed by GAAP, Commission rules, or a system of regulation of a government or governmental authority or self-regulatory organization that is applicable to the registrant.

b. **GAAP**. *GAAP* refers to generally accepted accounting principles in the United States, except that:
   1. In the case of foreign private issuers whose primary financial statements are prepared in accordance with non-U.S. generally accepted accounting principles, GAAP refers to the principles under which those primary financial statements are prepared; and
   2. In the case of foreign private issuers that include a non-GAAP financial measure derived from a measure calculated in accordance with U.S. generally accepted accounting principles, GAAP refers to U.S. generally accepted accounting principles for purposes of the application of the requirements of Regulation G to the disclosure of that measure.

c. **Registrant.** A *registrant* subject to this regulation is one that has a class of securities registered under Section 12 of the Securities Exchange Act of 1934, or is required to file reports under Section 15(d) of the Securities Exchange Act of 1934, excluding any investment company registered under Section 8 of the Investment Company Act of 1940.

d. **United States.** *United States* means the United States of America, its territories and possessions, any State of the United States, and the District of Columbia.

Rule 102 – No Effect on Antifraud Liability

Neither the requirements of this Regulation G nor a person's compliance or non-compliance with the requirements of this Regulation shall in itself affect any person's liability under Section 10(b) of the Securities Exchange Act of 1934 or Rule 10b-5 under such Act.

Regulation M

Rule 100 – Preliminary Note; Definitions

a. *Preliminary note:* Any transaction or series of transactions, whether or not effected pursuant to the provisions of Regulation M, remain subject to the antifraud and antimanipulation provisions of the securities laws, including, without limitation, Section 17(a) of the Securities Act of 1933 and Sections 9, 10(b), and 15(c) of the Securities Exchange Act of 1934.

b. For purposes of Regulation M the following definitions shall apply:

ADTV means the worldwide average daily trading volume during the two full calendar months immediately preceding, or any 60 consecutive calendar days ending within the 10 calendar days preceding, the filing of the registration statement; or, if there is no registration statement or if the distribution involves the sale of securities on a delayed basis pursuant to Rule 415 under the Securities Act, two full calendar months immediately preceding, or any consecutive 60 calendar days ending within the 10 calendar days preceding, the determination of the offering price.

Affiliated purchaser means:
1. A person acting, directly or indirectly, in concert with a distribution participant, issuer, or selling security holder in connection with the acquisition or distribution of any covered security; or
2. An affiliate, which may be a separately identifiable department or division of a distribution participant, issuer, or selling security holder, that, directly or indirectly, controls the purchases of any covered security by a distribution participant, issuer, or selling security holder, whose purchases are controlled by any such person, or whose purchases are under common control with any such person; or
3. An affiliate, which may be a separately identifiable department or division of a distribution participant, issuer, or selling security holder, that regularly purchases securities for its own account or for the account of others, or that recommends or exercises investment discretion with respect to the purchase or sale of securities; *Provided, however*, That this paragraph (3) shall not apply to such affiliate if the following conditions are satisfied:
   i. The distribution participant, issuer, or selling security holder:
      A. Maintains and enforces written policies and procedures reasonably designed to prevent the flow of information to or from the affiliate that might result in a violation of Rules 101, 102, and 104 of Regulation M; and
      B. Obtains an annual, independent assessment of the operation of such policies and procedures; and
   ii. The affiliate has no officers (or persons performing similar functions) or employees (other than clerical, ministerial, or support personnel) in common with the distribution participant, issuer, or selling security holder that direct, effect, or recommend transactions in securities; and

    iii.   The affiliate does not, during the applicable restricted period, act as a market maker (other than as a specialist in compliance with the rules of a national securities exchange), or engage, as a broker or a dealer, in solicited transactions or proprietary trading, in covered securities.

Agent independent of the issuer means a trustee or other person who is independent of the issuer. The agent shall be deemed to be independent of the issuer only if:

1. The agent is not an affiliate of the issuer; and
2. Neither the issuer nor any affiliate of the issuer exercises any direct or indirect control or influence over the prices or amounts of the securities to be purchased, the timing of, or the manner in which, the securities are to be purchased, or the selection of a broker or dealer (other than the independent agent itself) through which purchases may be executed; *Provided, however*, That the issuer or its affiliate will not be deemed to have such control or influence solely because it revises not more than once in any three-month period the source of the shares to fund the plan, the basis or determining the amount of its contributions to a plan, or the basis for determining the frequency of its allocations to a plan, or any formula specified in a plan that determines the amount or timing of securities to be purchased by the agent.

Asset-backed security has the meaning contained in General Instruction I.B.5. to Form S-3.

At-the-market offering means an offering of securities at other than a fixed price.

Business day refers to a 24 hour period determined with reference to the principal market for the securities to be distributed, and that includes a complete trading session for that market.

Completion of participation in a distribution. Securities acquired in the distribution for investment by any person participating in a distribution, or any affiliated purchaser of such person, shall be deemed to be distributed. A person shall be deemed to have completed its participation in a distribution as follows:

1. An issuer or selling security holder, when the distribution is completed;
2. An underwriter, when such person's participation has been distributed, including all other securities of the same class that are acquired in connection with the distribution, and any stabilization arrangements and trading restrictions in connection with the distribution have been terminated; *Provided, however,* That an underwriter's participation will not be deemed to have been completed if a syndicate overallotment option is exercised in an amount that exceeds the net syndicate short position at the time of such exercise; and
3. Any other person participating in the distribution, when such person's participation has been distributed.

Covered security means any security that is the subject of a distribution, or any reference security.

Current exchange rate means the current rate of exchange between two currencies, which is obtained from at least one independent entity that provides or disseminates foreign exchange quotations in the ordinary course of its business.

Distribution means an offering of securities, whether or not subject to registration under the Securities Act, that is distinguished from ordinary trading transactions by the magnitude of the offering and the presence of special selling efforts and selling methods.

Distribution participant means an underwriter, prospective underwriter, broker, dealer, or other person who has agreed to participate or is participating in a distribution.

Electronic communications network has the meaning contained in Rule 11Ac1-1(a)(8) under the Exchange Act.

Employee has the meaning contained in Form S-8.

Exchange Act means the Securities Exchange Act of 1934.

Independent bid means a bid by a person who is not a distribution participant, issuer, selling security holder, or affiliated purchaser.

NASD means the National Association of Securities Dealers, Inc. or any of its subsidiaries.

Nasdaq means the Nasdaq system electronic dealer quotation system owned and operated by The Nasdaq Stock Market, Inc.

Nasdaq security means a security that is authorized for quotation on Nasdaq, and such authorization is not suspended, terminated, or prohibited.

Net purchases means the amount by which a passive market maker's purchases exceed its sales.

Offering price means the price at which the security is to be or is being distributed.

Passive market maker means a market maker that effects bids or purchases in accordance with the provisions of Rule 103.

Penalty bid means an arrangement that permits the managing underwriter to reclaim a selling concession from a syndicate member in connection with an offering when the securities originally sold by the syndicate member are purchased in syndicate covering transactions.

Plan means any bonus, profit-sharing, pension, retirement, thrift, savings, incentive, stock purchase, stock option, stock ownership, stock appreciation, dividend reinvestment, or similar plan; or any dividend or interest reinvestment plan or employee benefit plan as defined in Rule 405 under the Securities Act.

Principal market means the single securities market with the largest aggregate reported trading volume for the class of securities during the 12 full calendar months immediately preceding the filing of the registration statement; or, if there is no registration statement or if the distribution involves the sale of securities on a delayed basis pursuant to Rule 415, during the 12 full calendar months immediately preceding the determination of the offering price. For the purpose of determining the aggregate trading volume in a security, the trading volume of depositary shares representing such security shall be included, and shall be multiplied by the multiple or fraction of the security represented by the depositary share. For purposes of this paragraph, depositary share means a security, evidenced by a depositary receipt, that represents another security, or a multiple or fraction thereof, deposited with a depositary.

Prospective underwriter means a person:
1.   Who has submitted a bid to the issuer or selling security holder, and who knows or is reasonably certain that such bid will be accepted, whether or not the terms and conditions of the underwriting have been agreed upon; or
2.   Who has reached, or is reasonably certain to reach, an understanding with the issuer or selling security holder, or managing underwriter that such person will become an underwriter, whether or not the terms and conditions of the underwriting have been agreed upon.

Public float value shall be determined in the manner set forth on the front page of Form 10-K, even if the issuer of such securities is not required to file Form 10-K, relating to the aggregate market value of common equity securities held by non-affiliates of the issuer.

Reference period means the two full calendar months immediately preceding the filing of the registration statement or, if there is no registration statement or if the distribution involves the sale of securities on a delayed basis pursuant to Rule 415, the two full calendar months immediately preceding the determination of the offering price.

Reference security means a security into which a security that is the subject of a distribution ("subject security") may be converted, exchanged, or exercised or which, under the terms of the subject security, may in whole or in significant part determine the value of the subject security.

Restricted period means:
1.   For any security with an ADTV value of $100,000 or more of an issuer whose common equity securities have a public float value of $25 million or more, the period beginning on the later of one business day prior to the determination of the offering price or such time that a person becomes a distribution participant, and ending upon such person's completion of participation in the distribution; and
2.   For all other securities, the period beginning on the later of five business days prior to the determination of the offering price or such time that a person becomes a distribution participant, and ending upon such person's completion of participation in the distribution.

3.   In the case of a distribution involving a merger, acquisition, or exchange offer, the period beginning on the day proxy solicitation or offering materials are first disseminated to security holders, and ending upon the completion of the distribution.

Securities Act means the Securities Act of 1933.

Selling security holder means any person on whose behalf a distribution is made, other than an issuer.

Stabilize or **stabilizing** means the placing of any bid, or the effecting of any purchase, for the purpose of pegging, fixing, or maintaining the price of a security.

Syndicate covering transaction means the placing of any bid or the effecting of any purchase on behalf of the sole distributor or the underwriting syndicate or group to reduce a short position created in connection with the offering.

30% ADTV limitation means 30 percent of the market maker's ADTV in a covered security during the reference period, as obtained from the NASD.

Underwriter means a person who has agreed with an issuer or selling security holder:
1.   To purchase securities for distribution; or
2.   To distribute securities for or on behalf of such issuer or selling security holder; or
3.   To manage or supervise a distribution of securities for or on behalf of such issuer or selling security holder.

Rule 101 – Activities by Distribution Participants

a.   **Unlawful Activity.** In connection with a distribution of securities, it shall be unlawful for a distribution participant or an affiliated purchaser of such person, directly or indirectly, to bid for, purchase, or attempt to induce any person to bid for or purchase, a covered security during the applicable restricted period; *Provided, however*, That if a distribution participant or affiliated purchaser is the issuer or selling security holder of the securities subject to the distribution, such person shall be subject to the provisions of Rule 102, rather than this section.

b.   **Excepted Activity.** The following activities shall not be prohibited by paragraph (a) of this section:
1.   Research. The publication or dissemination of any information, opinion, or recommendation, if the conditions of Rule 138 or Rule 139 under the Securities Act of 1933 are met; or

2.   Transactions complying with certain other sections. Transactions complying with Rule 103 or Rule 104; or

3.   Odd-lot transactions. Transactions in odd-lots; or transactions to offset odd-lots in connection with an odd-lot tender offer conducted pursuant to Rule 13e-4(h)(5) under the Securities Exchange Act of 1934; or

4.   Exercises of securities. The exercise of any option, warrant, right, or any conversion privilege set forth in the instrument governing a security; or

5.   Unsolicited transactions. Unsolicited brokerage transactions; or unsolicited purchases that are not effected from or through a broker or dealer, on a securities exchange, or through an inter-dealer quotation system or electronic communications network; or

6.   Basket transactions.
     i.   Bids or purchases, in the ordinary course of business, in connection with a basket of 20 or more securities in which a covered security does not comprise more than 5% of the value of the basket purchased; or
     ii. Adjustments to such a basket in the ordinary course of business as a result of a change in the composition of a standardized index; or

7.   De minimis transactions. Purchases during the restricted period, other than by a passive market maker, that total less than 2% of the ADTV of the security being purchased, or unaccepted bids; *Provided, however*, That the person making such bid or purchase has maintained and enforces written policies and procedures reasonably designed to achieve compliance with the other provisions of this section; or

8.   Transactions in connection with a distribution. Transactions among distribution participants in connection with a distribution, and purchases of securities from an issuer or selling security holder in connection with a distribution, that are not effected on a securities exchange, or through an inter-dealer quotation system or electronic communications network; or

9.   Offers to sell or the solicitation of offers to buy. Offers to sell or the solicitation of offers to buy the securities being distributed (including securities acquired in stabilizing), or securities offered as principal by the person making such offer or solicitation; or

10. Transactions in Rule 144A securities. Transactions in securities eligible for resale under Rule 144A(d)(3) under the Securities Act of 1933, or any reference security, if the Rule 144A securities are sold in the United States solely to:
     i.   Qualified institutional buyers, as defined in Rule 144A(a)(1) under the Securities Act of 1933, or to offerees or purchasers that the seller and any person acting on behalf of the seller reasonably believes are qualified institutional buyers, in transactions exempt from registration under section 4(a0(2) of the Securities Act or Rule 144A or Rule 500 *et seq.* under such Act; or
     ii. Persons not deemed to be "U.S. persons" for purposes of Rule 902(o)(2) or Rule 902(o)(7) under the Securities Act of 1933 [Editor's note: It appears this should be Rule 902(k)(2) and Rule 902 (k)(7).], during a distribution qualifying under paragraph (b)(10)(i) of this section.

c.   **Excepted Securities.** The provisions of this section shall not apply to any of the following securities:

1.   Actively-traded securities. Securities that have an ADTV value of at least $1 million and are issued by an issuer whose common equity securities have a public float value of at least $150 million; *Provided, however,* That such securities are not issued by the distribution participant or an affiliate of the distribution participant; or

2.   Investment grade nonconvertible and asset-backed securities. Nonconvertible debt securities, nonconvertible preferred securities, and asset- backed securities, that are rated by at least one nationally recognized statistical rating organization, as that term is used in Rule 15c3-1 under the Securities Exchange Act of 1934, in one of its generic rating categories that signifies investment grade; or

3.   Exempted securities. "Exempted securities" as defined in section 3(a)(12) of the Exchange Act; or

4.   Face-amount certificates or securities issued by an open-end management investment company or unit investment trust. Face-amount certificates issued by a face-amount certificate company, or redeemable securities issued by an open-end management investment company or a unit investment trust. Any terms used in this paragraph (c)(4) that are defined in the Investment Company Act of 1940 shall have the meanings specified in such Act.

d.   **Exemptive Authority.** Upon written application or upon its own motion, the Commission may grant an exemption from the provisions of this section, either unconditionally or on specified terms and conditions, to any transaction or class of transactions, or to any security or class of securities.

Rule 102 – Activities by Issuers and Selling Security Holders During a Distribution

a.   **Unlawful Activity.** In connection with a distribution of securities effected by or on behalf of an issuer or selling security holder, it shall be unlawful for such person, or any affiliated purchaser of such person, directly or indirectly, to bid for, purchase, or attempt to induce any person to bid for or purchase, a covered security during the applicable restricted period; *Except that* if an affiliated purchaser is a distribution participant, such affiliated purchaser may comply with Rule 101, rather than this section.

b.   **Excepted Activity.** The following activities shall not be prohibited by paragraph (a) of this section:

1.   Odd-lot transactions. Transactions in odd-lots, or transactions to offset odd-lots in connection with an odd-lot tender offer conducted pursuant to Rule 13e-4(h)(5) under the Securities Exchange Act of 1934; or

2.   Transactions by closed-end investment companies.

i.   Transactions complying with Rule 23c-3 under the Investment Company Act of 1940; or

ii.   Periodic tender offers of securities, at net asset value, conducted pursuant to Rule 13e-4 under the Securities Exchange Act of 1934 by a closed-end investment company that engages in a continuous offering of its securities pursuant to Rule 415 under the Securities Act of 1933; *Provided, however,* That such securities are not traded on a securities exchange or through an inter-dealer quotation system or electronic communications network; or

3. Redemptions by commodity pools or limited partnerships. Redemptions by commodity pools or limited partnerships, at a price based on net asset value, which are effected in accordance with the terms and conditions of the instruments governing the securities; *Provided, however,* That such securities are not traded on a securities exchange, or through an inter-dealer quotation system or electronic communications network; or

4. Exercises of securities. The exercise of any option, warrant, right, or any conversion privilege set forth in the instrument governing a security; or

5. Offers to sell or the solicitation of offers to buy. Offers to sell or the solicitation of offers to buy the securities being distributed; or

6. Unsolicited purchases. Unsolicited purchases that are not effected from or through a broker or dealer, on a securities exchange, or through an inter- dealer quotation system or electronic communications network; or

7. Transactions in Rule 144A securities. Transactions in securities eligible for resale under Rule 144A(d)(3) under the Securities Act of 1933, or any reference security, if the Rule 144A securities are sold in the United States solely to:
    i. Qualified institutional buyers, as defined in Rule 144A(a)(1) under the Securities Act of 1933, or to purchasers that the seller and any person acting on behalf of the seller reasonably believes are qualified institutional buyers, in transactions exempt from registration under section 4(a)(2) of the Securities Act or Rule 144A or Rule 500 *et seq.* under such Act; or
    ii. Persons not deemed to be "U.S. persons" for purposes of Rule 902(k)(2) during a distribution qualifying under paragraph (b)(7)(i) of this section.

c. **Plans.**
   1. Paragraph (a) of this section shall not apply to distributions of securities pursuant to a plan, which are made:
      i. Solely to employees or security holders of an issuer or its subsidiaries, or to a trustee or other person acquiring such securities for the accounts of such persons; or
      ii. To persons other than employees or security holders, if bids for or purchases of securities pursuant to the plan are effected solely by an agent independent of the issuer and the securities are from a source other than the issuer or an affiliated purchaser of the issuer.
   2. Bids for or purchases of any security made or effected by or for a plan shall be deemed to be a purchase by the issuer unless the bid is made, or the purchase is effected, by an agent independent of the issuer.

d. **Excepted Securities.** The provisions of this section shall not apply to any of the following securities:

1. Actively-traded reference securities. Reference securities with an ADTV value of at least $1 million that are issued by an issuer whose common equity securities have a public float value of at least $150 million; *Provided, however,* That such securities are not issued by the issuer, or any affiliate of the issuer, of the security in distribution.
2. Investment grade nonconvertible and asset-backed securities. Nonconvertible debt securities, nonconvertible preferred securities, and asset- backed securities, that are rated by at least one nationally recognized statistical rating organization, as that term is used in Rule 15c3-1 under the Securities Exchange Act of 1934, in one of its generic rating categories that signifies investment grade; or
3. Exempted securities. "Exempted securities" as defined in section 3(a)(12) of the Exchange Act; or
4. Face-amount certificates or securities issued by an open-end management investment company or unit investment trust. Face-amount certificates issued by a face-amount certificate company, or redeemable securities issued by an open-end management investment company or a unit investment trust. Any terms used in this paragraph (d)(4) that are defined in the Investment Company Act of 1940 shall have the meanings specified in such Act.

e. **Exemptive Authority.** Upon written application or upon its own motion, the Commission may grant an exemption from the provisions of this section, either unconditionally or on specified terms and conditions, to any transaction or class of transactions, or to any security or class of securities.

Rule 103 – Nasdaq Passive Market Making

a. **Scope of Section**. This section permits broker-dealers to engage in market making transactions in covered securities that are Nasdaq securities without violating the provisions of Rule 101; Except That this section shall not apply to any security for which a stabilizing bid subject to Rule 104 is in effect, or during any at-the-market offering or best efforts offering.

b. **Conditions to be Met**.
1. General limitations. A passive market maker must effect all transactions in the capacity of a registered market maker on Nasdaq. A passive market maker shall not bid for or purchase a covered security at a price that exceeds the highest independent bid for the covered security at the time of the transaction, except as permitted by paragraph (b)(3) of this section or required by a rule promulgated by the Commission or the NASD governing the handling of customer orders.
2. Purchase limitation. On each day of the restricted period, a passive market maker's net purchases shall not exceed the greater of its 30% ADTV limitation or 200 shares (together, "purchase limitation"); *Provided, however,* That a passive market maker may purchase all of the securities that are part of a single order that, when executed, results in its purchase limitation being equaled or exceeded. If a passive market maker's net purchases equal or exceed its purchase limitation, it shall withdraw promptly its quotations from Nasdaq. If a

passive market maker withdraws its quotations pursuant to this paragraph, it may not effect any bid or purchase in the covered security for the remainder of that day, irrespective of any later sales during that day, unless otherwise permitted by Rule 101.

3. Requirement to lower the bid. If all independent bids for a covered security are reduced to a price below the passive market maker's bid, the passive market maker must lower its bid promptly to a level not higher than the then highest independent bid; *Provided, however,* That a passive market maker may continue to bid and effect purchases at its bid at a price exceeding the then highest independent bid until the passive market maker purchases an aggregate amount of the covered security that equals or, through the purchase of all securities that are part of a single order, exceeds the lesser of two times the minimum quotation size for the security, as determined by NASD rules, or the passive market maker's remaining purchasing capacity under paragraph (b)(2) of this section.

4. Limitation on displayed size. At all times, the passive market maker's displayed bid size may not exceed the lesser of the minimum quotation size for the covered security, or the passive market maker's remaining purchasing capacity under paragraph (b)(2) of this section; *Provided, however*, That a passive market maker whose purchasing capacity at any time is between one and 99 shares may display a bid size of 100 shares.

5. Identification of a passive market making bid. The bid displayed by a passive market maker shall be designated as such.

6. Notification and reporting to the NASD. A passive market maker shall notify the NASD in advance of its intention to engage in passive market making, and shall submit to the NASD information regarding passive market making purchases, in such form as the NASD shall prescribe.

7. Prospectus disclosure. The prospectus for any registered offering in which any passive market maker intends to effect transactions in any covered security shall contain the information required in Items 502 and 508 of Regulation S-K.

c. **Transactions at Prices Resulting from Unlawful Activity.** No transaction shall be made at a price that the passive market maker knows or has reason to know is the result of activity that is fraudulent, manipulative, or deceptive under the securities laws, or any rule or regulation thereunder.

Rule 104 – Stabilizing and Other Activities in Connection with an Offering

a. **Unlawful Activity**. It shall be unlawful for any person, directly or indirectly, to stabilize, to effect any syndicate covering transaction, or to impose a penalty bid, in connection with an offering of any security, in contravention of the provisions of this section. No stabilizing shall be effected at a price that the person stabilizing knows or has reason to know is in contravention of this section, or is the result of activity that is fraudulent, manipulative, or deceptive under the securities laws, or any rule or regulation thereunder.

b. **Purpose**. Stabilizing is prohibited except for the purpose of preventing or retarding a decline in the market price of a security.

c. **Priority**. To the extent permitted or required by the market where stabilizing occurs, any person stabilizing shall grant priority to any independent bid at the same price irrespective of the size of such independent bid at the time that it is entered.

d. **Control of Stabilizing**. No sole distributor or syndicate or group stabilizing the price of a security or any member or members of such syndicate or group shall maintain more than one stabilizing bid in any one market at the same price at the same time.

e. **At-the-Market Offerings**. Stabilizing is prohibited in an at-the-market offering.

f. **Stabilizing Levels.**
    1. Maximum stabilizing bid. Notwithstanding the other provisions of this paragraph (f), no stabilizing shall be made at a price higher than the lower of the offering price or the stabilizing bid for the security in the principal market (or, if the principal market is closed, the stabilizing bid in the principal market at its previous close).
    2. Initiating stabilizing.
        i. Initiating stabilizing when the principal market is open. After the opening of quotations for the security in the principal market, stabilizing may be initiated in any market at a price no higher than the last independent transaction price for the security in the principal market if the security has traded in the principal market on the day stabilizing is initiated or on the most recent prior day of trading in the principal market and the current asked price in the principal market is equal to or greater than the last independent transaction price. If both conditions of the preceding sentence are not satisfied, stabilizing may be initiated in any market after the opening of quotations in the principal market at a price no higher than the highest current independent bid for the security in the principal market.
        ii. Initiating stabilizing when the principal market is closed.
            A. When the principal market for the security is closed, but immediately before the opening of quotations for the security in the market where stabilizing will be initiated, stabilizing may be initiated at a price no higher than the lower of:
                1. The price at which stabilizing could have been initiated in the principal market for the security at its previous close; or
                2. The most recent price at which an independent transaction in the security has been effected in any market since the close of the principal market, if the person stabilizing knows or has reason to know of such transaction.
            B. When the principal market for the security is closed, but after the opening of quotations in the market where stabilizing will be initiated, stabilizing may be initiated at a price no higher than the lower of:

1. The price at which stabilization could have been initiated in the principal market for the security at its previous close; or

2. The last independent transaction price for the security in that market if the security has traded in that market on the day stabilizing is initiated or on the last preceding business day and the current asked price in that market is equal to or greater than the last independent transaction price. If both conditions of the preceding sentence are not satisfied, under this paragraph (f)(2)(ii)(B)(2), stabilizing may be initiated at a price no higher than the highest current independent bid for the security in that market.

iii. Initiating stabilizing when there is no market for the security or before the offering price is determined. If no bona fide market for the security being distributed exists at the time stabilizing is initiated, no stabilizing shall be initiated at a price in excess of the offering price. If stabilizing is initiated before the offering price is determined, then stabilizing may be continued after determination of the offering price at the price at which stabilizing then could be initiated.

3. Maintaining or carrying over a stabilizing bid. A stabilizing bid initiated pursuant to paragraph (f)(2) of this section, which has not been discontinued, may be maintained, or carried over into another market, irrespective of changes in the independent bids or transaction prices for the security.

4. Increasing or reducing a stabilizing bid. A stabilizing bid may be increased to a price no higher than the highest current independent bid for the security in the principal market if the principal market is open, or, if the principal market is closed, to a price no higher than the highest independent bid in the principal market at the previous close thereof. A stabilizing bid may be reduced, or carried over into another market at a reduced price, irrespective of changes in the independent bids or transaction prices for the security. If stabilizing is discontinued, it shall not be resumed at a price higher than the price at which stabilizing then could be initiated.

5. Initiating, maintaining, or adjusting a stabilizing bid to reflect the current exchange rate. If a stabilizing bid is expressed in a currency other than the currency of the principal market for the security, such bid may be initiated, maintained, or adjusted to reflect the current exchange rate, consistent with the provisions of this section. If, in initiating, maintaining, or adjusting a stabilizing bid pursuant to this paragraph (f)(5), the bid would be at or below the midpoint between two trading differentials, such stabilizing bid shall be adjusted downward to the lower differential.

6. Adjustments to stabilizing bid. If a security goes ex-dividend, ex-rights, or ex-distribution, the stabilizing bid shall be reduced by an amount equal to the value of the dividend, right, or distribution. If, in reducing a stabilizing bid pursuant to this paragraph (f)(6), the bid would be at or below the midpoint between two trading differentials, such stabilizing bid shall be adjusted downward to the lower differential.

7. Stabilizing of components. When two or more securities are being offered as a unit, the component securities shall not be stabilized at prices the sum of which exceeds the then permissible stabilizing price for the unit.

8. Special prices. Any stabilizing price that otherwise meets the requirements of this section need not be adjusted to reflect special prices available to any group or class of persons (including employees or holders of warrants or rights).

g. **Offerings with no U.S. Stabilizing Activities**
    1. Stabilizing to facilitate an offering of a security in the United States shall not be deemed to be in violation of this section if all of the following conditions are satisfied:
        i.   No stabilizing is made in the United States;
        ii. Stabilizing outside the United States is made in a jurisdiction with statutory or regulatory provisions governing stabilizing that are comparable to the provisions of this section; and
        iii. No stabilizing is made at a price above the offering price in the United States, except as permitted by paragraph (f)(5) of this section.
    2. For purposes of this paragraph (g), the Commission by rule, regulation, or order may determine whether a foreign statute or regulation is comparable to this section considering, among other things, whether such foreign statute or regulation: specifies appropriate purposes for which stabilizing is permitted; provides for disclosure and control of stabilizing activities; places limitations on stabilizing levels; requires appropriate recordkeeping; provides other protections comparable to the provisions of this section; and whether procedures exist to enable the Commission to obtain information concerning any foreign stabilizing transactions.

h. **Disclosure and Notification**
    1. Any person displaying or transmitting a bid that such person knows is for the purpose of stabilizing shall provide prior notice to the market on which such stabilizing will be effected, and shall disclose its purpose to the person with whom the bid is entered.
    2. Any person effecting a syndicate covering transaction or imposing a penalty bid shall provide prior notice to the self-regulatory organization with direct authority over the principal market in the United States for the security for which the syndicate covering transaction is effected or the penalty bid is imposed.
    3. Any person subject to this section who sells to, or purchases for the account of, any person any security where the price of such security may be or has been stabilized, shall send to the purchaser at or before the completion of the transaction, a prospectus, offering circular, confirmation, or other document containing a statement similar to that comprising the statement provided for in Item 502(b) of Regulation S-K.

i. **Recordkeeping Requirements**. A person subject to this section shall keep the information and make the notification required by Rule 17a-2 under the Securities Exchange Act of 1934.

j.   **Excepted Securities**. The provisions of this section shall not apply to:
1.   Exempted Securities. "Exempted securities," as defined in section 3(a)(12) of the Exchange Act; or
2.   Transactions of Rule 144A securities. Transactions in securities eligible for resale under Rule 144A(d)(3) under the Securities Act of 1933, if such securities are sold in the United States solely to:
i.   Qualified institutional buyers, as defined in Rule 144A(a)(1) under the Securities Act of 1933, or to purchasers that the seller and any person acting on behalf of the seller reasonably believes are qualified institutional buyers, in a transaction exempt from registration under section 4(a)(2) of the Securities Act or Rule 144A or Rule 500 *et seq.* under such Act; or
ii. Persons not deemed to be "U.S. persons" for purposes of Rule 902(k)(2), during a distribution qualifying under paragraph (j)(2)(i) of this section.

k.   **Exemptive Authority**. Upon written application or upon its own motion, the Commission may grant an exemption from the provisions of this section, either unconditionally or on specified terms and conditions, to any transaction or class of transactions, or to any security or class of securities.

Rule 105 – Short Selling in Connection with a Public Offering

a.   **Unlawful Activity**. In connection with an offering of equity securities for cash pursuant to a registration statement or a notification on Form 1-A or Form 1-E filed under the Securities Act of 1933 ("offered securities"), it shall be unlawful for any person to sell short (as defined in Rule 200(a)) the security that is the subject of the offering and purchase the offered securities from an underwriter or broker or dealer participating in the offering if such short sale was effected during the period ("Rule 105 restricted period") that is the shorter of the period:
1.   Beginning five business days before the pricing of the offered securities and ending with such pricing; or
2.   Beginning with the initial filing of such registration statement or notification on Form 1-A or Form 1-E and ending with the pricing.

b.   **Excepted Activity.**
1.   Bona Fide Purchase. It shall not be prohibited for such person to purchase the offered securities as provided in paragraph (a) of this section if:
i.   Such person makes a bona fide purchase(s) of the security that is the subject of the offering that is:
A.   At least equivalent in quantity to the entire amount of the Rule 105 restricted period short sale(s);
B.   Effected during regular trading hours;
C.   Reported to an "effective transaction reporting plan" (as defined in Rule 600(b)(22)); and
D.   Effected after the last Rule 105 restricted period short sale, and no later than the business day prior to the day of pricing; and

ii.   Such person did not effect a short sale, that is reported to an effective transaction reporting plan, within the 30 minutes prior to the close of regular trading hours (as defined in Rule 600(b)(64)) on the business day prior to the day of pricing.

2.   Separate Accounts. Paragraph (a) of this section shall not prohibit the purchase of the offered security in an account of a person where such person sold short during the Rule 105 restricted period in a separate account, if decisions regarding securities transactions for each account are made separately and without coordination of trading or cooperation among or between the accounts.

3.   Investment Companies. Paragraph (a) of this section shall not prohibit an investment company (as defined by Section 3 of the Investment Company Act) that is registered under Section 8 of the Investment Company Act, or a series of such company (investment company) from purchasing an offered security where any of the following sold the offered security short during the Rule 105 restricted period:

i.   An affiliated investment company, or any series of such a company; or

ii.   A separate series of the investment company.

c.   **Excepted Offerings.** This section shall not apply to offerings filed under Rule 415 of this chapter or to offerings that are not conducted on a firm commitment basis.

d.   **Exemptive Authority.** Upon written application or upon its own motion, the Commission may grant an exemption from the provisions of this section, either unconditionally or on specified terms and conditions, to any transaction or class of transactions, or to any security or class of securities.

SCHEDULES
Schedules 14A

Schedule 14A – Information Required in Proxy Statement

Proxy Statement Pursuant to Section 14(a)
of the Securities Exchange Act of 1934
(Amendment No.)

Filed by the Registrant [ ]

Filed by a Party other than the Registrant [ ]

Check the appropriate box:
[ ] Preliminary Proxy Statement
[ ] Confidential, for Use of the Commission Only (as permitted by Rule 14a-6(e)(2))
[ ] Definitive Proxy Statement
[ ] Definitive Additional Materials
[ ] Soliciting Material under Rule 14a-12

Name of the Registrant as Specified In Its Charter

(Name of Person(s) Filing Proxy Statement, if other than the Registrant)

Payment of Filing Fee (Check the appropriate box):
[ ] No fee required.
[ ] Fee computed on table below per Exchange Act Rules 14a-6(i)(4) and 0-11.

1. Title of each class of securities to which transaction applies:

   ....

2. Aggregate number of securities to which transaction applies:

   ....

3. Per unit price or other underlying value of transaction computed pursuant to Exchange Act Rule 0-11 (Set forth the amount on which the filing fee is calculated and state how it was determined):

   ....

4. Proposed maximum aggregate value of transaction:

   ....

5. Total fee paid:

   ....

[ ] Fee paid previously with preliminary materials.

[ ] Check box if any part of the fee is offset as provided by Exchange Act Rule 0-11(a)(2) and identify the filing for which the offsetting fee was paid previously. Identify the previous filing by registration statement number, or the Form or Schedule and the date of its filing.

1. Amount Previously Paid:

   ....

2. Form, Schedule or Registration Statement No.:

   ....

3. Filing Party:

   ....

4. Date Filed:

   ....

Notes:

A. Where any item calls for information with respect to any matter to be acted upon and such matter involves other matters with respect to which information is called for by other items of this schedule, the information called for by such other items also shall be given. For example, where a solicitation of security holders is for the purpose of approving the authorization of additional securities which are to be used to acquire another specified company, and the registrants' security holders will not have a separate opportunity to vote upon the transaction, the solicitation to authorize the securities is also a solicitation with respect to the acquisition. Under those facts, information required by Items 11, 13 and 14 shall be furnished.

B. Where any item calls for information with respect to any matter to be acted upon at the meeting, such item need be answered in the registrant's soliciting material only with respect to proposals to be made by or on behalf of the registrant.

C. Except as otherwise specifically provided, where any item calls for information for a specified period with regard to directors, executive officers, officers or other persons holding specified positions or relationships, the information shall be given with regard to any person who held any of the specified positions or relationship at any time during the period. Information, other than information required by Item 404 of Regulation S-K, need not be included for any portion of the period during which such person did not hold any such position or relationship, provided a statement to that effect is made.

D. Information may be incorporated by reference only in the manner and to the extent specifically permitted in the items of this schedule. Where incorporation by reference is used, the following shall apply:

1. Any incorporation by reference of information pursuant to the provisions of this schedule shall be subject to the provisions of Item 10(d) of this chapter restricting incorporation by reference of documents which incorporate by reference other information. A registrant incorporating any documents, or portions of documents, shall include a statement on the last page(s) of the proxy statement as to which documents, or portions of documents, are incorporated by reference. Information shall not be incorporated by reference in any case where such incorporation would render the statement incomplete, unclear or confusing.

2. If a document is incorporated by reference but not delivered to security holders, include an undertaking to provide, without charge, to each person to whom a proxy statement is delivered, upon written or oral request of such person and by first class mail or other equally prompt means within one business day of receipt of such request, a copy of any and all of the information that has been incorporated by reference in the proxy statement (not including exhibits to the information that is incorporated by reference unless such exhibits are specifically incorporated by reference into the information that the proxy statement incorporates), and the address and telephone numbers to which such a request is to be directed. This includes information contained in documents filed subsequent to the date on which definitive copies of the proxy statement are sent or given to security holders, up to the date of responding to the request.

3. If a document or portion of a document other than an annual report sent to security holders pursuant to the requirements of Rule 14a-3 with respect to the same meeting or solicitation of consents or authorizations as that to which the proxy statement relates is incorporated by reference in the manner permitted by Item 13(b) or 14(e)(1) of this schedule, the proxy statement must be sent to security holders no later than 20 business days prior to the date on which the meeting of such security holders is held or, if no meeting is held, at least 20 business days prior to the date the votes, consents or authorizations may be used to effect the corporate action.

4. *Electronic filings.* If any of the information required by Items 13 or 14 of this Schedule is incorporated by reference from an annual or quarterly report to security holders, such report, or any portion thereof incorporated by reference, shall be filed in electronic format with the proxy statement. This provision shall not apply to registered investment companies.

E. In Item 13 of this Schedule, the reference to "meets the requirement of Form S-3" shall refer to a registrant which meets the following requirements:

1. the registrant meets the requirements of General Instruction I.A. of Form S-3; and

2. one of the following is met:

    i. The registrant meets the aggregate market value requirement of General Instruction I.B.1 of Form S-3; or

    ii. Action is to be taken as described in Items 11, 12 and 14 of this schedule which concerns non-convertible debt or preferred securities issued by a registrant meeting the requirements of General Instruction I.B.2 of Form S-3; or

    iii. The registrant is a majority-owned subsidiary and one of the conditions of General Instruction I.C. of Form S-3 is met.

Item 1. Date, time and place information.

a. State the date, time and place of the meeting of security holders, and the complete mailing address, including ZIP Code, of the principal executive offices of the registrant, unless such information is otherwise disclosed in material furnished to security holders with or preceding the proxy statement. If action is to be taken by written consent, state the date by which consents are to be submitted if state law requires that such a date be specified or if the person soliciting intends to set a date.

b. On the first page of the proxy statement, as delivered to security holders, state the approximate date on which the proxy statement and form of proxy are first sent or given to security holders.

c. Furnish the information required to be in the proxy statement by Rule 14a-5(e).

Item 2. Revocability of proxy.

State whether or not the person giving the proxy has the power to revoke it. If the right of revocation before the proxy is exercised is limited or is subject to compliance with any formal procedure, briefly describe such limitation or procedure.

Item 3. Dissenters' right of appraisal.

Outline briefly the rights of appraisal or similar rights of dissenters with respect to any matter to be acted upon and indicate any statutory procedure required to be followed by dissenting security holders in order to perfect such rights. Where such rights may be exercised only within a limited time after the date of adoption of a proposal, the filing of a charter amendment or other similar act, state whether the persons solicited will be notified of such date.

Instructions.
1. Indicate whether a security holder's failure to vote against a proposal will constitute a waiver of his appraisal or similar rights and whether a vote against a proposal will be deemed to satisfy any notice requirements under State law with respect to appraisal rights. If the State law is unclear, state what position will be taken in regard to these matters.
2. Open-end investment companies registered under the Investment Company Act of 1940 are not required to respond to this item.

Item 4. Persons Making the Solicitation

a. *Solicitations not subject to Rule 14a-12(c)*
 1. If the solicitation is made by the registrant, so state. Give the name of any director of the registrant who has informed the registrant in writing that he intends to oppose any action intended to be taken by the registrant and indicate the action which he intends to oppose.
 2. If the solicitation is made otherwise than by the registrant, so state and give the names of the participants in the solicitation, as defined in paragraphs (a)(iii), (iv), (v) and (vi) of Instruction 3 to this Item.
 3. If the solicitation is to be made otherwise than by the use of the mails or pursuant to Rule14a-16, describe the methods to be employed.. If the solicitation is to be made by specially, engaged employees or paid solicitors, state
    i. the material features of any contract or arrangement for such solicitation and identify the parties, and
    ii. the cost or anticipated cost thereof.
 4. State the names of the persons by whom the cost of solicitation has been or will be borne, directly or indirectly.
b. *Solicitations subject to Rule 14a-12(c)*
 1. State by whom the solicitation is made and describe the methods employed and to be employed to solicit security holders.
 2. If regular employees of the registrant or any other participant in a solicitation have been or are to be employed to solicit security holders, describe the class or classes of employees to be so employed, and the manner and nature of their employment for such purpose.
 3. If specially engaged employees, representatives or other persons have been or are to be employed to solicit security holders, state
    i. the material features of any contract or arrangement for such solicitation and the identity of the parties,
    ii. the cost or anticipated cost thereof and

      iii.   the approximate number of such employees of employees or any other person (naming such other person) who will solicit security holders).

4. State the total amount estimated to be spent and the total expenditures to date for, in furtherance of, or in connection with the solicitation of security holders.

5. State by whom the cost of the solicitation will be borne. If such cost is to be borne initially by any person other than the registrant, state whether reimbursement will be sought from the registrant, and, if so, whether the question of such reimbursement will be submitted to a vote of security holders.

6. If any such solicitation is terminated pursuant to a settlement between the registrant and any other participant in such solicitation, describe the terms of such settlement, including the cost or anticipated cost thereof to the registrant.

Instructions.

1. With respect to solicitations subject to Rule 14a-12(c), costs and expenditures within the meaning of this Item 4 shall include fees for attorneys, accountants, public relations or financial advisers, solicitors, advertising, printing, transportation, litigation and other costs incidental to the solicitation, except that the registrant may exclude the amount of such costs represented by the amount normally expended for a solicitation for an election of directors in the absence of a contest, and costs represented by salaries and wages of regular employees and officers, provided a statement to that effect is included in the proxy statement.

2. The information required pursuant to paragraph (b)(6) of this Item should be included in any amended or revised proxy statement or other soliciting materials relating to the same meeting or subject matter furnished to security holders by the registrant subsequent to the date of settlement.

3. For purposes of this Item 4 and Item 5 of this Schedule 14A:

    a.   The terms "participant" and "participant in a solicitation" include the following:

        i.   In the case of a solicitation made on behalf of the registrant, the registrant, each director of the registrant and each of the registrant's nominees for election as a director;

        ii.   In the case of a solicitation made otherwise than on behalf of the registrant, each of the soliciting person's nominees for election as a director;

        iii.   Any committee or group which solicits proxies, any member of such committee or group, and any person whether or not named as a member who, acting alone or with one or more other persons, directly or indirectly takes the initiative, or engages, in organizing, directing, or arranging for the financing of any such committee or group;

        iv.   Any person who finances or joins with another to finance the solicitation of proxies, except persons who contribute not more than $500 and who are not otherwise participants;

        v.   Any person who lends money or furnishes credit or enters into any other arrangements, pursuant to any contract or understanding with a participant, for the purpose of financing or otherwise inducing the purchase, sale, holding or voting of securities of the registrant by any participant or other persons, in support of or in opposition to a participant; except that such terms do not include a bank, broker or dealer who, in the ordinary course of business, lends money or executes orders for the purchase or sale of securities and who is not otherwise a participant; and

    vi.   Any person who solicits proxies.

  b.   The terms "participant" and "participant in a solicitation" do not include:

    i.   Any person or organization retained or employed by a participant to solicit security holders and whose activities are limited to the duties required to be performed in the course of such employment;

    ii.   Any person who merely transmits proxy soliciting material or performs other ministerial or clerical duties;

    iii.   Any person employed by a participant in the capacity of attorney, accountant, or advertising, public relations or financial adviser, and whose activities are limited to the duties required to be performed in the course of such employment;

    iv.   Any person regularly employed as an officer or employee of the registrant or any of its subsidiaries who is not otherwise a participant; or

    v.   Any officer or director of, or any person regularly employed by, any other participant, if such officer, director or employee is not otherwise a participant.

Item 5. Interest of Certain Persons in Matters to Be Acted Upon

  a.   *Solicitations not subject to Rule 14a-12(c).*

     Describe briefly any substantial interest, direct or indirect, by security holdings or otherwise, of each of the following persons in any matter to be acted upon, other than elections to office:

    1.   If the solicitation is made on behalf of the registrant, each person who has been a director or executive officer of the registrant at any time since the beginning of the last fiscal year.

    2.   If the solicitation is made otherwise than on behalf of the registrant, each participant in the solicitation, as defined in paragraphs (a)(iii), (iv), and (v) and (vi) of Instruction 3 to Item 4 of this Schedule 14A.

    3.   Each nominee for election as a director of the registrant.

    4.   Each associate of any of the foregoing persons.

    5.   If the solicitation is made on behalf of the registrant, furnish the information required by Item 402(t) of Regulation S-K.

    Instruction to paragraph (a).

    Except in the case of a solicitation subject to this regulation made in opposition to another solicitation subject to this regulation, this sub-item (a) shall not apply to any interest arising from the ownership of securities of the registrant where the security holder receives no extra or special benefit not shared on a pro rata basis by all other holders of the same class.

  b.   *Solicitation subject to Rule 14a-12(c).*

     With respect to any solicitation subject to Rule 14a-12(c):

    1.   Describe briefly any substantial interest, direct or indirect, by security holdings or otherwise, of each participant as defined in paragraphs (a)(ii), (iii), (iv), (v) and (vi) of Instruction 3 to Item 4 of this Schedule 14A, in any matter to be

acted upon at the meeting, and include with respect to each participant the following information, or a fair and accurate summary thereof:

   i.   Name and business address of the participant.

   ii.   The participant's present principal occupation or employment and the name, principal business and address of any corporation or other organization in which such employment is carried on.

   iii.   State whether or not, during the past ten years, the participant has been convicted in a criminal proceeding (excluding traffic violations or similar misdemeanors) and, if so, give dates, nature of conviction, name and location of court, and penalty imposed or other disposition of the case. A negative answer need not be included in the proxy statement or other soliciting material.

   iv.   State the amount of each class of securities of the registrant which the participant owns beneficially, directly or indirectly.

   v.   State the amount of each class of securities of the registrant which the participant owns of record but not beneficially.

   vi.   State with respect to all securities of the registrant purchased or sold within the past two years, the dates on which they were purchased or sold and the amount purchased or sold on each such date.

   vii.   If any part of the purchase price or market value of any of the shares specified in paragraph (b)(1)(vi) of this Item is represented by funds borrowed or otherwise obtained for the purpose of acquiring or holding such securities, so state and indicate the amount of the indebtedness as of the latest practicable date. If such funds were borrowed or obtained otherwise than pursuant to a margin account or bank loan in the regular course of business of a bank, broker or dealer, briefly describe the transaction, and state the names of the parties.

   viii.   State whether or not the participant is, or was within the past year, a party to any contract, arrangements or understandings with any person with respect to any securities of the registrant, including, but not limited to joint ventures, loan or option arrangements, puts or calls, guarantees against loss or guarantees of profit, division of losses or profits, or the giving or withholding of proxies. If so, name the parties to such contracts, arrangements or understandings and give the details thereof.

   ix.   State the amount of securities of the registrant owned beneficially, directly or indirectly, by each of the participant's associates and the name and address of each such associate.

   x.   State the amount of each class of securities of any parent or subsidiary of the registrant which the participant owns beneficially, directly or indirectly.

   xi.   Furnish for the participant and associates of the participant the information required by Item 404(a) of Regulation S-K.

   xii.   State whether or not the participant or any associates of the participant have any arrangement or understanding with any person-

       A.   with respect to any future employment by the registrant or its affiliates; or

       B.   with respect to any future transactions to which the registrant or any of its affiliates will or may be a party.

If so, describe such arrangement or understanding and state the names of the parties thereto.

2. With respect to any person, other than a director or executive officer of the registrant acting solely in that capacity, who is a party to an arrangement or understanding pursuant to which a nominee for election as director is proposed to be elected, describe any substantial interest, direct or indirect, by security holdings or otherwise, that such person has in any matter to be acted upon at the meeting, and furnish the information called for by paragraphs (b)(1)(xi) and (xii) of this Item.

3. If the solicitation is made on behalf of the registrant, furnish the information required by Item 402(t) of Regulation S-K.

Instruction to paragraph (b)

For purposes of this Item 5, beneficial ownership shall be determined in accordance with Rule 13d-3 under the Act.

Item 6. Voting Securities and Principal Holders Thereof

a. As to each class of voting securities of the registrant entitled to be voted at the meeting (or by written consents or authorizations if no meeting is held), state the number of shares outstanding and the number of votes to which each class is entitled.

b. State the record date, if any, with respect to this solicitation. If the right to vote or give consent is not to be determined, in whole or in part, by reference to a record date, indicate the criteria for the determination of security holders entitled to vote or give consent.

c. If action is to be taken with respect to the election of directors and if the persons solicited have cumulative voting rights:
1. Make a statement that they have such rights,
2. briefly describe such rights,
3. state briefly the conditions precedent to the exercise thereof, and
4. if discretionary authority to cumulate votes is solicited, so indicate.

d. Furnish the information required by Item 403 of Regulation S-K to the extent known by the persons on whose behalf the solicitation is made.

e. If, to the knowledge of the persons on whose behalf the solicitation is made, a change in control of the registrant has occurred since the beginning of its last fiscal year, state the name of the person(s) who acquired such control, the amount and the source of the consideration used by such person or persons; the basis of the control, the date and a description of the transaction(s) which resulted in the change of control and the percentage of voting securities of the registrant now beneficially owned directly or indirectly by the person(s) who acquired control; and the identity of the person(s) from whom control was assumed. If the source of all or any part of the consideration used is a loan made in the ordinary course of business by a bank as defined by section 3(a)(6) of the Act, the identity of such bank shall be omitted provided a request for confidentiality has been made pursuant to section 13(d)(1)(B) of the Act by the person(s) who acquired control. In lieu thereof, the material shall indicate that the identity of the bank has been so omitted and filed separately with the Commission.

Instructions.

1. State the terms of any loans or pledges obtained by the new control group for the purpose of acquiring control, and the names of the lenders or pledgees.

2.   Any arrangements or understandings among members of both the former and new control groups and their associates with respect to election of directors or other matters should be described.

Item 7. Directors and Executive Officers

If action is to be taken with respect to the election of directors, furnish the following information in tabular form to the extent practicable. If, however, the solicitation is made on behalf of persons other than the registrant, the information required need be furnished only as to nominees of the persons making the solicitation.

a.   The information required by Item 103(c)(2) of Regulation S-K with respect to directors and executive officers.

b.   The information required by Items 401, 404(a) and (b), 405, 407 and 408(b) of Regulation S–K, other than the information required by:

    i.   Paragraph (c)(3) of Item 407 of Regulation S–K; and

    ii. Paragraphs (e)(4) and (e)(5) of Item 407 of Regulation S–K (which are required by Item 8 of this Schedule 14A.

c.   If a shareholder nominee or nominees are submitted to the registrant for inclusion in the registrant's proxy materials pursuant to Rule 14a-11 and the registrant is not permitted to exclude the nominee or nominees pursuant to the provisions of Rule 14a-11, the registrant must include in its proxy statement the disclosure required from the nominating shareholder or nominating shareholder group under Item 5 of Rule14n-101 with regard to the nominee or nominees and the nominating shareholder or nominating shareholder group.

d.   If a registrant is required to include a shareholder nominee or nominees submitted to the registrant for inclusion in the registrant's proxy materials pursuant to a procedure set forth under applicable state or foreign law, or the registrant's governing documents providing for the inclusion of shareholder director nominees in the registrant's proxy materials, the registrant must include in its proxy statement the disclosure required from the nominating shareholder or nominating shareholder group under Item 6 of Rule 14n–101 with regard to the nominee or nominees and the nominating shareholder or nominating shareholder group.

e.   In lieu of the information required by this Item 7, investment companies registered under the Investment Company Act of 1940 must furnish the information required by Item 22(b) of this Schedule 14A.

f.   If a person is conducting a solicitation that is subject to Rule 14a–19, the registrant must include in its proxy statement a statement directing shareholders to refer to any other soliciting person's proxy statement for information required by Item 7 of this Schedule 14A with regard to such person's nominee or nominees and a soliciting person other than the registrant must include in its proxy statement a statement directing shareholders to refer to the registrant's or other soliciting person's proxy statement for information required by Item 7 of this Schedule 14A with regard to the registrant's or other soliciting person's nominee or nominees. The statement must explain to shareholders that they can access the other soliciting person's proxy statement, and any other relevant documents, without cost on the Commission's website.

Instruction to Item 7. The information disclosed pursuant to paragraphs (c) and (d) of this Item will not be deemed incorporated by reference into any filing under the Securities Act of 1933, the Securities Exchange Act of 1934, or the Investment Company Act of 1940, except to the extent that the registrant specifically incorporates that information by reference.

Item 8. Compensation of Directors and Executive Officers.

Furnish the information required by Item 402 of Regulation S-K and paragraphs (e)(4) and (e)(5) of Item 407 of Regulation S-K if action is to be taken with regard to:
   a.   The election of directors;
   b.   Any bonus, profit sharing or other compensation plan, contract or arrangement in which any director, nominee for election as a director, or executive officer of the registrant will participate;
   c.   Any pension or retirement plan in which any such person will participate; or
   d.   The granting or extension to any such person of any options, warrants or rights to purchase any securities, other than warrants or rights issued to security holders as such, on a pro rata basis.
        However, if the solicitation is made on behalf of persons other than the registrant, the information required need be furnished only as to nominees of the persons making the solicitation and associates of such nominees. In the case of investment companies registered under the Investment Company Act of 1940, furnish the information required by Item 22(b)(13) of this Schedule 14A.

Instruction

If an otherwise reportable compensation plan became subject to such requirements because of an acquisition or merger and, within one year of the acquisition or merger, such plan was terminated for purposes of prospective eligibility, the registrant may furnish a description of its obligation to the designated individuals pursuant to the compensation plan. Such description may be furnished in lieu of a description of the compensation plan in the proxy statement.

Item 9. Independent Public Accountants.

If the solicitation is made on behalf of the registrant and relates to: (1) The annual (or special meeting in lieu of annual) meeting of security holders at which directors are to be elected, or a solicitation of consents or authorizations in lieu of such meeting or (2) the election, approval or ratification of the registrant's accountant, furnish the following information describing the registrant's relationship with its independent public accountant:
   a.   The name of the principal accountant selected or being recommended to security holders for election, approval or ratification for the current year. If no accountant has been selected or recommended, so state and briefly describe the reasons therefor.
   b.   The name of the principal accountant for the fiscal year most recently completed if different from the accountant selected or recommended for the current year or if no accountant has yet been selected or recommended for the current year.
   c.   The proxy statement shall indicate:
        1.   Whether or not representatives of the principal accountant for the current year and for the most recently completed fiscal year are expected to be present at the security holders' meeting,
        2.   whether or not they will have the opportunity to make a statement if they desire to do so, and
        3.   whether or not such representatives are expected to be available to respond to appropriate questions.

d.   If during the registrant's two most recent fiscal years or any subsequent interim period,

    1.   an independent accountant who was previously engaged as the principal accountant to audit the registrant's financial statements, or an independent accountant on whom the principal accountant expressed reliance in its report regarding a significant subsidiary, has resigned (or indicated it has declined to stand for re-election after the completion of the current audit) or was dismissed, or

    2.   a new independent accountant has been engaged as either the principal accountant to audit the registrant's financial statements or as an independent accountant on whom the principal accountant has expressed or is expected to express reliance in its report regarding a significant subsidiary, then, notwithstanding any previous disclosure, provide the information required by Item 304(a) of Regulation S-K.

e.

    1.   Disclose, under the caption Audit Fees, the aggregate fees billed for each of the last two fiscal years for professional services rendered by the principal accountant for the audit of the registrant's annual financial statements and review of financial statements included in the registrant's Form 10-Q or services that are normally provided by the accountant in connection with statutory and regulatory filings or engagements for those fiscal years.

    2.   Disclose, under the caption Audit-Related Fees, the aggregate fees billed in each of the last two fiscal years for assurance and related services by the principal accountant that are reasonably related to the performance of the audit or review of the registrant's financial statements and are not reported under paragraph (e)(1) of this section. Registrants shall describe the nature of the services comprising the fees disclosed under this category.

    3.   Disclose, under the caption Tax Fees, the aggregate fees billed in each of the last two fiscal years for professional services rendered by the principal accountant for tax compliance, tax advice, and tax planning. Registrants shall describe the nature of the services comprising the fees disclosed under this category.

    4.   Disclose, under the caption All Other Fees, the aggregate fees billed in each of the last two fiscal years for products and services provided by the principal accountant, other than the services reported in paragraphs (e)(1) through (e)(3) of this section. Registrants shall describe the nature of the services comprising the fees disclosed under this category.

    5.

        i.   Disclose the audit committee's pre-approval policies and procedures described in Rule 2-01(c)(7)(i) of Regulation S-X.

        ii. Disclose the percentage of services described in each of paragraphs (e)(2) - (e)(4) of this section that were approved by the audit committee pursuant to Rule 2-01(c)(7)(i)(C) of Regulation S-X.

    6.   If greater than 50 percent, disclose the percentage of hours expended on the principal accountant's engagement to audit the registrant's financial statements for the most recent fiscal year that were attributed to work performed by persons other than the principal accountant's full-time, permanent employees

7.   If the registrant is an investment company, disclose the aggregate non-audit fees billed by the registrant's accountant for services rendered to the registrant, and to the registrant's investment adviser (not including any subadviser whose role is primarily portfolio management and is subcontracted with or overseen by another investment adviser), and any entity controlling, controlled by, or under common control with the adviser that provides ongoing services to the registrant for each of the last two fiscal years of the registrant.

8.   If the registrant is an investment company, disclose whether the audit committee of the board of directors has considered whether the provision of non-audit services that were rendered to the registrant's investment adviser (not including any subadviser whose role is primarily portfolio management and is subcontracted with or overseen by another investment adviser), and any entity controlling, controlled by, or under common control with the investment adviser that provides ongoing services to the registrant that were not pre-approved pursuant to Rule 2-01(c)(7)(ii) of Regulation S-X is compatible with maintaining the principal accountant's independence.

Instruction to Item 9(e).

For purposes of Item 9(e)(2), (3), and (4), registrants that are investment companies must disclose fees billed for services rendered to the registrant and separately, disclose fees required to be approved by the investment company registrant's audit committee pursuant to Rule 2-01(c)(7)(ii) of Regulation S-X. Registered investment companies must also disclose the fee percentages as required by item 9(e)(5)(ii) for the registrant and separately, disclose the fee percentages as required by item 9(e)(5)(ii) for the fees required to be approved by the investment company registrant's audit committee pursuant to Rule 2-01(c)(7)(ii) of Regulation S-X.

Item 10. Compensation Plans.

If action is to be taken with respect to any plan pursuant to which cash or noncash compensation may be paid or distributed, furnish the following information:

a.   *Plans subject to security holder action.*

1.   Describe briefly the material features of the plan being acted upon, identify each class of persons who will be eligible to participate therein, indicate the approximate number of persons in each such class, and state the basis of such participation.

2.

         i.   In the tabular format specified below, disclose the benefits or amounts that will be received by or allocated to each of the following under the plan being acted upon, if such benefits or amounts are determinable:

NEW PLAN BENEFITS Plan Name		
Name and Position	**Dollar Value ($)**	**Number of Units**
CEO		
#A		
#B		
#C		
#D		
Executive Group		
Non-Executive Director Group		
Non-Executive Officer Employee Group		

ii. The table required by paragraph (a)(2)(i) of this Item shall provide information as to the following persons:

 A. Each person (stating name and position) specified in paragraph (a)(3) of Item 402 of Regulation S-K;

 Instruction:

 In the case of investment companies registered under the Investment Company Act of 1940, furnish the information for Compensated Persons as defined in Item 22(b)(13) of this Schedule in lieu of the persons specified in paragraph (a)(3) of Item 402 of Regulation S-K.

 B. All current executive officers as a group;

 C. All current directors who are not executive officers as a group; and

 D. All employees, including all current officers who are not executive officers, as a group.

 Instruction to New Plan Benefits Table.

 Additional columns should be added for each plan with respect to which security holder action is to be taken.

iii. If the benefits or amounts specified in paragraph (a)(2)(i) of this item are not determinable, state the benefits or amounts which would have been received by or allocated to each of the following for the last completed fiscal year if the plan had been in effect, if such benefits or amounts may be determined, in the table specified in paragraph (a)(2)(i) of this Item:

 A. Each person (stating name and position) specified in paragraph (a)(3) of Item 402 of Regulation S-K;

 B. All current executive officers as a group;

 C. All current directors who are not executive officers as a group; and

 D. All employees, including all current officers who are not executive officers, as a group.

3. If the plan to be acted upon can be amended, otherwise than by a vote of security holders, to increase the cost thereof to the registrant or to alter the allocation of

the benefits as between the persons and groups specified in paragraph (a)(2) of this item, state the nature of the amendments which can be so made.

b. *Additional information regarding specified plans subject to security holder action.*

    1. With respect to any pension or retirement plan submitted for security holder action, state:

        i. The approximate total amount necessary to fund the plan with respect to past services, the period over which such amount is to be paid and the estimated annual payments necessary to pay the total amount over such period; and

        ii. The estimated annual payment to be made with respect to current services. In the case of a pension or retirement plan, information called for by paragraph (a)(2) of this Item may be furnished in the format specified by paragraph (h)(2) of Item 402 of Regulation S-K.

        Instruction.

        In the case of investment companies registered under the Investment Company Act of 1940, refer to instruction 4 in Item 22(b)(13)(i) of this Schedule in lieu of paragraph (h)(2) of Item 402 of Regulation S-K.

    2.

        i. With respect to any specific grant of or any plan containing options, warrants or rights submitted for security holder action, state:

            A. The title and amount of securities underlying such options, warrants or rights;

            B. The prices, expiration dates and other material conditions upon which the options, warrants or rights may be exercised;

            C. The consideration received or to be received by the registrant or subsidiary for the granting or extension of the options, warrants or rights;

            D. The market value of the securities underlying the options, warrants, or rights as of the latest practicable date; and

            E. In the case of options, the federal income tax consequences of the issuance and exercise of such options to the recipient and the registrant; and

        ii. State separately the amount of such options received or to be received by the following persons if such benefits or amounts are determinable:

            A. Each person (stating name and position) specified in paragraph (a)3 of Item 402 of Regulation S-K;

            B. All current executive officers as a group;

            C. All current directors who are not executive officers as a group;

            D. Each nominee for election as a director;

            E. Each associate of any of such directors, executive officers or nominees;

            F. Each other person who received or is to receive 5 percent of such options, warrants or rights; and

            G. All employees, including all current officers who are not executive officers, as a group.

c. *Information regarding plans and other arrangements not subject to security holder action.* Furnish the information required by Item 201(d) of Regulation S-K.

Instructions to paragraph (c):

1. If action is to be taken as described in paragraph (a) of this Item with respect to the approval of a new compensation plan under which equity securities of the registrant are authorized for issuance, information about the plan shall be disclosed as required under paragraphs (a) and (b) of this Item and shall not be included in the disclosure required by Item 201(d) of Regulation S-K. If action is to be taken as described in paragraph (a) of this Item with respect to the amendment or modification of an existing plan under which equity securities of the registrant are authorized for issuance, the registrant shall include information about securities previously authorized for issuance under the plan (including any outstanding options, warrants and rights previously granted pursuant to the plan and any securities remaining available for future issuance under the plan) in the disclosure required by Item 201(d) of Regulation S-K. Any additional securities that are the subject of the amendments or modification of the existing plan shall be disclosed as required under paragraphs (a) and (b) of this Item and shall not be included in the Item 201(d) disclosure.

Instructions

1. The term "plan" as used in this Item means any plan as defined in paragraph (a)(7)(ii) of Item 402 of Regulation S-K.
2. If action is to be taken with respect to a material amendment or modification of an existing plan, the item shall be answered with respect to the plan as proposed to be amended or modified and shall indicate any material differences from the existing plan.
3. If the plan to be acted upon is set forth in a written document, three copies thereof shall be filed with the Commission at the time copies of the proxy statement and form of proxy are first filed pursuant to paragraph (a) or (b) of Rule 14a-6. Electronic filers shall file with the Commission a copy of such written plan document in electronic format as an appendix to the proxy statement. It need not be provided to security holders unless it is a part of the proxy statement.
4. Paragraph (b)(2)(ii) does not apply to warrants or rights to be issued to security holders as such on a pro rata basis.
5. The Commission shall be informed, as supplemental information, when the proxy statement is first filed, as to when the options, warrants or rights and the shares called for thereby will be registered under the Securities Act or, if such registration is not contemplated, the section of the Securities Act or rule of the Commission under which exemption from such registration is claimed and the facts relied upon to make the exemption available.

Item 11. Authorization or Issuance of Securities Otherwise than for Exchange.

If action is to be taken with respect to the authorization or issuance of any securities otherwise than for exchange for outstanding securities of the registrant, furnish the following information:

a. State the title and amount of securities to be authorized or issued.
b. Furnish the information required by Item 202 of Regulation S-K. If the terms of the securities cannot be stated or estimated with respect to any or all of the securities to be authorized, because no offering thereof is contemplated in the proximate future, and if no further authorization by security holders for the issuance thereof is to be obtained, it should be stated that the terms of the securities to be authorized, including dividend

or interest rates, conversion prices, voting rights, redemption prices, maturity dates, and similar matters will be determined by the board of directors. If the securities are additional shares of common stock of a class outstanding, the description may be omitted except for a statement of the preemptive rights, if any. Where the statutory provisions with respect to preemptive rights are so indefinite or complex that they cannot be stated in summarized form, it will suffice to make a statement in the form of an opinion of counsel as to the existence and extent of such rights.

c. Describe briefly the transaction in which the securities are to be issued including a statement as to

1. the nature and approximate amount of consideration received or to be received by the registrant and

2. the approximate amount devoted to each purpose so far as determinable for which the net proceeds have been or are to be used.

If it is impracticable to describe the transaction in which the securities are to be issued, state the reason, indicate the purpose of the authorization of the securities, and state whether further authorization for the issuance of the securities by a vote of security holders will be solicited prior to such issuance.

d. If the securities are to be issued otherwise than in a public offering for cash, state the reasons for the proposed authorization or issuance and the general effect thereof upon the rights of existing security holders.

e. Furnish the information required by Item 13(a) of this schedule.

Item 12. Modification or Exchange of Securities.

If action is to be taken with respect to the modification of any class of securities of the registrant, or the issuance or authorization for issuance of securities of the registrant in exchange for outstanding securities of the registrant furnish the following information:

a. If outstanding securities are to be modified, state the title and amount thereof. If securities are to be issued in exchange for outstanding securities, state the title and amount of securities to be so issued, the title and amount of outstanding securities to be exchanged therefor and the basis of the exchange.

b. Describe any material differences between the outstanding securities and the modified or new securities in respect of any of the matters concerning which information would be required in the description of the securities in Item 202 of Regulation S-K.

c. State the reasons for the proposed modification or exchange and the general effect thereof upon the rights of existing security holders.

d. Furnish a brief statement as to arrears in dividends or as to defaults in principal or interest in respect to the outstanding securities which are to be modified or exchanged and such other information as may be appropriate in the particular case to disclose adequately the nature and effect of the proposed action.

e. Outline briefly any other material features of the proposed modification or exchange. If the plan of proposed action is set forth in a written document, file copies thereof with the Commission in accordance with Rule 14a-6.

f. Furnish the information required by Item 13(a) of this Schedule.

Instruction.

If the existing security is presently listed and registered on a national securities exchange, state whether the registrant intends to apply for listing and registration of the new or reclassified security on such exchange or any other exchange. If the registrant does not intend to make such application, state the effect of the termination of such listing and registration.

Item 13. Financial and Other Information. (*See* Notes D and E at the beginning of this Schedule.)

    a.   *Information required.* If action is to be taken with respect to any matter specified in Item 11 or 12, furnish the following information:

        1.   Financial statements meeting the requirements of Regulation S-X, including financial information required by Rule 3-05 and Article 11 of Regulation S-X with respect to transactions other than that pursuant to which action is to be taken as described in this proxy statement;

        2.   Item 302 of Regulation S-K, supplementary financial information;

        3.   Item 303 of Regulation S-K, management's discussion and analysis of financial condition and results of operations;

        4.   Item 304 of Regulation S-K, changes in and disagreements with accountants on accounting and financial disclosure;

        5.   Item 305 of Regulation S-K, quantitative and qualitative disclosures about market risk; and

        6.   A statement as to whether or not representatives of the principal accountants for the current year and for the most recently completed fiscal year:

            i.   Are expected to be present at the security holders' meeting;

            ii.   Will have the opportunity to make a statement if they desire to do so; and

            iii.   Are expected to be available to respond to appropriate questions.

    b.   *Incorporation by reference.* The information required pursuant to paragraph (a) of this Item may be incorporated by reference into the proxy statement as follows:

        1.   *S-3 registrants.* If the registrant meets the requirements of Form S-3 (*see* Note E to this Schedule), it may incorporate by reference to previously-filed documents any of the information required by paragraph (a) of this Item, provided that the requirements of paragraph (c) are met. Where the registrant meets the requirements of Form S-3 and has elected to furnish the required information by incorporation by reference, the registrant may elect to update the information so incorporated by reference to information in subsequently-filed documents.

        2.   *All registrants.* The registrant may incorporate by reference any of the information required by paragraph (a) of this Item, provided that the information is contained in an annual report to security holders or a previously-filed statement or report, such report or statement is delivered to security holders with the proxy statement and the requirements of paragraph (c) are met.

    c.   *Certain conditions applicable to incorporation by reference.* Registrants eligible to incorporate by reference into the proxy statement the information required by paragraph (a) of this Item in the manner specified by paragraphs (b)(1) and (b)(2) may do so only if:

        1.   The information is not required to be included in the proxy statement pursuant to the requirement of another Item;

        2.   The proxy statement identifies on the last page(s) the information incorporated by reference; and

        3.   The material incorporated by reference substantially meets the requirements of this Item or the appropriate portions of this Item.

Instructions to Item 13.

1.   Notwithstanding the provisions of this Item, any or all of the information required by paragraph (a) of this Item not material for the exercise of prudent judgment in regard to the matter to be acted upon may be omitted. In the usual case the information is deemed material to the exercise of prudent judgment where the matter to be acted upon is the authorization or issuance of a material amount of senior securities, but the information is not deemed material where the matter to be acted upon is the authorization or issuance of common stock, otherwise than in an exchange, merger, consolidation, acquisition or similar transaction, the authorization of preferred stock without present intent to issue or the authorization of preferred stock for issuance for cash in an amount constituting fair value.

2.   In order to facilitate compliance with Rule 2-02(a) of Regulation S-X, one copy of the definitive proxy statement filed with the Commission shall include a manually signed copy of the accountant's report. If the financial statements are incorporated by reference, a manually signed copy of the accountant's report shall be filed with the definitive proxy statement.

3.   Notwithstanding the provisions of Regulation S-X, no schedules other than those prepared in accordance with Rules 12-15, 12-28 and 12-29 (or, for management investment companies, Rules 12-12 through 12-14) of that regulation need be furnished in the proxy statement.

4.   Unless registered on a national securities exchange or otherwise required to furnish such information, registered investment companies need not furnish the information required by paragraph (a)(2) or (3) of this Item.

5.   If the registrant submits preliminary proxy material incorporating by reference financial statements required by this Item, the registrant should furnish a draft of the financial statements if the document from which they are incorporated has not been filed with or furnished to the Commission.

6.   A registered investment company need not comply with items (a)(2), (a)(3), and (a)(5) of this Item 13.

***

Item 15. Acquisition or Disposition of Property.

If action is to be taken with respect to the acquisition or disposition of any property, furnish the following information:

a.   Describe briefly the general character and location of the property.

b.   State the nature and amount of consideration to be paid or received by the registrant or any subsidiary. To the extent practicable, outline briefly the facts bearing upon the question of the fairness of the consideration.

c.   State the name and address of the transferer or transferee, as the case may be and the nature of any material relationship of such person to the registrant or any affiliate of the registrant.

d.   Outline briefly any other material features of the contract or transaction.

Item 16. Restatement of Accounts.

If action is to be taken with respect to the restatement of any asset, capital, or surplus account of the registrant furnish the following information:

a. State the nature of the restatement and the date as of which it is to be effective.

b. Outline briefly the reasons for the restatement and for the selection of the particular effective date.

c. State the name and amount of each account (including any reserve accounts) affected by the restatement and the effect of the restatement thereon. Tabular presentation of the amounts shall be made when appropriate, particularly in the case of recapitalizations.

d. To the extent practicable, state whether and the extent, if any, to which, the restatement will, as of the date thereof, alter the amount available for distribution to the holders of equity securities.

Item 17. Action with Respect to Reports.

If action is to be taken with respect to any report of the registrant or of its directors, officers or committees or any minutes of a meeting of its security holders, furnish the following information:

a. State whether or not such action is to constitute approval or disapproval of any of the matters referred to in such reports or minutes.

b. Identify each of such matters which it is intended will be approved or disapproved, and furnish the information required by the appropriate item or items of this schedule with respect to each such matter.

Item 18. Matters not Required to be Submitted.

If action is to be taken with respect to any matter which is not required to be submitted to a vote of security holders, state the nature of such matter, the reasons for submitting it to a vote of security holders and what action is intended to be taken by the registrant in the event of a negative vote on the matter by the security holders.

Item 19. Amendment of Charter, Bylaws or Other Documents.

If action is to be taken with respect to any amendment of the registrant's charter, bylaws or other documents as to which information is not required above, state briefly the reasons for and the general effect of such amendment.

Instructions.

1. Where the matter to be acted upon is the classification of directors, state whether vacancies which occur during the year may be filled by the board of directors to serve only until the next annual meeting or may be so filled for the remainder of the full term.

2. Attention is directed to the discussion of disclosure regarding anti-takeover and similar proposals in Release No. 34-15230 (October 13, 1978).

Item 20. Other Proposed Action.

If action is to be taken on any matter not specifically referred to in this Schedule 14A, describe briefly the substance of each such matter in substantially the same degree of detail as is required by Items 5 to 19, inclusive, of this Schedule, and, with respect to investment companies registered under the Investment Company Act of 1940, Item 22 of this Schedule.

Item 21. Voting Procedures.

As to each matter which is to be submitted to a vote of security holders, furnish the following information:

   a. State the vote required for approval or election, other than for the approval of auditors.

   b. Disclose the method by which votes will be counted, including the treatment and effect under applicable state law and registrant charter and bylaw provisions of abstentions, broker non-votes, and, to the extent applicable, a security holder's withholding of authority to vote for a nominee in an election of directors.

   c. When applicable, disclose how the soliciting person intends to treat proxy authority granted in favor of any other soliciting person's nominees if such other soliciting person abandons its solicitation or fails to comply with Rule 14a-19.

***

Item 23. Delivery of Documents to Security Holders Sharing an Address.

If one annual report to security holders, proxy statement, or Notice of Internet Availability of Proxy Materials is being delivered to two or more security holders who share an address in accordance with Rule 14a-3(e)(1), furnish the following information:

   a. State that only one annual report to security holders, proxy statement, or Notice of Internet Availability of Proxy Materials, as applicable, is being delivered to multiple security holders sharing an address unless the registrant has received contrary instructions from one or more of the security holders;

   b. Undertake to deliver promptly upon written or oral request a separate copy of the annual report to security holders, proxy statement, or Notice of Internet Availability of Proxy Materials, as applicable, to a security holder at a shared address to which a single copy of the documents was delivered and provide instructions as to how a security holder can notify the registrant that the security holder wishes to receive a separate copy of an annual report to security holders, proxy statement, or Notice of Internet Availability of Proxy Materials, as applicable;

   c. Provide the phone number and mailing address to which a security holder can direct a notification to the registrant that the security holder wishes to receive a separate annual report to security holders, proxy statement, or Notice of Internet Availability of Proxy Materials, as applicable, in the future; and

   d. Provide instructions how security holders sharing an address can request delivery of a single copy of annual reports to security holders, proxy statements, or Notices of Internet Availability of Proxy Materials if they are receiving multiple copies of annual reports to security holders, proxy statements, or Notices of Internet Availability of Proxy Materials.

Item 24. Shareholder Approval of Executive Compensation.

Registrants required to provide any of the separate shareholder votes pursuant to Rule 14a-21 of this chapter shall disclose that they are providing each such vote as required pursuant to section 14A of the Securities Exchange Act, briefly explain the general effect of each vote, such as whether each such vote is non-binding, and, when applicable, disclose the current frequency of shareholder advisory votes on executive compensation required by Rule 14a-21(a) and when the next such shareholder advisory vote will occur.

Item 25. Exhibits.

Provide the legal opinion required to be filed by Item 402(u)(4)(i) of Regulation S-K in an exhibit to this Schedule 14A.

Exchange Act – Forms 8-K, 10, 10-K, 10-Q

UNITED STATES SECURITIES AND EXCHANGE COMMISSION
Washington, D.C. 20549

FORM 8-K

CURRENT REPORT

Pursuant to Section 13 or 15(d) of The Securities Exchange Act of 1934

Date of Report (Date of earliest event reported) _____

_____
(Exact name of registrant as specified in its charter)

(State or other jurisdiction of incorporation or organization)	(Commission File No.)	(IRS Employer Identification No)

_____
(Address of principal executive offices)　　　　　　　　　(Zip Code)

Registrant's telephone number, including area code
_____
(Former name, former address and former fiscal year, if changed since last report)

Check the appropriate box below if the Form 8-K filing is intended to simultaneously satisfy the filing obligation of the registrant under any of the following provisions (see General Instruction A.2. below):

[ ]　Written communications pursuant to Rule 425 under the Securities Act
[ ]　Soliciting material pursuant to Rule 14a-12 under the Exchange Act
[ ]　Pre-commencement communications pursuant to Rule 14d-2(b) under the Exchange Act
[ ]　Pre-commencement communications pursuant to Rule 13e-4(c) under the Exchange Act

Securities registered pursuant to Section 12(b) of the Act:

Title of each class	Trading Symbol(s)	Name of each exchange on which registered

Indicate by check mark whether the registrant is an emerging growth company as defined in Rule 405 of the Securities Act of 1933 or Rule 12b-2 of the Securities Exchange Act of 1934.

Emerging growth company　　　　　　　❑

If an emerging growth company, indicate by check mark if the registrant has elected not to use the extended transition period for complying with any new or revised financial accounting standards provided pursuant to Section 13(a) of the Exchange Act.　　　❑

GENERAL INSTRUCTIONS

A.   **Rule as to Use of Form 8-K.**

    1.   Form 8-K shall be used for current reports under Section 13 or 15(d) of the Securities Exchange Act of 1934, filed pursuant to Rule 13 a-11 or Rule 15d-11 and for reports of nonpublic information required to be disclosed by Regulation FD.

    2.   Form 8-K may be used by a registrant to satisfy its filing obligations pursuant to Rule 425 under the Securities Act, regarding written communications related to business combination transactions, or Rules 14a-12 or Rule 14d-2(b) under the Exchange Act, relating to soliciting materials and pre-commencement communications pursuant to tender offers, respectively, provided that the Form 8-K filing satisfies all the substantive requirements of those rules (other than the Rule 425(c) requirement to include certain specified information in any prospectus filed pursuant to such rule). Such filing is also deemed to be filed pursuant to any rule for which the box is checked. A registrant is not required to check the box in connection with Rule 14a-12 or Rule 14d-2(b) if the communication is filed pursuant to Rule 425. Communications filed pursuant to Rule 425 are deemed filed under the other applicable sections. See Note 2 to Rule 425, Rule 14a-12 and Instruction 2 to Rule 14d-2(b)(2).

B.   **Events to be Reported and Time for Filing of Reports.**

    1.   A report on this form is required to be filed or furnished, as applicable, upon the occurrence of any one or more of the events specified in the items in Sections 1-6 and 9 of this form. Unless otherwise specified, a report is to be filed or furnished within four business days after occurrence of the event. If the event occurs on a Saturday, Sunday or holiday on which the Commission is not open for business, then the four business day period shall begin to run on, and include, the first business day thereafter. A registrant either furnishing a report on this form under Item 7.01 (Regulation FD Disclosure) or electing to file a report on this form under Item 8.01 (Other Events) solely to satisfy its obligations under Regulation FD must furnish such report or make such filing, as applicable, in accordance with the requirements of Rule 100(a) of Regulation FD, including the deadline for furnishing or filing such report. A report pursuant to Item 5.08 is to be filed within four business days after the registrant determines the anticipated meeting date.

    2.   The information in a report furnished pursuant to Item 2.02 (Results of Operations and Financial Condition) or Item 7.01 (Regulation FD Disclosure) shall not be deemed to be "filed" for purposes of Section 18 of the Exchange Act or otherwise subject to the liabilities of that section, unless the registrant specifically states that the information is to be considered "filed" under the Exchange Act or incorporates it by reference into a filing under the Securities Act or the Exchange Act. If a report on Form 8-K contains disclosures under Item 2.02 or Item 7.01, whether or not the report contains disclosures regarding other items, all exhibits to such report relating

to Item 2.02 or Item 7.01 will be deemed furnished, and not filed, unless the registrant specifies, under Item 9.01 (Financial Statements and Exhibits), which exhibits, or portions of exhibits, are intended to be deemed filed rather than furnished pursuant to this instruction.

3. If the registrant previously has reported substantially the same information as required by this form, the registrant need not make an additional report of the information on this form. To the extent that an item calls for disclosure of developments concerning a previously reported event or transaction, any information required in the new report or amendment about the previously reported event or transaction may be provided by incorporation by reference to the previously filed report. The term previously reported is defined in Rule 12b-2.

4. Copies of agreements, amendments or other documents or instruments required to be filed pursuant to Form 8-K are not required to be filed or furnished as exhibits to the Form 8-K unless specifically required to be filed or furnished by the applicable Item. This instruction does not affect the requirement to otherwise file such agreements, amendments or other documents or instruments, including as exhibits to registration statements and periodic reports pursuant to the requirements of Item 601 of Regulation S-K or Item 601 of Regulation S-B, as applicable.

5. When considering current reporting on this form, particularly of other events of material importance pursuant to Item 7.01 (Regulation FD Disclosure) and Item 8.01 (Other Events), registrants should have due regard for the accuracy, completeness and currency of the information in registration statements filed under the Securities Act which incorporate by reference information in reports filed pursuant to the Exchange Act, including reports on this form.

6. A registrant's report under Item 7.01 (Regulation FD Disclosure) or Item 8.01 (Other Events) will not be deemed an admission as to the materiality of any information in the report that is required to be disclosed solely by Regulation FD.

C. **Application of General Rules and Regulations.**

1. The General Rules and Regulations under the Act contain certain general requirements which are applicable to reports on any form. These general requirements should be carefully read and observed in the preparation and filing of reports on this form.

2. Particular attention is directed to Regulation 12B which contains general requirements regarding matters such as the kind and size of paper to be used, the legibility of the report, the information to be given whenever the title of securities is required to be stated, and the filing of the report. The definitions contained in Rule 12b-2 should be especially noted. See also Regulations 13A and 15D.

D. **Preparation of Report.**

This form is not to be used as a blank form to be filled in, but only as a guide in the preparation of the report on paper meeting the requirements of Rule 12b-12. The report shall contain the number and caption of the applicable item, but the text of such item may be omitted, provided the answers thereto are prepared in the manner specified in Rule 12b-13. To the extent that Item 1.01 and one or more other items of the form are applicable, registrants need not provide the number and caption of Item 1.01 so long as the substantive disclosure required by Item 1.01 is disclosed in the report and the number and caption of the other applicable item(s) are provided. All items that are not required to be answered in a particular report may be omitted and no reference thereto need be made in the report. All instructions should also be omitted.

E.   Signature and Filing of Report.

Three complete copies of the report, including any financial statements, exhibits or other papers or documents filed as a part thereof, and five additional copies which need not include exhibits, shall be filed with the Commission. At least one complete copy of the report, including any financial statements, exhibits or other papers or documents filed as a part thereof, shall be filed, with each exchange on which any class of securities of the registrant is registered. At least one complete copy of the report filed with the Commission and one such copy filed with each exchange shall be manually signed. Copies not manually signed shall bear typed or printed signatures.

F.   Incorporation by Reference.

If the registrant makes available to its stockholders or otherwise publishes, within the period prescribed for filing the report, a press release or other document or statement containing information meeting some or all of the requirements of this form, the information called for may be incorporated by reference to such published document or statement, in answer or partial answer to any item or items of this form, provided copies thereof are filed as an exhibit to the report on this form.

* * *

INFORMATION TO BE INCLUDED IN THE REPORT

Section 1 - Registrant's Business and Operations

Item 1.01 Entry into a Material Definitive Agreement.

(a) If the registrant has entered into a material definitive agreement not made in the ordinary course of business of the registrant, or into any amendment of such agreement that is material to the registrant, disclose the following information:

   (1) the date on which the agreement was entered into or amended, the identity of the parties to the agreement or amendment and a brief description of any material relationship between the registrant or its affiliates and any of the parties, other than in respect of the material definitive agreement or amendment; and

   (2) a brief description of the terms and conditions of the agreement or amendment that are material to the registrant.

(b) For purposes of this Item 1.01, a material definitive agreement means an agreement that provides for obligations that are material to and enforceable against the registrant, or rights that are material to the registrant and enforceable by the registrant against one or more other parties to the agreement, in each case whether or not subject to conditions.

Instructions.

1. Any material definitive agreement of the registrant not made in the ordinary course of the registrant's business must be disclosed under this Item 1.01. An agreement is deemed to be not made in the ordinary course of a registrant's business even if the agreement is such as ordinarily accompanies the kind of business conducted by the registrant if it involves the subject matter identified in Item 601(b)(10)(ii)(A) - (D) of Regulation S-K. An agreement involving the subject matter identified in Item 601(b)(10)(iii)(A) or (B) need not be disclosed under this Item.

2. A registrant must provide disclosure under this Item 1.01 if the registrant succeeds as a party to the agreement or amendment to the agreement by assumption or assignment (other than in connection with a merger or acquisition or similar transaction).

3. With respect to asset-backed securities, as defined in Item 1101 of Regulation AB, disclosure is required under this Item 1.01 regarding the entry into or an amendment to a definitive agreement that is material to the asset-backed securities transaction, even if the registrant is not a party to such agreement (e.g., a servicing agreement with a servicer contemplated by Item 1108(a)(3) of Regulation AB.

4. To the extent a material definitive agreement is filed as an exhibit under this Item 1.01, schedules (or similar attachments) to the exhibits are not required to be filed unless they contain information material to an investment or voting decision and that information is not otherwise disclosed in the exhibit or the disclosure document. Each exhibit filed must contain a list briefly identifying the contents of all omitted schedules. Registrants need not prepare a separate list of omitted information if such information is already included within the exhibit in a manner that conveys the subject matter of the omitted schedules and attachments. In addition, the registrant must provide a copy of any omitted schedule to the Commission or its staff upon request.

5. To the extent a material definitive agreement is filed as an exhibit under this Item 1.01, the registrant may redact information from the exhibit if disclosure of such information would constitute a clearly unwarranted invasion of personal privacy (e.g., disclosure of bank account numbers, social security numbers, home addresses and similar information).

6. To the extent a material definitive agreement is filed as an exhibit under this Item 1.01, the registrant may redact specific provisions or terms of the exhibit if the registrant customarily and actually treats that information as private or confidential and if the omitted information is not material, provided that the registrant intends to incorporate by reference this filing into its future periodic reports or registration statements, as applicable, in satisfaction of Item 601(b)(10) of Regulation S-K. If it does so, the registrant should mark the exhibit index to indicate that portions of the exhibit have been omitted and include a prominent statement on the first page of the redacted exhibit that certain identified information has been excluded from the exhibit because it is both not material and is the type that the registrant treats as private or confidential. The registrant also must include brackets indicating where the information is omitted from the filed version of the exhibit. If requested by the Commission or its staff, the registrant must promptly provide on a supplemental basis an unredacted copy of the exhibit and its materiality and privacy

or confidentiality analyses. Upon evaluation of the registrant's supplemental materials, the Commission or its staff may require the registrant to amend its filing to include in the exhibit any previously redacted information that is not adequately supported by the registrant's analyses. The registrant may request confidential treatment of the supplemental material submitted under this instruction pursuant to Rule 83 while it is in the possession of the Commission or its staff. After completing its review ..., the Commission or its staff will return or destroy it if the registrant complies with the procedures outlined in Rules 418 or 12b-4 .

Item 1.02 Termination of a Material Definitive Agreement.

(a) If a material definitive agreement which was not made in the ordinary course of business of the registrant and to which the registrant is a party is terminated otherwise than by expiration of the agreement on its stated termination date, or as a result of all parties completing their obligations under such agreement, and such termination of the agreement is material to the registrant, disclose the following information:

   (1) the date of the termination of the material definitive agreement, the identity of the parties to the agreement and a brief description of any material relationship between the registrant or its affiliates and any of the parties other than in respect of the material definitive agreement;

   (2) a brief description of the terms and conditions of the agreement that are material to the registrant;

   (3) a brief description of the material circumstances surrounding the termination; and

   (4) any material early termination penalties incurred by the registrant.

(b) For purposes of this Item 1.02, the term material definitive agreement shall have the same meaning as set forth in Item 1.01(b).

Instructions.

1. No disclosure is required solely by reason of this Item 1.02 during negotiations or discussions regarding termination of a material definitive agreement unless and until the agreement has been terminated.

2. No disclosure is required solely by reason of this Item 1.02 if the registrant believes in good faith that the material definitive agreement has not been terminated, unless the registrant has received a notice of termination pursuant to the terms of agreement.

Item 1.03 Bankruptcy or Receivership.

(a) If a receiver, fiscal agent or similar officer has been appointed for a registrant or its parent, in a proceeding under the U.S. Bankruptcy Code or in any other proceeding under state or federal law in which a court or governmental authority has assumed jurisdiction over substantially all of the assets or business of the registrant or its parent, or if such jurisdiction has been assumed by leaving the existing directors and officers in possession but subject to the supervision and orders of a court or governmental authority, disclose the following information:

   (1) the name or other identification of the proceeding;

(2) the identity of the court or governmental authority;

(3) the date that jurisdiction was assumed; and

(4) the identity of the receiver, fiscal agent or similar officer and the date of his or her appointment.

(b) If an order confirming a plan of reorganization, arrangement or liquidation has been entered by a court or governmental authority having supervision or jurisdiction over substantially all of the assets or business of the registrant or its parent, disclose the following;

(1) the identity of the court or governmental authority;

(2) the date that the order confirming the plan was entered by the court or governmental authority;

(3) a summary of the material features of the plan and, pursuant to Item 9.01 (Financial Statements and Exhibits), a copy of the plan as confirmed;

(4) the number of shares or other units of the registrant or its parent issued and outstanding, the number reserved for future issuance in respect of claims and interests filed and allowed under the plan, and the aggregate total of such numbers; and

(5) information as to the assets and liabilities of the registrant or its parent as of the date that the order confirming the plan was entered, or a date as close thereto as practicable.

Instruction.

The information called for in paragraph (b)(5) of this Item 1.03 may be presented in the form in which it was furnished to the court or governmental authority.

Item 1.04 Mine Safety – Reporting of Shutdowns and Patterns of Violations.

(a) If the registrant or a subsidiary of the registrant has received, with respect to a coal or other mine of which the registrant or a subsidiary of the registrant is an operator

- an imminent danger order issued under section 107(a) of the Federal Mine Safety and Health Act of 1977;

- a written notice from the Mine Safety and Health Administration that the coal or other mine has a pattern of violations of mandatory health or safety standards that are of such nature as could have significantly and substantially contributed to the cause and effect of coal or other mine health or safety hazards under section 104(e) of such Act; or

- a written notice from the Mine Safety and Health Administration that the coal or other mine has the potential to have such a pattern,

disclose the following information:

(1) The date of receipt by the issuer or a subsidiary of such order or notice.

(2) The category of the order or notice.

(3) The name and location of the mine involved.

Instructions to Item 1.04.

1. The term "coal or other mine" means a coal or other mine, as defined in section 3 of the Federal Mine Safety and Health Act of 1977, that is subject to the provisions of such Act.

2. The term "operator" has the meaning given the term in section 3 of the Federal Mine Safety and Health Act of 1977.

Section 2 - Financial Information

Item 2.01 Completion of Acquisition or Disposition of Assets.

If the registrant or any of its majority-owned subsidiaries has completed the acquisition or disposition of a significant amount of assets, otherwise than in the ordinary course of business, disclose the following information:

    (a) the date of completion of the transaction;

    (b) a brief description of the assets involved;

    (c) the identity of the person(s) from whom the assets were acquired or to whom they were sold and the nature of any material relationship, other than in respect of the transaction, between such person(s) and the registrant or any of its affiliates, or any director or officer of the registrant, or any associate of any such director or officer;

    (d) the nature and amount of consideration given or received for the assets and, if any material relationship is disclosed pursuant to paragraph (c) of this Item 2.01, the formula or principle followed in determining the amount of such consideration; and

    (e) if the transaction being reported is an acquisition and if a material relationship exists between the registrant or any of its affiliates and the source(s) of the funds used in the acquisition, the identity of the source(s) of the funds unless all or any part of the consideration used is a loan made in the ordinary course of business by a bank as defined by Section 3(a)(6) of the Act, in which case the identity of such bank may be omitted provided the registrant:

        (1) has made a request for confidentiality pursuant to Section 13(d)(1)(B) of the Act;

        (2) states in the report that the identity of the bank has been so omitted and filed separately with the Commission.

Instructions.

1. No information need be given as to:

(i)   any transaction between any person and any wholly-owned subsidiary of such person;

(ii) any transaction between two or more wholly-owned subsidiaries of any person; or

(iii) the redemption or other acquisition of securities from the public, or the sale or other disposition of securities to the public, by the issuer of such securities or by a wholly-owned subsidiary of that issuer.

2. The term acquisition includes every purchase, acquisition by lease, exchange, merger, consolidation, succession or other acquisition, except that the term does not include the construction or development of property by or for the registrant or its subsidiaries or the acquisition of materials for such purpose. The term disposition includes every sale, disposition by lease, exchange, merger, consolidation, mortgage, assignment or hypothecation of assets, whether for the benefit of creditors or otherwise, abandonment, destruction, or other disposition.

3. The information called for by this Item 2.01 is to be given as to each transaction or series of related transactions of the size indicated. The acquisition or disposition of securities is deemed the indirect acquisition or disposition of the assets represented by such securities if it results in the acquisition or disposition of control of such assets.

4. An acquisition or disposition shall be deemed to involve a significant amount of assets:
(i)   if the registrant's and its other subsidiaries' equity in the net book value of such assets or the amount paid or received for the assets upon such acquisition or disposition exceeded 10% of the total assets of the registrant and its consolidated subsidiaries; or
(ii) if it involved a business (see 17 CFR 210.11-01(d)) that is significant (see 17 CFR 210.11-01(b)).

Acquisitions of individually insignificant businesses are not required to be reported pursuant to this Item 2.01 unless they are related businesses (see 17 CFR 210.3-05(a)(3)) and are significant in the aggregate.

5. Attention is directed to the requirements in Item 9.01 (Financial Statements and Exhibits) with respect to the filing of:
(i)   financial statements of businesses acquired;
(ii) pro forma financial information; and
(iii) copies of the plans of acquisition or disposition as exhibits to the report.

Item 2.02 Results of Operations and Financial Condition.

(a) If a registrant, or any person acting on its behalf, makes any public announcement or release (including any update of an earlier announcement or release) disclosing material non-public information regarding the registrant's results of operations or financial condition for a completed quarterly or annual fiscal period, the registrant shall disclose the date of the announcement or release, briefly identify the announcement or release and include the text of that announcement or release as an exhibit.

(b) A Form 8-K is not required to be furnished to the Commission under this Item 2.02 in the case of disclosure of material non-public information that is disclosed orally, telephonically, by webcast, by broadcast, or by similar means if:
(1) the information is provided as part of a presentation that is complementary to, and initially occurs within 48 hours after, a related, written announcement or release that has been furnished on Form 8-K pursuant to this Item 2.02 prior to the presentation;
(2) the presentation is broadly accessible to the public by dial-in conference call, by webcast, by broadcast or by similar means;
(3) the financial and other statistical information contained in the presentation is provided on the registrant's website, together with any information that would be required under 17 CFR 244.100; and
(4) the presentation was announced by a widely disseminated press release, that included instructions as to when and how to access the presentation and the location on the registrant's website where the information would be available.

Instructions.

1. The requirements of this Item 2.02 are triggered by the disclosure of material non-public information regarding a completed fiscal year or quarter. Release of additional or updated material non-public information regarding a completed fiscal year or quarter would trigger an additional Item 2.02 requirement.

2. The requirements of paragraph(e)(1)(i) of Item 10 of Regulation S-K shall apply to disclosures under this Item 2.02.

3. Issuers that make earnings announcements or other disclosures of material non-public information regarding a completed fiscal year or quarter in an interim or annual report to shareholders are permitted to specify which portion of the report contains the information required to be furnished under this Item 2.02.

4. This Item 2.02 does not apply in the case of a disclosure that is made in a quarterly report filed with the Commission on Form 10-Q or an annual report filed with the Commission on Form 10-K.

Item 2.03 Creation of a Direct Financial Obligation or an Obligation under an Off-Balance Sheet Arrangement of a Registrant.

(a) If the registrant becomes obligated on a direct financial obligation that is material to the registrant, disclose the following information:

  (1) the date on which the registrant becomes obligated on the direct financial obligation and a brief description of the transaction or agreement creating the obligation;

  (2) the amount of the obligation, including the terms of its payment and, if applicable, a brief description of the material terms under which it may be accelerated or increased and the nature of any recourse provisions that would enable the registrant to recover from third parties; and

  (3) a brief description of the other terms and conditions of the transaction or agreement that are material to the registrant.

(b) If the registrant becomes directly or contingently liable for an obligation that is material to the registrant arising out of an off-balance sheet arrangement, disclose the following information:

  (1) the date on which the registrant becomes directly or contingently liable on the obligation and a brief description of the transaction or agreement creating the arrangement and obligation;

  (2) a brief description of the nature and amount of the obligation of the registrant under the arrangement, including the material terms whereby it may become a direct obligation, if applicable, or may be accelerated or increased and the nature of any recourse provisions that would enable the registrant to recover from third parties;

  (3) the maximum potential amount of future payments (undiscounted) that the registrant may be required to make, if different; and

  (4) a brief description of the other terms and conditions of the obligation or arrangement that are material to the registrant.

(c) For purposes of this Item 2.03, direct financial obligation means any of the following:

    (1) a long-term debt obligation, means a payment obligation under long-term borrowings referenced in FASB ASC paragraph 470-10-50-1 (Debt Topic) as may be modified or supplemented);

    (2) a financial lease obligationmeans a payment obligation under a lease that would be classified as a finance lease pursuant to FASB ASC Topic 842, Leases, as may be modified or supplemented;

    (3) an operating lease obligation means a payment obligation under a lease that would be classified as an operating lease pursuant to FASB ASC Topic 840, as may be modified or supplemented; or

    (4) a short-term debt obligation that arises other than in the ordinary course of business.

(d) For purposes of this Item 2.03, off-balance sheet arrangement means any transaction, agreement or other contractual arrangement to which an entity unconsolidated with the registrant is a party, under which the registrant has:

    (1) Any obligation under a guarantee contract that has any of the characteristics identified in FASB ASC paragraph 460-10-15-4 (Guarantees Topic), as may be modified or supplemented, and that is not excluded from the initial recognition and measurement provisions of FASB ASC paragraphs 460-10-15-7, 460-10-25-1, and 460-10-30-1.

    (2) A retained or contingent interest in assets transferred to an unconsolidated entity or similar arrangement that serves as credit, liquidity or market risk support to such entity for such assets;

    (3) Any obligation, including a contingent obligation, under a contract that would be accounted for as a derivative instrument, except that it is both indexed to the registrant's own stock and classified in stockholders' equity in the registrant's statement of financial position, and therefore excluded from the scope of FASB ASC Topic 815, *Derivatives and Hedging,* pursuant to FASB ASC subparagraph 815-10-15-74(a), as may be modified or supplemented; or

    (4) Any obligation, including a contingent obligation, arising out of a variable interest (as defined in the FASB ASC Master Glossary), as may be modified or supplemented) in an unconsolidated entity that is held by, and material to, the registrant, where such entity provides financing, liquidity, market risk or credit risk support to, or engages in leasing, hedging or research and development services with, the registrant.

(e) For purposes of this Item 2.03, short-term debt obligation means a payment obligation under a borrowing arrangement that is scheduled to mature within one year, or, for those registrants that use the operating cycle concept of working capital, within a registrant's operating cycle that is longer than one year, as discussed in Accounting Research Bulletin No. 43, Chapter 3A, Working Capital.

Instructions.

1. A registrant has no obligation to disclose information under this Item 2.03 until the registrant enters into an agreement enforceable against the registrant, whether or not subject to conditions, under which the direct financial obligation will arise or be created or issued. If there is no such

agreement, the registrant must provide the disclosure within four business days after the occurrence of the closing or settlement of the transaction or arrangement under which the direct financial obligation arises or is created.

2. A registrant must provide the disclosure required by paragraph (b) of this Item 2.03 whether or not the registrant is also a party to the transaction or agreement creating the contingent obligation arising under the off-balance sheet arrangement. In the event that neither the registrant nor any affiliate of the registrant is also a party to the transaction or agreement creating the contingent obligation arising under the off-balance sheet arrangement in question, the four business day period for reporting the event under this Item 2.03 shall begin on the earlier of (i) the fourth business day after the contingent obligation is created or arises, and (ii) the day on which an executive officer, as defined in Rule 3b-7, of the registrant becomes aware of the contingent obligation.

3. In the event that an agreement, transaction or arrangement requiring disclosure under this Item 2.03 comprises a facility, program or similar arrangement that creates or may give rise to direct financial obligations of the registrant in connection with multiple transactions, the registrant shall:

    (i) disclose the entering into of the facility, program or similar arrangement if the entering into of the facility is material to the registrant; and

    (ii) as direct financial obligations arise or are created under the facility or program, disclose the required information under this Item 2.03 to the extent that the obligations are material to the registrant (including when a series of previously undisclosed individually immaterial obligations become material in the aggregate).

4. For purposes of Item 2.03(b)(3), the maximum amount of future payments shall not be reduced by the effect of any amounts that may possibly be recovered by the registrant under recourse or collateralization provisions in any guarantee agreement, transaction or arrangement.

5. If the obligation required to be disclosed under this Item 2.03 is a security, or a term of a security, that has been or will be sold pursuant to an effective registration statement of the registrant, the registrant is not required to file a Form 8-K pursuant to this Item 2.03, provided that the prospectus relating to that sale contains the information required by this Item 2.03 and is filed within the required time period under Securities Act Rule 424.

Item 2.04 Triggering Events That Accelerate or Increase a Direct Financial Obligation or an Obligation under an Off-Balance Sheet Arrangement.

    (a) If a triggering event causing the increase or acceleration of a direct financial obligation of the registrant occurs and the consequences of the event, taking into account those described in paragraph (a)(4) of this Item 2.04, are material to the registrant, disclose the following information:

        (1) the date of the triggering event and a brief description of the agreement or transaction under which the direct financial obligation was created and is increased or accelerated;

        (2) a brief description of the triggering event;

        (3) the amount of the direct financial obligation, as increased if applicable, and the terms of payment or acceleration that apply; and

(4) any other material obligations of the registrant that may arise, increase, be accelerated or become direct financial obligations as a result of the triggering event or the increase or acceleration of the direct financial obligation.

(b) If a triggering event occurs causing an obligation of the registrant under an off-balance sheet arrangement to increase or be accelerated, or causing a contingent obligation of the registrant under an off-balance sheet arrangement to become a direct financial obligation of the registrant, and the consequences of the event, taking into account those described in paragraph (b)(4) of this Item 2.04, are material to the registrant, disclose the following information:

(1) the date of the triggering event and a brief description of the off-balance sheet arrangement;

(2) a brief description of the triggering event;

(3) the nature and amount of the obligation, as increased if applicable, and the terms of payment or acceleration that apply; and

(4) any other material obligations of the registrant that may arise, increase, be accelerated or become direct financial obligations as a result of the triggering event or the increase or acceleration of the obligation under the off-balance sheet arrangement or its becoming a direct financial obligation of the registrant.

(c) For purposes of this Item 2.04, the term direct financial obligation has the meaning provided in Item 2.03 of this form, but shall also include an obligation arising out of an off-balance sheet arrangement that is accrued under FASB Statement of Financial Accounting Standards No. 5 Accounting for Contingencies (SFAS No. 5) as a probable loss contingency.

(d) For purposes of this Item 2.04, the term off-balance sheet arrangement has the meaning provided in Item 2.03 of this form.

(e) For purposes of this Item 2.04, a triggering event is an event, including an event of default, event of acceleration or similar event, as a result of which a direct financial obligation of the registrant or an obligation of the registrant arising under an off-balance sheet arrangement is increased or becomes accelerated or as a result of which a contingent obligation of the registrant arising out of an off-balance sheet arrangement becomes a direct financial obligation of the registrant.

Instructions.

1. Disclosure is required if a triggering event occurs in respect of an obligation of the registrant under an off-balance sheet arrangement and the consequences are material to the registrant, whether or not the registrant is also a party to the transaction or agreement under which the triggering event occurs.

2. No disclosure is required under this Item 2.04 unless and until a triggering event has occurred in accordance with the terms of the relevant agreement, transaction or arrangement, including, if required, the sending to the registrant of notice of the occurrence of a triggering event pursuant to the terms of the agreement, transaction or arrangement and the satisfaction of all conditions to such occurrence, except the passage of time.

3. No disclosure is required solely by reason of this Item 2.04 if the registrant believes in good faith that no triggering event has occurred, unless the registrant has received a notice described in Instruction 2 to this Item 2.04.

4. Where a registrant is subject to an obligation arising out of an off-balance sheet arrangement, whether or not disclosed pursuant to Item 2.03 of this form, if a triggering event occurs as a result of which under that obligation an accrual for a probable loss is required under SFAS No. 5, the obligation arising out of the off-balance sheet arrangement becomes a direct financial obligation as defined in this Item 2.04. In that situation, if the consequences as determined under Item 2.04(b) are material to the registrant, disclosure is required under this Item 2.04.

Item 2.05 Costs Associated with Exit or Disposal Activities.
If the registrant's board of directors, a committee of the board of directors or the officer or officers of the registrant authorized to take such action if board action is not required, commits the registrant to an exit or disposal plan, or otherwise disposes of a long-lived asset or terminates employees under a plan of termination described in paragraph 8 of FASB Statement of Financial Accounting Standards No. 146 Accounting for Costs Associated with Exit or Disposal Activities (SFAS No. 146), under which material charges will be incurred under generally accepted accounting principles applicable to the registrant, disclose the following information:

> (a) the date of the commitment to the course of action and a description of the course of action, including the facts and circumstances leading to the expected action and the expected completion date;

> (b) for each major type of cost associated with the course of action (for example, one-time termination benefits, contract termination costs and other associated costs), an estimate of the total amount or range of amounts expected to be incurred in connection with the action;

> (c) an estimate of the total amount or range of amounts expected to be incurred in connection with the action; and

> (d) the registrant's estimate of the amount or range of amounts of the charge that will result in future cash expenditures,

provided, however, that if the registrant determines that at the time of filing it is unable in good faith to make a determination of an estimate required by paragraphs (b), (c) or (d) of this Item 2.05, no disclosure of such estimate shall be required; *provided further*, however, that in any such event, the registrant shall file an amended report on Form 8-K under this Item 2.05 within four business days after it makes a determination of such an estimate or range of estimates.

Item 2.06 Material Impairments.
If the registrant's board of directors, a committee of the board of directors or the officer or officers of the registrant authorized to take such action if board action is not required, concludes that a material charge for impairment to one or more of its assets, including, without limitation, impairments of securities or goodwill, is required under generally accepted accounting principles applicable to the registrant, disclose the following information:

(a) the date of the conclusion that a material charge is required and a description of the impaired asset or assets and the facts and circumstances leading to the conclusion that the charge for impairment is required;

(b) the registrant's estimate of the amount or range of amounts of the impairment charge; and

(c) the registrant's estimate of the amount or range of amounts of the impairment charge that will result in future cash expenditures,

provided, however, that if the registrant determines that at the time of filing it is unable in good faith to make a determination of an estimate required by paragraphs (b) or (c) of this Item 2.06, no disclosure of such estimate shall be required; *provided further*, however, that in any such event, the registrant shall file an amended report on Form 8-K under this Item 2.06 within four business days after it makes a determination of such an estimate or range of estimates.

Instruction.
No filing is required under this Item 2.06 if the conclusion is made in connection with the preparation, review or audit of financial statements required to be included in the next periodic report due to be filed under the Exchange Act, the periodic report is filed on a timely basis and such conclusion is disclosed in the report.

Section 3 - Securities and Trading Markets

Item 3.01 Notice of Delisting or Failure to Satisfy a Continued Listing Rule or Standard; Transfer of Listing.

(a) If the registrant has received notice from the national securities exchange or national securities association (or a facility thereof) that maintains the principal listing for any class of the registrant's common equity (as defined in Exchange Act Rule 12b-2 that:
- the registrant or such class of the registrant's securities does not satisfy a rule or standard for continued listing on the exchange or association;
- the exchange has submitted an application under Exchange Act Rule 12d2-2 to the Commission to delist such class of the registrant's securities; or
- the association has taken all necessary steps under its rules to delist the security from its automated inter-dealer quotation system,

the registrant must disclose:
   (i) the date that the registrant received the notice;
   (ii) the a rule or standard for continued listing on the national securities exchange or national securities association that the registrant fails, or has failed to, satisfy; and
   (iii) any action or response that, at the time of filing, the registrant has determined to take in response to the notice.

(b) If the registrant has notified the national securities exchange or national securities association (or a facility thereof) that maintains the principal listing for any class of the registrant's common equity (as defined in Exchange Act Rule 12b-2 that the registrant is aware of any material noncompliance with a rule or standard for continued listing on the exchange or association, the registrant must disclose:

    (i)   the date that the registrant provided such notice to the exchange or association;

    (ii) the rule or standard for continued listing on the exchange or association that the registrant fails, or has failed, to satisfy; and

    (iii) any action or response that, at the time of filing, the registrant has determined to take regarding its noncompliance.

(c) If the national securities exchange or national securities association (or a facility thereof) that maintains the principal listing for any class of the registrant's common equity (as defined in Exchange Act Rule 12b-2, in lieu of suspending trading in or delisting such class of the registrant's securities, issues a public reprimand letter or similar communication indicating that the registrant has violated a rule or standard for continued listing on the exchange or association, the registrant must state the date, and summarize the contents of the letter or communication.

(d) If the registrant's board of directors, a committee of the board of directors or the officer or officers of the registrant authorized to take such action if board action is not required, has taken definitive action to cause the listing of a class of its common equity to be withdrawn from the national securities exchange, or terminated from the automated inter-dealer quotation system of a registered national securities association, where such exchange or association maintains the principal listing, for such class of securities, including by reason of a transfer of the listing or quotation to another securities exchange or quotation system, describe the action taken and state the date of the action.

Instructions.

1. The registrant is not required to disclose any information required by paragraph (a) of this Item 3.01 where the delisting is a result of one of the following:

- the entire class of the security has been called for redemption, maturity or retirement; appropriate notice thereof has been given; if required by the terms of the securities, funds sufficient for the payment of all such securities have been deposited with an agency authorized to make such payments; and such funds have been made available to security holders;
- the entire class of the security has been redeemed or paid at maturity or retirement;
- the instruments representing the entire class of securities have come to evidence, by operation of law or otherwise, other securities in substitution therefore and represent no other right, except, if true, the right to receive an immediate cash payment (the right of dissenters to receive the appraised or fair value of their holdings shall not prevent the application of this provision); or
- all rights pertaining to the entire class of the security have been extinguished; *provided, however,* that where such an event occurs as the result of an order of a court or other governmental authority, the order shall be final, all applicable appeal periods shall have expired and no appeals shall be pending.

2. A registrant must provide the disclosure required by paragraph (a) or (b) of this Item 3.01, as applicable, regarding any failure to satisfy a rule or standard for continued listing on the

national securities exchange or national securities association (or a facility thereof) that maintains the principal listing for any class of the registrant's common equity (as defined in Exchange Act Rule 12b-2 even if the registrant has the benefit of a grace period or similar extension period during which it may cure the deficiency that triggers the disclosure requirement.

3. Notices or other communications subsequent to an initial notice sent to, or by, a registrant under Item 3.01(a), (b) or (c) that continue to indicate that the registrant does not comply with the same rule or standard for continued listing that was the subject of the initial notice are not required to be filed, but may be filed voluntarily.

4. Registrants whose securities are quoted exclusively (i.e., the securities are not otherwise listed on an exchange or association) on automated inter-dealer quotation systems are not subject to this Item 3.01 and such registrants are thus not required to file a Form 8-K pursuant to this Item 3.01 if the securities are no longer quoted on such quotation system. If a security is listed on an exchange or association and is also quoted on an automated inter-dealer quotation system, the registrant is subject to the disclosure obligations of Item 3.01 if any of the events specified in Item 3.01 occur.

Item 3.02 Unregistered Sales of Equity Securities.

(a) If the registrant sells equity securities in a transaction that is not registered under the Securities Act, furnish the information set forth in paragraphs (a) and (c) through (e) of Item 701 of Regulation S-K. For purposes of determining the required filing date for the Form 8-K under this Item 3.02(a), the registrant has no obligation to disclose information under this Item 3.02 until the registrant enters into an agreement enforceable against the registrant, whether or not subject to conditions, under which the equity securities are to be sold. If there is no such agreement, the registrant must provide the disclosure within four business days after the occurrence of the closing or settlement of the transaction or arrangement under which the equity securities are to be sold.

(b) No report need be filed under this Item 3.02 if the equity securities sold, in the aggregate since its last report filed under this Item 3.02 or its last periodic report, whichever is more recent, constitute less than 1% of the number of shares outstanding of the class of equity securities sold. In the case of a smaller reporting company, no report need be filed if the equity securities sold, in the aggregate since its last report filed under this Item 3.02 or its last periodic report, whichever is more recent, constitute less than 5% of the number of shares outstanding of the class of equity securities sold.

Instructions.
1. For purposes of this Item 3.02, "the number of shares outstanding" refers to the actual number of shares of equity securities of the class outstanding and does not include outstanding securities convertible into or exchangeable for such equity securities.

2. Smaller reporting company is defined in Item 10(f)(1) of Regulation S-K.

Item 3.03 Material Modification to Rights of Security Holders.

    (a) If the constituent instruments defining the rights of the holders of any class of registered securities of the registrant have been materially modified, disclose the date of the modification, the title of the class of securities involved and briefly describe the general effect of such modification upon the rights of holders of such securities.

    (b) If the rights evidenced by any class of registered securities have been materially limited or qualified by the issuance or modification of any other class of securities by the registrant, briefly disclose the date of the issuance or modification, the general effect of the issuance or modification of such other class of securities upon the rights of the holders of the registered securities.

Instruction.
Working capital restrictions and other limitations upon the payment of dividends must be reported pursuant to this Item 3.03.

Section 4 - Matters Related to Accountants and Financial Statements

Item 4.01 Changes in Registrant's Certifying Accountant.

    (a) If an independent accountant who was previously engaged as the principal accountant to audit the registrant's financial statements, or an independent accountant upon whom the principal accountant expressed reliance in its report regarding a significant subsidiary, resigns (or indicates that it declines to stand for re-appointment after completion of the current audit) or is dismissed, disclose the information required by Item 304(a)(1) of Regulation S-K, including compliance with Item 304(a)(3) of Regulation S-K.

    (b) If a new independent accountant has been engaged as either the principal accountant to audit the registrant's financial statements or as an independent accountant on whom the principal accountant is expected to express reliance in its report regarding a significant subsidiary, the registrant must disclose the information required by Item 304(a)(2) of Regulation S-K.

Instruction.
The resignation or dismissal of an independent accountant, or its refusal to stand for re-appointment, is a reportable event separate from the engagement of a new independent accountant. On some occasions, two reports on Form 8-K are required for a single change in accountants, the first on the resignation (or refusal to stand for re-appointment) or dismissal of the former accountant and the second when the new accountant is engaged. Information required in the second Form 8-K in such situations need not be provided to the extent that it has been reported previously in the first Form 8-K.

Item 4.02 Non-Reliance on Previously Issued Financial Statements or a Related Audit Report or Completed Interim Review.

    (a) If the registrant's board of directors, a committee of the board of directors or the officer or officers of the registrant authorized to take such action if board action is not required, concludes that any previously issued financial statements, covering one or more years or interim periods for which the registrant is required to provide financial statements under Regulation S-X should no longer be relied upon because of an error in such financial statements as addressed in Accounting Principles Board Opinion No. 20, as may be modified, supplemented or succeeded, disclose the following information:

(1) the date of the conclusion regarding the non-reliance and an identification of the financial statements and years or periods covered that should no longer be relied upon;

(2) a brief description of the facts underlying the conclusion to the extent known to the registrant at the time of filing; and

(3) a statement of whether the audit committee, or the board of directors in the absence of an audit committee, or authorized officer or officers, discussed with the registrant's independent accountant the matters disclosed in the filing pursuant to this Item 4.02(a).

(b) If the registrant is advised by, or receives notice from, its independent accountant that disclosure should be made or action should be taken to prevent future reliance on a previously issued audit report or completed interim review related to previously issued financial statements, disclose the following information:

(1) the date on which the registrant was so advised or notified;

(2) identification of the financial statements that should no longer be relied upon;

(3) a brief description of the information provided by the accountant; and

(4) a statement of whether the audit committee, or the board of directors in the absence of an audit committee, or authorized officer or officers, discussed with the independent accountant the matters disclosed in the filing pursuant to this Item 4.02(b).

(c) If the registrant receives advisement or notice from its independent accountant requiring disclosure under paragraph (b) of this Item 4.02, the registrant must:

(1) provide the independent accountant with a copy of the disclosures it is making in response to this item 4.02 that the independent accountant shall receive no later than the day that the disclosures are filed with the Commission;

(2) request the independent accountant to furnish to the registrant as promptly as possible a letter addressed to the Commission stating whether the independent accountant agrees with the statements made by the registrant in response to this Item 4.02 and, if not, stating the respects in which it does not agree; and

(3) amend the registrant's previously filed Form 8-K by filing the independent accountant's letter as an exhibit to the filed Form 8-K no later than two business days after the registrant's receipt of the letter.

Section 5 - Corporate Governance and Management

Item 5.01 Changes in Control of Registrant.

(a) If, to the knowledge of the registrant's board of directors, a committee of the board of directors or authorized officer or officers of the registrant, a change in control of the registrant has occurred, furnish the following information:

(1) the identity of the person(s) who acquired such control;

    (2) the date and a description of the transaction(s) which resulted in the change in control;

    (3) the basis of the control, including the percentage of voting securities of the registrant now beneficially owned directly or indirectly by the person(s) who acquired control;

    (4) the amount of the consideration used by such person(s);

    (5) the source(s) of funds used by the person(s), unless all or any part of the consideration used is a loan made in the ordinary course of business by a bank as defined by Section 3(a)(6) of the Act, in which case the identity of such bank may be omitted provided the person who acquired control:

        (i) has made a request for confidentiality pursuant to Section 13(d)(1)(B) of the Act; and

        (ii) states in the report that the identity of the bank has been so omitted and filed separately with the Commission.

    (6) the identity of the person(s) from whom control was assumed; and

    (7) any arrangements or understandings among members of both the former and new control groups and their associates with respect to election of directors or other matters.

(b) Furnish the information required by Item 403(c) of Regulation S-K.

Item 5.02   Departure of Directors or Principal Officers; Election of Directors; Appointment of Principal Officers.

    (a)(1) If a director has resigned or refuses to stand for re-election to the board of directors since the date of the last annual meeting of shareholders because of a disagreement with the registrant, known to an executive officer of the registrant, as defined in Rule 3b-7, on any matter relating to the registrant's operations, policies or practices, or if a director has been removed for cause from the board of directors, disclose the following information:

        (i) the date of such resignation, refusal to stand for re-election or removal;

        (ii) any positions held by the director on any committee of the board of directors at the time of the director's resignation, refusal to stand for re-election or removal; and

    (2) a brief description of the circumstances representing the disagreement that the registrant believes caused, in whole or in part, the director's resignation, refusal to stand for re-election or removal. If the director has furnished the registrant with any written correspondence concerning the circumstances surrounding his or her resignation, refusal or removal, the registrant shall file a copy of the document as an exhibit to the report on Form 8-K.

    (3) The registrant also must:

        (i) provide the director with a copy of the disclosures it is making in response to this Item 5.02 no later than the day the registrant files the disclosures with the Commission;

        (ii) provide the director with the opportunity to furnish the registrant as promptly as possible with a letter addressed to the registrant stating whether he or she agrees with the statements made by the registrant in response to this Item 5.02 and, if not, stating the respects in which he or she does not agree; and

(iii) file any letter received by the registrant from the director with the Commission as an exhibit by an amendment to the previously filed Form 8-K within two business days after receipt by the registrant.

(b) If the registrant's principal executive officer, president, principal financial officer, principal accounting officer, principal operating officer, or any person performing similar functions, or any named executive officer, retires, resigns or is terminated from that position, or if a director retires, resigns, is removed, or refuses to stand for re-election (except in circumstances described in paragraph (a) of this Item 5.02), disclose the fact that the event has occurred and the date of the event.

(c) If the registrant appoints a new principal executive officer, president, principal financial officer, principal accounting officer, principal operating officer, or person performing similar functions, disclose the following information with respect to the newly appointed officer:

(1) the name and position of the newly appointed officer and the date of the appointment;

(2) the information required by Items 401(b), (d), (e) and Item 404(a) of Regulation S-K; and

(3) a brief description of any material plan, contract or arrangement (whether or not written) to which a covered officer is a party or in which he or she participates that is entered into or material amendment in connection with the triggering event or any grant or award to any such covered person or modification thereto, under any such plan, contract or arrangement in connection with any such event.

Instruction to paragraph (c).

If the registrant intends to make a public announcement of the appointment other than by means of a report on Form 8-K, the registrant may delay filing the Form 8-K containing the disclosures required by this Item 5.02(c) until the day on which the registrant otherwise makes public announcement of the appointment of such officer.

(d) If the registrant elects a new director, except by a vote of security holders at an annual meeting or special meeting convened for such purpose, disclose the following information:

(1) the name of the newly elected director and the date of election;

(2) a brief description of any arrangement or understanding between the new director and any other persons, naming such persons, pursuant to which such director was selected as a director;

(3) the committees of the board of directors to which the new director has been, or at the time of this disclosure is expected to be, named; and

(4) the information required by Item 404(a) of Regulation S-K.

(5) a brief description of any material plan, contract or arrangement (whether or not written) to which the director is a party or in which he or she participates that is entered into or material amendment in connection with the triggering event or any grant or award to any such covered person or modification thereto, under any such plan, contract or arrangement in connection with any such event.

719

(e) If the registrant enters into, adopts, or otherwise commences a material compensatory plan, contract or arrangement (whether or not written), as to which the registrant's principal executive officer, principal financial officer, or a named executive officer participates or is a party, or such compensatory plan, contract or arrangement is materially amended or modified, or a material grant or award under any such plan, contract or arrangement to any such person is made or materially modified, then the registrant shall provide a brief description of the terms and conditions of the plan, contract or arrangement and the amounts payable to the officer thereunder.

Instructions to paragraph (e).

(1) Disclosure under this Item 5.02(e) shall be required whether or not the specified event is in connection with events otherwise triggering disclosure pursuant to this Item 5.02.

(2) Grants or awards (or modifications thereto) made pursuant to a plan, contract or arrangement (whether involving cash or equity), that are materially consistent with the previously disclosed terms of such plan, contract or arrangement, need not be disclosed under this Item 5.02(e), provided the registrant has previously disclosed such terms and the grant, award or modification is disclosed when Item 402 of Regulation S-K requires such disclosure.

(f)

(1) If the salary or bonus of a named executive officer cannot be calculated as of the most recent practicable date and is omitted from the Summary Compensation Table as specified in Instruction 1 to Item 402(c)(2)(iii) and (iv) of Regulation S-K, disclose the appropriate information under this Item 5.02(f) when there is a payment, grant, award, decision or other occurrence as a result of which such amounts become calculable in whole or part. Disclosure under this Item 5.02(f) shall include a new total compensation figure for the named executive officer, using the new salary or bonus information to recalculate the information that was previously provided with respect to the named executive officer in the registrant's Summary Compensation Table for which the salary and bonus information was omitted in reliance on Instruction 1 to Item 402(c)(2)(iii) and (iv) of Regulation S-K.

(2) As specified in Instruction 6 to Item 402(u) of Regulation S-K, disclosure under this Item 5.02(f) with respect to the salary or bonus of a principal executive officer shall include pay ratio disclosure pursuant to Item 402(u) of Regulation S-K calculated using the new total compensation figure for the principal executive officer. Pay ratio disclosure is not required under this Item 5.02(f) until the omitted salary or bonus amounts for such principal executive officer become calculable in whole.

Instructions to Item 5.02.

1. The disclosure requirements of this Item 5.02 do not apply to a registrant that is a wholly-owned subsidiary of an issuer with a class of securities registered under Section 12 of the Exchange Act, or that is required to file reports under Section 15(d) of the Exchange Act.

2. To the extent that any information called for in Item 5.02(c)(3) or Item 5.02(d)(3) or Item 5.02(d)(4) is not determined or is unavailable at the time of the required filing, the registrant shall include a statement to this effect in the filing and then must file an amendment to its Form

8-K filing under this Item 5.02 containing such information within four business days after the information is determined or becomes available.

3. The registrant need not provide information with respect to plans, contracts, and arrangements to the extent they do not discriminate in scope, terms or operation, in favor of executive officers or directors of the registrant and that are available generally to all salaried employees.

4. For purposes of this Item, the term "named executive officer" shall refer to those executive officers for whom disclosure was required in the registrant's most recent filing with the Commission under the Securities Act or Exchange Act that required disclosure pursuant to Item 402(c) of Regulation S-K.

Item 5.03 Amendments to Articles of Incorporation or Bylaws; Change in Fiscal Year.

(a) If a registrant with a class of equity securities registered under Section 12 of the Exchange Act amends its articles of incorporation or bylaws and a proposal for the amendment was not disclosed in a proxy statement or information statement filed by the registrant, disclose the following information:
   (1) the effective date of the amendment; and
   (2) a description of the provision adopted or changed by amendment and, if applicable, the previous provision.

(b) If the registrant determines to change the fiscal year from that used in its most recent filing with the Commission other than by means of:
   (1) a submission to a vote of security holders through the solicitation of proxies or otherwise; or
   (2) an amendment to its articles of incorporation or bylaws,

disclose the date of such determination, the date of the new fiscal year end and the form (for example, Form 10-K or Form 10-Q) on which the report covering the transition period will be filed.

Instruction to Item 5.03.
Refer to Item 601(b)(3) of Regulation S-K regarding the filing of exhibits to this Item 5.03.

Item 5.04 Temporary Suspension of Trading Under Registrant's Employee Benefit Plans.

(a) No later than the fourth business day after which the registrant receives the notice required by section 101(i)(2)(E) of the Employment Retirement Income Security Act of 1974, or, if such notice is not received by the registrant, on the same date by which the registrant transmits a timely notice to an affected officer or director within the time period prescribed by Rule 104(b)(2)(i)(B) or 104(b)(2)(ii) of Regulation BTR, provide the information specified in Rule 104(b) and the date the registrant received the notice required by section 101(i)(2)(E) of the Employment Retirement Income Security Act of 1974, if applicable.

(b) On the same date by which the registrant transmits a timely updated notice to an affected officer or director, as required by the time period under Rule 104(b)(2)(iii) of Regulation BTR, provide the information specified in Rule 104(b)(3)(iii).

Item 5.05 Amendments to the Registrant's Code of Ethics, or Waiver of a Provision of the Code of Ethics.

    (a) Briefly describe the date and nature of any amendment to a provision of the registrant's code of ethics that applies to the registrant's principal executive officer, principal financial officer, principal accounting officer or controller or persons performing similar functions and that relates to any element of the code of ethics definition enumerated in Item 406(b) of Regulation S-K.

    (b) If the registrant has granted a waiver, including an implicit waiver, from a provision of the code of ethics to an officer or person described in paragraph (a) of this Item 5.05, and the waiver relates to one or more of the elements of the code of ethics definition referred to in paragraph (a) of this Item 5.05, briefly describe the nature of the waiver, the name of the person to whom the waiver was granted, and the date of the waiver.

    (c) The registrant does not need to provide any information pursuant to this Item 5.05 if it discloses the required information on its Internet website within four business days following the date of the amendment or waiver and the registrant has disclosed in its most recently filed annual report its Internet address and intention to provide disclosure in this manner. If the registrant elects to disclose the information required by this Item 5.05 through its website, such information must remain available on the website for at least a 12-month period. Following the 12-month period, the registrant must retain the information for a period of not less than five years. Upon request, the registrant must furnish to the Commission or its staff a copy of any or all information retained pursuant to this requirement.

Instructions.
1. The registrant does not need to disclose technical, administrative or other non-substantive amendments to its code of ethics.

2. For purposes of this Item 5.05:
    (i) The term waiver means the approval by the registrant of a material departure from a provision of the code of ethics; and
    (ii) The term implicit waiver means the registrant's failure to take action within a reasonable period of time regarding a material departure from a provision of the code of ethics that has been made known to an executive officer, as defined in Rule 3b-7 of the registrant.

Item 5.07 Submission of Matters to a Vote of Security Holders. If any matter was submitted to a vote of security holders, through the solicitation of proxies or otherwise, provide the following information:

    (a) The date of the meeting and whether it was an annual or special meeting. This information must be provided only if a meeting of security holders was held.

    (b) If the meeting involved the election of directors, the name of each director elected at the meeting, as well as a brief description of each other matter voted upon at the meeting; and state the number of votes cast for, against or withheld, as well as the number of abstentions and broker non-votes as to each such matter, including a separate tabulation with respect to each nominee for office. For the vote on the frequency of shareholder advisory votes on executive compensation required by section 14A(a)(2) of the Securities Exchange Act of 1934 and Rule 14a-21(b), state the number of votes cast for each of 1 year, 2 years, and 3 years, as well as the number of abstentions.

(c) A description of the terms of any settlement between the registrant and any other participant (as defined in Instruction 3 to Item 4 of Schedule 14A) terminating any solicitation subject to Rule 14a-12(c), including the cost or anticipated cost to the registrant.

(d) No later than one hundred fifty calendar days after the end of the annual or other meeting of shareholders at which shareholders voted on the frequency of shareholder votes on the compensation of executives as required by section 14A(a)(2) of the Securities Exchange Act of 1934, but in no event later than sixty calendar days prior to the deadline for submission of shareholder proposals under Rule 14a-8, as disclosed in the registrant's most recent proxy statement for an annual or other meeting of shareholders relating to the election of directors at which shareholders voted on the frequency of shareholder votes on the compensation of executives as required by section 14A(a)(2) of the Securities Exchange Act of 1934, by amendment to the most recent Form 8-K filed pursuant to (b) of this Item, disclose the company's decision in light of such vote as to how frequently the company will include a shareholder vote on the compensation of executives in its proxy materials until the next required vote on the frequency of shareholder votes on the compensation of executives.

Instruction 1 to Item 5.07. The four business day period for reporting the event under this Item 5.07, other than with respect to Item 5.07(d), shall begin to run on the day on which the meeting ended. The registrant shall disclose on Form 8-K under this Item 5.07 the preliminary voting results. The registrant shall file an amended report on Form 8-K under this Item 5.07 to disclose the final voting results within four business days after the final voting results are known. *However*, no preliminary voting results need be disclosed under this Item 5.07 if the registrant has disclosed final voting results on Form 8-K under this Item.
Instruction 2 to Item 5.07. If any matter has been submitted to a vote of security holders otherwise than at a meeting of such security holders, corresponding information with respect to such submission shall be provided. The solicitation of any authorization or consent (other than a proxy to vote at a stockholders' meeting) with respect to any matter shall be deemed a submission of such matter to a vote of security holders within the meaning of this item.
Instruction 3 to Item 5.07. If the registrant did not solicit proxies and the board of directors as previously reported to the Commission was re-elected in its entirety, a statement to that effect in answer to paragraph (b) will suffice as an answer thereto regarding the election of directors.
Instruction 4 to Item 5.07. If the registrant has furnished to its security holders proxy soliciting material containing the information called for by paragraph (c), the paragraph may be answered by reference to the information contained in such material.
Instruction 5 to Item 5.07. A registrant may omit the information called for by this Item 5.07 if, on the date of the filing of its report on Form 8-K, the registrant meets the following conditions:

1. All of the registrant's equity securities are owned, either directly or indirectly, by a single person which is a reporting company under the Exchange Act and which has filed all the material required to be filed pursuant to Section 13, 14 or 15(d) thereof, as applicable; and

2. During the preceding thirty-six calendar months and any subsequent period of days, there has not been any material default in the payment of principal, interest, a sinking or purchase fund installment, or any other material default not cured within thirty days, with respect to any indebtedness of the registrant or its subsidiaries, and there has not been any material default in the payment of rentals under material long-term leases."

Item 5.08 Shareholder Director Nominations

(a) If the registrant did not hold an annual meeting the previous year, or if the date of this year's annual meeting has been changed by more than 30 calendar days from the date of the previous year's meeting, then the registrant is required to disclose the date by which a nominating shareholder or nominating shareholder group must submit the notice on Schedule 14N required pursuant to Rule 14a-11(b)(10), which date shall be a reasonable time before the registrant mails its proxy materials for the meeting. Where a registrant is required to include shareholder director nominees in the registrant's proxy materials pursuant to either an applicable state or foreign law provision, or a provision in the registrant's governing documents, then the registrant is required to disclose the date by which a nominating shareholder or nominating shareholder group must submit the notice on Schedule 14N required pursuant to Rule 14a-18.

(b) If the registrant is a series company as defined in Rule 18f-2(a) under the Investment Company Act of 1940, then the registrant is required to disclose in connection with the election of directors at an annual meeting of shareholders (or, in lieu of such an annual meeting, a special meeting of shareholders) the total number of shares of the registrant outstanding and entitled to be voted (or if the votes are to be cast on a basis other than one vote per share, then the total number of votes entitled to be voted and the basis for allocating such votes) on the election of directors at such meeting of shareholders as of the end of the most recent calendar quarter.

Section 6 – Asset-Backed Securities

* * *

Section 7 - Regulation FD

Item 7.01 Regulation FD Disclosure.
Unless filed under Item 8.01, disclose under this item only information that the registrant elects to disclose through Form 8-K pursuant to Regulation FD.

Section 8 - Other Events

Item 8.01 Other Events.
The registrant may, at its option, disclose under this Item 8.01 any events, with respect to which information is not otherwise called for by this form, that the registrant deems of importance to

security holders. The registrant may, at its option, file a report under this Item 8.01 disclosing the nonpublic information required to be disclosed by Regulation FD.

Section 9 - Financial Statements and Exhibits

Item 9.01 Financial Statements and Exhibits.
List below the financial statements, pro forma financial information and exhibits, if any, filed as a part of this report.

(a) Financial statements of businesses acquired.
  (1) For any business acquisition required to be described in answer to Item 2.01 of this form, financial statements of the business acquired shall be filed for the periods specified in Rule 3-05(b) of Regulation S-X.
  (2) The financial statements shall be prepared pursuant to Regulation S-X except that supporting schedules need not be filed. A manually signed accountant's report should be provided pursuant to Rule 2-02 of Regulation S-X.
  (3) With regard to the acquisition of one or more real estate properties, the financial statements and any additional information specified by Rule 3-14 of Regulation S-X shall be filed.
  (4) Financial statements required by this item may be filed with the initial report, or by amendment not later than 71 calendar days after the date that the initial report on Form 8-K must be filed. If the financial statements are not included in the initial report, the registrant should so indicate in the Form 8-K report and state when the required financial statements will be filed. The registrant may, at its option, include unaudited financial statements in the initial report on Form 8-K.

(b) Pro forma financial information.
  (1) For any transaction required to be described in answer to Item 2.01 of this form, furnish any pro forma financial information that would be required pursuant to Article 11 of Regulation S-X.
  (2) The provisions of paragraph (a)(4) of this Item 9.01 shall also apply to pro forma financial information relative to the acquired business.

* * *

(d) Exhibits. The exhibits shall be deemed to be filed or furnished, depending on the relevant item requiring such exhibit, in accordance with the provisions of Item 601 of Regulation S-K and Instruction B.2 to this form.

Instruction.
During the period after a registrant has reported a business combination pursuant to Item 2.01 of this form, until the date on which the financial statements specified by this Item 9.01 must be filed, the registrant will be deemed current for purposes of its reporting obligations under Section 13(a) or 15(d) of the Exchange Act. With respect to filings under the Securities Act, however, registration statements will not be declared effective and post-effective amendments to registrations statements will not be declared effective unless financial statements meeting the requirements of Rule 3-05 of Regulation S-X are provided. In addition, offerings should not be

made pursuant to effective registration statements, or pursuant to Rule 506 of Regulation D where any purchasers are not accredited investors under Rule 501(a) of that Regulation, until the audited financial statements required by Rule 3-05 of Regulation S-X are filed; *provided, however,* that the following offerings or sales of securities may proceed notwithstanding that financial statements of the acquired business have not been filed:

(a) offerings or sales of securities upon the conversion of outstanding convertible securities or upon the exercise of outstanding warrants or rights;
(b) dividend or interest reinvestment plans;
(c) employee benefit plans;
(d) transactions involving secondary offerings; or
(e) sales of securities pursuant to Rule 144.

SIGNATURES

Pursuant to the requirements of the Securities Exchange Act of 1934, the registrant has duly caused this report to be signed on its behalf by the undersigned hereunto duly authorized.

_____
(Registrant)

Date _____   _____
(Signature)*

*Print name and title of the signing officer under his signature.

UNITED STATES SECURITIES AND EXCHANGE COMMISSION
Washington, D.C. 20549

FORM 10

GENERAL FORM FOR REGISTRATION OF SECURITIES
Pursuant to Section 12(b) or (g) of The Securities Exchange Act of 1934

_____

(Exact name of registrant as specified in its charter)

(State or other jurisdiction of incorporation or organization)	(I.R.S. Employer Identification No.)

_____

(Address of principal executive offices)	(Zip Code)

Registrant's telephone number, including area code _____

Securities to be registered pursuant to Section 12(b) of the Act:

Title of each class to be so registered	Name of each exchange on which each class is to be registered

_____

_____

Securities to be registered pursuant to Section 12(g) of the Act:

_____

(Title of class)

_____

(Title of class)

Indicate by check mark whether the registrant is a large accelerated filer, an accelerated filer, a non-accelerated filer, a smaller reporting company, or an emerging growth company. See the definitions of "large accelerated filer," "accelerated filer," "smaller reporting company," and "emerging growth company" in Rule 12b-2 of the Exchange Act.

Large accelerated filer	❏	Accelerated filer	❏
Non-accelerated filer	❏	Smaller reporting company	❏
		Emerging growth company	❏

If an emerging growth company, indicate by check mark if the registrant has elected not to use the extended transition period for complying with any new or revised financial accounting standards provided pursuant to Section 13(a) of the Exchange Act. ❏

INFORMATION REQUIRED IN REGISTRATION STATEMENT

Item 1.   **Business.**

Furnish the information required by Item 101 of Regulation S-K.

Item 1A.   **Risk Factors.**

Set forth, under the caption "Risk Factors," where appropriate, the risk factors described in Item 105 of Regulation S-K applicable to the registrant. Provide any discussion of risk factors in plain English in accordance with Rule 421(d) of the Securities Act of 1933.

Item 2.   **Financial Information.**

Furnish the information required by Items 303 and 305 of Regulation S-K.

Item 3.   **Properties.**

Furnish the information required by Item 102 of Regulation S-K.

Item 4.   **Security Ownership of Certain Beneficial Owners and Management.**

Furnish the information required by Item 403 of Regulation S-K.

Item 5.   **Directors and Executive Officers.**

Furnish the information required by Item 401 of Regulation S-K.

Item 6.   **Executive Compensation.**

Furnish the information required by Item 402 of Regulation S-K and paragraph (e)(4) of Item 407 of Regulation S-K.

Item 7.   **Certain Relationships and Related Transactions.**

Furnish the information required by Item 404 of Regulation S-K and Item 407(a) of Regulation S-K.

Item 8.   **Legal Proceedings.**

Furnish the information required by Item 103 of Regulation S-K.

Item 9.   **Market Price of and Dividends on the Registrant's Common Equity and Related Stockholder Matters.**

Furnish the information required by Item 201 of Regulation S-K.

Item 10. Recent Sales of Unregistered Securities.

Furnish the information required by item 701 of Regulation S-K.

Item 11. Description of Registrant's Securities to be Registered.

Furnish the information required by Item 202 of Regulation S-K. If the class of securities to be registered will trade in the form of American Depositary Receipts, furnish Item 202(f) disclosure for such American Depositary Receipts as well.

Item 12. Indemnification of Directors and Officers.

Furnish the information required by Item 702 of Regulation S-K.

Item 13. Financial Statements and Supplementary Data.

Furnish all financial statements required by Regulation S-X and the supplementary financial information required by Item 302 of Regulation S-K.

Item 14. Changes in and Disagreements with Accountants on Accounting and Financial Disclosure.

Furnish the information required by Item 304 of Regulation S-K.

Item 15. Financial Statements and Exhibits.

(a) List separately all financial statements filed as part of the registration statement.
(b) Furnish the exhibits required by Item 601 of Regulation S-K.

SIGNATURES

Pursuant to the requirements of Section 12 of the Securities Exchange Act of 1934, the registrant has duly caused this registration statement to be signed on its behalf by the undersigned, thereunto duly authorized.

_____
(Registrant)

Date:_____   By:_____
                                          (Signature)*

*Print name and title of the signing officer under his signature.

GENERAL INSTRUCTIONS

A.   Rule as to Use of Form 10.

Form 10 shall be used for registration pursuant to Section 12(b) or (g) of the Securities Exchange Act of 1934 of classes of securities of issuers for which no other form is prescribed.

B.   Application of General Rules and Regulations.

(a) The General Rules and Regulations under the Act contain certain general requirements which are applicable to registration on any form. These general requirements should be carefully read and observed in the preparation and filing of registration statements on this form.

(b) Particular attention is directed to Regulation 12B which contains general requirements regarding matters such as the kind and size of paper to be used, the legibility of the registration statement, the information to be given whenever the title of securities is required to be stated, and the filing of the registration statement. The definitions contained in Rule 12b-2 should be especially noted.

C.   Preparation of Registration Statement.

(a) This form is not to be used as a blank form to be filled in, but only as a guide in the preparation of the registration statement on paper meeting the requirements of Rule 12b-12. The registration statement shall contain the item numbers and captions, but the text of the items may be omitted. The answers to the items shall be prepared in the manner specified in Rule 12b-13.

(b) Unless otherwise stated, the information required shall be given as of a date reasonably close to the date of filing the registration statement.

(c) Attention is directed to Rule 12b-20 which states: "In addition to the information expressly required to be included in a statement or report, there shall be added such further material information, if any, as may be necessary to make the required statements, in light of the circumstances under which they are made, not misleading.

D.   Signature and Filing of Registration Statement.

Three complete copies of the registration statement, including financial statements, exhibits and all other papers and documents filed as a part thereof, and five additional copies which need not include exhibits, shall be filed with the Commission. At least one complete copy of the registration statement, including financial statements, exhibits and all other papers and documents filed as a part thereof, shall be filed with each exchange on which any class of securities is to be registered. At least one complete copy of the registration statement filed with the Commission and one such copy filed with each exchange shall be manually signed. Copies not manually signed shall bear typed or printed signatures.

E.   Omission of Information Regarding Foreign Subsidiaries.

Information required by any item or other requirement of this form with respect to any foreign subsidiary may be omitted to the extent that the required disclosure would be detrimental to the registrant. However, financial statements, otherwise required, shall not be omitted pursuant to this instruction. Where information is omitted pursuant to this instruction, a statement shall be made that such information has been omitted and the names of the subsidiaries involved shall be separately furnished to the Commission. The Commission may, in its discretion, call for justification that the required disclosure would be detrimental.

F.   Incorporation by Reference.

Attention is directed to Rule 12b-23 which provides for the incorporation by reference of information contained in certain documents in answer or partial answer to any item of a registration statement.

UNITED STATES SECURITIES AND EXCHANGE COMMISSION
Washington, D.C. 20549

FORM 10-K

ANNUAL REPORT PURSUANT TO SECTION 13 OR 15(d)
OF THE SECURITIES EXCHANGE ACT OF 1934

GENERAL INSTRUCTIONS

A.   **Rule as to Use of Form 10-K.**

     (1)   This Form shall be used for annual reports pursuant to Section 13 or 15(d) of the Securities Exchange Act of 1934 (the "Act") for which no other form is prescribed. This Form also shall be used for transition reports filed pursuant to Section 13 or 15(d) of the Act

     (2)   Annual reports on this Form shall be filed within the following period:

         (a)   60 days after the end of the fiscal year covered by the report (75 days for fiscal years ending before December 15, 2006) for large accelerated filers (as defined in Rule 12b-2):

         (b)   75 days after the end of the fiscal year covered by the report for accelerated filers (as defined in Rule 12b-2); and

         (c)   90 days after the end of the fiscal year covered by the report for all other registrants.

     (3)   Transition reports on this Form shall be filed in accordance with the requirements set forth in Rule 13a-10 or Rule 15d-10 applicable when the registrant changes its fiscal year end.

     (4)   Notwithstanding paragraphs (2) and (3) of this General Instruction A., all schedules required by Article 12 of Regulation S-X may, at the option of the registrant, be filed as an amendment to the report not later than 30 days after the applicable due date of the report.

B.   **Application of General Rules and Regulations.**

     (1)   The General Rules and Regulations under the Act contain certain general requirements which are applicable to reports on any form. These general requirements should be carefully read and observed in the preparation and filing of reports on this Form.

     (2)   Particular attention is directed to Regulation 12B which contains general requirements regarding matters such as the kind and size of paper to be used, the legibility of the report, the information to be given whenever the title of securities is required to be stated, and the filing of the report. The definitions contained in Rule 12b-2 should be especially noted. *See also* Regulations 13A and 15D.

C.   **Preparation of Report.**

     (1)   This form is not to be used as a blank form to be filled in, but only as a guide in the preparation of the report on paper meeting the requirements of Rule 12b-12.

Except as provided in General Instruction G, the answers to the items shall be prepared in the manner specified in Rule 12b-13.

(2) Except where information is required to be given for the fiscal year or as of a specified date, it shall be given as of the latest practicable date.

(3) Attention is directed to Rule 12b-20, which states: "In addition to the information expressly required to be included in a statement or report, there shall be added such further material information, if any, as may be necessary to make the required statements, in the light of the circumstances under which they are made, not misleading."

D.   Signature and Filing of Report.

(1) Three complete copies of the report, including financial statements, financial statement schedules, exhibits, and all other papers and documents filed as a part thereof, and five additional copies which need not include exhibits, shall be filed with the Commission. At least one complete copy of the report, including financial statements, financial statement schedules, exhibits, and all other papers and documents filed as a part thereof, shall be filed with each exchange on which any class of securities of the registrant is registered. At least one complete copy of the report filed with the Commission and one such copy filed with each exchange shall be manually signed. Copies not manually signed shall bear typed or printed signatures.

(2) (a) The report must be signed by the registrant, and on behalf of the registrant by its principal executive officer or officers, its principal financial officer or officers, its controller or principal accounting officer, and by at least the majority of the board of directors or persons performing similar functions. Where the registrant is a limited partnership, the report must be signed by the majority of the board of directors of any corporate general partner who signs the report.

(b) The name of each person who signs the report shall be typed or printed beneath his signature. Any person who occupies more than one of the specified positions shall indicate each capacity in which he signs the report. Attention is directed to Rule 12b-11 concerning manual signatures and signatures pursuant to powers of attorney.

(3) Registrants are requested to indicate in a transmittal letter with the Form 10-K whether the financial statements in the report reflect a change from the preceding year in any accounting principles or practices, or in the method of applying any such principles or practices.

E.   Disclosure With Respect to Foreign Subsidiaries.

Information required by any item or other requirement of this form with respect to any foreign subsidiary may be omitted to the extent that the required disclosure would be detrimental to the registrant. However, financial statements and financial statement schedules, otherwise required, shall not be omitted pursuant to this Instruction. Where information is omitted pursuant to this Instruction, a statement shall be made that such information has been omitted and the names of the subsidiaries involved shall be separately furnished to the Commission. The Commission may, in its discretion, call for justification that the required disclosure would be detrimental.

F.   Information as to Employee Stock Purchase, Savings and Similar Plans.

Attention is directed to Rule 15d-21 which provides that separate annual and other reports need not be filed pursuant to Section 15(d) of the Act with respect to any employee stock purchase, savings or similar plan if the issuer of the stock or other securities offered to employees pursuant to the plan furnishes to the Commission the information and documents specified in the Rule.

G.   Information to be Incorporated by Reference.

(1) Attention is directed to Rule 12b-23 which provides for the incorporation by reference of information contained in certain documents in answer or partial answer to any item of a report.

(2) The information called for by Parts I and II of this form (Items 1 through 9A or any portion thereof) may, at the registrant's option, be incorporated by reference from the registrant's annual report to security holders furnished to the Commission pursuant to Rule 14a-3(b) or Rule 14c-3(a) or from the registrant's annual report to security holders, even if not furnished to the Commission pursuant to Rule 14a-3(b) or 14c-3(a), provided such annual report contains the information required by Rule 14a-3.
Note 1. In order to fulfill the requirements of Part I of Form 10-K, the incorporated portion of the annual report to security holders must contain the information required by Items 1-3 of Form 10-K; to the extent applicable.
Note 2. If any information required by Part I or Part II is incorporated by reference into an electronic format document from the annual report to security holders as provided in General Instruction G, any portion of the annual report to security holders incorporated by reference shall be filed as an exhibit in electronic format, as required by Item 601(b)(13) of Regulation S-K.

(3) The information required by Part III (Items 10, 11, 12, 13 and 14) may be incorporated by reference from the registrant's definitive proxy statement (filed or required to be filed pursuant to Regulation 14A) or definitive information statement (filed or to be filed pursuant to Regulation 14C) which involves the election of directors, if such definitive proxy statement or information statement is filed with the Commission not later than 120 days after the end of the fiscal year covered by the Form 10-K. However, if such definitive proxy statement or information statement is not filed with the Commission in the 120-day period or is not required to be filed with the Commission by virtue of Rule 3a12-3(b) under the Exchange Act, the Items comprising the Part III information must be filed as part of the Form 10-K, or as an amendment to the Form 10-K, not later than the end of

the 120-day period. It should be noted that the information regarding executive officers required by Item 401 of Regulation S-K (may be included in Part I of Form 10-K under an appropriate caption. See the Instruction to Item 401 of Regulation S-K.

(4) No item numbers of captions of items need be contained in the material incorporated by reference into the report. However, the registrant's attention is directed to Rule 12b-23(e) regarding the specific disclosure required in the report concerning information incorporated by reference. When the registrant combines all of the information in Parts I and II of this Form (Items 1 through 9A) by incorporation by reference from the registrant's annual report to security holders and all of the information in Part III of this Form (Items 10 through 14) by incorporating by reference from a definitive proxy statement or information statement involving the election of directors, then, notwithstanding General Instruction C(1), this Form shall consist of the facing or cover page, those sections incorporated from the annual report to security holders, the proxy or information statement, and the information, if any, required by Part IV of this Form, signatures, and a cross-reference sheet setting forth the item numbers and captions in Parts I, II and III of this Form and the page and/or pages in the referenced materials where the corresponding information appears.

H.   Integrated Reports to Security Holders.

Annual reports to security holders may be combined with the required information of Form 10-K and will be suitable for filing with the Commission if the following conditions are satisfied:

(1) The combined report contains full and complete answers to all items required by Form 10-K. When responses to a certain item of required disclosure are separated within the combined report, an appropriate cross-reference should be made. If the information required by Part III of Form 10-K is omitted by virtue of General Instruction G, a definitive proxy or information statement shall be filed.

(2) The cover page and the required signatures are included. As appropriate, a cross-reference sheet should be filed indicating the location of information required by the items of the Form.

(3) If an electronic filer files any portion of an annual report to security holders in combination with the required information of Form 10-K, as provided in this instruction, only such portions filed in satisfaction of the Form 10-K requirements shall be filed in electronic format.

I.   Omission of Information by Certain Wholly-Owned Subsidiaries.

If, on the date of the filing of its report on Form 10-K, the registrant meets the conditions specified in paragraph (1) below, then such registrant may furnish the abbreviated narrative disclosure specified in paragraph (2) below.

(1) Conditions for availability of the relief specified in paragraph (2) below.

    (a) All of the registrant's equity securities are owned, either directly or indirectly, by a single person which is a reporting company under the Act and which has filed all the material required to be filed pursuant to section 13, 14, or 15(d) thereof, as applicable, and which is named in conjunction with the registrant's description of its business;

    (b) During the preceding thirty-six calendar months and any subsequent period of days, there has not been any material default in the payment of principal, interest, a sinking or purchase fund installment, or any other material default not cured within thirty days, with respect to any indebtedness of the registrant or its subsidiaries, and there has not been any material default in the payment of rentals under material long-term leases; and

    (c) There is prominently set forth, on the cover page of the Form 10-K, a statement that the registrant meets the conditions set forth in General Instruction (I)(1)(a) and (b) of Form 10-K and is therefore filing this Form with the reduced disclosure format.

(2) Registrants meeting the conditions specified in paragraph (1) above are entitled to the following relief:

    (a) Such registrants may omit the information called for by Item 7, Management's Discussion and Analysis of Financial Condition and Results of Operations provided that the registrant includes in the Form 10-K a management's narrative analysis of the results of operations explaining the reasons for material changes in the amount of revenue and expense items between the most recent fiscal year presented and the fiscal year immediately preceding it. Explanations of material changes should include, but not be limited to, changes in the various elements which determine revenue and expense levels such as unit sales volume, prices charged and paid, production levels, production cost variances, labor costs and discretionary spending programs. In addition, the analysis should include an explanation of the effect of any changes in accounting principles and practices or method of application that have a material effect on net income as reported.

    (b) Such registrants may omit the list of subsidiaries exhibit required by Item 601 of Regulation S-K.

    (c) Such registrants may omit the information called for by the following otherwise required Items: Item 4, Submission of Matters to a Vote of Security Holders; Item 10, Directors and Executive Officers of the Registrant; Item 11, Executive Compensation; Item 12, Security Ownership of Certain Beneficial Owners and Management; and Item 13, Certain Relationships and Related Transactions.

(d) In response to Item 1, Business, such registrant only need furnish a brief description of the business done by the registrant and its subsidiaries during the most recent fiscal year which will, in the opinion of management, indicate the general nature and scope of the business of the registrant and its subsidiaries, and in response to Item 2, Properties, such registrant only need furnish a brief description of the material properties of the registrant and its subsidiaries to the extent, in the opinion of the management, necessary to an understanding of the business done by the registrant and its subsidiaries.

* * *

UNITED STATES SECURITIES AND EXCHANGE COMMISSION
Washington, D.C. 20549

FORM 10-K

(Mark One)

[ ] ANNUAL REPORT PURSUANT TO SECTION 13 OR 15(D) OF THE SECURITIES EXCHANGE ACT OF 1934

For the fiscal year ended _____

Or

[ ] TRANSITION REPORT PURSUANT TO SECTION 13 OR 15(d) OF THE SECURITIES EXCHANGE ACT OF 1934

For the transition period from _____ to _____

Commission file number _____

_____
(Exact name of registrant as specified in its charter)

_____

| (State or other jurisdiction of incorporation or organization) | (I.R.S. Employer Identification No.) |

(Address of principal executive offices)   (Zip Code)

Registrant's telephone number, including area code _____

Securities to be registered pursuant to Section 12(b) of the Act:

Title of each class   Name of each exchange on which registered
_____

Securities registered pursuant to Section 12(b) of the Act:

Title of each class	Trading Symbol(s)	Name of each exchange on which registered

Securities to be registered pursuant to Section 12(g) of the Act:

_____
(Title of class)

_____
(Title of class)

Indicate by check mark if the registrant is a well-known seasoned issuer, as defined in Rule 405 of the Securities Act.   ❑ Yes   ❑ No

Indicate by check mark if the registrant is not required to file reports pursuant to Section 13 or Section 15(d) of the Act.   ❑ Yes   ❑ No
Note: Checking the box above will not relieve any registrant required to file reports pursuant to Section 13 or 15(d) of the Exchange Act from their obligations under those Sections.

Indicate by check mark whether the registrant (1) has filed all reports required to be filed by Section 13 or 15(d) of the Securities Exchange Act of 1934 during the preceding 12 months (or for such shorter period that the registrant was required to file such reports), and (2) has been subject to such filing requirements for the past 90 days.   ❑ Yes   ❑ No

Indicate by check mark whether the registrant has submitted electronically and posted on its corporate Web site, if any, every Interactive Data File required to be submitted and posted pursuant to Rule 405 of Regulation S-T during the preceding 12 months (or for such shorter period that the registrant was required to submit and post such files).   ❑ Yes   ❑ No

Indicate by check mark if disclosure of delinquent filers pursuant to Item 405 of Regulation S-K is not contained herein, and will not be contained, to the best of registrant's knowledge, in definitive proxy or information statements incorporated by reference in Part III of this Form 10-K or any amendment to this Form 10-K.   ❑

Indicate by check mark whether the registrant is a large accelerated filer, an accelerated filer, a non-accelerated filer, a smaller reporting company, or an emerging growth company. See the definitions of "large accelerated filer," "accelerated filer," "smaller reporting company," and "emerging growth company" in Rule 12b-2 of the Exchange Act.

Large accelerated filer	❑	Accelerated filer	❑
Non-accelerated filer	❑	Smaller reporting company	❑
		Emerging growth company	❑

If an emerging growth company, indicate by check mark if the registrant has elected not to use the extended transition period for complying with any new or revised financial accounting standards provided pursuant to Section 13(a) of the Exchange Act.   ❑

Indicate by check mark whether the registrant has filed a report on and attestation to its management's assessment of the effectiveness of its internal control over financial reporting under Section 404(b) of the Sarbanes-Oxley Act by the registered public accounting firm that prepared or issued its audit report.   ❑

Indicate by check mark whether the registrant is a shell company (as defined in Rule 12b-2 of the Act).   ❑ Yes   ❑ No

If securities are registered pursuant to Section 12(b) of the Act, indicate by check mark whether the financial statements of the registrant included in the filing reflect the correction of an error to previously issued financial statements. ❑

Indicate by check mark whether any of those error corrections are restatements that required a recovery analysis of incentive-based compensation received by any of the registrant's executive officers during the relevant recovery period pursuant to Rule 10D-1(b). ❑

State the aggregate market value of the voting and non-voting common equity held by non-affiliates computed by reference to the price at which the common equity was last sold, or the average bid and asked price of such common equity, as of the last business day of the registrant's most recently completed second fiscal quarter.

Note: If a determination as to whether a particular person or entity is an affiliate cannot be made without involving unreasonable effort and expense, the aggregate market value of the common stock held by non-affiliates may be calculated on the basis of assumptions reasonable under the circumstances, provided that the assumptions are set forth in this Form.

APPLICABLE ONLY TO REGISTRANTS INVOLVED IN BANKRUPTCY
PROCEEDINGS DURING THE PRECEDING FIVE YEARS:

Indicate by check mark whether the registrant has filed all documents and reports required to be filed by Section 12, 13 or 15(d) of the Securities Exchange Act of 1934 subsequent to the distribution of securities under a plan confirmed by a court.   ❑ Yes   ❑ No

(APPLICABLE ONLY TO CORPORATE REGISTRANTS)

Indicate the number of shares outstanding of each of the registrant's classes of common stock, as of the latest practicable date.

DOCUMENTS INCORPORATED BY REFERENCE

List hereunder the following documents if incorporated by reference and the Part of the Form 10-K (e.g., Part I, Part II, etc.) into which the document is incorporated: (1) Any annual report to security holders; (2) Any proxy or information statement; and (3) Any prospectus filed pursuant to Rule 424(b) or (c) under the Securities Act of 1933. The listed documents should be clearly described for identification purposes (e.g., annual report to security holders for fiscal year ended December 24, 1980).

PART I
[See General Instruction G(2)]

Item 1.   **Business.**

Furnish the information required by Item 101 of Regulation S-K except that the discussion of the development of the registrant's business need only include developments since the beginning of the fiscal year for which this report is filed.

Item 1A.   **Risk Factors.**

Set forth, under the caption "Risk Factors," where appropriate, the risk factors described in Item 105 of Regulation S-K applicable to the registrant. Provide any discussion of risk factors in plain English in accordance with Rule 421(d) of the Securities Act of 1933.

Item 1B.   Unresolved Staff Comments.

If the registrant is an accelerated filer as defined in Rule 12b-2 of the Exchange Act or is a well-known seasoned issuer as defined in Rule 405 of the Securities Act and has received written comments from the Commission staff regarding its periodic or current reports under the Act not less than 180 days before the end of its fiscal year to which the annual report relates, and such comments remain unresolved, disclose the substance of any such unresolved comments that the registrant believes are material. Such disclosure may provide other information including the position of the registrant with respect to any such comment.

Item 2.   Properties.

Furnish the information required by Item 102 of Regulation S-K.

Item 3.   Legal Proceedings.

(a) Furnish the information required by Item 103 of Regulation S-K.

(b) As to any proceeding that was terminated during the fourth quarter of the fiscal year covered by this report, furnish information similar to that required by Item 103 of Regulation S-K, including the date of termination and a description of the disposition thereof with respect to the registrant and its subsidiaries.

Item 4.   Mine Safety Disclosures

If applicable, provide a statement that the information concerning mine safety violations or other regulatory matters required by Section 1503(a) of the Dodd-Frank Wall Street Reform and Consumer Protection Act and Item 104 of Regulation S-K is included in exhibit 95 to the annual report.

PART II
[(See General Instruction G(2)]

Item 5.   Market for Registrant's Common Equity, Related Stockholder Matters and Issuer Purchases of Equity Securities.

(a) Furnish the information required by Item 201 of Regulation S-K and Item 701 of Regulation S-K as to all equity securities of the registrant sold by the registrant during the period covered by the report that were not registered under the Securities Act. *Provided* that if the Item 701 information previously has been included in a Quarterly Report on Form 10-Q or in a current report on Form 8-K, it need not be furnished.

(b) If required pursuant to Rule 463 of the Securities Act of 1933, furnish the information required by Item 701(f) of Regulation S-K.

(c) Furnish the information required by Item 703 of Regulation S-K for any repurchase made in the fourth quarter of the fiscal year covered by the report.

Item 6.   **Selected Financial Data.**

Furnish the information required by Item 301 of Regulation S-K.

Item 7.   **Management's Discussion and Analysis of Financial Condition and Results of Operation.**

Furnish the information required by Item 303 of Regulation S-K.

Item 7A.   **Quantitative and Qualitative Disclosures About Market Risk.**

Furnish the information required by Item 305 of Regulation S-K.

Item 8.   **Financial Statements and Supplementary Data.**

Furnish financial statements meeting the requirements of Regulation S-X, except §210.3-05 and Article 11 thereof, and the supplementary financial information required by Item 302 of Regulation S-K. Financial statements of the registrant and its subsidiaries consolidated (as required by Rule 14a-3(b)) shall be filed under this item. Other financial statements and schedules required under Regulation S-X may be filed as "Financial Statement Schedules" pursuant to Item 13, Exhibits, Financial Statement Schedules, and Reports on Form 8-K, of this form.

Notwithstanding the above, if the issuer is subject to the reporting provisions of Section 15(d) and such obligation results solely from the issuer having filed a registration statement on Form S-18 which became effective under the Securities Act of 1933 during the last fiscal year, or such obligation applies as to the first or second fiscal year after the registration statement on Form S-18 became effective solely because the issuer had on the first day of the pertinent fiscal year 300 or more record holders of any of its securities to which the Form S-18 related, audited financial statements for the issuer, or for the issuer and its predecessors, may be presented as provided below. The report of the independent accountant shall in all events comply with the requirements of Article 2 of Regulation S-X.

(a) A Form 10-K filed for the fiscal year during which the registrant had a registration statement on Form S-18 become effective may include the following financial statements prepared in accordance with generally accepted accounting principles:

(1) A balance sheet as of the end of each of the two most recent fiscal years; and

(2) Consolidated statements of income, statements of cash flows, and statements of other stockholders' equity for each of the two fiscal years preceding the date of the most recent audited balance sheet being filed.

(b) A Form 10-K filed for the first fiscal year after the registrant had a registration statement on Form S-18 become effective may include financial statements prepared as follows:

(1) Financial statements for the most recent fiscal year prepared in accordance with Regulation S-X, Form and Content of and Requirements for Financial Statements; and

(2) Financial statements previously disclosed in accordance with paragraph (a) for the prior year. These statements do not need to include the compliance items and schedules of Regulation S-X, but should be recast to show the same line items as are set forth for the most recent fiscal year.

(c) A Form 10-K filed for the second fiscal year after the registrant had a registration statement on Form S-18 become effective may include financial statements for the two most recent fiscal years prepared in accordance with Regulation S-X.

Item 9.   Changes in and Disagreements With Accountants on Accounting and Financial Disclosure.

Furnish the information required by Item 304 of Regulation S-K.

Item 9A.   Controls and Procedures.

Furnish the information required by Item 307 and 308 of Regulation S-K.

Item 9B.   Other Information

(a) The registrant must disclose under this item any information required to be disclosed in a report on Form 8-K during the fourth quarter of the year covered by this Form 10-K, but not reported, whether or not otherwise required by this Form 10-K. If disclosure of such information is made under this item, it need not be repeated in a report on Form 8-K which would otherwise be required to be filed with respect to such information or in a subsequent report on Form 10-K.

(b) Furnish the information required by Items 408(a) and 408(d) of Regulation S-K.

PART III
[See General Instruction G(3)]

Item 10.   Directors and Executive Officers of the Registrant.

Furnish the information required by Items Items 401, 405, 406, 407(c)(3), (d)(4), (d)(5), and 408(b) of Regulation S-K.

Instruction
Checking the box provided on the cover page of this Form to indicate that Item 405 disclosure of delinquent Form 3, 4, or 5 filers is not contained herein is intended to facilitate Form processing and review. Failure to provide such indication will not create liability for violation of the federal securities laws. The space should be checked only if there is no disclosure in this Form of reporting person delinquencies in response to Item 405 and the registrant, at the time of filing the Form 10-K, has reviewed the information necessary to ascertain, and has determined that, Item 405 disclosure is not expected to be contained in Part III of the Form 10-K or incorporated by reference.

Item 11.   Executive Compensation.

Furnish the information required by Item 402 of Regulation S-K.

Item 12.   Security Ownership of Certain Beneficial Owners and Management.

Furnish the information required by Item 201(d) of Regulation S-K and Item 403 of Regulation S-K.

Item 13.   Certain Relationships and Related Transactions.

Furnish the information required by Item 404 of Regulation S-K.

Item 14.   Principal Accounting Fees and Services.

Furnish the information required by Item 9(e) of Schedule 14A.

(1) Disclose, under the caption Audit Fees, the aggregate fees billed for each of the last two fiscal years for professional services rendered by the principal accountant for the audit of the registrant's annual financial statements and review of financial statements included in the registrant's Form 10-Q or services that are normally provided by the accountant in connection with statutory and regulatory filings or engagements for those fiscal years.

(2) Disclose, under the caption Audit-Related Fees, the aggregate fees billed in each of the last two fiscal years for assurance and related services by the principal accountant that are reasonably related to the performance of the audit or review of the registrant's financial statements and are not reported under Item 9(e)(1)

of Schedule 14A. Registrants shall describe the nature of the services comprising the fees disclosed under this category.

(3) Disclose, under the caption Tax Fees, the aggregate fees billed in each of the last two fiscal years for professional services rendered by the principal accountant for tax compliance, tax advice, and tax planning. Registrants shall describe the nature of the services comprising the fees disclosed under this category.

(4) Disclose, under the caption All Other Fees, the aggregate fees billed in each of the last two fiscal years for products and services provided by the principal accountant, other than the services reported in Items 9(e)(1) through 9(e)(3) of Schedule 14A. Registrants shall describe the nature of the services comprising the fees disclosed under this category.

(5) (i) Disclose the audit committee's pre-approval policies and procedures described in paragraph (c)(7)(i) of Rule 2-01 of Regulation S-X.
    (ii) Disclose the percentage of services described in each of Items 9(e)(2) through 9(e)(4) of Schedule 14A that were approved by the audit committee pursuant to paragraph (c)(7)(i)(C) of Rule 2-01 of Regulation S-X.

(6) If greater than 50 percent, disclose the percentage of hours expended on the principal accountant's engagement to audit the registrant's financial statements for the most recent fiscal year that were attributed to work performed by persons other than the principal accountant's full-time, permanent employees.

Instruction to Item 14. A registrant that is an Asset-Backed Issuer (as defined in Rule 13a-14(g) and Rule 15d-14(g) of this chapter) is not required to disclose the information required by this Item.

PART IV

Item 15.   Exhibits, Financial Statement Schedules, and Reports on Form 8-K.

(a) List the following documents filed as a part of the report:
    (1) All financial statements;
    (2) Those financial statement schedules required to be filed by Item 8 of this form, and by paragraph (d) below.
    (3) Those exhibits required by Item 601 of Regulation S-K and by paragraph (c) below. Identify in the list each management contract or compensatory plan or arrangement required to be filed as an exhibit to this form pursuant to Item 14(c) of this report.

(b) Reports on Form 8-K. State whether any reports on Form 8-K have been filed during the last quarter of the period covered by this report, listing the items reported, any financial statements filed and the dates of any such reports.

(c) Registrants shall file, as exhibits to this form, the exhibits required by Item 601 of Regulation S-K.

(d) Registrants shall file, as financial statement schedules to this form, the financial statements required by Regulation S-X which are excluded from the annual report to shareholders by Rule 14a-3(b) including (1) separate financial statements of subsidiaries not consolidated and fifty percent or less owned persons; (2) separate financial statements of affiliates whose securities are pledged as collateral; and (3) schedules.

SIGNATURES

[See General Instruction D]

Pursuant to the requirements of Section 13 or 15(d) of the Securities Exchange Act of 1934, the registrant has duly caused this report to be signed on its behalf by the undersigned, thereunto duly authorized.

(Registrant) _____

By (Signature and Title)* _____

Date _____

Pursuant to the requirements of the Securities Exchange Act of 1934, this report has been signed below by the following persons on behalf of the registrant and in the capacities and on the dates indicated.

By (Signature and Title)* _____

Date _____

By (Signature and Title)* _____

Date _____

Supplemental Information to be Furnished with Reports Filed
Pursuant to Section 15(d) of the Act by Registrants Which Have Not Registered
Securities Pursuant to Section 12 of the Act

(a) Except to the extent that the materials enumerated in (1) and/or (2) below are specifically incorporated into this Form by reference, every registrant which files an annual report on this Form pursuant to Section 15(d) of the Act must furnish to the Commission for its information, at the time of filing its report on this Form, four copies of the following:

(1) Any annual report to security holders covering the registrant's last fiscal year; and

(2) Every proxy statement, form of proxy or other proxy soliciting material sent to more than ten of the registrant's security holders with respect to any annual or other meeting of security holders.

(b) The foregoing material shall not be deemed to be "filed" with the Commission or otherwise subject to the liabilities of Section 18 of the Act, except to the extent that the registrant specifically incorporates it in its annual report on this Form by reference.

(c) If no such annual report material has been sent to security holders, a statement to that effect shall be included under this caption. If such report or proxy material is to be furnished to security holders subsequent to the filing of the annual report of this Form, the registrant shall so state under this caption and shall furnish copies of such material to the Commission when it is sent to security holders.

UNITED STATES SECURITIES AND EXCHANGE COMMISSION
Washington, D.C. 20549

FORM 10-Q
GENERAL INSTRUCTIONS

A.   Rule as to Use of Form 10-Q.

1. Form 10-Q shall be used for quarterly reports under Section 13 or 15(d) of the Securities Exchange Act of 1934, required to be filed pursuant to Rule 13a-13 or Rule15d-13 of this chapter. A quarterly report on this form pursuant to Rule 13a-13 or Rule 15d-13 of this chapter shall be filed within the following period after the end of the first three fiscal quarters of each fiscal year, but no quarterly report need be filed for the fourth quarter of any fiscal year:

    a. 40 days after the end of the fiscal quarter for large accelerated filers and accelerated filers (as defined in 12b-2); and

    b. 45 days after the end of the fiscal quarter for all other registrants.

B.   Application of General Rules and Regulations.

1. The General Rules and Regulations under the Act contain certain general requirements which are applicable to reports on any form. These general requirements should be carefully read and observed in the preparation and filing of reports on this form.

2. Particular attention is directed to Regulation 12B which contains general requirements regarding matters such as the kind and size of paper to be used, the legibility of the report, the information to be given whenever the title of securities is required to be stated, and the filing of the report. The definitions contained in Rule 12b-2 should be especially noted. See also Regulations 13A and 15D.

C.   Preparation of Report.

1. This is not a blank form to be filled in. It is a guide copy to be used in preparing the report in accordance with Rules 12b-11 and 12b-12. The Commission does not furnish blank copies of this form to be filled in for filing.

2. These general instructions are not to be filed with the report. The instructions to the various captions of the form are also to be omitted from the report as filed.

D.   Incorporation by Reference.

1. If the registrant makes available to its stockholders or otherwise publishes, within the period prescribed for filing the report, a document or statement containing information meeting some or all of the requirements of Part I of this form, the information called for may be incorporated by reference from such published document or statement, in answer or partial answer to any item or items of Part I

of this form, provided copies thereof are filed as an exhibit to Part I of the report on this form.

2. Other information may be incorporated by reference in answer or partial answer to any item or items of Part II of this form in accordance with the provisions of Rule 12b-23.

3. If any information required by Part I or Part II is incorporated by reference into an electronic format document from the quarterly report to security holders as provided in General Instruction D, any portion of the quarterly report to security holders incorporated by reference shall be filed as an exhibit in electronic format, as required by Item 601(b)(13) of Regulation S-K.

E.   Integrated Reports to Security Holders.

Quarterly reports to security holders may be combined with the required information of Form 10-Q and will be suitable for filing with the Commission if the following conditions are satisfied:

1. The combined report contains full and complete answers to all items required by Part I of this form. When responses to a certain item of required disclosure are separated within the combined report, an appropriate cross-reference should be made.

2. If not included in the combined report, the cover page, appropriate responses to Part II, and the required signatures shall be included in the Form 10-Q. Additionally, as appropriate, a cross-reference sheet should be filed indicating the location of information required by the items of the form.

3. If an electronic filer files any portion of a quarterly report to security holders in combination with the required information of Form 10-Q, as provided in this instruction, only such portions filed in satisfaction of the Form 10-Q requirements shall be filed in electronic format.

F.   Filed Status of Information Presented.

1. Pursuant to Rule 13a-13(d) and Rule 15d-13(d), the information presented in satisfaction of the requirements of Items 1, 2 and 3 of Part I of this form, whether included directly in a report on this form, incorporated therein by reference from a report, document or statement filed as an exhibit to Part I of this form pursuant to Instruction D(1) above, included in an integrated report pursuant to Instruction E above, or contained in a statement regarding computation of per share earnings or a letter regarding a change in accounting principles filed as an exhibit to Part I pursuant to Item 601 of Regulation S-K, except as provided by Instruction F(2) below, shall not be deemed filed for the purpose of Section 18 of the Act or otherwise subject to the liabilities of that section of the Act but shall be subject to the other provisions of the Act.

2. Information presented in satisfaction of the requirements of this form other than those of Items 1, 2 and 3 of Part I shall be deemed filed for the purpose of Section 18 of the Act; except that, where information presented in response to Item 1 or 2 of Part I (or as an exhibit thereto) is also used to satisfy Part II requirements through incorporation by reference, only that portion of Part I (or exhibit thereto) consisting of the information required by Part II shall be deemed so filed.

G.   Signature and Filing of Report.

If the report is filed in paper pursuant to a hardship exemption from electronic filing (see Item 201 et seq. of Regulation S-T), three complete copies of the report, including any financial statements, exhibits or other papers or documents filed as a part thereof, and five additional copies which need not include exhibits must be filed with the Commission. At least one complete copy of the report, including any financial statements, exhibits or other papers or documents filed as a part thereof, must be filed with each exchange on which any class of securities of the registrant is registered. At least one complete copy of the report filed with the Commission and one such copy filed with each exchange must be manually signed on the registrant's behalf by a duly authorized officer of the registrant and by the principal financial or chief accounting officer of the registrant. (See Rule 12b-11(d).) Copies not manually signed must bear typed or printed signatures. In the case where the principal executive officer, principal financial officer or chief accounting officer is also duly authorized to sign on behalf of the registrant, one signature is acceptable provided that the registrant clearly indicates the dual responsibilities of the signatory.

H.   Omission of Information by Certain Wholly-Owned Subsidiaries.

If on the date of the filing of its report on Form 10-Q, the registrant meets the conditions specified in paragraph (1) below, then such registrant may omit the information called for in the items specified in paragraph (2) below.

1. Conditions for availability of the relief specified in paragraph (2) below:

    a. All of the registrant's equity securities are owned, either directly or indirectly, by a single person which is a reporting company under the Act and which has filed all the material required to be filed pursuant to Section 13, 14 or 15(d) thereof, as applicable;

    b. During the preceding thirty-six calendar months and any subsequent period of days, there has not been any material default in the payment of principal, interest, a sinking or purchase fund installment, or any other material default not cured within thirty days, with respect to any indebtedness of the registrant or its subsidiaries, and there has not been any material default in the payment of rentals under material long-term leases; and

    c. There is prominently set forth, on the cover page of the Form 10-Q, a statement that the registrant meets the conditions set forth in General Instruction H(1)(a) and (b) of Form 10-Q and is therefore filing this form with the reduced disclosure format.

2.   Registrants meeting the conditions specified in paragraph (1) above are entitled to the following relief.

a.   Such registrants may omit the information called for by Item 2 of Part I, Management's Discussion and Analysis of Financial Condition and Results of Operations, provided that the registrant includes in the Form 10-Q a management's narrative analysis of the results of operations explaining the reasons for material changes in the amount of revenue and expense items between the most recent fiscal year-to-date period presented and the corresponding year-to-date period in the preceding fiscal year. Explanations of material changes should include, but not be limited to, changes in the various elements which determine revenue and expense levels such as unit sales volume, prices charged and paid, production levels, production cost variances, labor costs and discretionary spending programs. In addition, the analysis should include an explanation of the effect of any changes in accounting principles and practices or method of application that have a material effect on net income as reported.

b.   Such registrants may omit the information called for in the following Part II Items: Item 2, Changes in Securities; Item 3, Defaults Upon Senior Securities; and Item 4, Submission of Matters to a Vote of Security Holders.

c.   Such registrants may omit the information called for by Item 3 of Part I, Quantitative and Qualitative Disclosures About Market Risk.

UNITED STATES SECURITIES AND EXCHANGE COMMISSION
Washington, D.C. 20549

FORM 10-Q

(Mark One)

[ ] QUARTERLY REPORT PURSUANT TO SECTION 13 OR 15(d) OF THE SECURITIES EXCHANGE ACT OF 1934

For the quarterly period ended _____

or

[ ] TRANSITION REPORT PURSUANT TO SECTION 13 OR 15(d) OF THE SECURITIES EXCHANGE ACT OF 1934

For the transition period from _____ to _____

Commission file number _____

_____
(Exact name of registrant as specified in its charter)

(State or other jurisdiction of incorporation or organization)	(I.R.S. Employer Identification No)
(Address of principal executive offices)	(Zip Code)

Registrant's telephone number, including area code

_____
(Former name, former address and former fiscal year, if changed since last report)

Securities registered pursuant to Section 12(b) of the Act:

Title of each class	Trading Symbol(s)	Name of each exchange on which registered

    Indicate by check mark whether the registrant (1) has filed all reports required to be filed by Section 13 or 15(d) of the Securities Exchange Act of 1934 during the preceding 12 months (or for such shorter period that the registrant was required to file such reports), and (2) has been subject to such filing requirements for the past 90 days.   ❑ Yes ❑ No

    Indicate by check mark whether the registrant has submitted electronically every Interactive Data File required to be submitted and posted pursuant to Rule 405 of Regulation S-T during the preceding 12 months (or for such shorter period that the registrant was required to submit and post such files).   ❑ Yes ❑ No

Indicate by check mark whether the registrant is a large accelerated filer, an accelerated filer, a non-accelerated filer, a smaller reporting company, or an emerging growth company. See the definitions of "large accelerated filer," "accelerated filer," "smaller reporting company," and "emerging growth company" in Rule 12b-2 of the Exchange Act.

Large accelerated filer	❑	Accelerated filer	❑
Non-accelerated filer	❑	Smaller reporting company	❑
		Emerging growth company	❑

If an emerging growth company, indicate by check mark if the registrant has elected not to use the extended transition period for complying with any new or revised financial accounting standards provided pursuant to Section 13(a) of the Exchange Act.   ❑

Indicate by check mark whether the registrant is a shell company (as defined in Rule 12b-2 of the Act).   ❑ Yes ❑ No

APPLICABLE ONLY TO ISSUERS INVOLVED IN BANKRUPTCY PROCEEDINGS DURING THE PRECEDING FIVE YEARS:

Indicate by check mark whether the registrant has filed all documents and reports required to be filed by Sections 12, 13 or 15(d) of the Securities Exchange Act of 1934 subsequent to the distribution of securities under a plan confirmed by a court.   ❑ Yes ❑ No

APPLICABLE ONLY TO CORPORATE ISSUERS:

Indicate the number of shares outstanding of each of the issuer's classes of common stock, as of the latest practicable date.

PART I—FINANCIAL INFORMATION

Item 1.   Financial Statements.

Provide the information required by Rule 10-01 of Regulation S-X.

Item 2.   Management's Discussion and Analysis of Financial Condition and Results of Operations.

Furnish the information required by Item 303 of Regulation S-K.

Item 3.   Quantitative and Qualitative Disclosures About Market Risk.

Furnish the information required by Item 305 of Regulation S-K.

Item 4.   Controls and Procedures.

Furnish the information required by Item 307 of Regulation S-K and Item 308(c) of Regulation S-K.

PART II—OTHER INFORMATION

Instruction. The report shall contain the item numbers and captions of all applicable items of Part II, but the text of such items may be omitted provided the responses clearly indicate the coverage of the item. Any item which is inapplicable or to which the answer is negative may be omitted and no reference thereto need be made in the report. If substantially the same information has been previously reported by the registrant, an additional report of the information on this form need not be made. The term "previously reported" is defined in Rule 12b-2. A separate response need not be presented in Part II where information called for is already disclosed in the financial information provided in Part I and is incorporated by reference into Part II of the report by means of a statement to that effect in Part II which specifically identifies the incorporated information.

Item 1.   **Legal Proceedings.**

Furnish the information required by Item 103 of Regulation S-K. As to such proceedings which have been terminated during the period covered by the report, provide similar information, including the date of termination and a description of the disposition thereof with respect to the registrant and its subsidiaries.

Instruction. A legal proceeding need only be reported in the 10-Q filed for the quarter in which it first became a reportable event and in subsequent quarters in which there have been material developments. Subsequent Form 10-Q filings in the same fiscal year in which a legal proceeding or a material development is reported should reference any previous reports in that year.

Item 1A.   **Risk Factors.**

Set forth any material changes from risk factors as previously disclosed in the registrant's Form 10-K in response to Item 1A. to Part I of Form 10-K.

Item 2.   **Unregistered Sales of Equity Securities and Use of Proceeds.**

(a) Furnish the information required by Item 701 of Regulation S-K as to all equity securities of the registrant sold by the registrant during the period covered by the report that were not registered under the Securities Act. If the Item 701 information previously has been included in a Current Report on Form 8-K, however, it need not be furnished.

(b) If required pursuant to Rule 463 of the Securities Act of 1933, furnish the information required by Item 701(f) of Regulation S-K.

(c) Furnish the information required by Item 703 of Regulation S-K for any repurchases made in the quarter covered by the report.

Instruction. Working capital restrictions and other limitations upon the payment of dividends are to be reported hereunder.

Item 3. Defaults Upon Senior Securities.

(a) If there has been any material default in the payment of principal, interest, a sinking or purchase fund installment, or any other material default not cured within 30 days, with respect to any indebtedness of the registrant or any of its significant subsidiaries exceeding 5 percent of the total assets of the registrant and its consolidated subsidiaries, identify the indebtedness and state the nature of the default. In the case of such a default in the payment of principal, interest, or a sinking or purchase fund installment, state the amount of the default and the total arrearage on the date of filing this report.

Instruction. This paragraph refers only to events which have become defaults under the governing instruments, i.e., after the expiration of any period of grace and compliance with any notice requirements.

(b) If any material arrearage in the payment of dividends has occurred or if there has been any other material delinquency not cured within 30 days, with respect to any class of preferred stock of the registrant which is registered or which ranks prior to any class of registered securities, or with respect to any class of preferred stock of any significant subsidiary of the registrant, give the title of the class and state the nature of the arrearage or delinquency. In the case of an arrearage in the payment of dividends, state the amount and the total arrearage on the date of filing this report.

Instruction. Item 3 need not be answered as to any default or arrearage with respect to any class of securities all of which is held by, or for the account of, the registrant or its totally held subsidiaries.

Item 4. Mine Safety Disclosures.

If applicable, provide a statement that the information concerning mine safety violations or other regulatory matters required by Section 1503(a) of the Dodd-Frank Wall Street Reform and Consumer Protection Act and Item 104 of Regulation S-K is included in exhibit 95 to the quarterly report.

Item 5. Other Information.

(a) The registrant may, at its option, report under this item any information, not previously reported in a report on Form 8-K, with respect to which information is not otherwise called for by this form. If disclosure of such information is made under this item, it need not be repeated in a report on Form 8-K which would otherwise be required to be filed with respect to such information or in a subsequent report on Form 10-Q; and

(b) Furnish the information required by Item 407(c)(3) of Regulation S-K.

(c) Furnish the information required by Item 408(a) and 408(d) of Regulation S-K.

Item 6.   Exhibits and Reports on Form 8-K.

(a) Furnish the exhibits required by Item 601 of Regulation S-K.

(b) Reports on Form 8-K. State whether any reports on Form 8-K have been filed during the quarter for which this report is filed.

SIGNATURES**

Pursuant to the requirements of the Securities Exchange Act of 1934, the registrant has duly caused this report to be signed on its behalf by the undersigned thereunto duly authorized.

_____

(Registrant)

_____   _____

            Date   (Signature) **

_____   _____

            Date   (Signature) **

SEC RULES OF PRACTICE

Rule 102 – Appearance and Practice Before the Commission.

A person shall not be represented before the Commission or a hearing officer except as stated in paragraphs (a) and (b) of this rule or as otherwise permitted by the Commission or a hearing officer.

   e. **Suspension and Disbarment**.

      1. Generally. The Commission may censure a person or deny, temporarily or permanently, the privilege of appearing or practicing before it in any way to any person who is found by the Commission after notice and opportunity for hearing in the matter:

          i. not to possess the requisite qualifications to represent others; or

         ii. to be lacking in character or integrity or to have engaged in unethical or improper professional conduct; or

       iii. to have willfully violated, or willfully aided and abetted the violation of any provision of the Federal securities laws or the rules and regulations thereunder.

       iv. with respect to persons licensed to practice as accountants, "improper professional conduct" under Rule 102(e)(1)(ii) means:

          A. intentional or knowing conduct, including reckless conduct, that results in a violation of applicable professional standards; or

          B. either of the following two types of negligent conduct:

             1. a single instance of highly unreasonable conduct that results in a violation of applicable professional standards in circumstances in which an accountant knows, or should know, that heightened scrutiny is warranted.

             2. repeated instances of unreasonable conduct, each resulting in a violation of applicable professional standards, that indicate a lack of competence to practice before the Commission.

      2. Certain Professionals and Convicted Persons. Any attorney who has been suspended or disbarred by a court of the United States or of any State; or any person whose license to practice as an accountant, engineer, or other professional or expert has been revoked or suspended in any State; or any person who has been convicted of a felony or a misdemeanor involving moral turpitude shall be forthwith suspended from appearing or practicing before the Commission. A disbarment, suspension, revocation or conviction within the meaning of this rule shall be deemed to have occurred when the disbarring, suspending, revoking or convicting agency or tribunal enters its judgment or order, including a judgment or order on a plea of nolo contendere, regardless of whether an appeal of such judgment or order is pending or could be taken.

      3. Temporary Suspensions. An order of temporary suspension shall become effective upon service on the respondent. No order of temporary suspension shall be entered by the Commission pursuant to paragraph (e)(3)(i) of this rule more than 90 days after the date on which the final judgment or order entered in a judicial or administrative proceeding described in paragraph (e)(3)(i)(A) or (e)(3)(i)(B) has become effective, whether upon completion of review or appeal

procedures or because further review or appeal procedures are no longer available.

   i.   The Commission, with due regard to the public interest and without preliminary hearing, may, by order, temporarily suspend from appearing or practicing before it any attorney, accountant, engineer, or other professional or expert who has been by name:

      A.   permanently enjoined by any court of competent jurisdiction, by reason of his or her misconduct in an action brought by the Commission, from violating or aiding and abetting the violation of any provision of the Federal securities laws or of the rules and regulations thereunder; or

      B.   found by any court of competent jurisdiction in an action brought by the Commission to which he or she is a party or found by the Commission in any administrative proceeding to which he or she is a party to have violated (unless the violation was found not to have been willful) or aided and abetted the violation of any provision of the Federal securities laws or of the rules and regulations thereunder.

   ii.   Any person temporarily suspended from appearing and practicing before the Commission in accordance with paragraph (e)(3)(i) of this rule may, within 30 days after service upon him or her of the order of temporary suspension, petition the Commission to lift the temporary suspension. If no petition has been received by the Commission within 30 days after service of the order, the suspension shall become permanent.

   iii.   Within 30 days after the filing of a petition in accordance with paragraph (e)(3)(ii) of this rule, the Commission shall either lift the temporary suspension, or set the matter down for hearing at a time and place designated by the Commission, or both, and, after opportunity for hearing, may censure the petitioner or disqualify the petitioner from appearing or practicing before the Commission for a period of time or permanently. In every case in which the temporary suspension has not been lifted, every hearing held and other action taken pursuant to this paragraph (e)(3) shall be expedited in accordance with Rule 500. If the hearing is held before a hearing officer, the time limits set forth in Rule 531 will govern review of the hearing officer's initial decision.

   iv.   In any hearing held on a petition filed in accordance with paragraph (e)(3)(ii) of this rule, the staff of the Commission shall show either that the petitioner has been enjoined as described in paragraph (e)(3)(i)(A) of this rule or that the petitioner has been found to have committed or aided and abetted violations as described in paragraph (e)(3)(i)(B) of this rule and that showing, without more, may be the basis for censure or disqualification. Once that showing has been made, the burden shall be upon the petitioner to show cause why he or she should not be censured or temporarily or permanently disqualified from appearing and practicing before the Commission. In any such hearing, the petitioner may not contest any finding made against him or her or fact admitted by him or her in the judicial or administrative proceeding upon which the proceeding under this paragraph (e)(3) is predicated. A person who has consented to the entry of a permanent injunction as described in paragraph (e)(3)(i)(A) of this rule without admitting the facts set forth in the complaint shall be presumed for all purposes under this paragraph (e)(3) to have been enjoined by reason of the misconduct alleged in the complaint.

4.   Filing of Prior Orders. Any person appearing or practicing before the Commission who has been the subject of an order, judgment, decree, or finding as set forth in paragraph (e)(3) of this rule shall promptly file with the Secretary a copy thereof (together with any related opinion or statement of the agency or tribunal involved). Failure to file any such paper, order, judgment, decree or finding shall not impair the operation of any other provision of this rule.

5.   Reinstatement.

   i.   An application for reinstatement of a person permanently suspended or disqualified under paragraph (e)(1) or (e)(3) of this rule may be made at any time, and the applicant may, in the Commission's discretion, be afforded a hearing; however, the suspension or disqualification shall continue unless and until the applicant has been reinstated by the Commission for good cause shown.

   ii. Any person suspended under paragraph (e)(2) of this rule shall be reinstated by the Commission, upon appropriate application, if all the grounds for application of the provisions of that paragraph are subsequently removed by a reversal of the conviction or termination of the suspension, disbarment, or revocation. An application for reinstatement on any other grounds by any person suspended under paragraph (e)(2) of this rule may be filed at any time and the applicant shall be accorded an opportunity for a hearing in the matter; however, such suspension shall continue unless and until the applicant has been reinstated by order of the Commission for good cause shown.

6.   Other Proceedings Not Precluded. A proceeding brought under paragraph (e)(1), (e)(2) or (e)(3) of this rule shall not preclude another proceeding brought under these same paragraphs.

7.   Public Hearings. All hearings held under this paragraph (e) shall be public unless otherwise ordered by the Commission on its own motion or after considering the motion of a party.

Rule 205 – Standards of Professional Conduct for Attorneys

Rule 1 – Purpose and Scope

This part sets forth minimum standards of professional conduct for attorneys appearing and practicing before the Commission in the representation of an issuer. These standards supplement applicable standards of any jurisdiction where an attorney is admitted or practices and are not intended to limit the ability of any jurisdiction to impose additional obligations on an attorney not inconsistent with the application of this part. Where the standards of a state or other United States jurisdiction where an attorney is admitted or practices conflict with this part, this part shall govern.

Rule 2 – Definitions

For purposes of this part, the following definitions apply:

a. **Appearing and practicing before the Commission**:
   1.   Means:
       i.   Transacting any business with the Commission, including communications in any form;
      ii.   Representing an issuer in a Commission administrative proceeding or in connection with any Commission investigation, inquiry, information request, or subpoena;
     iii.   Providing advice in respect of the United States securities laws or the Commission's rules or regulations thereunder regarding any document that the attorney has notice will be filed with or submitted to, or incorporated into any document that will be filed with or submitted to, the Commission, including the provision of such advice in the context of preparing, or participating in the preparation of, any such document; or
     iv.   Advising an issuer as to whether information or a statement, opinion, or other writing is required under the United States securities laws or the Commission's rules or regulations thereunder to be filed with or submitted to, or incorporated into any document that will be filed with or submitted to, the Commission; but
   2.   Does not include an attorney who:
       i.   Conducts the activities in paragraphs (a)(1)(i) through (a)(1)(iv) of this section other than in the context of providing legal services to an issuer with whom the attorney has an attorney-client relationship; or
      ii.   Is a non-appearing foreign attorney.

b. **Appropriate response** means a response to an attorney regarding reported evidence of a material violation as a result of which the attorney reasonably believes:
   1.   That no material violation, as defined in paragraph (i) of this section, has occurred, is ongoing, or is about to occur;
   2.   That the issuer has, as necessary, adopted appropriate remedial measures, including appropriate steps or sanctions to stop any material violations that are ongoing, to prevent any material violation that has yet to occur, and to remedy or otherwise appropriately address any material violation that has already occurred and to minimize the likelihood of its recurrence; or
   3.   That the issuer, with the consent of the issuer's board of directors, a committee thereof to whom a report could be made pursuant to Rule 3(b)(3), or a qualified legal compliance committee, has retained or directed an attorney to review the reported evidence of a material violation and either:
       i.   Has substantially implemented any remedial recommendations made by such attorney after a reasonable investigation and evaluation of the reported evidence; or
      ii.   Has been advised that such attorney may, consistent with his or her professional obligations, assert a colorable defense on behalf of the issuer (or the issuer's officer, director, employee, or agent, as the case

may be) in any investigation or judicial or administrative proceeding relating to the reported evidence of a material violation.

c. **Attorney** means any person who is admitted, licensed, or otherwise qualified to practice law in any jurisdiction, domestic or foreign, or who holds himself or herself out as admitted, licensed, or otherwise qualified to practice law.

d. **Breach of fiduciary duty** refers to any breach of fiduciary or similar duty to the issuer recognized under an applicable Federal or State statute or at common law, including but not limited to misfeasance, nonfeasance, abdication of duty, abuse of trust, and approval of unlawful transactions.

e. **Evidence of a material violation** means credible evidence, based upon which it would be unreasonable, under the circumstances, for a prudent and competent attorney not to conclude that it is reasonably likely that a material violation has occurred, is ongoing, or is about to occur.

f. **Foreign government issuer** means a foreign issuer as defined in Rule 405 under the Securities Act of 1933 eligible to register securities on Schedule B of the Securities Act of 1933.

g. **In the representation of an issuer** means providing legal services as an attorney for an issuer, regardless of whether the attorney is employed or retained by the issuer.

h. **Issuer** means an issuer (as defined in section 3 of the Securities Exchange Act of 1934, the securities of which are registered under section 12 of that Act, or that is required to file reports under section 15(d) of that Act, or that files or has filed a registration statement that has not yet become effective under the Securities Act of 1933, and that it has not withdrawn, but does not include a foreign government issuer. For purposes of paragraphs (a) and (g) of this section, the term "issuer" includes any person controlled by an issuer, where an attorney provides legal services to such person on behalf of, or at the behest, or for the benefit of the issuer, regardless of whether the attorney is employed or retained by the issuer.

i. **Material violation** means a material violation of an applicable United States federal or state securities law, a material breach of fiduciary duty arising under United States federal or state law, or a similar material violation of any United States federal or state law.

j. **Non-appearing foreign attorney** means an attorney:
   1. Who is admitted to practice law in a jurisdiction outside the United States;
   2. Who does not hold himself or herself out as practicing, and does not give legal advice regarding, United States federal or state securities or other laws (except as provided in paragraph (j)(3)(ii) of this section); and
   3. Who:
      i. Conducts activities that would constitute appearing and practicing before the Commission only incidentally to, and in the ordinary course of, the practice of law in a jurisdiction outside the United States; or

    ii. Is appearing and practicing before the Commission only in consultation with counsel, other than a non-appearing foreign attorney, admitted or licensed to practice in a state or other United States jurisdiction.

k. **Qualified legal compliance committee** means a committee of an issuer (which also may be an audit or other committee of the issuer) that:

1. Consists of at least one member of the issuer's audit committee (or, if the issuer has no audit committee, one member from an equivalent committee of independent directors) and two or more members of the issuer's board of directors who are not employed, directly or indirectly, by the issuer and who are not, in the case of a registered investment company, "interested persons" as defined in section 2(a)(19) of the Investment Company Act of 1940;

2. Has adopted written procedures for the confidential receipt, retention, and consideration of any report of evidence of a material violation under Rule 3;

3. Has been duly established by the issuer's board of directors, with the authority and responsibility:

    i. To inform the issuer's chief legal officer and chief executive officer (or the equivalents thereof) of any report of evidence of a material violation (except in the circumstances described in Rule 3(b)(4));

    ii. To determine whether an investigation is necessary regarding any report of evidence of a material violation by the issuer, its officers, directors, employees or agents and, if it determines an investigation is necessary or appropriate, to:

        A. Notify the audit committee or the full board of directors;

        B. Initiate an investigation, which may be conducted either by the chief legal officer (or the equivalent thereof) or by outside attorneys; and

        C. Retain such additional expert personnel as the committee deems necessary; and

    iii. At the conclusion of any such investigation, to:

        A. Recommend, by majority vote, that the issuer implement an appropriate response to evidence of a material violation; and

        B. Inform the chief legal officer and the chief executive officer (or the equivalents thereof) and the board of directors of the results of any such investigation under this section and the appropriate remedial measures to be adopted; and

4. Has the authority and responsibility, acting by majority vote, to take all other appropriate action, including the authority to notify the Commission in the event that the issuer fails in any material respect to implement an appropriate response that the qualified legal compliance committee has recommended the issuer to take.

l. **Reasonable or reasonably** denotes, with respect to the actions of an attorney, conduct that would not be unreasonable for a prudent and competent attorney.

m. **Reasonably believes** means that an attorney believes the matter in question and that the circumstances are such that the belief is not unreasonable.

n.   **Report** means to make known to directly, either in person, by telephone, by e-mail, electronically, or in writing.

Rule 3 – Issuer as Client

a.   **Representing an issuer.** An attorney appearing and practicing before the Commission in the representation of an issuer owes his or her professional and ethical duties to the issuer as an organization. That the attorney may work with and advise the issuer's officers, directors, or employees in the course of representing the issuer does not make such individuals the attorney's clients.

b.   **Duty to report evidence of a material violation.**
   1.   If an attorney, appearing and practicing before the Commission in the representation of an issuer, becomes aware of evidence of a material violation by the issuer or by any officer, director, employee, or agent of the issuer, the attorney shall report such evidence to the issuer's chief legal officer (or the equivalent thereof) or to both the issuer's chief legal officer and its chief executive officer (or the equivalents thereof) forthwith. By communicating such information to the issuer's officers or directors, an attorney does not reveal client confidences or secrets or privileged or otherwise protected information related to the attorney's representation of an issuer.
   2.   The chief legal officer (or the equivalent thereof) shall cause such inquiry into the evidence of a material violation as he or she reasonably believes is appropriate to determine whether the material violation described in the report has occurred, is ongoing, or is about to occur. If the chief legal officer (or the equivalent thereof) determines no material violation has occurred, is ongoing, or is about to occur, he or she shall notify the reporting attorney and advise the reporting attorney of the basis for such determination. Unless the chief legal officer (or the equivalent thereof) reasonably believes that no material violation has occurred, is ongoing, or is about to occur, he or she shall take all reasonable steps to cause the issuer to adopt an appropriate response, and shall advise the reporting attorney thereof. In lieu of causing an inquiry under this paragraph (b), a chief legal officer (or the equivalent thereof) may refer a report of evidence of a material violation to a qualified legal compliance committee under paragraph (c)(2) of this section if the issuer has duly established a qualified legal compliance committee prior to the report of evidence of a material violation.
   3.   Unless an attorney who has made a report under paragraph (b)(1) of this section reasonably believes that the chief legal officer or the chief executive officer of the issuer (or the equivalent thereof) has provided an appropriate response within a reasonable time, the attorney shall report the evidence of a material violation to:
      i.   The audit committee of the issuer's board of directors;
      ii.   Another committee of the issuer's board of directors consisting solely of directors who are not employed, directly or indirectly, by the issuer and are not, in the case of a registered investment company, "interested persons" as defined in section 2(a)(19) of the Investment Company Act of 1940 (if the issuer's board of directors has no audit committee); or

       iii.   The issuer's board of directors (if the issuer's board of directors has no committee consisting solely of directors who are not employed, directly or indirectly, by the issuer and are not, in the case of a registered investment company, "interested persons" as defined in section 2(a)(19) of the Investment Company Act of 1940).

4.   If an attorney reasonably believes that it would be futile to report evidence of a material violation to the issuer's chief legal officer and chief executive officer (or the equivalents thereof) under paragraph (b)(1) of this section, the attorney may report such evidence as provided under paragraph (b)(3) of this section.

5.   An attorney retained or directed by an issuer to investigate evidence of a material violation reported under paragraph (b)(1), (b)(3), or (b)(4) of this section shall be deemed to be appearing and practicing before the Commission. Directing or retaining an attorney to investigate reported evidence of a material violation does not relieve an officer or director of the issuer to whom such evidence has been reported under paragraph (b)(1), (b)(3), or (b)(4) of this section from a duty to respond to the reporting attorney.

6.   An attorney shall not have any obligation to report evidence of a material violation under this paragraph (b) if:

       i.   The attorney was retained or directed by the issuer's chief legal officer (or the equivalent thereof) to investigate such evidence of a material violation and:

           A.   The attorney reports the results of such investigation to the chief legal officer (or the equivalent thereof); and

           B.   Except where the attorney and the chief legal officer (or the equivalent thereof) each reasonably believes that no material violation has occurred, is ongoing, or is about to occur, the chief legal officer (or the equivalent thereof) reports the results of the investigation to the issuer's board of directors, a committee thereof to whom a report could be made pursuant to paragraph (b)(3) of this section, or a qualified legal compliance committee; or

      ii.   The attorney was retained or directed by the chief legal officer (or the equivalent thereof) to assert, consistent with his or her professional obligations, a colorable defense on behalf of the issuer (or the issuer's officer, director, employee, or agent, as the case may be) in any investigation or judicial or administrative proceeding relating to such evidence of a material violation, and the chief legal officer (or the equivalent thereof) provides reasonable and timely reports on the progress and outcome of such proceeding to the issuer's board of directors, a committee thereof to whom a report could be made pursuant to paragraph (b)(3) of this section, or a qualified legal compliance committee.

7.   An attorney shall not have any obligation to report evidence of a material violation under this paragraph (b) if such attorney was retained or directed by a qualified legal compliance committee:

       i.   To investigate such evidence of a material violation; or

      ii.   To assert, consistent with his or her professional obligations, a colorable defense on behalf of the issuer (or the issuer's officer, director, employee, or agent, as the case may be) in any investigation or judicial or